THE
COLLEGE
PRESS
NIV
COMMENTARY

JOB

THE COLLEGE PRESS NIV COMMENTARY

JOB

STEPHEN M. HOOKS

Old Testament Series Co-Editors:

Terry Briley, Ph.D.
Lipscomb University

Paul Kissling, Ph.D.
Great Lakes Christian College

COLLEGE PRESS
PUBLISHING COMPANY
Joplin, Missouri

Library of Congress Cataloging-in-Publication Data

Hooks, Stephen M.
    Job / by Stephen Hooks.
        p.   cm. — (The College Press NIV commentary.)
    Includes bibliographical references.
    ISBN 978-0-89900-886-8 (hardback)
    1. Bible. O.T. Job—Commentaries.   I. Title. II. Series.

  BS1415.53.H66 2006
  223'.1077–dc22

2006034644

A WORD FROM THE PUBLISHER

Years ago a movement was begun with the dream of uniting all Christians on the basis of a common purpose (world evangelism) under a common authority (the Word of God). The College Press NIV Commentary Series is a serious effort to join the scholarship of two branches of this unity movement so as to speak with one voice concerning the Word of God. Our desire is to provide a resource for your study of the Old Testament that will benefit you whether you are preparing a Bible School lesson, a sermon, a college course, or your own personal devotions. Today as we survey the wreckage of a broken world, we must turn again to the Lord and his Word, unite under his banner and communicate the life-giving message to those who are in desperate need. This is our purpose.

ABBREVIATIONS

AB . . . . *Anchor Bible*
AfO . . . . . . *Archiv für Orientforschung*
AJBA . . . . . *Australian Journal of Biblical Archaeology*
AJSL . . . . . *American Journal of Semitic Languages and Literature*
ANE . . . . . *Ancient Near East(ern)*
ANET . . . . *Ancient Near Eastern Texts*, J. Pritchard, ed.
Ang . . . . . . *Angelicum*
AnOr . . . . . *Analecta Orientalia*
AOS . . . . . . *American Oriental Society*
Arab. . . . . . *Arabic*
BA . . . . *Biblical Archaeologist*
BAR . . . . . *Biblical Archaeology Review*
BASOR . . . *Bulletin of the American Schools of Oriental Researh*
BBB . . . . . *Bonner biblische Beiträge*
BDB . . . . . *A Hebrew and English Lexicon of the Old Testament*, F.
Brown, S. Driver, C. Briggs, eds.
BHK . . . . . *Biblia Hebraica. Stuttgart*, R. Kittel, ed.
BHS . . . . . *Biblia Hebraica Stuttgartensia*, K. Elliger and W.
Rudolph, eds.
Bib . . . . . . *Biblica*
BibOr . . . . *Biblica et orientalia*
BJRL . . . . . *Bulletin of the John Rylands Library*
BKAT . . . . *Biblischer Kommentar: Altes Testament*
BSO(A)S . . *Bulletin of the School of Oriental (and African) Studies*
BTB . . . . . *Biblical Theology Bulletin*
BWANT . . *Beiträge zur Wissenschaft vom Alten und Neuen Testament*
BWL . . . . . *Babylonian Wisdom Literature*
BZ . . . . . . *Biblische Zeitschrift*
BZAW . . . . *Beihefte zur Zeitschrift für die alttestamentliche Wissenschaft*
CBQ . . . . . *Catholic Biblical Quarterly*

CTA . . . . . *Corpus des tablettes en cuneiformes alphabétiques découvertes à Ras-Shamra Ugarit de 1929 à 1939.*

DOTT . . . . *Documents from Old Testament Times*

ErIsr . . . . . *Eretz-Israel*

EstBib . . . . *Estudios bíblicos*

EvQ . . . . . . *Evangelical Quarterly*

EvT . . . . . . *Evangelische Theologie*

ExpTim . . . *Expository Times*

Fest. . . . . . . *Festschrift*

FOTL . . . . *Forms of Old Testament Literature*

FRLANT . . *Forschungen zur Religion und Literatur des Alten und Neuen Testaments*

GKC . . . . . *Gesenius' Hebrew Grammar, 2nd ed.,* E. Kautzsch and A. Cowley

HAT . . . . . *Handbuch zum Alten Testament*

HSM . . . . . *Harvard Semitic Monographs*

HTR . . . . . *Harvard Theological Review*

HUCA . . . . *Hebrew Union College Annual*

IB . . . . *The Interpreter's Bible*

ICC . . . . . . *International Critical Commentary*

IDB . . . . . . *The Interpreter's Dictionary of the Bible*

Int . . . . *Interpretation*

ISBE . . . . . *The International Standard Bible Encyclopedia*

JAOS . . . . . *Journal of the American Oriental Society*

JB . . . . *Jerusalem Bible*

JBL . . . . . . *Journal of Biblical Literature*

JJS . . . . *Journal of Jewish Studies*

JQR . . . . . . *Jewish Quarterly Review*

JRAS . . . . . *Journal of the Royal Asiatic Society*

JSOT . . . . . *Journal for the Study of the Old Testament*

JSOTSupp . *Journal for Study of the Old Testament Supplement Series*

JSS . . . . *Journal of Semitic Studies*

JTS . . . . . . *Journal of Theological Studies*

KAT . . . . . *Kommentar zum Alten Testament*

KB . . . . *Hebraisches und Aramaisches Lexicon zum Alten Testament, 3rd ed.,* L. Kohler, W. Baumgartner, et al.

LXX . . . . . *Septuagint*

mss. . . . . . . *manuscripts*

MT . . . . . . *Masoretic Text*

NEB ..... *New English Bible*
NICOT ... *New International Commentary on the Old Testament*
NIV ...... *New International Version*
OBO ..... *Orbis biblicus et orientalis*
Or .... *Orientalia*
OTL ..... *Old Testament Library*
OtSt ...... *Oudtestamentische Studiën*
PEFQS ... *Palestine Exploration Fund Quarterly Statement*
PEQ ..... *Palestine Exploration Quarterly*
PIBA ..... *Proceedings of the Irish Biblical Association*
PRU ..... *Le Palais royal d'Ugarit*
RA ...... *Revue d'assyriologie et d'archéologie orientale*
RB .... *Revue Biblique*
REJ ...... *Revue des études juives*
ResQ ..... *Restoration Quarterly*
RevExp ... *Review and Expositor*
RSP ...... *Ras Shamra Parallels, 3 vols. Analecta Orientalia 49, 50,*
          51, vols. 1-2 ed. L. Fisher; vol. 3 ed. S. Rummel
RSV ...... *Revised Standard Version*
SBL ...... *Society of Biblical Literature*
SBLMS ... *Society of Biblical Literature Monograph Series*
SBT ...... *Studies in Biblical Theology*
SJT ...... *Scottish Journal of Theology*
ST .... *Studia Theologica*
SVTQ .... *St. Vladimir's Theological Quarterly*
SWJT .... *Southwest Journal of Theology*
Syr. ...... *Syriac*
Targ. ..... *Targum*
T.B. ...... *Babylonian Talmud*
TBT ..... *The Bible Today*
TDOT .... *Theological Dictionary of the Old Testament*
THAT .... *Theologisches Handworterbuch zum Alten Testament*
TLZ ...... *Theologische Literaturzeitung*
TOTC .... *Tyndale Old Testament Commentaries*
UF .... *Ugarit Forschungen*
Ugar. ..... *Ugaritic*
UT ...... *Ugaritic Textbook*
VT .... *Vetus Testamentum*

VTSupp . . . *Vetus Testamentum, Supplements*
Vulg. . . . . . . *Vulgate*
WBC . . . . . *Word Biblical Commentary*
WMANT . . *Wissenschaftliche Monographien zum Alten und Neuen Testament*
WO . . . . . . *Die Welt des Orients*
WZKM . . . *Wiener Zeitschrift für die Kunde des Morgenlandes*
ZAW . . . . . *Zeitschrift für die altestamentliche Wissenschaft*
ZDMG . . . . *Zeitschrift der deutschen morgenländischen Gesellschaft*
ZTK . . . . . *Zeitschrift für Theologie und Kirche*

Simplified Guide to Hebrew Writing

Heb. letter	Translit.	Pronunciation guide
א	’	Has no sound of its own; like smooth breathing mark in Greek
ב	b	Pronounced like English B *or* V
ג	g	Pronounced like English G
ד	d	Pronounced like English D
ה	h	Pronounced like English H, silent at the end of words in the combination āh
ו	w	As a consonant, pronounced like English V or German W
וּ	û	Represents a vowel sound, pronounced like English long OO
וֹ	ô	Represents a vowel sound, pronounced like English long O
ז	z	Pronounced like English Z
ח	ḥ	Pronounced like German and Scottish CH and Greek χ (chi)
ט	ṭ	Pronounced like English T
י	y	Pronounced like English Y
כ/ך	k	Pronounced like English K
ל	l	Pronounced like English L
מ/ם	m	Pronounced like English M
נ/ן	n	Pronounced like English N
ס	s	Pronounced like English S
ע	‘	Stop in breath deep in throat before pronouncing the vowel
פ/ף	p/ph	Pronounced like English P *or* F
צ/ץ	ṣ	Pronounced like English TS/TZ
ק	q	Pronounced very much like כ (k)
ר	r	Pronounced like English R
שׂ	ś	Pronounced like English S, much the same as ס
שׁ	š	Pronounced like English SH
ת	t/th	Pronounced like English T *or* TH

Note that different forms of some letters appear at the end of the word (written right to left), as in כָּפַף (*kāphaph*, "bend") and מֶלֶךְ (*melek*, "king").

Vowels in Hebrew (except where the ו is used to represent a vowel sound), are represented by "vowel points" added to the consonant. For example: הַ (*ha*, "the"). The letter *yod* (', *y*) also becomes a *part of* certain vowel sounds, as in the conjunction כִּי (*kî*, "that"). Originally, Hebrew was written as "unpointed" text, with just the consonants. For convenience, the different vowel points are shown below on the letter Aleph (א).

אָ	ā	Pronounced not like long A in English, but like the broad A or AH sound
אַ	a	The Hebrew short A sound, but more closely resembles the broad A (pronounced for a shorter period of time) than the English short A
אֶ	e	Pronounced like English short E

אֵ	ē	Pronounced like English long A, or Greek η (eta)
אִ	i	Pronounced like English short I
אִ	î	The same vowel point is sometimes pronounced like אִ (see below)
אֹ	o	This vowel point sometimes represents the short O sound
אֹ	ō	Pronounced like English long O
אֻ	u	The vowel point ֻ sometimes represents a shorter U sound and
אֻ	ū	is sometimes pronounced like the ו (û, see above)
אֵי	ê	Pronounced much the same as אֵ
אֵי	ê	Pronounced much the same as אֵ
אִי	î	Pronounced like long I in many languages, or English long E
אְ	ə	An unstressed vowel sound, like the first E in the word "severe"
אֳ, אֲ, אֱ	ŏ, ă, ĕ	Shortened, unstressed forms of the vowels אֹ, אַ, and אֶ, pronounced very similarly to אְ

PREFACE AND
ACKNOWLEDGMENTS

Few works of literature have evoked more wonder from its readers than has the biblical book of Job. Virtually all who turn its pages feel they have had an encounter with the profound. Theologians, literary critics, poets, politicians, novelists, musicians, dramatists, sociologists. and psychologists have all been engaged by its provocative story of a pious man afflicted by God. Witness to its universal appeal is supplied by the vast amount of literature it has inspired.

Interpreting Job is no easy task. Its unpredictable plot, its cacophony of competing voices, and its provocative challenges to conventional theology all conspire to leave the reader both puzzled and provoked. To complicate matters, the Hebrew of the book of Job is some of the most difficult of the Old Testament. It is not surprising then that Job's interpreters have proposed such a wide variety of approaches to understanding its meaning and purpose.

This commentary attempts to read the book of Job *canonically* and *theologically*. We read the book canonically because the biblical version of Job is the only book of Job we have. Though numerous attempts have been made to reconstruct an "original" or rearrange the book into a more "consistent" and "readable" form, there is no agreement on just what such a form should take. Further, there is no evidence from any extant manuscript that the book of Job ever existed in any version other than the one found in the Bible. We read the book theologically because the book of Job is a "God-book" from cover to cover. God is the subject or the subject-behind-the-subject of every page. Through its compelling plot and exalted speeches the book of Job explores the mystery of God's ways to a depth and with an intensity that is unsurpassed in all of ancient religious literature.

The Book of Job has the power to engage its readers on different levels. Intellectually, it forces the reader to rethink traditional

theories of divine justice by exposing the inadequacy of the simplistic, fatalistic doctrine of retribution. Emotionally, it stirs feelings of
sympathy, anger, frustration, sorrow, and even laughter over its surprising plot and ironic language. Spiritually, it calls the believer to a
new and higher kind of piety—a piety that trusts God in spite of life's
cruel absurdities and loves God simply for who he is. It invites the
reader, like Job, on a journey of faith that ends with an unexpected
and life-transforming encounter with the sovereign Lord of the universe. It is my hope that this study of the book of Job will serve to
facilitate this journey to perfected faith for all who choose to read it.

I wish to thank my former students Chad and Deanna McDonald
for their assistance in the preparation of this manuscript and my col-
leagues at Atlanta Christian College for many helpful suggestions.
Finally, I wish to dedicate this book to Lois, Katherine, Stephanie,
and Kurtis, each of whom has faithfully endured suffering and
inspired my own spiritual pilgrimage.

Stephen M. Hooks

INTRODUCTION

Like other books of the Old Testament (e.g., Ruth, Esther) the Book of Job receives its name from its principal character. The Hebrew אִיּוֹב ('Îyôb), rendered in Greek by (Ιωβ) *Iob*, came through Latin into English as Job. Though the precise meaning of the name is uncertain, it was widely used by tribal leaders in Palestine and the surrounding territories in the second millennium B.C.[1]

The Book of Job is located in the third major division of the Hebrew Bible called the Writings (*Kethubim*). In some manuscripts Job follows Psalms and Proverbs, while in others it stands between them. In the Syriac Bible the book stands between Deuteronomy and Joshua, undoubtedly reflecting the early view that the book originated in the patriarchal age. The position of the book in our modern English Bibles (after the historical books and at the beginning of the poetic books) owes its origin to the Vulgate. Though the rabbis debated the canonicity of controversial books like the Song of Songs and Ecclesiastes until a century after Christ, Job's inclusion in the official list of biblical books was never seriously questioned. Jews and Christians alike recognized the book as Holy Scripture in spite of its challenging subject matter and language. The Jewish sect of Qumran (Dead Sea Scrolls) also accepted the book and even made an Aramaic translation of it.[2]

---

[1]Cf. discussion by M. Pope, *Job*, AB (New York: Doubleday, 1965), p. 6; D. Clines, *Job 1–20*, WBC (Dallas: Word Books, 1989), pp. 10-11.

[2]Cf. J. van der Ploeg and A. van der Woude, *Le Targum de Job de la grotte XI de Qumrân* (Leiden: Brill, 1960); C. Mangan, et al., *The Targum of Job* (London: T & T Clark, 1991); M. Sokoloff, *The Targum to Job from Qumran Cave XI* (Ramat Gan: Bar-Ilan University, 1974); D. Stec, *The Text of the Targum of Job: An Introduction and Critical Edition* (Leiden: Brill, 1994).

AUTHORSHIP

One of the many ironies of this great literary masterpiece is that its author remains anonymous. We can only speculate over who he was and when he lived. Evidence from his book suggests that he was one of the ancient sages (*hochamim*), a group of scribes, court administrators, and teachers who were regarded, along with the prophets and priests (cf. Jer 18:18), as one of the three authoritative sources of spiritual truth in Israel. A learned man, he was skilled in forensic rhetoric, the use of proverbs and riddles, and displayed a wide awareness of the culture, geography, and literature of the ancient Near Eastern world.

The author was almost certainly an Israelite, judged by his familiarity with other portions of the Hebrew Bible.[3] In places his writings echo the language and thought of the hymnic, prophetic, and wisdom literature of the Old Testament, especially the laments of the Psalms and Jeremiah. He was surely a strong monotheist and a devout servant of Yahweh. His portrayal of Yahweh as the uncontested Sovereign over his created world is one of the most exalted portraits of the one true God to be found in Scripture. The writer also valued the fear of the Lord as the foundation of true worship and the basis for all righteous behavior.

DATE

Suggested dates for the origin of Job span more than a millennium. The early rabbis dated the book to the time of the biblical patriarchs and its authorship to Moses.[4] In support of this early tradition

---

[3]Because of numerous difficulties in the language of the Hebrew version of Job some scholars have speculated that it had a non-Hebrew origin and was perhaps written by a non-Israelite. Without compelling evidence, however, it is difficult to imagine a book entering the Hebrew canon that did not have an Israelite origin. Cf. R. Pfeiffer, "Edomite Wisdom," *ZAW* 44 (1926): 13-15; A. Guillaume, "The Arabic Background of the Book of Job," in *Promise and Fulfillment: Essays Presented to Professor S.H. Hooke,* ed. by F.F. Bruce (Edinburgh: T. & T. Clark, 1963), pp. 106-127.

[4]T.B., *Baba Bathra*, 14b. In the apocryphal appendix to the Septuagint, Job is identified with Jobab the king of Edom, grandson of Esau. Cf. The discussion in Pope, *Job,* pp. xxx-xxxvii.

it is noted that the story of Job has a patriarchal setting. Like the patriarchs Job's wealth is measured in terms of cattle and servants. As in the time of the patriarchs there is no priesthood or central sanctuary and Job himself offers sacrifice. The kind of money referred to in Job 42:11 is found elsewhere in the Bible only in Genesis 33:19 and Joshua 24:32. Job's longevity is also similar to that of the patriarchs. The names that Job and the friends use for God (Shaddai, El, Eloah) are identical to those used by the patriarchs. Further, as noted below, Job shares several literary features with ancient Near Eastern works that date to the early second millennium B.C., the time when we believe the biblical patriarchs lived.[5]

A careful reading of the book, however, suggests that while the events of the story of Job are set in patriarchal times, the actual writing of the book must have taken place at a later date. The author was clearly familiar with other portions of the Old Testament and his frequent citation of the Israelite prophetic, poetic, and wisdom literature provides strong evidence that the book originated much later than the patriarchal period.[6] Noting this, modern scholars tend to assign the book to one of three eras: the seventh century B.C., during Hezekiah's reign;[7] the sixth century B.C., after the fall of Jerusalem;[8] and the fourth/third century B.C., during the time of the second temple.[9] The arguments for each position take into consideration evidence from Job's language, style, and subject matter as well as the aforementioned relationship to other biblical books.[10] The references to Job in Ezekiel 14:14,20 do establish that at least some version of the story of Job was known in Israel by the early sixth century B.C.

---

[5]Cf. N.M. Sarna, "Epic Substratum in the Prose of Job," *JBL* 76 (1957): 13-25; cf. also H.L. Ginsberg, "The Legend of King Keret," *BASORSupp.* 2-3 (1946) for a comparison with the story of Job.

[6]Cf. discussion, pp. 19-20; and n. 22 below.

[7]Cf. F.E. Andersen, *Job*, TOTC (London/Downers Grove, IL: Tyndale/InterVarsity, 1976).

[8]Cf. S. Terrien, "The Book of Job: Introduction and Exegesis," *IB* (Nashville: Abingdon Press, 1954), 3:885-888.

[9]Cf. G. Fohrer, *Das Buch Hiob*, KAT 16 (Gutersloh: Gerd Mohn, 1963), pp. 22-29.

[10]For discussion cf. J. Hartley, *The Book of Job*, NICOT (Grand Rapids: Eerdmans, 1988), pp. 17-20.

ANCIENT NEAR EASTERN PARALLELS

The book of Job is representative of a genre of literature attested throughout the ancient Near Eastern world. Philosophical and theological discussions of the meaning of suffering abound in the sacred writings of Egypt, Canaan, and Mesopotamia. Some of these works show striking affinities with the biblical Job.[11]

Among the most important of these works for the study of Job are:

1. "I Will Praise the Lord of Wisdom" — Akkadian[12]
2. "A Dialogue about Human Misery"— Akkadian[13]
3. "The Babylonian Theodicy"—Akkadian[14]
4. "Man and His God" — Sumerian[15]
5. "The Protests of the Eloquent Peasant" — Egyptian[16]
6. "A Dispute over Suicide" — Egyptian[17]

These and other ancient parallels[18] to Job illustrate that interest in the meaning of suffering and the role of the gods in the human sphere was widespread in the world from which the biblical Job emerged. The extent to which these works may have influenced Job is uncertain, but it is likely that the author of Job was conversant with at least some of them. Wisdom literature was widely circulated

---

[11]Cf. R. Albertson, "Job and Ancient Near East Wisdom Literature," in *Scripture in Context, II: More Essays on the Comparative Method*, ed. by W.H. Hallo, J.C. Moyer, and L.G. Perdue (Winona Lake, IN: Eisenbrauns, 1983), pp. 213-230; G. Mattingly, "The Pious Sufferer: Mesopotamia's Traditional Theodicy and Job's Counselors," in *The Bible in the Light of Cuneiform Literature*, ed. by W. Hallo, B. Jones, and G. Mattingly (Lewiston, NY: Edwin Mellen, 1990), pp. 305-348.

[12]Also known as "The Poem of the Righteous Sufferer" and "The Babylonian Job"; cf. *ANET*, pp. 434-437; W.G. Lambert, *Babylonian Wisdom Literature* (Oxford: Clarendon, 1960), pp. 21-62.

[13]*ANET*, pp. 438-440, also known as "The Babylonian Ecclesiastes."

[14]*ANET*, pp. 601-604; Lambert, *Babylonian Wisdom Literature*, pp. 63-91.

[15]*ANET*, pp. 589-591.

[16]*ANET*, pp. 407-410; cf. also W.K. Simpson, ed., *The Literature of Ancient Egypt*, rev. ed. (New Haven, CT: Yale University Press, 1973), pp. 31-49.

[17]*ANET*, pp. 405-407; Simpson, *Literature of Ancient Egypt*, pp. 201-209.

[18]Cf. J. Nougayrol, "Une version ancienne du 'juste souffrant,'" *RB* 59 (1952): 239-250; S. Rao and M. Reddy, "Job and His Satan—Parallels in Indian Scripture," *ZAW* 82 (1970): 251-269; and Pope, *Job*, pp. l-lxvi.

in the ancient Near Eastern world, and there is direct biblical evidence that the authors of Scripture were aware of it (cf., e.g, 1 Kgs 4:30-31).

The Book of Job, however, stands apart from the parallel literature in several ways. First, of course, is its unique theology. The monotheistic perspective of Job posed a special problem for the author's consideration of the role of God in human suffering. The book affirms faith in one true God, sovereign and just, maker of all things. Whence then the origin of undeserved suffering? No other ancient work goes as far as Job does in its search for an answer to the problem of theodicy. It's challenge to retributive justice as the sole model by which to understand how God governs his world is unapproached by any other ancient work.[19] Second, the Book of Job stands out as literature. Its characterization and employment of its protagonists, its balancing of lament and substantive debate, its blending of religious tradition and wisdom, and its powerful use of lyrical poetry are all without peer in the ancient literature.[20] Finally, the book of Job surpasses its ancient parallels in the lasting influence it has had in human intellectual history, especially on the thinking of the Western world. Theologians, philosophers, novelists, poets, and even psychologists have pondered the book through the centuries and offered their own interpretations of its meaning.[21]

PARALLELS TO OTHER
OLD TESTAMENT LITERATURE

As noted above, the author of Job was conversant with the Hebrew Scriptures. Numerous texts in the book of Job find parallels with the rest of the Old Testament. No less than fifty different texts in Job demonstrate interconnection with at least eleven other Old Testament books. The textual similarities of Job with Psalms, Prov-

---

[19]Cf. Andersen, *Job*, p. 32.

[20]Cf. J. Roberts, "Job and the Israelite Religious Tradition," *ZAW* 89 (1977): 13.

[21]Cf., e.g., N.A. Francisco, "Job in World Literature," *RevExp* 68 (1971): 521-533; M. Friedman, "The Modern Job: On Melville, Dostoyevsky, and Kafka," *Judaism* 12 (1963): 436-455.

erbs, and Isaiah are especially strong as are the parallels with Lamentations and Jeremiah.[22]

Some of these similarities are explainable on the basis of shared genres like the hymns found in Job, Psalms, and Isaiah and the laments found in Job, Jeremiah, and Lamentations. Other intertextual connections reveal a shared theology. This is especially true of texts in Job and Isaiah 40–55. God's transcendence (cp. Job 22:13-14 and Isaiah 40:22) and his sovereignty over nations (cp. Job 12:13-25 and Isaiah 40:15-17) and over nature (cp. Job 9:13; 41:1-34 and Isaiah 51:9-16) are described in very similar terms. But perhaps the most significant theme shared by these two great books is that of the righteous sufferer. The Suffering Servant songs of Isaiah 40–55 have several affinities with Job. Both the suffering servant and Job are innocent, having done no violence or spoken any deceit (Job 6:30; 16:17 and Isaiah 53:7,9); both plead their case to God (Isaiah 49:4; 50:8-10 and Job 13:15; 16:19); both are despised (Isaiah 53:2 and Job 19:18) and then deserted by their peers (Job 19:14 and Isaiah 53:3). One major difference between Isaiah and Job, however, must be noted. In Isaiah, the Servant's suffering is vicarious. It atones for the sins of his people. This theme is absent from the book of Job.[23]

The exact nature of the literary dependency or borrowing between Job and these other books is difficult to establish. Complicating the issue is the debate over the dating of Job and some of the other works in question. Suffice it to say that, with the exception of Job's strong challenge to retributive justice as the model by which God governs His world, the book of Job is demonstrably similar in subject matter and style to significant portions of the Old Testament literature.

---

[22]There are nine texts in Job that are identical to other biblical texts: Job 9:8a = Isaiah 44:24c; Job 9:8b = Amos 4:13d; Job 9:9a = Amos 5:8a; Job 9:18b = Lamentations 3:15a; Job 12:9b = Isaiah 41:20a; Job 12:21a = Psalm 104:40; Job 14:11 = Isaiah 19:5; Job 15:7b = Proverbs 8:25b; Job 15:35a = Isaiah 59:4d.

[23]Cf. R. Pfeiffer, "The Dual Origins of Hebrew Monotheism," *JBL* 46 (1927): 202-206; S. Terrien, "Quelques remarques sur les affinites de Job avec el Deutero-Esaie," *Volume du Congress:* Geneve 1965, VTSupp 15 (Leiden: Brill, 1966), pp. 295-310.

LITERARY CONSIDERATIONS

THE HEBREW TEXT

The Hebrew text (MT) of Job presents the reader with many philological and syntactical challenges.[24] There are, for example, more *hapax legomena* (words that occur only once) in Job than in any other book of the Old Testament. There are places in the book where the Hebrew text evidences heavy influence by Aramaic and Arabic, two related Northwest Semitic languages. So different is the language of Job from other Old Testament books that it has led some scholars to propose that the book is a translation of a non-Hebrew original.[25] Edomite,[26] Aramaic,[27] and Arabic[28] originals have all been suggested as the basis for the Hebrew version of Job. More recently, comparisons with Ugaritic, another Northwest Semitic language, have added to our understanding of the philology and syntax of biblical Job.[29]

THE VERSIONS

The Greek version (LXX) of Job generally follows the Masoretic Text (MT), but in some places there are significant differences. Most notable is the fact that LXX is some 400 lines shorter than MT.[30]

---

[24]See D. Freedman, "Orthographic Peculiarities in the Book of Job," *ErIsr* 9 (1969): 35-44.

[25]This was first suggested by Ibn Ezra in the twelfth century A.D.

[26]R. Pfeiffer, "Edomite Wisdom," pp. 13-25.

[27]N.H. Tur-Sinai, *The Book of Job: A New Commentary* (Jerusalem: Kiryath Sepher, 1957), pp. xxx-xl.

[28]A. Guillaume, "Arabic Background," pp. 106-127.

[29]See, e.g., M. Dahood, "Northwest Semitic Philology and Job," in *The Bible in Current Catholic Thought*, ed. by J. McKenzie (New York: Herder & Herder, 1962), pp. 55-74; A. Blommerde, *Northwest Semitic Grammar and Job*, BibOr 22 (Rome: Pontifical Biblical Institute, 1969); A. Ceresko, *Job 29–31 in the Light of Northwest Semitic*, BibOr 39 (Rome: Pontifical Biblical Institute, 1980); and M. Pope, *Job*, 1965.

[30]Origen's Hexapla used Theodotion's Greek translation to restore the lines missing from LXX. On the Hexapla and Origen's use of Theodotion cf. J.M. Dines, *The Septuagint* (Edinburgh: T & T Clark, 2004), pp. 97-103, esp. p. 100.

While it is possible that LXX had a different Hebrew text than MT as its basis, it is more likely that the Greek translators intentionally abridged certain parts of the book. This seems especially so in the speeches of Elihu (chs. 32–37) where many of the lines omitted in LXX are duplications and repetitions in the Hebrew. Though there is evidence that the Greek translators occasionally attempted to impose their theology on the Hebrew text,[31] their general goal seems to have been a faithful translation of the text before them.[32]

The early Aramaic translations and paraphrases known as Targums generally follow MT, only occasionally departing from the Hebrew, primarily on theological grounds. The oldest known Targum of Job comes from the Dead Sea Scrolls and is commonly dated in the second or first century B.C.[33] The early Christian-era Syriac version known as the Peshitta was translated directly from the Hebrew and sheds light on some of the more difficult language of the book.[34] Jerome's fourth-century Latin translation, though primarily from the Greek, employed insights from the Hebrew and the rabbinic traditions.

STRUCTURE[35]

The book of Job consists of a series of poetic speeches placed between a prose prologue and epilogue that together form the story of Job. This format, found elsewhere in the literature of the Bible and the ancient Near East, is made the vehicle of an intense theological debate over the role of God in human suffering. Dominant

---

[31]Cf. H. Gehman, "The Theological Approach of the Greek Translator of the Book of Job 1–15," *JBL* 68 (1949): 231-240.

[32]So concludes H. Orlinsky, "Studies in the Septuagint of the Book of Job," *HUCA* 28 (1957): 53-74; 29 (1958): 229-271; 30 (1959): 153-167; 32 (1961): 239-268; 33 (1962): 119-151; 35 (1964): 57-78.

[33]11QtgJob generally supports MT but at times seems not to understand it or to intentionally alter it for theological purposes. Cf. discussion in Pope, *Job*, pp. xlv-xlvii; Sokoloff, *Targum to Job*.

[34]Cf., L. Rignell, "Notes on the Peshitta of the Book of Job," *ASTI* 9 (1973): 98-106.

[35]Cf. R. Polzin, "The Framework of the Book of Job," *Int* 28 (1974): 182-200. Also P. Bowes, "The Structure of Job," *TBT* 20 (1982): 329-333; C.R. Seitz, "Job: Full Structure, Movement and Interpretation," *Int* 43 (1989): 5-17.

in the structure of Job is the literary feature of repetition.[36] This is not only true of repeated terms and themes, but of repeated patterns as well. The prologue, for example, features a repeated alternation between scene-in-heaven (1:6-12; 2:1-6) and scene-on-earth (1:7-22; 2:7-10). The speeches move forward through repeated cycles (4:1–14:22; 15:1–21:34; 22:1–26:14)[37] in which each of the friends speak and Job, in turn, responds. When Yahweh answers Job, he does so in a pair of related speeches (38:1–40:2; 40:6–41:34) to which Job, in turn, responds (40:3-5; 42:1-6). The prose epilogue (42:7-17) shows numerous connections with the prologue.[38] In addition, a wide variety of rhetorical and literary techniques are employed to develop the book's powerful plot. Wordplay, anticipation, irony, and parody are used masterfully to both build and resolve the tension of the story.[39] All of this suggests that the book of Job is a highly stylized and sophisticated piece of literature. Hardly a disparate collection of narrative and speech, as some have claimed, this masterful work displays significant internal cohesion and observable literary unity.

KINDS OF LITERATURE

There has been no shortage of suggestions concerning what kind of literature the book of Job represents. The following survey represents a sampling of suggested genres:

1. Job is *a lawsuit*. The רִיב (*rîb*; legal disputation) was a favorite genre of the biblical writers, especially the prophets. A number of scholars understand Job to be written in this style. According to Richter's analysis, the various sections of the book represent different stages of a lawsuit between Job and God. After a pretrial hearing (chs. 4–14) a formal trial follows (chs. 15–31). The absence of any reply by the friends to Job's oath of innocence

---

[36]Cf. Habel, *Job*, pp. 49-51.

[37]Most discussions of Job assign chs. 27–31 to the "dialogue" portion of the book. Our analysis understands the dialogue to end with chapter 26 and assigns chs. 27–31 (Job's final defense) to the "postdialogue."

[38]Cf. Hartley, *Job*, pp. 21-24.

[39]Cf. Habel, *Job*, pp. 49-60, 79-84.

(ch. 31) indicates that they concede the case to Job. The Elihu speeches (chs. 32–37) represent an appeal to this decision. Finally God appears to cross-examine Job (chs. 38–41). In response Job withdraws his complaint bringing about reconciliation between him and God (42:1-6).[40] In a similar treatment Gemser understands Job to be the plaintiff and prosecutor with God as defendant and then ultimately the judge. The friends are witnesses, as well as codefendants.[41] While there are legal forms and terms in Job, the lawsuit genre is insufficient to account for the form and content of the book as a whole.

2. Job is *a wisdom discourse*. Comparing Job to its ancient Near Eastern counterparts several scholars have identified Job as s specific kind of wisdom discourse known as "complaint and reconciliation." This genre is said to have the following components: account of human suffering; lamentation; divine intervention to heal the sufferer.[42] This view, however, fails to account for the controversy with the friends — the very heart of the present form of the book.

3. Job is *a dramatized lament*. Westermann and others argue that Job is too personal and poignant to be merely a wisdom discourse. Citing numerous parallels with the individual laments in the Psalms, they suggest that this is the genre most like the book.[43] These laments are given a dramatic setting in which the friends respond to Job's laments with disputations based upon orthodox theology. It is precisely on this point (the friends' disputations), however, where Job differs from the laments of the Psalms. This view also fails to properly account for the story of Job in the prologue and epilogue.

4. Job is *a parable* (מָשָׁל, *māšāl*). In the second century A.D. Rabbi Simeon ben-Laqish argued that Job was a fictional story designed

---

[40]H. Richter, *Studien zu Hiob: Der Aufbau des Hiobbuches dargestellt an den Gattungen des Rechtslebens* (Berlin: Evangelische Verlagsanstalt, 1959).

[41]B. Gemser, "The *Rib*- or Controversy-Pattern in Hebrew Mentality," *VTSupp* 3 (1955): 135.

[42]H. Gese, *Lehre und Wirtlichkeit in der alten Weisheit* (Tübingen: J.C.B. Mohr, 1958); also N.H. Snaith, *The Book of Job: Its Origin and Purpose* (Napierville, IL: A.R. Allenson, 1968).

[43]C. Westermann, *The Structure of the Book of Job: A Form-Critical Analysis*, trans. by C.A. Muenchow (Philadelphia: Fortress, 1981).

to convey a spiritual truth.[44] Some proponents of this theory understand the book to be a parable of Israel's struggle with the meaning of their national suffering under the Babylonians. It is true that Job's speeches are sometimes called *māšāl* (27:1–29:1) and that his great struggle is intended as spiritual instruction. However, the *māšāl* genre is never elsewhere applied to a work of such length and diversity in the Old Testament and, unlike most of the other parables of the Hebrew Bible, the "lesson" of Job is not explained.

5. Job is *a school lecture*. Job is seen by some to represent the instruction of a master teacher to his students concerning "God's supervision of the righteous and the wicked."[45] It is presumed that Israel's wisdom schools regularly discussed such issues as theodicy and the role of God in his world. The evidence concerning these schools, however, is scant, and we know virtually nothing about their curriculum. It should be further noted that, though the book of Job does teach, its genre is hardly didactic. For a didactic treatment of theodicy one would do better to consult a text like Psalm 37.

6. Job is *epic history*. Andersen compares Job to the stories of the patriarchs (Moses, David, Ruth) and identifies four characteristics that it shares with these "epics": economic presentation of events, objectivity in describing the actions of the major characters, restraint by the author in making moral judgments, and the use of speeches to reveal the struggle and faith of the characters.[46] None of these epics, however, come close to approaching Job when it comes to the length and intensity of its speeches. The proportion of speech to narrative is simply not comparable.

7. Job is *dramatic tragedy* in the pattern of the ancient Greeks.[47] While intriguing, this view is impossible to corroborate due to our lack of knowledge of dramatic presentation in ancient Israel

---

[44]Midrash *Gen.Rab. 67;* Talmud *B. Bat.*15a.

[45]M.B. Crook, *The Cruel God: Job's Search for the Meaning of Suffering* (Boston: Beacon Press, 1959), p. 5.

[46]Andersen, *Job*, pp. 36-37.

[47]H.M. Kallen, *The Book of Job as Greek Tragedy Restored* (New York: Moffat, Yard, and Co., 1918); also R.B. Sewall, *The Vision of Tragedy*, 2nd ed. (New Haven: Yale University Press, 1980), pp. 9-24. Cf. also, S. Terrien, "Book of Job."

prior to the second century B.C. Further, there are vast differences in content between Job and the Greek tragedies with regard to the role of the fates as compared to Job's God, as well as the moral flaws of the Greek protagonists in contrast with Job's integrity.

8. Job is *comedy*. Focusing on irony in the book, a number of scholars have suggested that Job represents an ancient form of comedy.[48] As such it is said to expose life's many absurdities and incongruities and the inability of conventional wisdom to satisfactorily account for them. A supposed comedic plot line ends with the hero ultimately finding happiness. This view, like the dramatic one, is difficult to corroborate from the biblical and ancient Near Eastern literature. Further, as Aharoni has argued, the so-called comedic elements in Job — irony, incongruity, and paradox — are also found in biblical tragedy.[49]

As this broad range of suggestions illustrates, attempts to assign Job to a specific genre have proven unsatisfactory. The book, in fact, employs a wide variety of literary forms. As Lasor eloquently argues:

> (Job) must not be fit into any preconceived mold. It does weep with complaint, argue with disputation, teach with didactic authority, excite with comedy, sting with irony, and relate human experience with epic majesty. But above all, Job is unique — the literary gift of an inspired genius.[50]

A careful analysis of Job reveals a diverse spectrum of literary devices employed by the author. The following list is merely representative of its multiple forms:

1. Lament: 6:2-27; 7:1-21; 9:17-28; 10:1-17; 13:13-28; 14:1-12,18-22; 16:2-17; 17:1-2,10-16; 19:2-20; 23:15-17; 26:2-4
2. Lawsuit: 9:2-4,14-16,19-20,29-33; 13:4-12,13-17,18-27; 23:3-7
3. Praise Hymn: 9:5-13; 10:8-12; 12:13-25; 23:8-9,13-14; 26:5-14; 28:1-28 (of wisdom)

---

[48]J.W. Whedbee, "The Comedy of Job," *Semeia* 7 (1977): 1-39; also J.A. Holland, "On the Form of the Book of Job," *AJBA* 2 (1972): 160-177.

[49]R. Aharoni, "An Examination of the Literary Genre of the Book of Job," *Tarbiz* 49 (1979): 1-13.

[50]W. Lasor, D. Hubbard, F. Bush, *Old Testament Survey* (Grand Rapids: Eerdmans, 1992), p. 487.

4. Petition (prayer): 6:8-10; 7:11-21; 14:13-17; 17:3-4; 19:23-24; 27:7-10
5. Disputation: 21:2-33; 24:1-17; 33:1-33; 34:5-33
6. Wisdom Instruction: 4:7-11; 12:7-12; 15:7-16; 34:10-30
7. Protest of Innocence: 6:28-30; 23:10-12; 27:2-6; 31:1-40 (oath of innocence)
8. Affirmation of Trust in God: 16:19-22; 19:25-27; 23:6-7
9. Proverb: 5:2,6ff; 6:14,25a; 12:5ff.; 13:28; 17:5; 22:2,21ff.
10. Interrogation: 38:4–39:30
11. Epic Narrative: 1:1–2:13; 42:7-17
12. Apology: 32:6-22; 33:1-7
13. Exhortation: 5:8,27; 8:5-7; 11:13-20
14. Numerical Saying: 5:19; 33:14,29-30; 40:5
15. Extended Metaphor: 6:15-21
16. Rhetorical Question: 4:7; 6:5f.,11f.,22f.; 7:12; 8:3,11; 9:12; 11:2f.,7f.,10f.; 12:9; 13;7-9; 15:2f.,7-9,11-14; 34:13,17-19,31-33; 36:19,22f.; 38:4-5,17,34.

UNITY

Is the book of Job the work of a single author, or is it a collection of once independent pieces from different authors? Those who argue for the latter have questioned the unity of Job along the following lines.

Prologue–Epilogue Narrative and the Poetic Speeches

It has long been argued that the story of Job found in the epilogue–prologue and the speeches that constitute the central portion of the book were once independent pieces of literature joined together by some editor.[51] Arguments for this distinction center first around differences in genre. The prologue–epilogue is narrative prose while the speeches are poetic dialogue. The joining of prose and poetry is not unique to Job in the Hebrew Bible, however, and

---

[51]Prevailing scholarly opinion treats the story of Job found in the prologue and epilogue to be an older legend about the hero; cf., e.g., Sarna, "Epic Substratum," pp. 13-25.

it is also attested in other ancient Near Eastern literature.[52] Further, the central position of dialogue in Hebrew narrative is a regular feature of this genre. It is also argued that the social setting of these two parts of the book conflict. In the story of Job he is portrayed as semi-nomadic, the owner of great herds, while in the speeches he is portrayed as a city dweller. This supposed tension disappears, however, when one considers that it was customary for many tribal chieftains to divide their time between the field and the city.[53] One should also remember that in the prologue all of Job's sons are said to have owned their own houses. Finally, it is argued that the Job of the prologue and the Job of the dialogue appear to be two entirely different persons with respect to their attitudes about God and life. The prologue ends with Job humbly submitting to the God who gives and takes away. But the speeches portray an angry and defiant Job who questions God's providence and curses the day of his birth.[54] The difference in Job's attitudes, however, can be accounted for on grounds other than different authors. As the rabbis first argued, the passage of time with its unrelenting suffering eventually took its toll on Job and resulted in his lashing out at God.

The story of Job, rather than conflicting with the speeches, is instead essential to our understanding of them. How can we fully appreciate the intensity of Job's suffering apart from knowing of his great loss? How can we understand his protest of innocence apart from God's evaluation of him as a good man? Indeed, who are these speakers and why have they come together to debate so intensely? Without the prologue we have difficulty even accounting for the rest of the book. The prologue not only introduces us to the speakers; it also lays the foundation for the very issue which they debate. Likewise, the verdict portion of the epilogue with its account of God's criticism of the friends and vindication of Job (42:7-9) confirms the

---

[52]Cf., e.g., the Egyptian "The Protests of the Eloquent Peasant," datable to the 21st century B.C.; also cf. discussion by N. Snaith, *The Book of Job: Its Origin and Purpose*, SBT 2/11 (London: SCM, 1966), pp. 2, 21, 27; G. Fohrer, "Zur Vorgeschichte und Komposition des Buches Hiob," *VT* 6 (1956): 249-267.

[53]Cf. M. Rowton, "Dimorphic Structure and the Tribal Elite," *Studia Instituti Anthropos* 28 (1976): 219-257.

[54]Cf., e.g., E. König, *Das Buch Hiob* (Gutersloh: C. Bertelsmann, 1929), pp. 3ff.

refutation of retributive justice established in the speeches and records the reconciliation of Job and the friends.

There are those who reject the final portion of the epilogue (42:10-17) as a later addition designed to make the book conform to more traditional theological models of divine justice. Its account of the restoration of Job is considered anticlimactic and is said to contradict the message of the speeches.[55] In large part this objection is the result of a misunderstanding of the basis for Job's restoration. Just as his initial suffering had nothing to do with any sin that he had committed, his restoration has nothing to do with any piety that he displayed. The divinely ordained suffering of the prologue was a "trial" of Job to determine if his piety was genuine. That trial is now ended and Job's piety has been proven true. The purpose of Job's affliction having been achieved, the epilogue appropriately concludes with an account of the end of Job's suffering and the restoration of his family and possessions. The epilogue closes the story of Job's epic struggle by bringing its hero full circle.[56] The Job of the prologue, righteous and blessed by God, is again the Job of the epilogue.[57] The importance of both the prologue and epilogue portions of the book is affirmed by the fact that both of the subsequent references to Job in the Bible emphasize information given about him in the narrative of the book. From the prologue we learn that Job is a righteous man (Ezek 14:14,20) and from the epilogue we learn that Job's patient endurance of his suffering resulted in God's gracious blessing of his life (Jas 5:11).

Hymn to Wisdom (Chapter 28)[58]

The Hymn to Wisdom found in chapter twenty-eight is viewed by several scholars as either unoriginal to the book or out of place in

---

[55]Cf., e.g., M. Buttenwieser, *Job* (New York: Macmillan, 1925), pp. 67ff.

[56]Cf. discussion by Rowley, *Job* (Grand Rapids: Eerdmans, 1978), pp. 8-9, 266-267.

[57]There are also obvious literary connections between the epilogue and prologue. Cf. discussion by N. Habel, *The Book of Job* (Philadelphia: Westminster, 1985), pp. 34-35; Fohrer, "Zur Vorgeschichte," pp. 249-267.

[58]The LXX version of the hymn is considerably shorter than the Hebrew version; cf. discussion of the potential reasons behind this by P. Zerafa, *The Wisdom of God in the Book of Job* (Rome: Herder, 1978), pp. 130-136.

its present location.[59] It differs from the speeches that precede and follow it in that it is not addressed to God or to the friends and seems to constitute an exalted, self-contained hymn in praise of wisdom. It is hard to see it coming from the lips of Job, for its contemplative nature seems a radical departure from Job's troubled laments or his very personal protests of innocence. It is likewise difficult to hear it on the lips of one of the friends whose speeches have to this point been rather terse and combative.

If, as the book seems to suggest, it was spoken by Job, then we may understand the hymn as Job's attempt to disqualify the friends as authoritative interpreters of God's designs by insisting that only God knows the way of wisdom. Alternatively, we could understand the hymn in its present location as a transitional poem attributable to the author, designed to bring formal closure to the debate by censuring the friends for their inability to comprehend God's management of his world. It is indeed this very point that is the focus of the poem. If, as many have argued, it is independent commentary offered by the author, it should be understood as a bridge connecting the dialogues (chs. 4–27) with the concluding speeches (29:1–42:6) by emphasizing the point which they will ultimately make: the eternal wisdom which lies behind the grand design of the cosmos simply cannot be comprehended by mortal men. The meaning of undeserved suffering or any other mystery of the universe can only be found in the God who gives wisdom and who "alone knows where it dwells" (28:23).

Speeches of Elihu (Chapters 32–37)

The speeches of Elihu (32:1–37:24) are rejected as interpolations by many critics who see them as having little literary value and contributing nothing to the book's message.[60] Evidence for Elihu as a late intruder is also adduced from the fact that he is not mentioned in either the prologue or the epilogue. It should be noted, however, that the prose introduction to his speeches (32:1-5) explains his

---

[59]Cf., e.g., A. Robert and A. Feuillet, *Introduction to the Old Testament* (New York: Scribner's and Sons, 1968), pp. 425ff.; Rowley, *Job,* pp. 13ff.

[60]Cf., e.g., J. Eichhorn, *Einleitung in das Alte Testament* (Leipzig: Weidmann, 1803), pp. 597ff.

omission from the prologue. When one considers his absence from the epilogue, it should be noted that Satan and Job's wife are likewise absent even though they too have played key roles in the drama. The fact that he does not receive censure like the other friends may be accounted for on the basis that he is presented as a more neutral figure criticizing both Job and the friends.

The Elihu speeches are also said to differ in language and style from those of the other friends. He prefers a different name for God, quotes from earlier portions of the book, and employs a number of Aramaic terms.[61] As Snaith has argued, however, these stylistic differences are not significant enough to posit another author. In fact numerous parallels between the speeches of Elihu and the other speeches can also be found.[62]

In their present location these speeches should be understood as preparation for the Yahweh speeches. After summarizing the arguments of Job and the friends and exposing their inability to adequately resolve the issue of God's role in Job's undeserved suffering, Elihu's speeches offer new perspectives on Job's dilemma that Yahweh himself will affirm. Further, through his use of the "storm" motif as a metaphor of how God "speaks," Elihu sets the stage for God to actually appear and speak in "the storm" (38:1) in what constitutes the climactic scene in this great drama.

Though challenges to the authenticity of the third cycle of speeches (chs. 22–27)[63] and the second Yahweh speech (40:15–41:34 [MT 26])[64] have also been made, the tendency of more recent scholarship is to take the book on its own terms and seek to understand it in its full and final form.[65]

---

[61]Cf., e.g., G. Fohrer, "Die Weisheit des Elihu (Hi 32–37)," *AfO* 19 (1959–60): 83-94.

[62]Snaith, *Job*, pp. 72-91.

[63]Cf., e.g., G. Barton, "The Composition of Job 24–30," *JBL* 30 (1911): 66-67.

[64]Cf., e.g., Westermann, *Structure*, pp. 105-123.

[65]Cf., e.g., Carol Newsom, *The Book of Job: A Contest of Moral Imaginations* (Oxford: Clarendon Press, 2003). Habel (*Job*, pp. 25–35) has argued convincingly from literary grounds that the structure and flow of the book suggest it was fashioned as a coherent unity with each part of the book advancing a common plot:

Movement I: God Afflicts the Hero – the Hidden Conflict (1:2-2:20)
Movement II: The Hero Challenges God – The Conflict Explored
    (2:11-31:40)

SUMMARY OF CONTENTS

Located outside of Israel in the land of Uz, the story of Job opens with a portrait of the hero as the most righteous and most wealthy man of his times. Blessed with flocks, herds, servants, and an ideal family, Job is in every way the pious man on whom God's blessing rests. The scene then shifts to a heavenly tribunal where an accuser appears before the Lord. In response to the Lord's approval of Job's righteousness the accuser challenges not Job's pious deeds but the motivation behind them. "Does Job fear God for nothing?" he impugns. The implication of his challenge is obvious. Job serves God only because it brings him personal benefit. "But stretch out your hand and strike everything he has, and he will surely curse you to your face." God accepts the challenge as proposed by the accuser, and this acceptance determines the plot of the book. God allows the accuser to afflict Job with great suffering in order to test the genuineness of his piety. On a single day Job loses all of his possession and his ten children. But instead of cursing God he falls to the ground in worship and praises the name of the Lord. Not dissuaded, the accuser approaches the Lord a second time, insisting that the test needed to be intensified. "Stretch out your hand and strike his flesh and bones, and he will surely curse you to your face." Again God agrees and allows the accuser to afflict Job with painful sores. Though chided by his wife, Job does not disavow his God but instead defends him.

But when three friends of Job — Eliphaz, Bildad, and Zophar — approach him to offer comfort, they are met by a man with a different temperament. From his opening speech Job is resentful of his dire situation and begins to question the propriety of God's actions toward him. Protesting his innocence he accuses God of being unjust, even cruel. Struck by Job's impious spirit the friends confront Job, relentlessly defending the appropriateness of God's

---

Movement III: God Challenges the Hero — The Conflict Resolved (32:1–42:17)

In this model the Elihu speeches are seen as a deliberate anticlimax intended to heighten the final, unexpected impact of the Yahweh speeches. As such they are consistent with the style, plot, and thematic progresssion of the rest of the book.

actions. "God sees to it that men get what they deserve," they argue. "If you suffer, it is because you have sinned. Repent and you will be restored." There follows an intense debate over the justice of God which, though long and protracted, produces no meeting of the minds. When Job and the friends have run out of words, a young man, Elihu, speaks up with some observations of his own. But when he finishes speaking, the dilemma created by Job's suffering remains unsolved. Finally the Lord himself appears in a great storm. Not directly addressing the issue of Job's suffering or God's role in it, he instead bombards Job with a series of questions about the world God has created and now rules. Unable to answer God, Job finally confesses his ignorance, affirms God's limitless power, and repents in dust and ashes.

After condemning the friends for misrepresenting him and commanding Job to pray for their forgiveness, God vindicates Job by restoring his health and family, giving him twice as many possessions as he had before. The story ends with Job living out the rest of his long life in happiness, dying "old and full of years."

THEOLOGICAL THEMES

The book of Job makes important contributions to our understanding of the faith of ancient Israel. The story of Job's undeserved suffering and his search for the meaning of God's role in it gives rise to a theological discussion that is as provocative as it is profound. Some of the issues explored by the book, though addressed elsewhere in the Old Testament, are discussed more fully and with greater intensity in Job than any other book of the Bible.

JOB AND THEODICY

Whether it be Yahweh's dialogue with Abraham over the impending destruction of Sodom (Gen 18:16-33) or the prophets explaining the reasons behind God's impending destruction of Jerusalem (cf., e.g., Jer 7:1-34; Ezek 8:1-18), the Old Testament abounds with efforts to explain or defend the justice of God. The book of Job likewise addresses this important subject. It does so by debating one of ancient Israel's most widely held models of divine justice — retribution. The Hebrew Scriptures claim that there is often a direct correlation between sin and suffering as the judgment of a righteous God against human sin (cf., e.g., Deut 11:13-17; 28; Hos 8:7; 10:12,13; Psalm 37; Prov 12:21; 22:8). Job's friends went so far as to argue that there are no exceptions to this rule and insisted that retributive justice was the exclusive moral principle by which God ruled his world.[66] By confronting us with the story of a good man who yet suffers, the book of Job takes exception to this teaching. It suggests that suffering is not always related to sin and that God does not always see to it that every human behavior is met by reward or punishment.[67]

This does not mean, however, that the book teaches that there is no such thing as divine justice or a moral order by which God governs the universe.[68] A careful reading of the entire book of Job simply does not support such a conclusion. In the prologue, for example, the author goes out of his way to explain the divinely sanctioned affliction of Job. While, from a retributive perspective, Job's suffering was not "deserved" as punishment for some sin (cf. 1:1,8; 2:3), neither was it purposeless or malevolent. It was specifically designed to "test" the genuineness of Job's piety (cf. 1:8-11; 2:3-6). Further, when Yahweh finally appears to "answer" Job, he repeatedly challenges Job's impugning of his just rule (40:2,8). Thus, while the book does indeed rebut the friends' extreme model of retribution, it also defends the propriety of God's presiding over Job's affliction. By portraying the suffering of Job as a divinely sanctioned test of Job's piety it offers an explanation of God's afflicting of the saints that is not contradictory to the Old Testament's larger definition of divine justice.[69]

---

[66]The Old Testament, however, is full of examples of exceptions to this rule. On the one hand it acknowledges that innocent people do suffer. Abel and Naboth committed no sins, yet God permitted them to suffer at the hands of others. On the other hand the Old Testament acknowledges that God does not always punish the guilty. Again and again he forgives wayward Israel and provides redemption for human sin through the ritual of animal sacrifice.

[67]Some interpreters go so far as to insist that the book was written for the specific purpose of refuting the doctrine of retribution and that it teaches that God is not "just"; cf., e.g., M. Tsevat, "The Meaning of the Book of Job," *HUCA* 37 (1966): 73-108.

[68]Contra Tsevat and many others.

[69]The portrayal of God in Genesis, for example, is likewise a portrait of a deity who is both just and a tester of the saints (Gen 22:1ff).

JOB AND PIETY

The theme of religious devotion to God is given a great deal of attention in the book of Job. Job is introduced as a pious man in the prologue (1:1,4-6), and God himself twice praises his righteousness (1:8; 2:3). Job's initial responses to his undeserved suffering are likewise noted to be free of any "sin" (1:22b; 2:10b). Throughout the speeches, Job vigorously defends his integrity (cf., e.g., 9:21; 13:17-24; 19:6-7) and even challenges God to show Job his sin in his final oath of innocence (31:1-40; esp. vv. 35-36). Though Yahweh takes exception to Job's ignorant and presumptuous challenges against his just rule (40:2,8), he nonetheless affirms Job's integrity in his final verdict (42:7-9) and, by restoring Job (42:10-17), vindicates him as a good man blessed by God.

Even more important for the book's discussion of religious devotion is its exploration of exactly what true piety is. In the event which sets the book's plot in motion, an "accuser" impugns Job's piety as self-serving and insincere. Satan charged that Job's devotion to God was driven purely by the desire for reward. He then proposed that God deprive Job of every tangible blessing as a means of exposing Job's religious self-interest (1:9-11). Yahweh's acceptance of this challenge affirms the legitimacy of the accuser's contention that if Job is pious only because it pays, he is not pious at all. The devastating suffering that follows is permitted by Yahweh to test this very issue. Job, of course, passes this test. Bewildered and even angered by his suffering, he questions God and even challenges God. But he never forsakes his faith in God (cf. 13:15; 19:23-27). In the end, without reward or rationale, he humbly resubmits himself to his Maker (42:1-6). In so doing he personifies what the book defines as true piety — to love and serve God simply for who he is regardless of what blessing or reward he might choose to offer the believer (cf. 1:20-21; 2:9-10).

JOB AND THE LIMITS OF HUMAN KNOWLEDGE

One of the major teachings of the book of Job is that the ways of God are beyond the capacity of humans to know and fully understand. According to the prologue the challenge which precipitated Job's suffering occurred in heaven, and neither Job nor the friends were aware of it. Nonetheless, in their speeches both the friends and Job boldly claimed to "know" the cause of Job's suffering. The friends "know" that Job is being punished for some sin (cf., e.g., 4:8; 11:6; 22:4-5). Job "knows" that God is unjustly afflicting him (cf., e.g., 9:21-22; 19:6-7). As Yahweh's speeches (cf. 38:2ff) and Yahweh's verdict (42:7-9) make clear, however, Job and the friends do not know the reason for Job's suffering, or, for that matter, virtually anything else about how God runs his world. The Hymn to Wisdom (ch. 28) proclaims that God alone "understands" the meaning behind his ways and he alone "knows" where wisdom "dwells" (28:23; cf. vv. 12,13). Elihu adds, "God does great things beyond our understanding" (37:5). Job finally acknowledges his ignorance of God's ways confessing, "I spoke of things which I did not understand, things too wonderful for me to know" (42:3). The friends, by their obedient response to Yahweh's verdict, likewise acknowledge the erroneous presumption of their claims to know what God was doing in Job's life (42:9). The emphasis given to the inscrutability of God's ways in the book suggests that believers should exercise great caution in their theological assumptions, especially when they apply them to the lives of others. Theology is an inexact science that should be practiced with the kind of humility that acknowledges that God's ways are beyond humankind.

JOB AND THE NATURE AND CHARACTER OF GOD

The book of Job is arguably the most theological book of the Old Testament. Whatever else it is about, it is about God. The book's portrait of God focuses on two different aspects of his nature. First and foremost, the God of Job is sovereign. He rules over the world he has made, and before him everyone and everything bows. In the prologue he is pictured as the king of a heavenly court to whom the "sons of god" (angels) report and give account (1:6; 2:1a). The "accuser," too, answers to God (2:1b) and can only do what God permits him to do (1:12b; 2:6b). In the speeches, both Job and the friends acknowledge God's uncontestable power to rule his world (cf., e.g., Eliphaz, 4:18-19; Job, 12:13-25; Bildad, 25:2-4; cf. also Elihu, 36:22-26). When Yahweh speaks he draws a contrast between his omnipotence and Job's impotence (40:9ff), insisting that it is he who presides over any encounter that he has with humans (38:3; 40:7). As Maker of heaven and earth and Lord of his creation he is not answerable to humans, obligated to explain his behavior to any mortal, or required to behave in accordance with anyone's systematic theology or self-righteous expectations (cf., e.g., 40:2,8; 41:11). Job, who in defense of his integrity presumed to challenge God and demand vindication from him (cf., e.g., 31:35-37), is finally reconciled to his Maker by acknowledging God's sovereignty and bowing before him in humble submission (40:3-5; 42:1-6).

This God who sits enthroned above the heavens is also intimately involved in the lives of his creatures. The transcendent God is also immanent. He is a God of providence. Though he will not be obligated by any mortal, he is, nonetheless, attentive to their world. He acknowledges Job's piety (1:8; 2:3), takes the "accuser's" challenge to that piety seriously, and personally presides over Job's "trials." He patiently endures Job's impugning of his ways, and in the end does appear to "answer" Job (38:1). He then goes on to vindicate Job (42:7-9) and restore his health and wealth (42:10-17). Job's belief that God had abandoned him was proved wrong, and, in the light of Yahweh's appearance, his understanding of God is transformed (42:5).

OUTLINE

BIBLIOGRAPHY

SELECTED BIBLIOGRAPHY

1. Commentaries and Major Works

Andersen, F.E. *Job*. Tyndale Old Testament Commentaries. London/Downers Grove, IL: Tyndale/InterVarsity, 1976.

Blommerde, A.C.M. *Northwest Semitic Grammar and Job*. Rome: Pontifical Biblical Institute, 1969.

Budde, K.R.R. *Das Buch Hiob*. Göttingen: Vandenhoeck & Ruprecht, 1913.

Buttenweiser, M. *The Book of Job*. Chicago: University of Chicago Press, 1922.

Clines, D. *Job 1–20*. Word Biblical Commentary 17. Dallas: Word Books, 1989.

_____. *Job 21–37*. Word Biblical Commentary 18. Dallas: Word Books, 2006.

Delitzsch, F. *Biblical Commentary on the Book of Job*. Trans. by F. Bolton. 2 vols. Grand Rapids: Eerdmans, 1949.

Dhorme, E. *A Commentary of the Book of Job*. London: Thomas Nelson & Sons, 1967.

Driver, S.R., and G.G. Gray. *The Book of Job*. International Critical Commentary. Edinurgh: T. & T. Clark, 1921.

Duhm, B. *Das Buch Hiob*. Tübingen: J.B.B. Mohr, 1897.

Fohrer, G. *Das Buch Hiob*. Kommentar zum Alten Testament 16. Gütersloh: Gütersloher Verlagshaus Gerd Mohn, 1963.

Gordis, R. *The Book of Job: Commentary, New Translation and Special Notes*. New York: Jewish Theological Seminary of America, 1978.

Grabbe, L.L. *Comparative Philology and the Text of Job*. SBL Dissertation Series 34. Missoula, MT: Scholars Press, 1977.

Greenberg, M., J.C. Greenfield, and N.H. Sarna. *The Book of Job: A New Translation according to the Traditional Hebrew Text*. Philadelphia: Jewish Publication Society of America, 1980.

Guillaume, A. *Studies in the Book of Job, with a New Translation*. Leiden: E.J. Brill, 1968.

Habel, N. *The Book of Job*. Philadelphia: Westminster, 1985.

Holscher, G. *Das Buch Hiob*. HAT. Tübingen: J.C.B. Mohr, 1937.

Horst, F. *Hiob*. Biblischer Kommentar Altes Testament 16/1 (Chs. 1–19). Neukirchen: Neukirchener Verlag, 1960.

Jansen, G. *Job*. Interpretation. Atlanta: John Knox, 1985.

Keel, O. *Jahwes Entgegnung an Iob*. Göttingen: Vandenhoeck & Ruprecht, 1978.

Kissane, E.J. *The Book of Job*. Dublin: Browne & Nolan, 1939.

Kubina, V. *Die Gottesreden im Buche Hiob*. Roma: Herder, 1979.

Léveque, J. *Job et son Dieu*. 2 vols. Paris: J. Gabalda, 1970.

Newsom, C.A. *The Book of Job: A Contest of Moral Imaginations*. Oxford: Oxford University Press, 2003.

Peake, A.A. *Job*. The Century Bible. London: T. C. & E. C. Jack, 1904.

Pope, M. *Job*. The Anchor Bible. 3rd ed. Garden City, NY: Doubleday, 1973.

Richter, H. *Studien zu Hiob*. Berlin: Evangelische Verlagsanstalt, 1959.

Rowley, H.H. *The Book of Job*. New Century Bible. Grand Rapids: Eerdmans, 1970.

Snaith, N. *The Book of Job: Its Origin and Purpose*. London: SCM Press, 1968.

Tur-Sinai, N.H. *The Book of Job*. Jerusalem: Kiryath Sepher, 1957.

Weiser, A. *Das Buch Hiob*. Göttingen: Vandenhoeck & Ruprecht, 1951.

Westermann, C. *The Structure of the Book of Job: A Form-Critical Analysis*. Trans. by C. Muenchow. Philadelphia: Fortress, 1981.

Wilde, A. de. *Das Buch Hiob*. Oudtestamentische Studiën 22. Leiden: E.J. Brill, 1981.

Zuckerman, B. *Job the Silent: A Study in Historical Counterpoint*. New York: Oxford University Press, 1991

2. Special Studies and Articles

Aharoni, R. "An Examination of the Literary Genre of the Book of Job." *Tarbiz* 49 (1979): 1-13.

Alt, A. "Zur Vorgeschichte des Buches Hiob." *ZAW* 55 (1937): 265-268.

Baker, J.A. "The Book of Job: Unity and Meaning." JSOTSupp 11 (1978): 17-26.

Barr, J. "The Book of Job and Its Modern Interpreters." *BJRL* 54 (1971–72): 28-46.

Boecker, H.J. *Redeformen des Rechtsleben im Alten Testament*. Neukirchen: Neukirchener Verlag, 1963.

Brenner, A. "God's Answer to Job." *VT* 31 (1981): 129-137.

_____ . "Job the Pious? The Characterization of Job in the Narrative Framework of the Book." *JSOT* 43 (1989): 37-52.

Ceresko, A.R. *Job 29–31 in the Light of Northwest Semitic*. Rome: Biblical Institute Press, 1980.

Clines, D. "False Naivety in the Prologue of Job." *HAR* 9 (1985): 127-136.

_____ . "Job 5:1-8: A New Exegesis." *Bib* 62 (1981): 185-194.

_____ . "Verbal Modality and the Interpretation of Job 4:20-21." *VT* 30 (1980): 354-357.

Cooper, A. "Reading and Misreading the Prologue of Job. "*JSOT* 46 (1990): 67-79.

Couroyer, B. "Qui est Behemoth?" *RB* 82 (1975): 418-443.

Cox, D. "Structure and Function of the Final Challenge: Job 29–31." *PIBA* 5 (1981): 55-71.

Crenshaw, J.L. "Popular Questioning of the Justice of God in Ancient Israel." *ZAW* 82 (1970): 380-393.

Curtis, J.B. "On Job's Witness in Heaven." *JBL* 102 (1983): 549-562.

Dahood, M. "Northwest Semitic Philology and Job." In *The Bible in Current Catholic Thought*, pp. 55-74. Ed. by J. McKenzie. New York: Herder & Herder, 1962.

_____. "Some Northwest-Semitic Words in Job." *Bib* 38 (1957): 306-320.

Dell, K.J. *The Book of Job as Sceptical Literature*. BZAW 197. Berlin: Walter de Gruyter, 1991.

Dick, M.B. "Job 31, the Oath of Innocence, and the Sage." *ZAW* 95 (1983): 31-51.

_____. "The Legal Metaphor in Job 31." *CBQ* 41 (1979): 37-50.

Driver, G.R. "Problems in the Hebrew Text of Job." *VTSupp* 3 (1960): 72-93.

Fishbane, M. "Jer. 4 and Job 3: A Recovered Use of the Creation Pattern." *VT* 21 (1971): 151-167.

Fohrer, G. "The Righteous Man in Job 31." In *Essays in Old Testament Ethics*, pp. 3-22. Ed. by J.L. Crenshaw and J.T. Willis. New York: KTAV, 1974.

_____. *Studien zum Buche Hiob*. Gütersloh: Güttersloher Verlagshaus Gerd Mohn, 1963.

Freedman, D.N. "The Elihu Speeches in the Book of Job." *HTR* 61 (1968): 51-59.

_____. "The Structure of Job 3." *Bib* 49 (1968): 503-508.

Fullerton, K. "Double Entendre in the First Speech of Eliphaz." *JBL* 49 (1930): 320-341.

Gammie, J.G. "Behemoth and Leviathan: On the Didactic and Theological Significance of Job 40:15–41:26." In *Israelite Wisdom*, pp. 217-231. Ed. by J.G. Gammie et al. Missoula, MT: Scholars Press, 1978.

Gard, D.H. *The Exegetical Method of the Greek Translator of the Book of Job*. SBL Monograph Series 8 (Philadelphia: SBL, 1952).

Geller, S.A. "'Where Is Wisdom?': A Literary Study of Job 28 in Its Settings." In *Judaic Perspectives on Ancient Israel*, pp. 155-188. Ed.

by J. Neusner, B. Levine, and E.S. Frerichs. Philadelphia: Fortress, 1987.

Glatzer, N.N., ed. *The Dimensions of Job: A Study and Selected Readings.* New York: Schocken Books, 1969.

Good, E.M. *In Turns of Tempest: A Reading of Job with Translation.* Stanford, CA: Stanford University Press, 1987.

Gordis, R. *The Book of God and Man: A Study of Job.* Chicago: University of Chicago Press, 1965.

_____ . "Virtual Quotations in Job, Sumer and Qumran." *VT* 31 (1981): 410-427.

Gordon, D. "Leviathan: Symbol of Evil." In *Biblical Motifs*, pp. 1-10. Ed. by A. Altmann. Cambridge, MA: Harvard University Press, 1966.

Gray, J. "The Book of Job in the Context of Near Eastern Literature." *ZAW* 82 (1970): 251-269.

Habel, N. "Of Things beyond Me: Wisdom in the Book of Job." *CTM* 10 (1983): 142-154.

_____ . "The Role of Elihu in the Design of the Book of Job." In *In The Shelter of Elyon: Essays on Palestinian Life and Literature in Honor of G.W. Ahlstrom.* JSOTSupp 31. Sheffield: JSOT Press, 1984.

Hoffman, Y. "The Relation between the Prologue and the Speech Cycles in Job: A Reconsideration." *VT* 31 (1981): 160-170.

_____ . "The Use of Equivocal Words in the First Speech of Eliphaz (Job 4–5)." *VT* 30 (1980): 114-118.

Hurvitz, A. "The Date of the Prose Tale of Job Linguistically Reconsidered." *HTR* 67 (1974): 17-34.

Irwin, W.A. "Job's Redeemer." *JBL* 81 (1962): 217-229.

Kallen, H. *The Book of Job as a Greek Tragedy.* New York: Moffat, Yard & Co., 1918.

Kluger, R.S. *Satan in the Old Testament.* Evanston, IL: Northwestern University Press, 1967.

Kramer, S.N. "'Man and His God': A Sumerian Variation on the 'Job' Motif." *VTSupp* 3 (1960): 179-182.

Laurin, R. "The Theological Structures of Job." *ZAW* 84 (1972): 86-92.

Lévêque, J. "Anamnèse et discupation: la conscience du juste en Job 29–31." In *La sagesse de l'Ancien Testament,* pp. 231-248. Ed. by M. Gilbert. Louvain: Leuven University Press, 1980.

Linafelt, T. "The Undecidability of *BRK* in the Prologue to Job and Beyond." *Biblical Interpretation* 4 (1996): 154-172.

Lugt, P. van der. *Rhetorical Criticism and the Book of Job.* Oudtestamentische Studien 32. Leiden: E.J. Brill, 1995.

Maag, V. *Hiob: Wandlung und Verarbeitung des Problems in Novelle, Dialogdichtung und Spätfassungen.* Göttingen: Vandenhoeck & Ruprecht, 1982.

MacDonald, D.B. "The Original Form of the Legend of Job." *JBL* 14 (1895): 63-71.

Mattingly, G.L. "The Pious Sufferer: Mesopotamia's Traditional Theodicy and Job's Counselors." In *The Bible in the Light of Cuneiform Literature: Scripture in Context III,* pp. 305-348. Ed. by W. Hallo, B. Jones, and G. Mattingly. Lewiston, ME: Edwin Mellen, 1990.

McKenzie, R.A.F. "The Purpose of the Yahweh Speeches in the Book of Job." *Bib* 40 (1959): 435-445.

Meek, T.J. "Job 19:25ff." *VT* 6 (1956): 99-103.

Mettinger, T.N.D. "The God of Job: Avenger, Tyrant, or Victor?" In *The Voice from the Whirlwind: Interpreting the Book of Job,* pp. 39-49. Ed. by L. Perdue, W. Gilpin. Nashville: Abingdon, 1992.

Michel, L.W. *The Ugaritic Texts and the Mythological Expressions in the Book of Job, Including a New Translation of and Philological Notes on the Book.* Ph.D. dissertation. Madison, WI: University of Wisconsin, 1970.

Moore, R.D. "The Integrity of Job." *CBQ* 45 (1983): 17-31.

Morrow, W. "Consolation, Rejection, and Repentance in Job 42:6." *JBL* 105 (1986): 211-225.

Mowinckel, S. "Hiobs *go'el* und Zeuge im Himmel." *BZAW* 41 (1925): 207-222.

Müller, H.-P. *Das Hiobproblem: seine Stellung und Entstehung im alten Orient und im alten Testament.* 3rd ed. Erträge der Forschung 84. Darmstadt: Wissenschaftliche Buchgesellschaft, 1995.

Nemo, P. *Job and the Excess of Evil*. Trans. by M. Kigel. Pittsburgh: Duquesne University Press, 1998.

Newsom, C.A. "The Book of Job: Introduction, Commentary, and Reflections." In *The New Interpreter's Bible*, 4:317-637. Nashville: Abingdon, 1996.

Nougayrol, J. "Une version ancienne du 'juste souffrant.'" *RB* 59 (1952): 237-250.

Orlinsky, H. "Studies in the Septuagint of Job." *HUCA* 28 (1957): 53-74; 29 (1958): 229-271; 30 (1959): 153-157; 32 (1961): 239-268; 33 (1962): 119-151; 35 (1964): 57-78; 36 (1965): 37-47.

Patrick, D. "The Translation of Job 42:6." *VT* 26 (1976): 369-371.

Reddy, M.P. "The Book of Job — A Reconstruction." *ZAW* 90 (1978): 49-94.

Richter, G. *Textstudien zum Buche Hiob*. Stuttgart: W. Kohlhammer, 1927.

Richter, H. "Die Naturweisheit des Alten Testaments im Buche Hiob." *ZAW* 70 (1958): 1-20.

Roberts, J.J. "Job and the Israelite Religious Tradition." *ZAW* 89 (1977): 107-114.

_____. "Job's Summons to Yahweh: The Exploitation of a Legal Metaphor." *ResQ* 16 (1973): 159-165.

Rowald, H.L. "Yahweh's Challenge to Rival: The Form and Function of the Yahweh-Speeches in Job 38–39." *CBQ* 47 (1985): 199-211.

Rowley, H.H. "The Book of Job and Its Meaning." *BJRL* 41 (1958): 167-207.

Ruprecht, E. "Das Nilpferd im Hiobbuch." *VT* 21 (1971): 209-231.

Sarna, N.M. "Epic Substratum in the Prose of Job." *JBL* 76 (1957): 13-25

_____. "The Mythological Background of Job 18." *JBL* 82 (1963): 315-318.

Scholnick, S.H. "Lawsuit Drama in the Book of Job." Ph.D. dissertation. Waltham, MA: Brandeis University, 1975.

Seitz, C. "Job: Full-Structure, Movement, and Interpretation." *Int* 43 (1989): 5-17.

Skehan, P. "Strophic Patterns in the Book of Job." *CBQ* 23 (1961): 125-142.

Stevenson, W.B. *Critical Notes on the Hebrew Text of the Poem of Job.* Aberdeen: Aberdeen University Press, 1951.

_____. *The Poem of Job.* Oxford: Oxford University Press, 1947.

Terrien, S. "The Book of Job: Introduction and Exegesis." *The Interpreter's Bible.* Vol. 3. Nashville: Abingdon Press, 1954.

_____. "The Yahweh Speeches and Job's Response." *RevExp* 58 (1971): 497-509.

Tsevat, M. "The Meaning of the Book of Job." *HUCA* 37 (1966): 73-106.

Urbrock, W. "Job as Drama: Tragedy or Comedy?" *CTM* 8 (1981): 35-40.

Von Rad, G. "Job 38 and Ancient Egyptian Wisdom." In *The Problem of the Hexateuch and Other Essays*, pp. 281-291. Edinburgh: Oliver & Boyd, 1966.

Waterman, L. "Note on Job 19:23-27: Job's Triumph of Faith." *JBL* 69 (1950): 379-381.

Weinfeld, M. "Job and Its Mesopotamian Parallels: A Typological Analysis." In *Text and Context: Old Testament and Semitic Studies for F.C. Fensham*, pp. 217-226. Ed. by W. Classen. Sheffield: JSOT Press, 1988.

Whedbee, W. "The Comedy of Job." *Semeia* 7 (1970): 1-39.

Wilcox, J.T. *The Bitterness of Job.* Ann Arbor, MI: University of Michigan Press, 1989.

Williams, R.J. "Theodicy in the Ancient Near East." *Canadian Journal of Theology* 2 (1956): 14-26.

Wilson, J.V. Kinnier. "A Return to the Problem of Behemoth and Leviathan." *VT* 25 (1975): 1-14.

Wolde, E.J. van. "Job 42, 1-6: The Reversal of Job." In *The Book of Job.* Ed. by W. Beuken. Louvain: Louven University Press, 1994.

Wolfers, D. "The Speech-Cycles in the Book of Job." *VT* 43 (1993): 385-402.

Zerafa, P.P. *The Wisdom of God in the Book of Job.* Roma: Herder, 1978.

Zink, J.K. "Impatient Job: An Interpretation of Job 19:25-27." *JBL* 84 (1965): 147-152.

JOB 1

I. THE PREDIALOGUE (1:1–3:26)

A. PROLOGUE (1:1–2:13)

The prologue introduces us to the poetic core of the book by telling us the story of Job. It does so in classic Hebrew prose. The account moves swiftly and powerfully through six scenes that depict Job's devastating suffering and his pious response. In a manner that is highly stylized and relentlessly efficient, the author masterfully develops the principal characters and the compelling plot of this great drama in the span of a few brief verses. In a story of epic proportions heaven looks down on the struggle for a human soul in whom God himself has a stake.

1. Job and His Family (1:1-5)

¹In the land of Uz there lived a man whose name was Job. This man was blameless and upright; he feared God and shunned evil. ²He had seven sons and three daughters, ³and he owned seven thousand sheep, three thousand camels, five hundred yoke of oxen and five hundred donkeys, and had a large number of servants. He was the greatest man among all the people of the East.

⁴His sons used to take turns holding feasts in their homes, and they would invite their three sisters to eat and drink with them. ⁵When a period of feasting had run its course, Job would send and have them purified. Early in the morning he would sacrifice a burnt offering for each of them, thinking, "Perhaps my children have sinned and cursed God in their hearts." This was Job's regular custom.

1:1 The opening line of the account departs from the normal formula for introducing historical narrative.[1] This construction, **there was a man** (lit., "a man there was") indicates the beginning of an independent narrative unconnected with what precedes it like Nathan's parable (2 Sam 12:1) and the stories of Micah (Judg 17:1) and Mordecai (Esth 2:5). The precise location of Job's home is unknown. Some biblical passages suggest a location near Edom (Gen 36:28; Lam 4:21). Other texts seem to connect **Uz** with Aram (Gen 10:22,23; 22:21). This northern location is supported by Josephus[2] who says that Uz founded Trachonitis and Damascus. The Greek appendix to Job locates his home "on the borders of Idumea and Arabia," while Byzantine and Arab tradition place it northeast of Palestine in Hauran.[3]

The meaning of Job's name (אִיּוֹב, 'Iyôb) has long been debated. One tradition connects it with the Hebrew אֹיֵב ('yb, "enmity, hostility"). Some who favor this etymology understand the name to be artificially constructed to characterize Job as one who actively opposes God, who sees himself as God's "enemy." The term has also been understood in a passive sense to describe Job as the victim, the object of God's enmity (cf. 13:24). Though this fits well with the story of Job, there is little philological evidence to support this view. Another theory connects 'Iyôb to Arabic 'wb, "return, repent." This is said to fit the epilogue of the book which portrays Job as "the penitent one." More recently scholars have connected 'Iyōb with the Northwest Semitic 'Ayyab and taken it to mean, "Where is Father?" It has been suggested that this name reflects Job's cry for God to reveal himself. Though the original meaning of "Job" is unclear, the name was a common one and is widely attested in the literature of the ancient Near Eastern world.[4]

---

[1]See M. Weiss, *The Story of Job's Beginning* (Jerusalem: Magness Press, 1983), pp. 17-20.

[2]Josephus, *Antiq.* I.6.4

[3]Cf. P. Dhorme, "Le pays de Job," *RB* 20 (1911): 102-107; G. Schmitt, "Die Heimat Hiobs," *Zeitschrift des deutschen Palestia-Vereins* 101 (1985): 56-63. LXX and Vulg. have Ausitidis in the place of Uz.

[4]The Egyptian Execration Texts (2000 B.C.) and a letter from Tell el-Amarna (14th cent. B.C.) attest the use of the name by princes in and around Palestine. The name is also found at Mari and Alalakh. Cf. the discussion in Pope, *Job*, pp. 5-6; Clines, *Job 1–20*, pp. 10-11.

It is also interesting to note that the author does not attach Job's genealogy to his name as is the custom when important biblical personalities are introduced (cf., e.g., Abraham, Gen 11:26-29; Jonah, Jonah 1:1). We do not know his family, his tribe, or, for that matter, even the time that he lived. This may be intentional. Just as the issue which Job addresses (undeserved suffering) is universal and timeless, so also is the principal character who personifies it. There is a sense in which Job is the archetype of the righteous sufferer. He is so remembered by the prophet Ezekiel (14:14,20) who puts him alongside Noah and Daniel as an exemplar of piety and by James (5:11) who lifts him up as a model of patience in the face of suffering.

More important than the name or home of Job was the quality of his character. The terms **blameless** (םָּת, *tām*) and **upright** (יָשָׁר, *yāšār*) are also used together in Psalm 25:21 and Psalm 37:37 to describe the epitome of moral excellence. The first word carries the idea of "completeness" and the second the idea of "straightness." When used together, they describe someone who has personal integrity, who faithfully adheres to God's laws, and who behaves fairly and justly in his treatment of others. These terms do not imply sinlessness or moral perfection, but they do characterize Job as someone who is above reproach.

The second pair of terms, **fearing God** and **shunning evil**, are distinctly more religious in character.[5] They describe Job's faith and piety. It has often been observed that the Hebrew language has no exact equivalent to our word "religion." The phrase "fear of God/the LORD" found here and often in the Wisdom literature comes closest to approximating this concept.[6] Reverence is the foundation of the proper human response to deity. Biblically speaking it is the proper basis for all piety. In a positive sense it manifests itself in trust, love, and obedience (Deut 10:12), and in a negative sense it motivates the God-fearer to conscientiously "shun evil" (Prov 3:7; 14:16).

This characterization of Job's piety appears no less than three times in the prologue — stated once by the author (1:1b) and twice by God himself (1:8b; 2:3b). This repetition is not accidental. The fact it establishes is crucial to the plot of the book and the issue debated in

---

[5]These terms also appear together in Prov 3:7; 14:16; 16:6.
[6]Cf. G. von Rad, *Wisdom in Israel* (London: SCM, 1972), pp. 65-68, and G.A. Lee, "Fear," *ISBE*, 2:289-291.

the dialogues between Job and his friends. In his suffering Job is not being punished by God for some sin. Job's passionate protests of innocence, his intense search for God's role in his suffering, and God's condemnation of his friends for presuming his guilt must all be understood in light of this fact. Job is not suffering because he has sinned. Upon this fact the plot of this epic struggle is built.

1:2-3 The vastness of Job's prosperity is characterized by the numbers "three," "seven," and "ten." These numbers are symbolic of completeness in the Hebrew Bible. The size of his flocks and herds is staggering. The pasturage they would have required suggests that he must have been an owner of much land as well. The listing of **oxen** in pairs ("yoke") suggests that he was also involved in the cultivation of his fields. The large number of **camels** is also interesting. It invites the speculation that Job might have been involved in the caravan trade of his day.

But Job's greatest asset was his family. The combination of **seven sons** (cf. 1 Sam 2:5; Ruth 4:15) and **three daughters** portrays the ideal family. Children (especially sons) are viewed as the ultimate blessing of God and are to be viewed as a sign of his favor (Ps 127:3,5). This combination of ideal family and vast holdings of flocks, herds,[7] and servants makes Job the **greatest** (i.e., wealthiest) of the ancient sheikhs who populated the fringes of the Arabian Desert. The fact that Job is numbered among the **sons of the East** (i.e., east of Palestine; Gen 29:1; Judg 6:33) suggests that he is either a non-Israelite or an Israelite living abroad and sets the story in a locale outside the "promised land."

The correlation of Job's righteousness with his wealth is important for our understanding of the book. Conventional wisdom taught that health and wealth were to be understood as God's reward for human righteousness. This opening portrait of Job as both the best man and the richest man reflects the prevailing theological view that God manages His world on a model of retributive justice (righteousness = reward and sin = suffering). Job, it seems, is living proof of this worldview. That is, until his great trials befall him.

---

[7]The reference to "three thousand camels" is interesting. According to Aristotle (*De Historia Animalia* 9.50.5) the ancient Arabs were known to possess such large herds. Cf. J.P. Free, "Abraham's Camels," *JNES* 3 (1944): 187-193; R. Walz, "Neue Untersuchungen zum Domestikationsproblem der altweltlichen Cameliden," *ZDMG* 104 (1954): 45-87; K.A. Kitchen, *IDB*, 1:228-230.

1:4-5 These verses complete the opening portrait of Job as both a righteous and wealthy man. His sons all owned their own **homes** in which they **took turns** entertaining. The term used to indicate these festive occasions (יוֹמוֹ, *yômô*, "his day") may refer to the respective birthdays of the sons (cf. 3:1) or to continual feasting every day of the week, one day for each of the seven sons. Whichever understanding is correct, only a family of great wealth could afford such a lifestyle.

As in the opening verses, so also here Job's wealth is connected to his piety. So scrupulous is he in his pursuit of righteousness that he seeks to expiate even some inadvertent sin that his children might have committed during their periods of feasting. He does so in the fashion of the usual acts of ancient ritual purity. First he has them **purified**, probably by ceremonial washings and fresh changes of garments. Then he offers a sacrifice, a whole **burnt offering** (עֹלָה, *'ōlāh*) designed to atone for any misdeed they may have even accidentally committed.[8]

One sin that Job fears his children might be guilty of is **cursing God**. The Hebrew term (בָּרַךְ, *brk*) for "curse" literally means "bless." This translational curiosity may best be understood as either a scribal euphemism or an intentional change to keep the word "curse" from coming into juxtaposition with the word "God." This phenomenon is observable elsewhere in Job 1:11; 2:5,9; 1 Kings 21:10,13, and Psalm 10:3.[9] This reference sets the stage for Satan's challenge that Job would willingly "curse God" in response to his loss (1:11; 2:5). It also anticipates what Job's wife will urge him to do in order to end his miserable existence (2:9).

2. The First Heavenly Assembly (1:6-12)

[6]One day the angels[a] came to present themselves before the LORD, and Satan[b] also came with them. [7]The LORD said to Satan, "Where have you come from?"

---

[8]For a psychological interpretation of Job's pious intervention on behalf of his children, see J. Kahn, *Job's Illness: Loss, Grief and Integration: A Psychological Interpretaion* (Oxford: Pergamon, 1975), p. 18.

[9]Cf. E. Tov, *Textual Criticism of the Hebrew Bible* (Minneapolis: Fortress, 1992), p. 272.

Satan answered the LORD, "From roaming through the earth and going back and forth in it."

[8]Then the LORD said to Satan, "Have you considered my servant Job? There is no one on earth like him; he is blameless and upright, a man who fears God and shuns evil."

[9]"Does Job fear God for nothing?" Satan replied. [10]"Have you not put a hedge around him and his household and everything he has? You have blessed the work of his hands, so that his flocks and herds are spread throughout the land. [11]But stretch out your hand and strike everything he has, and he will surely curse you to your face."

[12]The LORD said to Satan, "Very well, then, everything he has is in your hands, but on the man himself do not lay a finger."

Then Satan went out from the presence of the LORD.

[a]6 Hebrew *the sons of God*   [b]6 Satan means *accuser*.

The scene now shifts dramatically to a heavenly assembly over which the Lord presides. The repeating back-and-forth shift between earth and heaven in the prologue confronts the reader with the close interrelation between the two worlds with an emphasis on the one God who presides over both. Our first portrait of God is of a sovereign before whom the sons of God and the Satan are subordinate.

1:6 As in 2:1 the occasion for this heavenly assembly is not specified. The Jerusalem Targum places this meeting on New Year's Day while the second assembly (2:1) is assigned to the Day of Atonement. These designations undoubtedly reflect a postexilic Jewish theology that assigned preliminary judgment of the wicked to New Year's Day and a gracious, secondary judgment of the repentant wicked on the Day of Atonement. All that can be inferred from the language of Job is that this heavenly tribunal was a regular matter of course.

The Hebrew text of Job identifies the beings present at this assembly as "sons of God." The term refers to superhuman, celestial beings but does not imply any direct descent from God. The Septuagint identifies them as "angels" and this is probably correct. In the Bible the "sons of God" are portrayed as present at creation (Job 38:7) and residing in the heavens (Ps 82:6 [5]). In a most unusual text (Gen 6:1-4) the "sons of God" are censured by God for uniting in marriage with the "daughters of men." From this passage and others the theory of "fallen angels" developed.

These angels came **to present themselves before the LORD**. In this act they literally "stand" or "station themselves" before God as royal officials before a king (cf. Prov 22:29). In an act of subordination they come to give account of their activities and receive orders from the Lord who clearly functions as their sovereign. As a number of scholars have noted, the portrait presented here and in several other biblical texts (Ps 29:1; 82; 89:5-8; 1 Kgs 22:19-23) is much like that of the "assembly of the gods" motif found in the literature of the surrounding ancient Near Eastern world. In the Canaanite myths, for example, the gods are said to govern the world through a divine council.[10] If the biblical portraits are closely compared to their Canaanite counterparts, however, some important distinctions become evident. In the Bible the "sons of God" are never portrayed as independent deities. They are always placed on a completely different level from Yahweh, dependent upon him and in total submission to him. In this heavenly tribunal the Lord reigns uniquely and exclusively, not as one god among many. Hence this portrait of the enthroned Lord is consistent with the monotheism of the Hebrew Bible.

Joining the angels is the intriguing character **Satan**. The NIV transliterates (not translates) the Hebrew śāṭān (lit., הַשָּׂטָן, haśśāṭān, "the satan") here as a proper name, and those who read it commonly assume the author is speaking of the Evil One referred to so often by that name in the New Testament. Since the character described here is obviously some kind of spirit-being who has access to the heavenly realm, impugns righteousness, and inflicts harm upon a child of God, it is only natural to identify him with the infamous Satan mentioned so often in the New Testament and Judeo-Christian tradition. The phrase **and Satan also came with them** may even serve to further distinguish this "evil one" from the rest of the angels who had come to present themselves before the Lord. If, indeed, we identify this character with Satan, the Devil (διάβολος, *diabolos*) of the New Testament, then we should probably understand this negotiation between God and Satan over the fate of Job as an

---

[10]Cf. E.T. Mullen, Jr., *The Divine Council in Canaanite and Early Hebrew Literature*, HSM 24 (Chicago: Scholars Press, 1980).

exceptional case. Nowhere else in the Bible is such an encounter described, and it would be inappropriate to make this isolated case definitive for the biblical doctrine of Satan.

There is, however, another way to understand the identity of the *satan* of Job. For a number of reasons, grammatical and theological, many scholars question whether or not the character introduced here should be identified with the "Devil" of later Scripture. They see him as one of the angels ("sons of God") who regularly came before the Lord. Rather than God's enemy they understand him to be God's agent, whose specific duty it is to expose any disloyalty among God's subjects. This explains, they argue, God's willingness to permit the *satan* to inflict suffering on Job in order to test the purity of Job's devotion.[11] A fuller discussion of this view is offered in the following excursus.

---

[11]Cf., e.g., Pope, Habel, Clines.

EXCURSUS

THE SATAN OF JOB

There are several reasons to question that the "Satan" of Job's prologue is the same Satan or Devil we read of in the New Testament. In the Hebrew text of Job the term *satan* is presented as a title and not a personal name. As in Zechariah 3:1-2 the term here carries the definite article (*haśśāṭān*="*the* satan") and functions not as a personal name but as a common noun meaning simply "the accuser" or "the adversary."[12] The word is sometimes used in the Old Testament to refer to ordinary human adversaries. In fact, the only place in the Hebrew Bible where the term "Satan" is unquestionably used as a proper name is 1 Chronicles 21:1. In that text he is portrayed as a troublemaker, inciting king David to take an ill-advised and punitive census. It is possible to identify the "Satan" of the Chronicles account as the superhuman personification of evil spoken of in Judeo-Christian tradition.[13]

A different character, however, may to be described here. As one meaning of the Hebrew root (שׂטן, *stn*, "to oppose in court") suggests, "the satan" here may be understood simply as "the accuser, the opponent," functioning much like a prosecuting attorney who brings formal charges against someone (Ps 109:6; Zech 3:1-2). Some scholars even argue that in Job *the satan* is not portrayed as an enemy of God but as one of his servants.[14] They understand the line

---

[12]In the Hebrew Bible nouns are always written without capital letters. Normally the reader cannot tell by form alone whether the term is to be read as a proper name or simply as a common noun. The presence of the definite article "the" here, however, would suggest that *satan* should not be read as a proper name but a common noun.

[13]But even this supposed reference to "Satan" is not without problems because the parallel version of David's census found in 2 Sam 24:1-25 begins by saying, "The anger of the Lord burned against Israel, and he [not 'Satan'] incited David against them, saying, 'Go take a census of Israel and Judah.'" If *satan* in 1 Chron 21:1 refers to some divinely appointed "adversary" rather than the Evil One, this tension between the two accounts can be relieved; cf. M. Tate, "Satan in the Old Testament," *RevExp* 89 (1992): 461-475.

[14]Some scholars have argued that the *satan* functions like one of the secret service agents of the Assyrian or Persian royal courts whose duty it was to expose citizens who were secretly disloyal to the throne. Herodotus referred

"and Satan also came with them" to mean that he was one of the "sons of God," a spirit-being whose specific duty it was to report the misbehavior of any of the Lord's subjects. This model, it is argued, explains the Lord's question, "Where have you come from?" of verse 7 and *the satan's* reply of verse 8, "From roaming through the earth and going back and forth in it." In other words, *the satan* of Job is not cast in the role of the Evil One who opposes God and tempts man but as a royal agent whose sworn duty it was to expose any disloyalty to the king (Yahweh). This indeed is what he goes on to do in his questioning of the genuineness of Job's devotion to God.

This might explain some difficult theological questions raised by the conversation between the Lord and the Satan. If this is the Satan who is God's enemy and the personification of evil itself, what is he even doing here in God's court? Why does God grant him an audience and engage him in conversation? Why does God listen to his impugning of Job's righteousness? Why does God allow Satan to inflict such suffering upon one whom God himself has pronounced righteous? If, however, he is God's agent whose duty it is to test the loyalty of the Lord's subjects, all of these troublesome questions are resolved.

The Satan of the prologue of Job simply does not relate to God like the Satan of the New Testament. Here he regularly reports to the Lord in heaven, receives permission from him to act, and can only do to Job what God will allow. These actions are out of character with the Evil One we read of later in the New Testament. These observations serve to confirm what biblical scholars have long noted. Though the seeds of a biblical doctrine of Satan may be found in the Old Testament, one must consult the New Testament to find a full disclosure of his nature and work.[15]

---

to these agents as "the eyes and ears of the king." Cf. the discussion in Hartley, *The Book of Job*, pp. 71-72; also M.J. Gruenthaner, "The Demonology of the OT," *CBQ* 6 (1944): 6-27.

[15]The reader will also note that Job never blames the *satan* for the evil that has befallen him. If Job is even aware of some superhuman Satan who inflicts harm upon God's children, he never once mentions him. Instead, he consistently lays the responsibility for his suffering in the lap of God.

However we understand the identity of *the satan* of the prologue, the function of this initial scene in heaven is clear. The author is establishing the basis for the testing of Job. A "trial" of sorts is about to take place, in an open court witnessed by the "sons of God." Yahweh, who has complete confidence in the genuineness of Job's piety, will permit *the satan* to expose the alleged disloyalty of Job by means of inflicting suffering upon him.

1:8 In the dialogue between the accuser and Yahweh it is the Lord who first mentions Job. He honors Job by calling him his **servant**,[16] and then praises his extraordinary piety: **he is blameless and upright, a man who fears God and shuns evil.** Yahweh's characterization of Job's righteousness is identical to that of the author in the opening verse of the prologue. It is repeated by God yet again in his second dialogue with the *satan* (2:3). The purpose of this repetition becomes more apparent as the story unfolds. Job is about to suffer a great trial. These texts clearly establish the very point Job will later argue. His suffering is not punishment for any sin which he has committed. By the standard of retributive justice it is therefore undeserved and unfair.

1:9-11 "Does Job fear God for nothing?" With this accusation the trial of Job begins, and upon it the remainder of the story rests. Is Job's piety sincere, or is he merely exploiting a system that results in his personal gain? Is he righteous because he truly loves God, or is he righteous because it benefits him to be so? The clear implication of the accuser's questions is that Job is disingenuous in his devotion to God. Just how could Job's insincerity be exposed? **"Stretch out your hand and strike everything he has, and he will surely curse you to your face."** In other words, systematically take away from Job every tangible, self-serving reason for submitting to God, and he will instead publicly disavow him. From these words we learn the function of the suffering God permits the accuser to inflict upon Job. It is designed to test the genuineness of Job's piety. Will Job still serve a God who takes away as well as gives? Will he continue to love a God who brings pain in the place of prosperity?

---

[16]"Servant" is a title reserved for some of the most important leaders set apart by God: Abraham (Ps 105:6,42), Moses (Exod 14:31), Joshua (Josh 24:29), David (2 Sam 7:5,8).

1:12 "Very well, then, everything he has is in your hands." The Lord's reply surprises, even shocks the reader. The Lord is willing to permit the accuser to rain down undeserved suffering upon the life of one of his saints?! Why? What is it in the accuser's challenge that is so significant, so important to God that he will allow his faithful child to be put to such a test? To attempt to answer this question is to address the larger issue of the very purpose and meaning of the book of Job.

Whatever else the book of Job is about, it is certainly about piety. Job practices it, God values it, and the "accuser" impugns it. But what exactly is it? Is it about professing faith, performing liturgy, and living righteously, or is its essence found in something else? The challenge of the "accuser" and the subsequent response of God suggest that it involves not just these actions but the attitude behind these actions. The "accuser" said that Job's righteous acts were insincere. According to the "accuser" Job practiced piety because it was rewarded, it resulted in some tangible, personal benefit. God's response to that accusation shows that he accepts the basic premise of the "accuser's" challenge. He agrees that if Job's motives are purely selfish, his piety is insincere and invalid. In other words, to serve God because it serves self is not to serve God at all.

What then is genuine piety? What does it mean to truly live before God in faith and love? According to Job it is to love God simply for who He is and serve Him without reward or rationale. It is at last to sit on the ash heap of life denied every proof of God's existence and deprived of every good thing he is said to give and to love him anyway!

3. Job's First Trial (1:13-22)

[13]One day when Job's sons and daughters were feasting and drinking wine at the oldest brother's house, [14]a messenger came to Job and said, "The oxen were plowing and donkeys were grazing nearby, [15]and the Sabeans attacked and carried them off. They put the servants to the sword, and I am the only one who has escaped to tell you!"

[16]While he was still speaking, another messenger came and said, "The fire of God fell from the sky and burned up the sheep

and the servants, and I am the only one who has escaped to tell you!"

¹⁷While he was still speaking, yet another messenger came and said, "The Chaldeans formed three raiding parties and swept down on your camels and carried them off. They put the servants to the sword, and I am the only one who has escaped to tell you!"

¹⁸While he was still speaking, yet another messenger came and said, "Your sons and daughters were feasting and drinking wine at the oldest brother's house, ¹⁹when suddenly a mighty wind swept in from the desert and struck the four corners of the house. It collapsed on them and they are dead, and I am the only one who has escaped to tell you!"

²⁰At this, Job got up and tore his robe and shaved his head. Then he fell to the ground in worship ²¹and said:

"Naked I came from my mother's womb, / and naked I will depart.ᶜ / The LORD gave and the LORD has taken away; / may the name of the LORD be praised."

²²In all this, Job did not sin by charging God with wrongdoing.

ᶜ21 Or *will return there*

1:13-14 This third scene opens like the one before it with the indeterminate **one day**. The portrait here is one of serenity and ease. Completely unaware of the agreement between God and the "accuser," life for Job and his family goes on as it always has. As the Lord mandates in the latter part of verse 12, the adversary's attacks will be directed at Job's possessions and family, not his person. The account is moved along by the repeated phrase **a messenger came**[17] which punctuates the story of four successive disasters that deprive Job of nearly all that he holds dear. It is interesting to note that Job is deprived of his possessions in the exact opposite order that they are listed in the catalogue of his wealth in chapter one.[18] The number four is prominent in the account (four disasters strike from all four points of the compass, culminating with the great wind which struck the "four corners" of the house), a literary feature which else-

----

[17]In the Hebrew the noun מַלְאָךְ (*mal'āk*, "messenger") is in the emphatic position to dramatize the sudden interruptions to Job's peaceful world.

[18]This literary technique known as chiasm is a favorite of the biblical authors. Cf. A. Hakam, ספר איוב (Jerusalem: Mosad ha-Rab Quq, 1970), p. 76.

where in the Hebrew Bible signifies totality or completion. The verb "fell" (נָפַל, *nāphal*) is used to describe each of the four devastations. This is probably the author's way of focusing upon the supernatural origin of Job's suffering. Finally the repeated, **but while he was still speaking, another came** (vv. 16,17,18), completes the picture of a supernaturally orchestrated set of disasters.

1:15-17 He first loses his **donkeys** and **oxen** and the **servants** attending them at the hands of a marauding band of **Sabeans**. In the Old Testament Saba or Sheba is associated with Tema and Dedan. While most scholars locate their territory more than a thousand miles from Uz in southern Arabia (the place from which the queen of Sheba came; 1 Kgs 10:1-10), others have placed it in northern Arabia much closer to where we believe Uz to have been.[19] The extent of the loss in this and the three following disasters is epitomized by the recurring phrase of the sole surviving messenger, **"I am the only one who has escaped to tell you"** (cf. also vv. 16,17,18). **The fire of God**[20] is the source of the next disaster, most likely a devastating bolt of lightning (cf. Num 11:1-3; 1 Kgs 18:38) that wipes out his flock of sheep and their shepherds. This, in turn, is followed by an attack upon the camels and their keepers by the **Chaldeans**, not the imperial race of the neo-Babylonian empire but a nomadic people who roamed the deserts between north Arabia and the Persian Gulf in earlier times.[21] The strategy of dividing one's forces into three was a favorite of biblical times (Judg 7:16; 9:43: 1 Sam 11:11; 13:17).

1:18-19 But the worst of all imaginable disasters is yet to come. A fourth and final messenger brings the news that completes Job's devastating loss: **your sons and daughters are dead**. This time a **mighty wind** is the agent of destruction collapsing the four corners of the **house** in which Job's children were eating and drinking. In four swift strokes virtually all that Job holds dear has been taken from him in such striking concurrence that it cannot be attributed to mere coincidence. Though each disaster is human or natural, it is

---

[19]Cf. Pope, *Job*, p. 13.

[20]The LXX omits "of God." The Hebrew expression can also mean simply "a great fire."

[21]On the origin and use of the name Chaldeans, see A.R. Millard, "Daniel 1–6 and History," *EvQ* 49 (1977): 67-73.

obvious that a supernatural power is behind it. As we find elsewhere in the Bible, nature and nations are made the instruments of God's purging or punitive activity upon His people.

1:20 Job's reactions to his unspeakable loss are shaped by both his culture and his personal faith. In formal gestures of mourning he **tore his robe and shaved his head**. These expressions of grief are widely attested in the biblical and ancient Near Eastern literature.[22] In the manner of his day he faces the grim reality that has come upon him. But how will he face the God who has permitted it? Will he lose faith and abandon God? Will he angrily curse him to his face? No. In an act of incredible piety he **fell to the ground in worship**. This must be understood as nothing short of full surrender to the will of God. In this gesture of humble submission Job acknowledges God's sovereignty as he seeks his comfort.

1:21 What comes from Job's lips is one of the most amazing examples of unconditional faith in God to be found in Scripture. Quoting two proverbs and a liturgical formula, he faithfully places his life, his family, and his possessions beneath the lordship of Yahweh. **"Naked I came from my mother's womb and naked I will depart. The LORD gave and the LORD has taken away; may the name of the LORD be praised."** This is not fatalism. It is faith. In what amounts to a confessional[23] Job affirms that God owes him nothing and that all the things he has been privileged to enjoy in his life are nothing less than the gift of a gracious Sovereign. With these words Job addresses the very issue that the "accuser" had raised before the Lord: Job is pious because God rewards him (1:9-11). Job's reply shows that such is indeed *not* the case. The blessing of God is not a prerequisite for Job's devotion. He submits to God and praises him regardless of what he gives or takes away (cf. 2:10).

---

[22]First Sam 18:4; 24:5,11; Isa 15:2; Jer 7:29; Ezek 7:18. Cf. also Gilgamesh 8.2.21. A similar but different custom of cutting a bald spot or gashing the scalp was forbidden in the Mosaic law (Lev 21:5; Deut 14:1); see A.J. Wensinck, *Some Semitic Rites of Mourning and Religion* (Amsterdam: J. Müller, 1917), pp. 5-55.

[23]Notice that Job does not address God directly as he will do later in the speeches. Using the personal name of Yahweh three times he speaks of him in the third person in the style of confessional language. Cf. W.S. Towner, "'Blessed by YHWH' and 'Blessed Art Thou, YHWH': The Modulation of a Biblical Formula," *CBQ* 30 (1968): 386-399.

The LORD has taken away. It is important to note that Job attributes his great loss directly to Yahweh. He does not say, "The LORD gave and the *Chaldeans* took away," or "The LORD gave and the *whirlwind* took away." As Clines observes, "he (Job) sees his human enemies and the natural forces as secondary to the one who must ultimately be responsible."[24] Neither does he say, "The LORD gave and *the Satan* took away." If Job is even aware of the existence of such a being, he makes absolutely no reference to him anywhere. Nor do the friends acknowledge his existence. From Job's opening words to his final soliloquy he lays responsibility for his loss squarely in the lap of the Lord. It is the consistent theology of Job and his friends that God either causes or permits everything that happens. Both Job's praise and his later complaints are directed exclusively toward Yahweh.

Job concludes his great confessional with the unconditional affirmation **"May the name of the LORD be praised."** The Hebrew literally reads, "May the name of the LORD be *blessed*." The verb בָּרַךְ (*bārak*), which in normal usage means "to bless," never means that when used by humans of God. In such usage it becomes an expression of gratitude and praise.[25] In the Hebrew Bible "blessing" is something that a superior does to a subordinate. Fathers bless their children; kings bless their subjects; but theologically speaking, God's people cannot bless him. They can only praise him (hence the translation of the NIV). When Job praises God's **name** (cf. Ps 113:2), he is using a conventional liturgical formula that amounts to a call to worship. He is inviting all who witness God's management of Job's life to respond with adoration and praise.

1:22 The author ends his account of the first cycle of Job's suffering with a positive appraisal of Job's initial response. There is nothing in Job's actions or words that even hints at rebellion against God. A lesser man might have impugned God or accused him of **wrongdoing** (תִּפְלָה, *tiphlāh*).[26] To be sure, Job will later make just such an accusation. But in his initial response to his great loss Job is guilty of no irreverence.

---

[24]Clines, *Job*, p. 38.
[25]Cf. J. Scharbert, *TWOT*, 1:305.
[26]The meaning of this term is uncertain. It most likely refers to some kind of improper or unseemly behavior.

JOB 2

4. The Second Heavenly Assembly (2:1-6)

[1]On another day the angels[a] came to present themselves before the LORD, and Satan also came with them to present himself before him. [2]And the LORD said to Satan, "Where have you come from?"

Satan answered the LORD, "From roaming through the earth and going back and forth in it."

[3]Then the LORD said to Satan, "Have you considered my servant Job? There is no one on earth like him; he is blameless and upright, a man who fears God and shuns evil. And he still maintains his integrity, though you incited me against him to ruin him without any reason."

[4]"Skin for skin!" Satan replied. "A man will give all he has for his own life. [5]But stretch out your hand and strike his flesh and bones, and he will surely curse you to your face."

[6]The LORD said to Satan, "Very well, then, he is in your hands; but you must spare his life."

[a]1 Hebrew *the sons of God*

This second scene in heaven is modeled closely upon the first with much repetition. This is a regular feature of Hebrew narrative style[1] and represents the equivalent in prose of what parallelism represents in Hebrew poetry. Balancing similar or contrasting sounds, concepts, or story lines is characteristic of Semitic literature. Here, as it does in other narratives, it heightens the suspense for the reader and puts him on guard for any new developments. As is also typical of Hebrew narrative, it is these new developments that move the story forward.

---

[1]Cf. J. Muilenburg, "A Study of Hebrew Rhetoric: Repetition and Style," *VTSupp* 1 (1953): 97-111; R. Alter, *The Art of Biblical Narrative* (New York: Basic Books, 1981), pp. 88-113.

The first cycle of events has left the reader with numerous questions. What is heaven's reaction to Job's trial and response? Now that the Lord's confidence in Job's piety has been affirmed will the Satan relent and will Job be set free? It is upon these very issues that the second cycle of the narrative will turn.

2:1-2 The language here is identical to that of 1:6-7 with (*the*) **Satan** appearing, along with the **angels** (lit. "sons of God"), before the Lord. One phrase, however, is here added to tell us that the Satan also came specifically **to present himself before him** (the LORD). This language was used in the first account only of the angels. Its significance there was to suggest that they came in obeisance as courtiers before a sovereign. The application of the phrase to the Satan is similarly designed to establish his subordination and accountability before the Lord.[2] Given the liberties that Yahweh has allowed Satan to take with Job, it is important for the reader to remember that the Lord is still in charge of this encounter. The repeated question, **Where have you come from?** also serves to reinforce the Lord's sovereignty. It is interesting that in the Satan's reply to the Lord's question there is not a single word about the dramatic events that have already transpired.

2:3 If the Satan is not eager to speak of the foregoing events, the Lord certainly is. He immediately calls attention to Job — his **servant** Job; Job, the **blameless and upright**; Job, who **still maintains his integrity** in spite of all the evils that the Satan has heaped upon him. The Lord's delight in Job's faithfulness is made obvious by his repetition of the fourfold description of Job's character (cf. 1:8) and his specific reference to the trials intended to expose their disingenuousness. In the Lord's characterization of that trial three things are said about Job and God's role in his suffering. First, God says that the Satan **incited** him to afflict Job. This word (סוּת, *sûth*) means to "stir someone to a course of action they would not ordinarily take." By using this term the author informs us that God does not ordi-

---

[2]The suggestion of Gordis that the preposition "before" (עַל, *'al*) when used here of Satan means "stand over against God" or "in defiance of God" in rebelliousness is interesting (cf. Deut 7:24). If we read it this way, the Satan may be understood better as God's opponent rather than his servant (cf. R. Gordis, *The Book of Job: Commentary, New Translation and Special Notes* [New York: Jewish Theological Seminary of America, 1978], p. 64).

narily act this way towards his servants. God's affliction of Job is not to be understood as the norm. Second, God says that the Satan incited **me against him**. This point, too, is crucial to our understanding of Job's struggle. Though the Satan may have encouraged and even carried out the affliction of Job (cf. v. 7), it was God who actually authorized it. With these words Yahweh accepts responsibility for Job's suffering, and it is from Yahweh that Job seeks deliverance in the dialogue. Third, God characterizes his **ruin** of Job as **without any cause**. This finally establishes the very point on which the dialogue turns and which the book on the whole is written to address — Job has done nothing to deserve the suffering that has befallen him. God does not always operate on a principle of retribution. In his management of his world he does not always see to it that people get what they deserve. Life, as God presides over it, is not always just.

2:4-6 The Satan reacts to the Lord's affirmation of Job's faithfulness by calling for an even greater test. He begins by quoting a proverb, **"Skin for skin!"** Though the precise meaning of this proverb is uncertain,[3] the purpose of his quoting it is made clear by what follows. It is one thing to take away a man's possessions and family, but **a man will give all he has for his own life**. In other words Job has not been tested severely enough to expose the self-interest of his piety. The test will only be true if it strikes his person, **his flesh and bones**. The Satan remains convinced that if Job is threatened with his own demise, his faith and piety will indeed crumble. When he challenges God to **strike his flesh and bones**, it becomes clear that the Satan has a physical illness in mind. In the Hebrew Bible the bones are commonly referred to as the seat of disease (Ps 6:2; Prov 12:4).

"Very well, then, he is in your hands." Again the reader is surprised by the Lord's reply to the Satan's challenge. Why does God agree to doom his faithful servant to such terrible suffering? To win some heavenly wager? To prove a point to some spirit-being? To satisfy God's own curiosity? To teach a lesson to the heavenly beings?

---

[3]The proposed explanations of the proverb are many: "one skin for another skin" or "a man will give anyone else's skin to save his own," perhaps with the idea of *lex talionis* in mind (Exod 21:23-25, "life for life, eye for eye") implying here that Job would give up all his possessions or even his family to save his own life; or "an outer skin and an inner skin"; or "skin beneath skin," perhaps suggesting that God has only scratched the surface and needs to go deeper and afflict more harshly; cf. discussion in Clines, *Job,* pp. 44-45.

Or, more positively, is this divinely authored suffering designed to teach Job patience or to vindicate his servant against the insinuations of Satan? Though these two latter answers are more consistent with the goal of God's activity as revealed elsewhere in Scripture, they too fall short of explaining the role of suffering in the book of Job. The suffering God permits in this man's life should be understood as a "test." In response to the Satan's challenge that piety isn't really piety if it is based on some personal benefit, the genuineness of Job's devotion will be tested by systematically detaching it from any self-serving reward or rationale. Does Job (or anyone) truly believe in God? In the final analysis this great struggle is not for the benefit of God or the heavenly beings or the Satan. It is for the benefit of Job and those who ponder his incredible struggle. At least one purpose for the existence of the book of Job is to explore the issue of just what true piety constitutes. The challenge of the Satan and God's response to it clearly suggest that the issue of the genuineness of human piety is important enough to God to allow this difficult test of one of his children.[4]

But you must spare his life. The end of verse 6 remembers the language of the first scene in heaven where the Lord put limits on what the Satan could do to Job (1:12b). By this divinely imposed limitation Job's life is ultimately protected from whatever disease the Satan might inflict upon him. God's control over the affliction of Job is thus confirmed.

5. Job's Second Trial (2:7-10)

[7]**So Satan went out from the presence of the LORD and afflicted Job with painful sores from the soles of his feet to the top of his head. [8]Then Job took a piece of broken pottery and scraped himself with it as he sat among the ashes.**

---

[4]W. Brown argues that the *satan*'s accusation against Job is at the same time an accusation against Yahweh and the way he relates to humans. It implies that while Job is guilty of exploiting the practice of piety in order to serve some self-interest, Yahweh is also guilty of permitting it. Cf. W.P. Brown, *Character in Crises: A Fresh Approach to the Wisdom Literature of the Old Testament* (Grand Rapids: Eerdmans, 1996), p. 53.

⁹His wife said to him, "Are you still holding on to your integrity? Curse God and die!"

¹⁰He replied, "You are talking like a foolishᵃ woman. Shall we accept good from God, and not trouble?"

In all this, Job did not sin in what he said.

ᵃ*10* The Hebrew word *foolish* denotes moral deficiency.

2:7 So Satan went out . . . and afflicted Job. As in the first set of trials Satan is the agent of Job's suffering (though in the earlier trial it is only inferred; cf. 1:12). The reader should remember, however, that the Satan does this only by divine permission. As verse 3 makes clear, it is God himself who accepts the ultimate responsibility for Job's ruin. The Satan **afflicted Job with painful sores from the soles of his feet to the top of his head**. There is in this language another parallel with the first set of trials. Just as earlier he lost all of his possessions, Job is now smitten with a disease that afflicts the whole of his body (cf. similar language in Deut 28:35; Isa 1:6). The effect of the disease was to convince Job that his demise was imminent, to confront him with his mortality. Just what disease is being described here? The Hebrew term used here (שְׁחִין, *šᵊḥîn*) is a general one used to describe various diseases of the skin. It is mentioned in Leviticus 13:18-23 as a boil indicating the presence of leprosy, and this has led many interpreters to assume this is Job's disease. Another suggestion is that Job was afflicted with elephantiasis, the symptoms of which are blackened skin and swollen limbs. Pemphigus, scurvy, eczema, smallpox, and malignancy have also been suggested.[5] Though there is uncertainty over exactly which disease afflicted Job, information gleaned from the speeches reveals the devastating effect it had upon him. He suffered from disfiguration (2:12); running sores infected with worms (7:5); darkening and shriveling of the skin (30:30); red, swollen eyes (16:16); diarrhea (30:27); fever with chills (21:6; 30:30); choking (7:15); foul breath (19:17); emaciation (19:20); nightmares and sleeplessness (7:4,14); and excruciating pain (30:17). We also learn that this unrelenting illness afflicted him for months (7:3).

---

[5]Cf. E.V. Hulse, "The Nature of Biblical 'Leprosy'and the Use of Alternative Medical Terms in Modern Translations of the Bible," *PEQ* 107 (1975): 87-105. J.F.A. Sawyer, "A Note on the Etymology of *Sāra'at*," *VT* 26 (1976): 241-245.

2:8 The grammar of the Hebrew suggests that Job was already sitting **among the ashes** when he was afflicted by the disease. We do not know for sure if he was doing this near his own house or in some public place. Palestinian towns had such places, usually outside the city, called *mezbele* where the collection of the city's ashes, broken pots, and other refuse were thrown. It was the abode of outcasts. Ashes (and dust) were sometimes thrown on the head (2 Sam 13:19) or on the clothes (Esth 4:1) or rolled in (Jer 6:26) as signs of mourning.[6] The scene depicted here is that, as Job was mourning the loss of his children, he was subsequently smitten by this dreaded, painful disease. Since disease was generally associated with God's curse in ancient times, the reader is correct in assuming that people are beginning to think the worst of Job. As Clines observes, "the two trials of Job have now coalesced."[7] The ash-heap, the place of mourning, now becomes the place of humiliating suffering. The tears of his sorrow are now joined by the cries of his pain and sense of alienation.

2:9 In this verse a new character is briefly introduced. For the first time we hear from Job's wife.[8] From her words we get our first glimpse of the social implications of Job's trial. She, like Job, has lost much in the tragedies that have befallen them. In ancient times a wife looked to her husband for her identity in the community and for her financial security. If Job had lost everything, so had she. The LXX, which assigns to her a longer speech, calls attention to her deep sense of loss and her conclusion that Job is to blame.[9] Some

---

[6]Cf. M. Jastrow, "Dust, Earth, and Ashes as Symbols of Mourning among the Ancient Hebrews," *JAOS* 20 (1904): 133-150.

[7]Clines, *Job*, p. 50.

[8]The Targum names Job's wife Dinah based on the fact that Dinah is said to have acted foolishly in Gen 34:1-10. In the Testament of Job she is named Sitis.

[9]The LXX expands her speech in the following way: "After much time had passed his wife said to him, 'How long will you endure, saying, "Behold, I shall wait a little longer, expecting the hope of my salvation." Behold, your memory is already blotted out from the earth, the sons and daughters, the travail and pangs of my womb, whom I reared with toil in vain. And you sit in decay caused by worms, spending the nights outside, and I am a wanderer and a servant, going from place to place and from house to house, looking for the sun to set, in order that I might rest from my toils and pains which now oppress me. But say some word against the Lord and die.'" This expansion probably represents an example of the midrashic tendency to add additional information about biblical characters (cf. also the LXX on 42:17).

commentators have characterized her as "Satan's tool" (John Calvin) spared by the tempter in order to use her in this way against Job (Thomas Aquinas). Others have seen her in the stereotype of "woman as temptress" found in many biblical stories (Eve, Delilah, Jezebel, etc.). It is true that she echoes the Satan's words, "**Curse God and die!**" But she also echoes the words of God, marveling that Job was **still holding on to** (his) **integrity**. With these words she reveals that she believes Job has obviously wronged God, and it is only a matter of time before his inevitable demise. It is therefore foolish to continue to practice piety since it obviously will yield no blessing in the face of their great loss. What she is suggesting is a form of theological euthanasia — suicide by cursing God. If there is anger in her voice there may also be pity and wish for a merciful end to the whole ordeal.

The words of Job's wife anticipate the conclusion about Job that the friends will reach: Job suffers because he has sinned. Her words also anticipate the great sense of alienation that Job will feel when rejected by his friends and peers. Her suggestion that Job "curse God" only heightens the invitation for Job to abandon his piety and disavow God.

2:10 Whatever the intent of her remarks, Job takes great exception to them. His initial retort is strong, "**You are talking like a foolish woman.**" These words are very condemnatory in the Hebrew culture. The word for fool (נָבָל, *nābāl*) refers to someone who is disreputable, immoral, or irreligious. And so to Job did her counsel sound. It is his way of saying that he regards her suggestion as irreverent. He then counters with a question of his own, "**Shall we accept good from God and not trouble?**" The word for "trouble" (רַע, *ra'*) may refer to moral evil, but of course it does not mean that here. In this construction "good" (טוֹב, *ṭôb*) refers to the blessings God has bestowed while "trouble" refers to the deprivation of blessing or harm. With these words he implies that Job's wife is failing to trust God's providence, to surrender to his sovereignty. This question echoes the thought of his earlier confession, "The LORD gives and the LORD takes away," and reveals his theology that God is in charge of all that happens and it is the duty of humans to trust him to do what is appropriate.

There is no impiety in Job's speech. The author's appraisal makes it clear that the Satan's prediction did not come true. The

Satan said a suffering Job would curse God. Instead Job defends him and praises him. **In all this Job did not sin with his lips.** The ancient rabbis took this language to mean that, though Job did not sin with his lips, he did ponder rebellious thoughts in his mind and later these spilled over into his speech as well. It is more likely that this language is simply meant to parallel the author's judgment at the end of chapter one (v. 22). Both assessments of the propriety of Job's behavior begin with the identical "In all this Job did not sin" (1:22a = 2:10b), and the repetition invites a similar comparison between the qualifying phrases which follow. In other words, the phrase "with his lips" (2:10c) corresponds with "by charging God with wrongdoing" (1:22b) and together they exonerate Job of the specific sin of irreverent speech.

There may be a sense though in which the reference to Job's lips here foreshadows the irreverent speech he will soon make against God. Clines envisions a process in Job similar to that addressed by the Psalmist in Psalm 39:1-3: "I said, I will guard my ways, that I may not sin with my tongue; I will bridle my mouth . . . I was dumb and silent; I held my peace to no avail; my distress grew worse, my heart became hot within me. As I mused, the fire burned; then I spoke with my tongue."[10] Job, the victim of unrelenting suffering, is about to go down this path. From his lips will eventually come words of which he must finally repent.

6. The Arrival of the Three Friends (2:11-13)

[11]When Job's three friends, Eliphaz the Temanite, Bildad the Shuhite and Zophar the Naamathite, heard about all the troubles that had come upon him, they set out from their homes and met together by agreement to go and sympathize with him and comfort him. [12]When they saw him from a distance, they could hardly recognize him; they began to weep aloud, and they tore their robes and sprinkled dust on their heads. [13]Then they sat on the ground with him for seven days and seven nights. No one said a word to him, because they saw how great his suffering was.

---

[10]Clines, *Job*, p. 55.

2:11 Many scholars see these verses as transitional, but as Habel argues, they really signal the beginning of the second major movement of the story line.[11] We have introduced here the partners in a dialogue that will constitute the main portion of the book. We learn that they have **heard about all the troubles that had come upon** Job and **met together by agreement to go and sympathize with him and comfort him.** The fact that these men met by appointment suggests that they know one another as well as Job. How they have learned of Job's misfortune we are not told. News of Job must have spread far and wide. These developments imply the passing of some time, and information gleaned from the dialogues confirms this. In 7:3, for example, Job speaks of "months" of pain he has already endured. Sympathy (נוד, *nûd*, "to shake the head or rock the body back and forth") is indeed what Job needs. The practice of visiting mourners to console them is mentioned in several other biblical texts (cf., e.g., Gen 37:25; 2 Sam 10:2). Jeremiah 16:5,7 refers to the custom of providing food and drink.

Who are these **friends**[12] and from whence have they come? **Eliphaz,** whose name means "God is fine gold" or "God conquers,"[13] comes from **Teman,**[14] a site which the Bible locates near Edom (Ezek 25:13; Gen 36:34). Edom was known for its wisdom (Jer 49:7). **Bildad** ("son of Hadad") hails from **Shuah** which is variously located from the middle Euphrates to Dedan. In the patriarchal narratives of Genesis a Shuah was born to Abraham by Keturah (Gen 25:2). **Zophar** ("young bird") comes from **Naamah**[15] commonly located north of Israel between Beirut and Damascus. Like Job the friends live outside Israel.

2:12-13 When they saw him from a distance, they could hardly recognize him. The Hebrew is difficult here, but the NIV seems to

---

[11]Habel, *Job*, pp. 29-30.

[12]The term "friends" (רֵעַ, *rēaʿ*) can mean everything from confidant (1 Chr 27:33) to party in a legal dispute (Exod 22:9). Before this drama is over they will prove to be both.

[13]Cf. B. Moritz, "Edomitische Genealogiea," *ZAW* 44 (1926): 84.

[14]According to Gen 36:4-15 Eliphaz was the name of Esau's oldest son, and Teman was the son of Eliphaz (cf. also Jer 49:7; Amos 1:11-12; Obad 8).

[15]Gen 4:22 speaks of a female Naamah who descended from Cain and 1 Kgs 14:21 identifies an Ammonite princess by this name whom Solomon marries.

have caught the sense of the original language. They know it is Job, but they are aghast at the sight of him. Disfigured by his suffering, this outcast sitting in the ashes is but a shell of the man they once knew. When they see him, they immediately abandon their original purpose for coming. Instead of offering comfort to a mourner they begin to mourn him as one already dead. **They began to weep aloud, and they tore their robes, and sprinkled dust on their heads**. As noted above, these were formal, public gestures of mourning. It does not seem to be his children they mourn but Job himself. They regard his condition terminal and his situation desperate. The gesture of sitting **on the ground** is also a mourning rite (cf. Lam 2:10; Isa 3:26; Ezek 8:14; Ezra 9:3). It signifies identification **with him** and with the humiliating condition of his suffering. **Seven days** was the normal period for mourning for a person of note (Gen 50:10; 1 Sam 31:13; Ezek 3:15). The silence of the friends, a result of their being overwhelmed by Job's suffering and having respect for the sufferer, also has its roots in traditional mourning rites.[16]

With the completion of Job's two trials and his pious responses, the reader may have come to expect some immediate resolution of the entire ordeal. The appearance of the three friends, however, signals new developments in the story. Just as there had been interaction between Job and his heavenly testers, we now await further interaction between Job and the three friends. But there is no way we could be prepared for the stunning change in Job's demeanor and words which immediately follow.

---

[16]Cf. N Lohfink, "Einheilten die im Alten Testament bezeugten Klageriten eine Phase des Schweigens," *VT* 12 (1962): 260-277, and E. Haulotte, *Symbolique du vêtement selon la Bible* (Paris: Aubier, 1966), p. 128.

JOB 3

B. JOB'S OPENING SOLILOQUY (3:1-26)

Job's silence will now suddenly be broken. The pious sufferer who has been careful to avoid "charging God with wrongdoing" (1:22) will now begin to vent his anger over his great loss and question why God has let it happen (v. 23). His words will ignite a debate that will probe one of the most troubling issues of all theology: "Why does God preside over the suffering of the righteous?"

This speech, which is one of the most eloquent and powerful of the book, joins together two different but often related literary genres — the curse (3:3-10) and the lament (3:11-26). In so doing it shares several stylistic and thematic affinities with Jeremiah 20:14-18. Both speak of cursing the day of birth (Job 3:1,8=Jer 20:14a); announcement of a male child (Job 3:3=Jer 20:15); blocking the womb (Job 3:11=Jer 20:17); and seeing misery or trouble (עָמָל, 'āmāl, Job 3:10=Jer 20:18). Jeremiah, like Job, feels mistreated by God and vents his frustration in a curse-lament. While Jeremiah's curse-lament makes reference to specific historical events, however, Job's repeatedly refers to cosmological realities like light, darkness, and chaos.[1]

Job's opening speech moves forward by a series of contrasts, a series of reversals invoked by Job: from birth to unbirth, order to chaos, from light to darkness, from gloom in life to pleasure in the

---

[1]This has not escaped the attention of scholars. M. Fishbane ("Jeremiah IV 23-26 and Job III 3-13: A Recovered Use of the Creation Pattern," *VT* 21 [1971]: 151-167) argues that Job's curse constitutes a "counter-cosmic incantation" in which he seeks to reverse or undo the creation with his words as a means of expressing an absolute and unrestrained death wish for himself. He goes on to suggest correlation between this text and the creative days of Genesis 1.

underworld, from turmoil and confinement on earth to liberation and peace in Sheol.[2]

1. Introductory Word (3:1-2)

[1]**After this, Job opened his mouth and cursed the day of his birth. **[2]**He said:**

3:1 Job opened his mouth and cursed. "In this speech we are suddenly plunged out of the epic grandeur and deliberateness of the prologue into the dramatic turmoil of the poetry, from the external description of suffering to Job's inner experience."[3] The reader is as shocked as Job's friends must have been at Job's opening words. The consistent piety and reverence that Job has to this point manifested in his submissive response to the tragedies that have befallen him is suddenly broken by a painful cry that expresses resentment against the blessing of life and questions the motives of the God who gives it (v. 23). This unexpected turn of events sets in motion a struggle between Job and his God that is not resolved until Job's final words in 42:2-6. From this moment forward Job the pious becomes Job the protester. The Job who has humbly bowed before God now sets himself against God. Before he is through speaking, he will question God, impugn him, and demand vindication from him.

Recognizing this, the reader immediately asks, "What has happened to the Job of the prologue?" "What has come over this once reverent, submissive saint?" So radical is the difference between the Job of chapters 1–2 and the Job of chapter 3 that a number of scholars have argued that the speeches are from a different author and were only later joined to the prologue. More recent evaluations of Job have tended to explain the difference on literary grounds pointing to the author's desire to complicate the plot or develop the story line. Others have found in his words a hidden impiety that finally comes to light. Still others suggest that Job's earlier responses were canned or even catatonic in nature, the expected or stunned reply of a pious man. The simplest answer may be merely the passing of

---

[2]Habel, *Job*, p. 105.
[3]Clines, *Job*, p. 77.

time and the unrelenting nature of his suffering. At least months have passed by the time Job begins his debate with the friends (7:3). Is it possible that the trusting Job, once expecting imminent release from his torture, has now succumbed to the fear that he will die of his disease, remembered only as an outcast and one cursed of God?

What is the meaning and significance of uttering a "curse" in biblical times? While some interpreters suggest that curses were thought to have magical power to bring about actual events, such a notion is difficult to prove in the Hebrew Bible.[4] The term employed here for "curse" (קָלַל, *qll*, used in the Piel) simply means to "make light, treat as insignificant or worthless." It is a less offensive term than the stronger אָרוּר (*'ārûr*) which is sometimes used in the sense of "reviling" God or "cursing" a ruler. Neither term necessarily carries with it the idea of some magical incantation.[5] In this context Job's curse is in reality a death-wish, a malediction directed against **the day of his birth**[6] because it brought him into this world of misery and distress.

2. Job's Curse (3:3-10)

[3]**May the day of my birth perish, / and the night it was said, 'A boy is born!' / [4]That day—may it turn to darkness; / may God above not care about it; / may no light shine upon it. / [5]May darkness and deep shadow[a] claim it once more; / may a cloud settle over it; / may blackness overwhelm its light. / [6]That night—may thick darkness seize it; / may it not be included among the days of the year / nor be entered in any of the months. / [7]May that night be barren; / may no shout of joy be heard in it. / [8]May those who curse days[b] curse that day, / those who are ready to rouse Leviathan. / [9]May its morning stars become dark; / may it wait for daylight in vain / and not see the first rays of dawn, / [10]for it did not shut the doors of the womb on me / to hide trouble from my eyes.**

[a]*5 Or and the shadow of death*   [b]*8 Or the sea*

---

[4]Cf. A.C. Thiselton, "The Supposed Power of Words in the Biblical Writings," *JTS* 25 (1974): 283-299.

[5]Cf. H.C. Brichto, *The Problem of "Curse" in the Hebrew Bible*, JBLMS 13 (Philadelphia: SBL, 1963), pp. 105ff..

[6]יוֹם אִוָּלֶד בּוֹ (*yôm 'iwwāled bô*). It may refer to the day of his birth or more generally to his "lifetime."

3:3 Job wishes he could undo the past, that he could reverse the events that brought him into the world. He parallels the **day** of his **birth**, with the **night it was said, "A boy is born!"** Several interpreters regard the second **is born** (הֹרָה, *hōrāh*) as referring to conception and see this to be a reference to two separate events: birth and conception, one assigned to the day, the other to the night.[7] In this scenario this verse constitutes a double curse. Apart from the obvious problem of how they might have known **a boy** (גְּבוֹר, *gibbôr*, "strong one") had been conceived,[8] however, it is important to note also that nowhere in this chapter does Job even mention his conception. Reading with NIV we may see a different purpose in the repeated contrast between "day" and "night" (vv. 3-10). They are two different words for the same occasion, and their parallel use is intentional. His labeling of the day of his birth as night is ironic, intended to set the tone of the entire poem, that an occasion (his birth) which should have been a bright and joyous day has instead become a dark and tragic night. Note how the author consistently balances day and night, light and darkness throughout verses 3-10. In so doing he employs a common Hebrew motif of representing evil and malevolence with darkness (cf. Exod 10:22; Prov 4:19; Joel 2:2).

3:4-7 In this section the author uses no less than five different terms to characterize the "dark" day of his birth: **darkness** (חֹשֶׁךְ, *ḥōšek*, vv. 4a,5a); **deep shadow** (צַלְמָוֶת, *ṣalmāweth*, v. 5a);[9] **cloud** (עֲנָנָה, *'ănānāh*, 5b);[10] **blackness** (כַּמְרִיר, *kamrîr*, v. 5c);[11] **thick darkness**

---

[7]Cf., e.g., Clines, *Job,* p. 82; Hartley, *Job,* p. 91.

[8]Clines (*Job,* p. 67) and Hartley (*Job,* p. 90) understand the night in a personified sense to be announcing the conception of a boy. Clines then (following Habel and Strahan) suggests that the night knows and proclaims what a human could not — the sex of the child. But this rendering is unnecessary and undesirable if the entire verse is more naturally taken as synonymous parallelism of day with night.

[9]Lit., "darkness of death," but here carries a superlative force of "very deep darkness"; cf. D.W. Thomas, "צַלְמָוֶת in the Old Testament," *JSS* 7 (1962): 191-200. The term is elsewhere used in Job to describe the region of the dead (10:21-22; 38:17). Amos also uses this term to describe the darkness prior to creation (Amos 5:8).

[10]*'Anānāh* may be the black thundercloud (37:11) or perhaps, even more drastically, the cloud which eliminates all light (cf. Ezek 30:3; 32:7-8; 34:12; Joel 2:2).

[11]The etymology of this term is disputed but is here best understood to be from the root, כמר (*kmr*, "be black").

(אֹפֶל, 'ōphel, v. 6a). These terms, which are used in a wide variety of biblical contexts, exemplify the Old Testament metaphor of "disaster" or "evil" as "darkness." The same idea is carried forth in the New Testament in the writings of John (cf., e.g., John 1:5). Job begins by wishing that the day of his birth fade into oblivion, **may it turn to darkness** (lit., "let there be darkness"). There is in this language a reversal of the language of Genesis 1:3, "let there be light." A number of scholars see his choice of these words to signal a curse process by which he seeks to counter or undo the creation as described in Genesis 1. It is his way of expressing the wish that the day of his birth would have never been. He directs his wish to **God above**, for creation is exclusively the activity of the sovereign God. He asks that God **not care about it** (the day of his birth). The Hebrew here literally says, "May God above not seek [דָּרַשׁ, dāraš] it." That which God "seeks" he is "concerned about" and "provides for." The same term is used in Isaiah 62:12 where the new Jerusalem is called "Sought After, The City No Longer Deserted." The implications of God's seeking are the salvation, vindication, and glorification of the once-forsaken Holy City. By asking God not to "seek" the day of his birth, Job wishfully seeks that it be abandoned or eradicated and that somehow, therefore, he might not exist.

3:5,6 There are two different ways to understand these verses. When Job asks, **May darkness and deep shadow claim it once more**, he may be referring to the chaotic powers that presided over the world before God's creative activity (Gen 1:2). Cosmologically speaking day is the child of night. If night could just reclaim the day, then, Job reasons, his birth might also be reclaimed. This is, in a way, a cry to ultimately turn back the hands of time as an attempt to rewrite the story of his personal history. All of this then could represent a form of cosmological nostalgia — a longing to go back to when time began. By turning back the hands of the primeval clock Job seeks to undo his own existence. On the other hand by calling for the **darkness** to **seize** the day he may be referring simply to the sunset which ends the light of each day. Since light represents life (cf. vv. 16, 20,23) and darkness death (10:21-22; 23:17), in Job this may be just another way of desiring death as an end to his suffering. In other words he wishes that the day which brought him life be somehow forever swallowed up in the darkness that regularly overtakes the day.

He concludes this string of maledictions with two more metaphors of nonexistence. First he asks that his birthday be stricken from the calendar, that it **not be included among the days of the year**. Second he asks that that night **be barren** (גַּלְמוּד, *gālmûd*) like stony, infertile soil that yields no fruit (his birth). All of these death wishes have masterfully developed the "day that is really night" theme which opened the poem.

3:8 Of the wishes Job makes in his curse (vv. 3-10) this is the most difficult to comprehend. The verse is tied to what goes before by referring to **that day**. But who are **those who curse the day** and **those who are ready to rouse Leviathan**, and how do they figure into his singular wish that he had not been born. Most commentators see Job borrowing from the worlds of magic and mythology which surrounded ancient Israel. Those who **curse** and those who **rouse** are viewed as professional sorcerers who claimed the magical power to summon the malevolent forces of chaos that bring upheaval upon the world. Those who argue this often emend **day** (יוֹם, *yôm*) to read **sea** (יָם, *yām*) understanding it to be the biblical equivalent to the sea-god Yamm of the Canaanite myths.[12] The idea then is that the professional sorcerers who can summon the sea-god Yamm and the sea-serpent Leviathan are being enjoined by Job to return the night of his birth to the oblivion of chaos. In support of this interpretation an Aramaic inscription from Nippur is often cited:

> I enchant you with the spell of the sea [Yam],
> And the spell of Leviathan the sea-monster.[13]

This interpretation is further strengthened by evidence from the Canaanite literature of the sun and the sea-dragon being enemies and the dragon even swallowing up the sun or moon.[14] This would fit very nicely into the general wish that Job has that the day of his birth be swallowed up by some great darkness.

---

[12]First suggested by H. Gunkel in *Schopfung und Chaos in Urzeit und Endzeit* (Göttingen: Vandenhoeck & Ruprecht, 1985), p. 59.

[13]Cited by G.R. Driver, "Problems in the Hebrew Text of Job, "*VTSupp* 3 (1955): 72. Also in C.D. Isbell, *Corpus of the Aramaic Incantation Bowl*, SBLDS 17 (Missoula: SBL, 1975), 2:3-4.

[14]Cf. Ugaritic text *CTA* 6.6.44-52; also T.H. Gaster, *Myth, Legend, and Custom in the Old Testament* (New York: Harper and Row, 1969), pp. 787-788.

3:9-10 Continuing his curse against the day he wishes that darkness would also trap the **first rays of dawn** (lit., "eyelids of dawn"). With yet another invective he wishes away the day that brought him into the world. The **morning stars**, Mercury and Venus to us, signal the end of night and the dawning of the new day. By wishing that they never shine he poetically longs that the day of his birth would have never been allowed to dawn. That day is to be cursed because **it did not shut the doors of the womb** on Job. This expression is used elsewhere both in the sense of preventing conception (Gen 29:31; 1 Sam 1:5) and of keeping the fetus from being born (Job 38:8). However we understand its use here, the implication is the same: Job wishes that he had never existed.

3. Job's Lament (3:11-26)

[11]"Why did I not perish at birth, / and die as I came from the womb? / [12]Why were there knees to receive me / and breasts that I might be nursed? / [13]For now I would be lying down in peace; / I would be asleep and at rest / [14]with kings and counselors of the earth, / who built for themselves places now lying in ruins, / [15]with rulers who had gold, / who filled their houses with silver. / [16]Or why was I not hidden in the ground like a stillborn child, / like an infant who never saw the light of day? / [17]There the wicked cease from turmoil, / and there the weary are at rest. / [18]Captives also enjoy their ease; / they no longer hear the slave driver's shout. / [19]The small and the great are there, / and the slave is freed from his master. / [20]Why is light given to those in misery, / and life to the bitter of soul, / [21]to those who long for death that does not come, / who search for it more than for hidden treasure, / [22]who are filled with gladness / and rejoice when they reach the grave? / [23]Why is life given to a man / whose way is hidden, / whom God has hedged in? / [24]For sighing comes to me instead of food; / my groans pour out like water. / [25]What I feared has come upon me; / what I dreaded has happened to me. / [26]I have no peace, no quietness; / I have no rest, but only turmoil."

For the rest of the chapter Job's words constitute a Hebrew lament, differing from the traditional lament style found in the book of Psalms in that it does not address God directly through the use of the second person. His lament is punctuated by five "Why?" statements. The first three address Job's personal situation while the last two ponder the plight of all who suffer. This pattern of reasoning from the particular to the universal will come into play in several of Job's speeches as he considers the implications of his own suffering for his understanding of how God manages his world.

3:11-12 Job's first **"Why?"** continues the theme of the first part of the chapter by questioning the very propriety of his **birth**. This rhetorical question does not so much seek an answer as it makes an assertion. From the beginning it has been Job's contention that his life has been invalidated by his suffering, and from the perspective of his present peril it would have been better if he had not been born. This idea is not unique to Job. It can be found biblically in Ecclesiastes 4:2-3 and in the Hebrew intertestamental literature in 2 Baruch 10:6; 4 Ezra 7:116; Ecclesiasticus 30:17.[15] The **knees** that received Job were probably his mother's (cf. Isa 66:12) in preparation for nursing the child (3:12b); but fathers, too, were known to take a newborn on the knees as an act of acceptance and provision (cf. Gen 50:23).[16]

3:13-15 Beginning here and continuing through verse 19 the place Job desires to be is in Sheol. Though the term is not actually used in the passage, the references to **there** in verses 17 and 19 clearly suggest this as do the characterizations of those who reside there (vv. 14-15,17-19). Job envisions Sheol as a place to escape his miserable existence. From the beginning of his curse he has sought but one thing — release from his turmoil. With four well-chosen words — **lying down** (שָׁכַב, šākab), **peace** (lit., "quiet"; שָׁקַט, šāqaṭ), **sleep** (יָשֵׁן, yāšēn), and **rest** (נוּחַ, nûaḥ) — he portrays the perfect rest that the grave would bring him (cf. v. 26.). This portrayal of the netherworld is the opposite of how it is pictured elsewhere. Normally in the Bible Sheol is spoken of in terms of darkness and gloom, and those who go there are forgotten (Ps 88:11-13). Job, too, will later so describe it (10:21-22). But here he welcomes the oblivion of the grave as deliverance from his desperate circumstance. In

---

[15]For a review of this concept in Hebrew and Greek literature cf. D. Daube, "Black Hole," *Rechtshistorisches Journal* 2 (1983): 177-193.

[16]Cf. B. Stade, "Auf Jemandes Knieen gebaren," *ZAW* 6 (1886): 143-156.

such a place he would be in good company with others who have
fallen from high places to its inescapable grasp. Even **kings, counselors**, and **rulers**[17] end up there, those who had amassed **gold** and
silver and **built for themselves places now lying in ruins** (חֳרָבוֹת,
ḥŏrābôth).[18] In ancient times rulers commonly constructed great edi-
fices as testimony to their power and wealth (cf. Isa 44:26; 58:12).
This may be referring to tombs built by rulers to house the wealth
they intended to take with them to the realm beyond.[19] But such a
practice was primarily limited to Egyptian culture in biblical times.
However we take it, the meaning is the same. Even those whom death
has deprived of wealth and privilege are better off than the living.

3:16 Many commentators see this verse as out of place and argue
that it logically belongs with verses 11-12 which likewise focus on a
desire for miscarriage at birth. Note also that the **there** of verse 17
obviously refers to Sheol and picks up on the theme of verse 15.
Strictly speaking, though, the event portrayed here is not the miscarriage (as in 3:11-12) but the stillbirth.[20] Further, a connection with
Sheol can be found in the phrase **why was I not hidden in the ground**,
expressing his claim that had he been a **stillborn child** he would have
immediately been buried. Rather than having lived a full life and then
going to the netherworld, he wishes that he had gone directly from
the womb to the grave (as in 10:18-19). This, he feels, would have
spared him the misery that his life has brought him. Accordingly we
can understand how verse 16 fits into the overall lament.

3:17-19 Job now returns to his depiction of those who reside in
Sheol. The phrase **There the wicked cease from turmoil** does not
refer to some kind of annihilation of judgment which the wicked
have been suffering in this life and that death will relieve. The **turmoil**[21] is the grief they dispense upon the **weary**, or those whom they
exploit. In the next two verses he goes on to develop this idea of the
grave being the great leveler of opposing or competing classes.
Captives and **slave drivers, small** and **great**, all end up there. This

---

[17]Lit. "princes"; the same three terms appear in Ezra 7:28; 8:25.

[18]Some emend *ḥŏrābôth* to *ḥaramôth* and connect it with the Arabic *ḥrm*,
"be decayed," which is a term that refers to pyramid ruins.

[19]So Duhm and Fohrer.

[20]נֵפֶל, *nēphel*, "that which falls."

[21]רֹגֶז, *rōgez*, "raging." The term describes the upheaval which a violent
ruler causes upon the earth (Joel 2:11; Isa 23:11).

focus on socioeconomic and political opposites may reflect Job's comparison of the two different phases of his life. Once the greatest of the sons of the east, he has now been reduced to a poor outcast. That great sense of loss will be neutralized in the netherworld where there is no oppression, no conflict, no suffering.

3:20-22. Why is light given to those in misery? With these words Job takes a step in reasoning that he will repeat many times in his speeches. He moves from a consideration of his individual situation to an assessment of the larger arena of universal human suffering. When he asks why life is even given to those who suffer, he asks not only for himself but for suffering humanity in general. The "why?" question is typical of the Hebrew lament and is attested in several of the psalms. We should probably understand that here, as elsewhere in the book, it is being asked of God (cf. v. 23). He is the giver of life (1 Sam 2:6). There is in this question an implied challenge to the way God manages his world.[22] Job sees a cruel illogic in a providence that grants life only to have it lived out in **misery**.[23] Job's question is more than an intellectual quest for understanding. It amounts to a complaint, an accusation against God. The equation of **life**[24] with **light** is a familiar one in Scripture (Ps 56:14; Isa 53:11). Here it resurrects a theme sounded earlier in the chapter where Job desired darkness to consume the day of his birth. The **bitter of soul** (מָרֵי נָפֶשׁ, *mārê nāpheš*) are those who are deeply distressed. The phrase is used to describe the childless (1 Sam 1:10), the impoverished (Job 21:25), and the bereaved (Ezek 27:31). The use of the phrase **long for death** is ironic. Instead of longing for the Lord to deliver, these bitter ones long for death as their savior. They do not merely long for death; they **search for it** as if it were **hidden treasure**. They are prospectors searching for death, digging their own graves.[25] The irony is completed with the imagery of death bringing **gladness** instead of the sorrow that normally accompanies it.

---

[22]Cf. H.J. Boecker, *Redeformen des Rechtslebens im Alten Testament*, WMANT 14 (Neukirchen-Vluyn: Neukirchener Verlag, 1964), pp. 30-31.

[23]עָמָל, *'āmēl*, "conflict, turmoil, unease."

[24]The choice of the word "light" may also reflect a cosmic imagery that many scholars believe is behind this lament. Cf. note 1 above.

[25]The joining of the images of prospecting for treasure and the welcomeness of the grave makes one think of the grave robbers of the ancient world

Job's death wish echoes the thought of the sufferer who argues with his soul in the Egyptian text, *A Dispute over Suicide*:

> Death is in my sight today
>   [Like] the recovery of a sick man,
>   Like going out into the open after a confinement.
> Death is in my sight today
>   Like the odor of myrrh,
>   Like sitting under an awning on a breezy day. . . .
> Death is in my sight today
>   Like the longing of a man to see his house [again]
>   After he has spent many years held in captivity.[26]

3:23 The "Why?" which has punctuated Job's lament is asked again with a slightly different emphasis. Here Job is perplexed over his inability to discover the meaning of his life. The word **way** (דֶּרֶךְ, *derek*) here refers to Job's destiny. When he says that it is **hidden**, he confesses that he is now unsure of the purpose and destiny of his life and the path that he should pursue to find it. With these words Job addresses the psychological and even spiritual implications of his suffering. He has lost his way. The path that was once so clear to him has now been obscured by the tragedies which have befallen him. Paramount in his bewilderment is just where God is in all of this. That he is thinking of God is implicit in his string of "whys?" but now for the first time he actually mentions him. He feels that his life has been **hedged in** by God. Immediately the reader's mind is called back to the challenge of the Satan that God had **put a hedge around** Job. In that text God's hedge was viewed positively as a protective wall. Here that idea is ironically reversed to describe a wall that hems in or traps. With these words Job explicitly accuses God of creating a world in which life is cruelly invalidated by suffering.[27]

3:24-26 Job ends his lament with a description of the suffering he endures by focusing on the emotional consequences of his brokenness. In the place of the **food** and **water** that daily sustain human

---

who sought to rob the tombs of their treasures (cf. the discussion of v. 15 above).
[26]*ANET*, pp. 405-407.
[27]Against Clines, *Job*, pp. 104-105.

life, he consumes only **sighs** (אֲנָחָה, *'ănāḥāh*)[28] and **groans** (שְׁאָגָה, *š'āgāh*).[29] Job considers himself the victim of what he had **feared** and **dreaded**.[30] It is interesting to note that even before disaster struck him, Job had lived with a sense of dread that something disastrous might happen to his children. He had even offered sacrifices on behalf of his children to atone for some possible irreverence on their part (1:5). He punctuates his characterization of his distress by a trilogy of terms describing his loss of tranquility. He is without **peace**, without **quietness**, and without **rest**. Dhorme understands these terms to refer to the absence of mental rest (שָׁלָה, *šālāh*), physical rest (שָׁקַט, *šāqaṭ*), and rest in general (נוּחַ, *nûaḥ*). In the place of this lost serenity Job is possessed by **turmoil** (רֹגֶז, *rōgez*). With this final term Job thematically joins his lament with his opening curse by consigning himself to the chaos that possessed the world before God's creation.

---

[28]This term is elsewhere used to describe the anguishing sounds of those broken by some tragedy or exploited by slave labor (cf., e.g., Exod 2:23; Lam 1:4,8,11; Jer 45:3).

[29]This term is used to describe the "roaring" of a lion (Isa 5:29) as well as the loud cries of the afflicted (Ps 22:2[1]; 32:3).

[30]See R.L. Katz, "A Psychoanalytic Commentary on Job 3:23," *HUCA* 29 (1958): 377-383.

JOB 4

II. DIALOGUE BETWEEN JOB AND HIS FRIENDS (4:1–26:14)

The opening speech of Eliphaz begins a dialogue that will occupy the next twenty-three chapters of the book. These speeches, which employ a wide variety of rhetorical forms, essentially constitute a debate over the role of God in Job's suffering. They move forward in three cycles in which each of the friends will speak in turn followed by a reply from Job. The third cycle ends with Bildad making only a brief remark (25:1-6) and Zophar not speaking at all. After replying to Bildad (26:1-14) Job concludes his final defense in the longest speech of the book (27:1–31:40).

A. THE FIRST CYCLE OF SPEECHES (4:1–14:22)

1. The First Speech of Eliphaz (4:1–5:27)

Of the three friends who debate with Job, Eliphaz is arguably the most eloquent and theologically advanced.[1] His prominence among the friends is illustrated by the fact that he speaks first in each of the three cycles of speeches and that his discourses are significantly longer than those of the other comforters. His skill as a rhetorician is illustrated by his employment of a wide variety of rhetorical forms.[2] Over the course of his speeches he punctuates his arguments

---

[1]So argues R. Gordis in *The Book of God and Man: A Study of Job* (Chicago: University of Chicago Press, 1965), p. 77.

[2]K. Fullerton, "Double Entendre in the First Speech of Eliphaz," *JBL* 49 (1930): 320-374; Y. Hoffman, "The Use of Equivocal Words in the First Speech of Eliphaz," *VT* 30 (1980): 114-119.

with wisdom sayings, proverbs, parables, hymns, doxologies, a vision report, rhetorical questions, exhortations, and many analogies.

Eliphaz's argument, like that of the other friends, is built upon the premise that God governs his world by the principle of retributive justice. He believes that God prospers the righteous and inflicts suffering and premature death upon the wicked. Though Eliphaz speaks generally of all humankind, it is obvious that he believes that Job's suffering is the result of some sin he has personally committed. He is convinced that only if Job accepts God's chastening and repents of his sin can he find restoration and blessing from God. Eliphaz is caught between two conflicting roles. On the one hand he wants to extend sympathy to Job, but overriding that desire is his even greater determination to defend the God whose providence Job has called into question.

Eliphaz's Initial Response to Job (4:1-6)

¹Then Eliphaz the Temanite replied:
²"If someone ventures a word with you, will you be impatient? / But who can keep from speaking? / ³Think how you have instructed many, / how you have strengthened feeble hands. / ⁴Your words have supported those who stumbled; / you have strengthened faltering knees. / ⁵But now trouble comes to you, and you are discouraged; / it strikes you, and you are dismayed. / ⁶Should not your piety be your confidence / and your blameless ways your hope?

4:1-2 Following the author's formulaic introduction, Eliphaz's opening speech begins with a gentle rebuke of the ungrateful and irreverent language of Job's curse. In a conciliatory tone that shows sensitivity to Job's plight he asks a rhetorical question intended to prepare Job for the challenge he feels compelled to render: **If someone ventures a word with you, will you be impatient?** Eliphaz's dilemma as both comforter of Job and defender of Yahweh is evident in this question and the remark which follows: **But who can keep from speaking?** Eliphaz knows that his challenge to Job's death wish may only further agitate him, but he feels that Job's words cannot go unanswered. Eliphaz's compulsion to speak may be understood from three different perspectives. First, Job's words have expressed lack of gratitude for God's great gift of life and even impugned the propriety of God's management of his world. That

challenge demands a reply. Second, Eliphaz may have a broader concern over the possibility that Job's words will be heard by others who
might be led astray. If we presume, as many do, that these speeches
had an audience, the potential influence of a man as prominent as
Job would be great. To have a man once honored as the "greatest of
the sons of the East" say such negative things about life and God
may be viewed by the friends as a dangerous teaching that could be
misleading to the theologically naïve. Third, Eliphaz believes he has
received a revelation (vv. 12-17) and, like Jeremiah, may feel compelled to deliver that revealed word which "burns in his bones" (Jer
20:9). Restraint in speech is commonly urged by the sages (Prov
10:19; 12:23) among whom Eliphaz is surely to be numbered. But
after sitting a week in silence and then enduring Job's curse, this
sage must respond.

4:3-5 Think how you instructed many. With these words Eliphaz
assumes the role that Job once performed. In better times Job was
the "instructor," but now he needs the lesson Eliphaz has to teach.
The Hebrew word for **instructed** (יִסַּר, *yissēr*) refers to a disciplinary,
corrective teaching like that which a father might offer his son (Prov
19:18; Deut 8:5). By using this word Eliphaz is inviting the teacher
to become the pupil. Job's edifying words had once nurtured those
with **feeble hands** and **faltering knees**. These terms must be
thought of as metaphorical descriptions of those who have difficulty staying on the path of wisdom (cf. Prov 4:10ff). Job's **words** (מִלִּים,
millîm) have helped them stay on that path. Of the thirty-eight occurrences of this term in the Old Testament, thirty-four are in Job. This
word exhibits a wide range of meanings in Job from "argument" to
"message." To this point Eliphaz has been praising Job, portraying
him as a champion of the spiritually weak and religiously confused.
But in verse 5 he turns from compliment to censure: **But now trouble comes to you, and you are discouraged**. Job's response to his
current crisis contradicts his career of encouragement. These words
are commonly regarded as sarcastic, and indeed they may be so.
Other opinions suggest they are more motivated by Eliphaz's pity of
a man who once helped others but now is, himself, in need of help.[3]

4:6 Eliphaz continues his gentle rebuke with a rhetorical question built upon a tenet of biblical wisdom. The **piety** upon which

---

[3]Fullerton, "Double Entendre," p. 340.

Eliphaz suggests Job's **confidence**[4] should rest is in the Hebrew, literally, Job's "fear of the LORD." As noted above, this phrase approximates our concept of "religion." According to Proverbs this reverence for God is the source and basis of true wisdom (Prov 1:7,29; 2:5; 9:10).[5] More specifically in the book of Job it means to "trust God as faithful" (6:14; 22:4). Eliphaz's reference to this wisdom principal appears to assume that Job agrees with it. Evidently he does not yet realize that Job has lost confidence in the way of piety. Indeed, Job will later rebuke Eliphaz for failing to recognize Job's theological problem (cf. 6:14ff).

Ironically, Job's **blameless ways** (תֹּם, tōm, "integrity"), which Eliphaz suggests are the basis of Job's **hope**, have instead become the basis of his despair. Unaware that his piety is being tested, Job has wrongly concluded that God, by inflicting him with suffering, no longer honors his piety. Job's defense of his integrity will eventually lead him to accuse God of being unjust. Eliphaz's question illustrates the disconnection between him and Job and the different sets of presumptions behind their opposing views. Eliphaz believes that if Job recovers his integrity he will be restored. Job believes that the integrity he has never lost is no longer of any value in winning the favor of God.

Eliphaz's Doctrine of Retribution (4:7-11)

[7]"Consider now: Who, being innocent, has ever perished? / Where were the upright ever destroyed? / [8]As I have observed, those who plow evil / and those who sow trouble reap it. / [9]At the breath of God they are destroyed; / at the blast of his anger they perish. / [10]The lions may roar and growl, / yet the teeth of the great lions are broken. / [11]The lion perishes for lack of prey, / and the cubs of the lioness are scattered.

---

[4]כִּסְלָה (kislāh) is an interesting term. The root כסל (ksl) means, "be fat, thick," referring to the fat of the body. Since too much fat can rob one of vitality and health, the term often takes on a negative meaning in the Bible and can even be a synonym for "folly" (cf., e.g., Job 15:25-27). Here, however, it is used in a positive sense of "confidence" or "trust" (cf. also 8:14; 31:24), perhaps reflecting the concept that the fat on the liver was viewed as sustaining life. Cf. H. Wolff, *Anthropology of the Old Testament* (London: SCM, 1974), p. 64.

[5]Cf. R.E. Murphy, "Kerygma of the Book of Proverbs," *Int* 20 (1966): 3-14.

4:7-11 Who, being innocent, has ever perished? Eliphaz the comforter has now become Eliphaz the systematic theologian. The specific tenet he is rehearsing here is the doctrine of retribution. The
idea that the righteous are blessed by God while the wicked experience suffering and premature death is taught elsewhere in Scripture.[6]
The way Eliphaz states the doctrine suggests that he believes this
principle has no exceptions. Eventually he will attempt to force Job
and even God into his airtight theological box. As will be the case
throughout his speeches, Eliphaz bases his claim on what he has personally **observed**. The other sources of his theology are his religious
tradition and a special revelation he claims to have received (4:12-21).
These instructors have convinced him that the world is governed by
a fundamental law of harvest: **those who sow trouble reap it**. The
prophet Hosea, the writer of Proverbs, and the apostle Paul echo this
concept.[7] Some interpreters understand this language to describe a
"fate-determining deed," in the sense of a self-destructive behavior
pattern in which people, by their own ill-advised actions, set in
motion a set of consequences that are difficult, if not impossible, to
escape.[8] Others see this as a crime-and-punishment model governed
by God's direct and personal intervention.[9] That Eliphaz has the latter in mind is made clear by the next verse. The **breath of God** and
the **blast of his anger** (lit., "wind of his nostril") are the executors of
the guilty. This can mean nothing less than God's personal involvement in their judgment. In the Old Testament God's breath (נְשָׁמָה,
nᵉšāmāh, or רוּחַ, *rûaḥ*, "wind, spirit") is often used as a metaphor of
God's creative or life-giving activity.[10] But the idea of God's breath as
a destructive force is also to be found in several places (Exod 15:7f;
2 Sam 22:16; Hos 13:15; Ezek 17:10).[11]

---

[6]Cf., e.g., Deut 11:26-28; 28:1ff; Ps 37; Prov 12:21.

[7]Cf. Hos 8:7; Prov 22:8; Gal 6:7.

[8]Cf. K. Koch, "Gibt es ein Vergeltungsdogma im alten Testament?" *ZTK*
52 (1955): 1-42. According to Koch, God does not directly judge each individual action but, in a broader sense, guarantees the moral order.

[9]Cf. H. Graf Reventlow, "Sein Blut komme über sein Haupt," *VT* 10
(1960): 311-327. Also J.G. Gammie, "The Theology of Retribution in the
Book of Deuteronomy," *CBQ* 32 (1970): 1-12; P. Zerafa, "Retribution in the
OT," *Ang* 50 (1973): 464-490.

[10]Gen 2:7; Job 34:14; Ps 104:29-30; Amos 4:13; Jer 10:13.

[11]Cf. T.C. Mitchell, "The Old Testament Usage of *NeŠĀMÂ*," *VT* 11 (1961):
177-187.

Eliphaz closes his initial argument by citing a proverb in which five different terms for "lion" are employed.[12] The Hebrew here is difficult, but the idea seems to be that in spite of the lion's ferocity it is yet destined to perish, just like evil men. God breaks the strength of the wicked as he does the **teeth** of the mighty lion (cf. Ps 58:7[6]). Eliphaz's comparison of the wicked man with lions is echoed by several other biblical texts (Ps 7:3[2]; 17:12; 22:14[13],22[21]; Prov 28:15).[13]

Eliphaz's Vision Report (4:12-21)

[12]"A word was secretly brought to me, / my ears caught a whisper of it. / [13]Amid disquieting dreams in the night, / when deep sleep falls on men, / [14]fear and trembling seized me / and made all my bones shake. / [15]A spirit glided past my face, / and the hair on my body stood on end. / [16]It stopped, / but I could not tell what it was. / A form stood before my eyes, / and I heard a hushed voice: / [17]"Can a mortal be more righteous than God? / Can a man be more pure than his Maker? / [18]If God places no trust in his servants, / if he charges his angels with error, / [19]how much more those who live in houses of clay, / whose foundations are in the dust, / who are crushed more readily than a moth! / [20]Between dawn and dusk they are broken to pieces; / unnoticed, they perish forever. / [21]Are not the cords of their tent pulled up, / so that they die without wisdom?"[a]

[a]21 Some interpreters end the quotation after verse 17.

This vision report falls into two connected parts: 1) a description of his nocturnal vision experience (vv. 12-16) and 2) the message of the vision along with its implication for Job (vv. 17-21). This particular account demonstrates similarities with several other biblical passages (cf., e.g., Gen 15:12-19; Jer 1:4-9; Ezek 2:1–3:3; Isa 6:1-8). Like many of the prophets Eliphaz claims to have received a direct revelation of a prophetic word. And like Abraham he experienced this in a deep sleep. The content of Eliphaz's vision builds upon his earlier argument. In his initial words he explained why the wicked suffer. God is punishing them for their sins. In this part of his speech

---

[12]Cf. G. Botterweck, "ari," TDOT, 1:374-388.

[13]Cf. J.J.M. Roberts, "The Young Lions of Psalm 34,11," Bib 54 (1973): 265-267.

he explains why the righteous suffer. God corrects them of their imperfections (cf. 5:17). This correction is necessary because no mortal (not even a righteous man) is pure before his Maker. Humans are therefore worthy of any ill that God might bring upon their lives. Neither are they qualified to accuse God of any injustice in afflicting the saints. This or any other explanation of why the righteous suffer, argues Eliphaz, can only come by revelation.[14]

4:12-16 The instructive **word** (דָּבָר, *dābar*) that Eliphaz had promised to deliver to Job (v. 2) was **secretly brought** (יְגֻנַּב, *yᵉgunnāb*) to him.[15] These terms, used in tandem, are Eliphaz's way of suggesting he has had a supernatural revelation. **To me** (v. 12) is at the beginning of the sentence to emphasize the fact that this is his personal experience. The mention of **ears** and later **voice** (v. 16) informs the reader that, though this was a vision, it was what he heard that was most important. The connection of revealed word and vision is also attested in Amos 7-9. Eliphaz received his revelation during a night filled with **disquieting dreams** (שְׂעִפִּים, *śᵉ'ippîm*),[16] the biblical expression for nightmares. The **deep sleep** (תַּרְדֵּמָה, *tardēmāh*) into which he fell is used in the Bible to connote everything from unconsciousness (Gen 2:21; 1 Sam 26:12) to a terrifying dream (Gen 15:12; Job 33:15). Only rarely is it made the medium of revelation in the Old Testament.[17] Like Abraham (Gen 15:12) Eliphaz responds to his vision with a **fear and trembling** (v. 14) that made his **bones shake**. The bones as supporters of the body are often in Hebrew poetry made to represent it, including its emotions and affections. The eerie **spirit**[18] (v. 15) and the unrecognizable **form** (v. 16) which

---

[14]Cf. F. Asensio Nieto, "La visión de Elifaz y su proyección sapiencial," *EstBib* 35 (1976): 145-163.

[15]Cf. R.J. Werblowsky, "Stealing a Word," *VT* 6 (1956): 105-106; who argues that the term *gunnāb* here is a technical term for a nocturnal revelation.

[16]This term is commonly associated with *śar'appîm* (Ps 94:19; 139:23) and rendered "disturbing thoughts."

[17]Dreams were commonly regarded as revelations throughout the ancient world. This is why they were taken so seriously (cf. Genesis 40–41; Daniel 2). The infrequent use of them by Yahweh probably reflects God's desire to disassociate his word from the widespread superstitions of the time.

[18]There is a play here on the Hebrew word *rûaḥ* which can mean "wind" or "spirit." The same double meaning occurs in the NT with the Greek word *pneuma*. The properties of wind (invisible, yet powerful; life-giving; mysteri-

passed before Eliphaz refer to some manifestation of God. This is reinforced by the fact that God is also made the subject of the verb **glided** (חָלַף, *ḥālaph*, "pass by quickly") in 9:11 and 11:10. In Psalm 17:15 God's "form" (תְּמוּנָה, *tᵉmûnāh*) is parallel with God's "face" (פָּנִים, *pānîm*). The inability of Eliphaz to recognize God is similar to the experience of many others who saw God in the Old Testament.

4:17-21 The content of Eliphaz's mysterious revelation is not mysterious at all. It reflects the teaching of traditional theology: God is more righteous than man. The **voice**[19] that speaks out of the eerie silence asks two rhetorical questions: **Can a mortal be more righteous than God? Can a man be more pure[20] than his Maker?** The use of questions instead of simple declarations may be for the sake of emphasis. It might also anticipate the interrogation that Yahweh will later make of Job (40:8). One wonders why a revelation was needed to declare so common a truth. Perhaps it is Eliphaz's (or God's) way of addressing an argument implicit in Job's first speech (3:23) and vigorously stated in his subsequent addresses: God is not just. In support of this interpretation it should be noted that Eliphaz will repeat this doctrine in each of his two remaining speeches (15:15-16; 22:2), and each time in response to some challenge of God's justice by Job. Eliphaz's injecting this truth here allows him to correct Job's assertion that his innocence qualifies him to question God's justice from the outset without directly accusing Job of sin.[21] By this approach he is able to comfort Job and yet defend God.

According to Eliphaz what is true of humankind is also true of God's **servants** (עֲבָדִים, *'ăbādîm*) or **his angels** (מַלְאָכִים, *mal'ākîm*; cf. Ps 104:4). They too are charged with **error**.[22] Heavenly beings are

_____

ous in movement) make it suitable as a metaphor of the nonmaterial essence of God (or man).

[19]The Hebrew phrase דְּמָמָה וָקוֹל (*dᵉmamah waqōl*, "silence, then . . . a voice") is similar to the "still small voice" (קוֹל דְּמָמָה דַקָּה, *qôl demāmāh daqqāh*) Elijah received at Sinai (1 Kgs 19:12-18).

[20]The term טָהֵר (*ṭāhēr*) is often used in religious texts to refer to that which is ceremonially "pure" or "free from defect." Here, however, it refers to moral uprightness as it does in Prov 22:11; 30:12; Ps 12:7[6]; Hab 1:13; Zech 3:5.

[21]Cf. Hartley, *Job*, pp. 113-114.

[22]MT תָּהֳלָה (*toholāh*) is a *hapax legomenon* and we can only speculate over its meaning. Most scholars connect it with the Ethiopic *tahala* ("error") or Hebrew תִּפְלָה (*tiphlāh*, "folly"). Rashi and Ibn Ezra connect it to the root

referred to frequently in Job. In the dialogue they are called "holy ones" (קְדֹשִׁים, *qᵉdōšîm*; 5:1; 15:15). At first such a designation would seem to be at odds with this less positive assessment of them. But "holy" in the above texts does not mean "morally excellent" but "belonging to God." In the Old Testament sacred places and sacred objects are called "holy."[23]

If the angels are not righteous before God, how can those **who live in houses of clay** built on **foundations of dust** (v. 19) be righteous? Humans are not only impure, they are also transitory and vulnerable. The emphasis on "clay" and "dust" echoes the creation account of Genesis 2:7.[24] If the "houses" here refer to human bodies, as most commentators hold, this would be the first clear reference in Hebrew literature to the idea of the body as the residence of the human being.[25] Humans, like the **moth**, are on earth a relatively short time and can live and die without ever being noticed. As such they are simply too insignificant to challenge God or his management of his world.

Humans are but a **tent** (v. 21), a temporary structure that is soon **pulled up**. The breadth of human life is so short that humans may not even live long enough to gain **wisdom**. "Wisdom" is meant here and elsewhere in Job as reverence for God and insight into God's ways. To die without being noticed is one thing, but to die without gaining wisdom is to miss life's greatest gift (Prov 3:18). When Eliphaz raises the possibility of humans never acquiring wisdom, he touches on a theme that will be repeated several times in the book. The quest for some perspective on the meaning of Job's suffering and God's role in it is the very issue of this great debate. Though both Job and the friends will later declare that they have discovered its meaning, in reality they never do. This will reinforce the affirmation made in chapter 28 that God alone understands the way of wisdom (28:23).

הָלַל (*hālal*, "be mad" or "make a fool of"). Cf. Eccl 2:2; 7:7,25; 10:13. This suggestion has the support of LXX, Targ., and Vulg.

[23]Cf. M. Noth, "The Holy Ones of the Most High," in *The Laws in the Pentateuch* (Edinburgh: Oliver and Boyd, 1966), pp. 215-228; J. Milgrom, "The Compass of Biblical Sancta," *JQR* 65 (1975): 205-216.

[24]This idea is also attested in the ancient Near Eastern literature; cf. the Mesopotamian works Atrahasis and Enumah Elish.

[25]Cf. discussion by Clines, *Job*, pp. 134-135.

JOB 5

1. The First Speech of Eliphaz (4:1–5:27, continued)

No Mediator for Mortal Men (5:1-7)

[1]"Call if you will, but who will answer you? / To which of the holy ones will you turn? / [2]Resentment kills a fool, / and envy slays the simple. / [3]I myself have seen a fool taking root, / but suddenly his house was cursed. / [4]His children are far from safety, / crushed in court without a defender. / [5]The hungry consume his harvest, / taking it even from among thorns, / and the thirsty pant after his wealth. / [6]For hardship does not spring from the soil, / nor does trouble sprout from the ground. / [7]Yet man is born to trouble / as surely as sparks fly upward.

5:1-2 In this portion of his speech Eliphaz anticipates an approach that Job will later attempt to take in his dispute with God (9:33; 16:19-21). Is there some heavenly mediator to whom Job can plead his case? Eliphaz answers with a resounding "no." **Call if you will**, he suggests to Job, **but who will answer you?** The verbs "call" and "answer" reach back to Job's lament in which he begins his quest for some explanation for his suffering (cf. 3:22). Is Job hoping one of the **holy ones** will intervene on his behalf? If so, he has misplaced his hope. The "holy ones" (קְדֹשִׁים, *qᵉdōšîm*) most probably refer to angels (cf. 15:15).[1] They are called "holy ones" (lit., "set apart ones") because of their relationship with the holy God. This is one of only a few places in Scripture where angels are thought of as intercessors for humans (cf. 33:23-28). In postexilic times the belief in heavenly intercessors grew in Israelite theology and carried over

---

[1]Cf. also Deut 33:3; Ps 89:6-8[5-7]; Zech 14:5; Dan 4:14[17]; 8:13; 1 Enoch 1:9.

into Christian thought. This text and others in Job suggest that the
idea was present earlier as well. Eliphaz, however, strongly rejects
this possibility, probably on the grounds he has earlier argued that
not even the angels are guiltless before God (4:18).[2] Quoting a
proverb (v. 2) Eliphaz warns Job of the potentially disastrous consequences that can come of **resentment** (כַּעַשׂ, kā'aś, "burning anger")
and **envy** (קִנְאָה, qin'āh, "jealousy"). These attitudes are more typical
of the **fool** (אֱוִיל, 'ĕwîl) and the **simple** (פֹּתֶה, pōtheh) than they are of
the pious. The first of these two terms refers to the one who is
unrighteous or morally evil while the second refers to the naïve and
uninitiated. In these opening verses, then, Eliphaz has both denied
Job the possibility of an arbiter and condemned the kind of non-
pious attitude that might seek one.

5:3-7 In verses 3 and 4 Eliphaz traces out the destiny of the fool.
Giving his personal testimony (**I myself have seen**), Eliphaz insists
that though it may appear that fools **take root**,[3] in reality their lives
are doomed to collapse. The **curse** (קבב, qbb) which Eliphaz says the
fool's **house** is under carries with it the idea of being alienated from
God and his goodness. To be cursed is the equivalent of being cast
out or excommunicated from God's benevolence. Hence, **his children** are said to be **far from safety**. Extending the idea of such alienation to one's children was considered the ultimate punishment to
the ancient Semite. The fool, already dead (presumably at the hand
of God), leaves behind orphans who are vulnerable to exploitation.
The scene depicted here is that of the city gate where legal and commercial matters were decided. In such an arena the orphaned sur-
vivors of the fool are without a **defender** to protect their interests.
As a result (v. 5) such a family loses its wealth. The envious pounce
upon the wicked man's undefended possessions.[4] Some scholars
argue that the word translated **the hungry** (רָעֵב, rā'ēb) does not refer
to a class of the socially underprivileged but to a mythological des-

---

[2]David J.A. Clines in "Job 5,1-8: A New Exegesis," *Bib* 62 (1981): 185-194,
argues that the reason the angels can do Job no good is not because they
may have sinned but because they cannot break the nexus between Job's
actions and retributive justice.

[3]The tree is a symbol of prosperity and stability and so does the rich fool
at first seem (cf., e.g., Ps 1:3).

[4]The Hebrew of the first line of v. 5 is difficult, but the best rendering is
that of Gordis and Tur-Sinai: "His substances the starving will carry away."

ignation of the god death (Mot). This, they say, is supported by the Hebrew expression "sons of Reshef fly upward" (NIV, **sparks**[5] **fly upward**) in verse 7. Since Reshef was a well-known god in the ancient Near East and since this term is pared with Raeb ("hungry one") again in Job 18:12-13 and in Deuteronomy 32:24, it is arguable that the author is here referring to two deities believed in Job's day to wreak havoc on the unsuspecting.[6] Eliphaz again ties his argument to the doctrine of retribution when he reminds Job that **hardship does not spring from the soil**. In other words, trouble does not just spontaneously arise. It has causes. It is rooted in human sin. It is not nature which is the source of human suffering but humanity itself. There may be some allusion to the curse upon the soil as a consequence of Adam's sin here (cf. Gen 3:17-19).

The phrase **Yet man is born to trouble** should probably be read "Yet man begets trouble." Most interpreters render the verb **born** (יוּלָד, *yûllād*) actively and understand the phrase to mean that humans are the source of their own trouble.[7] This would make sense in view of the argument just made in verse 6. This rendering is also supported by similar wording in Isaiah 59:4b, "they conceive trouble and give birth to evil."

Eliphaz's Advice to Job (5:8-16)

[8]**"But if it were I, I would appeal to God; / I would lay my cause before him. / [9]He performs wonders that cannot be fathomed, / miracles that cannot be counted. / [10]He bestows rain on the earth; / he sends water upon the countryside. / [11]The lowly he sets on high, / and those who mourn are lifted to safety. / [12]He thwarts the plans of the crafty, / so that their hands achieve no success. / [13]He catches the wise in their craftiness, / and the schemes of the wily are swept away. / [14]Darkness comes upon them in the daytime; / at noon they grope as in the night. / [15]He saves the needy from the sword in their mouth; / he saves them from the clutches of the powerful. / [16]So the poor have hope, / and injustice shuts its mouth.**

---

[5]רֶשֶׁף, *rešeph* means "flame" in Cant 8:6 and metaphorically "sparks" (of the bow = lightning) in Ps 76:4[3].

[6]Cf. Habel, *Job*, p. 131. On the god Reseph cf. J.B. Burns, "The Mythology of Death in the Old Testament," *SJT* 26 (1973): 327-340; W. Fulco, *The Canaanite God Resep*, AOS 8 (New Haven: American Oriental Society, 1976).

[7]Cf., e.g., Duhm, Dhorme, Gordis.

5:8 Putting himself in Job's place, Eliphaz suggests a course of action which would be in keeping with the model of retributive justice he has just presented: **I would appeal to God, I would lay my cause before him**. Since no heavenly intercessors will come to Job's rescue (5:1) and since it is futile for a human to protest innocence before the holy God (4:17-18), the only remaining course of action is to throw oneself on the mercy of God. The verb **appeal** (דָּרַשׁ, dāraš) can refer to a formal approach for assistance or counsel (Gen 25:22; 1 Sam 9:9; 1 Kgs 22:8) or to seek deliverance from some peril (Amos 5:4,6). For Job, to appeal to God is to admit his dependency upon him and to invite his merciful intervention. Job, however, will take quite a different approach to God in his subsequent speeches.

5:9-10 The God to whom Job should appeal has both the power and the disposition to reverse Job's misfortunes. The attributes of God are set forth in a hymn of praise, a doxology honoring God as Creator (עֹשֶׂה, 'ōśeh, cf. also 4:17).[8] This hymn shares affinities with Amos 5:6-10.[9] The emphasis in both hymns is God's transforming power. This theme is illustrated in two arenas: creation and social justice. God **performs wonders that cannot be fathomed, miracles than cannot be counted**. The term for **miracles** (נִפְלָאוֹת, niphlā'ôth) is associated with the exodus (Ps 106:22); creation (Ps 107:24; 139:14); and with God's other saving acts in history (Ps 105:5; 106:7). If God can do this for his world and for his people, he can also do wonders for Job. The emphasis on God's provision of **rain** seems anticlimactic given what was said in the previous verse. But in the Near East rainfall, which is so scarce and so important for agriculture, is considered one of the greatest of God's wonders. In the thanksgiving hymn of Psalm 147 rain is the first of God's blessings to be mentioned. Rain also has the power to transform a desert landscape into a lush field. Such a blessing would be a fitting metaphor for Job's need of God's transforming power.[10]

5:11-16 The scene shifts here from the cosmological arena to the social arena. The God who governs the universe also governs human

---

[8]Westermann, *Structure*, pp. 75-76.

[9]Cf. J.L. Crenshaw, "The Influence of the Wise upon Amos: The 'Doxologies of Amos' and Job 5:9-16; 9:5-10," ZAW 79 (1967): 42-52.

[10]In the parallel hymn of Amos 5:9, God's sending of water is used as a metaphor of his judging activity, but that does not seem to be the idea here.

affairs. According to Eliphaz he does so with an interest in bringing justice to show whom society has wronged. **The lowly he sets on high and those who mourn are lifted to safety**. There are other biblical parallels to God's reversal of the "high" and "low" (Ps 18:28[27]; 113:7-8; 147:6). The portrait of God in these texts is one of a champion of the underprivileged and disenfranchised. These are the victims of the **crafty** and the **powerful**. The **poor** had few in ancient society to contend for them and plead their case. In Near Eastern culture earthly kings were enjoined to perform this function for their weaker subjects (cf. Prov 31:4-5).

Not only does God raise up the downtrodden, he also brings down their exploiters. The emphasis on the **craftiness** (v. 13; cf. also v. 12 and the **wily**, v. 13b) of these exploiters addresses the dishonesty of these manipulators. The **crafty** (עֲרוּמִים, *ărûmîm*) practice the cunning of the serpent in Genesis 3:1 (cf. also Ps 83:4[3]. They use their superior perceptions to mislead the **needy** (אֶבְיוֹן, *'ebyôn*). This term describes those who are destitute (Deut 15:7) and oppressed (Amos 2:6). To those who seek to exploit these simple ones God grants no **success**.[11] Instead, **he catches the wise in their craftiness**, seeing to it that they fall prey to their own schemes. This is the only verse in Job that is directly quoted in the New Testament. In 1 Corinthians 3:19 Paul declares the wisdom of God to be far superior to the wisdom of men and cites this line from Job to emphasize his point. The **wise** here are thus not the pursuers of righteousness so often referred to in the wisdom literature, but the practitioners of a proud and ungodly wisdom.[12]

In verses 15,16 Eliphaz returns to the central theme of his doxology: God's transforming power. As in verse 11 God is praised for reversing the fortunes of the underprivileged. Twice in these verses he emphasizes the God who **saves** (יָשַׁע, *yāša'*). As is so often the case in the Psalms, this term is used here in a decidedly nontheological way. It does not refer to God's forgiving of the **poor**'s iniquity or his

---

[11]תּוּשִׁיָה, (*tûšîyāh*) is one of the terms for wisdom in the OT. Here it carries the idea of enduring success which comes from practicing wisdom.

[12]W. Zimmerli in "The Place and Limit of the Wisdom Framework of the Old Testament Theology," *SJT* 17 (1964): 146-158, sees in this language a censure of the sages whose quest for meaning may lead them into areas that may improperly question God.

delivering them from the consequences of their sins, but to God's elevating of them from their oppressed condition. The phrase **sword in their mouth**[13] is parallel with **the clutches of the powerful**, and both refer to the attacks of their exploiters against them. God's saving acts also give the poor emotional deliverance. **Hope** for a brighter future free from threat and intimidation is set before them.

Eliphaz Offers Hope to Job (5:17-27)

[17]**"Blessed is the man whom God corrects; / so do not despise the discipline of the Almighty.**[a] / [18]**For he wounds, but he also binds up; / he injures, but his hands also heal. /** [19]**From six calamities he will rescue you; / in seven no harm will befall you. /** [20]**In famine he will ransom you from death, / and in battle from the stroke of the sword. /** [21]**You will be protected from the lash of the tongue, / and need not fear when destruction comes. /** [22]**You will laugh at destruction and famine, / and need not fear the beasts of the earth. /** [23]**For you will have a covenant with the stones of the field, / and the wild animals will be at peace with you. /** [24]**You will know that your tent is secure; / you will take stock of your property and find nothing missing. /** [25]**You will know that your children will be many, / and your descendants like the grass of the earth. /** [26]**You will come to the grave in full vigor, / like sheaves gathered in season. /** [27]**"We have examined this, and it is true. / So hear it and apply it to yourself."**

[a]*17 Hebrew Shaddai*; **here and throughout Job**

The hope that God offers the poor is now offered to Job. This hope, however, is rooted in Job's willingness to understand his suffering as some form of divine censure of his sin. Implicit in this word of encouragement is the expectation that Job will humbly submit to his plight as God's appropriate and just management of his life.

5:17 The Hebrew of this verse opens with "Behold" (הִנֵּה, *hinnēh*). It is Eliphaz's way of introducing a new and striking truth. That truth is offered in the form of a macarism:[14] **blessed is the man whom**

---

[13]The phrase is difficult in the Hebrew, but it seems to be referring to the verbal attacks inflicted upon the poor, perhaps slander, curse, or perjury. For the tongue as "sword" cf. Ps 57:5[4]; 64:4[3]; 52:4[3].

[14]A macarism is the secular counterpart to a beatitude. It is found many

God corrects.[15] Short of saying Job is being punished for his sins, Eliphaz offers a more positive analysis of the tragedy God has allowed to befall Job. Job is the special object of God's reproving activity. In a perspective only faith can generate, the child of God should rejoice in the trouble God brings to his life because it is being used as a negative means to a positive end. It is ultimately in the best interest of the saint because it will redirect his life to the path of God's approval. It should, therefore, be a source of happiness for him rather than grief. This phrase and the one following it are clearly related to Proverbs 3:11-12 and Psalm 94:12 which, in turn, are quoted in Hebrews 12:5-6. Together they represent one of the biblical models for understanding suffering in the life of a saint.

With the next phrase Eliphaz challenges the ungrateful and impious attitude of Job's first speech: **do not despise the discipline of the Almighty**. The conditions for Job's future hope have now been articulated (cf. also 5:8). The happiness that can come from God's chastening will be realized only when the afflicted saint humbly submits to it and will be instructed by it. The word for **discipline** (מוּסָר, *mûsar*) refers in general to the disciplined instruction wisdom offers (Prov 1:3; 23:12). At times, though, it takes the form of corrective pain (Prov 23:13; Isa 53:5). Typically it is the father or teacher who dispenses such discipline upon his son or pupil (Prov 1:8; 4:1; 13:1). As Habel notes, the discipline (instruction) of God is evidenced both in his redemptive acts (Deut 11:2) and his chastening of his children (Prov 3:11-12).[16] Later, Elihu will speak of discipline as the "warning" of God that he may bring through such things as nightmares (33:16).

The name for God, **Almighty** (שַׁדַּי, *šadday*), occurs here for the first time in Job. It is used a total of thirty-one times in the book and only 17 times in the rest of the Old Testament. Though the precise meaning of this name is debated,[17] it is commonly associated with

---

times in the wisdom literature (Prov 3:13; 8:32; 14:21; 16:20; Eccl 10:17) and twenty-six times in the Psalms. Cf. W. Janzen, "'*ASRÊ* in the Old Testament," *HTR* 58 (1965): 215-226.

[15]הוֹכִיחַ, *hôkîaḥ* means to "reprove" and is often used to describe a legal action taken against someone (13:15).

[16]Habel, *Job*, p. 134.

[17]The ancient rabbis associated the term with שַׁ + דַּי (*šed+day*), "the one who is self sufficient." Symmachus translates it ἱκανός (*ikanos*), "the sufficient one." The LXX renders παντοκράτωρ (*pantokrator*), "the almighty one."

the biblical patriarchs (Gen 17:1; 28:3; 35:11; cf. Exod 6:3) and reflects the patriarchal setting of the book.[18]

5:18 Eliphaz now cites an ancient formula that contrasts two different roles of God in his dealings with his creatures: **he wounds, but he also binds up; he injures but his hands also heal**. This line bears a strong resemblance to the theology of Deuteronomy 32:39 and Hosea 6:1. The contrast in each text is between God the disciplinarian and God the healer.[19] The idea here is that one of his individual children may over the course of his life experience either or both. It is obvious to Eliphaz that Job has already received the former. If Job will be instructed by his suffering, the same God who brought it will in turn respond and restore him.

5:19-22 To emphasize God's willingness to heal Job, Eliphaz employs a literary technique known as a septrain: **From six calamities he will rescue you; in seven no harm will befall you**. A septrain is an ascending numerical series ending in seven. Such numerical sayings are common to the wisdom and prophetic literature (Prov 6:16-19; 30:15-16,18-19,21-23,29-31; Eccl 11:2; Amos 1:3-13; 2:1-6; Isa 17:6).[20] Numerical sayings are not necessarily used to enumerate the exact number of things but are designed to add emphasis to the Lord's full awareness of the thing at issue. Attempts to enumerate seven calamities in the following verses have proven unsatisfactory.[21] It is interesting to note that the text does not say that God's children

---

Many scholars trace the term to Akk. *Šadû*, "mountain"; שַׁדַּי (*šadday*) means then the "mountain god." This view is further supported by F.M. Cross (*Canaanite Myth and Hebrew Epic: Essays in the History of the Religion of Israel* [Cambridge, MA: Harvard University Press, 1973], pp. 52-60), who identifies *šadday* as a warrior god. Cf. further W.F Albright, "The Names Shaddai and Abram," *JBL* 54 (1935): 173-193; W. Walker, "A New Interpretation of the Divine Name 'Shaddai,'" *ZAW* 72 (1960): 64-66, M. Weippert, "Erwagungen zur Etymologie des Gottesnames 'El Šaddaj," *ZDMG* 36 (1961): 42-62; V. Hamilton, *TWOT*, 2:907.

[18]When the author speaks as narrator, he uses the name Yahweh (cf., e.g., 1:6; 38:1), but when the characters speak, they use Shaddai or El which are typical of the patriarchal speeches.

[19]On God the "healer" cf. J. Hempel, "Ich in der Herr, dein Arzt (Ex 15,26)," *TLZ* 82 (1957): 9-26.

[20]Cf. W.M.W. Roth, *Numerical Sayings in the Old Testament: A Form-Critical Study*, VTSupp 13 (Leiden: Brill, 1965).

[21]Cf. discussion by Clines, *Job*, pp. 150-151.

will not experience any of these disasters, but that God will **rescue** them from the full effect of these calamities when they do come. Most notably God promises to **ransom** them from **death**. The term "ransom" (פָּדָה, *pādāh*) is an economic term describing a payment made to liberate someone from some oppressive situation. It is used frequently in the Psalms as part of the divine salvation vocabulary and included deliverance from famine (Ps 33:19; 105:16-17) and death (Ps 49:16[15]; 103:4). The combination of **famine** and **sword** (v. 20) is also found in Jeremiah 18:21 perhaps suggesting that the famine which the author had in mind was the result of a siege tactic against a city. The **lash of the tongue** in verse 21 may refer to the tongue of the false witness or the tongue of the sorcerer (Ps 31:21 [20]; 52:4,6[2,4]; 64:4[3]). Some commentators see this phrase and its parallel term **destruction** (v. 21b) to refer to the demon called the "Hungry One" (v. 4), the Ugaritic god of death (Mot) who ravenously consumes the living.[22] If so, the claim would be that God delivers his disciplined children from natural and supernatural enemies. The emphasis of verse 22 is that under God's care his people are no longer threatened by their environment whether in the form of **famine** or **wild beast**. The small villages of the ancient Near East could easily be put in danger by either.

5:23-26 The phrase **you will have a covenant with the stones of the field** has proven enigmatic to the interpreters. Pope emends "sons of the field" and understands it to refer to "field spirits." Rashi read "lords of the fields" and took it to refer to satyrs. Both of these suggestions would be in harmony with the "demon" interpretation of verse 21. A simpler solution would be to understand the threat that stones could pose to the agriculture necessary for human survival. In 2 Kings 3:19,25 casting stones into the fields of a defeated enemy was viewed as a means of ensuring lasting destruction. In Matthew 13:5 the stony soil is said to deny the seed from taking root. The term **covenant** (בְּרִית, *bᵊrîth*) is probably a metaphor of an assured relationship between farmer and stones that will keep them from hindering agriculture.[23] In

---

[22]Habel, *Job*, pp. 135-136. Gordis sees the phrase "lash of the tongue" (שׁוֹט לָשׁוֹן, *šôṭ lāšôn*) to be an ellipsis for *šôṭ lᵊšôn 'ēš*, "the scourging fire" (cf. Isa 5:24).

[23]Cf. A.S. Peake, "In League with the Stones of the Field," *ExpTim* 34 (1922): 42-43.

a similar portrait of Israel living in harmony with its environment under God's blessing, Hosea speaks of a covenant between them and the beasts of the field, the birds of the air and the creatures that crawl upon the ground (Hos 2:20[18]). Eliphaz closes his encouragement with the fourfold ideal of the divinely blessed man in the Old Testament: security (**your tent is secure**), **prosperity**, many **descendants**, and a long, full life lived in **vigor**[24] to the very end.

5:27 Eliphaz has framed his speech with an opening apology for any further grief he may cause Job (4:2) and now a closing exhortation to accept his counsel as true. As is his style throughout his speeches, he emphasizes his personal testing of his words, **we have examined this, and it is true** (cf. also 4:8; 5:3). The word "examined" (חָקַר, *ḥāqar*) refers to a process of intense exploration (13:9; 28:3,27; 29:16). The **we** refers to the sages among whom Eliphaz and his two associates number themselves. What remains for Job to do is **hear** (lit., "hearken"; שָׁמַע, *šāmaʿ*) and **apply** (lit., "acknowledge"; יָדַע, *yādaʿ*) these words.

A summary of Eliphaz's first speech reveals the delicate balance he has sought between being an encourager of Job and yet a defender of God. Rather than accusing Job of some blatant sin, he instead speaks more generally of the universal sinfulness of all people. Since no one is guiltless before the holy God, Job's desperate situation is no disgrace. It is typical of all humanity. What he must do is learn from it and use it as an occasion for seeking God's mercy. In so doing he will again experience God's blessing. The great and painful (for Job) irony of this speech is that Job sees God as his afflicter rather than his savior. Because Job believes that God has wronged him and no longer takes note of his piety, Eliphaz's counsel of throwing himself on the mercy of a just and responsive God falls on Job's ears with an empty, hollow ring.

---

[24]כֶּלַח, *kēlāḥ*. The meaning of the term is uncertain, but the idea of a ripe old age has the support of the Targ., "in the plenitude of your years." See discussion by Hartley, *Job*, p. 126, n. 24.

JOB 6

2. Job's Reply to Eliphaz (6:1–7:21)

Job's response (6:1–7:21) to Eliphaz's challenge is intended for
two different audiences. In chapter 6 his speech is directed primarily toward the friends who have come to counsel him.[1] In chapter 7
his words are aimed at the God from whom Eliphaz has urged him
to seek restoration. The tone of each speech is confrontational, even
accusational. Framed in the language of lament (cf., e.g., Ps 38, 88,
109), these speeches employ a variety of rhetorical forms (e.g., complaint [7:1-21]; appeal [6:28-29]; disputation [6:22-30]; parody [7:17-
18]; proverb [6:5-6]) designed to indict the friends for their unsympathetic and unsuccessful attempt to expose his supposed guilt and
to challenge God's unfair and cruel attack upon his servant. As
Eliphaz's speech lays out the primary position that the subsequent
speeches of the friends will argue, so now does Job's initial response
lay the foundation for the rebuttal that will be echoed in his remaining speeches. Fueled by his unrelenting pain and the added insult of
Eliphaz's accusation, Job lashes out at the friends and even God,
employing some of the most sarcastic and irreverent language to be
found in the Hebrew Bible.

Job's Explanation of His Desperate Plight (6:1-7)

¹Then Job replied:
**²"If only my anguish could be weighed / and all my misery be
placed on the scales! / ³It would surely outweigh the sand of the
seas— / no wonder my words have been impetuous. / ⁴The arrows**

---

[1]Clines (*Job 1–20*, p. 167) argues that 6:2-13 is a monologue aimed at neither the friends nor God. Habel (*Job*, p. 141), however, sees in 6:2-13 a clear
response to challenges raised by Eliphaz in 4:2-6 and 5:2-7.

of the Almighty are in me, / my spirit drinks in their poison; / God's terrors are marshaled against me. / ⁵Does a wild donkey bray when it has grass, / or an ox bellow when it has fodder? / ⁶Is tasteless food eaten without salt, / or is there flavor in the white of an egg^a? / ⁷I refuse to touch it; / such food makes me ill.

^a6 The meaning of the Hebrew for this phrase is uncertain.

Job's opening words seem to be a direct response to Eliphaz's assertion that Job should find blessing in God's correction and welcome his discipline (5:17). To the contrary, there is nothing good that Job can find in his affliction. Continuing the tone of his initial soliloquy (ch. 3) he can only lament his desperate condition.

6:1-4 Noting that Eliphaz has taken exception to his initial ingratitude (4:1-6), Job offers an explanation of the **impetuous**[2] nature of his previous language. If his words sound rash, it is because of the enormity of his suffering. Employing two powerful metaphors he seeks to refocus his friends' attention on the stark reality of his suffering rather than upon their theological speculation concerning its origin. First, he places his pain on a scale and proclaims it greater in weight that the **sand of the seas**. Job chooses the term **anguish** (כַּעַשׂ, kā'aś)[3] to describe his desperate plight, no doubt in response to Eliphaz's own use of the term where, speaking of Job, he suggested that **resentment** (kā'aś) **kills a fool** (5:2). Job will argue that his **anguish** is most understandable in light of the suffering he has endured. Job goes on to characterize his life as a target for the poison **arrows of the Almighty**. This phrase, coupled with the parallel **God's terrors**[4] **are marshaled against me**, explicitly states what Job has earlier (3:23) only intimated: it is God who is afflicting Job. On this point Job and Eliphaz are in agreement. The issue over which they sharply differ, however, is the

---

²לָעוּ (lā'û) is probably derived from לעע (l'') or לוע (lw') and means to "talk wildly." E.F. Sutcliffe ("Further Notes on Job, Textual and Exegetical: 6,2-3,13; 8,16-17; 19,20-26," *Bib* 31 [1950]: 365-378) translates "charged with grief." The only one other appearance of this term is in Prov 20:25 where it is used to describe a "rash" vow.

³*Kā'aś* refers to the resentful feelings aroused by the persecution of some enemy (Prov 27:3). God is said to be *vexed* by the sins of his people (1 Kgs 14:9; Jer 8:19).

⁴The term elsewhere refers to God's ability to overwhelm the foe (cf., e.g., Exod 23:27). Along with the term "arrows," this language portrays Job as the enemy of an assaulting God.

reason behind God's affliction of Job. It is on this crucial point that the lines for their great debate are being drawn.

6:5-7 In these verses Job employs two proverbs framed in the form of rhetorical questions and tied together by the common theme of unsatisfying food. Both questions are intended to address the absurd and expect a "No, of course not" answer. In the first question animal imagery is used to illustrate that if the **wild donkey** or the domesticated **ox** receive their normal food they have no reason to complain. Job, however, has received the very opposite of what he, as a righteous man, might expect from God. His complaint, therefore, is justified. The second question, also about sustenance, suggests that there are some foods which, though offered, are simply inedible. They are **tasteless** and without **flavor**. Whether Job is here referring to the bitter "pill" that God seeks to make him "swallow" (Clines) or to the insipid arguments of his friends (Duhm, Rowley, Habel), he insists that he is clearly justified in his rejection of what he has been "fed" (v. 7). Stung by the accusation of his friend and the unrelenting oppression of his God, Job vigorously defends his right to complain.

Job's Only "Hope" (6:8-13)

[8]"Oh, that I might have my request, / that God would grant what I hope for, / [9]that God would be willing to crush me, / to let loose his hand and cut me off! / [10]Then I would still have this consolation— / my joy in unrelenting pain— / that I had not denied the words of the Holy One.

[11]What strength do I have, that I should still hope? / What prospects, that I should be patient? / [12]Do I have the strength of stone? / Is my flesh bronze? / [13]Do I have any power to help myself, / now that success has been driven from me?

The second part of Job's reply is also tied to one of Eliphaz's assertions. According to Eliphaz, Job should find "hope" (תִּקְוָה, tiqwāh) in his "piety" (4:6) and in the God who "wounds but also binds up" (5:18). With an ironic twist Job asserts that his only hope is that the God who does not respect his piety but ruthlessly persecutes him will now mercifully finish him off.

6:8-10 In these verses Job returns to the death wish of his opening soliloquy (3:11ff). Giving no thought to taking his own life, he

eagerly waits for God himself to **let loose his hand and cut me off**.
The imagery here comes from the work of the ancient weaver who
finishes his carefully woven creation by cutting across the warp of the
fabric (cf. Isa 38:12). So Job invites God to finish the work he has
made of his life. This death wish is not the same as that advocated by
Job's wife ("curse God and die" [2:9]). Rather than cursing God, Job
is simply surrendering to the fate that God has obviously decreed for
him. As Weiser puts it: "Since Job can no longer see any possibility
of life with God, his last wish is that he should at least die at his
hand."[5] Verse 10 is difficult in the Hebrew and the subject of significant scholarly debate. Of special interest is what is meant by the
phrase, **I have not denied the words**[6] **of the Holy One**[7] and how this
brings Job **consolation**. The verb **denied** (כִּחֵד, *kiḥēd*) literally means
"hide, conceal." It is used elsewhere to refer to something that is not
"spoken" or "declared" (cf., e.g., Isa 3:9; Ps 78:4). Many interpreters
tie this verse back to the prologue where twice it is stated that Job did
not "sin" in "what he said" (2:10) or "by charging God with wrongdoing" (1:22). The idea is that, should Job die, he would still have the
consolation of knowing he has not died a sinner guilty of denying the
words of God. Other scholars, taking note of the urgent language of
the following verses, have suggested that Job wishes for God to take
him quickly before his suffering reaches the point where he might be
tempted to deny the "words of the Holy One."[8]

6:11-13 In these verses Job returns to the style of asking impossible questions[9] (cf. vv. 5,6) to express his sense of helplessness in
the face of unrelenting suffering. Deprived of **strength** and any

---

[5]A Weiser, *Das Buch Hiob* (Göttingen: Vandenhoeck & Ruprecht, 1951),
p. 141.

[6]אֲמָרִים, *'ămārîm* can refer either to the godly commands by which Job has
lived or to the "decrees" that God has dictated concerning the course of
Job's life (cf. 22:22,28).

[7]This epithet for God (cf. Isa 40:25; Hos 11:9) appears only here in Job.

[8]A different approach is taken by Habel (*Job*, p. 147). Given the defiant
tone of Job to this point, he takes Job's words to mean that he has refused
to conceal the unfair nature of what God has decreed for his life — cruel,
undeserved suffering. If this is so, then the title "Holy One" must be used
of God in a satirical way. Other scholars argue the entire line is a pious gloss
(a claim by Job of uncompromised righteousness) and omit it.

[9]Cf. the discussion in A. van Selms, "Motivated Interrogative Sentences in
the Book of Job," *Semitics* 6 (1978): 28-35.

prospects[10] of a brighter future, Job has simply lost hope. Hardly made of **stone** or **bronze** he is weak and powerless to change his tragic situation. **Success**[11] has been denied him, and his **patience**[12] has been exhausted. Habel sees in these words a sarcastic rejection of the strength God is said to offer as taught by Eliphaz (5:17ff) and traditional theology (cf. 9:19; also Ps 22:20; 33:20; 121:1-2; Gen 49:24).[13] Since Job feels that God has declared him an enemy, he sees God as his afflicter rather than his help. Later, speaking from the perspective of faith rather than frustration, Job will lay claim to such strength (19:25-27).

Job's Condemnation of His Friends (6:14-30)

[14]"A despairing man should have the devotion of his friends, / even though he forsakes the fear of the Almighty. / [15]But my brothers are as undependable as intermittent streams, / as the streams that overflow / [16]when darkened by thawing ice / and swollen with melting snow, / [17]but that cease to flow in the dry season, / and in the heat vanish from their channels. / [18]Caravans turn aside from their routes; / they go up into the wasteland and perish. / [19]The caravans of Tema look for water, / the traveling merchants of Sheba look in hope. / [20]They are distressed, because they had been confident; / they arrive there, only to be disappointed. / [21]Now you have proved to be of no help; / you see something dreadful and are afraid. / [22]Have I ever said, 'Give me something on my behalf, / pay a ransom for me from your wealth, / [23]deliver me from the hand of the enemy, / ransom me from the clutches of the ruthless?

[24]"Teach me, and I will be quiet; / show me where I have been wrong. / [25]How painful are honest words! / But what do your argu-

---

[10]קֵץ (qēṣ, "end"). Following NAB ("What is my limit that I should be patient?"), Clines (*Job*, p. 175) argues that Job is not referring to his future but to his limitations as a mortal and cites Ps 39:5-6[4-5] as echoing the same idea.

[11]תּוּשִׁיָּה (tušiyāh) is part of the "wisdom" vocabulary of the OT. It describes the positive outcomes that result from living wisely. Cf. J. Genung, "Meaning and Usage of the Term *TÛSIYYÂH*," *JBL* 30 (1911): 114-122.

[12]To be patient is literally in the Hebrew, "to make one's life ["soul," *nepheš*] long." By contrast, to be impatient in the Hebrew is "to be short of soul" (Judg 10:16; Num 21:4).

[13]Habel, *Job*, pp. 147-148.

ments prove? / ²⁶Do you mean to correct what I say, / and treat the words of a despairing man as wind? / ²⁷You would even cast lots for the fatherless / and barter away your friend.

²⁸"But now be so kind as to look at me. / Would I lie to your face? / ²⁹Relent, do not be unjust; / reconsider, for my integrity is at stake.ᵃ / ³⁰Is there any wickedness on my lips? / Can my mouth not discern malice?

ᵃ29 Or *my righteousness still stands*

In this criticism of his friends Job's frustration reaches full vent.[14] Disappointed by their disloyalty and lack of empathy he lashes out at them with a barrage of accusations. The sharpness of his attack surprises us. After all, these friends have traveled a great distance to be with Job (2:11), have wept over his condition (2:12), and sat for a week in respectful silence waiting for Job to speak (2:13). However, it becomes obvious from Eliphaz's opening words (4:1-11) that their estimation of Job has been greatly lowered by what they have seen of his pitiful condition and then heard from his opening soliloquy (ch. 3). Their conclusion has already been drawn. Job suffers because he has sinned. It is this judgment that stings Job to the core of his innermost being, and it is in view of this accusation that he now personally addresses the friends.

6:14 This opening salvo functions like a thesis sentence for his following argument. Unfortunately the Hebrew behind our English translations is difficult, resulting in at least two differing schools of thought on how it is to be rendered. To introduce the reader to the problem we offer the following translations:

> He who withholds kindness from a friend
>   forsakes the fear of the Almighty (RSV).

---

[14]Criticism of friends is a common theme in the ancient Near Eastern theodicies. As an example we may consider the complaint of the sufferer in Ludlul Bel Nemeqi:

My friend has become foe.
My companion has become a wretch and a devil.
In his savagery my comrade denounces me,
Constantly my associates furbish their weapons.
My intimate friend has brought my life into danger.
(I.84-88; *BWL*, p. 35)

> Grudge pity to a neighbor,
>> and you forsake the fear of Shaddai (JB).

The meaning suggested by these translations is that to deny a friend merciful love is equivalent to abandoning faith in God. It is the ultimate miscarriage of true religion (cf. Jas 1:27).

> A friend owes kindness to one in despair,
>> though he have forsaken the fear of the Almighty (NAB).

> Devotion is due from friends
>> to one who despairs and loses faith in the Almighty (NEB).

These renderings, like the NIV, suggest that Job expects unconditional love from his friends even if Job forsakes his faith in God. If this rendering is correct, it is unparalleled in the OT. For this reason, most commentators favor the former and understand Job to be accusing the friends of a failure so great that it rivals apostasy. Refusal to offer merciful love to fellow humans is the equivalent of being unfaithful to God (cf. 1 John 4:7-8).[15]

What Job has needed most from his pious brothers they have not been willing to give: **devotion** (חֶסֶד, *ḥesed*). This important term is often used in the OT to describe God's "steadfast love" or "lovingkindness" towards his people (Ps 25:10; 88:12[11]). It denotes the "loyalty" that God manifests as he keeps his covenant (Deut 7:9; Neh 1:5). When used of humans, it denotes similar ideas (Hos 4:1; Prov 3:3).[16] **Fear of the Almighty** means (as "fear of God" in 1:1,8; 2:3) reverence for God that expresses itself in pious behavior.[17] As Eliphaz was disappointed that Job's "fear of God" was not sustaining him in the face of his suffering (4:6), so now Job is equally disappointed that Eliphaz's "fear of the Almighty" is not motivating him

---

[15]Habel, however, favoring the other translations, argues that the language is calling for a true "loyalty" even "when all other support systems fail, including faith in God" (*Job*, p. 148).

[16]Cf. N. Glueck, *Hesed in the Bible* (Cincinnati: Hebrew Union College Press, 1967); K.D. Sakenfeld, *The Meaning of Hesed in the Bible: A New Inquiry* (Missoula: Scholars Press, 1978).

[17]Cf. previous discussion on pp. 57-58.

to manifest merciful love to Job. As Hartley observes, "both parties are thus attacking the center of the other's worship of God."[18]

6:15-20 Using a motif from the desert environs Job compares his friends to **intermittent streams**. The seasonal wadi of the Near East, while often a raging torrent in the rainy season, becomes a dry watercourse in the heat of summer. It offers no water just when it is needed most. **Caravans** of merchants, seeking precious water where they have found it before, go off in search of the wadis only to find them dry. Two famous trading centers are mentioned in this discourse. **Tema** (modern Teima) is a well-known oasis 250 miles southeast of Aqaba on the route between Medina and Damascus (cf. Isa 21:14; Jer 25:23). **Sheba** (Seba) was a market noted for its trading in precious metals and spices located in southwestern Arabia (cf. Isa 60:6; Jer 6:20; Ezek 27:22-23; Ps 72:10). Job, like a weary traveler, has sought life-giving sustenance from his friends, but they have proved cruelly unreliable. Job's use of the terms **brothers** and **undependable** is intended to sharpen Job's depiction of their failure. Desertion by one's kin in a time of crisis is considered the greatest of treacheries in the OT (cf., e.g., Ps 38:12; 88:8).

6:21 Job applies the metaphors of the wadis and the disappointed travelers in an attempt to shame his friends over their lack of sympathy. In the process he suggests at least one reason why they behaved toward him in this way. Seeing his **dreadful** condition they have recoiled in fear. Job may thus be describing their failure to identify with him because of his shameful, loathsome condition. More likely their fear stems out of a conclusion they have drawn that he has been cursed by God and that any association with him may expose them to the risk of also incurring God's wrath. Consequently, Job believes, they are holding him at "arm's length."

6:22-23 Pressing his point, Job says they are treating him as someone who seeks to financially obligate them or demand they **pay a ransom** on his behalf. Such a thing would not be unusual to ask of a friend, but Job has made no such request. He has not asked them to solve his problem, only to sympathize with it. Here we recall the complaint of Jeremiah, "I have not lent nor borrowed yet everyone curses me" (15:10). The term **ruthless** (עָרִיצִים, *'ārîṣîm*) is used in the OT to describe the proud and the rich who exploit the poor (Jer

---

[18]Hartley, *Job*, p. 138.

15:21) or a ruthless nation that plunders the weak (Ezek 28:7; Isa 49:25). We should not press the metaphor but, as will be observed from Job's language in chapter 7, he is not beyond speaking of even God in such terms.

6:24-30 In his conclusion to his first reply to Eliphaz, Job addresses the injustice that most offends him, the abuse which hurts him most deeply. Job has heard Eliphaz accuse him of being guilty of some sin worthy of the suffering God has brought upon him. In this bold retort Job demands that Eliphaz name his sin, **show me where I have been wrong.**[19] With this challenge Job lays the foundation for the position he will argue for the rest of the book: God has afflicted him without cause and in spite of his innocence. The stage for this claim was set in the prologue of the book where three times (once by the author and twice by God!) Job's integrity was praised. Job now assumes this same position and will not cease from defending it until he meets God at the climax of his great struggle.

How painful are honest words! This proverbial saying is not intended to praise the advice of his friends but to expose its inadequacy. It would be one thing for Job to endure the painful truth from the speech of his friends, but sadly he has found little truth in what they have said. The lack of substance in their arguments is challenged by Job's ironic retort, **but what do your arguments prove?** Not only are their arguments without merit, they totally ignore Job's heartfelt pleas, treating the **words of a despairing man as wind.** Focusing on the callousness of their accusations he casts them in the role of the hard-hearted exploiter of the weak and unsuspecting like those who **cast lots for the fatherless.**[20] In Job's day the orphan, with no father to defend him, was a favorite target of land-grabbing opportunists. Those who did such things are strongly condemned throughout the OT.

But now be so kind as to look at me. Job now shifts his approach from attack to appeal. Suggesting that they have completely forgot-

---

[19]Fohrer and Hartley suggest that Job's use of the term שָׁגָה (šāgāh, "sin, wrong") suggests that he is only asking his friends to expose some "unintentional" sin of which he is guilty. They take this to mean that Job only denies guilt of "high-handed, intentional" sin in the book. While it is true that šāgāh can refer more narrowly to "unintentional" sin, however, it need not mean this and the context does not suggest this narrower meaning.

[20]This conjures up the imagery of the situation described in 2 Kgs 4:1.

ten the person they are talking to (and about), he reminds them of
the honest man they have always known. It seems the friends have
fallen prey to the inevitable tendency of systematic theologians to
sacrifice people on the altar of their principles and ignore what *is* in
an attempt to articulate what *should be*. Job tries to help them
remember that they are dealing with a real person here, not just a
philosophical issue!

Can my mouth not discern malice?[21] Job insists that he is the
best judge of whether or not he has sinned, not his well-intentioned
friends. Their attempt to justify God at the expense of his personal
integrity is simply unfounded and even cruel. In their eagerness to
press their theological point they have done him a great injustice. Of
this unfair tactic, he insists, they must **relent!**[22]

---

[21]This line is difficult in the Hebrew. The term rendered "malice" (הַוּוֹת,
hawwôth) normally means "destruction." It has been variously understood
here to mean "windy words" or "magical curse," but the sense seems to be
that Job is the best judge of what is going on in his life. Cf. S. Erlandsson,
"*havvah*," *TDOT*, 3:357; A Guillaume, "Magical Terms in the OT," *JRAS*
(1942): 111-131; G.R. Driver, "Witchcraft in the OT *hwh*,"*JRAS* (1943): 6-16.

[22]שׁוּב (*šûb*) normally means "turn" or even "repent." In some contexts,
however, it is best rendered "stop, cease" Cf. W. Holladay, *The Root subh in
the Old Testament* (Leiden: Brill, 1958); R. Gordis, "Some Hitherto Unrecognized Meanings of the Root *SHUB*," *JBL* 52 (1933): 153-162.

JOB 7

2. Job's Reply to Eliphaz (6:1–7:21, continued)

Job's Complaint to God (7:1-21)

This chapter represents one of the strongest attacks upon God to be found in the Bible. Before he is through with his complaint, Job will argue against God's goodness, call him names, and even taunt him! Though in some ways this chapter bears resemblance to the cultic laments (e.g., Ps 17, 88) and the prophetic protests (e.g., Jer 20:7-12) of the OT, the extent to which Job carries his protest puts this complaint in a class by itself.[1] The chapter divides into three major units (vv. 1-8,9-16,17-21), each begun with a statement about the human condition and each concluded with a closing taunt. The taunts, in balanced style, are each concluded with an expression of the futile and fleeting nature of human existence ("I will be no more," [vv. 8,21] and "my days have no meaning," [v. 16]).[2]

Human Life Is Hard Service (7:1-8)

[1]**"Does not man have hard service on earth? / Are not his days like those of a hired man? / [2]Like a slave longing for the evening shadows, / or a hired man waiting eagerly for his wages, / [3]so I have been allotted months of futility, / and nights of misery have been assigned to me. / [4]When I lie down I think, 'How long before I get up?' / The night drags on, and I toss till dawn. / [5]My body is clothed with worms and scabs, / my skin is broken and festering.**

[6]**"My days are swifter than a weaver's shuttle, / and they come**

---

[1]The laments of the OT, though often critical of God, always balance protest with praise and usually conclude with a vow of adoration. This lament, by contrast, is punctuated by taunts against God.
[2]Habel, *Job*, pp. 153-156.

to an end without hope. / ⁷Remember, O God, that my life is but
a breath; / my eyes will never see happiness again. / ⁸The eye that
now sees me will see me no longer; / you will look for me, but I
will be no more.

7:1-2 Does not man have hard service³ on earth? Job's first portrait of the fate of humans employs the metaphor of the slave or
hireling. This language has both mythological and political ante-
cedents. In the ancient Near Eastern cosmogonies man is commonly characterized as an afterthought of the gods, created to relieve
them of hard work.⁴ In much of ancient Near Eastern society this
"man as underclass" worldview was actualized in a political system
that designated much of the population to corvée labor. In Israel it
was the kings who imposed this servitude. As Samuel warned (1 Sam
8:11-16) and as Solomon illustrated, the kings of Israel commonly
subjected their citizens to hard labor under their administrations
(1 Kgs 9:15-22; 2 Chr 26:11). Individual Israelite landowners also
"employed" the **hired man**⁵ in a more general form of corvée labor.
Though attempts were made to prevent the abuse of this system (cf.,
e.g., Exod 21:2-4; Lev 19:13; Deut 24:14-15), evidence from the
prophets makes it clear that these efforts were not always successful
(Jer 22:13; Mal 3:5). Job is employing this well-known model to
depict the human condition. Human existence is **slavery**⁶ (cf. 13:27)
and hard labor (cf. Gen 3:17-19).

7:3-6 Job now applies the slave model to his own condition, suggesting that his plight is even worse than that of the servant. Not
only does he toil in **futility** all the day, but his **nights** also are a
painful struggle. His **broken and festering** flesh, covered with
worms,⁷ torments him through endless, sleepless nights and traps

---

³צָבָא (*ṣābā'*) primarily refers to those forced into military service or labor
for the government (1 Kgs 5:27-28[13-14]).

⁴Cf., e.g., lines 195-197, 240-241, in W.G. Lambert and A.R. Millard, trans.
Atra-hasis: The Babylonian Story of the Flood (Oxford: Oxford University Press,
1969); and S. Kramer, *Sumerian Mythology* (New York: Harper & Row, 1964),
pp. 68-72.

⁵שָׂכִיר (*śākîr*) is usually used to describe domestic workers (Exod 12:45).

⁶עֶבֶד (*'ebed*) is the broadest of the three terms employed here. It refers to
people captured in war (Josh 16:10) or sold to pay a debt (Lev 25:44-46).

⁷The worm is a symbol of human mortality (cf. 25:6) and often used to
describe those doomed to Sheol (17:14; 21:26; 24:20; cf. also Isa 14:11).

him in a vicious cycle of insomnia. But his torment comes from more than physical maladies. There is also a psychological dimension to his suffering. Job feels that all of this has been **assigned**[8] to him. His suffering is the result of what God has arbitrarily fated him. As the remainder of the speech will reveal, it is this inescapable fact that undoes him most. Job also gives us a clue here concerning just how long he has been suffering. For **months**[9] he has endured this unrelenting pain. All of this has obviously led him to the conclusion that he will soon die of his dreaded disease, and his painful days will soon **come to an end without hope**. Once again, evoking the image of the **weaver's shuttle**, which with a sudden motion completes the garment, Job says that his days will swiftly pass.

7:7-8 This first part of Job's lament ends with a subtle taunt, a mock plea for God to act quickly before he cannot act at all. The cry, **Remember**, is Job's first direct address to God. It is full of irony. The term (זְכֹר, $z^ekōr$) is commonly directed toward God in the OT to invite him to show mercy according to the terms of his covenant with his people (Ps. 20:4[3]; 25:6; 79:8; Lam 5:1).[10] But, as becomes obvious from the context, Job's address to God is so filled with irony that it virtually amounts to a taunt.[11] Job suggests that God must have forgotten just how fragile Job's life is and how near to its end. By labeling God **the eye that now sees me** Job depicts God as having Job under his fierce gaze. He returns to this theme again in verse 20. In 10:4 Job will take this motif a step further by saying that God's eyes are no better than a human's, fallible and insincere. Rather than the benevolent God who protects his children, Job is portraying God as an "Evil Eye" who takes some kind of perverted pleasure in watching Job suffer. Job sarcastically reminds God that he will soon be deprived of the favorite target of his celestial surveillance: **you will look for me, but I will be no more**. This final phrase is not a claim of Job's anticipated nonexistence but of his impending absence. Similar language is used of Enoch in Genesis 5:24.

---

[8]מִנָּה (*minnāh*) "measured out" or "made to inherit."
[9]The *Testament of Job* states that Job's illness lasted seven years.
[10]Cf. B.S. Childs, *Memory and Tradition* (London: SCM, 1962).
[11]Cf. Habel, *Job*, p. 160; Clines, *Job*, p. 186.

Human Life Is Fleeting (7:9-16)

[9]As a cloud vanishes and is gone, / so he who goes down to the grave[a] does not return. / [10]He will never come to his house again; / his place will know him no more.

[11]"Therefore I will not keep silent; / I will speak out in the anguish of my spirit, / I will complain in the bitterness of my soul. / [12]Am I the sea, or the monster of the deep, / that you put me under guard? / [13]When I think my bed will comfort me / and my couch will ease my complaint, / [14]even then you frighten me with dreams / and terrify me with visions, / [15]so that I prefer strangling and death, / rather than this body of mine. / [16]I despise my life; I would not live forever. / Let me alone; my days have no meaning.

[a]*9* Hebrew *Sheol*

In this the second of three complaints to God, Job laments the transient nature of human existence and uses it as a pretext for his right to protest God's attack upon his life. The sarcasm builds as Job presses his complaint.

7:9-10 Job says that his life will end in the same way that a **cloud** moves across the sky and then disperses. So his life will pass quickly, and he will **go down to the grave**. The word for **grave** here is the famous Sheol of Scripture and the ancient Near Eastern literature. Sheol is the subterranean abode of the dead. It is mentioned here for the first time in the book (cf. also 11:8; 14:13; 17:13,16; 21:13; 24:19; 26:6). Elsewhere in Job it is described as deep in the earth (11:8), full of darkness (10:21-22), and the destiny of all living (30:23). Most importantly, it is a place from which no one ever returns (cf. 10:21).[12] The emphasis here is not that death ends human existence but that it forever ends all opportunity for a person to enjoy his earthly **place** and return to his **house**.

7:11 Therefore I will not keep silent. Job contends that he is justified in protesting against the way God is treating him. The tone of the language here is similar to that of the apology that he had earlier made to Eliphaz for speaking so rashly (6:3).[13] In Jewish tradition a

---

[12]This portrait of Sheol is consistent with Mesopotamian models (cf. "The Descent of Ishtar to the Nether World," *ANET*, pp. 106-109, where it is called the "land of no return").

[13]Eliphaz, too, knew the difficulty of restraining his words when compelled to speak out (4:2).

man in anguish is not held responsible for what he says.[14] But Job, keenly aware of how unconventional and even irreverent his protest must sound, feels the need to justify his speech. The brevity of life and the finality of death require that he be heard now. So **speak out** he will, and **complain** he must. This last term (שִׂיחַ, *śîaḥ*) denotes a specific kind of speech that expresses deep inner feelings (cf., e.g., Jer 20:9; 2 Kgs 9:11). In the context which follows, however, it will take on a narrower meaning of formal legal complaint (9:27; 10:1; 23:2).

7:12-14 The **sea** (Yamm) and the **monster** (Tannin) were symbols of chaos in ancient Canaan.[15] In Canaanite mythology, Yamm was the primordial sea god whom Baal conquered to establish order in the cosmos (cf. Ps 89:9-10). Tannin is used in the OT to refer to a mythological chaos deity (Ps 74:13) and is probably identical with Leviathan (41:1ff; Isa 27:1) and Rahab (9:13; 26:12; Isa 51:9). The point of introducing them here is to argue that God is treating Job as if he were some malevolent deity who challenges God's sovereignty and whom God is obliged to put **under guard** (cf. Jer 5:22; Ps 104:9).[16] Under God's detention Job is allowed no rest. If he seeks to take **comfort** on his **bed** even there he cannot escape God's terrors for God uses **dreams** and **visions** to deprive him of sleep. Dreams, regarded by the ancients as revelations from the gods, figure prominently in the dialogue portion of the book. Eliphaz claimed to have received a revelation in a dream (ch. 4), and Elihu will argue that God communicates in dreams (33:15-20).

7:15-16 Returning to the death wish of his earlier laments, Job sees the ending of his life to be his only escape. The reference to **strangling** may owe its origin to the symptoms of Job's illness.[17] Scholars disagree over what Job means by the cry **I would not live forever**.[18] Most likely it continues the thought of verse 15. He prefers

---

[14]*Baba Bathra* 16a-16b.

[15]יָם (*yām*) sometimes means only "sea" in a nonmythological sense and תַּנִּין (*tannîn*) sometimes refers to a nonmythological creature (cf., e.g., Gen 1:21; Exod 7:9). For further information cf. J. Day, *God's Conflict with the Dragon and the Sea* (Cambridge: Cambridge University Press, 1985).

[16]M. Dahood, "*Mišmār* 'Muzzle' in Job 7:12," *JBL* 80 (1961): 270-271, argues for the translation, "muzzle," on the basis of Ps 68:23b[22b] and Ps 39:2b[1b].

[17]Suffocation is one of the symptoms of elephantiasis, the disease that many identify with Job's affliction.

[18]Habel (*Job*, p. 163) compares this to Aqhat in the Canaanite myth who

death to life, and even if he could live forever, he would not choose to because his life is so miserable. Since his life has **no meaning**,[19] he asks only that it end. **Leave me alone**, he cries to God. Though some commentators see in this only a request for God to quit torturing him, the intent is really much stronger. This language is the equivalent to a rejection of life itself. What other biblical writers fear most (God's abandoning them) Job desires most. Echoed in 10:20 this Jobian cry is rare and radical, heard again in Scripture only once (Ps 39:13[14]). What Job seems to be saying at the close of this second part of his lament is that he is no godlike being trying to assault heaven and seize eternal life. In fact, if offered eternal life, he would not even take it from the hand of a God who undermines human life with such turmoil and pain. As in verse 8 the language here is very sarcastic and amounts to nothing less than a taunt of the Giver of life.

The God Who Mocks Humans Is to Be Mocked (7:17-21)

[17]"**What is man that you make so much of him, / that you give him so much attention, / [18]that you examine him every morning / and test him every moment? / [19]Will you never look away from me, / or let me alone even for an instant? / [20]If I have sinned, what have I done to you, / O watcher of men? / Why have you made me your target? / Have I become a burden to you?[a] / [21]Why do you not pardon my offenses / and forgive my sins? / For I will soon lie down in the dust; / you will search for me, but I will be no more.**"

[a]*20 A few manuscripts of the Masoretic Text, an ancient Hebrew scribal tradition and Septuagint; most manuscripts of the Masoretic Text I have become a burden to myself.*

Job's taunt of his God reaches a crescendo in this the third and final part of his lament. Employing a bitter parody of Psalm 8 Job chides God for his unjust treatment of his innocent servant. Moving from the general condition of humankind to the specific pain he

---

rejects the goddess Anath's offer of eternal life — a rejection which aroused her ire. Habel believes that Job, in similar fashion, is taunting God with a similar rejection, treating the offer of eternal life as mock gift not worth accepting.

[19]Lit., "my days are like vapor" (הֶבֶל, *hebel*). This term is used repeatedly by Job to denote a sense of futility (9:29; 21:34; 27:12). It is also a key term in the biblical book of Qoheleth (Eccl 1:2,14,17; 2:11,17,21).

personally bears, he bombards God with a series of sarcastic questions designed to expose the unfairness and cruelty of the Watcher's affliction of his creatures.

7:17-18 This parody of Psalm 8 stands as an excellent example of the use of irony in biblical literature.[20] It also serves to punctuate Job's protest against God's management of his world. To fully appreciate the clever irony of this parody it is important to remember the original language of the psalm:

> What is man that you are mindful of him,
>   the son of man that you care for him?
> You have made him a little lower than the heavenly beings
>   and crowned him with glory and honor.
>   (Ps 8:5-6[4-5])

According to Psalm 8 (cf. also Gen 1:26-28) humans, created in the image of God, stand just below God in honor and glory. But with an ironic twist Job reapplies the language of the psalm to argue that humans were created as God's target, not his exalted representatives. In Psalm 8 the psalmist marvels that mere humans should be given so much positive **attention** by their Creator. In this parody Job marvels that the Creator is so preoccupied with subjecting them to such merciless scrutiny and relentless examination. Job's parody plays on two key verbs found in Psalm 8 to which he then adds a third. The first is גִּדֵּל (giddēl, "exalt" = **make much of**). In Psalm 8 it means God has set man upon a pedestal, but in Job it means God has designated man as a target. The second is פָּקַד (pāqad, "visit" = **examine**). In Psalm 8 it denotes God's intervention for the good of humankind. In Job, by contrast, God intervenes to scrutinize human behavior as a pretext to unfairly judge them. To these terms Job adds a third verb בָּחַן (bāḥan, **test**) which also parodies the language of the Psalms. The psalmists sometimes invite God to test them because they are confident of their righteousness and God's justice (cf., e.g., Ps 17:3; 26:2; 139:23). But Job finds in God's testing only a cruel and unjust persecution.

7:19-21 Job ends his taunt of God with a flurry of rhetorical questions designed to expose what he believes to be God's cruel persecu-

---

[20]Cf. P.E Dion, "Formulaic Language in the Book of Job: International Background and Ironical Distortions," *SR* 16 (1987): 187-193; M. Fishbane, *Biblical Interpretation in Ancient Israel* (Oxford: Clarendon, 1985), pp. 285-286.

tion of his undeserving servant. **Will you never look away from me?**
In the Bible being under God's watchful eye is normally regarded a
positive thing (cf., e.g., Ps. 33:18-19; 34:16[15]). God's gaze (שָׁעָה,
šā'āh) usually portends blessing and deliverance. But here, just the
opposite is true. Job sees God's watching as surveillance, a relentless
scrutiny designed to catch him at some sin. It is not merciful, it is
malevolent. Job withers beneath this surveillance and pleads for relief
even for an instant.[21] Clearly Job expects no relief.

   If I have sinned, what have I done to you, O watcher of men?
The "if" is not present in the Hebrew but the sense demands it.[22]
With this question and an accompanying label that he pins upon
God, Job's taunt reaches a new level of irreverence. In a mocking
fashion he questions how the behavior of a mere mortal can threat-
en or injure God. Such language reduces God to the level of man
and is an assault upon his sovereignty. The label **watcher of men**
(נֹצֵר הָאָדָם, *nōṣēr hā'ādām*), like the name "Seeing Eye" (v. 8), is tinged
with sarcasm. Both are used to describe what Job believes to be God's
unjustified probing of human lives. Once again Job has reversed the
traditional view of the God who watches over his people (Deut 32:10)
and characterized him as Grand Inquisitor who takes some kind of
perverted pleasure in catching humans at their mistakes.

   Why have you made me your target [lit., "mark," מִפְגָּע,
miphgāh]? God is accused of taking target practice at Job, raining
blow after blow upon him as a form of cruel play. With the question
Have I become a burden to you? Job again raises the irreverent idea
that he has somehow become a problem or even a threat to God
demanding some kind of vindictive response. The final question
Why do you not pardon my offenses and forgive my sins? completes the taunt by suggesting that God is behaving in a small, igno-
ble way. If he were truly a great and noble God, nothing that Job has
done would reduce him to such vindictiveness. This should not be
taken as an admission of guilt by Job but as a hypothetical rebuttal
of the inappropriateness of God's affliction of Job. The God of reli-

---

[21]Lit., "let me be long enough to swallow my spittle," a well-known phrase
in Arabic.

[22]Andersen insists that the word should not be supplied and argues that
Job is here admitting his sin. But this flies in the face of his overall argument
that he has not done anything worthy of his suffering.

gious tradition is a merciful God who forgives the sin of his people. Why, then, does God continue to "punish" Job? If God is going to rise above his petty and unfair persecution of Job, he had better do it quickly, for Job is convinced he will **soon lie down in the dust**. Job is referring to the grave or Sheol which for him is a place of freedom and escape from turmoil (3:13-19). The taunt ends with a final caricature of God as a mortal desperately seeking to amend his ways and do right by Job only to find that it is too late. As in some of his other speeches Job ends his reply to Eliphaz with a focus on the imminence of his demise (cf., e.g., 10:21-22; 14:20-22; 17:13-16; 21:32-33). It is the belief that he will soon die that fuels the intensity of Job's cry for vindication.

JOB 8

3. Bildad's First Speech (8:1-22)

We do not know why the friends speak in the order that they do. It may be a matter of age, status, or eloquence.[1] Whatever their differences with regard to credentials and ability, however, their arguments are all essentially the same: Job suffers because he has sinned. Bildad builds upon Eliphaz's claim that God is just by arguing that there are no exceptions to this rule. Whereas Eliphaz claimed supernatural revelation as the source of his position, Bildad appeals to the traditions of the fathers and the lessons of nature. His language has a sharper tone than that of Eliphaz,[2] yet he does balance his criticisms of Job with the encouraging prospect of God's restoration of his broken servant. The speech breaks into three parts: 1) God is always just (8:1-7), 2) proofs of God's justice from tradition and nature (8:8-19), and 3) application of this principle to Job's life (8:20-22).

God Is Always Just (8:1-7)

[1]Then Bildad the Shuhite replied:
[2]"How long will you say such things? / Your words are a blustering wind. / [3]Does God pervert justice? / Does the Almighty pervert what is right? / [4]When your children sinned against him, / he gave them over to the penalty of their sin. / [5]But if you will look to God / and plead with the Almighty, / [6]if you are pure and upright, / even now he will rouse himself on your behalf / and restore you to your rightful place. / [7]Your beginnings will seem humble, / so prosperous will your future be.

---

[1]Cf. W.A. Irwin, "The First Speech of Bildad," *ZAW* 51 (1933): 204-216.
[2]Terrien calls him a "professor without charisma."

8:1-3 Bildad's opening words are more acrimonious than those of Eliphaz. Showing little patience (**How long**[3]) with Job he sharply dismisses his previous speech as so much **blustering wind**. Such language is a standard technique in the ancient disputes of the sages.[4] Job's criticisms of God were sharper in his second speech and **such things,** Bildad feels, demand a swift and strong response. Bildad's retort is issued in the form of two rhetorical questions, **Does God pervert justice?**[5] **Does the Almighty pervert what is right?** The divine names **God** and **Almighty** are in the emphatic position in the Hebrew conveying the shock that Bildad feels over Job's claim that God is unjustly persecuting him. To Bildad such a thing is simply unthinkable. Bildad's theology is built upon the principle of retributive justice, and to it he will permit no exceptions. Later in the book Elihu will make the same claim in a positive declaration, **It is unthinkable that God would do wrong, that the Almighty would pervert justice** (34:12). The term **pervert** (עִוֵּת, *'iwwēth*) means to "twist" or "bend" and is part of the "sin" vocabulary of the Old Testament (cf., e.g., Amos 8:5). We have here the articulation of an airtight theological system. Bildad has a static view of how God runs his world. God always sees to it that people get what they deserve. Before they are through, the friends will attempt to force Job and even God into this theological system.

8:4-7 According to Bildad, God's retributive justice is a double-edged sword. On the one hand it can mete out the harshest **penalty** for **sin**. By applying the negative side of this model to Job's children, Bildad does suggest a new idea for Job to ponder in the face of his great loss. Job's children did not die because God was punishing Job, but because God was punishing them. The reader may remember from the prologue that Job had some concern about his children's potential sinfulness and regularly made sacrifices on their behalf (1:5). It is doubtful that this argument provided Job any comfort over the loss of his children, but it does supply him with a poten-

[3]This question picks up on Job's earlier cry "How long" (7:19). The construction here is an abbreviated form of the normal Hebrew expression, perhaps itself an indication of Bildad's growing impatience with Job.

[4]Cf. examples given by Habel (*Job*, p. 173).

[5]Cf. S.H. Scholnick, "The Meaning of *Mišpat* in the Book of Job," *JBL* 101 (1982): 521-529.

tial rationale for their demise. Bildad does not name the sin of Job's children, but in his mind he does not need to do so. In his fixed model of retribution their death is proof of it. The result proves the cause. It should be noted, however, that the prologue does not even hint at the notion that Job's children died because of anything they had done. The suffering initiated by the Satan was a "test" of Job, not his children. So the reader, like Job, is afforded no logical, satisfactory explanation of their tragic deaths.

On the other hand, Bildad suggests, God's retributive justice has a positive side. It rewards the **pure** and **upright** with a **prosperous future**. With these words Bildad draws a contrast between Job and his children.[6] Whereas they have committed an unpardonable sin against God, Job obviously has not. He is still alive. For him there is still hope. This invites only one appropriate response: practice piety and expect piety's reward. Specifically Job should **look to** (lit., "seek," שָׁחַר, šiḥar) God. In the prophetic literature this verb is connected with repentance (cf., e.g., Hos 5:15). Here it carries the more general idea of "pray." This is supported by the companion term **plead** (הִתְחַנֵּן, hithḥānēn), a term often used with other Hebrew words for prayer (הִתְפַּלֵּל, hithpallēl, and קָרָא, qārā'). According to Bildad, however, the favor Job seeks is conditional. It can only be found in response to righteousness. **If you are pure** God will **rouse himself** (עוּר, 'ûr)[7] and **restore** (שִׁלֵּם, šillēm)[8] **you**. This, insists Bildad, is retribution's positive side, the reward it offers the pious. **Rightful place**, literally "place of the righteous," means "the place Job deserves," referring to the condition of ease and prosperity Job had once enjoyed and can enjoy again.[9]

Proofs of God's Justice (8:8-19)

[8]**"Ask the former generations / and find out what their fathers learned, / [9]for we were born only yesterday and know nothing, /**

---

[6]The "if you" of verse six is emphatic.

[7]This term is used in the liturgical language of the Psalms to describe God's "awakening" to deliver his people (cf., e.g., Ps 44:24[23]; 59:5-6[3-4]).

[8]שלם (šlm) in the Piel means to "repair, reestablish." It carries the idea of "make whole again."

[9]The expression is also used in the more literal sense, "abode of the righteous" to refer to the Temple mount (Jer 31:23).

and our days on earth are but a shadow. / [10]Will they not instruct
you and tell you? / Will they not bring forth words from their
understanding? / [11]Can papyrus grow tall where there is no marsh?
/ Can reeds thrive without water? / [12]While still growing and
uncut, / they wither more quickly than grass. / [13]Such is the destiny of all who forget God; / so perishes the hope of the godless.
/ [14]What he trusts in is fragile[a]; / what he relies on is a spider's
web. / [15]He leans on his web, but it gives way; / he clings to it, but
it does not hold. / [16]He is like a well-watered plant in the sunshine,
/ spreading its shoots over the garden; / [17]It entwines its roots
around a pile of rocks / and looks for a place among the stones. /
[18]But when it is torn from its spot, / that place disowns it and says,
'I never saw you.' / [19]Surely its life withers away, / and[b] from the
soil other plants grow.

[a]*14 The meaning of the Hebrew for this word is uncertain. [b]19 Or Surely
all the joy it has / is that*

8:8-10 Bildad turns first to the world of religious tradition[10] to
substantiate his claim that God is always just, **Ask**[11] **the former generations**.[12] The counsel of the **fathers**,[13] having stood the test of
time, was valued in Hebrew culture above the experience of the individual who is born **only yesterday** and **knows nothing** (cf. Deut
32:7).[14] Eliphaz appeals to a mysterious vision as his authority (4:12-
15) and Elihu to the "breath of the Almighty" which all humans possess (32:8; 33:4), but Bildad's authority goes all the way back to the
primordial wisdom of the distant past. In the world of these sages
no view could be more authoritative. The irony here is that it is precisely this view of the fathers (retributive justice) that the book of Job

---

[10]Cf. N.C. Habel, "Appeal to Ancient Tradition as a Literary Form," *ZAW*
88 (1970): 253-272.
[11]This expression is formulaic for appeal to the ancient traditions (cf.
Deut 4:32; Jer 18:13).
[12]"Generations" (דּוֹר, *dôr*) is singular in the Hebrew and refers to the continuous line of the patriarchs.
[13]The LXX translates simply "fathers" instead of "their fathers," and this
nicely parallels the first half of the verse. Cf. discussion of the grammar in
Blommerde, *Northwest Semitic Grammar and Job*, pp. 50-51.
[14]Cf. also Sirach 8:9-12, "Do not underrate the talk of old men, after all,
they themselves learned it from their fathers; from them you will learn how
to think, and the art of a timely answer."

will challenge. Job, who is most aware of what tradition teaches (9:2; 12:3; 13:1-2; 16:4), will deny it on the basis of his personal experience. Bildad preemptively asserts that the experience of an individual life that passes like a **shadow** (cf. Ps 102:12[11]; 109:23; 1 Chr 29:15) cannot compare with the collective wisdom of the ages. The meaning of life cannot be found in personal experience, he argues; it must be learned from others. He invites Job to allow the fathers to **instruct** him.

8:11-13 Turning to the world of nature, Bildad continues to build his case. Probably quoting from an Egyptian proverb, he characterizes the **godless**[15] as a **papyrus**[16] plant. The papyrus was a perennial rush that was found in rivers and lakes all over the ancient world. It grew to a height of fifteen feet and was valued as a raw material for mats, boats, and parchment. Though impressive, however, it was most unstable and quickly withered when deprived of its watery bed. Such, he argues, is the **destiny**[17] of those who **forget God** (cf. Ps 50:22). They appear to be substantial but actually are of no real significance. Denying God, they are like an aquatic rush cut off from its supply of water and destined to perish without **hope.**[18] Like the stately papyrus the godless are not self-sufficient and have no guarantee of ever coming to harvest. The idea of the pride of the wicked is also probably behind the author's choice of words here. Like the papyrus, he says, the godless **grow tall**. This term (גָּאָה, gā'āh) also means to "be exalted" and is one of the words used in the Bible to describe the arrogant.

8:14-15 The second image employed by Bildad to characterize the transitory and unstable nature of the wicked is the **spider's web**. The spider's house is a common metaphor for instability in the Bible and other ancient literature (cf., e.g., Isa 59:6). "Weaker than a spider's house" is a common Arabic proverb, and the Koran calls the spider's web the "frailest of all houses" (29:40). The godless place their **trust** in that which is most **fragile**. This expression (אֲשֶׁר־יָקוֹט,

---

[15]חָנֵף (ḥānēph), "profane."

[16]This term and the companion "reeds" (אָחוּ, 'āḥû) are probably Egyptian loanwords (cf. Gen 41:2; Exod 2:3).

[17]אָרְחוֹת ('orḥôth; lit., "paths") carries the idea of "fate" or "destiny" (v. 19; 3:23; Prov 1:19).

[18]תִּקְוָה (tiqwāh) refers to the renewing strength one needs to survive and flourish.

'ăšer yāqôṭ) is difficult in the Hebrew. Occurring only once in the Hebrew Bible it has been taken to mean "gossamer" or "threads." The versions and some commentators have connected it with the Hebrew word meaning "to cut off," and translate this line, "whose confidence is cut off."[19] Exactly in what the godless places his trust is not explicitly stated in the text. Perhaps it is in his possessions or his family. Having listened to Job's earlier words, however, Bildad may be referring more specifically to Job's reliance on his own right-eousness and his determination to demand vindication of God.

8:16-19 These verses are very difficult in the Hebrew and are the subject of some debate among the interpreters. First there is the issue of how these verses relate to what has just been said. Does this con-tinue the description of the godless, or is it a contrasting portrait of the godly man? Some scholars, following the medieval interpreter Saadiah, see this section as a portrait of the stable and substantial godly person.[20] The plant that wraps its roots **around a pile of rocks** contrasts the papyrus which grows from a fragile bed. Because of its inner strength this plant (the godly man) can endure any attempt to uproot it (v. 18) and spring back to life. Habel, for example, translates verse 19, "Such is the joy of its way that from the dust it shoots up else-where."[21] Those who hold this view point to verse 20 as a summary of the contrast between the **blameless man** and the **evildoers**. Most com-mentators, however, see this section as a continuation of the descrip-tion of the godless and understand this plant, like the papyrus, to have the appearance of stability when, in fact, it is easily uprooted and left to wither.[22] Some have even argued that it is God who does the uprooting in verse 18.[23] Though the readings of the text may differ, the point they make is essentially the same: the godless man, separat-ed from the one true source of life, simply has no future.

Application of the Principle (8:20-22)

[20]**"Surely God does not reject a blameless man / or strengthen the hands of evildoers. / [21]He will yet fill your mouth with laugh-**

---

[19]Cf. discussion in Hartley, *Job,* p. 159, n. 2.
[20]E.g., Hakam, Gordis, Habel.
[21]Habel, *Job,* p. 168; cf. his discussion on p. 177.
[22]E.g., Erlich, Duhm.
[23]E.g., Fohrer, cf. discussion in Clines, *Job,* p. 209.

ter / and your lips with shouts of joy. / ²²Your enemies will be
clothed in shame, / and the tents of the wicked will be no more."

8:20-22 Bildad's extended condemnation of the godless has been
pointed indirectly at Job in an "if the shoe fits wear it" manner. In
this concluding section he begins by reminding Job that the fate of
the wicked need not be his. **God does not reject the blameless man**.
Retributive justice also has a positive side. If you practice righteousness, you can expect righteousness' reward. It is not too late for Job.
Laughter and **joy** can still be his. Emotional and social restoration
are not beyond his reach. As Clines notes, this closing section is a fitting summary of Bildad's argument. All people are divided into two
classes: the **blameless** and the **evildoers**. God himself sees to it that
each group gets what they deserve. There are no exceptions to this
rule. This airtight summary also illustrates Bildad's disconnect with
what the readers know to be the truth about Job. It is he who is the
blameless one in this story. Yet it is he who suffers.

JOB 9

4. Job's Reply to Bildad (9:1–10:22)

If the intensity of the great debate between Job and his friends was heightened by the speech of Bildad, then Job's reply takes it to still higher levels. Unlike his reply to Eliphaz this speech of Job speaks exclusively of God. Impugning the justice of God, Job ponders the possibility of taking God to court. Recognizing that such a course of action would be impossible, he reverts first to despair and then to verbal assaults against God with language that can only be viewed as irreverent.[1] The speech employs a variety of literary genres including the hymn (9:5-10), the wish (10:18b-19), and the taunt 10:3-17). But the dominant genre of the speech is the legal dispute.[2] In the language of the ancient courtroom, Job seeks to "summon" God (9:16), "dispute" with him (9:14), and call him to "court" (9:32). He demands to know the "charges" (10:2) that God has against him and calls for a third party to "arbitrate" between them (9:33).

The Prospect of Taking God to Court (9:1-4)

¹Then Job replied:
²"Indeed, I know that this is true. / But how can a mortal be righteous before God? / ³Though one wished to dispute with him, / he could not answer him one time out of a thousand. / ⁴His wisdom is profound, his power is vast. / Who has resisted him and come out unscathed?

9:1-4 Job seems to open his speech with a concession: **Indeed, I**

---

[1] Cf. K. Fullerton, "On Job 9 and 10," *JBL* 53 (1934): 321-349; idem, "Job Chapters 9 and 10," *AJSL* 55 (1938): 225-269.

[2] For discussion cf. J.J.M. Roberts, "Summons to Yahweh: The Exploitation of a Legal Metaphor," *ResQ* 16 (1973).

know that this is true. **This** evidently refers to Bildad's assertion that God is just. This concession, however, may be nothing more than an ironic ploy to set the stage for a challenge to that claim. If this is so, then the emphatic **indeed**[3] may be viewed as a rhetorical tool intended to preface Job's desire to summon God to court. When Job follows with the query, **But how can a mortal be righteous before God?** (a restatement of Eliphaz's thesis [4:17] in the form of a question), it becomes apparent he has no plans to yield to the arguments of the friends. In this context the expression **be righteous before God** may more accurately be translated "be declared innocent in a contest with God."[4] In verse 3 Job makes clear his intentions to **dispute with him** (God). In the Hebrew this is the language of litigation. Job ponders the prospect of arguing his case against God in a court of law.[5] At this point, however, the difficulty of winning such a trial is acknowledged. Imagining a cross-examination by God, Job admits that he could not **answer** (עָנָה, *'ānāh*)[6] even one of God's questions **in a thousand**.[7] God is simply too formidable an opponent for a mere mortal. His **wisdom** and **power** make it impossible for any man to successfully **resist** him.[8]

God, the Formidable Opponent (9:5-13)

[5]**He moves mountains without their knowing it / and overturns them in his anger. / [6]He shakes the earth from its place / and makes its pillars tremble. / [7]He speaks to the sun and it does not shine; / he seals off the light of the stars. / [8]He alone stretches out the heavens / and treads on the waves of the sea. / [9]He is the Maker of the Bear and Orion, / the Pleiades and the constellations of the south. / [10]He performs wonders that cannot be fathomed, / miracles that cannot be counted. / [11]When he passes me, I cannot**

---

[3]אָמְנָם (*'omnām*, "surely") is also used with an ironic twist in 12:2.

[4]Habel, *Job*, p. 189.

[5]The legal metaphor in Job usually depicts Job as the defendant and God as the plaintiff. In this context, however, the roles are reversed. Cf. discussion by M.B. Dick, "The Legal Metaphor in Job 31," *CBQ* 41 (1979): 37-50.

[6]Also a legal term meaning to "respond to an allegation."

[7]This same expression occurs again in 33:23. Cf. also, Eccl 7:28. Another way to read this line is to understand God as the subject and render it, "God would not answer him, not one in a thousand times."

[8]Literally, "stiffen (the neck)" against him.

**see him; / when he goes by, I cannot perceive him. / [12]If he snatch-
es away, who can stop him? / Who can say to him, 'What are you
doing?' / [13]God does not restrain his anger; / even the cohorts of
Rahab cowered at his feet.**

9:5-10 The genre of this section is that of the ancient hymn. This
hymn, however, is not sung in the spirit of praise but of regret.[9] Job
laments the fact that God's immeasurable power makes it impossible to challenge him (cf. v. 14). The language of this hymn may be
regarded as a doxology to the irresistible ways of the Creator.[10] Job's
first depiction of God is as a terrifying Shaker of the earth. In
ancient cosmogony the **mountains** and the **pillars** constituted the
foundations of the cosmic order.[11] When God **shakes** them and
causes them to **tremble**, it threatens the world. With this language
Job hints at God's injustice. According to the OT it was when injustice was rampant that the foundations of the earth shook (Ps 82:1-
5). By contrast when God reigned with justice, the earth did not
move (Ps 96:10). Job is thus describing God as one who causes
chaos. He moves the mountains **without their knowing it**. As nature
remains ignorant of God's purposes, so also does the bewildered
Job. In verses 6-8 Job moves from the foundations of the earth to the
canopy above it. Here, too, his portrait of God's great power implies
its malevolent use. He commands the **sun** to **not shine**. This phrase
and the next (**seals off the light of the stars**) may refer simply to
heavy clouds or some other natural phenomenon that obscures the
light of the heavens. But the next verse suggests that Job has something more ominous in mind.[12] By paralleling **heavens** and **sea**[13] in
verse 8 Job may be suggesting that God is capable of some cosmic

---

[9]Cf. Fullerton, "On Job 9 and 10," pp. 330-331, and W. Whedbee, "The
Comedy of Job," pp. 1-39, regard this as a parody of a hymn of praise.
Against this interpretation cf. Clines, *Job*, p. 230.

[10]This hymn employs language typical of theophanies in the OT; cf. J.
Jeremias, *Theophanie* (Neukirchen: Neukirchener, 1965).

[11]Cf., e.g., Ps 75:4[3]; 104:5.

[12]The verb the author uses to describe God's preventing of the sun from
"shining" (זָרַח, *zāraḥ*) literally means to prevent it from "rising." This might
suggest God's power to disrupt the very cycles of the universe.

[13]The reference to God's "treading on the waves of the sea [*yām*]," may
allude to the ancient tradition of the conquest of the great sea monster
(Yamm) spoken of in the Canaanite myths.

chaos that threatens the world order. In the creation accounts of the
OT, God's primordial work is described in the realms of heaven,
earth, and sea. In each arena he brought order and fixed the boundaries that give creation its stability and predictability. But here just
the opposite is the case. As he brings upheaval to the earth (vv. 5-6),
God is likewise capable of bringing turmoil to the sky and sea. The
God who created the world can likewise destroy it. Job concludes his
survey of God's power in the universe by describing the constellations (vv. 9-10). These same three constellations are referred to in
the conventional hymnic language of the OT (cf., e.g., Amos 5:8; Job
38:31-32).[14] These great **wonders** of God's power **cannot be fathomed**. God's management of the universe is inscrutable as is his
management of Job's life. Interestingly enough, these same two
arenas will be placed alongside one another for a final climactic
time when God speaks from the whirlwind of his role in his world
and Job is somehow able to connect it to his own tragic experience
(38:1-42:6).

9:11-13 Job continues his characterization of his Opponent by
focusing on his mysterious, elusive nature. God's invisible nature
prevents Job from confronting him. The reference to the God who
goes by (חלף, ḥlp) may be an ironic allusion to the spirit who glided
(ḥlp) past Eliphaz in the night (4:15-16). Eliphaz claimed to receive a
revelation from this mysterious God. Job finds only frustration. He
cannot **see** (ראה, r'h) or **perceive** (בין, byn) him. Job uses these verbs
to describe his inability to comprehend the nature of God and the
inscrutability of his ways (cf. 13:1; 42:5; 14:21). The inability of humans to actually see God is a common feature of the theophany narratives of the Hebrew Bible. Even Moses is only allowed to see the
back of God as he **passes** (עבר, 'br, Exod 33:22-23 and here[15]). The
hiddenness of God is likewise a major theme of the book of Job.
Verse 12 focuses on the inability of humans to charge God with any
crime. The verb **snatches** (חתף, ḥtp) is commonly regarded as

---

[14]The actual identity of these constellations is debated. Cf. G. Schiaparelli,
Astronomy in the Old Testament (Oxford: Clarendon, 1905); N. Herz, "The
Astral Terms in Job ix 9, xxxviii 31-32," *JTS* 14 (1913): 575-577.

[15]Cf. also 1 Kgs 19:11-13. The references to Moses' speaking with God
"face to face" place the Lord in the pillar of cloud when this is taking place
(cf., e.g., Exod 33:9-11).

descriptive of violent, criminal behavior and is translated "abduct" or "steal."[16] Job may have in mind God's taking of Job's children or some personal assault upon him. The phrase **"What are you doing?"**[17] is the standard language of legal accusation.[18] By putting these two expressions together, Job is characterizing God as a criminal who is beyond the reach of the law. In verse 13 Job concludes his portrait of God by returning to a discussion of the **anger** (cf. v. 5) behind the reckless behavior of his Adversary. This anger is so great that even the **cohorts of Rahab** cower before him. In Canaanite mythology Rahab[19] was a sea monster who personified chaos. Job also mentions Leviathan (3:8; 40:25–41:26) and Tannin (7:12; 30:29) which were likewise thought by the ancients to be great dragons who inhabited the depths of the sea. The book of Job borrows from this popular mythology in order to portray God as one who is able to overpower even the most chaotic forces in the cosmos.[20]

The Difficulties of Winning a Dispute against God (9:14-20)

[14]**"How then can I dispute with him? / How can I find words to argue with him? / [15]Though I were innocent, I could not answer him; / I could only plead with my Judge for mercy. / [16]Even if I summoned him and he responded, / I do not believe he would give me a hearing. / [17]He would crush me with a storm / and multiply my wounds for no reason. /**

[18]**He would not let me regain my breath / but would overwhelm me with misery. / [19]If it is a matter of strength, he is mighty! / And if it is a matter of justice, who will summon him**[a]**? / [20]Even if I were innocent, my mouth would condemn me; / if I were blameless, it would pronounce me guilty.**

[a]*19* See Septuagint; Hebrew *me*.

9:14-16 How then can I dispute with him? In these verses Job returns to the challenge he raised at the beginning of his speech: How could a man possibly win a case against God (cf. v. 3)? The **I** is

---

[16]Cf. the discussion in Hartley, *Job*, p. 169, n. 9.

[17]A parallel may be found in Dan 4:32[35].

[18]Cf. Boecker, *Redeformen des Rechtslebens*, pp. 26-31.

[19]Cf. also 26:12; Ps 89:11[10]; Isa 51:9.

[20]Cf. J. Day, *God's Conflict with the Dragon and the Sea*.

in the emphatic position to emphasize Job's hopeless situation. If the chaotic powers of the universe cannot withstand God's wrath (v. 13), how can a mere man hope to do so? If God overthrows mountains (vv. 5-6), he can certainly overwhelm mortals. Even with right on Job's side (**though I were innocent**), the sheer power of God makes him unassailable. Normal legal recourse would be useless against such a sovereign. Delivering a defense (**answer**) or making countercharges (**words to argue**), he believes, would prove futile, not because God is in the right but because God will not give him a fair **hearing**. In any court God would never submit to becoming a defendant. He would always be the **judge** before whom Job could only **plead for mercy**. This conclusion must present Job with a painful irony. He is an innocent man whose only hope is to plead for mercy. He must beg for that to which he is entitled. Bildad has already suggested he do so (8:5). But Job will not. To do so would be to abandon his integrity by admitting to a crime he has not committed in order to win a release from a suffering he does not deserve. This, Job will resist until the end.

9:17-18 In these verses Job continues to insist that there is no justice in God's court. Driven by anger (v. 13) rather than righteousness God will sabotage any attempts for Job to find justice. To deny Job his day in court, God would **crush** him **with a storm**. The word for storm (שְׂעָרָה, *s⁽ᵉ⁾ārāh*) is unusual, and some scholars argue another meaning.[21] If the rendering of NIV be accepted, this verse does serve to tie together the beginning and end of the book. It remembers the storm which played a part in Job's tragic loss (1:16) and anticipates the resolution of Job's dilemma when God comes in a storm to speak with Job (Job 38–41). God assails Job **for no reason** (חִנָּם, *ḥinnām*). This term, too, serves a rhetorical purpose by cleverly tying Job's frustration to the events in heaven which brought it about. In the opening scene the satan had skeptically challenged that Job feared God "for nothing" (*ḥinnām*). In the second scene God looked down upon a devastated Job and charged that the *satan* had incited God to "ruin" Job "without any reason" (*ḥinnām*). This represents yet another claim within the book (albeit from Job's own

---

[21]Clines (*Job*, p. 235) and others read "for a hair" and see the expression as a good parallel with "for no reason" (17b). This has the support of Targ. and Syr. Comparison with Nahum 1:3, however, favors "storm" or "tempest."

mouth) that Job suffers innocently. This fact not only forms the plot of the book, it also lays the foundation for its inquiry into the nature of God.

9:19-20 These verses summarize the dilemma posed by the prospect of Job's challenging God. If winning depends upon a contest of strength, Job knows he is no match for the mighty God (cf. v. 4). If it depends upon a verdict of the courts, Job realizes he has no power to even **summon**[22] God much less convict him. God would never allow himself to be bound by the authority of some human legal proceeding. He is simply too powerful (vv. 3-10) and his ways too incomprehensible (vv. 11-12) to be judged by any earthly court. Thus even an **innocent**[23] man could not win against God in court. God is so great and his ways so inscrutable that any attempt by a mere mortal to accuse him of injustice would represent an irreverence, a sin. To even argue that God unfairly afflicts the righteous would prove the arguer to be unrighteous. Such a case would thus be lost before it even began.

Job's Charge against God (9:21-24)

[21]"Although I am blameless, / I have no concern for myself; / I despise my own life. / [22]It is all the same; that is why I say, / 'He destroys both the blameless and the wicked.' / [23]When a scourge brings sudden death, / he mocks the despair of the innocent. / [24]When a land falls into the hands of the wicked, / he blindfolds its judges. / If it is not he, then who is it?

9:21-24 Having acknowledged that God is not indictable and that no mortal could ever hope of winning against him in court, Job nonetheless barges headlong into where even angels fear to tread (4:18). He dares to protest his innocence before God and accuse

---

[22]MT reads "summon me [Job]." Most translators, following LXX, emend "summon him [God]." Gordis regards MT as a deliberate scribal alteration for reasons of reverence (though this text is not listed in the official list of *tiqqune sopherim* (cf. C. McCarthy, *The Tiqqune Sopherim and Other Theological Corrections of the Massoretic Text of the Old Testament*, OBO 36 [Freiburg: Universitätsverlag, and Göttingen: Vandenhoeck und Ruprecht, 1981], p. 168).

[23]תָּם (*tām*) appears three times in vv. 20-22 affirming the claims of the prologue that Job is an innocent man.

him of injustice. Job asserts unequivocally, **I am blameless**.[24] Such a claim might appear to us, as it did to Job's friends, arrogant and absurd. Indeed, if we the readers had not heard it from God's own lips (1:8; 2:3) we would regard it the ultimate presumption. As noted earlier, this is not a claim of moral perfection but describes someone who behaves with personal integrity and genuine piety.[25] The meaning it carries here is of an even more limited, legal sense. It means "I am innocent, not guilty." "I have committed no crime that merits such a sharp punishment from God." This, too, God has earlier affirmed (2:3b). In a series of terse, punctuated phrases Job continues to lament his plight. **I have no concern for myself**. The Hebrew reads "I do not know myself," and the interpreters have taken it to mean different things. The RSV ("I regard not myself") and Pope ("I care not for myself") read it much the same as the NIV. This would comport with the following **I despise my own life**.[26] Gordis takes it to mean "I am beside myself (with misery)."[27] S. Paul compares the phrase to a similar Akkadian expression and understands it to be a medical term describing a "loss of consciousness."[28] Elsewhere in this chapter, however, the verb "know" has a more cognitive sense of "be aware" or "understand" (cf. vv 2,5,28). Perhaps that is its meaning here. The issue that this term addresses may be the ultimate one of the book — Job's attempt to grasp the meaning of his suffering (and ultimately of his life). This may be Job's way of saying, "I can no longer comprehend the meaning of my life." If so, then the meaning of the three sequential phrases in verse 21 may be as follows: "I am blameless" (yet God afflicts me); "My life (of piety) no longer has meaning"; "I (therefore) despise my own life." Job's undeserved suffering has undone him more than physically. It has robbed him of his *raison d'etre*. Deprived of meaning his life is now without hope. He once thought God ruled his world by the principle of retributive justice. God rewarded the good and punished the evil. But his undeserved suffering has invalidated his worldview and

---

[24]Dhorme reads this assertion as a question, "Am I perfect?"

[25]Cf. discussion of 1:1.

[26]For a similar use of "know" cf. Gen. 39:6; Deut. 33:9. Cf. also D. Winton Thomas, "The Root *yada'* in Hebrew," *JTS* 35 (1935): 298-306.

[27]Cf. also Cant 6:12 where it may mean, "I am beside myself (with joy)."

[28]S.M. Paul, "An Unrecognized Medical Idiom in Canticles 6,12 and Job 9,21," *Bib* 59 (1978): 545-547.

led him to an inescapable conclusion: **He destroys both the blame-less and the wicked.** God is not just! He is arbitrary and indiscriminate in his treatment of his creatures. **It is all the same.**[29] His **scourge**[30] brings death to all. He is unremittingly hostile toward humans regardless of their piety. There is even a cruelty behind his actions. By refusing to intervene to save the **innocent**, he **mocks** the **despair** they feel over such injustice. And it is not just in the moment of their death that God does not discriminate between the blameless and wicked but also in their earthly existence.[31] He allows the land to **fall into the hands of the wicked**. He allows justice to be perverted in human affairs. It is unclear from Job's words whether he considers God as a direct agent of human injustice or an indirect encourager of it by his own injustice. This charge that God is the source of social disorder echoes his earlier claim that the malevolent God is the source of cosmic disorder (vv. 5-7). **If it is not he, then who is it?** This phrase reveals the problem that undeserved suffering poses for a monotheist. An atheist can look at life's injustices and declare, "There is no God." A polytheist can view the same and explain, "The bad gods are doing this." But the monotheist has a more difficult time. If there is but one God who made all things and who rules all things, what is the origin of life's cruel absurdities? Even the Satan of the prologue cannot take all the blame for such suffering for, as the story makes clear, he can do only what God permits. Job, if he knows of a Satan, never once indicts him. Instead, he lays responsibility for life's injustices squarely in the lap of God. All of this seems to be a direct refutation of Bildad's claim that God does not pervert justice (8:3). It also counters Eliphaz's assertion that God offers protection to the righteous in troubled times (5:19-22). The friends have argued God's justice on principle and tradition. Job seeks to refute it on the grounds of actual human experience.

---

[29]Some interpreters connect this phrase with the "blameless" and "wicked" of v. 22b while others connect it to Job's personal condition addressed in v. 21. Either way the ultimate meaning is the same. Blamelessness does not secure God's blessing.

[30]This term (שׁוֹט, *šôṭ*) means "whip" or "plague" and describes devastating destruction which brings widespread death (cf. Isa 10:5-19; 28:15-18).

[31]The phrase "blindfolds its judges" (lit., "covers the face [or eyes] of its judges") elsewhere refers to the giving of bribes (cf., e.g., Exod 23:8).

Job's Lament before God (9:25-31)

²⁵"My days are swifter than a runner; / they fly away without a glimpse of joy. / ²⁶They skim past like boats of papyrus, / like eagles swooping down on their prey. / ²⁷If I say, 'I will forget my complaint, / I will change my expression, and smile,' / ²⁸I still dread all my sufferings, / for I know you will not hold me innocent. / ²⁹Since I am already found guilty, / why should I struggle in vain? / ³⁰Even if I washed myself with soapᵃ / and my hands with washing soda, / ³¹you would plunge me into a slime pit / so that even my clothes would detest me.

ᵃ*30 Or snow*

At this point there is a distinct shift in the direction of Job's speech. In verses 1-24 Job has been speaking to the friends about God, consistently referring to him in the third person. Now he aims his words directly toward God (notice the use of the second person in verses 28 and 31). Job will continue this for the remainder of his speech.[32] This is a regular pattern in Job's speeches which typically move from monologue addressed to the friends to direct address of God. After lamenting the swift passing of his days (vv. 25-26), Job ponders three different alternatives to taking God to court: 1) dropping his complaint (vv. 27-29), cleansing himself of his iniquity (vv. 30-31), and finding an arbiter between him and God (vv. 32-35).

9:25-26 Job opens his lament by returning to a theme he has explored earlier, the fleeting nature of life (7:6,16). Three metaphors of life's swift passing are employed here. He declares his days **swifter than a runner**. This refers to ancient couriers who rushed on foot to bring their news (cf. 2 Sam 18:19ff.; Isa 41:27; 52:7). He then speaks of the **boats of papyrus** which used to ply the waters of Egypt (cf. Isa 18:1-2). These ancient boats were so light they seemed to skim over the water. The final image is that of the **eagles**[33] **swooping down on their prey** (cf. Deut 28:49; 2 Sam 1:23; Prov 23:5).[34] The sense of

---

[32]With the exception of vv. 32-35 which ponder the prospect of an arbiter between him and God.

[33]נֶשֶׁר (*nešer*) refers to birds of prey and may also mean "falcon" or "vulture."

[34]The bird and boat images of life's brevity are also present in Wisd. 5:10-11, where a third metaphor of the arrow is added.

urgency which pervades the speeches of Job grows out of Job's conviction that he is not long for this world.

9:27-29 In view of his imminent demise Job now urgently ponders the first of three alternatives to litigation against God. He considers dropping his **complaint**. His friends have already encouraged this. He could simply get a grip on his bitter feelings, change his demeanor, and just get on with his life. He remains convinced, however, that this will not end his **sufferings**. All along he has contended that his sufferings have nothing to do with his disposition toward God but are the result of God's unrelenting anger and unjust treatment of his subject. So what will silence and dishonest emotions get him? He believes that God has **already found him guilty** without even the formality of a trial and that there is, therefore, no hope for any acquittal. Any struggle to win God's approval would be **in vain**. This word (הֶבֶל, *hebel*; "breath, vapor") is the same word used in Ecclesiastes to refer to Qoheleth's (the "Teacher's") sense of futility.

9:30-31 Next Job ponders the prospect of some kind of ritual purification which might render him more pleasing to God. Job shares the sentiment of the Psalmist who, in view of his persecuted state, feels that he has "washed his hands in vain" (Ps 73:13b). The washing of hands was a well-known ritual of purification in ancient Israel (cf., e.g., Deut 21:6; Ps 26:6; Ps 51:7).[35] In similar fashion Pilate tried to exculpate himself from the guilt of shedding innocent blood by such a public rite (Matt 27:24). It is such a public ritual that Job is contemplating. The divine response he envisions is cynical and most striking. The angry God would take him fresh from his bath and **plunge** him **into a slime pit**. There is simply no appeasing this God, either by personal repentance or religious ritual.

Job's Desire for an Arbiter (9:32-35)

[32]**"He is not a man like me that I might answer him, / that we might confront each other in court. /** [33]**If only there were someone to arbitrate between us, / to lay his hand upon us both, /** [34]**someone to remove God's rod from me, / so that his terror would**

---

[35]Jeremiah (2:22) warns, however, that the affects of such washing are limited. Only God, not mere washing, can totally remove a man's guilt. For the possible influence of this prophetic theology on Job cf. Roberts, "Job and the Israelite Religious Tradition," pp. 107-114.

frighten me no more. / [35]Then I would speak up without fear of him, / but as it now stands with me, I cannot.

9:32-35 The third, and final, option to litigation Job considers is one of the most intriguing ideas raised by the book. Job seeks someone to **arbitrate** between him and God. Such arbitration seems necessary to Job for at least three reasons. First there is the vast difference between him and God. **He is not a man like me that I might answer him.** God is the creator and Job is the creature. God is so much greater than Job that he could never compel him to appear in court and answer charges (v. 19). Second, because of the aggressive manner of God, Job is intimidated by his power to harm him (vv. 14-17). Job wants someone to **remove God's rod**[36] from him and free him to **speak up without fear** against God's mistreatment of him. The third reason is suggested by the term **arbitrate** itself. An "arbiter" (מוֹכִיחַ, *môkîaḥ*)[37] was someone who was just and without bias. He was a neutral third party whose function was to provide a fair, impartial hearing. This, Job believes, is necessary if he is to have any chance in a contest with God. Since God has already treated him most unjustly in spite of Job's innocence (v. 20), Job believes he can get a fair trial only if some neutral party can **lay his hand** upon God and rein in his malevolent, overpowering might. At this point Job accepts the fact that no such person exists.[38] But he does not let the idea die (cf. 16:18-21; 19:23-27; 31:35).

---

[36]God's "rod" is the instrument of his anger (Lam 3:1; Isa 10:5).

[37]The term means "one who judges, reproves."

[38]Might Job be thinking of one of the "holy ones" (5:1) who might perform this role?

JOB 10

4. Job's Reply to Bildad (9:1-10:22, continued)

Knowing that he cannot win in a contest with God, Job is yet driven to state his case. He is ready to risk even his life in order to press charges against God's injustice. These words are spoken directly to God in the form of a complaint. Like so much that has already been said, the language here is that of the ancient courtroom.[1]

Job's Charge against God (10:1-17)

[1]"I loathe my very life; / therefore I give free rein to my complaint / and speak out in the bitterness of my soul. / [2]I will say to God: Do not condemn me, / but tell me what charges you have against me. / [3]Does it please you to oppress me, / to spurn the work of your hands, / while you smile on the schemes of the wicked? / [4]Do you have eyes of flesh? / Do you see as a mortal sees? / [5]Are your days like those of a mortal / or your years like those of a man, / [6]that you must search out my faults / and probe after my sin— / [7]though you know that I am not guilty / and that no one can rescue me from your hand?

[8]"Your hands shaped me and made me. / Will you now turn and destroy me? / [9]Remember that you molded me like clay. / Will you now turn me to dust again? / [10]Did you not pour me out like milk / and curdle me like cheese, / [11]clothe me with skin and flesh / and knit me together with bones and sinews? / [12]You gave me life and showed me kindness, / and in your providence watched over my spirit.

[13]"But this is what you concealed in your heart, / and I know

---

[1]רִיב (rîb, "go to court"; 10:2); רָשַׁע (rāša', "be guilty"; 10:7,15); צָדֵק (ṣādaq, "be innocent"; 10:15) are examples of this legal terminology.

that this was in your mind: / [14]If I sinned, you would be watching
me / and would not let my offense go unpunished. / [15]If I am
guilty—woe to me! / Even if I am innocent, I cannot lift my head,
/ for I am full of shame / and drowned in[a] my affliction. / [16]If I
hold my head high, you stalk me like a lion / and again display
your awesome power against me. / [17]You bring new witnesses
against me / and increase your anger toward me; / your forces
come against me wave upon wave.

[a]15 Or *and aware of*

10:1-2 When Job says **I loathe my very life** he not only vents his
feelings of disgust over his broken condition, he also tells us why he
is driven to speak so boldly. Simply put, he feels he has nothing to
lose. Since the grave obviously awaits him, there is no more harm
that anyone can do him. Released from fear of harm this condemned man will have his final say. He is able to give **free rein**[2] to
his **complaint**. Habel argues that this language is the equivalent of
making a formal presentation of a legal suit, and this seems to be
supported by the language of verse 2. The term used for **charges**
(רִיב, *rîb*) is the biblical word for "lawsuit."[3] What Job is demanding
is that he be formally charged so that he may have the opportunity
to defend himself. When Job says **do not condemn me**, he is not pre-
dicting the future outcome of the case but is calling upon God to
"not treat him as guilty." Job's charge is that the normal legal
process has been denied him. Without even being charged, he is
already being punished by God.

10:3-7 Through three rhetorical questions Job now explores the
possible motives that lie behind God's mistreatment of him. These
questions are not meant to inquire but to indict. **Does it please you
to oppress me?** This first question suggests that God stands to profit by Job's demise. Literally it asks, "Is it good for you to oppress
me?" The absurdity of such a motive is addressed in the next line, **to
spurn the work of your hands?**[4] Only some kind of masochist could

---

[2]Cf. M. Dahood, "The Root עוב II in Job," *JBL 78* (1959): 303-309.
[3]Cf. G. Liedke, *THAT*, 2:771-777.
[4]The phrase "work of your hands" (מַעֲשֵׂי יָדֶיךָ, *ma'ăśê yādêkā*) is elsewhere
positive in Scripture describing humans as the object of God's special concern (Ps 138:8). Here, however, Job uses a different word for "work" (יְגִיעַ,

find pleasure in destroying the very thing he had made. The idea of some perverted intention that God must have had when he made Job is again explored in verses 12-13. Job's indictment of the impropriety of God's disposition toward him is then sharpened by the contrast **while you smile on the schemes of the wicked**. The word **smile** literally means "shine" and is used in the Psalms to describe God's intervention to save (cf. Ps. 50:2; 80:3[2]; 94:1; also Deut 33:2). The thrust of the indictment is clear. God abuses the righteous Job while showing favor to the wicked.

The second question, **Do you have eyes of flesh?** charges that God's judgment is shortsighted and given to error like that of mere **mortals**. This charge flies in the face of what the Scriptures say about God's perception. As "spirit" his vision is not superficial but penetrates to the inner being (1 Sam 16:7; Prov 16:2; 21:2). Job knows that his charge is absurd, but the illogic of God's treatment of him yet invites it.

The third question hurls yet another challenge to God, **Are your days like those of a mortal?** The implication is that God is behaving like someone with a limited lifespan who feels some urgent pressure to expose Job's fault before it is too late (for God). The charge is that, acting quickly and under pressure, God is prone to error in judgment and behavior. Job is claiming to be the victim of God's rush to judgment. The verbs **search out** and **probe** revisit Job's earlier portrait of God as a malevolent "Seeing Eye" (7:8) and "Watcher of Humans" (7:20). Rather than looking favorably upon his children, God scrutinizes their lives looking for some error. When Job speaks of **my sin**, he is, of course, speaking hypothetically as the next line makes clear, **you know that I am not guilty.** Convinced that God is out to get him Job is now left with the desperate conclusion, **no one can rescue me from your hand**. The term **rescue** (מַצִּיל, *maṣṣîl*) commonly refers to deliverance in the sense of freeing a person from an oppressor. Often in Scripture, God is such a deliverer. Here, God is the oppressor. "If God be for us, who can be against us?" But if God be against us, there is, as Job realizes, none who can save.

---

yᵉgîaʿ) which carries the idea of "toil, painful effort to produce something" (e.g., Ps 78:46; 109:11). The stronger term heightens the absurdity of God destroying something he labored so hard to produce.

10:8-9 In these verses Job elaborates on the charge he raised in verse 3. **Your hands shaped[5] me.**[6] Job's depiction of God's creative activity is that of a potter shaping the embryo with care and skill. This, he says, is now absurdly contradicted by God's sudden decision to **destroy** him. This verb (בָּלַע, bala'; lit. "swallow, engulf") is ironically the same one used by God when he said to the Satan, "you incited me to ruin (bala') him (Job) without cause." Job blames his destruction on God, but God permitted it only to explore the challenge of the adversary that Job was disloyal to God. These words from the prologue show that God, too, was disturbed by the undeserved suffering of Job. Job, of course, has no knowledge of this. Job implores God to **remember** that he owed his existence to the personal, creative act of his Maker. This verb is used often in biblical prayers to invite God's mercy.[7] The common theme of mortals formed of **clay** and returned to the **dust** is found throughout Scripture.[8] In the prologue (1:21) Job proclaimed that he had come forth naked form the earth's womb and would thus return there. He has also repeatedly described humans as ephemeral creatures of dust destined to return there (4:19; 7:9-10,21). Here this concept is not used in the general sense of birth and death but specifically to God's purposeful act of destroying Job.

10:10-12 Job continues his metaphorical description of God's activity in the conception process. Semen, like **milk**, is **poured** into the womb and **curdles like cheese** into an embryo (cf. Ps 139:13-16; 2 Macc 7:22; Wis 7:2). This, in turn, is given form and structure by **bones and sinews** and **clothed with skin and flesh**. In Ezekiel's prophecy of the valley of the dry bones a similar metaphor is employed (Ezek 37:7ff.). To this carefully formed being is given **life** (חַיִּים, ḥayyîm). This term means more than the granting of Job's first breath. As the next term, **kindness** (חֶסֶד, ḥesed), makes clear, it describes Job's whole life experience before the disasters befell him. These same two terms appear together in Psalm 63:4[3]. The God

---

[5] עָצַב ('iṣṣēb) is also used to describe the making of an idol (עֹצֶב/עָצָב, 'ōṣēb/'āṣāb, Hos 8:4)

[6] For similar descriptions of the birth process cf. Ps 22:20[9]; 119:73; 139:13; Eccl 11:5.

[7] Cf. comment on 7:7 and the accompanying note.

[8] Cf., e.g., Gen 2:7; 3:19; Isa 64:7[8]; Rom 9:20-21; Ps 90:3; 104:29; 146:4.

who bestows life preserves it. Job's life has been protected by God's **providence** (פְּקֻדָּה, *pᵉquddāh*). This term literally means "visit, attend to, appoint" and describes God's personal intervention in human affairs to shape events to his desired end. In Jeremiah 29:10 God "visits" (פָּקַד, *pqd*) Israel to deliver them from captivity. In Psalm 80:15[14] God is petitioned to "care for" (*pqd*) the vine (his people) which he has planted.[9] In a similar sense God has **watched over** Job's **spirit**. This term (רוּחַ, *rûaḥ*), which can refer to the nonmaterial part of man, is here used in the more general sense of Job's "life." Notice the emphasis on God's personal involvement in Job's existence. This is played upon for the effect of demonstrating how illogical and cruel it is for God to destroy something he took such care to create.

10:13-14 Job sees in God's creative and providential activity a hidden agenda. God has made him, not to bless him and commune with him, but to spy on him and punish him. All along God's tender care had behind it a sinister purpose, **concealed** until God chose to make it known. God had set him up for this fall; he had created Job merely to destroy him. In developing this cynical view of God Job returns to a theme he has already sounded. God the "Watcher" (7:20) does not really **watch over** his creatures to protect them (as in v. 12) but to discover their **offenses** which he will not allow to **go unpunished**. Notice that Job does not actually admit to any such offenses ("*If* I sinned," v. 14; also "*If* I am guilty," v. 15).

10:15-17 As the object of God's scrutiny, Job sees himself caught in a no-win situation. Should he be **guilty**, he is without hope. The expression **woe to me** means "his fate is sealed." It occurs again in the Hebrew Bible only in Micah 7:1. If, on the other hand, Job is proved **innocent**, he still can find no vindication. The unjust, malevolent God has already condemned him to **drown in his affliction**. Since suffering was generally regarded as God's punishment for sin, Job appears guilty in the eyes of his society. It has brought him a stigma of **shame** that prevents him from confidently asserting his innocence. A raised **head** was a gesture of self-worth, while a lowered head expressed humiliation (cf. Judg 8:28; Zech 2:4[1:21]; Lam 2:10). Should Job dare to defend himself, the God who is out to get

---

[9]In a negative sense God sometimes "visits" (*pqd*) to punish (cf., e.g., Hos 9:7; Isa 10:3).

him would **stalk him like a lion.**[10] This is a common metaphor of victimization in the Psalms (cf., e.g., 7:3[2]; 10:9; 17:12; 22:14[13]; 35:17). God's wrath is described as that of a lion's in Hosea 5:14; 13:7. But there it is aimed at the guilty Israel. Job maintains God's anger is upon him even though he is innocent.[11] All of God's **power** is marshaled against Job. This term (הִתְפַּלֵּא, *hithpallā'*, "to work marvels") was used earlier in Job to describe God's creative activity (5:9; 9:10). That same power Job now believes is being used to destroy him.[12] The **new witnesses** (עֵד, *'ēd*) God brings upon Job must refer to his continuous sufferings which those around him regard as proofs of his guilt. A similar idea is expressed in 16:8 where Job's emaciated appearance is said to be a "witness" (*'ēd*) against him. Job says that an angry God, like a malicious, powerful commander, sends **wave upon wave** of assaults against him.

Job's Final Lament and Plea (10:18-22)

[18]**"Why then did you bring me out of the womb? / I wish I had died before any eye saw me. / [19]If only I had never come into being, / or had been carried straight from the womb to the grave! / [20]Are not my few days almost over? / Turn away from me so I can have a moment's joy / [21]before I go to the place of no return, / to the land of gloom and deep shadow,[a] / [22]to the land of deepest night, / of deep shadow and disorder, / where even the light is like darkness.**

[a]*21 Or and the shadow of death*; also in verse 22

Job ends his speech with a lament that echoes the sentiments of some of his earlier speeches. Resenting his very birth (as in 3:11ff.) he asks only for a brief respite from his interminable suffering (as in 7:19) before he meets his sad and inevitable end (cf. 7:16,21).

10:18-19 Why then did you bring me out of the womb? With this rhetorical question Job returns to the complaint of his opening speech (cf. 3:11,16). As Habel observes, however, he does so in a

---

[10]NEB makes Job the lion. But this reading is unlikely.

[11]For this animal imagery used of God cf. J. Hempel, "Jahwegleichnisse der israelitischen Propheten," *ZAW* 42 (1924): 74-104.

[12]A similar usage of this term occurs in Isa 29:14 where God's judgment of Israel is described as "astonishing."

more pointed way. In chapter 3 Job attributed his origins to some unseen force of destiny, while here the emphasis is upon God's personal role in bringing Job into this world (cf. 10:8-12). This is intentional and bespeaks the progression (or regression) of Job's theological struggle. Earlier (ch. 3) Job only spoke of God indirectly and merely inferred that he had acted unjustly (3:23). By now, not only is he blaming God for his undeserved suffering but charging that his entire life is nothing more than the result of a perverse divine plan of making him only to afflict him (10:13). As in his opening soliloquy, Job feels that it would have better if he had been stillborn, laid in the grave before **any eye**[13] saw him.

10:20-22 These verses blend the theme of brief respite (**a moment's joy**) before Job's demise (as in ch. 7) with the "resentment of birth" theme of chapter 3. Like other speeches of Job this one ends by staring death in the face. Four different words for "darkness" are employed to portray the gloom which death brings.[14] The portrait of death's hopeless and final state is completed with two additional metaphors. Death is **disorder.** The idea here is that death represents oblivion. It returns man to the state of primordial chaos from which creation was shaped. Death is a **place of no return** (cf. 7:10). It is final. Earlier Job had found solace in this. At least death would bring him some kind of rest from his suffering (3:16-22) or a place to hide from God (7:21). Here, however, the tone is one of complete despair. Death offers nothing but eternal darkness.

---

[13]Habel (*Job*, p. 200) speculates that the "eye" referred to here is God's eye. He argues that this resurrects the thought of God as the "Watcher" (cf. 10:14 and 7:8).

[14]"Darkness" (חֹשֶׁךְ, *ḥōšek*); "deep shadow" (צַלְמָוֶת, *ṣalmāweth*, twice); "gloom" (אֹפֶל, *'ōphel*, twice); "deepest night" (עֵיפָתָה, *'ēphātāh*).

JOB 11

5. Zophar's First Speech (11:1-20)

Of the three friends who address Job, Zophar is commonly regarded as either the youngest or the least in status. These assessments are based on the fact that he speaks last in the first two cycles
and does not speak at all in the third. Others see Zophar as the most
astute and creative of the friends and regard his words as the climax
to their arguments.[1] He does appear to be the least sympathetic of
the friends. Whereas Eliphaz condemns Job only for some small sin
and expects his suffering soon to pass (4:4-6); and Bildad calls attention to the fact that Job, unlike his children, still lives and thus still
possesses some righteousness (8:4-6); Zophar allows Job no positive
moral ground on which to stand. To the contrary, Zophar regards
Job to be deeply guilty as his sweeping condemnatory statement in
verse 6 affirms, "God has even forgotten some of your sin!" Zophar's
speech may also be distinguished from those of the other friends on
another ground. Eliphaz based his claims upon a personal revelation
(4:12-21) and Bildad upon the traditions of the fathers (8:8-10).
Zophar, however, bases his arguments solely upon what he calls the
"secrets of wisdom" (תַּעֲלֻמוֹת חָכְמָה, *tāʿălumôth ḥokmāh*, v. 6). More
than reasoned theology[2], this refers to hidden "mysteries" (v. 7) of
God's creative and providential activity that mere human intuition
and natural reasoning cannot comprehend (cf. 28:12ff.). It is insight
that only the initiated, those to whom God chooses to reveal it, can
know. So, from the outset Zophar is claiming the higher spiritual
and moral ground in his address to his suffering friend.

The speech, itself, may be divided into three parts: an indictment
of Job (vv. 1-4); the wisdom of God (vv. 5-12); a call to repentance

---

[1]Cf., e.g., Clines, *Job*, p. 262.
[2]Against Hartley, *Job*, p. 193.

(vv. 13-20). It is obvious from the language of the speech that Zophar has been carefully listening to Job. He responds to Job's arguments in three distinct ways typical of wisdom disputation. First, he quotes Job (as in v. 4) and directly refutes the claim. Second, he summarizes a key idea and develops a counterargument (cp. 11:10 to 9:11-12). Third, he employs ironic wordplay. No less than ten different terms prominent in Job's earlier speeches are played upon by Zophar in his rebuttal.[3] Zophar's disputation is also rich in the variety of literary genres it employs, featuring prophetic and wisdom sayings, the hymn, and the proverb.

Zophar's Indictment of Job (11:1-6)

[1]**Then Zophar the Naamathite replied:**
[2]**"Are all these words to go unanswered? / Is this talker to be vindicated? / [3]Will your idle talk reduce men to silence? / Will no one rebuke you when you mock? / [4]You say to God, 'My beliefs are flawless / and I am pure in your sight.' / [5]Oh, how I wish that God would speak, / that he would open his lips against you / [6]and disclose to you the secrets of wisdom, / for true wisdom has two sides. / Know this: God has even forgotten some of your sin.**

11:1-3 Zophar opens his speech in the conventional style of ancient disputation by dismissing his opponent's arguments and then refuting them. Many commentators see the sharper tone of Zophar's words as indicative of the growing frustration and anger of the friends over Job's audacious claims and their inability to force him to abandon them. In a more general sense it may be observed that throughout the three cycles of the speeches the rhetoric gradually intensifies. Zophar's response, phrased in a series of four rhetorical questions, seethes with sarcasm. **Are all these words to go unanswered?** The phrase **all these words** (lit., "multitude of words") may be intended to echo the thought of Proverbs 10:19, "When words are many, sin is not absent." The next question, **Is the talker to be vindicated?** would seem to affirm this. Zophar accuses Job of being verbose like a "chattering fool" (Prov 10:8). In the wisdom tradition there is a tendency to connect loquaciousness with the fool (cf., e.g.,

---

[3]Cf. the analysis of Habel, *Job*, pp. 204-205.

Eccl 5:2[3]). With his third question[4] Zophar is accusing Job of trying to filibuster his way to victory with an abundance of empty words. The expression **idle talk** (בַּד, *bad*) literally means "babbling." It sometimes carries the meaning of "boasting."[5] The word for **men** (מְתִים, *mᵊthîm*) means a "weak, powerless group."[6] Zophar asks, "Does Job think he can silence the friends as some glib boaster might silence the naïve listener?" In ancient disputation the silencing of an opponent was tantamount to proving one's case. In essence, Job will do this very thing before the speeches are over. But Job's words are more than an affront to the friends. They are also **mockery** of God. This term (לָעַג, *lā'ag*), which literally means to "speak rashly," is used here to accuse Job of impiety. When Job calls into question the justice of God, he is guilty of irreverence. Zophar stands ready to defend his God by **rebuking** such presumptions. The term **rebuke** means to "shame" or "humiliate" someone by proving him to be wrong. It is often used in legal contexts (cf. Job 19:3; Prov 25:8).

11:4 Here Zophar quotes Job's former claims as he prepares to refute them. As noted above, quotation of one's opponent was a common technique in ancient disputation.[7] Zophar's citing of Job, however, is an interpretive one and goes beyond what Job has actually said (9:20-21; 10:7). While it is true that Job has repeatedly claimed to be innocent, Zophar understands him to be making an even more sweeping claim when he says that his **beliefs are flawless. Beliefs** (לֶקַח, *leqaḥ*) is a common term for "teaching" or "doctrine" in the wisdom literature (Prov 1:5; 4:2; 98:9).[8] Most of the commentators are critical of Zophar over his "misrepresentation" of what Job has said. It should be noted, however, that Job has come close to making such a claim in his earlier indictment of God. He has moved

---

[4]It is possible to read this as an assertion in the Hebrew but the context suggests otherwise.

[5]Cf. Isa 16:6; Jer 48:30.

[6]Cf. A. Schoors, *I Am God Your Savior*, VTSupp 24 (Leiden: Brill, 1973), p. 60.

[7]This is especially true in legal disputations (cf., e.g., Isa 40:27; Ezek 12:21-22); cf. A.S. van der Woude, "Micha in Dispute with the Pseudo-Prophets," *VT* 19 (1969): 244-260.

[8]The term literally means "what is received." It can also mean "persuasive speech" (Prov 16:21,23) or even "testimony" in certain legal contexts (Deut 32:2).

beyond his own undeserved suffering to accuse God of presiding over a world where injustice rules (9:22-24). This claim of God's global malevolence and cruel injustice will be repeatedly argued as true and irrefutable by Job and could be understood as his "belief" or "teaching" (cf. ch. 24; esp. 24:25). More objectionable may be Zophar's rehearsal of Job's claim to innocence. Technically speaking, he misquotes Job as saying, **I am pure in your sight**. The word **pure** (בַּר, *bar*) is used in the OT to describe "moral purity" (cf., e.g., "pure in heart," Ps 24:4; 73:1). While Job has maintained his innocence (6:10,24,29-30; 7:20-21; 10:5-7), he has used another term, "blameless" (תָּם, *tām*). This term carries the more general meaning of "having integrity." Job has never claimed to be sinless. His contention is that he has not committed any sin worthy of the punishment that God has brought upon him. Zophar's exaggerated rehearsal of Job's claims is undoubtedly intended to heighten their absurdity for purposes of refutation.

11:5-6 Throughout his discourses Job has repeatedly spoken to God. He has leveled a barrage of accusatory questions against him, questions that ostensibly invite answers (7:12,17,19,20). He has even contemplated a day in court with God where God would be compelled to speak (9:3,14,16,35).[9] Zophar is confident that if **God would speak** Job would be immediately silenced. The word **God** ("Eloah") is put in the emphatic position here to punctuate Zophar's confidence in God's ability to defend himself. Like Job, Zophar does not think it likely that God will speak, so he chooses to speak on God's behalf. What Zophar wants God to disclose to Job are the **secrets of wisdom** (תַּעֲלֻמוֹת חָכְמָה, *tāʿalumôth ḥokmāh*).[10] By "wisdom" Zophar seems to be referring to the guiding principle by which God created and governs his world (15:9; Prov 8:22,30). It is **secret** because it is not discernible by human intuition or reasoning (28:12ff.). This phrase is paralleled by the comparable **true wisdom has two sides. True wisdom** (תּוּשִׁיָּה, *tûšîyāh*, "understanding"), carries the connotation of "abiding success" (5:12; 6:30). It refers to a perspective that enables one to solve problems which might threat-

---

[9]It is clear, however, from chapter 9 that Job really expects no answer from God.

[10]Pope takes "wisdom" (*hochmah*) to be a gloss designed to parallel *tushiyyah* ("true wisdom"), but his arguments are not compelling.

en harmony and peace. **Two sides** (כִּפְלַיִם, *kiphlayim*)[11] here is another way of saying the "fullness" or the "totality" of a matter (cf. Isa 40:2). These expressions are used in tandem to describe the mysteries of God's governance of his world. At one level God's activity might be judged unduly harsh or unjust. But at a deeper level, known only by God (and to those to whom he chooses to reveal it), it has a positive, even beneficent meaning. Zophar now applies this idea to Job's dilemma. Job believes that his suffering is unjust because he has committed no sin worthy of such punishment. What Job cannot see, insists Zophar, is that God has really been merciful, not harsh with him, for **God has even forgiven some of** (Job's) **sin**. Job should, therefore, be grateful to God for his mercies rather than critical of his punishments.[12] Though on a larger, biblical scale this is certainly true, it is not true in the specific case of Job. As the prologue has made clear, Job's suffering has nothing to do with God's judgmental or merciful responses to Job's behavior. Zophar is correct, however, in looking for the meaning of Job's suffering in the mysteries of God.[13]

The Unfathomable Wisdom of God (11:7-12)

[7]"Can you fathom the mysteries of God? / Can you probe the limits of the Almighty? / [8]They are higher than the heavens—what can you do? / They are deeper than the depths of the grave[a]—what can you know? / [9]Their measure is longer than the earth / and wider than the sea.

[10]"If he comes along and confines you in prison / and convenes a court, who can oppose him? / [11]Surely he recognizes deceitful men; / and when he sees evil, does he not take note? / [12]But a witless man can no more become wise / than a wild donkey's colt can be born a man.[b]

[a]8 Hebrew *than Sheol*   [b]12 Or *wild donkey can be born tame*

---

[11]Cf. discussion by G. von Rad, "כִּפְלַיִם in Jes 40:2 — Equivalent?" *ZAW* 79 (1967): 80-82.

[12]Clines (*Job*, pp. 261-262) even suggests the mercy and justice of God constitute the "two sides" which Zophar has in mind. He assigns the idea of justice trumped by mercy to the prophetic tradition and notes Zophar's creative introduction of this idea into the wisdom tradition of Israel.

[13]So Clines, *Job*, p. 262.

This section anticipates a theological concept developed more fully in chapter 28 (Praise of Wisdom) and the God-speeches (esp. Job 38–39; cf. also 23:3,8-9). Its focus on the inscrutable ways of God makes it prologue to a major theme of the book. Hymnic language is employed here comparable to that in Psalm 139:8-9 and Isaiah 40:12-14. The goal of this language seems to be to convince Job that he is not qualified to judge the actions of God.

11:7-9 The opening questions of verse 7 are designed to expose Job's inability to accurately discern the purposes of God. **Can you fathom the mysteries of God? Can you probe the limits of the Almighty?** The terms **fathom** and **probe** translate the same Hebrew verb (תִּמְצָא, *timṣā'*).[14] It describes the attempt to fully explore or apprehend something. **Mysteries** (חֵקֶר, *ḥēqer*) refer to the most profound issues of life (5:9; 9:10; Prov 25:3). Its companion term, **limits** (תַּכְלִית, *taklîth*) is elsewhere used in Job to describe the utmost edges of existence such as where light meets darkness (26:10). Elsewhere in the OT it has the meaning of "fullness" or "perfection" (Ps 139:22). The questions, of course, expect a "no" answer and serve to expose the limits of Job's knowledge of the ultimate designs of God. Job claims that he "knows" what God is doing in his life. Zophar refutes this presumption by reminding Job that human knowledge of God's ways is always incomplete. The separation between God and man is expressed in four dimensions: height, depth, length, and breadth. **Heavens** and **grave**[15] are parallel elsewhere in the OT (cf., e.g., Ps 139:8) as are **earth** and **sea** (cf., e.g., Hag 2:6). Comparing the inscrutability of God's ways with the limits of the universe is a common technique of the sages (Prov 25:3; 30:4). Such things are simply beyond human comprehension. Therefore, what Job can **know** (יָדַע, *yāda'*)[16] and **do** (פָּעַל, *pā'al*) are too limited to qualify him to criticize God. God himself will later challenge Job on these same two human limitations (chs. 38–41).

11:10-12 These verses apply the principles of the preceding claims to Job's particular situation. They represent an ironic rebuttal of Job's false charges against God. Job has claimed that he could

---

[14]LXX has תִּגַּע (*tiggā'*), "you reach" for the second occurrence.

[15]Or Sheol.

[16]Cf., M Granoth, "Deeper than Sheol: What Canst Thou Know?" *Beth Migra* 59 (1973–74): 572-588.

not "see" or "recognize" the elusive God as he "passes by" (חָלַף,
ḥālaph; cf. 9:11). But, insists Zophar, when God approaches (**comes
along**, ḥālaph) **deceitful men**[17] like Job, he has no trouble **recognizing** and **seeing** their evil. In other words, God's mysterious and irresistible ways, which Job interprets as cruel and unjust, actually qualify God to know the truth about even secret, deceptive sinners like
Job and to properly punish them. God's surveillance of humans,
rather than malicious (as Job has charged, 7:8; 10:14), is actually a
desirable and necessary part of his just management of his world. If
God has **imprisoned** Job, he has done so because Job deserves to be
there. As a just God who knows even the secret sins of his subjects,
his actions cannot be rightly **opposed**. It is God, not Job, who has
the high moral ground here. It is God, not Job, who has the right to
judge. Zophar concludes his rebuttal with a proverb that is difficult
to understand both in its meaning and in how it applies to his argument. If we read with NIV, then it means that one thing cannot be
changed into another. The **witless** cannot become **wise** any more
than a **wild donkey's colt** can become a **man**.[18] If this refers to the
preceding categories of what God knows and what man is able to
comprehend, then it serves to punctuate the impossibility of a mere
mortal ever hoping to be qualified to condemn God. If, on the other
hand, this phrase anticipates what follows, then the meaning is more
difficult to ascertain because the rest of the chapter (vv. 13-20) clearly invites Job to change. A solution can be found by comparing this
verse with verse 20 and taking them both to refer more generally to
the fate of the unrepentant sinner. The idea is that if Job keeps defy-
ing God he is without hope.

A Call to Repentance (11:13-20)

[13]**"Yet if you devote your heart to him / and stretch out your
hands to him, / **[14]**if you put away the sin that is in your hand / and
allow no evil to dwell in your tent, / **[15]**then you will lift up your face
without shame; / you will stand firm and without fear. / **[16]**You will
surely forget your trouble, / recalling it only as waters gone by. /
[17]Life will be brighter than noonday, / and darkness will become

---

[17]This expression literally means "men of nothingness" and is used to
identify those who have no moral scruples.

[18]Or "tame" with Pope.

like morning. / [18]You will be secure, because there is hope; / you will look about you and take your rest in safety. / [19]You will lie down, with no one to make you afraid, / and many will court your favor. / [20]But the eyes of the wicked will fail, / and escape will elude them; / their hope will become a dying gasp."

Zophar concludes his speech by inviting Job to deliver himself from the fate of the wicked through sincere repentance. Eliphaz (5:8-26) and Bildad (8:5-7) have already made similar appeals. Specifically, Zophar calls Job to renew his devotion to God and remove the sin that is in his life. This exhortation, of course, only serves to illustrate the disconnection that exists between the friends' perception of Job's problem and the true basis of Job's suffering. The two things Zophar says Job needs to do are the very things that the prologue says he has already done ("fearing God" and "shunning evil," 1:1,8; 2:3). Stuck in his airtight system of retributive theology, Zophar can connect Job's suffering only to some sin he must have committed.

11:13-14 The language here is that of conditionality, and the structure is similar to that of Bildad's invitation to repentance in 8:4-6. Zophar lists four conditions which Job must meet to be restored. First he must **devote** his **heart** to God. This is calling Job to "focus his thoughts" on the Lord. A similar call is extended to all Israel by the prophet Samuel (1 Sam 7:3). In the Samuel context it takes on the added dimension of loyalty to Yahweh as opposed to other gods. It also carries the connotation of "trust" (cf. Ps 78:8,37). The Mishnah uses the same term to describe the rabbinic practice of sitting quietly for an hour before praying, concentrating on God (*M. Ber.* 5:1). When Zophar makes this condition primary, he affirms the biblical principle that true righteousness comes from the inner being. Second, Job is to **stretch out** his **hands** (lit., "palm"; כַּף, *kaph*) to God. This, of course, is the language of prayer. In biblical times the conventional gesture of prayer was to raise the hands, palms upward presumably in supplication and petition to the deity.[19] Hands

---

[19]There is much speculation on the origin of this gesture. Some connect it with a military gesture of surrender, others with a claim of innocence, still others with an attempt to restrain a superior (cf. the discussion by Clines, *Job*, pp. 267-268).

raised to God must be pure (Isa 1:15-16). So in his third condition Zophar urges Job to **put away the sin** that is in his **hand**. Again we observe the disconnection between the friends and Job. All along it has been Job's contention that he has committed no sin worthy of such suffering. The word for sin (אָוֶן, *'āwen*) often depicts acts of exploitation and oppression by which the rich increase their wealth at the expense of the poor.[20] One wonders if Zophar believes that Job has become wealthy in this way. Job will later deny any such sin (31:16-21). Zophar concludes his list of conditions with a fourth requirement, **allow no evil to dwell in your tent**. The word for evil (עַוְלָה, *'awlāh*) refers to "injustice" of all kinds. Like the previous term it is used primarily to describe social sins. This expression, however, extends the call for righteousness to Job's household. As patriarch he was responsible not only for his own behavior but for that of his family as well. This, too, is ironic for all along Job has been dutiful in this role (1:5). Zophar's call for Job to distance himself from sin is typical of the language of the wisdom literature (Ps 1:1; Prov 1:10-15; 4:14,24).[21]

11:15-16 These verses constitute the second half of Zophar's conditional equation. They begin to enumerate the blessings that Job's repentance will yield. He will **lift up** his **face without shame**. Job's personal dignity and social status have suffered from the stigma of his suffering. His repentance, suggests Zophar, will bring an end to that. While the first suggested consequence of repentance addresses Job's social restoration, the second addresses his emotional healing. Job will **stand firm, without fear**. The expression **stand firm** means to be "cast" (as metal).[22] This language addresses the restored sense of security Job will have knowing he has nothing to fear from God or man. Job's **troubles** will be **forgotten** as something in the distant past. This does not mean that all memory of them will fade but that their power to torment him will be gone. The phrase **as waters gone by** is stronger than our expression "water under the bridge." It owes its origin to the flash floods so common to the Near East that suddenly threaten harm only then quickly to abate (Ps 69:3[2]; Isa 8:7,8). So the violent flood of Job's troubles will quickly subside.

---

[20]Cf. K. Bernhardt, *"'awen," TDOT*, 1:142-144.

[21]Cf. S. Porubean, *Sin in the Old Testament: A Soteriological Study* (Rome: Herder, 1963).

[22]Cf. NEB, "man of iron." Cf. also Jer 1:17-18; Ezek 3:8-9.

11:17-19 These verses complete the portrait of the restored Job. Job has characterized his fate as being doomed "to the land of gloom and deep shadow" (10:21). Zophar counters this with a portrait of the brightness of **noonday**. This is a common expression for the blessing of God (cf. Ps 37:6; Isa 58:10). The word for **life** (חֶלֶד, *ḥāled*) emphasizes its longevity. By contrast the troubled life is short and vain (Ps 39:5[6]; 89:48[47]). Verse 18 makes an interesting connection between **security** and **hope** (תִּקְוָה, *tiqwāh*). As in the New Testament "hope" in the Old Testament looks forward but not as far. While in the NT it is often connected with the life to come, in the OT it is more commonly located in this life. Hope is a commodity of which Job has been deprived. In fact the only hope he has clung to is that of the grave and the end it would bring to his misery (6:8-10). Zophar insists that he can again find it in the form of a long, secure, and enriched life by turning in humility and submission to God. He will **lie down with no one to make** him **fear**. The imagery here is that of sheep protected by their shepherd (Isa 17:2; Zeph 3:13). With these words Zophar seems to be countering Job's charge that God is hunting him like a lion (cf. 10:16). Instead, insists Zophar, God will be his Shepherd. Zophar completes his portrait of the restored Job with the image of many **courting** Job's **favor**. This phrase (וְחִלּוּ פָנֶיךָ, *wᵉḥilû phānêkā*) means to "sweeten the face" or "make the face smooth through stroking."[23] This expression describes the entreaty of a superior by subordinates.[24] While it is occasionally used of humans in the OT, it also appears with God as its object (cf., e.g., Exod 32:11; Jer 26:19; 1 Kgs 13:6; 2 Chr 33:12; Zech 8:21-22). Using this expression to portray the restored Job elevates him to the highest imagined social stature.

11:20 Zophar ends his speech on a negative note. If the previous verses (13-19) present positive reasons to repent, this verse balances all of that with what amounts to a threat.[25] Though speaking in generalities it is obvious that Zophar has Job specifically in mind as he revisits the fate of the unrepentant sinner. Bildad (7:11-19) and

---

[23]The exact meaning of the term is uncertain; see K. Seybold, "*chalah*," *TDOT*, 4:400, 403, 407-408.

[24]This often involved the offering of gifts (cf., e.g., Ps 45:13[12]).

[25]Some commentators compare this to the theme of the "two ways" in Psalm 1. The balancing of encouragement and warning is akin to the so-called "carrot-and-stick" approach of the Hebrew prophets.

Eliphaz before him (4:8-11) have not been remiss in warning Job of where his irreverent, rebellious spirit might take him. The portrait painted here, in contrast to the fate of the righteous, is one of perpetual insecurity, of life without hope. The phrase **eyes will fail** (lit., "grow dim") is used elsewhere to describe eyes wearied with tears or strained from searching for relief (Lam 2:11; 4:17; Ps 69:4[3]). The expression **dying gasp** is used in Jeremiah 15:9 to describe a mother's fainting upon hearing tragic news.

JOB 12

6. Job's Reply to Zophar (12:1–13:19)

Job's reply to Zophar completes the first cycle of speeches with some of the most powerful and passionate rhetoric of the book. Elements of wisdom instruction (12:7-12), legal dispute (ch. 13), hymn (12:13-25), and lament (ch. 14) are employed in the course of the speech as Job refutes the friends and presses his quest for a day in court with God. This sequence is important and anticipates the dominant rhetorical shift of the book as Job steadily moves away from debate with the friends to direct address to God. This monologue is the second longest of the speeches (only Job's final speech [chs. 29–31] is longer). It breaks down roughly into two major divisions:[1] 1) Job's rebuttal of the friends' claim to superior wisdom (12:1–13:19); 2) Job's complaint against God (13:20–14:22).

Job's Rebuttal of the Friends' Claim to Superior Wisdom (12:1-12)

[1]**Then Job replied:**

[2]**"Doubtless you are the people, / and wisdom will die with you! / [3]But I have a mind as well as you; / I am not inferior to you. / Who does not know all these things?**

[4]**"I have become a laughingstock to my friends, / though I called upon God and he answered— / a mere laughingstock, / though righteous and blameless! / [5]Men at ease have contempt for misfortune / as the fate of those whose feet are slipping. / [6]The tents of marauders are undisturbed, / and those who provoke God are secure— / those who carry their god in their hands.**[a]

[7]**"But ask the animals, and they will teach you, / or the birds of**

---

[1]For a discussion of how the speech should be divided cf. Clines, *Job,* pp. 285-286.

the air, and they will tell you; / [8]or speak to the earth, and it will teach you, / or let the fish of the sea inform you. / [9]Which of all these does not know / that the hand of the LORD has done this? / [10]In his hand is the life of every creature / and the breath of all mankind. / [11]Does not the ear test words / as the tongue tastes food? / [12]Is not wisdom found among the aged? / Does not long life bring understanding?

[a]6 Or *secure / in what God's hand brings them*

The first part of Job's speech is addressed to the friends and challenges their claim to superior insight on the meaning of Job's condition. Eliphaz had claimed supernatural revelation as the source of his knowledge (4:12ff). Bildad had based his arguments on the traditions of the fathers (8:8 ff). Zophar proclaimed himself privy to the deep things of God by virtue of superior insight that God had granted him (11:6). All three claimed to have "wisdom," or authoritative understanding of the causes behind Job's suffering. Job will now counter their claims by arguing that he, too, possesses such insight and that ultimate "wisdom" belongs only God.

12:1-3 Job's opening words seethe with sarcasm as his rhetoric rises to meet the escalating attacks of his friends. Addressing all of the friends,[2] Job exposes the arrogance of their authoritative claims. Opening with the bitterly ironic **doubtless** (אָמְנָם, *'omnām*), he accuses them of posing as the only people who possess true wisdom. Job suggests that they are setting themselves up as some kind of privileged class of spiritual and intellectual superiors. This may account for his choice of the word **people** (עָם, *'ām*), a term often used in the OT to denote an upper class of landed gentry.[3] Job follows with the even more sarcastic **wisdom will die with you.**[4] Though the friends have never claimed they are the repository of all wisdom, that is the way they appear to Job. They have consistently argued from an intellectually and morally superior position, and Job is determined to level the playing field of the debate. This he does with the reminder,

---

[2]The "you" of these verses is in the plural.

[3]Especially when used in the phrase "people of the land" (Jer 1:18; 34:19).

[4]J. Davies ("A Note on Job xii 2," *VT* 25 [1975]: 670-671) regards this line as a relative clause and translates, "No doubt you are the people with whom wisdom will die."

I have a mind as well as you. The word for **mind** (לֵבָב, *lēbāb*) is usually translated "heart" in the English versions. In the Hebrew Bible
it refers to the seat of human intellect and volition.[5] This language
seems to be in direct response to Zophar's earlier characterization
of Job as a "witless man" (11:12). So also is the following **I am not
inferior to you**,[6] which literally reads, "I have not fallen lower than
you." The word "inferior" (lit., "fallen"; נֹפֵל, *nōphēl*) is sometimes
used to refer to "birth" (Isa 26:18). With this choice of words Job is
saying he was born no lower than or, more precisely, no more of an
ass than they (cf. 11:12b).

12:4-6[7] The friends are not only arrogant, they are also insensi-
tive. In their eagerness to refute Job's claims against God, they seem
to completely overlook the humiliating devastation of his human
condition. For the first time, Job focuses on the social consequences
of his suffering. In ancient times suffering carried with it the stigma
of guilt. The sufferer is regarded as the object of God's punishment
and, therefore, worthy of reproach. The theme of a persecuted person being a **laughingstock** is found often in the Psalms of lament.[8]
That the derision heaped upon him is undeserved is claimed on two
fronts. First, Job characterizes himself as one who has **called upon
God and he answered**. In other words, Job was once in privileged
communication with God. Second, Job is mocked in spite of the fact
that he is **righteous and blameless**. This echoes the characterization
of Job found in the prologue. He is morally upright and religiously
pure. A similar description of Noah may be found in Genesis 6:9.[9] All
of this serves to underscore the essence of Job's case against God and
the disconnection between what the friends presume about Job and
what is actually going on. He is, he insists, an innocent sufferer.

---

[5]Cf. Wolff, *Anthropology*, p. 46; F. Stolz, *THAT*, 2:862-863.

[6]This same line occurs again at 13:2b. In tandem these repeated words
form a framework for Job's rebuttal of Zophar.

[7]These verses are difficult to understand in the Hebrew and some commentators regard them as not original to the book or misplaced. The goal
of the language seems to be to call the friends' attention to the reality they
refuse to acknowledge: Job, a righteous man, is yet being persecuted by
God.

[8]Cf., e.g., Ps 31:12-13[11-12]; 35:15; 41:10[9]; 69:11-13[10-12]; Jer 20:7;
Lam 1:7; 3:14.

[9]Note the comparison of Job and Noah in Ezek 14:14,20.

These verses are difficult in the Hebrew. The commentators understand them in two different ways. One approach is to take them as a
characterization of the friends who in their smug security act con-
temptuously of the fallen Job.[10] If this be so, Job's use of **men of ease**[11]
to describe the "self-righteous friends" may have an element of irony
in it. Elsewhere this term (שַׁאֲנָן, ša'ănān) denotes the godless who feel
secure in their prosperity (Amos 6:1; Isa 32:9; Zech 1:15). If, on the
other hand, we take these verses as referring to the godless in general, then this passage represents but another example of Job's leap
from claiming personal injustice done him by God to a claim of
God's general injustice in the world as a whole (cf. 9:21-24). The difficulty of the passage is heightened by the succeeding phrases. **Those
who provoke God** may refer to the friends who will later be charged
with "speaking deceitfully" of and for God (13:7-12). Or, as the parallel **tents of marauders**[12] suggests, this may be referring to violent
criminals. Finally, there is the most difficult, **those who carry their
god in their hand**.[13] This phrase has received numerous suggestions.[14] Habel sees it referring to the friends and takes it to be a
description of their supposed ability to manipulate God. Andersen
and Doederlein, on the other hand, take it to be yet another characterization of the godless and understand it to be a depiction of their
idolatrous ways. This seems preferable and agrees with Job's earlier
claim that God's injustice exists on a global scale (9:21-24). Job's argument then seems to be that while he, the righteous, is the object of
humiliating scorn, the wicked remain smug and secure.

   12:7-8[15] The strong adversative **but** (אוּלָם, 'ûlām) signals a radical
shift in Job's tactics. He will now ironically turn the claims of traditional wisdom on the very friends who defend it. The genre employed

---

[10]Cf. Ps 123:4.

[11]The phrase "men at ease have contempt for misfortune" may be an
ancient proverb.

[12]Or "plunderers," Jer 6:26; 12:12; 48:8. Is Job referring to the Sabeans
and Chaldeans who plundered his camp (1:15,17)?

[13]Cf. Micah 2:1 and Gen 31:29 where a similar expression means something like "their hand serves as their god" and refers to trusting in one's own
strength.

[14]Cf. the discussion in Clines, *Job*, p. 279, n.6b, pp. 291-292.

[15]Verses 7-11 are regarded by many commentators as out of place or not
original to the book. They are addressed to an individual rather than a
group and they employ the divine name Yahweh, which is done nowhere

here is that of wisdom instruction. In such lessons comparisons are often made between animals and humans (Prov 6:6; 27:8; 30:18-19). These words may be seen as a refutation of Zophar's claim that Job is too ignorant to comprehend the ways of God. Job responds to this attack by suggesting even the dumb beasts of nature could confirm his arguments. Since Zophar has compared Job to an ignorant beast (11:12), Job now cleverly suggests that Zophar himself might learn from the beasts. **Animals**, **birds**, and **fish** in the Hebrew Bible represent the three divisions of animal life (cf. Gen 1:20-25). In similar fashion, **earth**,[16] **air**, **sea** represent the three arenas of the created world. By employing these broad categories Job is saying, "all of nature affirms my claim." Bildad had earlier used an illustration from nature to instruct Job (8:11-19). Now Job will in similar fashion suggest that nature has something to teach the friends. It is interesting to note that the appeal to the natural order for clues to the meaning of God's purposes is a technique that God himself will ultimately employ in the climax of the book (chs. 38–41).

12:9-10 Just what is it that even the creatures **know** and can **teach** the friends? It is the very thing that Job has been arguing. The **hand of the LORD**[17] **has done this**[18] (that is, has unfairly caused Job's suffering). Elsewhere in Job, the "hand of God" is a negative, threatening power (6:9; 10:3,7,8; 13:21; 19:21). This is its meaning here. All things happen beneath the sovereign will of the Creator. On this Job and the friends agree. The friends have suggested that Job's suffering is God's sovereign and just response to Job's sin. Job has claimed that it is rather an expression of his irresistible and malevolent

---

else in the dialogue. R. Gordis ("Quotations as a Literary Usage in Biblical, Oriental and Rabbinic Literature," *HUCA* 22 [1949]: 157-219) suggests they are an ironic employment of traditional wisdom used to refute the claims of the friends that Job does not know enough to challenge God.

[16]There is an unusual use of "earth" (אֶרֶץ, *'ereṣ*) here, almost in the sense of our "mother earth" or "planet." Some scholars see this as an abbreviated expression for the fuller "creeping things of the earth" in parallel with "fish of the sea" (Gen 1:24,25; 7:1).

[17]As noted above (n. 15), this represents the only use of the name Yahweh in the speeches. It may be here as a citation of the standard phrase "hand of Yahweh" which appears over thirty times in the Hebrew Bible. By contrast, "hand of God" is quite rare.

[18]The phrase "the hand of the LORD has done it" also occurs in Isa 41:20 and Ps 109:27.

power. The God who controls the **life of every creature** and the **breath of all mankind** presides over a world that cannot resist his will. This closed universe makes sense to the friends, for they see it as something ordered, just, and providentially beneficial to all. Job, by contrast, has had a different experience at the "hand of God." He considers himself a hapless victim of a predetermined fate, a casualty of a cruel and arbitrary world order.

12:11-12 By the use of three rhetorical questions Job presses home his claim to having knowledge equal to that of the friends. In so doing, he revisits his earlier claim (v. 3) that critical thinking can arrive at truth just as effectively as quoting tradition. Job appeals to the sensory receptors of **ear** and **tongue** as metaphors of human discernment. Just as the palate discriminates between tasty and unsavory food, so does the ear discern between true and false claims. Job's discriminating taste has already rejected the arguments of his friends as nauseous food (6:6-7). By the questions of verse 12 Job is not so much agreeing with the friends (cf. 8:8-10) that the tradition of the fathers (lit. "aged ones"; יְשִׁישִׁים, *yᵉšîšîm*)[19] is the ultimate authority on truth as he is insisting that as an experienced, thoughtful person he, too, can legitimately pass judgment on the meaning of his life. In fact, as the next verse will make clear, only God (not the fathers) knows the true meaning of life.

A Hymn of "Praise" to God's Power (12:13-25)

[13]**"To God belong wisdom and power; / counsel and understanding are his. / [14]What he tears down cannot be rebuilt; / the man he imprisons cannot be released. / [15]If he holds back the waters, there is drought; / if he lets them loose, they devastate the land. / [16]To him belong strength and victory; / both deceived and deceiver are his. / [17]He leads counselors away stripped / and makes fools of judges. / [18]He takes off the shackles put on by kings / and ties a loincloth[a] around their waist. / [19]He leads priests away stripped / and overthrows men long established. / [20]He silences the lips of trusted advisers / and takes away the discernment of**

---

[19]This term appears only in Job in the OT (15:10; 29:8; 32:6). Hartley (*Job*, p. 210) takes it to be a plural of excellence and believes it to be an attribute of God. In each of the other occurrences, however, it clearly refers to humans.

elders. / [21]He pours contempt on nobles / and disarms the mighty. / [22]He reveals the deep things of darkness / and brings deep shadows into the light. / [23]He makes nations great, and destroys them; / he enlarges nations, and disperses them. / [24]He deprives the leaders of the earth of their reason; / he sends them wandering through a trackless waste. / [25]They grope in darkness with no light; / he makes them stagger like drunkards.

[a]*18 Or shackles of kings / and ties a belt*

Job's rhetorical strategy of quoting traditional wisdom as a prelude to refuting it takes another dramatic turn in verses 13-25. Employing a technique he used earlier, he now recites a hymn to the power of God (12:13-25). His recitation is not pious but ironic. Rather than praising God's power as a benevolent force that ensures justice, he instead assails it as a malevolent force that arbitrarily subverts human life. As noted by Clines, this hymn invites comparisons with that of 9:5-16.[20] In both, Job sarcastically turns the language of praise into criticism. Both hymns share the common theme of God's power to reverse the normal course of events. While the hymn in 9:5-16 focused on God's power to disrupt the *natural* order, this hymn focuses on God's power to disrupt the *social* order. The political, social, intellectual, and sacerdotal leaders of the world are undone by the irresistible power of the all-powerful sovereign. Literarily and thematically this hymn shares many affinities with Psalm 107 and Isaiah 44:24-28. There is, however, at least one major difference in Job's hymn. Unlike the prophet and the psalmist, Job sees absolutely no salvific or socially redeeming purpose in God's power to bring down the mighty. For Job there is not an ounce of justice in anything that God does.

12:13-14 To God (not men) **belong wisdom and power**. This introductory phrase is further rebuttal against the friends' claim that they are more qualified than Job to fathom God's purposes. True wisdom belongs only to God.[21] When it comes to human attempts to comprehend it, Job insists that he is the equal of the friends.[22] The

---

[20]Clines, *Job*, pp. 296-297.

[21]This same assertion is made in the famous hymn to wisdom (28:23).

[22]In fact this entire section (12:1–13:2) is framed by the repeated claim, "I am not inferior to you."

connection of **wisdom** and **power** here is interesting. In the Hebrew Bible wisdom is seldom regarded as purely theoretical. It is active. It has implications for life. It makes sense of life's absurdities and facilitates solutions to life's difficulties. The coupling of **wisdom** and **power** here speaks of God's ability to design and execute a plan beyond human power to understand or resist. In verse 14 Job begins to expose just what that plan is. What follows is a most unflattering portrait of God. An irrepressible tyrant, the Almighty **tears down** what humans have built and **imprisons** any whom he will. With these words Job opens his theme of God as capricious intervener and disrupter of the social order. His sovereignty overpowers human achievement and freedom. Job's choice of these verbs to open his characterization of divine activity may be more existential than philosophical. They represent an accurate summation of what Job believes God has done to him.

12:15-16 This part of Job's hymn represents a departure from the larger theme of God's power over human affairs. It focuses on the power of nature to wreak havoc on the earth. Unlike Psalm 107 where God's control of nature is the instrument of his justice and mercy (cf. Ps 107:33-37), Job's hymn sees God's manipulation of the forces of nature to be yet another example of his reckless behavior against men. The extremes of **drought** and flood which **devastate**[23] **the land** illustrate the destructive power of nature's God, not his benevolent provision. The phrase **strength and victory** (v. 16; the same words for "power" and "wisdom" in v. 13) repeats the thought of the opening line of the hymn but in reverse order. The word **victory** (תוּשִׁיָּה, *tûšîyāh*) is one of several Hebrew terms for "wisdom" and carries the meaning of "abiding success." Sarcastically, Job suggests that God's success is seen in his ability to cause humans to fail. Job categorizes the sum of humanity into two classes: the **deceived** and the **deceiver**. It is an interesting selection of terms. It may be only another example of his use of *merismus* (expressing the whole by the sum of its parts) as in "small and great" (3:19).[24] More likely it classes humanity into two different moral groups. There are those who lead people astray and those who are led. The Hebrew term

---

[23]This verb is also used in Gen 19:21,25,29 to describe the overthrow of Sodom and Gomorrah.

[24]Cf. also "slave and free" (Deut 32:36; 1 Kgs 14:10).

used here (שגג, *šgg*) sometimes refers to inadvertent sin in a religious sense.[25] But sometimes it carries the sense of "those who deliberately deceive" as in Proverbs 28:10 ("He who leads the upright along an evil path"). If, as some commentators suggest, the **deceivers** are the influential people listed in the following verses (17-25), then Job's choice of terms here reflects his cynical view of conventional wisdom and those who articulate it. Any true meaning of life taught by kings, counselors, priests or judges is rendered a deception by God's irresistible and arbitrary power to undo them and the political, social, legal, and religious structures they represent. Ironically the deceivers become the deceived by trusting in their life philosophies which, in the end, God causes to fail them.

12:17-21 In these verses Job runs through a laundry list of influential people whom God causes to fall. This portion of the hymn, too, is an ironic adaptation of one of God's great attributes: his power to bring down the mighty and confound the wise. Whereas in other biblical texts this attribute is offered as a positive demonstration of his justice and mercy (cf. Psalm 10; Isa 44:24-28), here it is touted as yet another example of his malevolence. **Counselors** and **judges** are royal court officials who advise the king like Ahithophel in David's administration (2 Sam 16:23).[26] Such important officials God **strips**[27] of status and mind. The Hebrew for **makes fools of** (יְהוֹלֵל, *yᵉhôlēl*) literally means to "make mad." The image portrayed here is of once great leaders parading naked like madmen. **Kings**, also, are brought down by God. Due to the difficulty of verse 18 in the Hebrew the precise meaning is unclear. Most scholars regard the **shackles** and **loincloth** to refer to royal garments worn by the king and take the verse to mean that God removes these symbols of power from kings.[28] Others understand this to be God's loosening of the bonds imposed by kings upon others.[29] Gordon understands this to be a biblical example of the ancient custom of belt-wrestling

---

[25]Cf. J. Milgrom, "The Cultic *ŠeGĀGĀ* and Its Influence in Psalms and Job," *JQR* 58 (1967): 115-125.

[26]For more on this office cf. W. McKane, *Prophets and Wise Men*, SBT 44 (London: SCM, 1965).

[27]שׁוֹלָל (*šôlāl*). For a similar use cf. Micah 1:8 "stripped and barefoot."

[28]Cf. discussion by Clines, *Job*, p. 300.

[29]With NIV, NEB, Gray, Rowley.

where the victor removes the belt of the vanquished opponent.[30]
Whatever the background of this language, the general idea is that
God strips kings of their status and power. Religious functionaries
are not exempt from God's power to overthrow. **Priests** and **men
long established** (אֵתָנִים, *'ēthānîm*, "temple functionaries")[31] are **over-
thrown** and **lead away stripped**. It is interesting to note that this is
the only place in the book of Job where religious functionaries are
mentioned. Cultic matters, too, are generally ignored in the dialogues. Local magistrates, the **trusted advisors**, and the **elders**, are
also objects of God's malevolent and unpredictable use of his sovereign power. They are deprived of their **discernment** (lit., "taste")
and their rhetorical skills (lit., "**lip**"). The aristocracy (**nobles**[32]) and
the warriors (**mighty**) complete the list of those whom God brings
down. The first line of verse 21 is identical to Psalm 107:40a
(40b=Job 12:24) further illustrating the backdrop to this ironic hymn
which the Psalm provides. In the psalm the princes who are made
contemptible are being judged by God for oppressing the people of
the Lord. In Job's hymn, however, no apparent reason is given for
God's **pouring contempt**[33] upon them other than the sovereign's
arbitrary power to do so. **Disarms** captures well the sense of the
original (lit., "loosens the belt") which describes a situation where
the soldier is no longer girded for war (cf. 2 Sam 20:8; Judg 3:21).

12:22-25 At first reading verse 22 seems to be out of place. All
along Job has been describing God's power over the mighty men of
the earth, a theme he picks up again in the next verse. But here he
appears to digress into cosmological issues. This digression may be
accounted for by way of allusion to one of Zophar's earlier claims
that God's mysteries are "deeper than the depths of Sheol" (11:8).

---

[30]C.H. Gordon, "Belt-Wrestling in the Bible World," *HUCA* 23 (1950–51):
131-136.

[31]N. Sarna, ("*'ytnym*, Job 12:19," *JBL* 74 [1955]: 272-273) ties this term to
Ugar. *ytnm* and understands the term to refer to cultic personnel. The title
is similar to *netinim* mentioned in 1 Chronicles, Ezra, Nehemiah. Others see
this as connected to אֵיתָן (*'êthān*, "perpetual") and take it to refer to the
nature of the priests' status and the ancient orders which they perpetuate.

[32]This term, נְדִיבִים (*neḏîḇîm*), may be parallel to the "mighty" and both
refer to military leaders. This term is used in Judg 5:2,9 to refer to those
who "volunteer" for military service.

[33]This is not referring to some verbal attack by God but to his making
them contemptible by bringing them down to some low estate.

Job's expression, **deep things of darkness**, is likewise part of the Sheol vocabulary of the Hebrew Bible. Some commentators think this refers to the evil plans of earthly leaders, which God brings to light. Others explain it as another ironic reversal of Psalm 107:10,14[34] and take it to mean that God is obscuring the counsel of the world's leaders by bringing up the darkness of Sheol to overpower it. In such an understanding God's wisdom is demonized as **darkness** and **shadow** which obscure and frustrate the rulers rather than enlighten them.[35] Still another explanation may be offered. Throughout the Old Testament there is a common connection between God's control of the cosmos or nature and God's control of the nations (cf., e.g., Psalm 107; Nahum 1:2-8). Verses 22 and 23, taken together, make the same connection. The God who extends his sovereignty over Sheol also extends it over the great men of the earth. Actually the entire stanza (vv. 22-25) frames the nations and their rulers with references to the cosmological "darkness."[36] In verse 23 the theme of God as "nation-builder" and "nation-destroyer" is developed. This, too, is a common theme of the Old Testament (cf. Hab 1:6; Jer 1:10; Isa 45:1-3). Here, however, the emphasis is upon the control which God exerts over the **reason** of the earth's leaders. By depriving them of their "reason" (לֵב, *lēb*; lit., "heart") God condemns them to flounder without any bearings. They are left to wander in a **trackless waste**. Like disoriented **drunkards** they **stagger** aimlessly through life. The idea of divine confusion of his foes is a motif found, among other places, in the book of Joshua (cf., e.g., Josh 10:10).

---

[34]In Psalm 107, "darkness" and "gloom" are the place from which God sets the captives free. Here they are the frustrating conditions God imposes on the world's leaders.

[35]Cf. Clines, *Job*, pp. 301-302.

[36]Notice the reference to "darkness" in v. 22 and in v. 25 with reference to nations in 23-24.

JOB 13

6. Job's Reply to Zophar (12:1–13:19, continued)

Job's Indictment of the Friends (13:1-12)

[1]"My eyes have seen all this, / my ears have heard and understood it. / [2]What you know, I also know; / I am not inferior to you. / [3]But I desire to speak to the Almighty / and to argue my case with God. / [4]You, however, smear me with lies; / you are worthless physicians, all of you! / [5]If only you would be altogether silent! / For you, that would be wisdom. / [6]Hear now my argument; / listen to the plea of my lips. / [7]Will you speak wickedly on God's behalf? / Will you speak deceitfully for him? / [8]Will you show him partiality? / Will you argue the case for God? / [9]Would it turn out well if he examined you? / Could you deceive him as you might deceive men? / [10]He would surely rebuke you / if you secretly showed partiality. / [11]Would not his splendor terrify you? / Would not the dread of him fall on you? / [12]Your maxims are proverbs of ashes; / your defenses are defenses of clay.

13:1-3 In chapter 13 Job continues to address the friends and counter their claim that he is incompetent to criticize God. These opening verses bring closure to the rebuttal he began in chapter 12 by echoing the sentiments of his initial retort to Zophar (12:1-2). Like his opening statement in chapter 12 Job makes a distinction between what he knows experientially and what tradition teaches. The references to his **eyes** and **ears**[1] as empirical instructors of truth reiterate Job's claim that his own intellect and his own life experience qualify him to challenge the claims of traditional wisdom and to accuse God of being unjust. By **all this** Job is not making some

---

[1]For the coupling of "seeing" and "hearing," cf. Isa 52:15; Eccl 1:8.

claim of omniscience but is specifically referring back to the content of the earlier part of his speech (12:13-25) where he cited a catalogue of examples of how God arbitrarily intervenes to bring chaos to the world order. The phrase **What you know, I also know** is not so much a claim of equal knowledge or comparable intellect as it is an affirmation of the equal validity of Job's perspective.[2] The issue between Job and the friends here is their insistence that they have a superior insight — a superior understanding of what God is doing in his management of his world. The friends, appealing to traditional wisdom, argued that God acts justly and even benevolently towards his creatures. Job, by contrast, claims that God acts recklessly and even malevolently. Far from being the defender of the moral order and sustainer of men, God cares nothing about justice and commonly acts against the best interests of his subjects. Job is arguing that the perspective of God gained from reason and empirical observation is truer than the portrait of him painted by religious tradition. Frustrated by the friends' inability to see the obvious, Job announces his intent to personally **argue** his **case with God**.[3] The verb **speak** (דָּבַר, *dābar*) here should be taken in the legal sense of "state one's case." This Job will indeed proceed to do in verses 20ff. All of this, of course, represents a reversal of his earlier conclusion that such litigation would be futile (chs. 9–10). Traditional theology teaches that God will not answer to man. But Job has long abandoned the canned tenets of traditional theology and is instead driven by the lessons he has gained by his own personal experience. Getting nowhere in the court of public opinion (his dialogue with the friends), he now wishes to take his case to a higher court.

13:4-5 Before Job takes his case directly to God, he will offer yet another scathing criticism of the friends. He accuses them of **smearing** him **with lies**. The expression in the Hebrew is literally "plasterers of lies" (cf. Ps 119:69) and may refer to the false accu-

---

[2]With Clines, *Job*, p. 305.

[3]Clines argues that the language here represents a change in posture in Job's request for a trial found in chs. 9–10. There he acknowledged the impossibility of charging God with wrong and holding him accountable for his actions. Job's new approach will now be altered to one of inviting God to charge him and prove the wrong that Job has done against God. Job is confident that this will work because he is convinced that it will result in his vindication (v. 18).

sations of sin they have made against him. But, as the following charges suggest (vv. 7ff), Job may have an even more ominous falsehood in mind. They have been offering a theologically dishonest explanation of Job's suffering. Like **worthless physicians**[4] they have applied a false remedy to Job's condition. Ignoring the real issue (the unfairness of what has happened to Job) they keep treating Job's pressing problem by plastering it over with inaccurate theological platitudes about God's never-failing justice. In short, the friends are "frauds, offering false answers to honest questions."[5] Job calls for them to be **altogether silent**. With this suggestion Job may be delivering the friends an even sharper blow by equating them with the "fool," the morally bankrupt, godless man. As Proverbs 17:28a puts it, "Even a fool is thought wise if he keeps silent." From Job's perspective silence is the only wisdom that could possibly come from the friends.

13:6-8 Job now turns from criticizing the friends to interrogating them. The language used here is litigious and constitutes nothing less than a formal cross-examination. **Hear now** is used by wisdom teachers (Prov 4:1; 7:24) and prophets (Isa 1:2) when they initiate a new teaching or oracle. Here it functions as the opening to Job's new legal strategy of cross-examining the friends.[6] Suddenly the tables are turned. The accused becomes the accuser. It is not the integrity of Job but the integrity of the friends which is now submitted to scrutiny. The series of rhetorical questions which follow indict the friends on two counts: dishonesty and partiality. They are accused of speaking **wickedly** and **deceitfully** for God. In other words, they are twisting the truth in a dishonest defense of God. The charge of **partiality** is issued in the form of a Hebrew idiom "lifting up the face" which is sometimes connected to bribes and is strictly forbidden in legal proceedings (cf. Lev 19:15).[7]

---

[4]The expression is comparable to the phrase "worthless shepherds" in Zech 11:17.

[5]Habel, *Job*, p. 223.

[6]The genre employed here is that of the Hebrew *rîb*, which can range in meaning from "quarrel" to "lawsuit," with the latter being the meaning here. Envisioned is the formal complaint and argument leading to some kind of verdict. For more on this rhetorical technique cf. B. Gemser, "The RIB- or Controversy Pattern in Hebrew Mentality," *VTSupp* 3 (1955): 120-137; J. Limburg, "The Root *RÎB* and the Prophetic Lawsuit Speeches," *JBL* 88 (1969): 291-304.

13:9-11 Any further testimony from the friends, Job's insists, must be impartial and committed to a search for the truth. He raises the specter that the friends, if they testify falsely, can expect to be cross-examined by God and have their deceit exposed. God's ability to expose the true intents of men has already been suggested by Zophar in his indictment of Job (11:11). Job now turns this scrutinizing tendency of the Almighty[8] upon the friends. The friends cannot assume that because they argue on God's behalf that he will automatically and indiscriminately approve of what they say. Rather than reward them, God might instead **terrify**[9] them. His scrutiny will expose them and his **splendor** (שְׂאֵת, *śᵊʾēth*; lit. his "lifted-up-ness") will overpower them and they will be undone. God himself will see to it that the accusers will become the accused. This is, of course, exactly what God does in his final verdict. (42:7).

13:12 Verse 12 proves that it is more than the friends' accusations against Job that are false. It is their very argument (God sees to it that justice is always done on earth) that is dishonest. Their **maxims** are **proverbs of ashes**. The term **maxims** (זִכְרֹן, *zikkārôn*) has as its root idea, "things remembered." They represent the cherished traditions of the past often expressed in pithy sayings. Here as empty platitudes they crumble before the reality of Job's undeserved suffering. **Ashes**, when not used in the context of mourning rites, connote that which is insubstantial (Isa 44:20; Gen 18:27). So have the arguments of the friends proven to be. The phrase, **defenses of clay** implies, as in 4:19, brittle pottery that is easily destroyed. The insubstantial and transitory nature of the friends' arguments will later be contrasted by Job's desire to have his defense carved in stone (19:24).

Job's Determination to Press His Case with God (13:13-19)

[13]**"Keep silent and let me speak; / then let come to me what may. / [14]Why do I put myself in jeopardy / and take my life in my**

---

[7]In nonlegal contexts, "lifting up the face" or partiality shown to certain groups (like the poor) is not necessarily wrong; cf. M.I. Gruber, "The Many Faces of Hebrew *nāśāʾ pānîm*, 'lift up the face,'" *ZAW* 95 (1983): 252-260.

[8]Cf. Ps 7:10[9]; Jer 11:20 on God's ability to expose the true intents of the human heart.

[9]For the idea of God's awesomeness terrifying his enemies cf. Ps 105:38; Isa 2:10,19,21. On פָּחַד (*pāḥad*, "dread") cf. H.-P. Stahli, *THAT*, 2:411-413.

hands? / [15]**Though he slay me, yet will I hope in him; / I will surely**[a] **defend my ways to his face.** / [16]**Indeed, this will turn out for my deliverance, / for no godless man would dare come before him!** / [17]**Listen carefully to my words; / let your ears take in what I say.** / [18]**Now that I have prepared my case, / I know I will be vindicated.** / [19]**Can anyone bring charges against me? / If so, I will be silent and die.**

[a]*15 Or He will surely slay me; I have no hope—/ yet I will*

13:13-16 This language may be viewed as a formal announcement by Job that he intends to go forward with a legal suit against God. Addressed to the friends it anticipates the next great rhetorical shift in the book away from debate with the friends to direct address to God. With the emphatic **keep silent** and **let me speak**, Job bluntly dismisses the friends and their failed efforts to argue God's justice. He relegates them to the role of bystanders as he takes his case to a higher court. **Let come to me what may,** he boldly cries. Job is keenly aware of the dangers of summoning God (Job 9–10). He understands it may put him at great risk. But rather than portraying this as an act of desperation he claims it instead serves to demonstrate his innocence. Instead of ending his life Job believes this **might turn out for my deliverance.**[10] Job begins his defense in the same manner he ends it. Both this preamble which begins the suit, and his final oath (Job 29–31) which ends it openly invite God to do with Job as he will. Job welcomes the verdict of the Lord because he is absolutely convinced that he is innocent. He will now proclaim it and later swear to it all in an effort to force God to respond justly to it. To be sure, this whole suit against God seems contradictory to Job's repeated claims about God. He is seeking justice from a God whom he has portrayed as unjust and even cruel toward his subjects. This can only be explained as the paradox of faith. His bold profession of unconditional trust, **though he slay me, I will hope in him**, anticipates his grand affirmation of faith in his second reply to Bildad (19:23-27).

---

[10]This language has been borrowed by Paul in Phil 1:19 (J.H. Michael, "Paul and Job: A Neglected Analogy," *ExpT* 36 [1924–25]: 67-70; R. Hays, *Echoes of Scripture in the Letters of Paul* [New Haven and London: Yale University Press, 1989], pp. 21-24).

13:17-19 With these words Job concludes his address to the friends. He summons them to take note of his intent to make a formal case against God. His parting words brim with confidence that his case is already won. His case has already been carefully **prepared.**[11] Confident that he will be **vindicated** (צָדַק, *ṣādaq*, "declared innocent"), Job issues what amounts to a taunt, **Can anyone bring charges against me?** The answer to his rhetorical question is, of course, "No, no one, not even God!" The defiant spirit of **If so, I will be silent and die,** anticipates the same bold attitude of his final oath of defense (Job 31). In what amounts to a most ironic outcome, Job is finally defeated by his legal opponent and "puts his hands over his mouth," canceling his suit with God (40:4-5). Rather than dying, however, he is, by the mercy of God (Jas 5:11), restored to health and prosperity (42:10-16).

7. Job's Complaint against God (13:20–14:22)

At this point in the dialogue, Job formally announces his intention to "take God to court." After acknowledging the difficulties of prevailing in a trial against God (9:14-24) he nonetheless moves forward with his case. This legal approach to his dispute with God will reach its culmination in Job's final speech when he will take an oath of innocence and demand vindication from God (cf. 31:1-40, esp. vv. 35-37).

The Opening of Job's Case against God (13:20-28)

[20]**"Only grant me these two things, O God, / and then I will not hide from you: / **[21]**Withdraw your hand far from me, / and stop frightening me with your terrors. / **[22]**Then summon me and I will answer, / or let me speak, and you reply. / **[23]**How many wrongs and sins have I committed? / Show me my offense and my sin. / **[24]**Why do you hide your face / and consider me your enemy? / **[25]**Will you torment a windblown leaf? / Will you chase after dry chaff? / **[26]**For you write down bitter things against me / and make**

---

[11]עָרַךְ (*'ārak*) literally means to "arrange in order." Here it refers to carefully arranged legal arguments as in Ps 50:21.

me inherit the sins of my youth. / ²⁷You fasten my feet in shackles; / you keep close watch on all my paths / by putting marks on the soles of my feet.

²⁸"So man wastes away like something rotten, / like a garment eaten by moths.

Job now turns from refuting the friends to a direct address to God. This part of the speech breaks down into two major parts. First he issues God a summons to court (13:20-28) and then follows with a lament on the brevity and difficulty of human life (14:1-22). Job does not directly address God again until his closing speech (30:20-23) and his final replies to God's interrogations (40:4-5; 42:1-6). This speech, then, is very important for determining exactly what it is that Job seeks from God.

13:20-22 The language Job uses here is that of the ancient courtroom. He begins by requesting two conditions that he believes will ensure him a fair trial against God. First, he asks of God: **Withdraw your hand far from me**. This represents a request for God to remove the undeserved suffering Job is experiencing so that the trial would not be prejudiced against him. God's **hand** is often used in Scripture as the instrument of his affliction of men (Ps 32:4; 38:3[2]; Exod 9:3). Second, he asks that God's **terrors** cease **frightening** him. This refers to God's awesome power that has such a demoralizing and intimidating effect on those who experience it (cf. Exod 23:27; Josh 2:9). Job had made a similar request of God earlier as he entertained the idea of some arbiter stepping in between him and his heavenly opponent (9:34). Job does not believe he can possibly receive a fair trial if he is constantly threatened by God's overwhelming power. Next Job defers to God as to how the trial should proceed. He invites God to act either as plaintiff (**summon me**) or defendant (**you reply**). It may be that Job already considers God the plaintiff because of the suffering he has brought upon Job. But Job, too, has adopted the plaintiff's role in his accusations against God (7:11-12,17-19; 10:3-7,18-19). At any rate, since God has yet to offer even a single reply, Job will be the first to speak.

13:23-24 Job's opening question presses to the very heart of the dispute between him and God. **How many wrongs and sins have I committed?** As the next phrase suggests (**show me my offense and my sin**), this question should not be taken as an admission of guilt but as a rhetorical question designed to protest Job's innocence (cf. Jer 2:5; Gen 31:36). Job is confident that no sins can be enumerated, or at least none worthy of the devastating punishment that God has brought upon him.[12] The terms that Job uses for "sin" here constitute all the possible ways of breaking God's law.[13] The same combination of terms is found in the high priest's confession of Israel's sins on the Day of Atonement (Lev 16:21). Job is pressing God to formally indict him for some specific crime. Confident that he has committed no crime, he can then proceed to plead that a great injustice has been done him. The **Why?** which follows must be taken as "reproachful."[14] Found often in the Psalms it seeks no explanation but serves to challenge the one at whom it is aimed.[15] The **hiding** of God's **face** can express his anger (Jer 33:5; Micah 3:4) or his refusal to acknowledge (Ps 30:8[7]; 69:18[17]).[16] Both ideas fit Job's impression of God's disposition toward him. When Job calls himself God's **enemy** (אֹיֵב, 'ôyēb), he may be making a play on his own name (אִיּוֹב, 'îyôb).

13:25-27 Will you torment a windblown leaf?[17] Will you chase after dry chaff?[18] The purpose of these two questions is to shine the bright light of accusation upon God's disproportionate response to any offense that Job might have committed against him. Job claims that he is no threat to God, no substantial opponent. To the contrary, he is powerless before God's onslaught. God's awesome power **torments** (עָרַץ, 'āraṣ, "intimidates") Job (cf. 31:34). This term is elsewhere used to describe the fear or dread of humans before some terrifying display of God's power (Ps 89:8[7]; Isa 29:23). This image of the helpless Job weathering the overpowering blows of the Almighty further strengthens Job's charge of injustice. There is no shortage of suggestions concerning precisely what is meant by the phrase **you write down bitter things against me.** Clines and Habel understand

---

[12]Note the "sins of my youth" in v. 26.

[13]עָוֹן ('awōn), "iniquity"; חַטָּאת (ḥaṭṭā'th), "sins"; פֶּשַׁע (pešaʻ), "rebellion."

[14]Clines, *Job*, p. 319.

[15]Cf., e.g., Ps 10:1; 22:2[1]; 74:1, and C.C. Broyles, *The Conflict of Faith and Experience in Psalms: A Form-Critical and Theological Study*, JSOTSupp 52 (Sheffield: JSOT, 1989).

[16]Cf. S.E. Balentine, *The Hidden God: The Hiding of the Face of God in the Old Testament* (Oxford: Oxford University Press, 1983).

[17]Cf. Isa 1:30; 34:4; 64:5[6]; Jer 8:13; Lev 26:36.

[18]Cf. Job 41:20,21[28,29]; Jer 13:24; Ps 83:14[13].

"write down against" to be a judge's sentence. Hitzig understands it in the sense of a physician prescribing bitter medicine. Dahood compares the expression to a similar one found in Ugaritic economic texts and takes it to mean "charge against the credit of." Of particular interest is the suggestion of Tur-Sinai who argues that the expression refers to "the assignment of property to an heir."[19] This would fit nicely with the parallel **make me inherit** of the next line. **Bitter things** may refer to acts of violence which Job believes have been unfairly done against him (cf. Hab 1:6). The commentators also differ over what exactly Job means by the **sins of my youth**. It could be that this refers to careless or inadvertent sins (cf. 1:5) of youth, the seriousness of which must be viewed advisedly given the indiscretions of that phase of life. In other words, they are sins for which one is not entirely responsible. It seems unlikely that Job is confessing some actual, intentional sin here given the fact that he has everywhere steadfastly argued his innocence. The goal in all of this language is to make God appear overreactive and disproportionate in his treatment of Job. If, hypothetically, Job were guilty of some youthful indiscretion, it still could not justify the level of suffering God has brought upon him. As Dhorme puts it, "It would indicate rancour on the part of God to persecute Job on account of these youthful errors, supposing them to have existed." Job closes his accusation by returning to his familiar theme of God as cruel scrutinizer and oppressor of humanity (cf. 7:20; 10:13-14). God has imprisoned him, putting his **feet in shackles**.[20] This conjures up the image of a prisoner closely watched and strictly confined. In Job's view God obsessively **keeps close watch** on him looking for some occasion to afflict him. The last phrase of verse 27 (**putting marks on the soles of my feet**) is curious and the subject of much speculation. Some commentators think it refers to some kind of brand on the foot identifying the slave with his owner. Others translate "smear the soles of my feet" and take it to refer to some means of tracking an escaped slave. Though the exact image escapes us, the general

---

[19]Tur-Sinai references the Babylonian Talmud, *Babba Qamma* 88a.

[20]סַד (*sad*, "stocks"). The term occurs only here and in 33:11 where Elihu quotes this line. The term does appear in Syriac and Aramaic and seems to refer to notched beams of timber placed between the legs.

sense does not. Job feels unfairly hemmed in by God to the extent that he cannot mount a fair defense.

13:28 This verse seems more connected with what follows it (14:1-2) than what precedes it. Some scholars even argue that it is out of its original position (after 14:2). Yet the strophic structure of the poetry argues for its inclusion with the end of chapter thirteen. It literally begins "so he" (וְהוּא, *wᵉhû'*) without explaining exactly to whom the "he" refers. NIV understands it to refer to mankind in general (**so man**). Others take it to refer to Job himself. More probably it refers back to the **windblown leaf** or **dry chaff** of verse 25. In such a reading verses 26-27 may be taken as parenthetical with verse 28 completing the thought of verse 25 (Gordis). Job, like a dry leaf or worthless chaff, **wastes away** (cf. Gen 18:12; Isa 50:9; Ps 32:3; 49:15[14]) beneath the unending onslaught of God.

JOB 14

7. Job's Complaint against God (13:20–14:22, continued)

God's Mistreatment of Mortal Humans (14:1-6)

[1]"Man born of woman / is of few days and full of trouble. / [2]He springs up like a flower and withers away; / like a fleeting shadow, he does not endure. / [3]Do you fix your eye on such a one? / Will you bring him[a] before you for judgment? / [4]Who can bring what is pure from the impure? / No one! / [5]Man's days are determined; / you have decreed the number of his months / and have set limits he cannot exceed. / [6]So look away from him and let him alone, / till he has put in his time like a hired man.

[a]3 Septuagint, Vulgate and Syriac; Hebrew *me*

14:1-2 Job now makes a rhetorical shift which he will make many times in his speeches (for earlier examples cf. 3:20; 7:1-10). He moves from talking solely about his limited, personal situation to discussing humankind in general.[1] The purpose of this lament is to further establish the unfairness of God's withering gaze upon someone so inconsequential as man. The phrase, **Man, born of woman** is found only in Job (15:24; 25:4). The expression, as the New Testament usage would indicate[2], simply means "mortal."[3] **Of few days** is undoubtedly an intentional reversal of the standard language for a fulfilled life, "full of days," or "satisfied by days" (cf., e.g., Gen 25:8; 1 Chr 29:28). Though empty of days, life is **full of turmoil** or emotional stress over life's difficult blows (3:26). The analogies of **flower** and **shadow** are apt depictions of the transitory nature of human

---

[1]אָדָם (*'ādām*, "man") is in the emphatic position.
[2]Matt 11:11; Luke 7:28; cf. also Eccl 10:18; Sir 10:18.
[3]Tur-Sinai takes it as a reference to the ritual impurity that comes with childbirth (cf. Lev 12:2-5).

existence. The flowers of Palestine could spring up quickly after a rain only to **wither** before the hot desert winds (Isa 40:6-8; Ps 103:15). Likewise, the shadow, which disappears with the sunset, proves to be of no real substance (Ps 102:12[11]; Eccl 6:12).

14:3 Given the inconsequential nature of human existence, why does God so scrutinize (**fix your eye**) man (**on such a one**)? This is Job's indicting question. Here he is returning to his familiar theme of God as "Watcher of Man" (7:20) and the "Evil Eye" (7:8). The divine scrutiny evidenced in God's unrelenting affliction of Job is a totally disproportionate response to any offense he might have committed. In the Hebrew the disproportion is further highlighted by the presence of the introductory particle אַף ('aph, "surely, indeed"). This divine scrutiny, Job insists, is true of God's disposition toward humanity in general. God's attention is fixed on man only to find fault with him (10:12-14). The **judgment** into which God brings them is not some final, eschatological judgment but the suffering he inflicts upon humans in this life.

14:4 At first reading this verse seems inappropriate or out of place. The context focuses on the brevity of human life not its corruption (vv 1-6). One way to make sense of it here is by comparing it with Job's words in 7:19-21. The argument he raised there he returns to here. Given how insignificant and brief human existence is, it is difficult for Job to understand why God is so preoccupied with human sin. Since impurity is characteristic of the human race, why does God go to such lengths to scrutinize and punish it? Surely God does not expect humans to be flawless. The church fathers quoted this verse more than any other in Job to support their doctrine of original sin and total depravity.[4] This, however, does not seem to be the intent of Job's assertion. He does not tie human impurity to parents or birth in the form of some kind of inherited guilt but speaks more from the perspective of the obvious fact of human propensity to evil. The words for **pure** (טָהוֹר, ṭāhōr) and **impure** (טָמֵא, ṭāmē') are the language of ancient Hebrew ritual, but here they mean "moral purity" and "moral impurity."[5]

---

[4]Cf. also the Targum of Job, "None but God can make man clean who is naturally unclean."

[5]Against J.K. Zink, "Uncleanness and Sin: A Study of Job xiv 4 and Psalm li 7," *VT* 17 (1967): 354-361.

14:5-6 Job now returns to his theme of the brevity of human life. **Man's days are determined**, he says, **the number of his months** are **decreed**. This comports with the larger biblical teaching on human longevity. As a consequence of human rebellion against God, immortality is denied them (Genesis 3; cf. also Gen 6:3). "The length of our days is seventy years—or eighty, if we have the strength . . . ." (Ps 90:10a). Though some people lived longer in biblical times, these exceptions must be seen as the result of God's blessing and providential intervention. Generally speaking, though, the human lifespan has been **determined** (חָרוּץ, *ḥārûṣ*; "decreed"; Isa 10:22; Dan 9:26,27) with **set limits he cannot exceed**. The emphasis here is not that each man's days are specifically numbered but that human longevity has limits that God himself has set. In view of this human finitude, Job asks, "Why do you make his brief life so miserable?" God should **look away from him and let him alone**[6] (cf. 7:16; 10:20). If God would spare humans his scrutinizing gaze, at least they could find some comfort during their short time on earth. Like a **hired man**, a person could at least enjoy a little pleasure while he **puts in his time**.

Job's Acknowledgment of Death's Finality (14:7-12)

[7]"At least there is hope for a tree: / If it is cut down, it will sprout again, / and its new shoots will not fail. / [8]Its roots may grow old in the ground / and its stump die in the soil, / [9]yet at the scent of water it will bud / and put forth shoots like a plant. / [10]But man dies and is laid low; / he breathes his last and is no more. / [11]As water disappears from the sea / or a riverbed becomes parched and dry, / [12]so man lies down and does not rise; / till the heavens are no more, men will not awake / or be roused from their sleep.

14:7-12 This powerful poem contrasts the hope of a tree with the hope of a man for life after death.[7] The poem extends the thought

---

[6]MT has "and let him cease" or "let him die," (וְיֶחְדָּל, *wᵉyeḥdāl*), but most read with NIV the imperative "leave alone," (וַחֲדָל, *waḥădāl*). P. Calderone ("*HDL II* in Poetic Texts," *CBQ* 23 [1961]: 451-460) suggests *ḥadal* II, "to be fat, to fill oneself with food, to be prosperous." He takes the next word עַד (*'ad*) to mean "food" and reads the entire line "that he may be filled with food."

[7]For a discussion of the structure and language of this poem cf. J. Krasovec, *Antithetic Structures in Biblical Hebrew Poetry*, VTSupp 35 (Leiden: Brill, 1984).

of verses 1-6 and its emphasis on the finitude of man while it anticipates verses 13-17 with its speculation that men could somehow live
beyond the grave. In contrast to Job, **at least there is hope for a
tree**. The word **hope** (תִּקְוָה, *tiqwāh*) refers to an inner ability to face
disaster with confidence.[8] It is a quality of which Job has been
deprived (7:6; cf. also 17:15; 19:10). A tree has hope because it has
the prospect of being revived. Even though **cut down** with its **stump**
left to **die in the soil**,[9] at the mere **scent of water** it will **bud and put
forth shoots**. Death does not claim the tree. By contrast, **man dies**
and **is no more**. There is considerable debate among interpreters
about the precise meaning of this last term (חָלַשׁ, *ḥālaš*, lit., "be
weak"). NIV and RSV take it to mean "be prostrate" and hence to be
laid low. Others have suggested "be snatched away," "be driven
away," or "disappear." It is preferable to keep its basic meaning of
"weak" and see it as contrasting the companion term for **man** earlier in the verse. גִּבּוֹר (*gibbôr*, "mighty man") when used with the verb
ḥālaš ("defeat") should be taken to mean "death deprives mighty
man of his power."[10] This fits the biblical and extrabiblical descriptions of the inhabitants of Sheol (the grave) as weaklings or subhuman "shades" (Ps 88:5[4]). Unlike for the tree, for humans death dis-
sipates all vitality. When the tree is felled, it springs to life yet again.
But when a man is laid low in the grave, he **is no more**. This last
expression is literally stated as a question in the Hebrew. It reads,
"He breathes his last and *where is he?*" That is, he is "nowhere to be
seen." He has forever disappeared from the land of the living. Job
punctuates his belief in the finality of death with yet another analogy. Like water that drains or evaporates and is no more, so is man
who goes down to the dust. The first part of verse 11 is very similar
to Isaiah 19:5 and may be a quotation. In Isaiah God is said to be
drying up the Nile as part of his punishment of Egypt. Even as a life-
giving river can totally disappear, so can the vitality of man be
drained by death. Job completes his poem with what appears to be
a powerful denial of human immortality: **so man lies down and**

---

[8]Habel, *Job*, p. 241.

[9]עָפָר (*'āphār*, "dust"), the domain of death and the place where men ultimately rest (7:5; 17:16; 21:26).

[10]Cf. M. Dahood, "The Conjunction *WN* and Negative *'Î* in Hebrew," *UF*
14 (1982): 51-54, who translates "diminished vigor."

does not rise. He compares death to a **sleep** from which men **will not awake**.[11] Many scholars take this to mean that Job does not believe in any form of human immortality. They take the phrase, **till the heavens are no more**, to mean that humans stay dead forever.[12] Citing such passages as Psalm 41:9[8] and Ecclesiastes 3:19-20, they understand Job's statement to be typical of the standard Israelite teaching that death ends human existence.[13] "Human resurrection is considered as likely as the disappearance of the heavens; death is as permanent as the ancient structures of the cosmos."[14] This Jewish tradition about death was still held in Jesus' day by the Sadducees (Matt 22:23).[15] Other commentators, noting clear references to belief in immortality in the Old Testament (cf., e.g., Isa 26:19; Dan 12:2) understand the phrase **till the heavens are no more** to qualify Job's denial of human immortality. As long as the normal rhythms of the cosmos abide, humans will not rise from the grave. But the Old Testament (like the New Testament) does envisage an eschaton, an end to the universe in a cosmic catastrophe (Isa 34:4; Ps 102:26-27[25-26]).[16] Perhaps this is what Job means by his reference to the passing of the heavens. Notice that Job does go on to speculate about the prospect of encountering God after death (vv. 13-15). This being so, Job's statement here is not necessarily in conflict with the New Testament doctrine of the resurrection of the dead. In the final analysis, however, Job's concerns here are not so much driven by eschatological considerations as they are by his immediate, personal needs. Facing his imminent demise and knowing that people do not come back from the grave, he feels the urgent need to press his case for vindication.

---

[11]For a discussion of this metaphor cf. J.G.G.S. Thompson, "Sleep: An Aspect of Jewish Anthropology," *VT* 5 (1955): 421-433; T.H. McAlpine, *Sleep, Divine and Human, in the Old Testament*, JSOTSupp 38 (Sheffield: JSOT, 1987).

[12]For this meaning of the phrase cf. Deut 11:21; Ps 72:5,7,17; 89:30[29], 38[37].

[13]Cf. Habel, *Job*, pp. 241-242; L. Bailey, *Biblical Perspectives on Death* (Philadelphia: Fortress Press, 1979); H.H. Rowley, *The Faith of Israel* (London: SCM; Philadelphia: Westminster, 1956), pp. 150-176.

[14]Habel, *Job*, p. 242.

[15]Cf. also Sir 38:16-24.

[16]Cf. also 1 Enoch 45:4-5; 51:1-2.

Job's Hope for Life after Death (14:13-17)

[13]"If only you would hide me in the grave[a] / and conceal me till your anger has passed! / If only you would set a time / and then remember me. / [14]If a man dies, will he live again? / All the days of my hard service / I will wait for my renewal[b] to come. / [15]You will call and I will answer you; / you will long for the creature your hands have made. / [16]Surely then you will count my steps / but not keep track of my sin. / [17]My offenses will be sealed up in a bag; / you will cover over my sin.

[a]*13 Or Sheol*　　[b]*14 Or release*

14:13-15 In this passage Job clearly entertains the idea of resurrection from the grave. He envisages a time when he might return from a temporary asylum in Sheol to encounter a God whose anger toward him has abated. In language that is intensely personal (notice the exclusive use of "me" and "I"), Job pleads with God to **hide me in the grave** (lit., "Sheol") **and conceal me till your anger has passed.**[17] Since there is no place on earth for Job to hide from God's wrath, he seeks that refuge in Sheol. The concept of people in Sheol yet being the object of God's attention can also be found in Psalm 139:8 and Amos 9:2-3.[18] But since Sheol is commonly regarded as the land of no return, Job asks God to **set me a time and then remember me.** After God's anger has cooled, Job wishes to be brought back from Sheol to encounter a God more disposed to hearing his pleas.

The often quoted, **If a man dies, will he live again?** has been the subject of great debate among interpreters. If we take it as a rhetorical question expecting a "no" answer, it seems out of place here. For this reason some commentators have labeled it a gloss (Fohrer) or repositioned it after verse 19 (Dhorme). As commonly translated it does not seem to fit Job's exploration of the possibility of returning from Sheol. Complicating the matter is the alternative rendering of the Septuagint. This early Greek version reads it as an affirmation instead of a question and translates, "If a man dies, he will live

---

[17]For the idea of God's anger having limits cf. Isa 54:8.

[18]For God hiding people from danger cf. also Isa 26:20; 49:2; Ps 27:5; 31:21[20].

again."[19] Other commentators make the "dying" and "living" dependent upon the "if" clause and translate, "If man, once dead, could live
again . . . ." (Terrien) or "When a man has died, were he to live again
. . . ." (NAB). This would suit the context nicely. Yet another solution would be to take the traditional reading as a rhetorical question
that expects a "yes" answer. Since Job is exploring this very possibility, this too would fit the context. Clearly verses 14b-15 envision a
return from the grave. After doing **hard service** (צָבָא, *ṣābā'*,
"appointed time")[20] in Sheol[21] Job would experience **renewal** (חֲלִיפָה,
ḥălîphāh; "release"). God will **call** and Job will **answer** perhaps in the
legal sense of going to court (Habel; 9:15-16; 13:22a) or in a more
personal sense of God's desire to be in fellowship with his creature
(Clines; 12:4; 19:16; 30:20). The latter seems more probable in view
of 15b, **you will long for the creature your hands have made**. The
verb **long** (כָּסַף, *kāsaph*, "be pale") describes an intense desire (Pope)
that God has to be with the man he has made.[22]

In view of the preceding passage (14:7-12) most commentators
view this language as "dream" or "fanciful wish." Job, convinced that
death is permanent, that Sheol is a land of misery and no return,
and that God has permanently abandoned him, yet fantasizes about
reencountering God after death. How else could we harmonize it
with the overt rejection of life after death in 14:7-12? But there is
another way to account for these contradictory statements. It is
found in the language of lament. The Hebrew lament is regularly
given to juxtaposed statements that seem to be logical opposites. As
an example we may take Jeremiah 20:7-18. The prophet, who like
Job also feels mistreated by God, alternates between complaint and
accusation on the one hand (vv. 7-10,15-18) and praise on the other
(vv. 11-13).[23] Rather than the result of the editing in of nonoriginal

---

[19]Cf. D.H. Gard, "The Concept of the Future Life according to the Greek
Translator of the Book of Job," *JBL* 73 (1954): 137-143, who argues the
translators of LXX intentionally changed the original Hebrew to make it
more compatible with their belief in immortality.

[20]The term refers to military service or corvée labor.

[21]Against Fohrer who insists the "hard service" can only refer to this present life. This language should rather be taken as a metaphorical description
of time served in Sheol.

[22]An idea raised in 10:3,8-12.

[23]Cf. also Eccl 3:16,18-20 in contrast with v. 17.

material, such contrasts can be explained by a spiritual and psychological process commonly exercised by struggling saints. It is the
process by which believers reconcile faith to life. It is the process by
which they reconcile what reason teaches and empiricism observes
to what belief systems affirm. It is possible that such a process is
going on in Job. His reason and his life experience teach him that
people do not return from the grave. But his faith teaches him that
such is indeed possible. This process can explain other seemingly
contradictory passages in the book. In chapter 19, Job complains for
twenty verses that God has "wronged" him and unjustly "struck"
him, then suddenly confesses his belief that he will yet "see God"
and find vindication from the vicious accusations of the friends
(vv. 23-29). Also noteworthy are those passages, where on the heels
of accusing God of the grossest injustice, Job yet appeals to God's
just nature for vindication (cf., e.g., 13:15-16). Most decisively this
principle is demonstrated in the climax of the book where Job finally has his encounter with God. Given no explanation of his suffering
and without hope of any vindication, Job, in the light of a fresh
vision of the sovereign God, yet ends his struggle against the
Almighty and resubmits himself to the obedience of faith (40:3-5;
42:1-6). It seems that these passages which pit empiricism against
faith anticipate the very resolution of Job's great dilemma.

14:16-17 These verses are best understood as a continuation of
the faith perspective of verses 13-15. Job, envisioning a time in the
future life[24] when vindication will finally be his, anticipates God's forgiveness of his sin. To **count** Job's **steps** is to closely scrutinize his
behavior (cf. 31:4; 34:21). Typically in Job and the rest of the
Hebrew Bible, God's scrutiny is a negative thing (7:17-19; 13:27).
But in this vision of a forgiving God it is viewed positively and providentially as it is in Psalm 8:4 (cf. also Job 31:4; 43:21). Again, it is
best to see Job's reference to his **sins** and **offenses** as hypothetical
or ostensible and not take this as an overt admission of any misbehavior meriting his suffering. Job's characterization of God's for-

---

[24]NIV, "Surely then" (כִּי־עַתָּה, kî-‘attāh) is preferable here to "But now"
(Duhm, Fohrer), which would shift the focus back to Job's present dilemma.
To do so would put v. 16b, "but not keep track of my sin," in direct conflict
with Job's repeated complaint that God is keenly observing his sin in this
present life (cf. 10:14; also 7:20; 13:26).

giveness in verse 17 is interesting. He refers to his offenses being **sealed up in a bag**. M. Pope sees in this language a reference to the ancient accounting method of sealing pebbles in a bag.[25] Tur-Sinai connects the language to the practice of sealing papyrus texts. This explanation could be supported by the parallel **cover over my sins** in 17b. This verb (טָפַל, *ṭāphal*), adds Tur-Sinai, could refer to "daubing" soft wax on the document. It is unclear, however, if the verb ever takes this meaning in the Hebrew Bible. In Job 13:4 it has to do with "concealment," and that is probably it's meaning here. A better explanation is offered by Clines who sees this language as reversal of the normally negative language of sins being "sealed up" and "hidden away" for future punishment (Deut 32:34-35; Hos 13:12).

Human Hope Is Crushed by God (14:18-22)

[18]**"But as a mountain erodes and crumbles / and as a rock is moved from its place, / [19]as water wears away stones / and torrents wash away the soil, / so you destroy man's hope. / [20]You overpower him once for all, and he is gone; / you change his countenance and send him away. / [21]If his sons are honored, he does not know it; / if they are brought low, he does not see it. / [22]He feels but the pain of his own body / and mourns only for himself."**

14:18-19 In the traditional fashion of Hebrew lament Job now abandons his flight of faith and returns to earth in the somber words of complaint. It is that classic shift from what faith affirms to what reality teaches. With clever irony Job takes classic Hebrew metaphors of stability (**mountain, rock**, Gen 49:26), and vitality (**water**, Ps 1:3) and uses them to characterize God's relentless assault upon undeserving humans. **Hope** is leached from the human heart in the manner that raging **torrents**[26] **erode** even the most substantial **rocks** and **soil**. This language seems to remember the characterization of God's destructive power in 9:5-10. The **you** of verse 19 (cf. also v. 20) lays the gradual destruction of human hope directly in the lap of God.

---

[25]Cf. also A.L. Oppenheim, "On an Operational Device in Mesopotamian Bureaucracy," *JNES* 18 (1959): 121-128.

[26]Reading סָפִיחַ (*sāphîaḥ*) with Budde and others as סְחִיפָה (*sᵊḥîphāh*) = "cloudburst" (cf. Prov 28:3 [סֹחֵף, *sōḥēph*] and Arabic *saḥîfeh*, "rainstorm.").

14:20-22 Job concludes this speech, as he does several others, with a discussion of death. It is the tragic end to the sad struggle that God ordains for humankind. As man's adversary, God is directly responsible for his demise (again note the "you" of v. 20). After the ravages of aging disfigure human **countenance**[27] man is finally **gone**.[28] Some commentators have taken verse 21 as proof that the Hebrews believed death ends all conscious existence (**he does not know . . . he does not see**). But verse 22 makes it clear that such is not the case. In Sheol he **feels pain** and **mourns**.[29] So what verse 21 is saying is that the dead have no knowledge of the living once they move on to the abode of the dead. It also serves as yet another denial of any kind of retributive justice in which a man is rewarded or punished through his progeny (**sons are honored . . . brought low**, v. 21).

---

[27]Ibn Ezra suggests this is a reference to *rigor mortis* but it is more likely a description of the aging process that precedes death.

[28]The verb הָלַךְ (*hālak*, "go, walk") is one of many euphemisms for death (cf. 19:10; Ps 39:14[13]).

[29]Against Clines, with Peake and Rowley.

JOB 15

B. THE SECOND CYCLE OF SPEECHES (15:1–21:34)

This chapter begins the second cycle of the debate between Job and the friends (15:1–21:34). As in the first cycle, all three of the friends deliver a speech and Job, in turn, responds. To the casual reader of Job, the second and third cycles of the speeches seem repetitive and redundant. By the end of the first cycle the basic arguments have already been stated, and few, if any, new ideas are advanced in the subsequent words of the friends. Some students of the book have even questioned the authenticity of these later speeches regarding them as unoriginal or misplaced.

More recent studies of the literary features of Job, however, have yielded fresh perspective on the purposes of this portion of the book. We should note first that repetition is a regular feature of both Hebrew narrative and poetry. Rather than an indicator of multiple sources, poor editing, or sloppy transmission of the text, it is an intentional tool of the Hebrew writer, often providing an important clue to the author's meaning and purpose. This is not only true for repeated terms and themes but for repeated structures and patterns as well. In the prologue, for example, we have the highly structured pattern of scene-in-heaven followed by scene-on-earth repeated in a nearly verbatim style. Other repeated patterns are also readily observed throughout the book.[1]

What possible purposes do the repeated cycles of speeches serve for the meaning of the book? First, from a rhetorical perspective the redundant speeches clearly intensify the debate and heighten the tension of the plot. In the course of the three cycles the friends move from gentle persuaders to vehement indictors of Job. The ris-

---

[1]Cf. discussion on pp. 22-23.

ing level of recrimination and accusation against Job, the inability of
the friends to counter the arguments put forth by Job, and the wan-
ing length of their speeches in the face of Job's ever-escalating rhetoric give the reader the author's desired impression that Job is winning the debate. This, in turn, raises the frustration of the reader
over Job's unanswered charges of injustice on the part of God and
thus prepares us for the angry outburst of Elihu. Second, from a theological perspective, the fact that the friends are reduced to slavish-
ly repeating their stated positions in the second and third cycles
illustrates the trite and intractable nature of their arguments. The
theological bankruptcy of their position is thus exposed, and we are
indirectly prepared for Yahweh's final verdict against them (42:7-9).
The prolonged debate thus anticipates the indictment of Yahweh
that the tenets of traditional theology are simply inadequate to
account for the meaning of Job's suffering.

Convinced that Job is suffering because he has sinned, the
friends intensify their call for Job to repent. In this cycle their focus
shifts to the terrible fate of the wicked as warning of what Job might
expect should he persist in claiming that he has no sin. Job, however, steadfastly clings to his integrity and refuses to repent. He contends that in the real world the wicked simply do not always get their
just punishment. He thus rejects retributive justice as the operative
model of how God runs his world.

1. Eliphaz's Second Speech (15:1-35)

This second speech of Eliphaz divides fairly evenly into two
major parts: a refutation of Job's claim of wisdom (2-16) and a treatise on the fate of the wicked (17-35). The speech represents a continuation of Eliphaz's earlier counsel (Job 4–5) but takes on a sharper tone in its rebuke of Job's "arrogant" claims.

A Refutation of Job's Claim of Wisdom (15:1-16)

¹**Then Eliphaz the Temanite replied:**
²**"Would a wise man answer with empty notions, / or fill his
belly with the hot east wind? / ³Would he argue with useless words,
/ with speeches that have no value? / ⁴But you even undermine
piety / and hinder devotion to God. / ⁵Your sin prompts your**

mouth; / you adopt the tongue of the crafty. / ⁶Your own mouth condemns you, not mine; / your own lips testify against you.

⁷"Are you the first man ever born? / Were you brought forth before the hills? / ⁸Do you listen in on God's council? / Do you limit wisdom to yourself? / ⁹What do you know that we do not know? / What insights do you have that we do not have? / ¹⁰The gray-haired and the aged are on our side, / men even older than your father. / ¹¹Are God's consolations not enough for you, / words spoken gently to you? / ¹²Why has your heart carried you away, / and why do your eyes flash, / ¹³so that you vent your rage against God / and pour out such words from your mouth?

¹⁴"What is man, that he could be pure, / or one born of woman, that he could be righteous? / ¹⁵If God places no trust in his holy ones, / if even the heavens are not pure in his eyes, / ¹⁶how much less man, who is vile and corrupt, / who drinks up evil like water!

15:1 Eliphaz begins his speech with a series of rhetorical questions (typical of Eliphaz) and pointed statements designed to expose the presumptuousness of Job's claims. Whereas Eliphaz's first speech might be characterized as an exhortation, his second is clearly a rebuke.[2] Job is addressed in the second person and is directly accused of subverting piety and falsely claiming to have the wisdom of God.

15:2-3 Would a wise man answer with empty notions . . . ? In his first speech Eliphaz had treated Job as a peer, as one wise man to another. Here he takes a decidedly less conciliatory approach. Having heard Job's stubborn defense of his integrity and irreverent criticism of God, he no longer sees him as a **wise man** (חָכָם, *ḥākām*).[3] By denying him this status, Eliphaz is doing more than challenging Job's intellect. He is also questioning his character. Job is acting and speaking like a "fool" (עֱוִיל, *'ăwîl*), a morally bankrupt person who lives as if there is no God.[4] His arguments are **empty notions**, literally, "knowledge of wind" (דַּעַת־רוּחַ, *da'ath-rûaḥ*). This could mean that his claims are without substance or consequence (Rowley,

---

[2]Contra Clines, who reads Eliphaz's language as "encouragement" rather than indictment (*Job*, pp. 345-346).

[3]Job has claimed to be "wise" (12:3;13:2).

[4]Eliphaz had already warned Job of the dangers of such spiritual regression in 5:2-3.

Fohrer) or, as in 8:2, that they are volatile and dangerous.[5] Job is behaving like a man who has **filled his belly with the hot east wind**. The word **belly** (בֶּטֶן, *beṭen*) in the Hebrew Bible is said to be the seat of feelings (Prov 18:8; Job 20:20), and a place where deceit is fashioned (v. 35). The **east wind** (קָדִים, *qādîm*) is the withering sirocco that blows in violently from the desert. Used in combination these terms convey the notion that Job is speaking irrationally from too much uncontrolled emotion. Job's words are **useless** and of **no value** in the view of Eliphaz, both in their lack of substance and in their ineffectiveness in resolving Job's dilemma.

15:4-6 Eliphaz now moves from questioning Job to directly accusing him. In the Hebrew Bible there are few crimes worse than the one for which Eliphaz indicts Job: **You undermine piety and hinder devotion to God.** What exactly does Eliphaz mean by this charge? The term **piety** (lit., "fear") is commonly thought to be elliptical for "fear of God/the LORD" (cf. 4:6) which is the Hebrew equivalent of "religion." In the prologue it is used in definition of Job's piety and in 28:28 it is said to be the essence of "wisdom." The Hebrew word, which the NIV translates **undermine** (פָּרַר, *pārar*), literally means to "break, violate." By accusing Job of "violating devotion" Eliphaz may have in mind Job's own breach of faith, the loss of his own personal devotion to God. This would seem to be the thought of verses 5,6 where it is said that **your** (Job's) **sin prompts your mouth** and **your own lips testify against you.**[6] It is likewise possible that Eliphaz has an even broader crime in mind. He may be accusing Job of **undermining piety** and **hindering devotion**[7] in others. Job's words are an attack on religion itself (Fohrer), seeking to do away with devoutness among men (Davidson) and thus a danger to society (Rowley). Verse 5 seems to join both ideas. The phrase **your sin prompts your mouth** seems to suggest that Eliphaz believes that Job's impious speech is inspired by some inner guilt while the phrase **you adopt**[8] **the tongue**

---

[5]Clines, *Job*, p. 347. Note the parallelism with "east wind" (*qadim*) v. 2b and also Hos 12:2[1].

[6]So Weiser, Habel. Job had anticipated that in a dispute with God his own speech would condemn him (9:20).

[7]Lit., "diminish meditation." The latter term (שִׂיחָה, *śîhāh*) refers to conversation with God or meditative prayer (תְּפִלָּה, *tephillāh*); cf. Ps 102:2[1] where the two terms are parallel.

[8]בָּחַר (*bāḥar*), "choose."

of the crafty (עֲרוּמִים, *'ărûmîm*) seems to cast Job in the role of the clever schemers who epitomize the enemies of God (5:12-13).

15:7-8 With sarcasm Eliphaz bombards Job with a series of rhetorical questions designed to challenge his claim to superior wisdom. **Are you the first man ever born?** The simplest interpretation of this language is to treat it as a metaphor of Job's exaggerated sense of his own importance.[9] Some scholars argue that the backdrop to this question is the ancient myth of the Primal Human (אָדָם, *'ādām*, but not the Adam of Genesis 2-3).[10] Note that, unlike Adam, this "man" was **born,** was **brought forth before the hills,**[11] and had access to **God's** (heavenly) **council.** This **council** (סוֹד, *sôd*) is the group of heavenly beings referred to in 1:6-12; 2:1-6 (cf. also 2 Kings 22).[12] This was the place where those present could directly hear God speak.[13] Eliphaz is thus accusing Job of assuming the role of the First Man and claiming to possess a superior wisdom to that of the friends which he gained directly through some privileged access to the heavenly council of God.

15:9-10 To the contrary, insists Eliphaz, **What do you know that we do not know?** It is the claim of the friends that the wisdom that comes from years of experience is on their side. This struggle over who truly "knows" (יָדַע, *yāda'*)[14] is at the heart of the debate between Job and the friends. It is an epistemological debate of sorts, an

---

[9]E.g., Hakam, סֵפֶר אִיּוֹב, who takes the line to mean that Job regards all other men born before him to be but beasts.

[10]Though the whole story of the Primal Human is not told in the OT, evidence of its influence may be found in Prov 8:22-31(= Wisdom); Ezek 28:11-19 (= the king of Tyre [not Satan!]). This First Man (אָדָם הַקַּדְמוֹן, *'ādām haqqadmôn*) story played a major role in apocryphal and rabbinic literature (cf., e.g., Sir 49:16; cf., also H. Schmidt, *Die Erzählung von Paradies und Sündenfall* [Tübingen: J.C.H. Mohr, 1931]; R. Gordis, "The Significance of the Paradise Myth," *AJSL* 52 [1936]: 86-94).

[11]The identical phrase is used of "Wisdom" in Prov 8:25b. The phrase connotes a primordial time when only God (Ps 90:2) and Wisdom were present. It is interesting to note that in chapters 38-39 God asks Job if he was indeed present at creation.

[12]Such councils are common in Mesopotamian and Canaanite mythology (cf. F. Cross, "The Council of Yahweh in Second Isaiah," *JNES* 12 [1953]: 274-277).

[13]According to Jeremiah (23:18,22) the false prophets claimed to be privy to the plans of God as if they had stood in this heavenly council.

[14]The root ידע (*yd'*, "to know") occurs over eighty times in Job.

argument over how humans "know." The book regularly pits knowledge taught by tradition (**The gray-haired and the aged are on our side.** cf., also, Bildad's claim in 8:8) against knowledge gained by empirical observation (what Job has seen and heard, 13:1-2). The final verdict of the book is that neither Job nor the friends "know." Yahweh pronounces Job "without knowledge" (38:2) and the friends "wrong" in what they have said of him (42:7,8). As affirmed in 28:23, only God knows the way of wisdom.

15:11-13 Eliphaz continues his assault against Job's irreverent attitude with more barbed rhetorical questions: **Are God's consolations not enough for you, words spoken gently to you?** "God's consolations" (תַּנְחֻמוֹת אֵל, *tanḥumôth 'ēl*) are the "words spoken" by the friends who have been acting as God's representatives. Earlier Eliphaz had attempted to offer an empathetic word (דָּבָר, *dābar*; 4:2,12) to Job. The tone of his question here echoes a sense of personal affront he feels over Job's sharp rebuff of Eliphaz's attempt to comfort him. This was the comfort that Eliphaz believed had come directly from God in the form of a vision (4:12-16). So, as Eliphaz says, it is God's comfort that Job is rejecting.

In verses 12-13 Eliphaz speculates over what has caused Job to become such a critic of God. First he focuses on Job's **heart** (לֵב, *lēb*) which, for the ancient Hebrews, was the seat of intellect and volition. His probing question suggests that Job has willfully turned against God. Next Eliphaz speaks of Job's **eyes** (עַיִן, *'ayin*) which send information to the heart and reflect the heart's disposition (31:1,7). Something has clouded Job's perspective. That something, Eliphaz suggests, is a **rage against God**. The word **rage** (רוּחַ, *rûaḥ*; lit., "wind," "spirit") is sometimes used to connote "anger" in the Hebrew Bible (cf. Judg 8:3; Prov 16:32). Finally, and most obviously, Eliphaz indicts Job's speech. The **words from** Job's **mouth** most betray him as God's opponent. His irreverent ranting and impious accusations reveal a Job who has radically changed and Eliphaz wants to know why.[15] This indictment of what Job says contrasts the positive assessment of Job's speech made earlier by the author: "In all this Job did not sin in what he said" (2:10b).

---

[15]The reader first notices this in the dramatic shift in the tone and substance of Job's speech between chapters two and three.

15:14-16 Eliphaz now reiterates the basic theme of the "revelation" he had shared earlier with Job (4:17). There are some changes in this reformulation of his view of human nature and the commentators are divided over the significance of the differences.[16] **What is man, that he could be pure or one born of woman, that he could be righteous?** As in chapter 4 Eliphaz argues that moral purity is simply not characteristic of human beings. This assertion is, of course, in direct rebuttal of Job's claims to such purity (12:4). **Born of woman** simply means "mortal" (cf. Job's own words, 14:1) and does not carry with it the idea that the woman or birth are the source of man's uncleanness (with Clines, against Dhorme, Rowley, Peake). Again, as in chapter four, Eliphaz reminds Job that even in the heavenly realm there are none who can claim righteousness before God. The **holy ones** are the angels (cf. 5:1) and the **heavens** may refer either to the realm itself or, more likely, to the beings who inhabit it (the "heavenly ones").[17] Humans, by contrast, are **vile** (נִתְעָב, *nith'āb*)[18] or "disgusting" and **corrupt** (נֶאֱלָח, *ne'ĕlāḥ*) or "filthy." The evidence of this corruption is the tendency of humans to **drink up evil like water.** The term **evil** (עַוְלָה, *'awlāh*, "injustice, deception") is the opposite of צֶדֶק (*ṣedek*, "righteousness"; cf. 6:29) and connotes lack of integrity.[19]

---

[16]זָכָה (*zākah*, "be pure") is substituted for טָהַר (*ṭāhar*, "be clean"), and the verbs are inverted. In the place of גֶּבֶר (*geber*, "strong man") the phrase יְלוּד אִשָּׁה (*yᵉlûd 'iššāh*, "born of woman") is used. "His holy ones" (קְדֹשִׁים, *qᵉdōšîm*) is substituted for "his servants" (עֲבָדִים, *'ăbādîm*) and "heavens" (שָׁמַיִם, *šāmayim*) replaces "his messengers" (מַלְאָכָיו, *mal'ākāyw*). Habel understands the differences as intentionally designed to shift the emphasis from the imperfection of mortals in comparison to their creator (4:17ff) to the inner impulses that are characteristic of humans like Job (15:14-16). Clines sees in the language a shift from a legal emphasis (4:17ff) to an ethical one (15:14-16). L.R. Fisher, however, has argued convincingly that *zakah* was a legal expression ("An Amarna Age Prodigal," *JSS* 3 [1958]: 11-22).

[17]For a similar usage cf. 38:7 and 25:2.

[18]Cf. P. Humbert, "Le substantif *to'ēbā* et le verbe *t'b* dans l'A.T.," *ZAW* 72 (1960): 217-237.

[19]As Habel notes, this section of Eliphaz's speech has some resemblance to the Babylonian Theodicy with its claim that the gods endowed the human race with perverse speech and lies forever (*BWL*, p. 89).

A Treatise on the Fate of the Wicked (15:17-35)[20]

[17]"Listen to me and I will explain to you; / let me tell you what I have seen, / [18]what wise men have declared, / hiding nothing received from their fathers / [19](to whom alone the land was given / when no alien passed among them): / [20]All his days the wicked man suffers torment, / the ruthless through all the years stored up for him. / [21]Terrifying sounds fill his ears; / when all seems well, marauders attack him. / [22]He despairs of escaping the darkness; / he is marked for the sword. / [23]He wanders about—food for vultures[a]; / he knows the day of darkness is at hand. / [24]Distress and anguish fill him with terror; / they overwhelm him, like a king poised to attack, / [25]because he shakes his fist at God / and vaunts himself against the Almighty, / [26]defiantly charging against him / with a thick, strong shield.

[27]"Though his face is covered with fat / and his waist bulges with flesh, / [28]he will inhabit ruined towns / and houses where no one lives, / houses crumbling to rubble. / [29]He will no longer be rich and his wealth will not endure, / nor will his possessions spread over the land. / [30]He will not escape the darkness; / a flame will wither his shoots, / and the breath of God's mouth will carry him away. / [31]Let him not deceive himself by trusting what is worthless, / for he will get nothing in return. / [32]Before his time he will be paid in full, / and his branches will not flourish. / [33]He will be like a vine stripped of its unripe grapes, / like an olive tree shedding its blossoms. / [34]For the company of the godless will be barren, / and fire will consume the tents of those who love bribes. / [35]They conceive trouble and give birth to evil; / their womb fashions deceit."

[a]*23 Or* about, looking for food

The fate of the wicked is a popular theme of traditional Hebrew wisdom[21] and a particular favorite of the friends (cf., e.g., Eliphaz in

---

[20]The interpreters differ over the purpose of this section with assessments ranging from "encouragement" (Clines) to "warning" (Weiser) to "Job's inescapable fate" (Gray).

[21]Westermann identifies this literary form as a typical "end of the world" motif often found in the psalms of lament. This particular portrait of the wicked, however, lacks several features common to the lament psalms.

5:12-14; Bildad in 8:8-19). The dominant theme in this particular portrait is that of an enemy of God petrified by his impending doom.

15:17-19 In these introductory verses, Eliphaz offers an apology
for his claim to speak true wisdom. The opening challenge, **Listen
to me**, and the testimony to his personal experience, **what I have
seen**, are typical of his earlier style (4:7,8; 5:1,3,17,27). The latter
may be a reference to his earlier visionary experience (4:13) or a
claim to a new vision he has received concerning the fate of the
wicked. The next phrase, **what wise men have declared**, now adds
the additional claim that his instruction is consistent with the wisdom handed down by the **fathers**. To the ancient "wise men"
(חֲכָמִים, *ḥăkāmîm*) there was no truth more authoritative than that
which has stood the test of time and been handed down through the
generations. Verse 19 has been the source of extensive scholarly
debate. Many scholars consider it a gloss (Holscher, DeWilde) and
the NEB treats it as a secondary addition. Still others have seen it a
clue to the date of the book referring to a time before the fall of
Samaria or the destruction of Jerusalem (Duhm). A careful reading
of the Hebrew Bible, however, calls the claim **when no alien passed
among them** into serious question. For it is the consistent testimony of the biblical writers that from patriarchal times forward other
races were present with Israel in Canaan. Whatever the historical
background to the language, its function in the passage is to heark-
en back to a time when true wisdom had not been polluted by competing ideologies of other people groups.[22]

15:20-24 Eliphaz's opening portrait of the **wicked man** (רָשָׁע, *rāšā'*)
is that of a besieged foe awaiting his inevitable demise. Like a **ruthless
tyrant** (עָרִיץ, *'ārîṣ*) dreading his just reward, he is overwhelmed by **torment**. This latter term (הִתְחוֹלֵל, *hithḥôlēl*) is often used in the OT to
describe the plight of a woman in childbirth. The emphasis here is on
the mental anguish suffered by the wicked. Even when **all seems well**,
he is yet vexed by **terrifying sounds**.[23] Never able to relax, he lives in
constant fear of his deserved end. He is **marked**[24] **for the sword** and

---

[22]For the idea of "alien" (זָר, *zār*), cf. L.A. Snijders, "The Meaning of *zr* in
the OT," *OTS* 10 (1954): 1-154.

[23]This term, פְּחָדִים (*pᵉḥādîm*), may refer to evil spirits over whom the king
of terrors ruled (18:14).

[24]Reading with Gordis, the Ketib, וְצָפוּ (*wᵉṣāphû*), as a passive participle of
the Qal (cf. also 41:25[33]).

he knows it. **Darkness**, a metaphor of death, awaits him and the **day of darkness is at hand** (cf. Amos 5:18-20).[25] **Vultures**, omens of death, are ready to pounce on him. **Distress** (צַר, *ṣar*) and **anguish** (מְצוּקָה, *mᵊṣûqāh*) have entrapped him. These final two terms carry as their root ideas, "confined," and "constrained" and are commonly used in the OT to characterize a conquered foe.[26] With this portrait of the desperate wicked, Eliphaz has strongly countered Job's claim that the "tents of the marauders are undisturbed, and those who provoke God are secure" (12:6).

15:25-27 Now Eliphaz identifies the reason the wicked are so tormented. Like a deluded hero **vaunting himself against the Almighty**,[27] the wicked man foolishly attempts to take on God as his personal opponent. Fohrer and Pope see in this a reference to the high-handed attitude of Job in challenging God to a legal disputation. It may also be a veiled reference to Job's own assertion that God is singling him out as some formidable foe (7:12; 13:24; so Habel). It is interesting to note that when God finally addresses Job, he challenges him to gird his loins like a "hero" (גִּבּוֹר, *gibbôr*) and demonstrate his power (40:7-9).[28] Habel correctly places verse 27 with what precedes it rather than with what follows. It completes the satirical portrait of a once formidable warrior now grown fat on easy living, a comical caricature of the foolish tyrant who would dare rush headlong into a battle with God.[29]

15:28-30 In these verses Eliphaz again discusses the fate of the wicked. Here, the evil man's ultimate destiny is his interest. According to Eliphaz, the wicked will be systematically deprived of all that

---

[25]The Hebrew of 22a literally reads "He does not hope to return [שׁוּב, *šûb*] from darkness." The wicked is thus portrayed as one already in the grasp of death with no hope of escape.

[26]Cf. Zeph 1:15. By contrast, one who is victorious occupies a broad, open place.

[27]The Hebrew of this line literally reads "act the hero [יִתְגַּבָּר, *yithgabbār*] toward Shaddai."

[28]Zophar also portrays Job as an insolent tyrant attempting to threaten the heavens (20:6ff).

[29]Rowley also reads v. 27 in this way. Clines, however, puts v. 27 with what follows and sees it as an ironic contrast. Even though the wicked lives the indulgent, prosperous life, he will end up an inhabitant of a devastated city (v. 28). Still another view is offered by Tur-Sinai and Terrien. They see in vv. 24-26 allusions to a mythological warrior doing battle with the gods.

he enjoyed in this life. First he will lose the security of his domicile. Driven from his home he will be forced to live among the houses of an ancient ruin.[30] Whether this refers to his own town and house (NEB) or more generally to any ruin, the motif of the abandoned city is widely used in the Bible and the ancient Near East to characterize the destiny of those worthy of judgment (cf., e.g., Isa 13:19-22; 34:9-17). Such places are considered cursed and are to be avoided by passersby. Second, the wicked man will forfeit his possessions. Though Eliphaz acknowledges that the wicked may become wealthy for a season, **his wealth will not endure**. The word **wealth** (חַיִל, *ḥayil*) can also mean "power." This may allude to yet a third characterization of the wicked man's demise, his loss of influence. As the following phrase, **nor will his possessions spread over the land**, implies his once dominant empire will diminish and eventually come crashing down around him. But an even greater adversity awaits him, death. With three powerful metaphors Eliphaz characterizes the wicked man's final end. **Darkness**, his enemy (v. 22) and his appointed fate ("day of darkness," v. 23), is once again used to describe the death he will experience. The **flame** (שַׁלְהֶבֶת, *šalhābeth*) probably refers to the sirocco which blows in off the desert to **wither his shoots**[31] or, more generally, to the **fire** (v. 34) which rises to **consume** the wicked.[32] The **breath of** (God's) **mouth**, likewise, may refer to the strong desert winds or, as some commentators have suggested, a supernatural blast designed to blow away the wicked.

15:31-35 After warning the godless not to trust in false hopes raised by the temporary prosperity of his evil lifestyle (v. 31), Eliphaz returns to his extended metaphor of the wicked man's final end as that of an ill-fated plant. Like a prematurely felled tree his **branches will not flourish**. This refers to his future descendents (cf. 5:25) who

---

[30]Other interpretations see this verse as a continuing description of the tyrant's arrogant actions. That is, he fearlessly visits such sites (Fohrer) and rebuilds the sites for his own use (Gray, Peake) even in defiance of some divine curse placed upon them (DeWilde).

[31]Hakam sees the dangers confronting the wicked to be like three successive hazards that confront a tree: darkness, that takes away the sun; hot dry winds that scorch the vegetation; and violent winds that can topple the strongest tree.

[32]Cf. Ps 106:17-18; Num 16:31-35 (Dathan and Abiram are consumed by a "flame" of death).

would ordinarily perpetuate his line. The depictions of the **vine stripped**[33] **of its unripe grapes** and the **olive tree shedding its blossoms** complete the portrait of a miscarried life, robbed of lasting achievement and any sense of fulfillment. Denied a "harvest" the wicked man's fate is the opposite of those blessed by God (5:26). Finally, Eliphaz turns to a proverb to punctuate his doctrine of retribution for the ungodly: **They conceive trouble and give birth to evil.** This "reap what you sow" idiom dominates the speeches of the friends and articulates their essential view of how God runs his world. He sees to it that people get what they deserve.[34] Even in **company**[35] the **godless** and **those who love bribes** cannot escape their just end and will be consumed by the **fire** of death. The final word **deceit** (מִרְמָה, *mirmāh*) is undoubtedly aimed at Job and returns to the initial charge against him with which Eliphaz began his speech (vv. 2,5).

In this speech Eliphaz offers Job little consolation. From the beginning his purpose has been to convince Job that he is suffering the fate of the ungodly. He has sinned, and God is seeing to it that the inevitable consequences of his behavior fall upon him. Though no invitation to repentance is offered Job in this speech, we may yet assume that this is the ultimate goal of Eliphaz's rhetoric.

---

[33]Lit., "lets fall" (חָמַס, *ḥāmas*), thereby indicating the violent, unnatural nature of this miscarriage.

[34]Though, unlike in his previous speech, Eliphaz does not specifically name God as the cause of the wicked man's downfall.

[35]This assembly (עֵדָה, *ʿēdāh*) is the essential opposite of the council of God's holy ones (v. 8).

JOB 16

2. Job's Reply to Eliphaz (16:1–17:16)

This fifth major speech of Job (16:1–17:16) is structurally complex. Wedged between sharp replies to the friends (16:1-6; 17:10-16) are complaints, laments, and appeals primarily aimed at God (16:7–17:9). This alternation between speech to friends and speech to God echoes the earth-and-heaven format of the prologue and reminds the reader that Job's struggle exists on two distinct levels. The dominant literary genre employed by Job is the lament, with elements of oath and legal disputation also present. In his previous speech (chs.12–14) Job had summoned God to issue a formal charge against him. Job, still awaiting God's reply, now presses his case by sounding the same familiar themes of unfair treatment at the hands of God coupled with strong protests of his personal innocence.

Job's Rebuke of His "Comforters" (16:1-5)

¹**Then Job replied:**
²**"I have heard many things like these; / miserable comforters are you all! / ³Will your long-winded speeches never end? / What ails you that you keep on arguing? / ⁴I also could speak like you, / if you were in my place; / I could make fine speeches against you / and shake my head at you. / ⁵But my mouth would encourage you; / comfort from my lips would bring you relief.**

16:1-3 In these opening verses Job's reply takes on the same sarcastic tone as that used earlier by the friends toward him (8:2; 11:2-3; 15:2). He belittles both what they say and the motives behind their speech. First, he accuses them of speech without substance. Job insists that their **long-winded speeches** are unoriginal (**I have heard many things like these**). They shed no new light, offer no fresh per-

spective on the meaning of his desperate plight. In explanation of
his intense suffering the friends can only offer the well-worn platitudes of theological tradition. Second, he suggests that though the
stated purpose of their words was to "sympathize with him and comfort him" (2:11), they really have another agenda.[1] The label **miserable comforters** (עֲמָל מְנַחֲמֵי, *mᵊnaḥămê ʿāmāl*) is an interesting one.[2]
"Troublesome comforters," "torturer-comforters," "trouble-making
comforters" are just a few of the ways the translators render this
phrase. The expression speaks directly to Job's perception of the
actual role of the friends. Instead of comforting his misery they only
add to it. Instead of bringing him relief from his troubles their
words only heap more trouble upon him. This they have done by
observing in Job's words and behavior "proof" of his sinfulness, thus
undermining his entire appeal to God.

16:4-5 Job will not be "spoken down to" by the friends. He possesses the same theological knowledge and rhetorical gifts as they.
Job has compared himself to the friends in other places (cf., e.g.,
12:3; 13:2), insisting that he is their intellectual and moral equal.
But here the comparison serves another purpose. He is saying that
if he were in their position he would use his knowledge and gifts to
encourage and offer **comfort** rather than to indict and condemn.
The expression **make fine speeches**[3] can also be translated "make
noise, harangue"[4] and "unite, join words."[5] It describes Job's self-
acclaimed abilities as an orator to do to them what they have been
doing to him. The next phrase, **shake my head at you,** most likely
refers to an act of contempt or scorn (Ps 22:8[7]; Jer 18:16). Conversely, the same gesture can at times denote sympathy (Job 2:22;
42:11).

---

[1]Job had earlier condemned the friends for their failure to comfort
(6:5ff).

[2]Cf., also, 13:4 where Job calls them "worthless physicians."

[3]Cf. KB, p. 276 which takes אַחְבִּירָה (*ʾaḥbîrāh*) as a derivative from Arab.,
ḥarbaru, "beautify, adorn."

[4]From Ugar., *ḥbr*, "make noise, harangue." Cf. J.J. Finkelstein, "Hebrew
ḥbr and Semitic *ḫbr*," *JBL* 7 (1956): 328-331; O. Loretz, "*Ḥbr* in Job 16:4,"
CBQ 23 (1961): 93-94.

[5]From חבר (*ḥbr*), "unite, join" (Gordis).

Job's Complaint against God (16:6-17)

⁶"Yet if I speak, my pain is not relieved; / and if I refrain, it does not go away. / ⁷Surely, O God, you have worn me out; / you have devastated my entire household. / ⁸You have bound me—and it has become a witness; / my gauntness rises up and testifies against me. / ⁹God assails me and tears me in his anger / and gnashes his teeth at me; / my opponent fastens on me his piercing eyes. / ¹⁰Men open their mouths to jeer at me; / they strike my cheek in scorn / and unite together against me. / ¹¹God has turned me over to evil men / and thrown me into the clutches of the wicked. / ¹²All was well with me, but he shattered me; / he seized me by the neck and crushed me. / He has made me his target; / ¹³his archers surround me. / Without pity, he pierces my kidneys / and spills my gall on the ground. / ¹⁴Again and again he bursts upon me; / he rushes at me like a warrior.

¹⁵"I have sewed sackcloth over my skin / and buried my brow in the dust. / ¹⁶My face is red with weeping, / deep shadows ring my eyes; / ¹⁷yet my hands have been free of violence / and my prayer is pure.

16:6-7 Having dismissed the friends as **miserable comforters**, Job returns to his complaint against God.[6] He begins by lamenting the fact that his repeated protests to God have resulted in absolutely no relief from his suffering. But neither does he get relief by remaining silent. So speak he will, and not further to the friends but to the one who is his real opponent. Before he is through, Job will characterize God as a wild animal (vv. 9-10), a traitor (v. 11), a wrestler (v. 12), an archer (vv. 12c-13a), and a swordsman (vv. 13b-14). God[7] has **worn** Job **out**, taking away all of his strength. More than this he has **devastated** Job's **entire household**. This latter term

---

[6]Some interpreters put v. 6 with what precedes and see it as an apology for why his speech is so provocative.

[7]The grammar does not clearly indicate the subject to be God. Rowley, following the Vulg., understands "pain" (v. 6) to be the subject, but the context (v. 7b) suggests God is the subject. There is also a grammatical problem involving the changing of persons between v. 7a (third person), "he/it has worn me out," and v. 7b (second person), "you have devastated," leading some to emend the text. However, as Gordis has shown, such shift in person is normative in Hebrew poetry.

(lit., "company"; עֵדָה, 'ēdāh) may refer to Job's friends and associates as well as to his family. Indeed, Job's entire world has been rocked by his suffering.

16:8-9 Speaking of God in both the second and third person Job continues his indictment of his Oppressor. Through God's mistreatment of him Job has been **bound**. This term (קָמַט, qāmaṭ) occurs only here and in 22:16. Many scholars connect it to Syriac qmt and take it to mean "shriveled" (AV). This fits nicely with the context and is paralleled by the term **gauntness**. God's reducing of Job to a shell of what he once was bears **witness** against Job and **testifies against** him. This claim owes its meaning to the ancient view that a person's physical devastation is clear evidence that God is punishing him. As the friends have already argued, Job's very appearance is proof of his guilt. In verse 9 Job characterizes God as a wild animal that **tears** and **gnashes his teeth** at Job.[8] God does this **in his anger** (אַף, aph).[9] Job had earlier asked to be hidden in Sheol until God's anger had passed (14:13). But that anger continues to hound Job. As a relentless **opponent** (צָר, ṣār)[10] God keeps Job under his piercing gaze. God's **eyes** refer to his scrutinizing surveillance of Job (7:8; 10:4,14,18; 13:27; 14:3). Interestingly, the verb **assails** with which Job began his characterization of God's assault, is שָׂטַם (śāṭam), similar and related to שָׂטָן (śāṭan, "accuser, adversary"). Not escaping the notice of the commentators, Job's use of this term has been taken by some to be a veiled reference to the Satan of the prologue.[11] If this be so, then this would constitute one of the ultimate impieties of Job's speeches. God is cast in the role of the Satan (cf. 1 Pet 5:8).

16:10-11 In these verses Job returns to the social implications of his suffering. He portrays himself as an object of **scorn**. They **open their mouth to jeer** (not to "gape," RSV) at Job (cf. Ps 35:21; Lam 2:16; Isa 57:4). This gesture, along with **striking the cheek**, is intended to insult and disgrace (cf. 1 Kgs 22:24; Micah 4:14[5:1]). In the

---

[8]Habel makes a comparison between God and the bloodthirsty goddess Anath in the myths of Canaan. Cf. also Hos 5:14; 6:1; and J. Hempel, "Jahwegleichnisse der israelitischen Propheten," pp. 74-104.

[9]The term 'aph can also mean "nose" or "snout." Such may be preferable here fitting the image of a raging, biting beast.

[10]Cf., also, Lam 2:4, where the same term is used to describe God as Israel's enemy.

[11]Terrien and Hartley.

language of lament Job blames God for this humiliation. His complaint against God is tinged with a claim of injustice. It is to **evil men** and the **wicked** that God has surrendered Job. This is a direct rebuttal to the claims of the friends that God punishes the wicked (8:22b;11:20; 15:20-34).

16:12-14 Job's lament reaches its crescendo in these verses. The poetry parallels two intensive and assonant verbs, **shattered**[12] and **crushed** to punctuate the extent of God's assault against Job.[13] The image is that of a **warrior**.[14] This term (גִּבּוֹר, *gibbôr*)[15] is consistently used of Yahweh in a positive, salvific sense elsewhere in the Hebrew Bible (cf., e.g., Isa 42:13; Jer 20:11; Zeph 3:17; Ps 24:8; 78:65). But here, as is done so often in the book, the image is reversed to portray God as a violent, malevolent assaulter of the innocent. This is God as storm trooper (Clines) in a full-bore attack upon Job.[16] This attack came upon an unsuspecting Job (**All was well with me**). The passage abounds with other militaristic metaphors. Seizing the enemy **by the neck** is equivalent to defeating him (Gen 49:8; Exod 23:27). Job has been made the **target** of the celestial **archers** who, at God's command, pierce Job's vital organs, leaving him mortally wounded.[17] All of this is said in direct rebuttal to Eliphaz's claim that Job is an armed warrior attacking God (15:26).

16:15-17 Job now moves to a graphic description of his pitiful physical condition. Like a person in mourning he covers himself with **sackcloth**. This was either a large grain sack (2 Kgs 19:12; 1 Chr 21:16) or a loincloth made of coarse material (2 Sam 3:31; Jer 4:8). There is no other reference in the OT to **stitching** such a garment. Perhaps it refers to his shaping of the garment as permanent attire,

---

[12]The verb פָּרַר II is used elsewhere of conquering the Sea (Ps 74:13) and shattering the earth (Isa 24:19).

[13]וַיְפַרְפְּרֵנִי (*wayᵉpharpᵉrēnî*) and וַיְפַצְפְּצֵנִי (*wayᵉphaṣpᵉṣēnî*).

[14]With Dhorme. Peake understands the imagery to be that of a wrestler and Driver that of a wild beast.

[15]Some scholars argue that this characterization of Yahweh as Israel's warrior God may owe its origin to Canaanite mythology. Cf. Cross, *Canaanite Myth and Hebrew Epic*, ch. 2.

[16]For a discussion of this imagery cf. R. de Vaux, "Single Combat in the Old Testament," in *The Bible and the Ancient Near East*, trans. J. McHugh (Garden City, NY: Doubleday, 1971).

[17]This recalls the earlier image of El Shaddai, the archer, similar to the Canaanite god Reshef (cf. 6:4).

believing he would wear it to the grave. The word for **skin** (גֶּלֶד, *geled*) may refer to crusty scabs that have formed over his sores.[18] Broken and humiliated, Job has **buried** his **brow** (lit., "horn") **in the dust.**[19] All of this suffering has taken an emotional toll on Job. With **dark shadows ringing his eyes** and a **face red with weeping** he awaits his inevitable death.[20] But Job's deepest pain has yet to be described. All of this has been done to him in spite of the fact that his **hands have been free of violence** and his **prayer is pure.** These words address the real source of his grief. It is more than the loss of his children and his health that undoes him. It is the fact that God has wrought this against him without any moral grounds. The **hands** (lit., "palms") are often used to signify innocence (Ps 7:4[3]; Gen 20:5). **Free of violence** here probably refers more broadly to innocent of "unscrupulous infringement of the personal rights of others."[21] Job's **prayer** refers to his piety in the sense of the opening portrait of Job the righteous in the prologue.[22] The irony of Job's complaint is thus complete. Job the nonviolent has been attacked by a violent God, and Job the pious has been abandoned by God to the wicked (Clines).

Job's Appeal to a Heavenly Witness (16:18-22)

[18]**"O earth, do not cover my blood; / may my cry never be laid to rest! /** [19]**Even now my witness is in heaven, / my advocate is on high. /** [20]**My intercessor is my friend**[a] **/ as my eyes pour out tears to God; /** [21]**on behalf of a man he pleads with God / as a man pleads for his friend.**

[22]**"Only a few years will pass / before I go on the journey of no return.**

---

[18]Cf. A. Cohen, "Studies in Hebrew Lexicography," *AJSL* 40 (1923-24): 167 and J.V. Kinnier Wilson "Leprosy in Ancient Mesopotamia," *RA* 60 (1966): 47-58.

[19]Conversely, "raising one's horn" is a symbol of victory and confidence (Ps 73:5-6[4-5]).

[20]Cf. T. Collins, "The Physiology of Tears in the Old Testament: Part I," *CBQ* 33 (1971): 18-38.

[21]H. Haag, *TDOT*, 4:478-487; Cf. G. von Rad, *Old Testament Theology*, trans. by D.M.G. Stalker (New York: Harper, 1962–65), 1:170.

[22]Against Gray, who emends "my way," and Habel, who sees it as "formal plea" in a legal sense.

16:18 Job concludes his speech with a cry for vindication. It is first directed to the **earth**. Interpreters have suggested a variety of reasons why Job invokes the earth. We should note first that such language is not unique in the Old Testament. Isaiah (1:2) and Micah (6:1-2), using the metaphor of a legal suit, call upon "heaven" and "earth" as witness to God's legal proceedings against his people. Since the language here is also that of the ancient courtroom, this alone is sufficient to account for this rhetorical device.[23] **Do not cover my blood** recalls Genesis 4:10 where the innocent spilled blood of Abel cries out for vindication. Upon this the interpreters agree. There is a debate, though, over just what kind of vindication Job envisages. Some connect this passage to 14:13-17 where Job longed for a postmortem vindication from Sheol (Andersen, Clines).[24] Fohrer and Habel, by contrast, argue that Job is crying for this-worldly vindication from a celestial court presided over by a heavenly witness (v. 19). To Fohrer the **cry** of verse18b is a cry for help, that is, while Job is still alive (as in Hab 1:2; Jer 20:8). To Clines it is a cry for vindication after death ("let the cry of it [Job's innocent blood] wander through the world" [citing Moffatt]). Whichever is correct, be it noted that "earth" (v. 18) and "heaven" (v. 19) are placed in contrast by Job, not in tandem (as the interpreters tend to do). This comports with one of the consistent rhetorical models of the book — the contrast between the events of earth and the events of heaven (cf. the prologue).

16:19-22 These verses present us with one of the most challenging interpretive issues of the book. Just who is Job's **witness in heaven**, his **advocate on high**?[25] There are four major views that have been proposed. 1) Job's witness is a rival deity who will oppose the God (Eloah) who is unfairly persecuting Job.[26] This view can be dismissed quickly as completely incompatible with the monotheistic theology of the book. The God of the book of Job is consistently

---

[23]This technique was also used in the world surrounding ancient Israel (Cf. D. Hillers, *Covenant* [Baltimore: John's Hopkins Press, 1969], pp. 37, 125ff.)

[24]Andersen suggests that the reader consider heaven and earth here as "sleepless watchers of men's actions and guardians of ancient covenants."

[25]Cf. 9:33; 19:25-27; and W. Irwin, "Job's Redeemer," *JBL* 81 (1962): 217-224.

[26]J.B. Curtis, "On Job's Witness in Heaven," *JBL* 102 (1983): 549-562.

presented as without peer or competitor. 2) Job's witness is an angel in the heavenly court.[27] Though Eliphaz has denied the possibility of such an angelic intercessor (5:1), Elihu does entertain the idea (33:23) of an "angel on his [Job's] side." As Habel points out already, we have been introduced to such a heavenly figure in the person of Job's accuser, the Satan of the prologue.[28] Job's angel-advocate would constitute a rhetorical opposite to the Satan and serve to help Job find deliverance from the devastation set in motion by this accusatory angel. This would fit the model of Zechariah 3:1 where an "angel of Yahweh" defends the high priest Joshua against the charges of the Satan. 3) Job's witness is God himself. Though logically difficult, this view has many advocates.[29] Gordis, appealing to the lack of delineation of personalities in Ancient Near Eastern thinking, argues that Job believes that the God of terror and the God of mercy are one and the same and that the righteousness and love of God will eventually rein in his malevolence.[30] In support of this view it should be noted that in the Old Testament it is usually God who avenges innocent blood (v. 18; cf. Gen 4:8-12; Isa 26:21; Ezek 24:6-9) and that, in the end, it is God himself who does rise as Job's vindicator (42:7-9). As Fohrer notes, the idea of God giving thought "to his own character and recognizing his true duty as protector of justice," is also entertained in Jeremiah 31:20 and Hosea 11:8-9. As Habel notes, however, the language of the context seems to envision a third party. Job's **witness** (עֵד, *'ēd*) is an **advocate** (שָׂהֵד, *śāhēd*; cf. 33:23) and an **intercessor** (מֵלִיץ, *mēlîṣ*; cf. 9:32-35) who will **plead with God as a man pleads for his friend**. This language makes it difficult to see this as something God does against himself. 4) Job's witness is his legal case against God. This view, suggested by JB ("my own lament is my advocate before God") and taken up by Clines, argues that Job's own words will take up his case before God.[31] Like innocent blood staining the earth (v. 18) Job's claims against God will eventually force God to give him a day in court that

---

[27]S. Mowinckel, "Hiobs *go'el* und Zeuge im Himmel," in *Vom Alten Testament, BZAW* 41 (Giessen: Töpelmann, 1925), pp. 207-212.

[28]Habel, *Job*, p. 275.

[29]Cf., e.g., Dhorme, Fohrer, Rowley.

[30]Gordis, *Book of Job*, p. 527, n. 15.

[31]Clines, *Job*, pp. 389-391. Clines translates v. 20a, "It is my cry that is my spokesman."

will result in his vindication. Though a novel idea, there is precedence in the context for something other than a distinct personality functioning as a "witness." In verse 8b Job says that his own "gauntness rises up and testifies against (him)." Similarly, it may be argued, his protest of innocence now rises up to testify on his behalf.

Whomever or whatever Job appeals to as his "witness" he does so with a sense of urgency. The expression **few years**,[32] literally "years of number" refers to a time of relative insignificance. By comparison, that which "cannot be numbered" is endless (5:9; 9:10). Job believes that his days on earth are numbered and death inevitably awaits him. The **journey of no return** is the road to Sheol. A similar idea is found in Babylonian literature where the underworld is called "the land of no return."[33]

---

[32]Nothing should be made of his choice of the word "years" (against Clines). It does not suggest that Job imagines several more years of his current condition (cf. 17:1).

[33]*ANET*, p. 106.

JOB 17

2. Job's Reply to Eliphaz (16:1–17:16, continued)

Job's Complaint against His Accusers (17:1-10)

[1]My spirit is broken, / my days are cut short, / the grave awaits me. / [2]Surely mockers surround me; / my eyes must dwell on their hostility.

[3]"Give me, O God, the pledge you demand. / Who else will put up security for me? / [4]You have closed their minds to understanding; / therefore you will not let them triumph. / [5]If a man denounces his friends for reward, / the eyes of his children will fail.

[6]"God has made me a byword to everyone, / a man in whose face people spit. / [7]My eyes have grown dim with grief; / my whole frame is but a shadow. / [8]Upright men are appalled at this; / the innocent are aroused against the ungodly. / [9]Nevertheless, the righteous will hold to their ways, / and those with clean hands will grow stronger.

[10]"But come on, all of you, try again! / I will not find a wise man among you.

17:1 This verse more naturally belongs with chapter 16 and completes the thought of 16:18-22. When Job says, **my spirit is broken**, by **spirit** (רוּחַ, *rûaḥ*), he does not mean either his soul or his emotions, but the life-force that gives him vitality. Used with the verb **broken** (חָבַל, *ḥābal*) it represents a characterization of his physical condition, not his spiritual one.[1] His existence is in jeopardy and his days are **cut short**. This expression (זָעַךְ, *z'k*) occurs only here in the Hebrew Bible and is commonly understood to be related to דָּעַךְ

---

[1]R. Albertz and C. Westermann, *THAT*, 2:726-753. Cf. also J Gamberone, "*chabal* III," *TDOT*, 4:185-186.

(*dā'ak*, "extinguish"), which is read in some manuscripts (cf. *BHS*).[2]
Now only the **grave awaits** (him). The noun **grave** (קְבָרִים, *qᵊbārîm*)
is plural in the Hebrew, perhaps suggesting "graveyard, cemetery."

17:2 In this verse Job returns to his condemnation of the unfair
treatment he is receiving at the hands of his accusers. He begins by
acknowledging the social implications of his desperate condition
referring to the **mockers** who **surround** him. In the Psalms this
expression refers to the response of the wicked to the suffering of
the righteous (Ps 22:8[7]; 35:15-16) and such an idea would fit here.
Most immediately Job is probably referring censoriously to the
friends who have accused him of wrongdoing.

17:3-5 Job now personally addresses God. Though **O God** (NIV)
does not actually appear in the Hebrew text, the pronoun **you** makes
it clear that Job is speaking to God. Less clear is actually what Job is
asking. Most emend the difficult Hebrew text (which literally says
"take me on pledge" to read "set my pledge with you."[3] A **pledge** was
a piece of personal property (or even a person) put on deposit with
a creditor as guarantee that the borrower would repay the debt (Gen
38:17ff; Deut 24:10-14).[4] The debt Job has accumulated is presumably his perceived sin against God which has resulted in his suffering. Is Job asking God to put up pledge for him (since no one else
can or will, v. 17:3b)[5] or to accept some kind of pledge from Job?[6]
Those who read with the NIV and argue the former tend to see Job's
"witness" as God himself. That is to say, Job is appealing to the
mercy of God to buy him some time until that same God will ultimately vindicate him. This, of course, is exactly what God finally
does. Verse 4 gives Job's perception of just why the friends remain
unsympathetic to him. God has **closed their minds to understanding**. God's power to do this is also addressed in 39:17 (cf. also Isa
6:10; 44:18). Job is making God responsible for both his undeserved
suffering and the seeming inability of the friends to sympathize with

---

[2]The JPS translation renders "run out."
[3]Reading עֶרְבֹנִי (*'ērᵊbōnî*) for MT עָרְבֵנִי (*'orbēnî*). Cf. Gordis.
[4]Cf. G.A. Barrois, "Debt," "Surety," *IDB*, 1:809-810; 4:446.
[5]NIV, Hartley; NEB, "Be thou [God] my surety with thyself."
[6]Note Clines' translation of verse 3: "Keep my pledge close by you [O
God], for there is no one who will stand surety for me." Clines argues that
Job himself or his declarations of innocence will constitute his "pledge."

him. The meaning of the phrase **therefore you will not let them triumph** hinges upon the rendering of a difficult Hebrew text. The NIV understands the friends to be the object of the verb **triumph** (רום, *rwm*) suggesting that the result of God's blinding of the friends is their ultimate defeat. Others take the verb as a passive and understand it to mean "you [God] are not exalted." If this be so, then Job is telling God that this confusion of the friends does God no good.[7] Verse 5 can best be explained as a proverb condemning those who act with ulterior motives and is directed at the friends. Like a false witness who **denounces his friends for reward**, the friends have acted like greedy mercenaries against Job, but it will not succeed.

17:6-7 In the language of lament Job returns to the theme of verse 2 to characterize the social implication of his suffering. Job depicts himself as a **byword** (Ps 69:12-13[11-12]). By this is meant that Job's situation has been turned into a popular saying, something like "a sinner as great as Job" (Gray). Job's scandalous circumstance is known to **everyone** (lit., "the peoples"), not just his family and friends. To **spit** in someone's **face** is one of the strongest expressions of contempt in Job's world (Deut 25:9; Isa 50:6; Matt 26:67; 27:30). Job has become an object of scorn. Next, the physical dimensions of Job's suffering are revisited (cf. 17:1). His **eyes have grown dim with grief**. In the OT the eyes are commonly said to grow dim because of advancing age (Gen 27:1; Deut 34:7). This particular expression is akin to the language of Psalm 6:8[7]. Job's emotional stress has sapped him of his strength. His suffering has left his **frame a shadow**.[8] He has wasted away to nothing.

17:8-10 These lines are so difficult to understand (especially vv. 9-10) in their present context that many scholars view them as misplaced.[9] They interrupt the language of lament begun in verses 6-7 and picked up again in verse 11. Yet they can be understood as coming from the mouth of Job as a further condemnation of the friends in several different ways. One way is to follow NIV and take verse 9

---

[7]So Gordis. Another option is offered by Dhorme who reads "their hand is not raised." This is said to continue the thought of v. 3b that the friends will not strike Job's hand in pledge.

[8]An alternative reading, "all shapes seem to me like shadows" (NJPS), has this line carrying on the thought of v. 7a, suggesting that Job cannot see well with his dim eyes.

[9]So Duhm, de Wilde, Fohrer, Gray.

as contrasting verse 8. In this interpretation the **upright men** and the **innocent** of verse 8 are the truly pious, appropriately indignant against the abuse of Job by ungodly mockers (v. 2). By contrast (**nevertheless**, v. 9)[10] the **righteous** and **those with clean hands** (v. 9) are sarcastic characterizations of the friends whose status as pious men is strengthened by their unsympathetic condemnation of Job. It is also possible to see both of these verses as referring to the friends. Verse 8 would then be describing their initial reaction to **this** (Job's suffering) as evidenced in their first meeting (2:11-12) and verse 9 their subsequent role as judgmental accusers and pious critics of Job (Job 4ff). Yet another possibility is that Job is simply quoting a traditional characterization of the pious (vv. 8-9), and then sarcastically contrasting it to the behavior of the friends (v. 10). The **you** of verse 10 may refer to the friends and other mockers whom, Job insists, are **not wise**, that is, not truly pious. This interpretation fits nicely with the defiant tone of verse 10, **But come on, all of you, try again!** The truly pious **grow stronger** in their response to the ungodly, but Job's critics are only growing weaker as the inadequacy of their arguments becomes more and more obvious.[11]

Job's Loss of Hope in the Face of Death (17:11-16)

[11]**My days have passed, my plans are shattered, / and so are the desires of my heart. /** [12]**These men turn night into day; / in the face of darkness they say, 'Light is near.' /** [13]**If the only home I hope for is the grave,ª / if I spread out my bed in darkness, /** [14]**if I say to corruption, 'You are my father,' / and to the worm, 'My mother' or 'My sister,' /** [15]**where then is my hope? / Who can see any hope for me? /** [16]**Will it go down to the gates of deathª? / Will we descend together into the dust?"**

ª 13, 16 Hebrew Sheol

17:11-12 Though Job is defiant toward his accusers, he is yet resigned to his ultimate fate. Returning to the language of lament he

---

[10]Reading the *waw* as a conversive rather than a conjunction.

[11]Davidson offers yet another explanation. He understands Job to be referring to himself as "upright," "righteous," and "innocent." He sees this as Job's determination to hold on to his righteousness even though opposed by God or the traditionally pious and believing that ultimately he will prevail.

ends his speech with a poignant cry of hopelessness. Job's life has miscarried. His **plans are shattered**. Though elsewhere, the term for **plans** (זִמָּה, *zimmāh*) refers negatively to "device" or "wickedness,"[12] it does not here. It refers more neutrally to Job's life agenda that has been rudely interrupted by his undeserved suffering. This is also what is meant by **desires of my heart**. All of Job's hopes and dreams for the future have been swept away by his expected untimely death. The change to third person plural in verse 12 (**these** [**men**]) suggests that Job is quoting what the friends have been saying. Throughout their speeches they have repeatedly suggested to Job that his suffering is merely temporary and that upon his repentance the **night** and **darkness** of his present condition will soon turn to **day** (5:17-26; 8:20-22; 11:13-19).[13]

17:13-16 For Job this has been a false hope. In his future he sees nothing but the **grave** (lit., "Sheol"). Here Job seems to be returning to the theme of chapter 14 where he envisions Sheol as his final resting place. Verses 13-14 are the apodosis of a conditional sentence (**if**) and verses 15-16 constitute the protasis in the form of rhetorical questions. In his despair Job imagines Sheol as his **home**[14] (or "house"; cf. Ps 49:12[11]; Eccl 12:5) complete with a family of **corruption**[15] (bodily decay) and consuming **worms**. Three times in this concluding section Job speaks of his **hope** (קְוֹה, *qwh*; 13a,15a,15b). As to how the grave can be Job's hope, one need only recall his opening soliloquy where he celebrates the prospect of death as relief from his suffering (3:13-14,17-19). But something else seems to be at work here. Whereas earlier the rest that death would bring was viewed positively by Job, now it is viewed negatively. As the rhetorical questions of verse 15 imply, the prospect of dying means the end of Job's hope — hope for health, hope for family, or, perhaps most importantly for Job, hope for vindication. The final wistful question

---

[12]S. Steingrimsson, "*zmm*," *TDOT*, 4:87-90.

[13]Dhorme and Gordis see this language as referring to Job's plans and that v. 12 is a continuation of v. 11. In other words, Job's "plans" and "desires" that "night would turn to day" and that "light would be near" have been crushed.

[14]On the idea of Sheol as a "house" cf. J. Reider, "Contributions to the Scriptural Text," *HUCA* (1952–53): 102-103; E.M. Meyers, "Secondary Burials in Palestine," *BA* 33 (1979): 2-29.

[15]Or "pit" (שַׁחַת, *šaḥath*) cf. KB, BDB.

of verse 16 tantalizingly raises the prospect of some postmortem vindication that Job entertained in 14:7,14. Does death end all hope or is there still an opportunity for vindication beyond Sheol? The open-ended nature of the question may leave room for the future hope of faith.[16] The most natural reading of the text, however, seems to favor a "no" answer to all of these rhetorical questions and has Job ending his speech with the lament that death will end his hope. This also fits the pattern of his earlier speeches (7:21b; 10:21-22; 14:20-22) where Job bemoans the fact that death ends all.

----

[16]So Habel.

JOB 18

3. Bildad's Second Speech (18:1-21)

Bildad's second speech is devoted to the fate of the wicked, by
now a well-worn theme. Why are the friends so preoccupied with
this subject? A clue may be found in Bildad's question, "Is the earth
to be abandoned for your sake?" (v. 4). The friends have been listening to Job. They fully understand the implications of his arguments: "God is not just; he does not see to it that people get what
they deserve." Reasoning from the particular (Job's personal experience) to the universal (the moral order by which God runs the
world), Job has concluded that God's governance of the universe is
not built upon a model of retributive justice. Such a position, Bildad
believes, will not only prove disastrous to Job but misleading to any
who hear it (an audience?). Such a view is also personally threatening to the friends (as defenders of traditional theology). It must be
rebutted.

Bildad's reply breaks into two parts: a personal criticism of Job
(18:2-4); and a discourse on the fate of the wicked (18:5-21). The
dominant literary genre is that of wisdom discourse. Also present
are mythopoetic images of Sheol.[1] The language shows connection
with other parts of the Hebrew Bible, most notably Proverbs[2] and
Psalms.[3] Certain themes in the speech relate to some of Job's earlier
assertions: light and darkness (3:4-5; 10:22; 17:12); trapped/hunted
(6:4; 10:13-16; 13:27); terror (7:14; 9:34; 13:11,21); using the rhetorical technique of reversal (of the way Job has used them).

---

[1]Cf. Westermann, *Structure of the Book of Job*, p. 85; N.M. Sarna, "The
Mythological Background of Job 18," *JBL* 82 (1963): 315-318.
[2]Prov 10:24a; 11:5b; 12:13; 13:9b; 14:11; 21:12; 22:5; 24:16b,20.
[3]Ps 7:15-17[14-16]; 10:2-11; 49:14-15[13-14]; 64:2-10[3-11].

Bildad's Criticism of Job (18:1-4)

¹Then Bildad the Shuhite replied:
²"When will you end these speeches? / Be sensible, and then we
can talk. / ³Why are we regarded as cattle / and considered stupid
in your sight? / ⁴You who tear yourself to pieces in your anger, /
is the earth to be abandoned for your sake? / Or must the rocks
be moved from their place?

18:1-3 Typical of the speeches, Bildad's initial words come in the
form of a personal attack upon Job. **When**[4] **will you end**[5] **these
speeches?** The **you** is plural in the Hebrew and this has spawned
numerous suggestions regarding to whom Bildad is referring.[6] Perhaps Bildad is grouping Job with the wicked, whose fate he will go
on to describe (Ewald, Pope). Perhaps it is a mark of politeness at
the beginning of the speech (Guillaume, Diaz). The context makes it
obvious that Job is the primary one being addressed. Bildad's sharp
question accuses Job of being verbose, a trait which proves him not
to be among the "wise." Not only are Job's words too many, they
also lack sense. **Be sensible**, Bildad says, **then we can talk**. Bildad
also takes exception to Job's intellectual arrogance. He resents the
fact that Job is talking down to the friends, treating them like **dumb
cattle**. This may be a direct reference to Job's earlier suggestion that
the friends "Ask the cattle and they will teach you" (12:7). Job himself had earlier objected to what he felt was an intellectual arrogance
on the part of the friends (12:3; 13:1,2).

18:4 In Bildad's eyes, Job is behaving in a foolishly self-destructive manner. Out of control and driven by rage he **tears** himself **to
pieces**. Job had just blamed God for "tearing" him in his divine
anger (16:9). Bildad counters by asserting his anguish is his own
doing rather than God's. By railing against the Sovereign who controls his destiny Job can only expect to hasten his own disintegra-

---

[4]Lit., "How long," (עַד־אָנָה, 'ad-'ānāh). Bildad began his first speech this
way (8:2). Job will similarly begin his next reply (19:2).

[5]Pope connects this term קִנְצֵי (qinṣê, "an end of") to Akk. qinṣu ("trap"),
suggesting that Job is being accused of setting a trap with his words.

[6]For a survey of the options cf. Clines, *Job*, pp. 409-410. Many interpreters,
following LXX, change the plurals to singulars in vv. 2,3.

tion. It is Job, Bildad insists, who is behaving like a dumb animal biting himself. The pair of rhetorical questions that follow demonstrate that Bildad has a handle on the theological and philosophical implications of Job's protests against God. Job's claim of God's injustice threatens the entire order of the universe. **Is the earth to be abandoned for your sake? Or must the rocks be removed from their place?** Bildad is saying that "If the retributive order of the moral universe is abandoned, as Job demands it should be for his sake, the cosmic order of stability goes with it" (Clines). This connection of moral order and cosmic order is interesting and is echoed several times in the book. Most notably the speeches of Elihu (cf. Job 36–37) and the speeches of God (Job 38–41) make a similar connection. The idea here is that the same God who creates order in the physical universe also creates order in the moral universe. To the friends, of course, retributive justice is that order. Does Job actually expect this divinely ordained order to be reversed for his sake? Such an expectation, Bildad asserts, is arrogant insanity and brings Job to the brink of self-destruction.

The Fate of the Wicked (18:5-21)

[5]**"The lamp of the wicked is snuffed out; / the flame of his fire stops burning. / [6]The light of his tent becomes dark; / the lamp beside him goes out. / [7]The vigor of his step is weakened; / his own schemes throw him down. / [8]His feet thrust him into a net / and he wanders into its mesh. / [9]A trap seizes him by the heel; / a snare holds him fast. / [10]A noose is hidden for him on the ground; / a trap lies in his path. / [11]Terrors startle him on every side / and dog his every step. / [12]Calamity is hungry for him; / disaster is ready for him when he falls. / [13]It eats away parts of his skin; / death's firstborn devours his limbs. / [14]He is torn from the security of his tent / and marched off to the king of terrors. / [15]Fire resides[a] in his tent; / burning sulfur is scattered over his dwelling. / [16]His roots dry up below / and his branches wither above. / [17]The memory of him perishes from the earth; / he has no name in the land. / [18]He is driven from light into darkness / and is banished from the world. / [19]He has no offspring or descendants among his people, / no survivor where once he lived. / [20]Men of the west are appalled at his fate; / men of the east are seized with horror. /**

²¹**Surely such is the dwelling of an evil man; / such is the place of one who knows not God."**

ª*15* Or *Nothing he had remains*

This part of Bildad's speech is closely related to Eliphaz's speech on the same subject (Job 15). Both speeches are designed to censure Job for what the friends consider to be his irreverent attitude and perverse speech. Whereas in his earlier speech Bildad had offered Job some hope of restoration (8:20-22), this time no such reassurances are entertained. Interpreters differ over the degree to which Bildad's words refer specifically to Job or more generally to the wicked as a group who will reap God's judgment,[7] but several statements in the speech are especially suited to Job's particular condition (vv. 11,13,15b,19). It is curious to note (with Weiser and others) that reference to God is strikingly sparse in this speech with Bildad mentioning him only at the end, and this probably in the quotation of a proverb, "such is the place of one who knows not God" (v. 21). Some commentators see this as an indication of Bildad's view that retributive justice is a self-regulating mechanism with God having established it and guaranteeing it.[8]

18:5-6 Bildad's opening portrayal of the fate of the wicked is a stock phrase of conventional Hebrew wisdom: **The lamp of the wicked is snuffed out** (Prov 13:9b; 20:20; 24:20). Light/darkness are used throughout the book of Job as symbols of life/death (3:5,20), gain/loss (22:28; 15:30). Eliphaz had earlier made a similar claim about the wicked, "He despairs of escaping the darkness" (15:22). The parallel **The light in his tent becomes dark** does not, as some interpreters offer, suggest a nomadic setting for the book, but should be seen as merely a metaphor for the habitation of the wicked. So also should be understood the phrase, **the lamp beside him[9] goes out.**[10]

---

[7]The Septuagint understood this part of the speech to be a pious wish for the destruction of the wicked (cf. G. Gerleman, *Studies in the Septuagint: I. Book of Job* [Lunds Universitets Arsskrift: N.F. Avd. 1. Bd 43. Nr2; Lund: Gleerup, 1946], pp. 50-52.

[8]Cf., e.g., Clines, *Job,* p. 413.

[9]Or "above him," (עָלָיו, *'ālāyw*).

[10]On this subject cf. R.H. Smith, "The Household Lamps of Palestine in Old Testament Times," *BA* 27 (1964): 1-31.

18:7 As is so often the case in Hebrew rhetoric, Bildad now switches metaphors, **The vigor of his step is weakened**. By "is weakened" Bildad probably means "is shortened."[11] The shortening of the wicked man's stride is yet another way to portray his vulnerability and fading strength. It may also portray his being hemmed in or ensnared as the following context suggests (cf. also Ps 18:37[36]; Prov 4:12). Bildad depicts the wicked man as on a journey that he begins with vigorous, confident strides. **His own schemes,**[12] however, **throw him down.**[13] No evil man will enjoy success forever. His self-determinism will not sustain him in the end.

18:8-10 In these verses Bildad uses six different terms for **trap** to drive home his claim that the wicked face an inescapable punishment. Like a minefield the wicked man's path is strewn with dangerous snares. The terms used here describe a wide variety of devices used to snare birds and game (cf. Hos 7:12; Ezek 19:8). The **net** is suspended above the ground and collapses on unsuspecting prey (cf. Ps 9:16[15]; 35:7-8). The **mesh** is spread over a pit into which the prey fall. The **noose** is set to spring upward when an animal strays into it. As to exactly what these "traps" are in the wicked man's life the interpreters disagree. It is possible, looking at the following verses, to regard them all to be characterizations of the inescapable death that all wicked men will face.

18:11-13 Surrounded by traps the wicked man is **startled** by **terrors**. These "terrors" may be feelings of dread (Hartley) or remorse (Dhorme) aroused by the prospect of meeting the "King of Terrors" (v. 14), death itself. A number of scholars, comparing this language to that of the Canaanite myths, have suggested that the terrors Job is referring to are demonic forces unleashed by the ruler of the underworld.[14] If this be so, this would be another example of Job's use of mythology as a rhetorical tool. The context suggests, however, that he is referring more directly to disaster (v. 12) and disease (v. 13), two of the "terrors" that actually precipitate death. As is so often the case in the Hebrew Bible, these threatening forces come

---

[11]צָרַר (ṣārar), "narrow, restricted, confined."

[12]עֲצָתוֹ (ʿăṣāthô); cf. 38:2. G.R. Driver ("Mistranslations," *ExpTim* 57 [1945-46]: 192-193) argues that it means "disobedience" (cf. NEB).

[13]Reading with LXX; cf. Prov 4:12; Ps 64:9[8].

[14]Cf. Sarna, "Mythological Background," pp. 315-319.

in pairs (cf., e.g., Ps 25:21; 43:3).[15] The language of verse 12 is similar to that of Jeremiah's prediction of the fate of Pashhur, "terrors
on every side." There, as here, some threatening physical circumstance is what is envisioned.[16] The idea of death as **hungry** for its
prey is present elsewhere in the Hebrew Bible (Deut 32:24; Hab 2:5;
Ps 141:7).[17] Like a ravenous beast, death **eats away**[18] the wicked
man's **skin**. This is probably a direct reference to the physical disease which has afflicted Job. The parallel **death's firstborn devours
his limbs** is also probably a reference to the effects of disease.[19] For
Bildad, Job's devastated physical condition is proof that he is among
the "wicked."

18:14-15 In the biblical world a man's **tent** was a symbol of his
ease and security. Conversely, the destruction of one's tent is often
the symbol of his violent death (4:21; Isa 33:20). The image of being
torn from one's **tent** and **marched off to the king of terrors** is a mil-
itary/political one. It depicts a violent entry of a man's domicile by
agents of some tyrant to drag him away to some terrible, irresistible
fate. In this case the "king of terrors" is death itself, a possible allusion

---

[15]For a possible mythological background cf. H.L. Ginsberg, "Baal's Two
Messengers," *BASOR* 95 (1944): 25-30.

[16]The Hebrew at the beginning of v. 12 is very difficult, spawning a number of translations: "His strength is hunger-bitten" (Terrien); "with his
wealth he is famished" (Pope); "his progeny hunger" (NJPS); "he is hungry
amid his wealth" (Dhorme); NIV follows the suggestion of BHK's emendation, "(his) trouble is hungry for him" (cf. Jer 42:14). Pope and Habel, following Dahood, see in this a title of the death god Mot, "Hungry One" (cf.
Dahood, *Psalms I*, AB, p. 203).

[17]Cf. T.H. Gaster, *Thespis* (Garden City, NY: Doubleday, 1961), p. 206,
who regards this to be a mythological motif of the Canaanite death god,
Mot.

[18]Also difficult in the Hebrew. RSV, NEB, and JB follow Dhorme and others in revocalizing the text to read "By disease his skin is eaten."

[19]Dhorme thinks the "firstborn of death" refers to plague, comparable to
the Babylonian plague god Namtaru. He also sites the Arab reference to diseases as "the daughters of death." Hitzig thinks it refers to starvation. Some
scholars (Pope, Habel) believe the expression "first born of death" (מָוֶת,
mûth) should be read "firstborn of Mot" (the Canaanite god of the underworld) and refers to death itself. Cf. W.L. Michel, *The Ugaritic Texts and the
Mythological Expression in the Book of Job*, Ph.D. diss. University of Wisconsin,
1970. For another view cf. J.B. Burns, "The Identity of Death's First-Born,"
VT 27 (1987): 363-364.

to the Canaanite god of the underworld, Mot.[20] The **fire**[21] mentioned in verse 15 is not the fire and brimstone that rained down on Sodom and Gomorrah but subterranean fire such as that which destroyed Dathan and Abiram (Num 15:31-35; cf. Ps 106:17-18). Fire, like darkness, is associated with the underworld (Sheol) as an agent of death. Coupled with **burning sulphur** (brimstone) it is a symbol of supernatural destruction (Ps 11:6; Isa 30:33).

18:16-19 Through a series of proverblike sayings, Bildad now portrays the total annihilation of the wicked man. The death of **root** and **branch** as a metaphor of total destruction is well known in biblical times (cf. Ezek 17:9; Mal 3:19[4:1]). The opposites (merismus) of **below** and **above** complete the all-encompassing nature of the wicked man's demise. Verses 17-19 address the two greatest tragedies which could befall a man in the ancient world: to be forgotten by posterity (Ps 109:15) and to die without progeny (Ps 9:6[5]). Both were believed to threaten one's immortality.[22] To be remembered and leave behind a good reputation was considered a great blessing (Prov 10:7). The wicked man is deprived of both. **Memory**[23] of him **perishes from the earth** and **he has no name in the land**. A man's ultimate memorial, of course, was the perpetuation of his name through his **offspring** or **descendants**.[24] In ancient times descendants not only carried on the name of the father but perpetuated his memory through memorials that sometimes involved ancestor worship. There was even a popular belief that a person literally "lived on" through his offspring. So, to die without a **survivor** was to cease to exist altogether. These characterizations of the wicked come

---

[20]Cf. note 14.

[21]Reading with Dahood מבל (*mbl*) = Akk. *Nablu*, Ug. *Nblat*. Dahood, "Some Northwest-Semitic Words in Job," *Bib* 38 (1957): 79.

[22]Cf. C. Brichto, "Kith, Kin, Cult and Afterlife—A Biblical Complex," *HUCA* 44 (1973): 22ff.; Childs, *Memory and Tradition in Israel*; W. Schottroff, *"Gedenken" im Alten Orient und im Alten Testament*, WMANT 50 (Neukirchen-Vluyn: Neukirchener Verlag, 1964).

[23]זָכַר (*zākar*) can refer to more than remaining in the consciousness of others. It can also mean a "memorial" in the form of an inscription (2 Sam 18:18; Isa 56:5) or a written account of one's accomplishments (Neh 5:19; 6:14; 13:14,22,29,31).

[24]נִין וָנֶכֶד (*nîn wāneked*), an alliterative wordplay also found in Gen 21:23 and Isa 14:22.

painfully close to Job's actual situation. The destruction of his possessions and the reputation that has come with them threaten the
"name" he once had as the "greatest of the sons of the East." The
loss of all of his children leaves him without heir and even hope of
future existence. According to Bildad's doctrine of retribution these
disasters prove Job's guilt and seal his fate. Like all wicked men **He
is driven from light into darkness and is banished from the world**.
The "darkness" is the gloom of Sheol (17:13) and the "world" is the
land of the living from which Job and his descendants will never be
allowed to return.

18:20-21 These verses form a conclusion to Bildad's argument.
Verse 20 looks at the destiny of the wicked from the perspective of
his peers. Job will not just quietly fade away but depart in complete
disgrace. **Men of the west** and **east** (merismus for all men)[25] are
appalled at his fate. The word "appalled" is frequently used in Job
and refers to the utter shock that people feel toward some disaster
(16:7; 17:8; 21:5).[26] The perspective of verse 21 is that of Bildad's and
serves as final summary of his argument (cf. 5:27; 8:19; 20:29). It
closes his speech much in the way it began with a reference to **place**
(מָקוֹם, *māqôm*, cf. v. 4), by which he means "its appointed locus in the
order of things (28:12, 23; 38:12, 19)."[27] In God's world everything
has its appointed "place" or "destiny." For the wicked, those who
know not God, that can only be total annihilation. The fact that
Bildad does not invite Job to repent or plead for mercy here may
suggest that he believes Job's fate is already sealed.

---

[25]Cf. also UT, *'nt*, II:78. Some scholars read the Hebrew more literally to
refer to those generations "coming before" and "coming after."

[26]Cf. D.R. Hillers, "A Convention in Hebrew Literature: The Reaction to
Bad News," *ZAW* 77 (1965): 86-90.

[27]Habel, *Job*, p. 289.

JOB 19

4. Job's Reply to Bildad (19:1-29)

This famous poem is one of the most impassioned speeches of the book. It comprehensively addresses Job's disappointment with the friends, his complaint against God, and his undying hope for eventual vindication. It differs from his most recent speeches in that it does not directly address God. Rhetorically the speech is dominated by the genre of lament, with elements of legal dispute, wish, hope, and threat also present. The speech breaks down into at least three major sections: 1) Job's condemnation of the friends (2-6); 2) Job's complaint against God's destruction of his life (7-20); 3) Job's hope for a redeemer (21-29).

Job's Condemnation of the Friends (19:1-6)

¹**Then Job replied:**
²**"How long will you torment me / and crush me with your words? / ³Ten times now you have reproached me; / shamelessly you attack me. / ⁴If it is true that I have gone astray, / my error remains my concern alone. / ⁵If indeed you would exalt yourselves above me / and use my humiliation against me, / ⁶then know that God has wronged me / and drawn his net around me.**

In the pattern of Job's previous responses he begins with an indictment of the friends. Before he is through, he will accuse them of cruelty, self-exaltation at his expense, and failure to recognize the obvious fact that God has done him wrong.

19:1-3 With his opening words Job takes his criticism of the friends to a new level. The **how long,** with which he begins this reply, is a direct quote of Bildad's earlier attacks (8:2; 18:2). Job plays on Bildad's words to impugn him just as Bildad had done to Job. Earlier

Job had accused the friends of being "miserable comforters" who did him more harm than good. But here he accuses them of intentionally **tormenting** and **crushing** him (v. 2). The former term (יָנָה, *yāgāh*) addresses the mental anguish they are causing Job (cf. Lam 1:12; 3:32,33) and the latter (דָּכָא, *dikkā'*) his status in society.[1] The **ten times** of verse 3 probably should not be taken literally but as the equivalent of "full measure."[2] Their **reproach** of Job refers to their relentless attempt to discredit him as a sinner, guilty before God. Their attacks are **shameless** because they are done in total insensitivity of his suffering out of a motive of self-exaltation (v. 5).

19:4-6 Job's statement, **If it is true that I have gone astray**, should not be taken as an admission of guilt (Rowley). Job has repeatedly stated his innocence (9:21; 10:7; 16:17), and he is not contradicting that here. This statement should rather be compared with the one he made to God in 7:20, "If I have sinned, what have I done to you?" In both places he is making a hypothetical statement for the purpose of arguing the point that any offense he may have committed does not merit the totally disproportionate response he has received from God (7:20) and from the friends (19:4). The friends are treating Job as an enemy who has attacked or threatened them when, in reality, he is a victim of God's attacks and their slander.[3] Job sarcastically suggests the friends are **exalting**[4] themselves by unfairly using his **humiliation** against him. From the beginning the friends have taken the high moral ground in their condemnation of Job and defense of God (cf., e.g., 12:2; 13:3). All of this has grown out of their presumption of Job's guilt. Job, in rebuttal, restates his claim that he has not done anything against God. To the contrary, **God has wronged** him. The verb **wronged** (עִוֵּת, *'iwweth*) in legal contexts refers to an unjust decision that denies a defendant his rights (Ps 119:78; Lam 3:36). When Job adds the charge that God has

---

[1]Cf., e.g., Job 5:4; Prov 22:22, where it refers to abuse of the judicial system to attack the poor and weak.

[2]Delitzsch; cf. Num 14:22; Gen 31:7; Lev 26:26.

[3]J. Milgrom, "The Cultic ŠeGĀGĀ," pp. 115-125, argues from the term used for "gone astray" that Job is speaking only of some inadvertent or accidental sin he may have committed.

[4]Gordis and Guillaume connect הִגְדִּיל (*higdîl*, "make great") to Arab. *jadala* ("quarrel") and think Job is accusing them of unreasonable quarrelling. NIV's rendering is preferable; cf. R. Mosis, "*gadhal*," *TDOT*, 2:405.

unfairly **drawn his net around me**, he is directly refuting Bildad's claim that God "traps" the wicked (18:8-10). In reality, it is Job the innocent whom God has "netted."

Job's Complaint against God (19:7-20)

[7]**"Though I cry, 'I've been wronged!' I get no response; / though I call for help, there is no justice. / [8]He has blocked my way so I cannot pass; / he has shrouded my paths in darkness. / [9]He has stripped me of my honor / and removed the crown from my head. / [10]He tears me down on every side till I am gone; / he uproots my hope like a tree. / [11]His anger burns against me; / he counts me among his enemies.**

[12]**"His troops advance in force; / they build a siege ramp against me / and encamp around my tent. / [13]He has alienated my brothers from me; / my acquaintances are completely estranged from me. / [14]My kinsmen have gone away; / my friends have forgotten me. / [15]My guests and my maidservants count me a stranger; / they look upon me as an alien. / [16]I summon my servant, but he does not answer, / though I beg him with my own mouth. / [17]My breath is offensive to my wife; / I am loathsome to my own brothers. / [18]Even the little boys scorn me; / when I appear, they ridicule me. / [19]All my intimate friends detest me; / those I love have turned against me. / [20]I am nothing but skin and bones; / I have escaped with only the skin of my teeth.**[a]

[a]**20** Or *only my gums*

19:7 Job's lament opens with a claim of unjust treatment by God. All along Job has sought a day in court with God (9:19; 13:22). But God does not answer. The verb **cry** (צָעַק, *ṣāʿaq*) is not a cry for deliverance[5] but for vindication.[6] Job has been **wronged** (lit., "done violence"; חָמָס, *ḥāmās*) by God. Job had earlier portrayed God as a warrior who had done him "violence" (*ḥāmās*, 16:9-14). Now he is formally charging God with such a crime. God has doubly wronged Job by attacking him then denying him any legal recourse.

---

[5]As in Hab 1:2.

[6]G. von Rad, *Old Testament Theology*, 1:157, n 34; H. Stoebe, *THAT*, 1:583-587.

19:8-12 This section employs a rich diversity of images to portray God's assault against Job.[7] Like a traveler (v. 8) whose **way** has been **blocked**, Job's pilgrimage has been interrupted and frustrated by God. This is similar to Hosea's description of what God did to faithless Israel after she turned to other gods (Hos 2:8[6]). By **shrouding** Job's **path in darkness** God adds to the obstacles hindering Job's successful journey through life. The use of **darkness** here may yet be another reference to the pall that the prospect of death has put upon Job's future (cf. 18:18). Like a dethroned prince (v. 9) Job has been **stripped of** his **honor** and deprived of his **crown**.[8] Job has worn his righteousness like a garment (29:14) but through his suffering has been reduced to sackcloth (16:15). His status as the greatest of his peers has been taken from him. Like a pulverized building (v. 10a) the once impressive Job has been **torn down on every side**. This may be part of a siege metaphor picked up again in verses 11-12 (Weiser, Fohrer). Like a fallen tree (v. 10b) Job's **hope** has been **uprooted**. A tree that has been cut down can grow again from its roots (14:7-9) but for the uprooted tree there is no future. The term for **hope** (תִּקְוָה, *tiqwāh*) most commonly refers to Job's desire for vindication (cf. v. 25). Like a besieged foe (vv. 11-12) Job is relentlessly assaulted by God.[9] Returning to the image of God as a "Mighty Warrior" (cf. ch. 16), Job says God has, in overkill fashion, marshaled his forces against Job's meager **tent**.[10]

19:13-16 In a rhetorical shift Job moves from a metaphorical (vv. 7-12) to an actual description of his plight (vv. 13-20). The common theme to these verses is Job's sense of isolation and humiliation before his peers. He feels **alienated** and **estranged** from family and friends alike. Using language common to the Psalms (Ps 38:12[11]; 88:9[8]), Job laments the fact that his **brothers** (or clansmen), his **kinsmen** (lit., "near ones" or closest blood relatives) have **gone away**. In patriarchal culture the bond between kin was strong. What then is the reason for this abandonment? The answer lies in the retributive theology of the day. Someone who became ill or experienced

---

[7]Parts of this section are similar to Lamentations 3.
[8]This language does not imply that Job was actually royalty (so Terrien).
[9]Cf. Y. Yadin, *The Art of Warfare in Biblical Lands* (London: Weidenfeld and Nicolson, 1963), pp. 314-315.
[10]Perhaps an allusion to Bildad's use of "tent" (18:5-6).

some disaster was believed to be guilty of some sin that God was punishing (Ps. 32:4; 1 Sam 5:5; cf. John 9:2). Given the gravity of all that has happened to Job, his peers have concluded he must be "cursed of God." It is not just unpleasant to be around him, it is dangerous. Like the leper who passes on the other side and shouts "unclean," Job's suffering has resulted in social rejection and isolation. It is not just intimacy that Job has lost, but also respect. Those who once owed Job a debt of hospitality (his **guests**) treat him like a **stranger** and an **alien**. These latter two terms refer to the resident alien (זָר, *zār*) and the foreigner (נָכְרִי, *nokrî*). Such people were considered outsiders who had few rights and could live[11] in the society only by the good graces of some member of the clan. The Job who once extended hospitality now needs it. The portrait of the fall of the once great Job is completed by the inclusion of the **maidservant** and the **servant** in the list of those who show Job no respect. These female and male attendants who once existed to serve even the whims of their master (cf., e.g., Ps 123:2) now treat him with contempt.

19:17-20 What exactly Job means by the phrase "my spirit, wind is strange" (רוּחִי זָרָה, *rûḥî zārāh*) is unclear. NIV takes *rûaḥ* as **breath**[12] and *zārāh* as **offensive**[13] and understands this to be a description of halitosis. Most commentators agree with this rendering. Some older commentators prefer to render *rûḥî* as "my spirit" = "my life, me" (cf. 6:4; 10:12; 17:1). Understood this way, Job's relatives' rejection of Job is not over his breath but his perceived spiritual condition (cursed of God). A similar problem arises over the second half of verse 17 regarding exactly to whom Job is referring with the phrase בְּנֵי בִטְנִי (*bᵉnê biṭnî*; lit., "sons of my belly/womb"). NIV renders **my brothers** taking the phrase to mean "sons who came from the same womb as I," and this is probably correct. A number of alternative suggestions have been proposed including: 1) other children Job has fathered (by another wife/concubine); 2) grandchildren; 3) orphans whom Job has raised (cf. 31:18-19); 4) poetic hyperbole.[14] The **little**

---

[11]Cf. L. Snijders, "The Meaning of *zr*," pp. 1-154.

[12]For *rûaḥ* meaning "breath," cf. Ps 135:17.

[13]P. Wernberg-Moeller, "The Old Accusative Case Ending in Biblical Hebrew," *VT* (1954): 322-325, proposes a root *zur* III, "be abhorrent, stink." Cf., also, Blommerde, *Northwest Semitic Grammar and Job*, p. 87.

[14]Some scholars cite this as proof that the speeches and prologue/epilogue are from two different authors, one not aware of the work of the other.

boys of verse 18 are either street urchins or small children who live in Job's household. In patriarchal culture children and even young men where expected to hold their elders in the highest esteem. For Job the social order has been turned upside down. This idea is continued in verse 19 on an even sadder note. His **intimate friends** (or "men of my council") have betrayed him and **loved** ones (another term for family) have not returned his love. At his most needful time the ones he considered closest to him, in whom he has made his deepest emotional investment, have turned their backs on him. Finally (v. 20) Job ends his lament with a characterization of his broken physical condition. **I am nothing but skin and bones** (NIV) catches the sense of the Hebrew "my bones cleave to my flesh."[15] The phrase **I have escaped with only the skin of my teeth** appears nowhere else in the Hebrew Bible and has become proverbial for barely escape. **Escape** here must be taken in the sense "survive."

Job's Hope for a Redeemer (19:21-29)

[21]"Have pity on me, my friends, have pity, / for the hand of God has struck me. / [22]Why do you pursue me as God does? / Will you never get enough of my flesh?

[23]"Oh, that my words were recorded, / that they were written on a scroll, / [24]that they were inscribed with an iron tool on[a] lead, / or engraved in rock forever! / [25]I know that my Redeemer[b] lives, / and that in the end he will stand upon the earth.[c] / [26]And after my skin has been destroyed, / yet[d] in[e] my flesh I will see God; / [27]I myself will see him / with my own eyes—I, and not another. / How my heart yearns within me!

[28]"If you say, 'How we hound him, / since the root of the trouble lies in him,'[f] / [29]you should fear the sword yourselves; / for wrath will bring punishment by the sword, / and then you will know that there is judgment.[g]"

[a]24 Or *and*　　[b]25 Or *defender*　　[c]25 Or *upon my grave*　　[d]26 Or *And after I awake, / though this body has been destroyed, / then*　　[e]26 Or */apart from* [f]28 Many Hebrew manuscripts, Septuagint and Vulgate; many Hebrew manuscripts *me*　　[g]29 Or */ that you may come to know the Almighty*

---

[15]For a discussion of the expression cf. Clines, *Job*, pp. 450-452.

19:21-22 For the first time in his dialogue with the friends Job asks them to show him **pity**.[16] This constitutes a major departure from Job's demeanor toward the friends. To this point he has consistently berated them as stupid (12:2-3; 13:2), treacherous (6:15; 19:2), and dishonest (13:7). Now, to play upon their compassion seems somehow uncharacteristic and out of place. Also unusual is the content of his request. All along, it is "justice" that Job has consistently sought, not "mercy." So unexpected is this desperate cry that some interpreters take it as a sarcastic barb (Habel) or an appeal for "silence" (Clines). The expression may be understood best as an ironic accusation. It has the rhetorical effect of punctuating the failure of the friends to treat him with the consideration due him, a theme he has just addressed (vv. 13-20). This explains, then, the basis for Job's appeal in the latter half of the verse (**for the hand of God has struck me** [21b]). To offer this as a reason that the friends should give Job "pity" is nonsensical given their understanding of what God is doing in his affliction of Job. God, they believe, always acts justly, and if he has struck Job, it is surely deserved. Why should they **pity** Job for getting exactly what he deserves? That Job's words are an accusation, rather than a petition is clarified by the following verse, **Why do you pursue me as God does?** that is, unfairly, cruelly. By equating the friends with God as vicious consumers of his **flesh**, Job summarizes the substance of his entire lament (vv 1-20). He has been wronged by God and men alike.

19:23-24 Convinced that he will not get justice before he dies, Job now expresses his confidence in ultimate vindication. Verses 23-27 are some of the most discussed in the book. Challenged by linguistic difficulties and different presumptions concerning what Job (and the ancient Israelites) believed about immortality, the interpreters have offered no shortage of suggestions for the meaning of the passage. We will attempt first to understand what the Hebrew text says and then survey and critique the most widely held interpretations of what it means.

The **Oh that**,[17] with which this section begins, is a recurring phrase in Job used to announce some wish Job expresses or some

---

[16]The line literally reads: "Have pity on me, have pity on me, you, my friends . . . ." The repletion of the verb חָנֻּנִי (ḥonnunî), along with the use of the emphatic "you" (אַתֶּם, 'attem) creates a mood of urgency.

[17]מִי־יִתֵּן (mî-yittēn).

hope that he entertains. In each of the other four places where it appears, it begins an invitation for God to appear or intervene in a way that will bring some decisive end to Job's predicament. In 6:8-9 it announces Job's desperate hope that God would crush him and end his misery. In 14:13 it initiates his hope that God would hide Job in Sheol until some future time when God's wrath would pass and he could meet him on better terms. In 23:3-4 it expresses his desire to find God's dwelling where he might personally state his case. In Job's final soliloquy (31:35) it expresses his intense desire for God to hear his case. Here, too, it begins a statement of hope that he will yet have some decisive encounter with God (vv. 26-27). It becomes apparent from what follows that Job believes this encounter will result in his final vindication. The **words** that Job wants **recorded** are the arguments of the case he has been making (cf. 13:17; 32:11,14). Fearful that he might die, Job wants his claims to innocence to survive him in some permanent form. In the custom of his day he wants them **written on a scroll**[18] or, even better, **engraved in rock forever**. The phrase **inscribed with an iron tool on lead**, is difficult in the Hebrew. It literally reads "inscribed with a tool of iron and lead." NIV (cf. Moffatt) alters the text to read "iron on lead" suggesting that the lead refers not to the pen but to the tablet. It is true that lead tablets were used in antiquity.[19] An alternative suggestion, first offered by Rashi, retains the original Hebrew and argues that lead or lead paint was used to fill in the incised letters.[20] Such inscriptions were, likewise, known in ancient times.

19:25-27 These verses have proved an enigma to the interpreters and the subject of much debate.[21] **I know**, most likely means "I

---

[18]סֵפֶר (sēpher) often means "book, scroll, tablet." Pope, following Dhorme and others, connects sēpher to Akk. siparru, "copper." As the famous copper scroll of Qumran attests, copper was used as a writing material for important documents.

[19]Cf. G.R. Driver, *Semitic Writing* (Oxford: Oxford University Press, 1976), p. 84. Also A. Deissmann, *Light from the Ancient East* (London: Hodder and Stoughton, 1910), pp. 304-305.

[20]Also argued by Dillmann, Delitzsch, Duhm. Cf. also C.R. Conder, "Notes on Biblical Antiquities," *PEFQS* (1905): 155-158.

[21]For a discussion of these verses cf.: J. Speer, "Zur Exegese von Hiob 19,25-27," *ZAW* 25 (1905): 47-140; C. Bruston, "Pour l'exegese de Job 19,25-27," *ZAW* 26 (1906): 143-146; A. Hudal, "Die Auslegung von Job 19,25-27 in der katholischen Exegese," *Der Katholik* 95 (1916): 331-345; S. Mowinckel,

believe" or "I am convinced" here as it does in earlier texts (9:2,28; 10:13; 13:18). In the face of persecution by his friends and his God (v. 22) Job rises to meet his desperate plight with a deep conviction: **my Redeemer lives**. Job's choice of the term **redeemer** (גֹּאֵל, $gō'ēl$)[22] provides us our first clue to what it is that he hopes. In ancient Israelite society the $gō'ēl$ was a near kinsman of some victimized member of the clan who intervened to see that justice was done. His intervention might mean buying back family property to keep it in the clan (Lev 25:25-34; Jer 32:6-15); redeeming a family member from slavery (Lev 25:47-54); raising up an heir to inherit the estate of a dead kinsman (Ruth 3:12; 4:1-6); or avenging a murdered relative (Num 35:12,19-27; Deut 19:6,11-12; Josh 20:2-5,9). The $gō'ēl$ becomes known as the defender of the orphan and the widow, the champion of the oppressed (Prov 23:10-11). The term is sometimes used to characterize Yahweh as Israel's deliverer from the Egyptian bondage (Exod 6:6; 15:3) and the Babylonian exile (Jer 1:34). Occasionally it describes God as the rescuer of an individual from imminent death (Ps 103:4; Lam 3:54). By attaching the term **lives** (lit., "is alive"; חַי, $ḥay$) Job is saying more than that his redeemer "exists." He is expressing his belief that this deliverer is ready and able to come to his aid.[23] Job is confident that somehow, some day, someone will rise (**stand**; קוּם, $qûm$)[24] in his defense to secure his vindication and restoration.

"Hiobs *go'el* und Zeuge im Himmel," pp. 207-212; W. Vischer, "God's Truth and Man's Lie," *Int* 11 (1961): 138-139; J. Lindblom, "Ich weiss, dass mein Erlöser lebt. Zum Verständnis der Stelle Hi. 19,25-27," *ST* 2 (1940): 65-77; L. Waterman, "Note on Job 19:23-27: Job's Triumph of Faith," *JBL* 69 (1950): 379-380; T. Meek, "Job xix, 25-27," *VT* 6 (1956): 100-103; Irwin, "Job's Redeemer," pp. 217-229; J. Zink, "Impatient Job," *JBL* 84 (1965): 147-152; L. Krinetzki, "Ich weiss, mein Anwalt lebt," *Bibel und Kirche* 20 (1965): 8-12; M. Barre, "A Note on Job xix, 25," *VT* 29 (1979): 107-109.

[22]Cf. H Ringgren, *TDOT*, 2:350-355; A.R. Johnson, "The Primary Meaning of *g'l*," *VTSupp* 1 (1953): 67-77.

[23]Some scholars argue that the expression "my redeemer lives" is the equivalent of a legal oath. Still others see it as a confessional statement descriptive of God, comparing it to the parallel Ugaritic line "I know (*yd'*) that mightiest Baal lives (*ḥy*), that the prince lord of earth exists" (*CTA* 6.3.8-9).

[24]This term most likely means here, as in Deut 19:15-16; Ps 27:12; 35:11, to "rise as a witness in court." Some scholars, believing God to be the "redeemer," see this term as referring to an anticipated theophany (an appearance of God) or, more specifically, God's coming forth from heaven

But just who is this "redeemer"? The voluminous attempts to answer this question have exercised some of biblical scholarship's greatest ingenuity and produced two major views:

1) Job's redeemer is God (Gordis, Dhorme). In support of this view it is argued that: a) God is known as a "redeemer" (gō'ēl) elsewhere in the Bible; b) the person Job expects to "see" in verse 26 (= "God"; אֱלוֹהַ, 'Elôah) is the same one he believes will "arise" in verse 25; c) "lives" (ḥāy) is used of God throughout the Bible, and the expression "my Redeemer lives" is the equivalent to "as God lives" in 27:2 with both constituting confessional formulas used to speak of the divine; d) the monotheistic perspective of the book prevents the consideration of a third party (e.g., a heavenly witness, 16:19) who could reconcile the dispute between God and Job; e) it is God who ultimately vindicates Job.[25]

This view is widely held and has much to commend it. The obvious problem with it is the logical "absurdity" of Job believing his "redemption" will come from the same God he has accused of brutally wronging him (9:14-20; 13:19-23). This paradox is said to be resolved by the language of faith. Job is caught in a struggle between two conflicting views of God. His reason teaches him that God is his unjust, ruthless accuser. His faith insists that God is good and just and that somehow, someday, that will be made manifest.

2) Job's redeemer is some heavenly being like the celestial "witness" (עֵד, 'ēd, 16:19) and "arbiter" (מוֹכִיחַ, môkîaḥ, 9:33) Job hoped for in his earlier speeches (Mowinckel, Pope, Habel). In support of this view it has been argued: 1) references to God as "redeemer" in other biblical texts are not relevant for the book of Job since they come from a different literary genre; 2) the "redeemer" (gō'ēl) Job expects to "arise" (v. 25) is not necessarily identical to

---

to render justice on earth (cf.. Zeph 3:8; Ps 76:10[9] and discussion by Hartley, Job, p. 294, n. 14).

[25]It is also argued that אַחֲרוֹן ('aḥărôn, "last"; taken adverbially by NIV "in the end," v. 25b) is really a noun and parallel to go'ēl, "redeemer," as an epithet of God. This expression is often compared to Isaiah's use of רִאשׁוֹן (ri'šôn, "first") with 'aḥărôn ("last") as a title of Yahweh (Isa 41:1; 48:12). M. Barre, "Note of Job xix, 25," pp. 107-108, suggests (with Pope) that 'aḥărôn may be related with the Mishnaic term אַחֲרָאִי ('aḥărā'î, "guarantor") and, likewise, constitutes an epithet of God.

the "God" (*'Ĕlôah*) he expects to "see" in verse 26; 3) the term "lives" (*ḥāy*) is a common expression and not necessarily an epithet of God; 4) since the monotheistic perspective of Job includes the existence of "satan" and the "sons of god" (Job 1, 2) it could also include the idea of a heavenly being who might act as Job's redeemer; 5) throughout the book Job has labeled God his afflicter and adversary at law and it is illogical to assume that Job now expects God to save him from God.

This view has much to offer and serves the plot of the book nicely. The story of Job begins with the accusation of a heavenly being (*śāṭan*) against Job that sets in motion his horrific trial. Job, who believes God is his real accuser, now wishes for some heavenly being to vindicate him. Though Eliphaz regarded such an appeal unlikely to succeed (5:1), Elihu considers it at least possible that some "angel" might arise to plead Job's case (33:23,24).[26] In the legal setting of the book this "redeemer"(19:25)/"witness"(16:19)/"arbiter" (9:33) is the advocate whom Job hopes will successfully plead his case against God. In response to those who remind us that such an advocate never rises in the book, it should be pointed out that Job's desire for a "redeemer"/"witness"/"arbiter" is his *wish* and not necessarily an anticipated reality. Job has been wrong on the reason for his suffering and the nature of the God who presides over it. He will likewise be proved wrong on who will ultimately rescue him from it. The fact that God himself will ultimately rise to vindicate Job will be the final and most dramatic irony of the book.

Whichever of the above views is correct, we see clearly from Job's words that he holds a deep conviction that he will ultimately be vindicated. But when will this redemption come? In an attempt to answer this question we will focus on four specific expressions Job uses. The first is the phrase **in the end** (אַחֲרוֹן, *'aḥărôn*, v. 25). This ambiguous term can mean "at last," "afterward," "at a later time." In the legal setting of the context it could refer to "the last one" to rise and speak in court.[27] The second expression is **will stand upon the**

---

[26]Could we have here a scene akin to what we find in Zech 3:1-5 where the "angel of the LORD" opposes "Satan" as he attempts to accuse Joshua, the high priest of postexilic Judah?

[27]Cf. G.R. Driver, "Problems of the Hebrew Text and Language: I. Scenes

earth. The verb **stand** (קוּם, *qûm*) elsewhere in Job means "rise as a witness"[28] and that is probably its meaning here. The phrase **upon the earth** (עַל־עָפָר, *'al-'āphār*) is more difficult. Noting that *'āphār* commonly means "dust," several commentators argue that it means' Job's dust, or his decayed remains, his grave.[29] It can also mean simply "on earth" as in Job (41:25[33]).[30] The next expression, **after my skin has been destroyed** (אַחַר עוֹרִי נִקְּפוּ, *'aḥar 'ôrî niqq²phû*, v. 26) is likewise difficult. It probably means "after my skin has been stripped off" (Kissane, Pope). It could also mean "after my skin has been shriveled up" or "marred beyond recognition" (Hartley). Finally, there is the enigmatic **yet in my flesh** (מִבְּשָׂרִי, *mibb²śārî*, v. 26) which can mean "from my flesh" or "without my flesh."[31]

The ambiguity of the language in verses 25-26 and differing perspectives on Job's view of the afterlife have led to three major views on the meaning of the passage:

1) Job will receive vindication and see God after his death and bodily resurrection. This view was first suggested by the church fathers and has many modern adherents.[32] The NIV ("in my flesh," v. 26) and most major western translations support this view. This interpretation also makes good sense of the following verse, in which Job insists that he will see God "with (his) own eyes." Habel, while not arguing for a general resurrection, connects this passage to 14:13-17, which he interprets as Job's envi-

---

in Court," *Alttestamentliche Studien*, ed. by H. Junker and J. Botterweck, BBB 1 (Bonn: Hanstein, 1950), pp. 46-61.

[28]Cf. 16:8; also Ps 27:12; 35:11; Deut 19:16.

[29]So Duhm, Janzen. For this meaning elsewhere in Job cf. 7:21; 17:16; 20:11; cf. N. Ridderbos, "'*pr* als Staub des Totenreiches," *OtSt* 5 (1948): 174-178.

[30]Some have even argued that it refers to the "underworld" (Pope).

[31]Terrien argues convincingly that the preposition מִן (*mtn*), when used with verbs expressing vision or perception, always refers to the point of vantage or the place from which the function of sight operates (Ps 33:13-14; Cant 2:9).

[32]Jerome's Vulgate reads: "For I know my redeemer lives and that on the last day I will be raised from earth; and I will again be surrounded by my skin, and in my flesh I will see my God; whom I myself will see; and my eyes will behold, and not another; this hope is fixed in my breast." Clement and Origen also held this view, though Chrysostom opposed it; cf. Speer, "Zur Exegese von Hiob 19,25-27," pp. 49-107. Among the moderns who support this view are Leveque, E.J. Young, G.L. Archer, Pope, Terrien, and Habel.

sioning of a future time when he will be personally raised from the grave to encounter a more forgiving God.[33]

2) Job expects a postmortem, disembodied encounter with God. This is the view of the early Jewish interpreters and, likewise, has many modern supporters.[34] Those who favor this view render *mibbᵉśārî* (v. 26) as "without my flesh" (RSV) and understand Job to be envisioning some kind of "spiritual" existence after death. Duhm interprets, "Job will rise from the earth as a spirit, rather like Samuel (I Sam 28)." The "see" of verse 27 is understood metaphorically to refer to the perspective of faith (Dillman, Weiser).

3) Job expects vindication before his death. Job "from his weak, emaciated body ('from my flesh') will see God's appearing to vindicate him" (Hartley). Those who hold this view emphasize that throughout the book Job has seen death as final and the grave as a place from which there is no return (7:9; 10:21; 14:10-12). Any vindication that Job foresees, therefore, must come in this life. He is thus hoping for his healing and return to prosperity.[35]

With whom then does Job believe he will have a vindicating encounter, and when does he believe it will happen? The most likely answer, both from the immediate context and from the larger context of the book, is that Job believes he will be personally vindicated by God after he has died. In support of this view we invite the reader to consider the following: 1) the **Oh that**, with which this hope passage begins, is always used in the book to invite some divine intervention; 2) the passage most similar to this (14:13-17) envisions a postmortem vindication by God; 3) the fact that Job wants his plea of innocence **engraved in rock forever** (v. 24) places his hope in the realm of the distant future; 4) the phrases **in my flesh** and **with my own eyes** suggest that Job believes he will be in some kind of bodily form when God appears; 5) whoever the **redeemer** of verse 25 is, it is clearly **God** whom Job believes he will some day **see** (v. 26).

The interpreters are correct when they say that such an understanding of Job's hope places him in contradiction with his own

---

[33]Habel, *Job*, p. 307.

[34]Traceable to the *Book of Jubilees* (23:19-31), which envisions the bones of the dead resting in the earth but then proclaims that the just will "see" that God is defeating their enemies. Cf. G. Holscher, "Hiob 19,25-27 and Jubil 23,30-31," *ZAW* 53 (1935): 277-283.

[35]Cf. Lindblom, "'Ich weiss, dass mein Erlöser lebt,'" pp. 100-103.

words which have proclaimed that death is final and accused God of being his unjust persecutor. It should be noted, however, that Job has already engaged in this same contradiction earlier in the book. After calling God his "enemy" and "tormenter" (13:24-28) and then insisting that the dead "do not rise" (14:7-12), this same Job paradoxically hopes that he might be "hidden in the grave" until God's "anger has passed" and a more forgiving God "calls" him (14:13-17). Nor is the presence of such contradictory language unique to the book of Job. In a passage most instructive to the meaning of Job, the prophet Jeremiah, also feeling mistreated by God, alternates between accuser of God and devotee in the span of a few words (20:7-13). On an even larger scale it is typical of the genre of biblical lament to observe complaint juxtaposed with confession. The psalms, in particular, abound with the contradictory language of protest and praise (cf., e.g., Psalm 102).

What do we make then of this biblical phenomenon of accusation against God contrasted by adoration of God? How can we account for the preponderance of biblical passages where protest and praise emerge from the same lips? What theology does this tension between complaint and confession teach? It is the theology of faith reconciling itself to life. It is the inevitable struggle that emerges within the mind of a suffering believer who is trying to comprehend how a loving God can preside over human misery. It is the agonizing process of reconciling the benevolence of God to the relentless malevolence of human experience. The believer, stunned and broken by life's absurd cruelties, honestly vents his disappointment with God and then struggles to rediscover him. Gradually, and sometimes grudgingly, the broken pilgrim regains his spiritual bearings to find rest in the very God who has disappointed him. Paradoxically and redemptively his frustration is met and finally overcome by faith. These great hope passages in Job, which some interpreters dismiss as mere "wishes" or "flights of fancy" are something far greater. They are the language of faith. So understood they provide the reader with one of the keys to understanding the theology of the book.

19:28-29[36] Convinced that God will ultimately vindicate him, Job closes his reply to Bildad with a warning to the friends. By **hound-**

---

[36]It is interesting to note that this speech does not close like Job's previous ones which were concluded with a reflection on death and Sheol (3:20-

ing (רָדַף, *rādaph*; lit., "persecute, pursue") Job with false accusations (**the root of the trouble lies in him** [Job]), they are placing themselves in jeopardy of **punishment**. The persecution of the righteous was a serious crime.[37] Once Job's righteousness is vindicated, it will become clear that they have unjustly persecuted him. The **sword**, symbolic of the death God brings upon his enemies (Deut 32:41-42; Isa 66:16), is what they will receive from a just God. This warning is akin to an earlier warning Job had issued to the friends that the "dread" of God might fall upon them for making false charges against Job (13:7-12). The Job who has repeatedly called God's justice into question now becomes its advocate, **then you will know there is a judgment.**[38] Though Job is convinced there has been a miscarriage of divine justice in his case, he does not seem to abandon the idea altogether.

26; 7:21b; 9:18-22; 14:20-22; 17:13-16). This omission could be seen as further evidence that in this "faith" passage Job envisions a day of vindication beyond the grave.

[37]Cf. A. Phillips, *Ancient Israel's Criminal Law* (Oxford: Blackwell, 1970), pp. 23-27.

[38]Lit., "that you may come to know *shaddayan*." Most interpreters take this final term to be a form of the root דִּין (*dyn*) and translate it "judgment" or "judge," and this view has the support of the Vulg., Syr., and the Targums. Others see it as a form of שַׁדַּי (*šādday*, "the Almighty") and translate "that you may come to know God"; cf. L.R. Fisher, "*sdyn* in Job xix 29," *VT* 11 (1961): 342-343; Walker, "A New Interpretation of the Divine Name 'Shaddai,'" pp. 64-66.

JOB 20

5. Zophar's Second Speech (20:1-29)

In this speech Zophar takes exception to Job's previous words on both a personal and theological level. Personally, he is insulted over Job's indictment of the friends as malicious persecutors of an innocent man. Theologically, Zophar remains absolutely convinced that Job's hope for vindication is misplaced and that there is but one inescapable fate of the wicked — they will "perish forever." As in the earlier speeches there is a strong element of satire in this poem. Using the technique of reversal Zophar plays upon Job's own words to refute him and offers an alternative meaning to his plight.[1] The poem breaks into two parts: 1) a brief personal attack of Job (20:1-3); 2) an extended discourse on the fate of the wicked (20:4-29). The main body of the poem is a disputation speech based upon an appeal to ancient tradition.[2]

Zophar's Personal Attack of Job (29:1-3)[3]

[1]Then Zophar the Naamathite replied:
[2]"My troubled thoughts prompt me to answer / because I am greatly disturbed. / [3]I hear a rebuke that dishonors me, / and my understanding inspires me to reply.

20:1-3 Zophar is vexed and insulted by Job's stinging accusations. His **troubled thoughts**[4] motivate his opening reply. Zophar's words

---

[1]Cf. J. Holbert, "'The Skies Will Cover His Iniquity': Satire in the Second Speech of Zophar (Job xx)," *VT* 31 (1981): 171-179; also Habel, *Job*, pp. 314-315.

[2]Cf. N.C. Habel, "Appeal to Ancient Tradition as a Literary Form," *SBL* 1973 *Seminar Papers*.

[3]The literary form of this exordium is a chiasm (ab-ba).

[4]שְׂעִפִּים (śə'ippîm) occurs only here and 4:13 in Job. It seems to refer to some kind of mental disorientation.

remind the reader that this debate is not without passion. Playing upon Job's own words Zophar vents his frustration in ironic fashion. Job had earlier accused the friends of "humiliating" (כלם, *klm*) him (19:5). Zophar insists that just the opposite is true by claiming that it is Job who **dishonors** (כְּלִמָּה, *kᵊlimmāh*) him. Zophar calls Job's attack a **rebuke** (מוּסָר, *mûsar*). This term often appears in a positive light in Proverbs referring to "correction" that comes from a parent or from God. Eliphaz has also used the term with this sense (5:17). It is one of the ways God "warns" those in danger of his judgment (cf. Elihu, 33:16). In this context Zophar is evidently using the term to refer to Job's warning that the friends may be in danger of judgment if they do not cease persecuting him (19:28-29). Though stunned by Job's sharp attacks, Zophar insists that it is his **understanding**,[5] not merely his passion that will inform his reply.

Zophar's Discourse on the Fate of the Wicked (20:4-29)

[4]"Surely you know how it has been from of old, / ever since man[a] was placed on the earth, / [5]that the mirth of the wicked is brief, / the joy of the godless lasts but a moment. / [6]Though his pride reaches to the heavens / and his head touches the clouds, / [7]he will perish forever, like his own dung; / those who have seen him will say, 'Where is he?' / [8]Like a dream he flies away, no more to be found, / banished like a vision of the night. / [9]The eye that saw him will not see him again; / his place will look on him no more. / [10]His children must make amends to the poor; / his own hands must give back his wealth. / [11]The youthful vigor that fills his bones / will lie with him in the dust.

[12]"Though evil is sweet in his mouth / and he hides it under his tongue, / [13]though he cannot bear to let it go / and keeps it in his mouth, / [14]yet his food will turn sour in his stomach; / it will become the venom of serpents within him. / [15]He will spit out the riches he swallowed; / God will make his stomach vomit them up. / [16]He will suck the poison of serpents; / the fangs of an adder will kill him. / [17]He will not enjoy the streams, / the rivers flowing with honey and cream. / [18]What he toiled for he must give back uneaten; / he will not enjoy the profit from his trading. / [19]For he has

---

[5]בִּינָה (*bînāh*) is a synonym of חָכְמָה (*ḥokmāh*, "wisdom").

oppressed the poor and left them destitute; / he has seized houses he did not build.

²⁰"Surely he will have no respite from his craving; / he cannot
save himself by his treasure. / ²¹Nothing is left for him to devour; /
his prosperity will not endure. / ²²In the midst of his plenty, distress will overtake him; / the full force of misery will come upon
him. / ²³When he has filled his belly, / God will vent his burning
anger against him / and rain down his blows upon him. / ²⁴Though
he flees from an iron weapon, / a bronze-tipped arrow pierces him.
/ ²⁵He pulls it out of his back, / the gleaming point out of his liver.
/ Terrors will come over him; / ²⁶total darkness lies in wait for his
treasures. / A fire unfanned will consume him / and devour what
is left in his tent. / ²⁷The heavens will expose his guilt; / the earth
will rise up against him. / ²⁸A flood will carry off his house, / rushing watersᵇ on the day of God's wrath. / ²⁹Such is the fate God allots
the wicked, / the heritage appointed for them by God."

ᵃ4 Or *Adam*   ᵇ28 Or *The possessions in his house will be carried off, /
washed away*

This highly metaphorical speech is devoted to a single topic —
the inescapable fate of the wicked. Its purpose seems to be a direct
counter to Job's misplaced hope (so Zophar believes) that God will
eventually vindicate him (19:23-27). To the contrary, insists Zophar,
nothing but destruction awaits the wicked, a truth to which no less
than time (v. 4) and the cosmic order testify (v. 27). Job's hope, then,
is a false one that will only further ensure his demise.

20:4-5 The sarcastic **surely you know** with which Zophar begins
is actually a rhetorical question in the Hebrew.[6] It is structured in
such a way that, should Job deny its claim, it would expose him as
an opponent of wisdom's oldest truth. Following the example of
Bildad (8:8) and Eliphaz (15:18-19), Zophar grounds the doctrine of
the inescapable fate of the wicked in the moral order of the created
universe (**it has been from of old**). As ancient as the creation of **man**
(אָדָם, *'ādām*), it is a fixed law, established by God at the beginning of
time. As such, there can be no exceptions to it, not even in Job's
case. Surely Job must know that, though the evil man may prosper

---

[6]Cf. R. Gordis, "A Rhetorical Use of Interrogative Sentences in Biblical
Hebrew," *AJSL* 49 (1932–33): 212-217.

for a short time, **the mirth of the wicked is brief**. There is simply no way they can escape their ultimate destiny. It is thus fanciful and dangerous for Job to oppose God and then entertain any hope of vindication from him.

20:6-7 In language that is rich in metaphor, Zophar now begins his characterization of the ill-fated wicked man. Driven by a **pride** that **reaches to the heavens**[7] the evil man is consumed by a hunger for self-exaltation that leads him to assault the very abode of God. Like Adam, the first man who is also the first rebel, he denies the creator's claim upon his life and tries to become God himself. The language used here is similar to that of Isaiah 14 and Ezekiel 28 which condemn the king of Babylon (not Satan) and the king of Tyre (not Satan) for trying to become gods. One is also reminded of the motive behind the building of the tower "that reaches to the heavens" by the people at Babel (Gen 11:1-9). But the higher the wicked man climbs, the farther he falls (cf. Amos 9:2; Obad 4). He will **perish forever**. Like his own **dung** (cf. Ezek 4:12,15) he will quickly disappear from view, and the once great man will have people asking of him, '**Where is he?**' As several commentators have suggested, Zophar may be alluding to Job himself who was once the "greatest man among the people of the East" but who has now been reduced to "ashes."

20:8-9 Zophar portrays the wicked man as a phantom (cf. Isa 29:7; Ps 73:20). Like a character in a **dream** he appears to be real only quickly to **fly away** (or "die"; cf. Ps. 90:10). The wicked man's life seems for a while to be of substance, but it has no lasting significance. As the morning light chases away the **night vision**, the apparently happy wicked man is suddenly **banished**. Once the center of attention among his peers, the wicked man's contemporaries will in the end **look on him no more**.

20:10-11 The difficulty of verse 10 has resulted in some translators omitting it (NAB) or moving it elsewhere in the text (NEB). Part of the problem has to do with how to render רָצָה (*rāṣāh*, **make amends**). NIV understands the verb in its usual sense of "pay off" or "satisfy a debt," and this is probably correct. The idea would be that any wealth the wicked had accumulated would not be enjoyed by

---

[7]Dhorme sees this language as a metaphorical portrait of a king as a tree raising its head into the clouds.

their children but be returned to the ones from whom it was improperly taken. RSV connects *rāṣāh* with another Hebrew root and takes it to mean, "seek the favor of" (**the poor**). Following this translation the idea is that the wicked man's children are so impoverished they will be reduced to begging from the poor. Also difficult to understand is the following phrase **his own hands must give back his wealth**. The translation is clear enough, but the reader wonders why the author refers back to the wicked man after moving on to his children in the first half of the verse. Gordis offers a solution by proposing that his **hands** (יָדָיו, *yādāyw*) figuratively refer to his "offspring"[8] and that both lines refer to the economically deprived state of his children. Though the exact meaning of the text may elude us, the general meaning seems clear enough. Zophar is refuting the idea that a wicked man's children might continue to benefit by the wealth he has illicitly acquired. This is clearly how Job understood it, for he goes on to challenge this very point in his reply (21:8). To Zophar, premature death is the judgment of God upon the wicked. His **youthful vigor** is consigned to the **dust**. Any joy he experiences is short-lived. He will die before his time and his children will be reduced to poverty.

20:12-15 Zophar now begins an extended metaphor on the "food of the wicked." **Evil** is portrayed as a tasty morsel savored in the **mouth** of the wicked man. He enjoys this meal so intensely that he **hides it under his tongue** and **keeps it in his mouth**. This is the author's way of describing the enticing nature of evil. The reader is reminded of the words of Proverbs: "stolen water is sweet" (9:17a) and "food gained by fraud tastes sweet" (20:17). The same idea is present in the story of the temptation of Eve (Gen 3:6). But the irony of divine judgment rises to frustrate the consuming appetite of the evil man. The meal that was so **sweet in his mouth** turns **sour in his stomach**. It becomes like the **venom of serpents within him**.[9] The food that he once thought was the source of his vitality instead becomes the cause of his death. The wicked man is destroyed by the very thing he has consumed. Again, one is reminded of the portrait of the intoxicated man found in Proverbs who drinks wine that

---

[8]R. Gordis, "A Note on *Yad*," *JBL* 62 (1943): 341-344.

[9]Cf. D. Pardee, "*Merôrat-Petanim* 'Venom' in Job 20:14," *ZAW* 91 (1979): 401-416, who argues that this refers to the bile produced by the liver.

"goes down smoothly" but then "bites like a snake, and poisons like a viper" (Prov 23:31-32). The **food** that so pleases the evil man's palate is the ill-gotten **riches** he has **swallowed** from dishonest gain. Such a meal, insists Zophar, will never satisfy. Not circumstance, not the courts, but **God** himself will intervene to force him to **vomit them up**.[10]

20:16-22 So driven is the wicked by his insatiable hunger for illicit gain that he unwittingly **sucks the poison of serpents**. It is Zophar's way of saying that the wicked man is destroyed by the very thing he pursues. The man who lives by the cunning of a serpent dies by its bite. The term **fangs** (NIV) literally means "tongue" in the Hebrew. The language owes its origin to the ancient belief that the serpent's tongue was the source of its venom (Ps 140:4[3]). Verses 17-18 continue the theme of God's frustration of the ravenous tendencies of the wicked. In a manner of financial regurgitation the wicked man will **give back uneaten** (cf. v. 15) all that he has sought to consume. Not only will the **profits from his trading** be forfeited, he will not even be allowed to enjoy the basic fruits of the land. **Rivers** (of oil) **with honey** and **cream** are among the staples of Palestinian agriculture. Even these basic commodities will be denied the greedy rich. They will be denied because the wicked man has **oppressed the poor**. Such was considered the most egregious of social sins in ancient Israel. The book of Job reflects this opinion. Eliphaz will finally accuse Job of this offense (22:5-9). In his self-defense Job will spend more time seeking to acquit himself of this crime than of any other (29:12-16; 31:13-23). The verb **oppressed** here refers to a form of fraud by which the wicked man has deprived the poor of their homes (cf. Micah 2:1-2).[11] The economic component of the wicked man's craving is the emphasis of verses 20-22. It is greed that fuels the wicked man's **craving**.[12] But his **treasure** cannot save him and his

---

[10]It is interesting to note that the LXX, evidently finding the idea of God causing a man to vomit offensive, has an "angel" do it. In another version it changes the vomiting to "expulsion" of the evil man from his house (cf. D.H. Gard, *The Exegetical Method of the Greek Translator of the Book of Job*, SBLMS 8 [Philadelphia: SBL. 1952], p. 26).

[11]For a discussion of how this may have been done, cf. B. Lang, "The Social Organization of Peasant Poverty in Biblical Israel," *JSOT* 24 (1982): 47-63.

[12]חֲמוּד (ḥămûd), normally rendered "desire," is better translated, "appetite," here (cf. Dhorme).

prosperity will not endure. The compulsive quest for more leaves him with nothing. In the very **midst of plenty**, **misery**[13] **will come upon him**. Zophar's use of the term **misery** is especially telling. This is the very word Job has repeatedly chosen to describe the "trouble" that God has brought upon him (3:10,20). Zophar insists that such misery is the fruit of a wicked man's behavior.

20:23-26 The irony of the wicked man being destroyed by the very thing he pursues is picked up again here by means of a different metaphor, the warrior God. Aggressive evil is met by the even greater aggression of divine judgment. In his **anger**, God **rains down his blows**[14] upon the sinner. This difficult phrase is probably meant to connote that God is marshalling a heavenly arsenal of weapons against the evil man. From these weapons there is no escape. Though the wicked man might seek to run from a short-ranged **iron weapon** (a sword), he will yet be struck by a long-ranged **bronzed-tipped arrow**.[15] It is shot with such force that it completely penetrates his body coming **out his back**. Like a lightening bolt, its **gleaming point**[16] destroys his vital organs. The wicked man, locked in mortal combat with God, is doomed. Death, like an inescapable **darkness** and an unquenchable **fire**, will overtake him, his wealth, and even his children.[17] Darkness is a common symbol of death and destruction in the book of Job (3:4-5; 12:25; 15:22-23; 18:18). The expression "unfanned fire" means a fire not made with human

---

[13]עָמֵל (*'āmēl*, "sufferer") should be rendered (with LXX) עָמָל (*'āmāl*, "misery").

[14]This phrase is difficult and has resulted in a wide variety of translations. RSV takes MT בִּלְחוּמוֹ (*bilḥûmô* from לחם, *lḥm*, "food") and understands it to mean that God is raining down his anger as food upon the wicked. This would nicely complete the earlier motif of evil as food met with a manna of judgment from heaven. The Hebrew root (*lḥm*) can also mean "warfare," and this is the direction most translators have gone. Driver connects it with yet another root (לְחוּם, *lᵉḥûm*) meaning "buffeting" and believes this is the origin of LXX ὀδύνας (*odynas*, "pains") ("Problems in the Hebrew Text," pp. 72-93). M. Dahood, "Some Northwest-Semitic Words in Job," pp. 306-320, connects it to yet another term מבל (*mbl*, "fire").

[15]קֶשֶׁת נְחוּשָׁה (*qešeth nᵉḥûšāh*, "a bronze bow"); but the phrase is used to refer to the arrow as well.

[16]בָּרָק (*bārāq*) literally means a "lightning flash" (cf. Deut 32:41; Hab 3:11; Ps 18:15[14]; 144:6 where God's weapons are described as "bolts of lightning").

[17]The word for "treasures," צְפוּנָיו (*sᵉphûnāyw*), can also mean his "treasured ones," that is, his family.

hands. The wicked man's judgment comes directly from God. The verbs **consume** and **devour** complete the "evil as poisonous food" theme of verses 12-26. Evil has run its full course. The irony is complete. The wicked man is devoured by the very thing he sought so greedily to consume.

20:27-29 Cosmic elements are introduced here to punctuate the fact that the fate of the wicked man is sealed. In the imagery of a divine lawsuit,[18] Zophar says the **heavens** and the **earth** will **rise up** as witnesses and testify against the sinner.[19] Responding to Job's request for a trial before a heavenly court, Zophar insists that any "witness in heaven" (16:19) or testimony by the "earth" (16:18) would **expose** (Job's) **guilt** rather than acquit him. The wicked, like Job, have no hope for any mediation of their fate. For them there awaits only a **day of God's wrath**. In the Hebrew Bible this expression may more generally refer to an eschatological day of God's judgment against a nation (Ezek 7:19) or more specifically to a day of retribution against some individual (Prov 11:4). Here, as in Isaiah 30:28, God's wrath is characterized as a torrent of **rushing waters** washing away the sinner's **house**. "House" here may mean everything from his body ("house of clay," 4:19) to his possessions and even his family. The final verse summarizes Zophar's theological position. In the order that God has created, everything has its own **fate**. This term (חֵלֶק, ḥēleq) primarily means someone's rightful share as in an inheritance.[20] No doubt, Zophar chooses it to solidify his argument that, in God's world, people get exactly what they deserve. As Bildad had done earlier (Job 18), Zophar concludes his speech with the word "God," adding even more emphasis to his theology of retributive justice as the divinely established principal that governs the moral universe.

---

[18]Cf. K. Nielsen, *Yahweh as Prosecutor and Judge*, JSOTSupp 9 (Sheffield: JSOT Press, 1978); cf. also, Deut 32:1; Isa 1:2.

[19]Such language is common in the legal documents of the ancient world (cf. D. Hillers, *Treaty-Curses and the Old Testament Prophets* [Rome: Pontifical Biblical Institute, 1964], p. 4).

[20]Cf. M. Tsevat, "*chalaq* II," *TDOT*, 4:447-451.

JOB 21

6. Job's Reply to Zophar (21:1-34)

This discourse by Job closes the first cycle of speeches with a compelling rejection of the doctrine of retributive justice.[1] In rebuttal of the friends' simplistic assertion that God always sees that people get what they deserve in life, Job invites the friends to take an honest look at the world. In the real world, Job argues, wicked men live long, prosperous lives in spite of the fact that they openly deny God. This powerful discourse is a disputation speech employing numerous quotations and allusions to the earlier speeches of the friends (Eliphaz, 15:20ff; Bildad, 18:5ff; Zophar, 20:5ff). It divides into two major parts: 1) an appeal for a sympathetic hearing (21:1-6); and 2) a refutation of the doctrine of retributive justice (21:7-34). In many ways the arguments of Job echo the complaints of Jeremiah (cf., e.g., Jer 12:1-2) and the Psalmist (73:1-12).

Job's Appeal for a Sympathetic Hearing (21:1-6)

¹**Then Job replied;**
²**"Listen carefully to my words; / let this be the consolation you give me. / ³Bear with me while I speak, / and after I have spoken, mock on.**

⁴**"Is my complaint directed to man? / Why should I not be impatient? / ⁵Look at me and be astonished; / clap your hand over your mouth. / ⁶When I think about this, I am terrified; / trembling seizes my body.**

21:1-3 Unlike some of Job's earlier speeches this discourse is directed exclusively toward the friends. **Listen carefully to my**

---

[1]Many scholars considered this chapter to be one of the most important of the book. Cf., e.g., C. Westermann, *Structure of the Book of Job*, pp. 87-90.

words is the biblical equivalent of "read my lips!" It bristles with sarcasm. At the same time it vents Job's frustration over the friends' unwillingness to offer him any **consolations**. Though their attempts to "console" him had begun with a sympathetic silence (2:13), they had quickly degenerated into an intense verbal assault on Job's irreverent attitude. It is true that Eliphaz had earlier offered Job what he called "God's consolations" (15:11), but his trite theological statements had only intensified Job's pain. In response to the sharp, condemnatory words of the friends Job has labeled them all "miserable comforters" (16:2). The comfort he now seeks from them is a fair and honest consideration of this argument. After that, he says, you can **mock on.**[2]

21:4-6 The rhetorical question, **"Is my complaint against man?"** functions to both reintroduce Job's argument that God is not just and to condemn the unsympathetic friends for their unjustified personal attacks upon Job. Job's **complaint** (שִׂיחַ, *śîaḥ*) is the legal charge that Job has lodged against God (cf. 10:1; 23:2). Job is **impatient** with God for his refusal to give him vindication, or even an explanation, for his undeserved suffering. He is also impatient with the friends for their refusal to even give him a fair hearing. Rather than attacking him they should be **astonished** over what he has suffered. To **clap the hand over the mouth** is to be dumbstruck and overcome with awe (cf. Micah 7:16).[3] When Job considers his condition and his frustrating attempts to get justice from God or sympathy from the friends, he **trembles** with personal dread. For Job this is no mere intellectual exercise or theological debate; it is a great struggle that consumes his whole being.

Job's Refutation of the Doctrine of Retributive Justice (21:7-34)

Job's rebuttal to the claim of the friends that the just God sees to it that wicked men get what they deserve is built upon two compelling questions: 1) Why do the wicked live long, prosperous lives?

---

[2]MT תַּלְעִיג (*tal'îg*) is singular in form perhaps suggesting that Job is aiming his remarks toward Zophar in particular. Zophar had used this same term (לַעַג, *l'g*) in one of his earlier speeches to characterize Job's speech (11:3). The LXX, Syr., and Vulg. render the verb in the plural form, taking it to refer to all of the friends.

[3]Cf. M. Dahood, "Northwest Semitic Philology and Job," p. 64.

(21:7-16); and 2) Where is the proof that God causes the wicked to suffer? (21:17-33). Throughout the speeches the friends have based their claims for a just God on theological tradition, personal revelations, and what they believe to be the moral laws of the universe. Job counters their arguments with empirical evidence from what can actually be observed in the arena of everyday human life.

Why Do the Wicked Live Long, Prosperous Lives? (21:7-16)

[7]**Why do the wicked live on, / growing old and increasing in power? / [8]They see their children established around them, / their offspring before their eyes. / [9]Their homes are safe and free from fear; / the rod of God is not upon them. / [10]Their bulls never fail to breed; / their cows calve and do not miscarry. / [11]They send forth their children as a flock; / their little ones dance about. / [12]They sing to the music of tambourine and harp; / they make merry to the sound of the flute. / [13]They spend their years in prosperity / and go down to the grave[a] in peace.[b] / [14]Yet they say to God, 'Leave us alone! / We have no desire to know your ways. / [15]Who is the Almighty, that we should serve him? / What would we gain by praying to him? / [16]But their prosperity is not in their own hands, / so I stand aloof from the counsel of the wicked.**

[a]*13* Hebrew *Sheol*   [b]*13* Or *in an instant*

21:7 With the question, **"Why do the wicked live on?"** Job directly refutes Zophar's claim that the lives of the wicked are cut short by God (20:5,11). Long life is traditionally regarded as one of God's blessings upon the righteous.[4] But Job observes that the wicked, too, **grow old and increase in power**. This later expression (גָּבְרוּ חָיִל, *gabᵊru ḥāyil*; cf. Ps 73:12) may refer to those who "increase in health and virility," those who "gain the upper hand" in military and political power, or even those who "increase in wealth."[5] Contrary to the assertions of Eliphaz (5:5; 15:20) and Zophar (20:15-18) that the prosperity of the wicked is taken from them, Job observes that it often establishes them as the prominent people of the land.

---

[4]Cf., e.g., Abraham (Gen 25:7-8) and the vindicated, restored Job (42:16,17).

[5]Cf. H. Kosmala, "*gabhar*," *TDOT*, 2:368.

21:8-13 Job now continues his argument with a compelling portrait of the prosperity of the wicked in ways that specifically refute earlier claims of the friends. One such claim was that the **offspring** of the wicked will perish or be struck by some calamity (15:33; 18:12,19; 20:19,26,28). To the contrary, says Job, the wicked **see their children established around them**. Unlike Job, who has lost all of his offspring, the wicked get to personally enjoy their children.[6] Eliphaz had once suggested to Job that if he accepted God's discipline his "tent would be secure" (5:24). But, Job says, it is the wicked whose **homes are safe and free from fear**. The **rod of God**, a symbol of God's punishment or discipline is **not upon them**.[7] Returning to the theme of the wicked man's[8] continually increasing wealth, Job observes that their livestock never fail to successfully reproduce.[9] Again, the fertility of the flock and herd was generally regarded as evidence of God's blessing of the righteous man (cf. Deut 28:11; Psalm 144:13-14; Gen 30:29-30). But Job observes that it is the wicked man who often enjoys this benefit. Like lambs playing in the fields their **little ones dance about** and **sing** to the sound of the **tambourine**, the **harp**, and the **flute** (cf. Gen 31:27; Isa 24:8). This is yet another portrait of the unbridled joy and leisure of the wicked man's family (cf. Zech 8:5). The wicked live comfortable lives and then **go down to the grave in peace**.[10] This last expression literally means they die "in an instant," without trauma or lingering illness. The **grave** (lit., "Sheol") was not thought to be a place of punishment in ancient times but a domain to which all men, good and evil, finally descend (30:23).

21:14-16 What bothers Job most is that the wicked enjoy this blissful life in spite of the fact that they openly defy God. It is not as if their lack of piety is cleverly hidden or escapes the notice of a just God. To the contrary, feeling smugly secure in their own prosperity

---

[6]Dahood takes the first half of v. 8 to be a reference to the ancestors of the wicked and reads, "their progeny is secure with them," *Job*, p. 142; cf. also idem., "The Metaphor in Job 22:22," *Bib* 47 (1966): 411.

[7]The very rod by which Job believes he was struck (19:21).

[8]Now described in the singular in the Hebrew.

[9]The verbal root used here, נעל (*g'l*), evidently carries a technical meaning of "impregnate without fail"; cf. H. Fuhs, "*ga'al*," *TDOT*, 3:47.

[10]The NIV reads with Gordis who connects רֶגַע (*rega'*) to Arab. *raja'a*, "return to rest."

they publicly disavow God, admitting they have **no desire to know** (his) **ways**. In language that is clearly defiant they shout, **"Who is the Almighty, that we should serve him?"** This blasphemous speech was so offensive to the authors of the LXX that they omitted verse 15 in their translation. Taking a purely utilitarian approach to piety the wicked go on to ask, **"What would we gain by praying**[11] **to him?"** They believe they already have everything they wish and they feel no need for God. One is reminded of the words of Agur who asked not to be given too much lest he "disown God and say, 'Who is the LORD?'" (Prov 30:9). The power of wealth to dull the sense of need for God is lamented elsewhere in Scripture (cf., e.g., Matt 19:23-24; Mark 10:17-24; Luke 12:13-18). Verse 16 is difficult to comprehend where it now stands. RSV and NEB take the sentence as a question[12] meaning that God does not concern himself with the wicked but leaves them their prosperity as their own achievement. The LXX omits the "not" to get much the same meaning. Others see this as a parenthetical disclaimer by God who wishes to disassociate himself from the blasphemous attitude of the wicked.[13]

Where Is the Proof That God Causes the Wicked to Suffer? (21:17-34)

[17]**"Yet how often is the lamp of the wicked snuffed out? / How often does calamity come upon them, / the fate God allots in his anger? /** [18]**How often are they like straw before the wind, / like chaff swept away by the gale? /** [19]**It is said, 'God stores up a man's punishment for his sons.' / Let him repay the man himself, so that he will know it! /** [20]**Let his own eyes see his destruction; / let him drink of the wrath of the Almighty.**[a] / [21]**For what does he care about the family he leaves behind / when his allotted months come to an end?**

[22]**"Can anyone teach knowledge to God, / since he judges even the highest? /** [23]**One man dies in full vigor, / completely secure and at ease, /** [24]**his body**[b] **well nourished, / his bones rich with marrow. /** [25]**Another man dies in bitterness of soul, / never having enjoyed anything good. /** [26]**Side by side they lie in the dust, / and worms cover them both.**

[27]**"I know full well what you are thinking, / the schemes by**

---

[11]נִפְגַּע־בֹּו (*niphga'-bô*), which means to "implore" or "entreat."

[12]Reading with Dhorme, Duhm, and Gray.

[13]Cf., e.g., Habel, Hartley.

which you would wrong me. / [28]You say, 'Where now is the great man's house, / the tents where wicked men lived?' / [29]Have you never questioned those who travel? / Have you paid no regard to their accounts— / [30]that the evil man is spared from the day of calamity, / that he is delivered from[c] the day of wrath? / [31]Who denounces his conduct to his face? / Who repays him for what he has done? / [32]He is carried to the grave, / and watch is kept over his tomb. / [33]The soil in the valley is sweet to him; / all men follow after him, / and a countless throng goes[d] before him.

[34]"So how can you console me with your nonsense? / Nothing is left of your answers but falsehood!"

[a]*17-20* Verses 17 and 18 may be taken as exclamations and 19 and 20 as declarations.   [b]*24* The meaning of the Hebrew for this word is uncertain.   [c]*30* Or *man is reserved for the day of calamity, / that he is brought forth to*   [d]*33* Or / *as a countless throng went*

21:17-18 Having demonstrated that the wicked often live long and prosperous lives, Job now refutes the other side of the retributive equation, asking "Where is the proof of God's punishment of the wicked?" He does so through a series of rhetorical questions aimed at specific assertions of the friends. Bildad had claimed that "darkness" overpowers the wicked and that their "lamp" goes out (18:5-6). Yet Job questions **how often** this really happens. Zophar had claimed that "calamity" overtakes the wicked and that their allotted "fate" is the "day of God's wrath" (20:22-29). Yet Job observes that this seldom happens in real life. Challenging the oft-used agricultural metaphor of the wicked as **straw before the wind** or **chaff swept away by a gale**, Job finds little proof of this in human affairs (cf. Ps 1:4; 35:5; 83:14 [13]; Isa 17:13; 29:5; Jer 13:24). An honest look at the real world yields little or no evidence that God always punishes the wicked.

21:19-21 Job now preemptively rebuts the standard answer of the traditional theologians to the undeniable fact that wicked men do not always experience God's punishment: **"God stores up a man's punishment for his sons."** Job's challenge to this assertion is to insist that for true justice to be done God should see to it that the one who sins personally suffers the consequences. **"Let him** [God] **repay the man himself, so that he will know it!"**[14] says Job. Though

---

[14]For the meaning of עָדַ‎ (*yāda'*) here cf. D.W. Thomas, "The Root *yd'* in Hebrew, II," *JTS* 66 (1947): 317.

in places the Scriptures suggest that there may be generational consequences for the "sins of the fathers" (cf. Exod 20:5; Deut 5:9),
other passages make it clear that children do not innocently suffer
for their parents' sin.[15] This comports with Job's assertion that
delayed retribution is no retribution at all. The wicked man's **eyes**
should **see his** own **destruction**,[16] insists Job, for he will know or
care nothing of the family he **leaves behind**. If the theory of retribution really works, the sinner should **drink the wrath of the
Almighty**[17] in his own lifetime.

21:22-26 The rhetorical question, **"Can anyone teach knowledge
to God since he judges even the highest?"**[18] of course, expects a
"no" answer. What Job means by asking this question here is less
clear.[19] Gordis takes it as a quotation of an accusation made against
him by the friends that Job presumed to instruct God (cf. Eliphaz in
4:17 and 15:8-14; Zophar in 11:5-9). What Job may be doing is ironically turning the friends' accusation against them. It is the friends,
with their airtight doctrine of retribution, who are now presuming
to teach God and their efforts are woefully inadequate.[20] This explanation would make sense of the following verses, for as verses 23-26
argue, there seems to be no correlation between one's behavior and
the timing or nature of his death. To the contrary, Job argues, death
makes no distinction based on what happens in one's life. Comparing a man of prosperity and leisure (vv. 23-24) to one who has
never enjoyed anything good, Job observes that the inequities

---

[15]Cf., e.g., Jer 31:29-30; Ezek 18:1ff. Jesus, too, refutes this idea in John
9:1-3.

[16]כִּיד (*kîd*) occurs only here. Dhorme reads פִּיד (*pîd*), "destruction," as in
12:5; A. Guillaume (*Studies in the Book of Job, with a New Translation* [Leiden:
E.J. Brill, 1968], p. 104) connects the term to Arab. *ka'dā'*, "calamity, loss"
(also Pope). Cf. also, L.L. Grabbe, *Comparative Philology and the Text of Job*
SBLDS 34 (Missoula, MT: Scholars Press, 1977), pp. 77-79.

[17]The image of drinking from the cup of God's wrath appears frequently
in the prophets (Isa 51:17; Jer 25:15; 49:12; Ezek 23:31-34; cf. also Ps 75:9[8]).

[18]רָמִים (*rāmîm*) has received a variety of interpretations. Tg. and Ps 78:69
take it as the "heavens" or those who occupy them, the "angels." Blommerde
sees it as an epithet for God, "the All-high" or "the Exalted."

[19]The same question is asked in Isa 40:14 as part of the prophet's argument that God is without peer, far above the nations and the false gods they
worship. But this does not appear to be the purpose of the question here.

[20]So Habel, *Job*, p. 329.

allowed to exist in life simply are not addressed in death. **Side by side** the vigorous[21] and the frustrated **lie in the dust**, says Job, proof that death has nothing to do with justice. It is interesting that Job does not here explicitly contrast the wicked and the good, but compares the fortunate and the unfortunate.[22] However, as verses 27-33 suggest, Job may have in mind the "evil rich" when he speaks of the man **at ease** and the "pious poor" when he describes the man who **dies in bitterness of soul**.

21:27-34 In this final section of the speech Job preemptively rebuts the corollary that God sees to it that the wealth and influence of the wicked do not survive them. Job begins by characterizing the friends' doctrine of retribution as a **scheme**[23] that they have maliciously devised to **wrong**[24] him. The claim of the friends is that the **great man's**[25] (= **evil man**, v. 30) **house** has long vanished, its ruin a symbol of God's judgment (cf. 8:14-15; 15:34; 18:15-21; 20:26-28). Job counters with the same approach he used earlier. He invites them to honestly look at what really happens in the world. **Those who travel**,[26] who actually see the real world, offer numerous **accounts** of **evil men spared from the day of calamity**. Contrary to the assertions of the friends, during the lifetime of the wicked man no one (not men, not even God) **denounces his conduct to his face** or **repays him for what he has done**. Even in death they are **carried to the grave** with great pomp and ceremony by a **countless throng**.

---

[21]The characterization of the vigorous man as one whose "body [is] well nourished," literally, "with intestines (עֲטִינָיו, *'ăṭînāyw*) full of cream" (v. 24), is interesting. *'ăṭînāyw* occurs only here and has received a wide variety of translations: LXX and Vulg., "intestines"; Targ., "breasts"; Syr., "sides." Gordis thinks it refers to the male genitals and the "cream" his semen.

[22]As compared to Eccl 9:2-6 where the contrast is between the good man and the evil man.

[23]מְזִמָּה (*mᵉzimmah*) can also refer to positive ideas or plans (Prov 3:21; 5:2). Here it carries the meaning of "mischief" (cf. Ps 21:12[11]).

[24]תַּחְמֹסוּ (*taḥmōsû*) is probably from the root, חמס (*ḥms*, "violence"), and means "do harm" or "plot violence." Another possibility is to connect it to Arab. *hamasa*, "speak" or Syr. *ḥms*, "think"; cf. B. Jacob, "Erklärung einer Hiob-Stellen," *ZAW* 32 (1912): 286-287.

[25]נָדִיב (*nādîb*), "nobleman, prince."

[26]The "wayfarers" who are eyewitnesses to the sights of far lands (Lam 1:12; Ps 80:13[12]). In ancient times their words were highly valued as a source of information on the otherwise unknown distant lands; cf. Ben Sira: "A much traveled man knows many things" (Sir 34:9a).

Guards **watch over** the tombs that perpetuate their memory. The evil tyrant is happy in life and honored in death. In a final complaint against the friends Job argues that their assertion that God governs his world by the principle of retributive justice is just so much **nonsense**.[27] Even worse, it is **falsehood** (מַעַל, *ma'al*, "treachery"), a strong term by which he accuses them of violating the sacred (Lev 5:5) and abandoning devotion to God (Deut 32:51).

---

[27] הֶבֶל (*hebel*), "vanity, nothingness."

JOB 22

C. THE THIRD CYCLE OF SPEECHES (22:1–26:14)

Up to this point the speeches of Job and the friends have unfolded in a repeated pattern. Eliphaz, Bildad, and Zophar have each spoken (in that order) and Job, in turn, has responded to each. But this third cycle, at least in the form we now have it, does not follow this pattern. Most notably in this cycle Bildad's speech (25:1-6) is but ten lines and Zophar does not speak at all. Further, Job is credited with speaking, without interruption, all the material from chapters 26–31. We may respond to this break in the earlier pattern on the basis of two different assumptions. First, we may assume that the book has retained its original form and the changes are intentional. As to what meaning, if any, the break in the pattern might suggest, it could be argued that the deterioration of the cycle merely indicates that Job is winning the debate. The friends are reduced to a few words or even silence while the victorious Job eloquently continues to press his point. This view would comport with Yahweh's final verdict on the debate (42:7-9) which labels the friends "wrong" and Job "correct" in what they have said about God and his role in Job's suffering.

Many scholars, however, have found evidence that the third cycle has suffered some corruption in the history of the text's transmission and needs to be reconfigured to match the pattern of the first two cycles. Basing their reconstructions on thematic, linguistic, and rhetorical factors they offer a variety of suggestions concerning the original structure of this cycle. The fact that such disagreement exists over exactly what form that pattern should take, however, only serves to illustrate the difficulty of the process.[1] Consistent with our

---

[1] Habel, for example, identifies the third cycle as chs. 21–28 and assigns as follows: ch. 21 = Job; 22=Eliphaz; 23 = Job; 24=Zophar; 25:1-6, 26:5-14 =

reading of Job we will follow the canonical form which appears to assign all the material in 26:1–31:40 to Job.

1. Eliphaz's Third Speech (22:1-30)

In his final speech Eliphaz directly accuses Job of specific sinful behaviors and attitudes that, Eliphaz believes, God is punishing by means of the suffering he has inflicted upon Job. He portrays Job as one of the proud rich who profit by exploiting the poor and then arrogantly reject God's claim upon their lives. More sarcastic and accusatory than in his previous speeches, Eliphaz counters Job's claim that God does not judge the wicked (Job 21) by portraying the suffering Job as living proof that he does. The speech breaks down into three major sections: 1) the charge of sins against the poor (22:1-11); 2) the charge of siding with the wicked (22:12-20); 3) a call to repentance (22:21-30).

The Charge of Sins against the Poor (22:1-11)

¹Then Eliphaz the Temanite replied:
²"Can a man be of benefit to God? / Can even a wise man benefit him? / ³What pleasure would it give the Almighty if you were righteous? / What would he gain if your ways were blameless?
⁴"Is it for your piety that he rebukes you / and brings charges against you? / ⁵Is not your wickedness great? / Are not your sins endless? / ⁶You demanded security from your brothers for no reason; / you stripped men of their clothing, leaving them naked. / ⁷You gave no water to the weary / and you withheld food from the hungry, / ⁸though you were a powerful man, owning land— / an honored man, living on it, / ⁹And you sent widows away empty-handed / and broke the strength of the fatherless. / ¹⁰That is why snares are all around you, / why sudden peril terrifies you, / ¹¹why it is so dark you cannot see, / and why a flood of water covers you.

Bildad; 26:1-4, 27:1-2 = Job; 27:13-23 =Zophar; 28 = Closure (by author). Hartley takes 27:13-23 and adds it to 25:1-6 and credits it to Bildad. Pope credits Bildad with 25:1-6 and 26:5-14 and assigns 27:8-23; 24:18-20,22-24 to Zophar.

22:1-3 With a series of four rhetorical questions Eliphaz sarcastically rejects Job's presumptuous attempts to make God accountable to his piety. What could Job possibly be or do that would be of any **benefit to God**?[2] All along Job has been demanding vindication from God on the basis of his faithfulness and innocence. Eliphaz counters by insisting that human righteousness does not obligate God in any way. The **blameless ways** of humans contribute nothing to God giving him neither **pleasure** nor **gain**.[3] God is transcendent, unaffected by the good or evil that men do. Even his heavenly servants (4:18) expect nothing from him. Job, therefore, should not entertain any hope of forcing God to give him a day in court.

Is Eliphaz correct in his assessment of God's response to human piety? A careful reading of the book of Job would suggest an answer of both "yes" and "no." On the one hand, the book of Job does affirm that God takes note of the righteous behavior of his children. In the prologue of Job, for example, it is God who acknowledges Job's extraordinary piety and invites the Satan to consider him (1:8; 2:3). So the suggestion that God is totally disinterested in human spirituality goes beyond what the story of Job suggests. On the other hand, the notion that the righteous behavior of humans does not obligate God or require a certain response from him is certainly consistent with the teaching of the book. In what appears to be the climax of the book, God appears to Job and directly challenges Job's presumption to judge God (38:2; 40:2; 40:8). Job's responses constitute a clear admission that he, even in his innocence, is not worthy to question God's providence or demand his vindication (40:3-5; 42:1-6).

22:4-9 After exposing the fallacy of Job's assumption that his piety has the power to obligate God to vindicate him, Eliphaz's speech takes a dramatic turn in tone and tact. He now directly refutes Job's claims of innocence and accuses him of specific sins. Again employing a set of rhetorical questions he sharply claims that Job's **wickedness** is **great** and his **sins** are **endless**. This accusatory language represents a departure from Eliphaz's approach in his ear-

---

[2]סָכַן (*sākan*) is variously interpreted (cf. Gordis). The usage in 34:9 seems to suggest a meaning of "benefit, profit." Cf. also Lipinski, "Punic *hkkbm* 1 and Isaiah 14,13," *UF* 5 (1973): 191-192, who translates "Can a man endanger God?" on the basis of Talmudic and Aramaic usage.

[3]Elihu will later make the same claim (35:7-8).

lier speeches. In his first speech, Eliphaz had praised Job for his piety (4:3-4) and suggested that his suffering represented God's efforts to discipline him for some indiscretion. Then, in his second speech, he compared Job to all humans, who by nature are given to sin (15:14-16). Now convinced that Job still mistakenly and dangerously labors from a false presumption of innocence, Eliphaz indicts Job with a list of specific crimes against humanity. Eliphaz has determined, presumably by deduction and without any empirical evidence, that Job is guilty of exploiting the poor and of demonstrating total lack of compassion for the disenfranchised. Abusing his status as a **powerful man**, Job has extorted illicit gain by **demanding** unreasonable **security** from his brothers and by **stripping men of their clothing**. These two phrases probably refer to the same crime. To take a garment as collateral for some loan (usually made in relief of poverty) and then not return it by evening was considered a crime against the poor according to the Mosaic legislation (Exod 22:25-26[26-27]). By **sending widows away empty-handed**[4] and **breaking the strength of the fatherless** Job is guilty of the lowest form of hard-hearted selfishness (Jer 7:6; Zech 7:10).[5] In the Bible lack of compassion for the poor is an indication of a lack of genuine piety.[6]

It is interesting to note that the four crimes of which Job is accused are all what might be called "sins of the wicked rich." They constitute what Habel describes as a "standard roster" of the crimes that the rich and powerful visit upon the poor.[7] But why does Eliphaz deduce that Job must be guilty of these particular sins? The answer lies in both who Job is and what he has been arguing. According to the prologue Job was one of the wealthiest and most powerful men of his day. Observing what Job has owned and what in turn has been taken from him, Eliphaz has concluded that Job's sins must have something to do with his misuse of this wealth and power. This would fit the retributive justice model in which a just

---

[4]Fohrer understands this to be referring to the act of illegally forcing a widow from her home (cf. Gen 31:42; Deut 15:13).

[5]The "widow" and the "orphan" were prime targets for economic and political exploitation in the ancient world because they had no male relative to defend them (cf. H. Hoffner, "*'almanah*," *TDOT*, 1:288.

[6]In the Bible, God himself is the champion of the widow, orphan, and stranger (cf., e.g., Deut 10:18).

[7]Habel, *Job*, p. 338.

God sees to it that the nature of the punishment matches the nature of the crime. Further, in his most recent speech (ch. 21), it was Job himself who spoke of the wealth and power of the wicked rich insisting that they escaped judgment for their evil behavior.[8] Seeking to counter Job's argument, Eliphaz identifies Job with this very group and argues that the **snares** and **peril** Job is experiencing is nothing less than God's **rebuke** of Job's sins and, therefore, proof that such people are indeed punished.[9]

The Charge of Siding with the Wicked (22:12-20)

[12]**"Is not God in the heights of heaven? / And see how lofty are the highest stars! /** [13]**Yet you say, 'What does God know? / Does he judge through such darkness? /** [14]**Thick clouds veil him, so he does not see us / as he goes about in the vaulted heavens.' /** [15]**Will you keep to the old path / that evil men have trod? /** [16]**They were carried off before their time, / their foundations washed away by a flood. /** [17]**They said to God, 'Leave us alone! / What can the Almighty do to us?' /** [18]**Yet it was he who filled their houses with good things, / so I stand aloof from the counsel of the wicked.**

[19]**"The righteous see their ruin and rejoice; / the innocent mock them, saying, /** [20]**"Surely our foes are destroyed, / and fire devours their wealth.'**

22:12-14 According to Eliphaz, not only is Job guilty of practicing the behavior of the wicked, he is also guilty of taking up their attitude of defiance toward God. Quoting a hymnic line (**"Is not God in the heights of heaven?"**[10]) that celebrates God's exalted greatness, Eliphaz begins his refutation of Job's claim that God's exalted station in the **zenith of the heavens** results in his ignorance of or indifference toward the affairs of men. When Job asks, **"What does God know?"** he is repeating the standard cry of evil men (cf. Ps 73:11; Isa 29:15). He takes up their claim that the transcendent

---

[8]Eliphaz too has already spoken of the wicked rich (15:20-35).

[9]It is interesting that in his final defense Job refers to some of these same sins and protests his innocence of them (cf. 31:16-23,31-32).

[10]Dahood interprets גֹּבַה שָׁמָיִם (gōbah šāmāyim) as a title for God, "the Lofty One of Heaven" ("Kühne, Cord, Randnotizen zu PRU VI," Or 34 [1965]: 171); cf. also his *Psalms I*, p. 62.

God is so remote and detached in his heavenly abode that he does not even know what mortals are doing, much less actively engage in judging them. Job goes on to charge that the **thick clouds** which are designed to "**veil** God's glory" (cf. Ps 18:12-13[11-12]) in reality only obscure his view of the world.[11] These ancient arguments sound a lot like the approach of modern deism which portrays God as a creator or first cause who then retreats from the world he has made and leaves it to run its own course.

22:15-18 Such arguments, asserts Eliphaz, are typical of the well worn, age-**old path**[12] that **evil men** have long **trod**. By repeating the claims of the wicked Job is proving himself to be one of them. He joins that vast throng of practical atheists who feel free to pursue their evil plans without any fear of divine reprisals. These are the ones who say to God, **"Leave us alone! What can the Almighty do to us?"** This defiance is yet another ingratitude they manifest toward the God who has blessed their lives with **good things**. But those who hold this irreverent attitude are sadly mistaken, reminds Eliphaz. They are on a collision course with disaster. They die prematurely, **carried off before their time**. Their **foundations**, their evil philosophies and the lifestyle it has produced, are **washed away by a flood**. This latter phrase is probably not a direct reference to the flood of Noah as some have suggested, but echoes the "destruction as a flash flood" theme of Zophar's second speech (20:28). The last half of verse 18 should be read as a parenthetical comment by Eliphaz explaining why he personally rejects the **counsel of the wicked**. Such comments are typical of his style (cf. 5:3,27).

22:19-20 Eliphaz now prepares Job for the call to repentance he is about to issue (vv. 21-30) by reminding him who the real winners and losers are in the world God rules. In the end the **righteous** people who have been victimized by wicked men will gain the upper

---

[11]Eliphaz's characterization of Job's position illustrates the rhetorical technique of reversal that Job has repeatedly employed in his rebuttal of traditional wisdom. Quoting statements originally meant to praise God, Job turns them into an occasion to attack God.

[12]The "old path," (אֹרַח עוֹלָם, 'ōraḥ 'ôlām), commonly describes the positive ways of good men (cf. Jer 6:16). Noting this, Pope and Blommerde (*Northwest Semitic Grammar*, p. 97) connect 'ôlām with עלם ('lm), "hide," and Ug. glm, "grow dark," and translate "dark path." Cf. also, Dahood, "Northwest Semitic Philology and Job," pp. 65-66.

hand. In what amounts to a victory celebration the **innocent** will **rejoice** over the **ruin** of the wicked and even **mock** them in their dramatic fall.[13] The **wealth**[14] that was gained as illicit profit by the wicked rich will be **devoured** by **fire**. This last line may have been intended as a direct attack of Job who lost some of his wealth in a "fire of God" that "fell from the sky" (1:16).

A Call to Repentance (22:21-30)

[21]"**Submit to God and be at peace with him; / in this way prosperity will come to you. / [22]Accept instruction from his mouth / and lay up his words in your heart. / [23]If you return to the Almighty, you will be restored: / If you remove wickedness far from your tent / [24]and assign your nuggets to the dust, / your gold of Ophir to the rocks in the ravines, / [25]then the Almighty will be your gold, / the choicest silver for you. / [26]Surely then you will find delight in the Almighty / and will lift up your face to God. / [27]You will pray to him, and he will hear you, / and you will fulfill your vows. / [28]What you decide on will be done, / and light will shine on your ways. / [29]When men are brought low and you say, 'Lift them up!' / then he will save the downcast. / [30]He will deliver even one who is not innocent, / who will be delivered through the cleanness of your hands.**"

22:21-22 Ever the counselor, Eliphaz ends his condemnatory speech on a positive note. Having indicted Job of specific sins and having refuted his claim that God does not punish the wicked, Eliphaz now exhorts Job to repent (cf. 5:8ff) of his evil ways and **return**[15] (v. 23) to God. Eliphaz suggest that this will first require Job to re**submit**[16] himself **to God**. In Job's refusal to admit his sin (so

---

[13]This language is similar to that of several Psalms (cf., e.g., 2:4; 52:7[6]; 107:42).

[14]קִימָנוּ (*qîmānû*) is either from the noun קִים (*qîm*) which can mean either "adversary" or "wealth" or from the noun יְקוּם (*yᵉqûm*), "substance" (cf. Gordis, Pope).

[15]שׁוּב (*šûb*) is the term commonly used by the prophets to invite Israel to repent (cf., e.g., Jer 4:1-2).

[16]For this translation of הַסְכֶּן (*hasken*) cf. W. Bishai, "Notes on *hskn* in Job 22:21," *JNES* 20 (1961): 258-259. Pope suggests it means, "come to terms with."

Eliphaz believes) and in his criticism of God's "injustice" Eliphaz sees in Job a defiant attitude that puts him in direct rebellion against God. If he ever hopes to **be at peace** with God, he must yield again to God's sovereignty over his life. One of the great ironies of the book is that this is exactly how Job's great dilemma will finally be solved. After hearing God reassert himself as Creator and Lord of the universe (Job 38–41) his struggle with God ends with Job "repenting in dust and ashes" (42:6). Though guilty of no sin worthy of the suffering he has experienced (as Eliphaz and the other friends have wrongly assumed), Job does subsequently become guilty of a "sin" in the midst of his vigorous defense of his integrity: the sin of irreverent pride, the sin of "charging God with wrongdoing" (2:22), the sin of demanding that God answer to him. Of this he will need to "repent."

Eliphaz, of course, is arguing from another assumption, a false one. Believing that the once prosperous Job became wealthy by exploitation and selfishness and that the loss of his health and wealth are God's judgment upon these sins, he contends that the only way **prosperity will come to** Job again is by his willingness to **accept** God's **instruction**[17] and **lay up**[18] God's **words** in his **heart**. This particular phrase is typical of the wisdom sayings of the Bible which frequently call the young and naïve to submit to the counsel of the wise teacher (Prov 2:1; 4:10; 8:10). Job needs to become "teachable," to learn the lessons that God has been teaching him through his disciplinary experience of suffering (cf. 5:17).

22:23-26 The first lesson Job needs to learn is the lesson of repentance. If Job is willing to **return** (שׁוּב, šûb) **to the Almighty**, he will **be restored** or "built up" (בָּנָה, bānāh). The repentance Eliphaz invites will require Job to **remove wickedness** from his **tents**. The term **wickedness** (עַוְלָה, 'awlāh) is used elsewhere in Job to describe "deceptive speech" (cf. 6:30; 27:4). Its employment here appears to be Eliphaz's way of characterizing Job's slanderous claims of divine

---

[17]תּוֹרָה (tôrāh), "law, instruction." Here it does not refer to the Law of Moses but to wisdoms' truth (Prov 4:2; 13:14).

[18]שִׂים (śîm), "put, place." Dahood argues it means, "write down, inscribe," here and is all part of a metaphor of making a covenant with God. Cf. Dahood, "Metaphor in Job 22:22," pp. 108-109. Dahood also argues that שׁלם (šlm, "be at peace") of verse 21 is a technical term meaning "make a covenant and agreement" (as in 5:23); cf. Dahood, *Psalms I*, pp. 42-43.

injustice. Job used this same term to describe the dishonest apologia
of the friends in his first reply to Zophar (13:7). According to
Eliphaz Job's repentance will also require him to divest himself of
his wealth which the friends believe Job has obtained illicitly. He
must return his **nuggets** to the **dust** and his **gold** to the **rocks**. The
term **Ophir** refers to the place famous for its precious metals (cf.
1 Chr 29:4; Isa 13:12).[19] Once Job returns his ill-gotten wealth to its
proper place, says Eliphaz, the **Almighty** will become his **gold**[20] and
his **choicest silver**.[21] No longer distracted or misled by his illicit
money, Job will find his **delight** in God and live life with his **face lifted up to God**.[22] This last expression is the opposite of letting one's
face "fall" (Gen 4:6) and describes the freedom from shame and fear
that comes from being devoted to God (cf. 11:15).

22:27-30 Eliphaz goes on to promise that, when Job learns to
repent, his supplications to God will begin to receive a favorable
response. When he **prays** (עָתַר, 'āthar), God will **hear**. Job's health
and wealth will be restored, and he will be able to **fulfill** his **vows** in
thanksgiving for answered prayer (cf. Jonah 2:10[9]). Submissive
before God and again in his will, the repentant Job will see his plans
blessed and his **ways** leading to abiding success. Beyond this he will
experience a newfound ability to bless others. He will be able to medi-
ate with God on behalf of those who are **brought low** (i.e., the
oppressed). When Job says (to God): "Lift them up!" God will answer
and **save the downcast**.[23] Job's recovered piety will put him in such
good standing with God that even those who are **not innocent**[24] will

---

[19]The exact location of Ophir is debated with East Africa and Southern
Arabia as the most likely locales; cf. R.L. Omanson, "Ophir," *ISBE*, 3:607-
608.

[20]It is interesting to note that Eliphaz's name means "my God is gold."

[21]For a discussion of תּוֹעָפוֹת (tôʿāphôth, "choicest?") see L. Grabbe,
Comparative Philology and the Text of Job, pp. 81-83.

[22]Later, perhaps in response to this charge by Eliphaz, Job will disavow
putting his trust in gold instead of God (31:24-25).

[23]For a discussion of this concept including the later Jewish belief that
saints had the power to influence even the most important divine decisions
see R. Gordis, "Corporate Personality in the Book of Job," *JNES* 4 (1945):
54-55.

[24]אִי־נָקִי ('î-nāqî). Because the friends typically see God as a deliverer of the
innocent, many interpreters ignore the negative particle אִי 'î or emend it to
אִישׁ ('îš) = "innocent man"; cf., e.g., Fohrer, Dhorme.

be **delivered through the cleanness of** Job's hands. Eliphaz's claim that Job's righteousness can have a vicarious effect for the guilty probably represents an exaggeration (cf. Ezek 14:12-20). Like the other friends (e.g., Zophar, 11:17) Eliphaz tends to overstate both the degree of Job's sinfulness and the expected blessings of his repentance.

JOB 23

2. Job's Third Response to Eliphaz (23:1–24:25)

In this speech Job does not directly reply to Eliphaz. He neither answers the charges that Eliphaz has brought against him nor responds to his call for Job's repentance. Instead, he chooses to renew his wish for a day in court with God and express his continued frustration with God's "injustice." Two conflicting themes are balanced in Job's words: 1) an intense desire to "see" God and 2) disappointment and anxiety over God's abuse of his intimidating power. The speech divides nicely into four major parts: 1) Job's desire to face God in court (23:1-7); 2) Job's frustration with his heavenly judge (23:8-17); 3) the failure of God to punish the wicked (24:1-17); 4) discourse on the fate of the wicked (24:18-25).

Job's Desire to Face God in Court (23:1-7)

[1]Then Job replied:
[2]"Even today my complaint is bitter; / his hand[a] is heavy in spite of[b] my groaning. / [3]If only I knew where to find him; / if only I could go to his dwelling! / [4]I would state my case before him / and fill my mouth with arguments. / [5]I would find out what he would answer me, / and consider what he would say. / [6]Would he oppose me with great power? / No, he would not press charges against me. / [7]There an upright man could present his case before him, / and I would be delivered forever from my judge.

[a]2 Septuagint and Syriac; Hebrew / *the hand on me*   [b]2 Or *heavy on me in*

23:1-3 As he has done before, Job ignores Eliphaz's words and takes his **complaint**[1] directly to God. Job's use of the word **today** does

---

[1]שִׂיחַ (*sîaḥ*, "complaint") here means more technically a "legal complaint" against God (cf. 9:27).

not inform us of the time frame of the debate but speaks instead to its urgency. It is Job's way of saying, "even now," "this very moment."[2] Frustrated with the friends' unwillingness to give his **bitter** cries of "injustice" a fair hearing, Job reaffirms his desire to appear personally before God in some kind of heavenly court. There is in this strategy an indirect reply to Eliphaz's list of Job's supposed "sins" and his call for Job to "return" to God. Job is saying that he wishes to appear before God not to repent of any supposed sins but to protest his innocence of them. Eliphaz believes Job needs God's forgiveness. By contrast Job seeks God's vindication. Job charges that God's **hand**[3] continues to oppress him **in spite of** his **groanings**. It is yet another way for Job to protest what he believes to be God's unfair treatment of him. The expression **if only** (v. 3) expresses Job's "wish" to **present** his **case** before God. He uses this expression (מִי־יִתֵּן, *mî-yitten*) five different times in the book, and in each case it expresses some "wish" or "hope" that he might encounter God in a way that would end his torment (6:8-9; 14:13; 19:22-25; 23:7-9; 31:35-37).[4] Here, it is God's **dwelling** that Job seeks. This term (תְּכוּנָה, *t³kûnāh*) literally means "a fixed place" and refers to the "foundation" upon which a structure is built. In this particular usage it refers to God's heavenly throne from which he rules his world (cf. 1 Kgs 8:39,43,49; Ps 33:14). Job envisions going where the "sons of God" are said to have presented themselves before God (1:6; 2:1). Of its precise location Job is not sure. Job's inability to **find him** (God) sounds a familiar theme of the book that God's ways, his wisdom, and his motives cannot be discovered by humans (cf. 11:7-9; 28:12ff).

23:4-7 Imagining his day in God's court, Job lays out his plans. He would persuasively argue his **case**[5] supporting it with a full array of **arguments**. After resting his case he would wait for God to

---

[2]So Fohrer, Delitzsch.

[3]Most interpreters read with LXX and Syr. יָדוֹ (*yādô*), "his [God's] hand" while MT literally has יָדִי (*yādî*), "my hand." Blommerde argues that the final *yod* of *yādî* is an alternative form of the 3rd pers. masc. sing. ending, and he is followed by Andersen in this. A. de Wilde ("Eine alte Crux Interpretum, Hiob xxiii.2," *VT* 22 [1972]: 368-374) proposes reading אָזְנוֹ (*'oznō*, "his ear") for *yādî* and takes the passage as referring to God's ear being "heavy" and not hearing Job's complaint.

[4]Cf. the analysis of Habel, *Job*, p. 347.

[5]מִשְׁפָּט (*mišpāṭ*), "justice" here carries the idea of "lawsuit."

answer. Would it be by overwhelming Job with his **great power**[6]? Earlier Job had expressed his fear that such might happen (cf. 9:16-19). This time, though, he imagines a more positive result. He is now convinced God **would not press charges**[7] against him. In the next verse Job tells us why he expects to receive a favorable hearing from God. Because he is an **upright man**, Job believes he not only can survive an encounter with God, he can secure an acquittal of the charges against him. God will be forced to answer Job because he is an innocent man. Job's righteousness is something God will simply not be able to ignore in a face-to-face meeting. Once Job's innocence is established he will be **delivered forever**[8] from his **judge**.[9] Once again we are confronted by the contradiction of Job expecting justice from a God he has repeatedly accused of being unjust. As Peake puts it, "The magnanimity he here ascribes to God contrasts remarkably with the pettiness of which he had before accused him."

Job's Frustration with His Heavenly Judge (23:8-17)

[8]"But if I go to the east, he is not there; / if I go to the west, I do not find him. / [9]When he is at work in the north, I do not see him; / when he turns to the south, I catch no glimpse of him. / [10]But he knows the way that I take; / when he has tested me, I will come forth as gold. / [11]My feet have closely followed his steps; / I have kept to his way without turning aside. / [12]I have not departed from the commands of his lips; / I have treasured the words of his mouth more than my daily bread.

[13]"But he stands alone, and who can oppose him? / He does whatever he pleases. / [14]He carries out his decree against me, / and many such plans he still has in store. / [15]That is why I am terrified before him; / when I think of all this, I fear him. / [16]God has made my heart faint; / the Almighty has terrified me. / [17]Yet I am

---

[6]כֹּחַ (kōaḥ) here means "legal power" as it does in Mishnaic Hebrew.

[7]On this expression, cf. Reider, "Contributions to the Scriptural Text," p. 104. Reider emends the text to read "He is not cruel that he should attack me."

[8]G.R. Driver ("Problems in Proverbs," *ZAW* 50 [1933]: 140-141) renders לָנֶצַח (lāneṣaḥ, "forever") as "successfully." Cf. also, D.W. Thomas, "The Use of *netsach* as Superlative in Hebrew," *JSS* 1 (1956): 106-109.

[9]מִשֹּׁפְטִי (miššōphṭî, "from my judge"; MT) is read by some as מִשְׁפָּטִי (mišpāṭî, "my case"; LXX, Syr., Vulg.), and taken to mean Job is cleared of his suit.

not silenced by the darkness, / by the thick darkness that covers my face.

23:8-10 Having expressed his wish to encounter God in court, Job now vents his frustration with his heavenly judge. He begins by returning to a theme he introduced earlier (v. 3), his inability to **find** God. As noted above, the idea of God's inaccessibility is also addressed elsewhere in the book (Job 11, 28). It is the consistent testimony of the wisdom literature that mortals simply cannot apprehend God nor can they discover the hidden principle by which he governs his world (cf. Prov 25:3; 30:4).[10] Job claims that he has been trying to find God. He has looked in all directions — **east, west, north,** and **south** only to find his search frustrated at every turn.[11] Earlier Job had spoken of God as inescapable (7:17-20; 13:27; cf. also Ps 139:7-12; Amos 9:2-3). Now he charges him with being hidden and elusive. Does Job believe God has been intentionally "dodging" him, in order to avoid answering Job's accusations? The verbs **behold** and **see** express Job's desire to have a face-to-face encounter with God. This of course will eventually happen though not with the outcome Job imagines (42:1-6). It is not Job who will question God, but God who will question him. Though Job does not know the "way" of God, he is convinced that God knows his **way.** Job believes God is fully aware of Job's true character, and once he has been able to make his case with God, Job's righteousness will be apparent to all; he will **come forth as gold.** Eliphaz had suggested that the "Almighty" would become Job's "gold" (22:24), the thing of ultimate value that would give Job fulfillment and a positive sense of worth. Job counters that his own character is the thing he trusts in and values most. It is interesting that Job characterizes his impending trial as a **test.**[12] Earlier Job had charged that God maliciously "tests" mortals for no legitimate reason (7:18). But now he seeks God's testing in the form of a formal trial, convinced that with any kind of fair hearing he will easily pass the test.

---

[10]For the theological implications of the "hiddenness" of God cf. Balentine, *The Hidden God*; S. Terrien, *The Elusive Presence: Toward a New Biblical Theology* (San Francisco: Harper & Row, 1978).

[11]These four directions in the Hebrew are literally "before," "behind," "left," and "right." In Israel directions were based on an orientation of facing east.

[12]The psalmists also speak of God "testing" his children (Ps 7:9[8]; 17:3-5).

23:11-12 Job's confidence rests in his own righteousness. Throughout the speeches he affirms his integrity, defends it, and then tries to hold God accountable to it. In some places he characterizes his piety in terms of his innocence of sin (cf., e.g., Job 31). Here he defines it in terms of faithful obedience to the **commands** of God. Job is not referring specifically to the law of Moses but to any and all **words** that come from God's **mouth** (cf. Jer 9:19[20]). More than just being obedient, Job has **treasured** God's words more than his **daily bread**.[13] This emphasis on Job's obedience to God's commands may be an indirect answer to Eliphaz's call for Job to "accept instruction from his [God's] mouth and lay up his words in your heart" (22:22). It is also consistent with the covenant model of the Old Testament that those who obey God are counted as righteous and may expect his blessing.

23:13-17 Job now tempers his confidence in his own righteousness by a consideration of the absolute power of God to respond to it as he chooses. In language that sounds confessional, Job says that God **stands alone**.[14] Job's purpose is not to affirm God's uniqueness but to establish the fact that as sovereign of the universe he is accountable to no one and carries out his decisions as he wills. It is apparent to Job that God has already issued a verdict or **decree** of suffering for him and that God alone is in control of his ultimate destiny. This leaves Job **terrified** and makes his **heart faint**. It is with the greatest trepidation that he ponders the prospect of challenging such a God. Nonetheless, compelled to plead his case before him, Job will not be **silenced**. Though the risks are great he will have his say.[15]

---

[13]This last phrase is difficult in the Hebrew. The debate centers around the term מֵחֻקִּי (mēḥuqqî), "from, more than my statute, portion." Pope and others follow LXX and read בְּחֵקִי (bᵉḥēqî, "in my bosom") and translate, "in my bosom I have treasured the words of his mouth." Cf. also, Blommerde, *Northwest Semitic Grammar*, pp. 100-101.

[14]Literally, "God is one," as in the Shema, the famous creedal statement of Deut 6:4. Cf. C. Gordon, "His Name Is 'One,'" *JNES* 29 (1970): 198-199, who argues that this refers to God's "name." Dahood, citing an Ugaritic text translates אֶחָד ('eḥād) as "only ruler" ("Northwest Semitic Philology and Job," p. 67).

[15]Verse 17 is notoriously difficult in the Hebrew. MT reads "Because I was not cut off before the darkness." Dhorme renders צמת (ṣmt; lit., "put an end to, cut off") with "be silent," a meaning it has in Arabic and Aramaic (also Fohrer and NIV). Gordis omits the negative לֹא (lō', "not") and renders, "Indeed, I am destroyed by darkness" (also RSV). Pope reads לִאׁ (lû') for lō' and renders, "Would that I could vanish in darkness" (also NAB).

JOB 24

2. Job's Reply to Eliphaz (23:1–24:25, continued)

Job continues his reply to Eliphaz by returning to one of the most problematic issues raised by Job's great struggle: "Where is the evidence of God's justice in this world?" After making a compelling case that wicked men go unpunished (vv. 1-17), Job surprisingly does an about-face and insists that the wicked are yet doomed to destruction (vv. 18-24). He then ends the speech by challenging anyone to prove his argument false (v. 25). This chapter has proved difficult for interpreters on at least two grounds. First, the speech is full of linguistic difficulties. This has resulted in a wide range of renderings by the translators.[1] Second, the issue of who spoke these words (especially vv. 18-24) has also been widely disputed. This has resulted in numerous attempts to reconstruct the "original" speech.[2] The merits of these arguments will be discussed below. If we take this chapter as it appears in the book and treat it as a unity spoken by Job, it can be divided into the following sections: 1) the miscarriage

---

[1]Cf. O. Loretz, "Philologische und textologische Probleme in Hi 24,1-25," *UF* 12 (1980): 261-266.

[2]The tendency among scholars has been either to reassign portions of the speech to other speakers or to regard certain portions of the speech as interpolations. For a discussion cf. Rowley, *Job*, pp. 161-162; Habel, *Job*, pp. 357-358; cf. also David Wolfers, "The Speech-Cycles in the Book of Job," *VT* 43 (1993): 385-402 and Markus Witte, *Vom Leiden zur Lehre: Der dritte Redegang (Hiob 21–27) und die Redaktionsgeschichte des Hiobbuches*, BZAW 230 (Berlin: Walter de Gruyter, 1994). Most notable in this debate is the issue of who spoke vv. 18-24. The very point of these verses, that God does indeed punish the wicked, is contradictory to the argument of the first seventeen verses and seems more like something one of the friends might say than anything Job would speak. Some scholars assign vv. 18-24 to Bildad or Zophar (Dhorme, Pope) while others believe it to be a quotation of the friends by Job (Gordis).

of God's justice on earth (24:1-17) and 2) a reaffirmation of the ultimate fate of the wicked (24:18-25).

The Miscarriage of God's Justice on Earth (24:1-17)

[1]"Why does the Almighty not set times for judgment? / Why
must those who know him look in vain for such days? / [2]Men move
boundary stones; / they pasture flocks they have stolen. / [3]They
drive away the orphan's donkey / and take the widow's ox in
pledge. / [4]They thrust the needy from the path / and force all the
poor of the land into hiding. / [5]Like wild donkeys in the desert, /
the poor go about their labor of foraging food; / the wasteland provides food for their children. / [6]They gather fodder in the fields /
and glean in the vineyards of the wicked. / [7]Lacking clothes, they
spend the night naked; / they have nothing to cover themselves in
the cold. / [8]They are drenched by mountain rains / and hug the
rocks for lack of shelter. / [9]The fatherless child is snatched from
the breast; / the infant of the poor is seized for a debt. / [10]Lacking
clothes, they go about naked; / they carry the sheaves, but still go
hungry. / [11]They crush olives among the terraces[a]; / they tread the
winepresses, yet suffer thirst. / [12]The groans of the dying rise from
the city, / and the souls of the wounded cry out for help. / But God
charges no one with wrongdoing.

[13]"There are those who rebel against the light, / who do not
know its ways / or stay in its paths. / [14]When daylight is gone, the
murderer rises up / and kills the poor and needy; / in the night
he steals forth like a thief. / [15]The eye of the adulterer watches for
dusk; / he thinks, 'No eye will see me,' / and he keeps his face concealed. / [16]In the dark, men break into houses, / but by day they
shut themselves in; / they want nothing to do with the light. / [17]For
all of them, deep darkness is their morning[b]; / they make friends
with terrors of darkness.[c]

[a]*11 Or* olives between the millstones; *the meaning of the Hebrew for this
word is uncertain.*   [b]*17 Or* them, their morning is like the shadow of death
[c]*17 Or* of the shadow of death

24:1 "Why does the Almighty not set times for judgment?"[3]
With this question Job returns to the most problematic theological

[3]The LXX renders this line, "Why are times hidden [צפן, *spn*] from the

issue raised by the book: If God is all-powerful and just, why is there so much injustice in his world (cf., e.g., 9:22-24; 12:5-9; 21:1-34)?[4] Eliphaz had argued that God has decreed a "day of darkness" for the wicked (15:23). Zophar called it a "day of God's wrath" (20:28). But Job countered that there is no real evidence of this in human life (Job 21) and now questions why the righteous have to look **in vain** for the **times** or **days** of God's judgment to finally come.

24:2-3[5] Job now offers an exhaustive list of unpunished crimes that were plaguing his society. Focusing first on economic injustice he begins by addressing the problem of widespread theft. People were stealing land by **moving boundary stones.** In ancient times stones placed at the corners of fields were the means of marking the official property lines of landowners. By moving the stones the greedy were able to encroach on the property of their neighbors. Eventually the expression "move the boundary stone" seems to have become a byword for describing all forms of land theft. As such it was universally condemned in the Bible (Deut 19:14; 27:17; Hos 5:10; Prov 22:28; 23:10).[6] Not only land but also the **flocks**[7] that grazed them were being **stolen.** Even the **orphan's donkey** and the **widow's ox** were being targeted by thieves. The parallelism of verse 3

Almighty?" Dhorme takes this to mean that God is either unaware of or indifferent to the events of earth, good or bad. *Ṣpn*, though, can mean "stored up, reserved" (cf. 15:20; 21:19) and this is most likely its meaning here.

[4]Interest in this issue was widespread in the ancient Near Eastern world. The language in this text with its protest of societal injustice is very similar to that found in Egyptian works like "The Protests of the Eloquent Peasant" (*ANET*, pp. 407-410), "The Admonitions of Ipu-wer" (*ANET*, pp. 441-444) and Mesopotamian works like "A Dialogue about Human Misery" (*ANET*, pp. 438-440).

[5]The first line of v. 2, "They move boundary stones" is shorter than most lines of this poem and seems to be missing its subject. LXX adds "the wicked" as the subject and this is followed by some translators.

[6]Another way of abusing boundary stones in order to steal land was to alter specifications about the property inscribed on the stones (cf. A. Oppenheim, *Ancient Mesopotamia* [Chicago: University of Chicago Press, 1964], pp. 123, 159; also P.C. Craigie, *The Book of Deuteronomy*, NICOT [Grand Rapids: Eerdmans, 1976], pp. 332-333).

[7]LXX has translated the Hebrew word וְרֹעוּ (*wᵊrōʻû*), as "and [lit., 'along with'] its shepherd" suggesting men are stealing land and kidnapping those who maintain the flocks. MT וְיִרְעוּ (*wāyyirʻû*, "and they pasture") is followed by NIV and is the preferred reading.

suggests that these animals were not being taken by violent crime (as the verb **drive away** might imply) but were being seized by wealthy financiers who accepted them as collateral (**in pledge**) for loans they issued to the poor. Such loans were not made in Israel for capital investment but for the relief of poverty.[8] The law of Moses prohibited taking and keeping basic necessities from the poor as collateral for these loans (e.g. "garments"; Exod 22:26; Deut 24:17). If it was wrong to take and keep a garment as collateral from the poor, how much greater an evil was it to keep the animals that supplied their livelihood? Because the orphan and the widow were among Israel's most exploitable classes, they were easy prey for callous and unscrupulous financiers. Those who perpetrated these very public crimes against the poor were obviously guilty of the most brazen kinds of theft. This, of course, is Job's point. Widespread theft is going unpunished, and God is doing nothing about it (v. 12b).

24:4-8 It is unclear what specific crime is being characterized by the phrase, **they thrust the needy from the path** (v. 4a). The second half of the verse would seem to suggest it is a way of saying that the normal access that the poor have to the land and its public roads is being denied them (cf. Judg 5:6; Amos 5:11-12). Constantly harassed and threatened at every turn they must go about in secretive, clandestine fashion and live as exiles in their own land.[9] They are reduced to the status of mere animals having to **forage food**[10] and **gather fodder**.[11] The picture here is that of desperate people seeking a meager existence from an inhospitable barren land. The verb

---

[8]Cf. E. Neufeld, "The Prohibition against Loans at Interest in Ancient Hebrew Laws," *HUCA* 26 (1955): 357-399. This is why "Taking [excessive] interest" from such loans was prohibited.

[9]Some interpreters have suggested a wider meaning for the word "path" (דֶּרֶךְ, *derek*) and understand the phrase to be describing the deprivation of the "rightful portion" due the poor.

[10]טֶרֶף (*ṭereph*), normally means "prey" or "carrion" but here carries the idea of "food" found by scavenging.

[11]Some think this means they can only get the food of cattle to eat. LXX and Vulg. read בְּלִי לֹו (*bᵉlî lô*) for בְּלִילֹו (*bᵉlîlô*), "They reap (in a field that is) not his." Still others emend to read, "They reap in the night" (בַּלַּיְלָה, *bal-laylāh* for *bᵉlîlô*). Taken this way the phrase might suggest that they either must steal food under the cover of darkness or work as common laborers in another man's field.

glean (לְקֵשׁ, *liqqēš*) is a hapax and its meaning is uncertain;[12] the following phrase, **in the vineyards of the wicked**, fits the rendering "glean" nicely. Such was the normal and legitimate practice of the poor in ancient Israel (Lev 19:10; Deut 24:21; Ruth 2:2ff). By identifying the fields in which they are forced to glean as those belonging to the **wicked**, Job is suggesting that the dependent status of the poor has been forced upon them by the exploitation of evil men. Job's portrait of the exploited poor is completed in verses 7,8. Not only are they without food, they are also deprived of proper **clothes** and shelter. **Naked** and exposed to the **cold**, they are reduced to **hugging rocks** in a desperate effort to stay warm.

24:9-12 The crimes perpetrated by the wicked rich upon the poor have reached beyond the illegal seizure of their land and livestock. They are also guilty of seizing their **fatherless children**.[13] As the next line explains this was being done by **snatching** young children from their widowed mothers in payment for a **debt**. This was the cruelest of all injustices suffered by the poor. In what amounted to an act of bartering in human flesh, fatherless children were being forced to leave their families and serve creditors as lifetime slaves. The description of the exploited poor in verses 10,11 is similar to that in verses 5-7, and some interpreters believe these verses are misplaced.[14] The duplication may be explained, however, in terms of whom the respective verses are describing. In verses 5-7 it is the poor in general who are being described, while in verses 10,11, it is the exploited worker or slave Job now characterizes. Irony is in play in this description of the rural poor. These exploited harvesters **carry sheaves** but **still go hungry.** They **crush olives**[15] and **tread**

---

[12]Various forms of the root לקשׁ (*lqš*) are associated with harvest in the Hebrew Bible, and in the Gezer Calendar it stands opposite זרע (*zr'*, "sow"). In Aramaic it means "do [something] late"; interpreters have seen this phrase as a description of unauthorized gleaning of another's field under the cover of darkness.

[13]Because this verse interrupts the flow of the immediate context and resurrects the theme of v. 3, many scholars omit it or relocate it (Gray, Dhorme, Fohrer). But as Andersen observes, such emendations destroy the poetic contrast of the oppressor and the oppressed.

[14]Cf., e.g., Gray.

[15]The meaning of this line in MT is uncertain. "They crush olives between the rows" or "between the millstones" or "between their songs" have all been suggested. Cf. the discussion by Gordis, *God and Man*, p. 165.

winepresses but still **suffer thirst**. Things are no better for the poor in the **city**. The **groans of the dying**[16] and the cries of the **wounded** are heard at every turn. The oppression of these workers and slaves threatens their very **souls.** This term (נֶפֶשׁ, *nepheš*) does not here refer to the nonmaterial, spiritual essence of a person but to his physical "being," his embodied "life."[17] In spite of the fact that the very existence of these exploited workers is being threatened by their evil taskmasters, **God charges no one with wrongdoing.**[18] Job is charging God with letting the wicked rich get away with murder.

24:13-17 Building upon his case that God does not punish the wicked, Job now begins to describe the criminal activity of those who **rebel against the light.** By choosing this phrase Job seems to be addressing two different but related ideas. At the most obvious level Job is merely observing that it is during the **night** (v. 13b), **when the daylight is gone** (v. 13a) and the **dusk** (14a) approaches, that **murderers, adulterers,** and **thieves**[19] perpetrate their crimes. At a deeper level this may also be Job's way of saying that such crimes and those who commit them are enemies of God's righteous rule and personify evil itself. Throughout the book of Job in particular and the wisdom literature in general "light" stands for righteousness and those who practice it while "darkness" stands for evil and those who commit it (e.g., 12:25; 18:5,18; cf. Prov 4:10-19). This being so, the wicked **want nothing to do with the light.** Enemies of goodness, they reverse the normal order of society and live by an opposing standard of values. Whereas the wicked rich abused the legal system to perpetrate crimes against the defenseless poor, these criminals flagrantly violate the recognized standards of proper behavior. Job's point, of course is that God lets them get away with it.

---

[16]MT מְתִים (*mᵉthîm*, "men"). Syr. has *metim*, "dying," and LXX has οἴκων (*oikōn*) ≡ בָּתִּים (*bātîm*), "houses." The reading of Syr. parallels nicely the term "wounded" (חֲלָלִים, *ḥălālîm*) in 12b and explains why they would be "groaning" (נָאַק, *nā'aq*); cf. Ezek 30:24 for a similar usage.

[17]This is also the meaning it carries in the story of God's creation of Adam (Gen 2:7).

[18]MT תִּפְלָה (*tiphlāh*, "error," "crime," "unseemly act"). Some Hebrew manuscripts and Syr. point תְּפִלָּה (*tᵉphillāh*, "prayer") and understand the line as God refusing to hear the prayers of the dying.

[19]These same three criminal acts are found together in Hos 4:2.

A Reaffirmation of the Certain Fate of the Wicked (24:18-25)

The words of Job now take a dramatic turn. After spending the first half of his speech accusing God of failing to punish the wicked, he now begins to describe their certain downfall. After challenging the doctrine of retribution, Job now seems to be defending it. The solution to this apparent contradiction proposed by many interpreters is to put these words on the lips of one of the friends rather than Job. Since the argument presented in verses 18-25 is clearly in tune with that offered by the friends, this is an attractive proposal. It is commonly suggested that perhaps this is the rest of Bildad's brief final speech (25:1-6) or is part of the third and (now) "misplaced" speech of Zophar.[20]

Is it possible, though, to see the final part of Job 24 as coming from the mouth of Job (as the book presents it) and still make sense of it? Joining with those who answer in the affirmative, we should begin by noting that this is not the only place in Job's speeches where he seems to contradict himself. In fact the book begins with a dramatic contradiction between the Job who piously submits to God in the prologue (1:20-21; 2:10) and then in his opening soliloquy immediately proceeds to express resentment toward God's gift of life and to challenge God's management of his world (3:1-26). This phenomenon continues throughout the book. In the speeches we find Job accusing God with one breath and then expressing his trust in him with the next.[21] We hear him quoting the arguments of the friends and the teachings of traditional wisdom and then immediately proceeding to refute them.[22] We find him denying the possibility of human immortality and then longing for it as a solution to his dilemma.[23] Everywhere else that Job has spoken contradictory language, it has been intentional and purposeful. It is, therefore,

---

[20]Such suggestions are offered in an attempt to "reconstruct" a "once complete" third cycle of Job thought to have been corrupted during the editing or transmission of the text. Peake considers the entire passage a "pious gloss" designed to make Job appear more orthodox. Snaith, Fohrer, and Habel think it is an independent poem of the author. Cf. the discussion by Gordis, *God and Man*, pp. 169-170, and Habel, *Job*, pp. 357-358.

[21]Compare 10:1-22 to 10:23-27; cf. also 9:1-20 to 9:21-24.

[22]Compare 12:13-25 to 13:1ff.

[23]Compare 14:1-12,19-22 to 14:13-17.

logical to assume that he has such a purpose here.[24] What purpose might that be? Perhaps the best answer is given by Gordis who suggests that this is yet another example of Job "quoting" traditional theology as a means of countering it.[25] Job has effectively employed this technique before, and he may be doing it again here.

[18]**"Yet they are foam on the surface of the water; / their portion of the land is cursed, / so that no one goes to the vineyards. / [19]As heat and drought snatch away the melted snow, / so the grave[a] snatches away those who have sinned. / [20]The womb forgets them, / the worm feasts on them; / evil men are no longer remembered / but they are broken like a tree. / [21]They prey on the barren and the childless woman, / and to the widow show no kindness. / [22]But God drags away the mighty by his power; / though they become established, they have no assurance of life. / [23]He may let them rest in a feeling of security, / but his eyes are on their ways. / [24]For a little while they are exalted, and then they are gone; / they are brought low and gathered up like all others; / they are cut off like heads of grain. / [25]If this is not so, who can prove me false / and reduce my words to nothing?"**

[a]*19* Hebrew *Sheol*

---

[24]It is interesting to observe here that the same tension between apparently contradictory or disconnected statements also exists in other biblical books that explore themes and employ genres like those found in Job. Cf., e.g., the laments of Jeremiah (Jer 12:1-4; 20:7-18) and the Psalms (Ps 22:1-5; 13:1-6; 77:1-16; 88:1-18) and the unconventional wisdom of Ecclesiastes (Eccl. 3:16,17; 8:11-13; 11:9; 12:9-14). It is possible to argue from these and other such texts that there is in Hebrew rhetoric an intentional technique that allows two opposing perspectives to stand together unreconciled and awaiting a final answer. A view similar to this is offered by Carol Newsom. Building on the work of literary critic Mikhail Baktin, she has suggested that Job should be read as a polyphonic text that intentionally juxtaposes competing views; cf. Newsom, *The Book of Job, A Contest of Moral Imaginations*.

[25]Gordis, *Job*, p. 322. Andersen suggests that Job is anticipating the destruction of the wicked he deems so worthy of judgment while the GGS translation takes it as some kind of "curse" which invites the destruction of the wicked; cf. M. Greenberg, J.C. Greenfield, and N.H. Sarna, *The Book of Job: A New Translation according to the Traditional Hebrew Text* (Philadelphia: Jewish Publication Society of America, 1980).

24:18-24[26] To this point in the chapter Job has been arguing that the wicked literally get away with murder while God stands by and does nothing. Now suddenly these claims are countered by a lengthy discourse on the sad and inevitable fate of the wicked. In what will amount to a reversal of fortunes, those evil men who have temporarily enjoyed lives of great substance are said to be doomed to fade away into nothingness. Like **foam**[27] **on the surface of the water** their lives will quickly dissipate. The wealthy **portion** they have illegally amassed will be **cursed**[28] and made useless. Those who once preyed upon **widows** will themselves become the prey of **God.** Those who abused their power to exploit the poor will be taken away by the **power** of God. In the same way that **heat and drought** quickly claim the **snow,** the **grave** (Sheol) will **snatch away**[29] **those who have sinned.** In a form of delayed justice God may allow them to become **exalted** for a **little while,** letting them **rest in a feeling of security** only suddenly to **bring** them **low** and **cut** them **off** like **heads of grain.** The metaphor in play here is that of the harvest. It is a common figure for judgment in the prophetic literature (cf. Isa 5:1-7). The basic idea here is that God, whose **eyes are on their ways,** will inevitably punish evil men for their ways. The concept of delayed judgment is entertained elsewhere in the Hebrew Bible in a form that reaches into the distant future (Gen 15:13-16; Dan 8:23-25; 11:36) or perhaps even unto an eschatological end time (Dan 12:2). This does not seem to be the idea here. In this context God's judgment is said to come in the evil man's own lifetime.

24:25 Having made his point, Job closes with a challenge to his opponent to **prove** his argument **false** (v. 25). But which argument does he mean? Is it the charge that God does not hold the wicked

---

[26]Verses 18-24 are very difficult in the Hebrew but the rendering of NIV captures what appears to be the essential meaning. For a discussion of the difficulties in translating this passage cf. Loretz, "Philologische und textologische Probleme," pp. 261-266; Rowley, *Job*, pp. 167-169. Hartley reads much of the language as a curse that Job is pronouncing upon the wicked: "Let the womb forget them, let the worm feast on them" (cf. *Job*, pp. 350-351).

[27]קַל (*qal*),"light" here probably means "light thing" (Cf. Hos 10:7).

[28]קלל (*qll*) seems to be a wordplay on *qal*.

[29]גזל (*gzl*), "snatch, steal." This is probably a wordplay on the charges made against wicked men earlier in the chapter that they "stole" (*gzl*, v. 2) livestock from the poor and "snatched" (*gzl*, v. 9) infants from the breasts of widows.

accountable which Job made in the first half of his speech (cf. v. 12b)? Or is it the opposite claim that God drags away evil men and dooms them to oblivion made in the second half of the speech (vv. 20-22)? Given the consistent challenge to God's justice that Job has voiced throughout his speeches, it is most likely that he is doing it here as well. If this is so, then verses 18-24, with their depiction of God's judgment of the wicked, should be read as a sarcastic quotation or parody of the arguments offered by the friends.[30] By juxtaposing his observations of real life (vv. 1-17) over against the empty claims of the friends (vv. 18-24) Job once again proves those claims to be false.

---

[30]This is a technique that Job has already employed (cf., e.g., 21:19a). As noted above some scholars treat vv. 18-24 as a prayer or curse that Job utters in his desire to see the wicked get their just rewards (cf. n. 26). But if Job is affirming his faith that God will somehow yet punish the wicked, it is even more difficult to explain the challenge he issues in v. 25. The view that Job is calling for the destruction of the wicked in vv. 18-24, however, should not be rejected out of hand. Job could be calling on God to destroy them as a kind of taunt, daring God to prove him wrong by bringing the wicked to judgment. Job has issued similar challenges to God in his earlier speeches (cf., e.g., 7:19-21; 10:8,9; 21:19b; cf. also 31:5-34). By calling on God to make good his threats against the wicked and knowing he will get no answer, Job strengthens his argument that God simply does not intervene in life to punish evil men. It is thus, even more difficult to prove Job wrong (v. 25).

JOB 25

3. Bildad's Third Speech (25:1-6)

This last speech of Bildad is different from his previous speeches in at least two ways. First, it has an abbreviated introduction. Bildad began each of his earlier discourses with a personal rebuff of Job's words and attitudes (cf. 8:2-3; 18:2-4), but this is missing here. Second, this speech is especially brief, consisting of a total of but five verses. Observing this, a significant number of scholars have argued that this speech has suffered some corruption of its original form and is in need of restoration. While there is no general agreement on exactly what form such a reconstruction should take,[1] the most popular suggestion is to join 25:1-6 to 26:5-14 and read this as the original speech of Bildad.[2] There is, however, no textual evidence to support any such emendation.[3]

It has long been argued that the brevity of Bildad's speech and the absence of one by Zophar in this third cycle is intentional and serves a specific rhetorical purpose. It should be noted that the general pattern of the speeches exhibits a progressive shortening of the discourses of the friends leading up to and including the so-called "broken" third cycle. Job's speeches, by contrast, get progressively longer. This could be the author's way of suggesting that the friends

---

[1]For a discussion of the wide variety of proposals cf. Rowley, *Job*, p. 169, and Markus Witte, *Vom Leiden zur Lehre*.

[2]With Dhorme, Terrien, Pope, Rowley, Habel.

[3]It is interesting to note, though, the presence of two additional introductions in Job's final speech (chs. 26–31). The expression, "Job continued his discourse," appears only in the third cycle (27:1; 29:1). These insertions appear to be redundant if Job is speaking everything in chs. 26–31. This could be taken as evidence that chs. 27 and 29 originally followed one of the speeches of the friends or, as some have suggested for ch. 28, a poem written by the author.

have run out of arguments and that Job has won the debate.[4] Such an understanding is consistent with the eventual judgment of the book itself. Elihu is said to be "angry" at the friends "because they had found no way to refute Job" (32:3), and Yahweh himself is "angry" at them "because [they] have not spoken of me [God] what is right, as my servant Job has" (42:7,8). Yahweh even goes so far as to label what the friends have been saying as "folly" (נְבָלָה, *nᵊbālāh*, 42:8).

As it stands, this brief speech of Bildad contrasts the majesty and holiness of God with the lowliness and impurity of humans (25:1-6). It employs a hymnic genre[5] coupled with an indicting use of rhetorical questions to challenge Job's qualifications as a self-appointed critic of the Almighty.

The Greatness of God and the Insignificance of Mortals (25:1-6)

[1]Then Bildad the Shuhite replied: / [2]"Dominion and awe belong to God; / he establishes order in the heights of heaven. / [3]Can his forces be numbered? / Upon whom does his light not rise? / [4]How then can a man be righteous before God? / How can one born of woman be pure? / [5]If even the moon is not bright / and the stars are not pure in his eyes, / [6]how much less man, who is but a maggot— / a son of man, who is only a worm!"

25:1-3 Too much should not be made of the fact that Bildad does not begin this speech with his normal exordium against Job (as in 8:2-3 and 18:2-4).[6] In an indirect way the entire speech is designed as just such a rebuke of Job. Though he speaks in the most general of terms, it seems clear that all along Job is the specific person at whom Bildad's words are aimed. In this speech Bildad directly challenges Job's right to criticize God. He does so in two ways. First, he reminds Job of who God is. Though Job has dared to challenge God as if he were just some ordinary opponent (cf. most recently 24:1), Bildad is

[4]Cf. A. Schultens, *Liber Jobi, II*, (1737), p. 729; K. Budde, *Beitrage zur Kritik des Buches Hiob* (1876), pp. 132ff.; R.K. Harrison, *Introduction to the Old Testament* (Grand Rapids: Eerdmans, 1969), pp. 1032-1033.

[5]Cf. C. Westermann, *Praise and Lament in the Psalms*, trans. K Crim (Atlanta: John Knox Press, 1981 repr.), pp. 15-35; S. Mowinckel, *The Psalms in Israel's Worship*, trans. D. Ap-Thomas (New York: Abingdon Press, 1979 repr.), 1:81ff.

[6]Against Habel, Rowley.

quick to point out that God is in a class by himself. **Dominion and awe**[7] **belong to God**, says Bildad. It is his way of confronting Job with the awe-inspiring power of the one whom Job has been challenging. Job, insists Bildad, is not giving God his proper due. Not only does he rule on earth, he also **establishes order in the heights of heaven**. The word translated **order** (שָׁלוֹם, *šālôm*) literally means "peace" in Hebrew, and some scholars have suggested that this may refer to God's power to quell conflicts between heavenly powers which have rebelled against God (cf. Ps 82:1; Isa 14:12-14; 24:21-22).[8] NIV is probably correct to understand it here to refer more generally to God's establishment of a celestial order (cf. 38:33). In verse 3 Bildad employs two rhetorical questions to complete his portrait of the incomparable greatness of God. The reference to God's **forces** (גְּדוּדִים, *gᵊdûdîm*) speaks of God in militaristic terms. God the warrior can summon a host of troops to enforce his rule. Here the term refers specifically to the celestial bodies[9] that populate his heavenly realm and emanate **his light**.[10] The reference to God's **light** is about his power to scrutinize humans and expose their impurity. It anticipates the rhetorical question of verse 4 concerning how a mortal could ever hope to be righteous before God and also explains that part of Job's reply which refers to the power of God's light to scrutinize even the abode of the dead (26:5-6).

25:4-6 In these verses Bildad gives the second part of his rebuttal of Job's repeated attempts to judge God. Having celebrated God's incomparable majesty (vv. 2-3) and the power of his light to expose the sins of mortals, Bildad now asks: "How could a mere **man** possibly think of himself as **righteous** or **pure** before such a God?" The inadequacy of humans as self-appointed judges of God is

---

[7] הַמְשֵׁל וָפַחַד (*hamšēl wāphahad*) is interpreted as a hendiadys for "awe-inspiring rule" by Duhm and Gordis.

[8] Cf. Habel, *Job*, p. 368.

[9] Cf. Judg 5:31 where the term is used to speak of the sun's might. In similar fashion the "hosts" (צְבָאוֹת, *ṣᵊba'ôth*, "armies") of heaven often refer to the celestial bodies in the Hebrew Bible (Deut 4:19; Isa 34:4; Ps 33:5[6]). The divine title "LORD of Hosts" carries the same militaristic idea of God as a warrior (cf., e.g., 1 Sam 15:2; 1 Chr 11:9.

[10] MT אוֹרֵהוּ (*'ôrēhû*). LXX reads ἔνεδρα παρ' αὐτοῦ = אָרְבוֹ (*'ōrᵊbô*, "his ambush"), which seems to be an attempt to continue the militaristic theme of v. 3a and is adopted by some (Duhm, Dhorme, Fohrer). Given the reference to "moon" and "stars" in v. 5 the emendation is unnecessary.

emphasized by Bildad's choice of terms to describe frail humanity. The term for **man** (אֱנוֹשׁ, 'ĕnôš) and the expression **one born of woman** (יְלוּד אִשָּׁה, yᵉlûd 'iššāh)[11] carry with them the idea of human weakness in contrast with the all-powerful God. According to Bildad it is simply impossible for a feeble human to regard himself as pious in the presence of such a holy God. Having listened to Job, Bildad knows that this is exactly what Job has been doing. In his rebuttal Bildad is echoing the sentiments first expressed by Eliphaz in his opening speech (4:17-18; cf. also 15:14-15).[12] Bildad continues his argument by declaring that even the **moon** and **stars**, so bright and dominant in the ancient sky, pale in comparison to the splendor of the Almighty. If they, in their brilliant perfection, do not impress God, how could a lowly man with his inherent imperfection ever hope to be favorably judged by God? Pressing his case of just how lowly a mere human is in God's sight, Bildad calls man a **maggot** and a **worm**. These terms are commonly used as symbols of death and decay in the book of Job (cf., e.g., 7:5; 17:14; 21:26; 24:20). But here they take on an additional meaning. According to Bildad humans are not merely weak and doomed to the grave, they are at the very bottom of the created order. This low view of man is a far cry from that expressed in Psalm 8 which honors man as made just "a little lower than the heavenly beings" and the **son of man**[13] as "crowned with glory and honor" (Ps 8:5[4]). Bildad's goal in his unflattering portrait of humans is to rebuff Job's attempt to judge God and to show the "sinful" Job that his determination to defend his integrity before a God of such absolute holiness is patently absurd.

---

[11]Dhorme and Rowley see in this language a negative view of the low estimate of women in ancient culture and suggest that humans, because they were birthed by women, were viewed as inherently "unclean."

[12]As noted above, some interpreters have seen in this kind of language biblical evidence for the doctrines of original sin and the total depravity of humans. It is interesting to note that such an idea is echoed outside of Israel. In the Sumerian wisdom text, "A Man and His God," there is a line that reads: "They say, the sages, a word righteous and straightforward: 'Never has a sinless child been born to its mother . . .'" (*ANET*, p. 590).

[13]An expression that means "of the class=human" both here and in Psalm 8.

JOB 26

4. Job's Reply to Bildad (26:1-14)

At this point in the dialogue the friends cease to speak. Job, by contrast, now launches into the single longest speech of the book (Job 26–31). Before he is through, he will: condemn the friends (26:1-4; 27:11-12); long for days gone by (29:1-25); lament his present condition (30:1-31); defend his integrity (27:1-6; 31:1-34); offer a traditional description of the fate of the wicked (27:13-23); acknowledge God's absolute power (26:5-14); affirm God as the exclusive possessor of wisdom (28:1-28); and call on God to "answer" him (31:35-40). Though there are portions of Job 26–31 which are difficult to comprehend as having been spoken by Job,[1] the book nonetheless assigns all of this material to him.[2] Assuming the existing form of the book to be the original one, we will attempt to understand these words in their present context and, with the possible exception of Job 28, treat all of this material as Job's final response to the friends.

Job's Rebuke of Bildad (26:1-4)

¹**Then Job replied:**
²**"How you have helped the powerless! / How you have saved the arm that is feeble! / ³What advice you have offered to one without wisdom! / And what great insight you have displayed! / ⁴Who**

---

[1]Most notably 26:6-14; 27:13-23; 28:1-28. For a discussion of scholarly opinion on who said what in chs. 26–28 cf. Rowley, *Job*, pp. 169-171, 175; also on ch. 28, H.H. Rowley, "The Book of Job and Its Meaning," *BJRL* 41 (1958): 191. Cf. also Barton, "The Composition of Job 24–30," pp. 66-77; and Witte, *Vom Leiden zum Lehre*.

[2]It does so, however, with the curious insertion of two additional headings (27:1; 29:1).

has helped you utter these words? / And whose spirit spoke from your mouth?

26:1-4 Job has regularly opened his replies to the friends with personal condemnations of their unsympathetic and untrue speech (cf., e.g., 12:2-3; 16:2-5; 19:2-6; 21:2-3). Whereas in his other rebukes he has tended to address the friends collectively,[3] here he speaks directly to Bildad.[4] These remarks are personal. For the "friend" who has just called him a "maggot" Job has saved his sharpest reply. With words full of sarcasm, he mocks Bildad's performance as self-appointed defender of God and comforter of the downtrodden. The translation of the NIV understands the expressions **the powerless** (v. 2a), **the arm that is feeble** (v. 2b), and **one without wisdom** (v. 3a) to be ironic self-characterizations of Job as Bildad views him and consequently "talks down" to him. They sarcastically condemn the superior moral ground that Bildad assumes as he condescendingly seeks to **help**, **save**, or **offer advice** to the "sinful" and "ignorant" Job.[5] The NEB and some interpreters,[6] however, believe these expressions are Job's characterizations of Bildad. Thus taken, Job is understood as accusing Bildad of being a "helper without power," a "savior with a feeble arm," a "counselor without wisdom." Whichever translation is correct, the meaning of the passage is essentially the same. Job is accusing Bildad of being a total failure as a counselor. As Job sees it, Bildad's **great insight**, is just so much "meaningless babble" and "pious pap." It is such misguided dribble that Job wonders just who or what could be the source of it. So he questions with **whose help** or by **whose spirit** Bildad was able to speak.[7] By using the term "spirit" (lit., "breath"; נְשָׁמָה, *nᵉšāmāh*) Job seems to

---

[3]Job regularly employs plural pronouns and suffixes in these speeches. There are, however, a few notable exceptions (10:3, spoken to Eliphaz; 12:7-8; 21:3b, spoken to Zophar).

[4]The "you" of v. 2a,b is in the second person, singular.

[5]Job has already condemned the friends for thinking lightly of him and speaking from the assumption of being on a higher intellectual and moral ground (12:2-3; 16:3-4; 19:5)

[6]Habel, *Job*, pp. 375, 376.

[7]RSV and ASV render v. 4a, "To whom do you utter these words?" and this is possible. If this is correct, then this would be yet another way by which Job is asserting that he is as well informed as the friends (cf. 12:3; 13:2).

be challenging Bildad's assumed role as a recipient of divine inspiration and qualified defender of God. The same term is used in 32:8 to describe the "breath of the Almighty" that "gives understanding." Job is suggesting that Bildad certainly could not be getting his words from God. They must, therefore, be coming from his own mind — from the mind of one of those lowly mortals he has just called a "maggot" and a "worm" (25:6).

Job's Affirmation of God's Great Power (26:5-14)

[5]"The dead are in deep anguish, / those beneath the waters and all that live in them. / [6]Death[a] is naked before God; / Destruction[b] lies uncovered. / [7]He spreads out the northern ⌞skies⌟ over empty space; / he suspends the earth over nothing. / [8]He wraps up the waters in his clouds, / yet the clouds do not burst under their weight. / [9]He covers the face of the full moon, / spreading his clouds over it. / [10]He marks out the horizon on the face of the waters / for a boundary between light and darkness. / [11]The pillars of the heavens quake, / aghast at his rebuke. / [12]By his power he churned up the sea; / by his wisdom he cut Rahab to pieces. / [13]By his breath the skies became fair; / his hand pierced the gliding serpent. / [14]And these are but the outer fringe of his works; / how faint the whisper we hear of him! / Who then can understand the thunder of his power?"

[a]6 Hebrew *Sheol*   [b]6 Hebrew *Abaddon*

These words represent an abrupt shift from Job's opening rebuke of Bildad and, at first reading, seem inexplicable in their present context. Sounding more like a praise of God than a protest against him, it is hard to hear them on the lips of Job. A closer examination of their actual meaning, however, can help us understand Job's purpose in this hymnlike recitation. The key is to read this text in the light of two separate but related contexts. The first context is the immediate one of Bildad's last speech (25:1-6). In that speech Bildad argued that God exercises great power to establish order in the heavens (25:2-3) and exposes the impurity of the mortals who inhabit the earth (25:4-6). This portion of Job's speech (26:5-14) touches on those same concepts and, outdoing Bildad, credits God with even greater scrutiny (of the dead, 26:5-6) and even greater power to order the cosmic forces of sky and sea and the regions beneath them (25:7-14). The second context to consider is that of Job's reply to Zophar's first speech (cf. 12:13-25). Job responded to Zophar's arguments about God in a manner very similar to this response to the speech of Bildad. Zophar had said God's "unfathomable mysteries" were "higher than the heavens" and "deeper than the grave" and that he could easily expose and punish "deceitful men" (11:7-11). In language that sounded more like a hymn than a lament, Job responded to Zophar's claims by outdoing him with his own praise of the unlimited "wisdom" and "power" of God (12:13-25). He then went on to explain why he did so. It was to prove that he knew everything the friends knew (and more) and that he was neither their intellectual nor their moral inferior (cf. 12:3; 13:1-2). This seems likewise to be Job's purpose here (cf. 27:11-12). It is as if Job is saying to Bildad, "You want to talk to me about how dominating and scrutinizing God is? I know this far better than you. In fact, I am living proof of it!"

26:5-6 As noted above, these words of Job directly relate to one of the arguments raised by Bildad's last speech. In 25:3b-6 Bildad made the point that God's light has the power to expose the flawed nature of the moon and stars as well as the impurity of lowly humans. In ironic and instructive fashion Job now picks up on that theme and takes it to another level. According to Job not only are the celestial and terrestrial inhabitants exposed by the scrutiny of God's penetrating light, but so also are the nether regions and those who inhabit them. With the term **the dead** (v. 5a) the NIV is translating רְפָאִים (rᵊphāʾîm).[8] This term refers here to the inhabitants of the grave and is sometimes translated "shades" because of the subhuman, shadowy existence that the departed dead are said to experience (Ps 88:11[10]; Isa 14:9-11; 26:14; Prov 2:18,19; 9:18). This term, along with the names **Death** (שְׁאוֹל, šᵊʾôl; v. 6a) and **Destruction** (אֲבַדּוֹן, ʾăbaddôn; v. 6b) are all borrowed from an ancient Near Eastern concept of a netherworld to which the dead are said to

---

[8]Cf. R. Schnell, "Rephaim," *IDB*, 4:35; S. Parker, "Rephaim," *IDBS*, p. 739. For the Canaanite background cf. C.L. Heureux, "The Ugaritic and Biblical Rephaim," *HTR* 67 (1974): 265-274, and J. de Moor, "Rapiuma — Rephaim," *ZAW* 88 (1976): 323-345. The term is also used in the Hebrew Bible to refer to a giantlike race that occupied Canaan before the Israelites (Deut 2:10-11,20-21).

descend. Job and other biblical authors appropriate this language in their poetic descriptions of death and the grave. Even though Sheol is deep (11:8), dark (17:13), and sealed (7:9), God's scrutinizing light **uncovers** it. There is nothing that escapes God's scrutiny.

26:7-9 Having spoken of God's dominion over the netherworld, Job now begins to characterize God's sovereign activity in the skies. In the manner of a Bedouin pitching a tent[9] God **spreads out the northern skies over the empty space.** The term for "north" (צָפוֹן, *ṣāphôn*) does not refer to a direction but to a place in the high heavens, where God's throne is said to reside.[10] When used with the verb "stretch out" (נָטָה, *nāṭāh*) it means the "heavens" (cf. 9:8; Isa 40:22). When Job says that God **suspends the earth over nothing**, he is more in tune with the cosmology of the modern scientific age than he is with the teachings of his own time. In the ancient Near Eastern world the earth was thought to stand on "pillars" (perhaps mountains) anchored in the watery depths (cf. 9:6; Ps 75:4[3]; 104:5; 1 Sam 2:8). Job's poetic description of an earth suspended in empty space (lit., "nothing"; בְּלִימָה, *bᵉlîmāh*) anticipates by centuries what science will later discover. Adding to this mystery is the phenomenon of **clouds**[11] full of **waters** that yet **do not burst under their weight** (cf. 37:11; 38:37; Ps 104:3). "Clouds" are a favorite subject of the biblical authors. Among other things they are said to "veil" or "mask" the glory of the Lord (Exod 19:16; 33:17-23)[12] and serve as God's celestial chariot (Ps 104:3). In the book of Job the clouds are used as symbols of the mysterious ways of God and his creation (36:29; 37:15-16; 38:37). Job goes on to say, "**He covers the face of**

---

[9]Cf. Habel, "He Who Stretches Out the Heavens," *CBQ* 34 (1972): 417-430.

[10]Cf. J.J.M. Roberts, "*ṢĀPÔN* in Job 26:7," *Bib* 56 (1975): 554-557; R. Reymond, *L'eau, sa vie, et sa signification dans l'Ancien Testament*, VTSupp 6 (Leiden: Brill, 1958), pp. 15, 175-176. In Canaanite mythology Mount Saphon was the dwelling place of the god Baal and in places the Hebrew authors appropriate this concept to speak of the throne of Yahweh (Ps 48:3[2]).

[11]Cf. R. Scott, "Meteorological Phenomena and Terminology," *ZAW* 64 (1952): 22-23, who defines עָבִים (*'ābîm*; v. 8) as a "rain cloud" or "thunderhead" and עָנָן (*'ānān*; v. 9) as a "dense cloud cover," "fog" or "mist."

[12]Cf. G. Mendenhall, *The Tenth Generation* (Baltimore: Johns Hopkins University Press, 1973), pp. 56ff.

the full moon,[13] **spreading his clouds over it**" (v. 9). If this translation is correct, then the language is exploring yet another mystery of the cosmos: the same clouds that contain rain and yet do not burst can also veil the light of the moon in the night sky. Since Bildad had just made reference to the "moon" (25:5) in his last speech, Job could be playing upon the theme of God's sovereignty over the celestial bodies. The Hebrew term translated "full moon," however, could also mean "throne"[14] or "his throne"[15] and refer to God "covering the appearance of his throne." The idea conveyed by this reading is that God shrouds his throne in a cloudbank to keep mortals from being consumed by his glory. Earlier in the book Eliphaz entertained a similar idea when he argued that though the clouds veil God in his heavenly abode, he can still see through them to judge the world (22:12-14).

26:10-11 Job extends his portrait of the awesome God by describing his creation of an important cosmic boundary — the **boundary between light and darkness**. God did this, Job says, by **marking out the horizon** or literally "drawing a boundary circle" (חֹק־חָג, *ḥōqḥag*)[16] **on the face of the waters** (v. 10). This seems to be Job's depiction of what Genesis 1 calls the "expanse" or "sky," the vault of heaven which separates the waters above from the waters beneath (Gen 1:6-8). This distant "boundary" (תַּכְלִית, *taklîth*) was regarded as the edge of the known cosmos where sky meets sea and day turns into night. Beneath this cosmic dome the **pillars of the heavens**, known elsewhere as the "pillars of the mountains" which were believed to support the huge canopy of the sky, are said to **quake** before the sound of God's **rebuke** (cf. Ps 18:8[7] = 2 Sam 22:8).[17]

26:12-13 In several of the ancient Near Eastern myths there is a description of creation as a great cosmic battle. Order is established through the defeat of the sea god (or goddess) whose waters represent malevolence and chaos.[18] Job is echoing those widely known sto-

---

[13]כֶּסֶה (*kissēh*), possibly a variant of כֶּסֶה (*keseh*), "full moon" (NEB, Dhorme following Ibn Ezra).

[14]ASV, RSV reading *kissēh* as a variant of כִּסֵּא (*kissē'*).

[15]Driver & Gray reading *kissēh* as a variant of כִּסֹה (*kisōh*).

[16]A variation of בְּחֻקוֹ חוּג (*bᵉḥûqô ḥûg*), "inscribe a circle" (cf. Prov 8:27).

[17]For a discussion of this theme in the Hebrew Bible cf. Jeremias, *Theophanie*, pp. 67-68.

[18]In the Babylonian myth of Enuma Elish, Marduk conquers Tiamat (the

ries in the language of these verses. By his **power** God **churned up the sea**.[19] By his **wisdom** he **cut Rahab to pieces**. Job had mentioned God's power over this mythological creature in an earlier speech (9:13). It is the sea-monster which personified chaos (cf. also Ps 89:11; Isa 51:9) said to be slain by God in primordial combat.[20] When Job describes causing the **skies** to become **fair** by his **breath**, he is probably appropriating imagery from the story of Enuma Elish where Marduk is said to have opened the mouth and distended the belly of Tiamat by a violent wind before he fatally shot her with an arrow.[21] God's **piercing** of the **gliding serpent**[22] is probably reminiscent of the Baal myth where the "crooked serpent" Leviathan (cf. Job 3:8; 41:1ff; Isa 27:1) is slain by Baal.[23]

26:14 Functioning as a summary of Job's praise of God's power (vv. 5-13) this line helps to understand, at least in part, why Job may have spoken these words in the first place. As noted above, the recitation of this traditional hymn was not about praise for the sake of praise, but praise in service of a rhetorical purpose. All along, Job's goal has been to demonstrate that he is the intellectual equal of Zophar and knows just as much (and more) as the friends do about the power of God (cf. 27:11). Building upon what Zophar had said about God's great power over the world he has made, Job makes an even greater case for this than Zophar. Then, as if to say "I have only scratched the surface of what I know about God's power," Job concludes his summary of these examples of God's power by claiming that they represent but the **outer fringe of his works**. The term

---

deep sea) and splits open her belly to form the world. (*ANET*, pp. 66-67). In the Canaanite myth of Baal, Baal conquers the sea god (Yamm) to establish his kingship over the earth (*ANET*, pp. 130-131). For other biblical adaptations of these myths cf. Ps 74:12-17; Hab 3:8-15 and B.W. Anderson, *Creation versus Chaos* (Philadelphia: Fortress Press, 1987).

[19]The verb רָגַע (*rāgaʿ*) can mean both "stir up" (Isa 51:15) and "quiet, calm" (Jer. 50:34). The translation "calmed" is probably to be preferred here in the model of creation as the establishment of order out of chaos.

[20]Cf. Day, *God's Conflict with the Dragon and the Sea.*

[21]Marduk then used a north wind to scatter her body parts (*ANET*, p. 67).

[22]נָחָשׁ בָּרִיחַ (*nāḥāš bᵊrîaḥ*), "fleeing serpent" (RSV). C. Gordon argues from comparison with the Ugaritic *brḥ* that *bariaḥ* means "evil" ("Leviathan, Symbol of Evil," *Orientalia* 22 [1951], 243).

[23]*UT*, 67:I:1-4. The imagery of the slain dragon is also employed in Rev 12:3ff.

"works" (דֶּרֶךְ, *derek*; lit., "way") has been variously interpreted[24] but its usage elsewhere in the book (38:19-20,24-25; 28:26 [used synonymously with חֹק, *ḥōq*; "law, rule"]) would suggest that it refers to God's "cosmic design" or the "principle" or "law" by which he governs his created world.[25] The created order (which Job knows even more about than the friends) constitutes but a **whisper** of God's grand design, a scheme simply beyond human ability to **understand** it. Job's argument has thus been made. When the friends authoritatively speak of what God is doing in his world (= punishing the evil, rewarding the good), they simply do not know what they are talking about.

---

[24]Andersen renders "realm," NEB renders "power," and GGS, "rule." Dahood ("Hebrew-Ugaritic Lexicography II," *Bib* 45 [1964]: 393-412) renders it "dominion, power."

[25]Cf. Habel, "The Symbolism of Wisdom in Proverbs 1-8," *Int* 26 (1972): 154-155; also Dhorme.

JOB 27

III. THE POST DIALOGUE (27:1–42:17)

A. JOB'S FINAL DEFENSE (27:1–31:40)

With the close of Job 26 the dialogue portion of the book of Job comes to an end. Through a prolonged series of speeches the three friends and Job have exhaustively debated the meaning of Job's suffering and the moral order by which God governs his world. They are no closer to agreement now than they were when the debate began. The friends remain convinced that Job's suffering is the result of a just God punishing him for some sin. Job is equally convinced that an unjust God is unfairly and maliciously afflicting him.

In a series of speeches beginning in chapter 27 and continuing through the end of chapter 31, Job will now offer his final argument. In order to appreciate why Job says what he does in his final defense, it is important that the reader remember what Job is trying to accomplish. Throughout the dialogue Job has been fighting two battles. The first battle has been fought against the friends. It has been fought rhetorically, in the form of an intense theological debate over the meaning of Job's suffering. Claiming the high moral ground, the friends have labeled Job a "sinner" who is appropriately reaping his just punishment from a God who always sees to it that people get what they deserve. Refusing to be treated as their inferior, Job has countered the friends by defending his integrity and arguing that their retributive model of divine justice is disproved by his own experience and by an honest observation of the real world.

Job's second and even more important battle has been fought against God. It has been fought spiritually in the form of a series of provocative charges and impassioned pleas offered up to a God whom Job believes has wronged him. Shattered by his undeserved suffering, Job has desperately sought vindication or, at least, an explanation from the God who seems to have inexplicably and unfairly turned against him.

In this, his final defense, Job now musters his last and best effort to win both of these battles. Fearlessly and with extraordinary rhetorical and forensic skill, Job will now attempt to win the debate with the friends and, at the same time, win vindication from God. Like a skilled lawyer concluding his case he makes his final summation through a series of well-designed arguments and legal maneuvers. Through a pair of discourses, each introduced with a new heading, the process unfolds as follows:

1. The First Discourse: Job Silences the Friends (27:1–28:28)

1. First, Job invokes a solemn oath in defense of his integrity (27:1-6).
2. He immediately follows this by threatening his enemies with a curse (27:7-10). By assigning them the fate of the "wicked" Job turns the tables on his accusers, suggesting that they, not he, are in danger of God's judgment.
3. He then claims the high ground in the debate with the friends by announcing his intentions to instruct them (27:11-12).
4. By restating their position with even greater eloquence and theological precision he proves himself their intellectual superior (27:13-23). At the same time he sets the stage for a final refutation of the claim that the "fate of the wicked" model is at work in his life (cf. 29:1–31:40).
5. Next, he disqualifies the friends as authoritative interpreters of God's designs by insisting that only God knows the way of wisdom (28:1-28). By reciting the traditional teaching that God gives wisdom to the pious (28:28), Job lays the groundwork for his rebuttal of this claim. Job the pious (1:1) has received no insight from God concerning the reason for his suffering (cf. 30:20; 31:35-37).

2. The Second Discourse: Job Demands Vindication from God (29:1–31:40)

1. By comparing his once-respected status as a righteous and compassionate man to the tragic suffering he now endures, Job repeats his claim to be an innocent sufferer unjustly afflicted by God (29:1–31:4).

2. Finally, in a climactic avowal of innocence, he boldly invites God to immediately punish him if he is guilty of any sin. He then dramatically closes his case by challenging God to personally indict him of any offense that merits the suffering God has inflicted upon his life (31:5-40).

1. The First Discourse: Job Silences the Friends (27:1–28:28)

Chapter 27 begins the postdialogue portion of the book in the form of Job's final defense (27:1–31:40). This portion of Job's final address consists of the following parts: 1) Job's avowal of innocence (27:1-6); 2) Job's curse upon his enemies (27:7-10); 3) Job's intention to instruct the friends (27:11-12); 4) Job's discourse on the fate of the wicked (27:13-23). As noted above, the second half of this chapter, with its traditional language regarding the destiny of the wicked, is thought by some to have been spoken by one of the friends. There is, however, no textual evidence to support this claim and, as will be shown, it is certainly possible to understand these words as having been spoken by Job.

Job's Final Words to the Friends (27:1-23)

Job's Avowal of Innocence (27:1-6)

¹And Job continued his discourse:
²"As surely as God lives, who has denied me justice, / the Almighty, who has made me taste bitterness of soul, / ³as long as I have life within me, / the breath of God in my nostrils, / ⁴my lips will not speak wickedness, / and my tongue will utter no deceit. / ⁵I will never admit you are in the right; / till I die, I will not deny my integrity. / ⁶I will maintain my righteousness and never let go of it; / my conscience will not reproach me as long as I live.

27:1-2 The reader is confronted with a new heading at this point in the dialogue. The phrase **and Job continued his discourse** (lit., "Then Job added, taking up his proverb [מָשָׁל, *māšāl*], saying") differs from the standard introductions to the other speeches and is similar to the one that will introduce Job's words in 29:1. What, if anything, might this new heading indicate? Some have seen it as an indication that an intervening speech by one of the friends (Zophar?) has been lost or misplaced. Others have suggested it proves that the preceding words (26:5-14) were not really spoken by Job and that this heading is needed to identify the beginning of Job's reply to words really spoken by one of the friends. More likely is the view that it acknowledges an obvious break in the third cycle and serves to identify Job as the speaker in a place where we would ordinarily expect here the words of Zophar.[1]

It is quite possible that this heading, like the one in 29:1, signals a new development or transition in the dialogue portion of the book.[2] The terminology used in this introduction suggests that something new and different is going on here. Elsewhere in the Hebrew Bible the expression "take up a discourse" (*māšāl*; lit., "proverb, parable")[3] is used to introduce an independent and formal statement rather than a continuation of some existing theme.[4] By choosing to introduce Job's words with this phrase, the author seems to be telling us that some new stage of this great drama is now upon us. The dialogue is over, and Job is about to begin his final summation. In a pair of discourses (27:1-28:28 and 29:1-31:40), each introduced with the heading *māšāl*, Job will conclude his debate with the friends and complete his case against God.

Job's new discourse opens with a formal oath. **As surely as God lives,** is a standard formula by which oaths were sworn in biblical times (cf. 1 Sam 14:39,45; 2 Sam 2:27). By implication the deity is called upon to curse the speaker if his words are false.[5] As he will do

---

[1]Cf. Wolfers, "Speech-Cycles," pp. 385-402.

[2]Cf. discussions by Hartley, *Job*, pp. 24-26; Habel, *Job*, pp. 377-378.

[3]*Māšāl* can refer to short proverbs as well as longer parables, discourses, and poems (cf. Johnson, "משׁל," *VTSupp* 3 [1960], 162-169.

[4]Cf. e.g., Balaam's attempted curse on Israel (Num 23:7,18); prophetic pronouncements of judgment (Isa 14:4; Micah 2:4; Hab 2:6). Habel (*Job*, p. 378) argues that this expression signals the introduction of a new unit in the plan of the book of Job. He identifies four distinct functions which 27:1-6 performs to create a transition between the dialogues with the friends and Job's final plea (chs. 29-31). Not only does this speech: 1) refer back to the prologue, 2) close the speeches, and 3) introduce Job's final testimony, but it is also 4) the one public statement of Job to which Yahweh later makes explicit reference (40:8).

[5]Verse 4 opens with an untranslated אם (*'im*, "if") which invites God to curse Job if he should ever "utter deceit."

later in his final appeal to heaven (Job 31), Job is taking this extreme measure in a desperate attempt to convince his critics of the truthfulness of his claims of innocence. This strategy may also represent an attempt by Job to provoke God to respond to Job's charges against him. The radical nature of this oath evokes two separate responses in the book. Elihu will rise up to contest it in 34:5ff, and God himself will rebuke it in 40:8. With the next phrase, **who has denied me justice**, the reader is again confronted by one of the major ironies of Job's predicament: Job seeks justice from the very God whom he has charged with injustice. In a contradiction only faith can permit, Job makes an appeal both against God and to him.

27:3-4 Most interpreters do not treat verse three as part of the content of Job's oath but see it as parenthetical (RSV). The language, however, does nicely fit the theme of Job's determination to **utter no deceit**. Taken along with the subsequent language of this entire declaration (e.g., **till I die**, v. 5b; **as long as I live**, v. 6b) the phrase, **as long as I have life within me, the breath of God in my nostrils**, echoes the sentiment of Job's unconditional commitment to maintain his innocence to the bitter end. The parallel terms **life** (lit., "breath"; נְשָׁמָה, *nᵉšāmāh*, v. 3a) and **breath** (lit., "spirit, wind"; רוּחַ, *rûaḥ*, v. 3b) refer to the animating force which comes from God (cf. Gen 2:7; 7:22; Isa 42:5). As long as Job is breathing, he will continue to protest his innocence. The essence of Job's oath is articulated in verse four. He will **speak no wickedness** and **utter no deceit**. Taken in the context of Job's legal complaint these words express Job's desire to "speak the whole truth and nothing but the truth."[6] Though the word **utter** (הָגָה, *hāgāh*) can mean "meditate," it can also mean "utter, murmur" and, in parallel with **speak** (דִּבֵּר, *dibbēr*), it carries that force here.[7] The emphasis on what Job "says" reminds the reader of the author's assessment of Job's initial responses to the tragedy Yahweh had brought to Job's life (1:22; 2:10b). Job's determination to speak only the truth contrasts with his earlier assessment of the kind of testimony that the friends might offer to God. He seriously questioned if it would indeed be free from "wickedness" (עַוְלָה, *'awlāh*) and "deceit" (רְמִיָּה, *rᵉmîyāh*) (13:7).

---

[6]So Habel, *Job*, p. 380.
[7]Cf. H. Ringgren, *TDOT*, 3:321-323.

27:5-6 Job concludes his declaration with another oathlike statement. **I will never** (v. 5a, NIV) literally reads "far be it from me"
(הָלִילָה לִי, *hālîlāh lî*) in the Hebrew and constitutes a form of self-
imprecation. It is grounded in Job's own fate in the same way that
the former oath ("as God lives") is grounded in God's very existence.
Job's determination to **not deny** (his) **integrity** and to **maintain** (his)
innocence reminds the reader of yet another irony in Job's tortur-
ous plight. The friends have repeatedly urged Job to confess his sin.
According to their model of retributive justice such a confession
would make God appear just and facilitate Job's restoration. Yet Job
knows (and so does the reader) that to make such a false confession
would itself constitute a sin and compromise the very integrity that
has been the hallmark of Job's life. This he will not do.

In the prologue the author has made the reader privy to a fact
that neither Job nor the friends can conceive. God has permitted the
suffering of Job for some other reason than justice — namely, as a
test of the genuineness of Job's piety. Job and the friends, each oper-
ating on a purely retributive model of how God runs his world, have
now come to two equally wrong conclusions. Applying the standard
of retributive justice to Job's condition the friends have wrongly concluded that Job has sinned. The error of this claim God will expose
in the epilogue of the book (42:7-9). Applying the same standard Job
has also wrongly concluded that God has treated him unfairly and
has "denied [him] justice" (27:2a). This claim, raised here to the level
of an oath, will likewise be challenged by God in his second speech
to Job (40:8).

Job's Curses upon His Enemies (27:7-10)

[7]"**May my enemies be like the wicked, / my adversaries like the
unjust! / [8]For what hope has the godless when he is cut off, / when
God takes away his life? / [9]Does God listen to his cry / when distress comes upon him? / [10]Will he find delight in the Almighty? /
Will he call upon God at all times?**

27:7-10[8] Job's final words to the friends now move from an oath
to a curse.[9] Identifying them as his **enemies**,[10] he utters an impreca-

---

[8]Many interpreters assign 27:7-23 to Zophar to account for his so-called
"missing speech" in the third cycle; cf., e.g., Rowley, *Job*, pp. 17, 5-78.

tion against them that would consign them to the fate of the **wicked**. That fate is described briefly in verses 8-10 where Job describes the wicked man as **cut off**[11] and without **hope** in his **distress**. When he **calls upon God**, he will get no response. The general portrait here is that of a helpless person abandoned by God. It is interesting to note that Job has thought of himself in such terms in his earlier speeches (cf., e.g., 14:19; 17:15; 19:7,10).

By identifying the friends with the "wicked" Job is clearly attempting to take the offensive in the debate. Throughout the speeches the friends have claimed the moral high ground by numbering Job among the wicked and by threatening him with their fate. In this his final defense, Job turns the tables on the friends. The accused becomes the accuser, the judged one takes on the role of the judge. Putting the friends on the defensive, Job now suggests that they, not he, should stand in fear of God's judgment. In the following verses he will continue this strategy of reversal by insisting that it is he who has something to teach the friends.

Job's Intention to Teach the Friends (27:11-12)

[11]**"I will teach you about the power of God; / the ways of the Almighty I will not conceal. / [12]You have all seen this yourselves. / Why then this meaningless talk?**

27:11-12[12] Job now speaks directly to the friends for the final time. His words serve to announce the agenda of his closing remarks (27:13–31:40). First, Job seeks to reverse the positions held by the

---

[9]"May my enemies be like" is a curse formula.

[10]"Enemy" is singular in the Hebrew. Habel thinks Job is referring here to God, his opponent in court (*Job*, pp. 379-380). But this would create an idea of Job's identifying God with the "wicked" and calling their fate upon him. God would be called upon to punish himself.

[11]יִבְצַע (*yibṣāʿ*), "gain by extortion or violence," is usually read in the Piel/Pual "cut off" (Driver & Gray). Gordis treats it as a Qal intransitive, meaning "is cut off." The parallel term יֵשֶׁל (*yēšel*), lit., "take as prey" (NIV "takes away his life") is also difficult. Duhm takes it as defective for יִשְׁאַל (*yišʾal*), "when God asks for his life." Others see it as from יִשָּׂא לְ (*yiśśāʾ lᵉ*), "[when] he lifts life to [God]," or "prays" (cf. Tur-Sinai).

[12]Though some scholars question the location of these words, there is little doubt that they are spoken by Job. He uses the familiar second person plural "you" by which he has regularly addressed the friends.

respective parties in the debate. All along the friends have considered themselves Job's teachers. Presuming the status of Job's moral and intellectual superiors, they have authoritatively instructed him of the divine purpose behind his suffering. Job now claims the intellectual and moral high ground from them by declaring, **I will teach you.**[13] Second, Job seeks to offer a final refutation of the friends' charge that God is punishing him for some sin. This he will do by instructing them on the **power** (lit., "hand"; יָד, *yad*) **of God.** For the friends this has meant the power of God to punish the wicked. But for Job the "hand of God" is a symbol of God's unjust treatment of him (10:7; 12:9; 13:21; 19:21). Now, through a series of powerful arguments Job intends to press this point in a way that will both silence the friends and win vindication from God. Unlike the friends Job **will not conceal** anything but expose God's true **ways.**[14] At the same time he intends to expose the folly of the friends' groundless accusations against him as so much **meaningless talk.**

The Fate of the Wicked (27:13-23)

[13]**"Here is the fate God allots to the wicked, / the heritage a ruthless man receives from the Almighty: /** [14]**However many his children, their fate is the sword; / his offspring will never have enough to eat. /** [15]**The plague will bury those who survive him, / and their widows will not weep for them. /** [16]**Though he heaps up silver like dust / and clothes like piles of clay, /** [17]**what he lays up the righteous will wear, / and the innocent will divide his silver. /** [18]**The house he builds is like a moth's cocoon, / like a hut made by a watchman. /** [19]**He lies down wealthy, but will do so no more; / when he opens his eyes, all is gone. /** [20]**Terrors overtake him like a flood; / a tempest snatches him away in the night. /** [21]**The east wind carries him off, and he is gone; / it sweeps him out of his place. /** [22]**It hurls itself against him without mercy / as he flees headlong from its power. /** [23]**It claps its hands in derision / and hisses him out of his place.**

---

[13]In a similar fashion, Yahweh will reverse roles with Job from the questioned to the questioner at the beginning of each of his two speeches ("I will question you" 38:3; 40:7).

[14]Lit., the preposition, "if," *'im*, conveying the thought of "what is on the mind of" God (Dhorme, Gordis).

Job continues his final defense by demonstrating that he is as knowledgeable as the friends concerning what traditional theology says about how God judges the wicked. The most challenging interpretive issue of this passage is to understand how these words could have been spoken by Job. Given the tone and content of this speech it sounds like something the friends would say rather than Job. In fact, Job has already spoken in direct rebuttal of this very kind of teaching in his earlier speeches (Job 21, 24).

The key to understanding this speech as the words of Job is 1) to read it in the context of what Job has just said he intends to do (27:11-12) and 2) to discover the role that it plays in Job's final defense (27:1–31:40). In 27:11-12 Job clearly states the purpose of what he is about to say. As noted above Job seeks first to claim the intellectual and moral high ground in the debate and then to prove the friends' model of retributive judgment wrong. By stating his opponents' position (on the fate of the wicked) with even greater eloquence and theological precision he achieves his goal of demonstrating that he is clearly their intellectual superior. Job's attempt to prove the friends wrong will unfold along the following sequence of argumentation: 1) He will restate the argument of the friends that supposedly proves the justice of God (the "fate of the wicked," 27:13-23). 2) He will undermine the friends' claim that they "know" God is punishing Job for some sin by arguing that the meaning of God's ways is beyond the ability of mortals to grasp (28:1-27). 3) By reciting the traditional teaching that God gives wisdom to the pious (28:28) Job will expose the invalidity of this claim. Job though pious (1:1) has been given no insight on the meaning of his suffering (cf. 30:20; 31:35-37). 4) He will rehearse his once-respected status as a righteous and compassionate man (29:1-25). 5) He will decry God's ruthless treatment of him (30:1–31:4). 6) He will directly challenge God to name any sin of which he is guilty thereby proving that God's treatment of him is unjust (31:5-40).

27:13-15 Job begins his final defense by demonstrating that he is just as knowledgeable as the friends concerning what traditional theology says about how God judges the wicked. The emphatic **Here** (lit., "this"; זֶה. *zeh*) announces Job's intention to "teach" them (v. 11) as they have repeatedly tried to teach him. The "fate of the wicked" has been a popular theme of the friends. It is the centerpiece of their argument for a just God. Job is now restating it for the purpose of refuting it. He has already used this rhetorical technique earlier. In language that also sounded more like the friends than Job, Job has already declared the power of God to bring down the mighty (12:13-25). He then went on to explain why he had spoken the language of traditional theology. First, it was to demonstrate that he was not the friends' intellectual inferior and could spout traditional theology with the best of the sages (13:1-2). Second, Job was seeking to prove, using his own life as an example, that the theology of retributive justice is simply inadequate to account for what God does in his world (13:3ff). Job's rehearsal of the traditional theology of the fate of the wicked serves the same purpose here.

Job 27:13 appears to be a paraphrase of Zophar's closing words in 20:29.[15] Both Job and the friends have quoted from each other throughout the debate as a technique of refutation. Job begins his discourse on the wicked by emphasizing the fixed destiny that God has set for them. The terms **fate** (חֵלֶק, *ḥēleq*) and **heritage** (נַחֲלָה, *naḥălāh*) carry the idea of an inheritance that the wicked have earned and are destined to receive.[16] The terms **wicked** (רָשָׁע, *rāšā'*) and **ruthless** (עָרִיצִים, *'ārîṣîm*)[17] often appear in tandem when speaking of God's enemies (cf., e.g., 15:20). The judgment of the wicked is first described as it relates to their **children**. Though they may be many, their lives are prematurely cut short by violence (**the sword**) or starvation (**they will never have enough to eat**) or disease (**the plague**). Since progeny were considered the ultimate blessing of God upon a man's life, so the loss of them is his ultimate curse.

27:16-19 Having spoken of what becomes of a wicked man's children, Job now speaks of what becomes of his possessions. Though the wicked amass great wealth, they will not keep it. God will see to it that the **righteous** and the **innocent** ultimately inherit it (cf. Prov 13:22; 28:8). The wicked man's **silver** will be spent by someone else, and his clothes will be worn by someone else. In a model of true

---

[15]This observation has led several interpreters to assign this speech to Zophar (cf., e.g., Habel, Pope, Gordis, Rowley).

[16]By the expression "God allots" NIV is translating עִם־אֵל (*'im-'ēl*; lit., "from God"). For a discussion on this particular form in the context of Job cf. M. Dahood, *Ugaritic-Hebrew Philology*, BibOr 17 (Rome: Pontifical Biblical Institute, 1965), p. 32.

[17]*'ārîṣîm* is plural in the Hebrew. The fluctuation between the singular and the plural in terms for the "wicked" in Job is common.

justice, the innocent people whom the wicked commonly exploit to get such things will ultimately enjoy them (cf. Eccl 2:20-21). The **house** that the wicked man builds will not stand. Though it may appear stately and impressive, in reality it is as flimsy as **a moth's cocoon**[18] or **a hut made by a watchman.** Such huts were constructed of straw and sticks as temporary shelters at harvestime (cf. Isa 1:8). All of the wicked man's wealth is illusory. One night he goes to bed rich and in the morning awakens a pauper.

27:20-23 The wicked man loses more than his children and his possessions. **Terrors**[19] (death) dramatically sweep him away like a **flood,** like a **tempest** or the ever-threatening **east wind.** These metaphors of swift judgment are used elsewhere in the Hebrew Bible (cf., e.g., 2 Sam 5:20; Isa 28:17; Hos 5:10). Of particular note in the book of Job is the use of storm/wind both as an instrument of the Satan's/God's affliction of Job (1:19) and an arena of God's self-disclosure (38:1; 40:6). The subject of verse 23 is disputed. It could be a continuation of the wind metaphor of verses 20-22 in the form of a personification or, as some interpreters suggest, refer to men[20] or God, himself.[21] The idea of these two views is that the people of the land and/or God rejoice in the demise of the wicked man.[22]

More than an "ironic parody" of the friends, this eloquent

---

[18]For a discussion of this expression see Rowley, *Job*, p. 178.

[19]For the idea that this term refers to a malevolent underworld figure see Habel's comment on 18:24.

[20]Dhorme.

[21]Andersen.

[22]It is easy to see how most readers wonder how Job could have possibly spoken these words. The position the speaker rehearses is exactly like that of the friends. In fact, Job has elsewhere refuted some of these very claims (cf., e.g., ch. 21). Noting this, most interpreters see this passage as evidence of a "broken" third cycle of the book of Job and reassign these words to Zophar or Bildad. A number of scholars, however, have attempted to interpret these words as having been spoken by Job. Accordingly they are viewed as: 1) sarcastic quotations of the friends; 2) preemptive citations of the friends for the purpose of refutation; 3) a parodic homage to a generic convention (the "fate of the wicked" poem); or 4) evidence of Job's acceptance of the friends' point of view. For a thorough discussion of the scholarly debate on this issue cf., Witte, *Vom Leiden zur Lehre*. Also, Seitz, "Job: Full-Structure, Movement, and Interpretation," pp. 5-17; Newsom, *The Book of Job*, pp. 164-168; H. Graf Reventlow, "Tradition und Redaktion in Hiob 27 im Rahmen der Hiobreden des Abschnittes Hi 27-27," *ZAW* 94 (1982): 279-293.

rehearsal of the "fate of the wicked" doctrine serves to silence the friends by implying that the fate God reserves for his enemies may be the very fate the friends should fear. Job takes full and final control of the debate by suggesting that they, not he, are the ones who are in violation of God's will and stand in danger of his judgment.

JOB 28

1. The First Discourse: Job Silences the Friends
(27:1–28:28, continued)

The Wisdom Hymn (28:1-28)[1]

This poem on the search for wisdom is one of the great literary gems of the book. Though there is significant dispute over who may have spoken it and what specific role it plays in the structure and purpose of Job,[2] nearly all who have read it agree on its essential theme: God alone has direct access to wisdom. Whereas precious metals and gems yield their secret locations to the persistent and ingenious quests of men, wisdom does not. It cannot be mined or bought or discovered in any way. It is available to humans only through pious submission to the Lord. The poem breaks down nicely into three stanzas: 1) wisdom cannot be mined (28:1-11); 2) wisdom cannot be bought (28:12-19); 3) God alone knows the way to wisdom and gives it to the pious (28:20-28). Though this poem differs somewhat in style and tone from the rest of Job, it does have connections with other parts of the book. Bildad has already addressed the theme of wisdom's inaccessibility (Job 11) and Yahweh will later assert his exclusive knowledge of the grand design of the universe (Job 38–39).[3]

The book makes Job the speaker of this poem, and in our view he recites it for two distinct but related purposes. The first purpose

---

[1] The LXX version of this speech is shorter. The translator's alterations may have been intentional to make it more appealing to his Greek readers (cf. P. Zerafa, *The Wisdom of God in the Book of Job* [Rome: Herder, 1978], pp. 130-136.

[2] For a discussion of these issues see the Introduction.

[3] Rowley considers this poem and the speeches of Yahweh to be in such agreement the he believes chapter 28 renders the Yahweh speeches unnecessary and offers this as proof that it is not original to the book (*Job*, p. 179).

is directed toward the friends. By claiming that humans cannot discover wisdom (the "design" or "purpose" behind God's creation and
management of his world), Job disqualifies the friends as authoritative interpreters of what God is doing in Job's life. The second purpose is directed toward God. By rehearsing the biblical claim that
God gives wisdom to the pious (28:28), Job will lay the groundwork
for adding to his charge that God has not been fair to him. Job the
pious (1:1; 2:3; cf. 29:1-25) has not been given any insight on the
meaning of the suffering in his life (3:20-23; cf. 31:35-37).

Wisdom Cannot Be Mined (28:1-11)

[1]**"There is a mine for silver / and a place where gold is refined.
/ **[2]**Iron is taken from the earth, / and copper is smelted from ore.
/ **[3]**Man puts an end to the darkness; / he searches the farthest
recesses / for ore in the blackest darkness. / **[4]**Far from where people dwell he cuts a shaft, / in places forgotten by the foot of man;
/ far from men he dangles and sways. / **[5]**The earth, from which
food comes, / is transformed below as by fire; / **[6]**sapphires**[a]** come
from its rocks, / and its dust contains nuggets of gold. / **[7]**No bird
of prey knows that hidden path, / no falcon's eye has seen it. /
[8]Proud beasts do not set food on it, / and no lion prowls there. /
[9]Man's hand assaults the flinty rock / and lays bare the roots of the
mountains. / **[10]**He tunnels through the rock; / his eyes see all its
treasures. / **[11]**He searches**[b]** the sources of the rivers / and brings
hidden things to light.**

[a]*6 Or* lapis lazuli; *also in verse 16*   [b]*11 Septuagint, Aquila and Vulgate;
Hebrew* He dams up

28:1-4[4] The frequent references to metals in the Hebrew Bible
illustrate the high value that was placed upon them by the ancient
Israelites. **Silver** and **gold** were not native to Israel and had to be
imported from distant places like Tarshish (Jer 10:9), Ophir (Isa
13:12; 1 Kgs 10:11), and Sheba (1 Kgs 10:2). **Copper** was mined at

---

[4]Though the NIV does not choose to translate it, the opening verse begins
in the Hebrew with the particle כִּי (*kî*), "for, because." Duhm sees this as evidence of a missing refrain like that found in vv. 12 and 20. Better is the view
of Gordis that *kî* is here functioning as an introductory particle with an
emphatic force meaning "surely." Such usage is found biblically in Isa 15:1
and extrabiblically in Ugaritic texts (cf., e.g., *UT* 1184).

Ezion-geber in Solomon's time, and Israel began to use **iron** extensively in David's time.[5] Various kinds of **mining** and **refining** were practiced from ancient times, including the cutting of deep **shafts** into the earth.[6] These technologies were heralded as examples of human ingenuity. With torches and lamps men were able to penetrate the **farthest recesses** and **blackest darkness**. These terms conjure up images of the netherworld, the abode of the dead (cf. 10:21-22). At great risk of personal injury the miner **dangles and sways** from ropes in the search of precious metals. In this text the author is seeking to compare the mining of the natural domain to the human pursuit of meaning (wisdom) in the cosmic domain.[7]

As Habel has observed, one of the keys to understanding this entire poem is the author's use of the term **place** (מָקוֹם, *māqôm*).[8] It is introduced in the first verse and appears again in verses 6,12, 20,23. In the book of Job everything has a "place" in the grand design of the universe (cf., e.g., humans, 7:10; 8:18; the earth, 9:6; the wind, 27:23). In these opening verses the author celebrates the ability of humans to find the **place** where precious metals can be found. By contrast the precise location of the world's most precious commodity (wisdom) is known only to God (v. 23).

28:5-11 While the earth's surface yields **food,** its **rocks** and **dust** also produce precious gems and metals. The term **sapphires** may refer to *lapis lazuli*, a dark blue stone.[9] The **nuggets of gold** referred to here may actually have been iron pyrites associated with this precious stone.[10] Commentators disagree over what is meant by the phrase **transformed below as by fire.** Some think it is a description of a mining technique of combining fire and water to shatter rock and extract its minerals.[11] Pope believes it reflects the ancient belief that gems were produced by volcanic activity and connects this phrase with the expression "stones of fire" found in Ezekiel 28:14.[12]

---

[5]Cf. discussion by Pope, *Job*, pp. 177-178.

[6]Cf. R. Forbes, *Studies in Ancient Technology VII* (Leiden: Brill, 1963); S. Singer, "From These Hills, " *BAR* 4/2 (1978): 16-25.

[7]Habel, *Job*, p. 396.

[8]Ibid., pp. 393, 395.

[9]According to Gordis, the sapphire was not known until Roman times.

[10]Rowley, *Job*, p. 181.

[11]L. Waterman, "Notes on Job 28:4," *JBL* 71 (1952): 167-170.

[12]Pope, *Job*, p. 179.

The point of verses 7-8 is that while the **bird of prey** with its keen eyesight and the **lion**[13] with its great ability to roam about in search for food cannot find these precious gems, humans with their superior ingenuity can. The mastery of mining thus illustrates the superiority of humans over the animals. While the birds of the sky and the wild beasts survey the face of the earth, humans are able to even **tunnel** beneath its surface in search of its **treasures**. In their search for riches men **lay bare the roots of mountains** and **assault the flinty rock** and **bring hidden things to light**. Such acts are normally attributed to God in the Hebrew Bible (Job 9:5; 12:22; Ps 78:15; Hab 3:9). Humans are depicted here as even rivaling God in their ingenuity and power. Unlike God, however, they cannot successfully locate wisdom.

Wisdom Cannot Be Bought (28:12-19)

[12]**"But where can wisdom be found? / Where does understanding dwell? /** [13]**Man does not comprehend its worth; / it cannot be found in the land of the living. /** [14]**The deep says, 'It is not in me'; / the sea says, 'It is not with me.' /** [15]**It cannot be bought with the finest gold, / nor can its price be weighed in silver. /** [16]**It cannot be bought with the gold of Ophir, / with precious onyx or sapphires. /** [17]**Neither gold nor crystal can compare with it, / nor can it be had for jewels of gold. /** [18]**Coral and jasper are not worthy of mention; / the price of wisdom is beyond rubies. /** [19]**The topaz of Cush cannot compare with it; / it cannot be bought with pure gold.**

28:12 But where can wisdom be found? This query, repeated in verse 20, poses the essential question raised by the poem and addresses one of the central issues addressed by the book of Job. The term **wisdom** (lit., "the wisdom"; הַחׇכְמׇה, *haḥokmāh*) is paralleled here by the term **understanding** (בִּינׇה, *bînāh*) as is common in the Wisdom literature (cf., e.g., Prov 1:2; 4:5; 9:10; 16:16). This latter term, with its root meaning of "discernment," helps us comprehend what the author means here by the broader concept of "wisdom." In this poem the search for wisdom is the search for "the plan" or the

---

[13]Some translate שׇׁחַל (*šāḥal*) as "lizard." Cf. S. Mowinckel, "*sahal*," in *Hebrew and Semitic Studies,* Fest. G.R. Driver, eds. D. Thomas and W. McHardy (Oxford: Clarendon, 1963), p. 97.

"grand design" by which the universe is governed.[14] In the book of Job this issue is explored on both a cosmic and moral level. This poem joins a chorus of voices in the book proclaiming that the answer to this mystery is beyond the grasp of humans. Though ingenious and skillful, humans cannot "discover" the "meaning" or "purpose" behind God's world. God alone knows it, and he grants it only to those who live in reverence before him.

In this poem wisdom is personified and described as having a place or **dwelling**. Such personifications of wisdom (always a woman in the OT) are common to the biblical Wisdom literature (c.f., e.g., Prov 1:20-33; 8:1-36; 9:1-6). In such texts wisdom is treated as having its own persona, separate from God (cf. Sir 1:1-10). Described in Proverbs as God's first "creature" it is commonly associated with creation and is said to be instrumental in the ordering of the created world (Prov 8:22-23,30-31).

28:13-14 Wisdom, the hidden principle that lies behind creation, is simply beyond human comprehension. NIV renders the opening line of verse 14, **Man does not comprehend its worth**, but it is probably better translated, "Man does not know its abode/place."[15] The idea of the "worth" or "value" of wisdom is not taken up until verses 15-19. Not only is the way of wisdom not known **in the land of the living,** the primordial **deep** (תְּהוֹם, *tᵊhôm*) or **sea** (יָם, *yām*) cannot find it either.[16] According to Proverbs 8:24,28 wisdom was present when the deep emerged and the boundaries of the sea were set. Here, as in Proverbs, wisdom is portrayed as something other than a mere part of the created world.

---

[14]In Yahweh's initial response to Job (38:2) he accuses Job of ignorantly obscuring or misrepresenting God's "design" (NIV, "counsel"; עֵצָה *'ēṣāh*) with his impious accusations of God's "injustice."

[15]NIV has the support of MT (עֶרְכָּהּ, *'erkāh*) and this reading is followed by Andersen. The LXX, however, reads דַּרְכָּהּ (*darkāh*, "its way") here. Noting that the next line has the verb "find" (מָצָא, *māṣa'*) and that this line is repeated again in v. 23 with the idea of "place," most commentators (Duhm, Dhorme, Fohrer, Habel) follow LXX. Gordis reads with MT but still renders *'erkāh* with "its place" on the basis of the use of this term in Exod 39:37 and 1 Sam 4:2. Dahood interprets MT as "house" by comparison with Ug. *'rl/bt* ("Hebrew-Ugaritic Lexicography VII," *Bib* 50 [1969]: 355).

[16]In the mythology of the ANE, *Tehom* and *Yamm* were deities (cf. Cross, *Canaanite Myth and Hebrew Epic*, ch. 6).

28:15-19[17] The theme of this section is the incomparable value of wisdom. In language similar to that of the book of Proverbs, wisdom is portrayed as a commodity of such supreme worth, that it **cannot be bought** for the price of even the most precious metal or gem (Prov 3:13-15). Wisdom, in the sense of knowledge of the grand design by which God created and governs his world, is simply not for sale at any price. The valuable commodities listed here represent the most prized metals and jewels of the ancient world. The terms for **gold** (סְגוֹר, *s⁽ᵉ⁾gôr*, v. 15; פָּז, *pāz*, v. 17) mean "solid gold" and "pure gold." The word for **crystal** (v. 17; זְכוֹכִית, *z⁽ᵉ⁾kôlîth*) can also be translated "glass." In biblical times Egypt and Phoenicia were famous for glassware. **Onyx** was used in the breastplate of the high priest (Exod 28:20). The term for **coral** (רָאמוֹת, *rā'môth*) could also mean "pearls." The **topaz of Cush** was probably yellow chrysolite found on the island of Zarbaqad off the coast of Egypt (Pope).

God Alone Knows the Way to Wisdom (28:20-28)

[20]"Where then does wisdom come from? / Where does understanding dwell? / [21]It is hidden from the eyes of every living thing, / concealed even from the birds of the air. / [22]Destruction[a] and Death say, / 'Only a rumor of it has reached our ears.' / [23]God understands the way to it / and he alone knows where it dwells, / [24]for he views the ends of the earth / and sees everything under the heavens. / [25]When he established the force of the wind / and measured out the waters, / [26]when he made a decree for the rain / and a path for the thunderstorm, / [27]then he looked at wisdom and appraised it; / he confirmed it and tested it. / [28]And he said to man, / 'The fear of the Lord—that is wisdom, / and to shun evil is understanding.'"

[a]22 Hebrew *Abaddon*

28:20-22 The refrain, **Where does wisdom come from?** is but a slight variation of verse 12.[18] Some interpreters suggest that the difference is intentional and is designed to reflect first the inability of humans to discover wisdom (v. 12) and second the inability of

---

[17]Some scholars see these verses as an insertion. LXX omits vv. 14-16.

[18]תָּבוֹא (*tābô'*), "it will come," is used in the place of תִּמָּצֵא (*timmāṣē'*), "it will be found" (v. 12).

humans to acquire wisdom (v. 20).[19] Whether or not this is so, verses 21-22 do add something to the idea of wisdom's inaccessibility
introduced earlier in the poem (vv. 12-13). By the use of the terms
hidden and **concealed** the author is suggesting that God has deliberately hidden his purposes from humans. Wisdom's inaccessibility
is not just an accidental phenomenon of the cosmos, it is itself part
of God's design. So deeply is this mystery hidden that even the birds
with their superior perspective cannot detect it. The remote regions
called **Destruction** (אֲבַדּוֹן, *'ăbaddôn*) and **Death** have heard **only a
rumor of it.** The Hebrew Abaddon is derived from a root (אָבַד,
'ābad) that means "perish" and is commonly used to refer to the
abode of the dead in the Wisdom literature (cf. 26:5; 31:12; Prov
15:11; 27:20). The deep recesses of the netherworld only know of
wisdom by hearsay.

28:23-27 These verses announce the essential theological teaching of the poem: God alone has firsthand knowledge of wisdom.[20]
He alone **understands** the meaning and purpose of the created
order. He comprehends what humans cannot because of two distinct qualifications he possesses. First, he has a unique perspective
of his world. He **sees everything under the sun** and **views the ends
of the earth.** Second, God created the world. He **established the
force of the wind** and **measured out the waters.**[21] Because he made
all things, he understands how all things fit together and the proper
role they perform in the created world. This is the very point that
Yahweh himself will make in his response to Job (Job 38–41).

The language of verse 27 is important for understanding the
author's view of wisdom's relationship to God. Depicting much
more than God's discovery of wisdom,[22] this verse rather describes

---

[19]Cf. Zerafa, *The Wisdom of God in the Book of Job*, p. 146.

[20]The association of wisdom with deity is also known in the ANE world.
The Mesopotamian deities Enki, Shamash, Ea, and Marduk are all praised
for their wisdom (cf. M. Eliade, *Patterns in Comparative Religion* [New York:
Meridian Books, 1963], ch. 2, and Habel, *Job*, p. 399). It is interesting to
note that in the Garden of Eden story of Genesis 2–3, the forbidden fruit
with its capacity to "make one wise" is associated with the desire of Eve to
"become like God."

[21]The forces of "wind," "waters," "thunderstorm," and "rain" are not said
to be chaotic but controlled and measured as part of God's creative design.

[22]Contra Habel.

God's sovereign control over wisdom. When the author says God **appraised** (סָפַר, *sippēr*), **confirmed** (הֵכִין, *hēkîn*), and **tested** (חָקַר, *ḥāqar*) wisdom, he is describing a God who both created wisdom and then determined its role in the rest of creation.[23] This echoes the thought of Proverbs 8:22-31 where wisdom is described as the first of God's creatures who plays an important role in the rest of the creation process (cf. also Prov 3:19-20). Though personified in this poem, wisdom is not presented as a self-existent entity totally independent of God.

With his eloquent claim that God alone knows the way of wisdom Job has successfully disqualified the friends as authoritative interpreters of God's purposes in his life. Like miners and merchants the friends have sought to take hold of the mystery behind God's management of his world through their theological speculation. Job has now invalidated that entire process. The first of his two purposes in reciting this elegant poem has now been achieved. The self-appointed interpreters of God's role in Job's life (the friends) have now been reduced to silence. Job's final purpose (directed toward God) will become apparent in the concluding statement of the poem (v. 28).

28:28[24] The same God who alone knows the way of wisdom and who has established wisdom as the primary principle behind his creation of the world offers it to **man** (אָדָם, *'ādām*).[25] He does so on the following terms: **'The fear of the Lord—that is wisdom, and to shun evil is understanding.'** Nothing is more central to the biblical doctrine of wisdom than this orthodox teaching (cf., e.g., Prov 1:7).

---

[23]Cf. von Rad, *Wisdom in Israel*, p. 147. For an alternative view cf. S. Harris, "Wisdom or Creation: A New Interpretation of Job 28:27," *VT* 33 (1983): 419-427.

[24]Some scholars believe this verse to be a later addition to the poem. But as Zuckerman and others have convincingly argued, the poem would end abruptly and be incomplete without it. Cf. Bruce Zuckerman, *Job the Silent: A Study in Historical Counterpoint* (Oxford: Oxford University Press, 1991), p. 143; Peter van der Lugt, *Rhetorical Criticism and the Book of Job*, OtSt 32 (Leiden: E.J. Brill, 1995), p. 324; Newsom, *The Book of Job*, pp. 180-182; Habel, *Job*, pp. 392-393. Habel goes so far as to argue that this verse is crucial to our understanding of the intent and purpose of the poem.

[25]Tur-Sinai believes this is referring to the first man, Adam. He makes this claim on the basis of references to creation in the immediate context (vv. 25-26).

According to the traditional teaching of the Wisdom literature, humans receive wisdom when they piously submit to the sovereign, holy God. But how exactly does this work? How do reverence and obedience lead to **wisdom** or **understanding**? The central premise of the Hebrew Bible (ethical monotheism) is that there is one good God who made all things and who rules them by his sovereign will. By revering God and pursuing good, humans actively acknowledge this truth and align themselves with the operative principle by which he governs his universe. Life takes on meaning and purpose because it is being lived in harmony with the will of a sovereign, holy God.[26]

Except for Job, of course! For Job, who has devoted his life to "fearing God" and "shunning evil" (1:1), life has been deprived of all meaning and purpose by the inexplicable suffering that has overtaken him. Why then does he say this? Why does he spout this pious rhetoric at this crucial point in his case against God? He says it in order to refute it. This final verse punctuates Job's second purpose for reciting this poem on the search for wisdom. After rehearsing the traditional claim that God alone possesses wisdom and gives it to those who revere him, Job will go on to charge that God has failed to do this in his life. In spite of the fact that he has lived a pious life, God has granted him no explanation, no understanding of why his life has so brutally miscarried (31:35-37). Job is thus building his case against an "unjust" God to a dramatic climax.

---

[26]This emphasis on submission to God may account for Job's choice of the term אֲדֹנָי (*'ădōnāy*) to speak of God in this text. This term, which means, "lord," carries with it the basic idea of sovereignty and is used commonly alongside of or synonymously with the term, *Yahweh*, the personal name of God in the Hebrew Bible (cf. Eissfeldt, *TDOT*, 1:59-72). For alternative theories to explain the appearance of the term *'ădōnāy* in 28:28 cf. Habel, *Job*, pp. 400-401.

JOB 29

2. The Second Discourse:
Job Demands Vindication from God (29:1-31:40)

The second "discourse" (מָשָׁל, *māšāl*, 29:1; cf. 27:1) of Job's final defense (29:1-31:40) opens with Job's recollection of his once favored status as a righteous man blessed by God (29:1-25). This autobiographical piece is not so much about gratitude for a once-blessed life as it is about laying a foundation for a protest of innocence.[1] More than mere nostalgia, this rehearsal of Job's former glory is designed to prove that the suffering Job is currently experiencing is undeserved and the result of ruthless persecution by an unjust God (30:1-31). Through this remembrance of his former state Job clearly seeks to establish the fact that he deserved God's blessings as a reward for his righteous behavior (vv. 11-17). On the basis of his virtue Job expected to continue to live a blessed life (vv. 18-20). Instead, he has received only humiliating suffering from God (30:1-31).

In his zealous rehearsal of his own virtues Job describes himself as an ideal ruler whose administration of justice is virtually equivalent to the role performed by God.[2] By elevating himself to almost godlike status, Job is positioning himself to challenge God for his "unjust" behavior.[3] As he claimed the high ground in his struggle with the friends in his first summation (27:1-28:28), he now seeks to claim a position of strength in his struggle with God (29:1-31:40).

---

[1]As such, it bears resemblance to the language of some of the psalms of lament (cf., e.g., 44:2-9[1-8]); cf. Westermann, *Structure of the Book of Job*, p. 39.

[2]A. Lévêque, *La sagesse de l'Ancien Testament*, ed. by M. Gilbert (Louvain: Leuven University Press, 1980), pp. 234-235.

[3]As Habel observes, Job's claims in this chapter serve to provoke Yahweh's challenge of Job's ability to administer justice (cf. 40:9-14).

This part of Job's closing speech may be outlined in the following way: 1) the Job once blessed by God (29:1-6); 2) the Job once honored as savior of the oppressed (29:7-25).

The Job Once Blessed by God (29:1-6)

[1]Job continued his discourse:
[2]"How I long for the months gone by, / for the days when God watched over me, / [3]when his lamp shone upon my head / and by his light I walked through darkness! / [4]Oh, for the days when I was in my prime, / when God's intimate friendship blessed my house, / [5]when the Almighty was still with me / and my children were around me, / [6]when my path was drenched with cream / and the rock poured out for me streams of olive oil.

29:1 The introductory formula, **Job continued his discourse** (lit., "Then Job added, taking up his proverb [*māšāl*], saying") is identical to that of 27:1. As noted above, this language breaks from the normal pattern in the speeches and suggests that something new and distinct is about to be said.[4] According to our interpretation, the two "discourses" introduced by this title (27:2–28:28; 29:1–31:40) signal the end of the dialogue portion of the book and announce the beginning of Job's final argument. Whereas the first discourse is designed to silence the friends, this discourse is designed to settle Job's dispute with God.

29:2-3 The expression **How I long for** (lit., "Oh, if only it was given to me"; מִי־יִתְּנֵנִי, *mî-yittᵊnēnî*) has been used earlier by Job to announce his desire to approach God in search of vindication (19:23; 23:3). It is used at the beginning and end (31:35) of this final speech as Job seeks to press God for a day in court. Job remembers his former days as a time when **God watched over** him. Elsewhere in the Hebrew Bible this expression (שָׁמַר, *šāmar*) refers to God's compassionate protection of his servant (Num 6:24-26; Ps 91:11). This is the kind of care that the Satan described as God's protective "hedge" about Job (1:10). **Lamp** and **light** are also symbols of God's protection and blessing (33:28-30; cf. Ps 18:29[28]; 36:10[9]). They guided Job through the **darkness** of difficult times.

---

[4]Cf. discussion of 27:1.

29:4-6 Job refers to his earlier days as being in his **prime** (lit., "his autumn"; חֹרֶף, *ḥōreph*).[5] Autumn, the time of harvest, was when the ancient peoples enjoyed the fruit of their labor. It was a time of abundance and joy. Job saw the felicity of his former days to be the result of **God's intimate friendship**.[6] Job understood that his life was full of goodness because God was **with** him. This is consistent with the Old Testament teaching that God's presence is the source of blessing (Exod 3:12; Josh 1:5,9). The greatest gift of God's providence was Job's **children**. Hebrew נַעַר (*na'ar*) is a broad term used to describe the period of life from small child to young adult. **Cream** and **oil** were symbols of abundance in ancient times. The expression **when my path was drenched in cream** can also be translated "when my feet were bathed in cream" and represent an even more exaggerated portrait of luxury. The **rocks** that **poured out** oil for Job may refer to the rock presses set up near the olive orchards. **Olive oil** was an especially valuable commodity used for cooking, ointments, and fuel for lamps.

The Job Once Honored as Savior of the Oppressed (29:7-25)

[7]**"When I went to the gate of the city / and took my seat in the public square, / [8]the young men saw me and stepped aside / and the old men rose to their feet; / [9]the chief men refrained from speaking / and covered their mouths with their hands; / [10]the voices of the nobles were hushed, / and their tongues stuck to the roof of their mouths. / [11]Whoever heard me spoke well of me, / and those who saw me commended me, / [12]because I rescued the poor who cried for help, / and the fatherless who had none to assist him. / [13]The man who was dying blessed me; / I made the widow's heart sing. / [14]I put on righteousness as my clothing; / justice was my robe and my turban. / [15]I was eyes to the blind / and feet to the**

---

[5]Pope translates the root חרף (*ḥrp*), "be early, young," by comparison with Arabic and Akkadian and notes that in the ancient calendar autumn was at the beginning of the year, not the end.

[6]MT בְּסוֹד (*bᵉsôd*), "intimacy, friendship" (Prov 3:32; Ps 25:14); cf. Gordis. Duhm emends בְּסוֹךְ (*bᵉsôk*, "when God protected"); cf. D.W. Thomas, "The Interpretation of BSÔD in Job 29:4," *JBL* 65 (1946): 63ff. Pope connects בְּסוֹד (*bᵉsôd*) with the root יסד (*ysd*) which means "find, establish," and reads בִּיסוֹד (*bîsôd*, "when God founded").

lame. / ¹⁶I was a father to the needy; / I took up the case of the
stranger. / ¹⁷I broke the fangs of the wicked / and snatched the victims from their teeth.

¹⁸"I thought, 'I will die in my own house, / my days as numer-
ous as the grains of sand. / ¹⁹My roots will reach to the water, / and
the dew will lie all night on my branches. / ²⁰My glory will remain
fresh in me, / the bow ever new in my hand.'

²¹"Men listened to me expectantly, / waiting in silence for my
counsel. / ²²After I had spoken, they spoke no more; / my words
fell gently on their ears. / ²³They waited for me as for showers /
and drank in my words as the spring rain. / ²⁴When I smiled at
them, they scarcely believed it; / the light of my face was precious
to them.^a / ²⁵I chose the way for them and sat as their chief; / I
dwelt as a king among his troops; / I was like one who comforts
mourners.

^a*24 The meaning of the Hebrew for this clause is uncertain.*

29:7-10 In the prologue Job was introduced as the "greatest man
among all the people of the East" (1:3). Here Job begins to characterize the great respect that was afforded him as a leader among his
peers. The **gate of the city** was the center of political, judicial, and
commercial life in the ancient Near East. Merchants spread their
wares there and the local elders would sit there to deliberate over
legal disputes between citizens of the community (Deut 21:19; Amos
5:10). Job identifies himself as "chief of the elders" (29:25). As such
he was accorded the greatest deference. Not only the **young men**,
but also **old men**, **chief men,** and **nobles** deferred to his authority.
When Job took his seat he was met with awe and hushed silence. The
legal approach that Job takes with God (13:13-23; 31:35-37) may
grow out of his familiarity with the procedure of seeking justice at
the city gate.

29:11-13 Job was so respected because of the righteous administration of justice over which he presided. In the ancient Near East,
the **poor**, the **orphan,** and the **widow** represented the powerless
members of society, who were commonly exploited by the rich and
powerful. The ideal ruler was one who made a special effort to protect the underprivileged.[7] God himself took up their case in his

---

[7]Ps 72:2,4,12; cf. also Aqhat II, 5-7.

administration of justice (cf. Isa 3:14-15). Earlier Eliphaz had specifically charged Job with the exploitation of the poor (22:5-9). Job will
later repeat his claim to having been their defender (31:16-23). The
man who was dying[8] had nothing but praise for Job because he
knew his widow and children would be cared for by this righteous,
compassionate man.

29:14-17 These words of self-praise are said with a purpose. Job
is building his case that the suffering God has inflicted upon him
was "unjust" and "undeserved" (30:21). That is why Job describes
himself as **clothed** with **righteousness** and **justice** (cf. Isa 59:17; Ps
132:9,16.). He means by this that these attributes are a part of his
very nature. Like a righteous king or priest he wears the **robe** and
turban as vestments of his integrity. He not only possessed these
qualities, he exercised them to the benefit of the disenfranchised
and exploitable people of his day. He took the side of the disabled
(the **blind** and the **lame**) and even the **stranger** had an advocate in
Job.[9] As **father to the needy** (cf. Isa 22:21) Job protected them from
the **fangs of the wicked** who sought to victimize the poor to their
own profit. By laying claim to the role of righteous protector of the
weak Job assumes a status given to righteous rulers and even God
himself. As such, he is positioned to legitimately challenge God for
the unjust and unrighteous behavior he has displayed toward Job.

29:18-20 On the basis of what is "fair" and "deserved" Job sees
himself as destined to be a lifelong recipient of God's favor.
Through a series of metaphors he depicts his expectation of living a
long and prosperous life. Of considerable debate among the translators is what Job means by the expression, **I will die in my own
house, my days**[10] **as numerous as the grains of sand** (v. 18). The
word rendered "house" by the NIV literally means "nest" (קֵן, *qēn*).
It can also mean "nestlings" and refer to one's household or family
(Deut 32:11; Isa 16:2). The LXX reads, "I will die in my old age" and

---

[8]Lit., "one who was destitute and at the point of dying" (אֹבֵד, *'ōbēd*).

[9]In ancient times, "strangers" were looked upon with the greatest of suspicion. There was no concept of international law, and those who traveled
beyond their traditional territories did so at great risk of exploitation and
even harm.

[10]Blommerde ("The Broken Construct Chain: Further Examples," *Bib* 55
[1974]: 550-551) reads יַמִּים (*yammîm*, "seas") for יָמִים (*yommîm*, "days") and
understands the line to be referring to the "sands of the seas."

this is followed by Dhorme.[11] The LXX also reads "like a palm tree" (φοίνιξ, *phoinix*) for "as grains of sand," and this is followed by many interpreters.[12] Rabbinic tradition connected this passage with the legendary phoenix which was said to rise from the ashes of its nest.[13] The ideas of resurrection and immortality, however, do not seem to be the subject of this section. It is better to read with MT and understand this statement to reflect Job's expectation of living a long life and then dying surrounded by his children. This, indeed, is the fate decreed for the righteous (cf. Deut 5:30[33]; Prov 10:27). Job's second metaphor of the well-watered tree (v. 19) is also a standard biblical model for the stable, productive life of a godly man (Ps 1:1-3). Job's third depiction of the God-blessed life is one of perpetual vigor. The term translated **glory** (כָּבוֹד, *kābôd*) can also mean "liver" and is used in Scripture to refer to the inner being (cf. Ps 16:9).[14] The **bow** is a symbol of manly strength (cf. Gen 49:24).[15]

29:21-25 In this final section of the chapter Job returns to the theme of the respect given him by his peers (cf. vv. 7-10).[16] His purpose is to compare the high esteem he once enjoyed to the disdain and contempt which he now endures (30:1-15). The emphatic **to me** of verse 21 calls attention to Job's unparalleled status in the city council. The respect paid to Job's **counsel** was a tribute to his superior wisdom and rhetorical skill. Throughout the debate the friends have been critical of Job's rhetoric, dismissing it as "empty notions" (15:2), "idle talk" (11:3), "a blustering wind" (8:2) prompted by "sin"

---

[11]Cf. also Pope. Driver, citing an Egyptian cognate translates "in my full strength" ("Birds in the Old Testament: II. Birds in Life," *PEQ* 87 [1955]: 138ff.).

[12]Reading כַּנַּחַל (*kannaḥal*) for MT כַּחוֹל (*kaḥôl*); cf. discussion by Rowley, *Job*, pp. 188-199. Cf. also R. van den Broek, *The Myth of the Phoenix according to Classical and Early Christian Tradition* (Leiden: E.J. Brill, 1972).

[13]This view has been upheld more recently by M. Dahood, "Nest and Phoenix in Job 29:18," *Bib* 48 (1967): 542-544; and by Grabbe, *Comparative Philology*, pp. 98-101. Pope, however, challenges the Ugaritic evidence.

[14]Cf. Ceresko, *Job 29–31*, p. 27.

[15]Conversely, to have one's bow "broken" is the equivalent to becoming impotent (cf. Ps 46:10[9]).

[16]Some interpreters relocate these verses to follow vv. 7-10 (Duhm, Dhorme, Fohrer). But as Kissane and Gordis argue, vv. 21-25 should be read as repetition for emphasis in order to prepare the reader for the contrast presented in 30:1ff.

and sounding like the "tongue of the crafty" (15:5). Job, by contrast, remembers when even the most respected men of the community **waited in silence** for him to speak. His word was considered final. After he had his say, **they spoke no more**. His words nourished the community like the **spring rain**. In ancient Israel the "spring rain" ripened the crops and produced a bountiful harvest (Jer 3:3; Zech 10:1). The language of verse 24 portrays Job as a benevolent ruler, almost godlike in the eyes of the people. They considered his favorable glance (**the light of my face**) to be a great blessing (cf. Prov 16:15; Num 6:25; Ps 44:4[3]). Job was not only a dispenser of justice (vv. 11-17), he was a sustainer of life. Verse 25 completes Job's self-portrait as the unquestioned leader of his people. He **sat as their chief**[17] and **chose the way for them**. With the absolute authority of a **king among his troops** he determined the destiny of his people to their fulfillment and **comfort**. All of this is said to set the stage for Job's protest of the frustrating and tormenting destiny that God has decreed for him.

---

[17]The verb שׁב (yšb, "preside") is used in the OT to describe the role of judge (Exod 18:14) and king (Ps 29:10).

JOB 30

2. The Second Discourse:
Job Demands Vindication from God (29:1–31:40, continued)

Job's Lament of His Present Condition (30:1-31)

The purpose of Job's rehearsal of his once-glorious past (30:1-25) is now revealed in this his final lament. Here he compares his present miserable and humiliating condition to the happiness and respect he once enjoyed and then charges God with being the cause of it. The dominant genre of this chapter is the lament, and it bears resemblance in tone and content to Psalm 38.[1] The first half of this chapter looks backward to Job 29 through the use of three exclamations, "but now" (וְעַתָּה, *wᵊ'attāh*, 1,9,16), while the second half looks forward to Job's final appeal for justice (Job 31) by addressing God with the repeated use of the accusatory "you" (vv. 20-22). Thematically the chapter unfolds along two major divisions: 1) the humiliation of Job by his enemies (30:1-15); 2) God's mistreatment of Job (30:16-31).

The Humiliation of Job by His Enemies (30:1-15)

[1]"But now they mock me, / men younger than I, / whose fathers I would have disdained / to put with my sheep dogs. / [2]Of what use was the strength of their hands to me, / since their vigor had gone from them? / [3]Haggard from want and hunger, / they roamed[a] the parched land / in desolate wastelands at night. / [4]In the brush they gathered salt herbs, / and their food[b] was the root of the broom tree. / [5]They were banished from their fellow men, / shouted at as if they were thieves. / [6]They were forced to live in the dry stream beds, / among the rocks and in holes in the ground.

---

[1]Cf. Westermann, *Structure*, pp. 40-42.

343

/ [7]They brayed among the bushes / and huddled in the under-growth. / [8]A base and nameless brood, / they were driven out of the land.

[9]"And now their sons mock me in song; / I have become a byword among them. / [10]They detest me and keep their distance; / they do not hesitate to spit in my face. / [11]Now that God has unstrung my bow and afflicted me, / they throw off restraint in my presence. / [12]On my right the tribe[c] attacks; / they lay snares for my feet, / they build their siege ramps against me. / [13]They break up my road; / they succeed in destroying me— / without anyone's helping them.[d] / [14]They advance as through a gaping breach; / amid the ruins they come rolling in. / [15]Terrors overwhelm me; / my dignity is driven away as by the wind, / my safety vanishes like a cloud.

[a]3 Or *gnawed*   [b]4 Or *fuel*   [c]12 The meaning of the Hebrew for this word is uncertain.   [d]13 Or *me.* / '*No one can help him,*' *[they say].*

30:1 With vitriolic language Job recoils against the attacks of the "rabble" who mock him. The opening **but now** (cf. also vv. 9,16) draws a contrast between the respect once afforded him (29:1-25) and the ridicule he now endures. The contrast is heightened by the lowly status of Job's detractors. In ancient Near Eastern society the **young** deferred to the aged, showing them utmost respect. But the Job who once had the admiration of the leaders of his community now faces contempt from even the children of those once scorned as outcasts. The reference to **dogs** is somewhat typical of the portrayal of "enemies" in the laments of the Old Testament (cf. Ps 22:13,17[12,16]). In ancient Israel dogs were viewed as filthy scavengers (Exod 22:31; Isa 56:10-12).[2] The ironic contrast with Job's former state is completed by a wordplay on the Hebrew term for **mock** (שָׂחַק, *śāḥaq*). Whereas Job had "smiled" (*śāḥaq*) beneficently on the citizens of his community (29:24), the lowest elements of that community now "smile" derisively at him.

30:2-8 Job goes on to expose the degraded character of his detractors. He reflects upon how insignificant and lowly was their

---

[2]Job's harsh words should not be seen as some bias against the poor in general. To the contrary, Job had respect and compassion for those who existed at the lower end of the socioeconomic spectrum (cf. 31:16-23).

status when he once ruled the land. They were so poor and powerless that they were of absolutely no benefit to Job. **Haggard**[3] **from
want and hunger,** they **roamed**[4] about as scavengers in a **parched
land.** Denied the produce of the land, they are forced to eat **salt
herbs,** the leaves of a shrub eaten only in times of great deprivation.[5]
They also sought to subsist on the **root of the broom tree.** This
shrub was one of the larger bushes of the Sinai and Dead Sea and
was the tree under which Elijah lay (1 Kgs 19:4).[6] Considered outcasts and **thieves** by the sedentary people, Job's detractors were **banished** from the community.[7] They were forced to seek shelter in **dry
stream beds** and **holes in the ground.**[8] There, like animals **huddled
in the undergrowth,** they **brayed** like wild donkeys. Job concludes
his portrait by calling them **a base** (בְּנֵי־נָבָל, *bᵊnê-nābāl*; lit., "sons of
a fool") **and nameless brood.** The former term is reserved for those
of the lowest character in the Old Testament (cf. Isa 32:5-6; Prov
17:7).[9] They are moral reprobates who have no honor ("nameless")
and no legitimate place in civil society.

30:9-11 Those who were once mocked by the society which held
Job in such high esteem have now become the mockers of Job. This
unbearable irony is deepened further by the fact that even the children (**sons**) of these scoundrels have made Job into a scorned caricature, a **byword** immortalized in mocking **song** (cf. Lam 3:14).
They ostracize Job (**keep their distance**) and add to his humiliation

---

[3]גַּלְמוּד (*galmûd*, "gaunt") is also used in Job to describe rocky, barren soil
(cf. 3:7; 15:34).

[4]עָרַק (*'āraq*) is a hapax legomenon. In Aramaic it can mean either "roam"
or "gnaw." Dhorme opts for the latter meaning and translates the line, "they
gnaw the roots of the dry ground."

[5]The Talmud calls this the "food of the poor" (T.B. *Qiddushin* 66a).

[6]NIV translates MT לַחְמָם (*laḥmām*, "their food"), but the roots of the
broom tree are apparently inedible. Tur-Sinai treats this as a reference to eating their "berries." Some scholars translate *laḥmām* "their warmth" and see
this as a reference to gathering firewood (cf. Hartley, *Job*, p. 396).

[7]The meaning "fellow men, community" for גֵּו (*gēw*) is supported by Phoeni-
cian inscriptions (cf. C.-F. Jean & Jacob Hoftijzer, *Dictionnaire des inscriptions
semitiques de l'ouest* (Leiden: E.J. Brill, 1965), p. 48).

[8]This group should not be confused with the oppressed poor who had
been victimized by the wicked rich (24:5-8). These people have earned their
exile by virtue of their dishonest behavior.

[9]Job had identified his wife with this group in response to her suggestion
that he "curse God" (2:10).

by **spit**ting **in** [his] **face**. In Job's time this was considered the sign of
ultimate contempt (cf. Isa 50:6). In verse 11 Job sounds a note that
will become dominant in the second half of the chapter. He begins
to identify **God** as his ultimate "afflicter," the one who has **unstrung**
Job's **bow** (literally his "cord"; יֶתֶר, *yether*). If we follow NIV and read
"bowstring" as in Psalm 11:2, this is another way of saying God has
broken Job's strength. It could also mean that God has "loosened
Job's belt," rendering him unable to defend himself or undertake a
difficult task. Still another possibility is that it means "loosened Job's
tent cord," which in biblical language means to bring one near to
death (cf. 4:21). Whatever the precise meaning of this metaphor, it
is clear that Job has been left defenseless inviting his enemies to
throw off all **restraint** in their assaults against him.[10]

30:12-15 The image depicted here is one of a full-scale military
assault. Like an army besieging a fortified city Job's enemies press
their **attacks**. Job has used this metaphor earlier in the speeches to
speak of God's attacks against him (cf. 13:25-27; 16:9-14; 19:6-12).
Here the enemy is described as an aggressive **tribe**. This term (פִּרְחָה,
piṛḥah) occurs only here in the Old Testament. It seems to be related to a similar term in 39:30 meaning "young bird." Gordis connects
it with an Arabic root (*farḥ*) that can mean "young bird" or "base
man." Some interpreters understand the term to be referring to
Job's enemies mentioned earlier in the chapter, while others believe
this to be a veiled reference to the terrors of death. The context
seems to favor the view that it is the assaults of Job's detractors that
are being described here. Like an invading army they break through
Job's defenses and then pour through the **gaping breach**. The last
line of verse 13 has proved challenging for the interpreters. The NIV
understands the phrase to be referring to the attackers of Job being
able to advance against him **without anyone's helping them.** But
others believe this phrase is meant to describe Job as one who is
"without a helper against them (the attackers)."[11] If this view is correct, then this phrase could be understood as an expression of Job's
sense of disappointment with God. The one who is known as the
helper and deliverer of the oppressed has abandoned Job and left

---

[10]Cf. discussion by Hartley, *Job*, p. 400.

[11]Cf. Blommerde, *Northwest Semitic Grammar*, p. 113. Some scholars read
עֹצֵר (*'ōṣēr*), "one who stops or hinders" for MT עֹזֵר (*'ōzēr*), "helper."

him defenseless (cf. v. 20). In verse 15 Job describes himself as being **overwhelmed** by **terrors** (בַּלָּהוֹת, *ballāhôth*). Bildad used this term to refer to the agents of death, whom he called the "king of terrors" (18:11,14). Such "terrors" are said to await the wicked (27:20), and now they have come upon Job. A number of scholars believe this borrows from mythological texts that refer to a legion of demons who serve the evil god Death. If so, this same Death could be the subject of verses 18-20. Like an army of evil spirits, Death and its evil troops advance against Job. It is not just the loss of his life that Job fears, but also the loss of his **dignity** or his once-respected position as a leader of his community (cf. Isa 32:8). He will die in humiliation, believed to be a sinner abandoned by God.

God's Mistreatment of Job (30:16-31)

[16]"And now my life ebbs away; / days of suffering grip me. / [17]Night pierces my bones; / my gnawing pains never rest. / [18]In his great power [God] becomes like clothing to me[a]; / he binds me like the neck of my garment. / [19]He throws me into the mud, / and I am reduced to dust and ashes.

[20]"I cry out to you, O God, but you do not answer; / I stand up, but you merely look at me. / [21]You turn on me ruthlessly; / with the might of your hand you attack me. / [22]You snatch me up and drive me before the wind; / you toss me about in the storm. / [23]I know you will bring me down to death, / to the place appointed for all the living.

[24]"Surely no one lays a hand on a broken man / when he cries for help in his distress. / [25]Have I not wept for those in trouble? / Has not my soul grieved for the poor? / [26]Yet when I hoped for good, evil came; / when I looked for light, then came the darkness. / [27]The churning inside me never stops; / days of suffering confront me. / [28]I go about blackened, but not by the sun; / I stand up in the assembly and cry for help. / [29]I have become a brother of jackals, / a companion of owls. / [30]My skin grows black and peels; / my body burns with fever. / [31]My harp is tuned to mourning, / and my flute to the sound of wailing.

[a]18 Hebrew; Septuagint [God] grasps my clothing

30:16-19 It is the unrelenting approach of death that Job now laments, laying blame for it squarely upon God. Racked by **gnawing**

pains Job is able to find no **rest**. Returning to the theme of rest-deny-
ing suffering (cf. 7:3-5,14) Job characterizes death's approach as that
of a wild beast tearing at his broken body. At issue in this section is
who or what exactly is the subject of the verbs. The term "God" never
appears in the text but is inserted by many translators for the more
general "he, it," and it is commonly assumed that Job is blaming God
for the suffering that pains him and threatens his very existence.[12]
The assumption has the support of the context (vv. 11:20-23) where
God is clearly identified as Job's assailant.[13] Throughout the speeches Job has seen God as his ultimate enemy who inexplicably and cruelly attacks him (cf., e.g., 9:31). In verse 18 God is described as choking Job like a tight collar in a constraining garment. Job is caught in
a straightjacket of pain with God pulling the straps tighter as Job
helplessly resists. With an ironic twist Job ends this part of the lament
by accusing God of casting him down into the **mud** from which he
was created, consigning him to the **dust and ashes** of lifeless matter
which he once was and to which he now expects to return.

30:20-23 Employing a series of accusatory "you's" Job lashes out
at God for his mistreatment of his righteous servant. His goal is to
expose God's injustice. First Job accuses God of failing to give him
a fair hearing. The language of verse 20 is more than a call for help,
it is a call for justice. Whereas Job had been responsive to the cries
of the poor and intervened to deliver them from their oppressors
(29:12,17), Job's cries to God for justice fall on deaf ears. When Job
stands up ("takes his stand")[14] in search of justice, God refuses even
to acknowledge him. With this accusation Job is resurrecting a
theme he has used throughout his laments (9:16-19; 13:19-24; 19:6-
9; 23:3-9). Second, Job accuses God of **ruthless**[15] oppression. God
has cruelly **attacked**[16] him for no apparent reason. This, too, has

---

[12]NIV takes "night" to be the subject of the verb "pierces" (נִקַּר, *niqqar*)
then supplies the name "God" as a subject of the ms. sg. verbs (cf. Pope).

[13]It is also possible that Job thinks of "pain" or "death" as his afflicter in
this section.

[14]A legal metaphor (cf. Habel, *Job*, p. 421).

[15]Literally "grown cruel" (אַכְזָר, *'akzār*), a term used commonly in the context of war (Jer 6:23; 30:14) and motivated by anger (Prov 27:4). The same
term is applied to Leviathan in 41:2[10].

[16]Lit., "acted hatefully" (שָׂטַם, *śāṭam*) against Job. This may be a wordplay
on the title *śāṭān* in the prologue. God has become Job's "adversary."

been an oft-repeated theme in Job's earlier discourses (6:4; 13:24-25; 16:9-14; 19:11). Verses 22-23 may be a parody on Psalm 18:11[10] where God is pictured as riding on the wings of the **wind** to deliver his people. Here the opposite is true. God uses the wind to **snatch up** Job and **toss** him **about in the storm.** God, the "cloud rider" (Ps 68:5,34[4,33]) uses the **might of** his **hand** to disrupt Job's life and **bring** him **down**[17] **to death.** The accusatory **I know** of verse 23 stands in sharp contrast to Job's great statement of faith in 19:25: "I know my redeemer lives." Here, God is not Job's deliverer but the one responsible for his demise. He will deliver Job only to the **place appointed for all the living**.

30:24-26 In these verses Job directly contrasts his compassion and justice toward the poor with God's lack of either toward him. The text of verse 24 is very difficult in the Hebrew leading to a wide variety of emendations and translations.[18] According to the translation proposed by NIV Job is expressing his incredulity over the thought that God would continue to persecute a **broken man.**[19] This is exactly what Job believes God has done to him. In spite of Job's **cries for help** God continues to **lay his hand** of persecution upon him. Through a pair of rhetorical questions Job calls attention to the compassion he has displayed toward the unfortunate. (v. 25). He has **wept for those in trouble** and **grieved**[20] **for the poor.** As a result he expected some kind of reciprocation from God. Indeed, such seemed to be at work in his earlier life when he enjoyed extraordinary wealth and happiness. But then he experienced a complete reversal of fortune. When he **hoped for good,** only **evil came.**[21] As Rowley notes, "while Job disputes the view of the friends that virtue leads to happiness, he shares with them the view that it ought to."[22]

---

[17]This verb (תָּשִׁיב, *t²šîb*) normally means to "restore, bring back" in the sense of "rescue." Here it is used sarcastically to depict God's devious and malevolent ways.

[18]Cf. Driver & Gray, Rowley, Gordis.

[19]עִי (*'î*, "heap"). Pope and Dhorme read עָנִי (*'ānî*, "afflicted, needy"). LXX makes the subject "I" and takes it as some statement Job is making about himself ("Have I not given a helping hand to the poor?").

[20]עָגַם (*'āgam*) found only here in OT. The meaning "grieved" is attested in Mishnaic Hebrew and is also attested in Ugaritic (*Krt* 26-27); cf. A. Ceresko, *Job 29–31*, pp. 91-92.

[21]"Good" (טוֹב, *ṭôb*) and "evil" (רָע, *rā'*) here are not moral categories but refer to good fortune and the lack of it.

[22]Rowley, *Job*, p. 198.

30:27-31 Job closes his complaint with a haunting lament of his deplorable condition. He describes an array of psychological and physiological maladies that plague him. The ceaseless **churning** of which Job speaks is literally "the boiling of his bowels." In the Old Testament the bowels were regarded to be the seat of emotions and this expression refers to emotional anguish caused by Job's **suffering.** Job's skin has been **blackened** by his disease. Leprosy and elephantiasis are among the many diseases proposed as the cause of Job's skin discoloration.[23] The expression **not by the sun** has been taken by some interpreters to mean that Job is covering his face and does not see the sun.[24] The man who once stood up in the assembly to defend the oppressed now gets no hearing when he attempts to **stand up** for himself. Given the fact that Job's disease has excommunicated him from the arena of normal social discourse and consigned him to the town "ash heap," Job's reference to **standing up in the assembly** is best understood as a metaphorical depiction of his attempt to get justice from God. The **jackal** and the **owl** (perhaps "ostrich") are solitary creatures that produce haunting cries.[25] By calling himself their **brother** Job is lamenting the social isolation that he feels. In one of the most powerful lines in the entire book, Job concludes his lament with the haunting refrain, **My harp is tuned to mourning and my flute to the sound of wailing.** Job has but one song and knows but one tune. He is reduced to bewailing his brokenness.

---

[23]Cf. discussion on 2:7 and footnote.

[24]Hakam. Duhm, Budde, and Forher read בְּלֹא נֶחָמָה (bᵊlō' neḥāmāh), "where there was not comfort," for בְּלֹא חַמָּה (bᵊlō' ḥammāh), "without the sun." LXX favors MT and supports the translation of NIV.

[25]Cf. Micah 1:8 where the same two animals are paired due to these moaning sounds.

JOB 31

2. The Second Discourse: Job Demands Vindication from God
(29:1–31:40, continued)

Job's Oath of Innocence (31:1-40)

Job concludes his final defense with a dramatic legal maneuver designed to prove his innocence and end the "unjust" persecution he believes he is receiving from the hands of God. Job seeks to achieve this by declaring an oath that boldly calls upon God to directly punish him if he is guilty of some specific sin. By taking this "oath of innocence" Job seeks to leverage God, to force him to appear and answer the charges that Job has leveled against him.

Such oaths were well known in the biblical world.[1] In formulaic language the swearer typically declared: "If I am guilty of such-and-such a sin, then do so-and-so to me." If God refused to punish the swearer, then this was considered proof of his innocence. Similar oaths may have been taken by worshipers who were preparing to enter the courts of the sanctuary (Deut 26:12-15; Ps 15; 24:3-6).

The long list of sins of which Job avows his innocence is intriguing. Though variously numbered by scholars, depending upon how specific verses are grouped together, the essential list may be summarized as follows:

1. Lust (vv. 1-4)
2. Falsehood (vv. 5-6)
3. Covetousness (vv. 7-8)
4. Adultery (vv. 9-12)

---

[1]Cf. Ps 7:4-7[3-6]; 137:5-6; cf. also S. Blank, "The Curse, the Blasphemy, the Spell and the Oath," *HUCA* 23 (1950–51): 87-92; *idem*, "An Effective Literary Device in Job XXXI," *JJS* 4 (1951): 105-107; J. Murtagh, "The Book of Job and the Book of the Dead," *Irish Theological Quarterly* 35 (1965): 166-173.

    5. Mistreatment of servants (vv. 13-15)
    6. Lack of concern for the poor (vv. 16-23)
    7. Trust in wealth (vv. 24-25)
    8. Worship of sun and moon (vv. 26-28)
    9. Vindictiveness (vv. 29-30)
   10. Inhospitality (vv. 31-32)
   11. Concealment of sin (vv. 33-34)

There is nothing quite like this list elsewhere in the Hebrew Bible or in any other ancient Near Eastern literature. Of all the evils Job may have disavowed, why does he focus on these specific sins? Attempts have been made to trace the origin of this list of offenses to ancient legal or wisdom traditions or to ancient liturgical texts but none of these comparisons have yielded an exact match.[2] Perhaps the answer can be found in the list itself, most notably: 1) in what all of these sins have in common and 2) in how the list is concluded. A careful consideration of this list of offenses reveals that they do have one thing in common. They are all sins that could be hidden. Some of the offenses are "sins of the mind," knowable only to the one committing them. Others, though overt acts, are private or family behaviors that could have easily been concealed and thus escaped detection by the community.

Taking note of this, the reader is now in a better position to understand why Job concluded the list as he did. In verses 33-34 Job disavows himself of having "concealed" his sin from others. Though scholars have traditionally regarded verses 33-34 as simply the last in the series of sins that Job disavows, this final entry may rather be understood as Job's summary of the entire list and, therefore, an explanation of the specific sins of which he has declared himself innocent. Throughout the speeches Job has challenged the friends to name the sin of which he is guilty and for which he is presumably being punished. Unable to do so, Eliphaz finally decided to invent one. In his final speech he accused Job of the very kind of sin con-

---

[2]Fohrer, for example, argues that it is derived from the ethical teaching of Israel's wisdom tradition; cf. G. Fohrer, "The Righteous Man in Job 31," in *Essays in Old Testament Ethics*, Fest. J.P. Hyatt, eds. J. Crenshaw and J Willis (New York: Ktav, 1974), pp. 1-22; cf. also, P. Humbert, *Recherches sur les sources égyptiennes de la littérature sapientiale d'Israël* (Neuchâtel: Secrétariat de l'Université, 1929), pp. 75-106; Dick, "Legal Metaphor in Job 31," pp. 37-50.

tained in this list — a sin that would be known only to Job's household — exploitation of and lack of compassion for the poor (22:5-
11). Since no one would be able to confirm or deny Job's guilt or
innocence, it was a perfect "crime" to postulate as the basis for
God's "judgment" of Job.[3] In his "oath of innocence" Job disavows
himself of this crime (cf. 31:13-23) and others that might have
escaped detection by the community.

The Sin of Lust (31:1-4)

[1]**"I made a covenant with my eyes / not to look lustfully at a
girl. / [2]For what is man's lot from God above, / his heritage from
the Almighty on high? / [3]Is it not ruin for the wicked, / disaster for
those who do wrong? / [4]Does he not see my ways / and count my
every step?**

31:1 Job begins his avowal of innocence by citing a **covenant** that
he has entered into designed to protect him from the sin of lust. Job
has made this covenant not with his wife but with his own **eyes**.[4] By
guarding his eyes no doubt Job seeks to guard his heart as well (cf.
Matt 5:28; Num 15:39). By announcing this long-standing commitment to his personal purity Job lays the foundation for his final and
most dramatic defense of his integrity. Not only will he now declare
himself innocent of overt, public sins but also of private, internal
sins, difficult to detect by others and knowable only by God. In biblical times sexual violation of a **girl** (בְּתוּלָה, *bᵉthûlāh*; "virgin") was a
serious crime (cf., e.g., Exod 22:15-16[16-17]). In a similar way Ben
Sira warns against the same danger: "Look not at a virgin, lest you
be trapped into sin with her" (Sir 9:5).

31:2-4 In the next three verses Job asks three questions designed
to explore his high sense of accountability before God and explain
why he made his covenant in the first place. The view of God suggested by these questions sounds much like that espoused by the

---

[3]Eliphaz, of course, has no evidence of such a sin, or he would have
charged Job with this much earlier. It is, however, just the kind of sin which
a wealthy man like Job might have committed and been able to successfully
conceal.

[4]Ceresko suggests that לְעֵנָי (*lᵉʿēnāy*), "with my eyes" should be rendered
"in his [God's] presence" understanding the suffix as 3.m.sg. rather than
1.c.sg. (cf. Gen 23:11).

friends and once held by Job. According to the doctrine of retributive justice God scrutinizes human behavior and apportions a fixed lot (חֵלֶק, *ḥēleq*), a **heritage** (נַחֲלָה, *naḥălāh*) to all people on the basis of how they live their lives. For the wicked this destiny could be only **ruin** and **disaster**[5] (cf. 20:29; 27:13). Having himself once believed that God **saw** all his **ways** and **counted** his **every step** (cf. Ps 33:13-15; Prov 5:21; Sir 15:17), Job is suggesting that this is what motivated him to pledge himself to a life of moral purity.[6] Confident that he has lived up to that commitment, Job will later end his oath of innocence by claiming that, if God would only grant him a hearing, Job would gladly give him account of his "every step" (31:37).

The Sin of Falsehood (31:5-6)

[5]"If[7] I have walked in falsehood / or my foot has hurried after deceit— / [6]let God weigh me in honest scales / and he will know that I am blameless—

31:5-6 Job has already uttered a similar pledge of honesty in defense of his integrity (27:4-6). Here he says he has avoided **falsehood** throughout his life. The word for **falsehood** (שָׁוְא, *šāw'*) refers to anything without worth or substance.[8] It is used in the Hebrew Bible to refer to false testimony (Exod 23:1), false prophecy (Ezek 12:24), and more generally to describe all forms of false worship (Isa 1:13; Jer 18:15). When he adds that he has kept his **foot** off the path of **deceit**, he is echoing the language of Hebrew wisdom literature that often speaks of a person's feet (how and where they walk) as a symbol of their ethical behavior (Ps 119:59,101; Prov 1:15-16; 4:26).

---

[5]The meaning of נֵכֶר (*neker*) is uncertain. Dhorme takes the root, נכר (*nkr*), to mean "to be alien" or "to be hostile" (cp. Akk. *nakaru*) or "to be harsh, hateful" (cp. Arab. *nakura*).

[6]In fact, Job had once believed that he would be rewarded by this very system (29:18-20; 30:26a).

[7]Gordis argues that אִם (*'im*) throughout this chapter (e.g., vv. 13,15,24, 25,26,33) should not be translated, "if," and understood as the protasis of an oath formula, noting that in several verses there is no corresponding apodosis (כִּי, *kî*; "then"). He treats *'im* in all these verses as a simple interrogative expecting a "no" answer. But as Blank points out, the apodosis is implied by the use of *'im* in such curse formulas (Blank, "Curse," p. 90).

[8]Cf. J. Sawyer, *THAT*, 2:882-884.

It is interesting to note that a similar pairing of **falsehood** (*šāw'*) and **deceit** (מִרְמָה, *mirmāh*) may be found in Psalm 24:4 as part of the declaration of innocence offered by the worshiper who is preparing to enter the temple. When Job invites God to **weigh** him in **scales**, he is also echoing a Wisdom motif that speaks of the scale as a symbol of God's testing of humans (Prov 16:2; 21:2; 24:12).[9] **Honest** scales are those which offer a true measure of weight, as opposed to the "dishonest scales" sometimes used in the marketplace and universally condemned in Scripture (Amos 8:5; Prov 11:1). Job is convinced that if his integrity is fairly weighed he will be found **blameless** when it comes to telling the truth.

The Sin of Covetousness (31:7-8)

[7]If my steps have turned from the path, / if my heart has been led by my eyes, / or if my hands have been defiled, / [8]then may others eat what I have sown, / and may my crops be uprooted.

31:7 The exact sin that is being described here has been variously explained. Some scholars, focusing on the term that the NIV has rendered **defiled** (MT מְאוּם, *m'ûm*), compare Job's statement with the prohibition found in Deuteronomy 13:18[17] and take this to be a denial of any ceremonial defilement. It is, however, more likely here to be referring more generally to the "stain" of any sin (cf. 16:17). The specific reference to Job's **heart** being led by his **eyes** (v. 7a) suggests that Job has some kind of covetousness in mind here which might, in turn, lead to some improper touching or taking (theft?) by the **hand**. In fact one could reconstruct the following process of temptation and sin from Job's words: the **eye** covets, the **heart** schemes, the **feet** turn aside, and the **hand** takes.[10]

31:8 For the first time in this list Job invites a specific sanction upon himself should he be guilty of sin. The probable meaning of the punishment that Job invokes upon himself is that he might lose his harvest, that his **crops be uprooted**. The word translated "crops"

---

[9]Some scholars suggest that Job has in mind the language of the Egyptian Book of the Dead that speaks of weighing the heart of the dead against a feather (the symbol of *maat*, "truth, justice"); cf. S. Morenz, *Egyptian Religion* (London: Methuen & Co., 1973), pp. 126-127.

[10]Cf. Hartley, *Job*, p. 412.

(צֶאֱצָא, ṣe'ĕṣā'), however, can refer both to the produce of the field (Isa 34:1; 42:5) and to human progeny (Isa 48:19; Job 5:25; 21:8; 27:14). Since his children are already dead, the former meaning is more likely here.[11] Having lost his flocks and herds, the loss of his crops could deprive him of his only remaining assets.

The Sin of Adultery (31:9-12)

[9]"If my heart has been enticed by a woman, / or if I have lurked at my neighbor's door, / [10]then may my wife grind another man's grain, / and may other men sleep with her. / [11]For that would have been shameful, / a sin to be judged. / [12]It is a fire that burns to Destruction[a]; / it would have uprooted my harvest.

[a]12 Hebrew Abaddon

31:9-12 As Job disavows himself of the sin of adultery, he employs subtle wordplay. The term for **entice** (פתה, pth) sounds like the word for **door** (פֶּתַח, pethaḥ). This latter term further carries a double entendre used to refer both to the entrance to a man's house and the entrance to a woman's womb (Cant 4:12). There is in biblical literature a common theme of the woman as temptress, whose enticements are to be avoided at all costs (Prov 2:16-19; 6:23-32). The curse Job specifies as punishment for such a sin is that his own wife be sexually violated by **other men**. The phrase **may my wife grind another man's grain** could refer to her enslavement (Exod 11:5; Isa 47:2), but most likely here it is a euphemism for sexual subservience.[12] Violation of another man's wife was a serious crime (**shameful**; זִמָּה, zimmāh)[13] in Israel and a **sin to be judged**.[14] When Job calls it a **fire that burns to Destruction** (אֲבַדּוֹן, 'ăbaddôn; "the grave"), he is either referring to

---

[11]Hakam cites Deut 28:18: "Cursed by the fruit of your body and the fruit of your ground," and argues that the term could refer to both crops and offspring.

[12]Cf. Gordis.

[13]This term is used in Leviticus to refer to a variety of sexual sins and is often translated "heinous crime" (Lev 18:27; 19:29; 20:14). Cf. S. Steingrimsson, "zmm," TDOT, 4:89-90.

[14]פְּלִילִי (pĕlîlî), "punishable offence"; cf. D. Ap-Thomas ("Some Notes on Terms Relating to Prayer," VT 6 [1956]: 233) who traces it to the verb פָּלַל (pālal, "cut off") and takes the noun to refer to a sin that outlaws the sinner from society.

the fire of lust burning out of control or poetically describing the legal consequence of adultery, execution (Lev 20:14).

Mistreatment of Servants (31:13-15)

[13]"If I have denied justice to my menservants and maidservants / when they had a grievance against me, / [14]what will I do when God confronts me? / What will I answer when called to account? / [15]Did not he who made me in the womb make them? / Did not the same one form us both within our mothers?

31:13-15 In ancient Near Eastern culture slavery was universally practiced and an accepted part of the economic structure of society. In this system slaves had very few if any rights. Israelite law, while accepting the practice, attempted to impose a more humanitarian standard upon the institution (cf., e.g., Exod 21:2-11,20-21,26-27; Lev 25:39-55). Even in Israel, however, servants remained politically vulnerable and legally exploitable. Masters, who held great power over their servants, were in a position to take advantage of those under their charge if they so chose. Job, however, claims that he has always treated his servants justly, even when they might have had a **grievance** against him (cf. 29:7-17). Job feels responsible in this matter for two distinct but related reasons. First, he sees this as his God-given responsibility, viewing God as the ultimate advocate of the poor and the one to whom he must give **account** (cf. Isa 3:14-15). When Job envisions God **confronting** him over this matter, he is imagining having to stand in God's court and defend his own behavior.[15] Second, he sees himself and his servants to share a common origin and status as mortals made by the same God, **Did not he who made me in the womb make them?** A similar egalitarian perspective can be found in Proverbs 22:2.

Lack of Concern for the Poor (31:16-23)

[16]"If I have denied the desires of the poor / or let the eyes of the widow grow weary, / [17]if I have kept my bread to myself, / not

---

[15]As Gordis explains, the verb קוּם (*qûm*, "arise"; NIV, "confront") literally means to "rise in court" in legal contexts. It can refer to a witness offering evidence (Deut 19:15-16), a plaintiff presenting his case (Micah 6:1), or a judge passing sentence (Ps 76:10[9]; 82:8).

sharing it with the fatherless— / ¹⁸but from my youth I reared him
as would a father, / and from my birth I guided the widow— / ¹⁹if
I have seen anyone perishing for lack of clothing, / or a needy man
without a garment, / ²⁰and his heart did not bless me / for warm-
ing him with the fleece from my sheep, / ²¹if I have raised my hand
against the fatherless, / knowing that I had influence in court, /
²²then let my arm fall from the shoulder, / let it be broken off at
the joint. / ²³For I dreaded destruction from God, / and for fear of
his splendor I could not do such things.

31:16-17 This extended disavowal of any failure toward the poor
captures the ancient Israelite ethic of responsibility toward the disenfranchised of society. In a culture controlled by male landowners, **widows** and **the fatherless**, deprived by death of their protectors, were
especially vulnerable to exploitation. They were often reduced to begging for even the simplest needs. To have ignored this and denied
bread to these "least of the poor" would have been the worst kind of
selfishness for such a wealthy man as Job. So sensitive is Job to even
being accused of such a moral failure that in hyperbolic language he
contends that he has been a compassionate man from the days of his
youth, even from his **birth**.[16] Job's defensiveness on this issue grows
both out of his innocence and out of his sensitivity to the charges leveled against him by Eliphaz in his final speech (cf. 22:1-11). Eliphaz is
probably reasoning that, since Job has been deprived of his great
wealth by God, he must have acquired that wealth like so many others
of his day — through illicit exploitation of the poor. Job has already
vigorously defended himself against this charge (29:7-16). By taking
this specific oath of innocence Job now adds to that defense.

31:18-20 The hyperbolic language of verse 18, by which Job
claims to have been a champion of the orphan and the widow from
his **youth** or even from his **birth**, echoes the tone of his earlier
claims to be the ideal protector of the poor (29:11-17).[17] By charac-

---

[16]Verse 18 is judged out of place by some interpreters and deleted
(Holscher). Complicating the matter is the difficulty of the Hebrew in MT.
Duhm understands v. 18 to be describing God as the compassionate one
and Job as his protected child. NIV, however, seems to capture the intent of
the original Hebrew (cf. Hakam, Gordis).

[17]Some commentators treat the *yodh* suffixes in v. 18 as 3.m.sg. rather than
1.c.sg. and take them to be referring to "*his* youth" and "*his* birth," recalling

terizing himself as a **father** to the orphan Job takes the role of the ideal ruler in ANE thought (cf. 29:16). One of the qualities of a righteous king was his duty to defend the poor and restore the underprivileged (cf. Psalm 72).[18]

31:21-23 In verses 21-23 Job disavows himself of any miscarriages of justice against the **fatherless** — those who personify the poor and defenseless in patriarchal society. The Hebrew of verse 21 makes specific reference to the "city gate," the place where most legal action took place in ancient Hebrew culture (cf. 2 Kgs 7:1,18; Ruth 4:1,11). Job insists that he never abused the **influence** that he wielded there. Job, whose wealth had given him great power in the court, insists that he never abused that power. To do so, he believed, would have put him at risk of **destruction from God**, who is the ultimate protector of the poor.[19] The specific punishment Job invites upon himself is expressed in irony. If he has **raised** his **hand** (in unfair indictment of the poor [cf. Zech 2:9; Isa 19:16]), **then let my arm fall from the shoulder**. In the Hebrew Bible a broken arm symbolizes the loss of power. God's punishment of the wicked is often described by such language (Jer 48:25; Ezek 30:21-22; Ps 10:15; 37:17).

Trust in Wealth and Idolatry (31:24-28)

[24]**"If I have put my trust in gold / or said to pure gold, 'You are my security,' / [25]if I have rejoiced over my great wealth, / the fortune my hands have gained, / [26]if I have regarded the sun in its radiance / or the moon moving in splendor, / [27]so that my heart was secretly enticed / and my hand offered them a kiss of homage, / [28]then these also would be sins to be judged, / for I would have been unfaithful to God on high.**

31:24-28 In the prologue of the book Job was introduced as a man of great wealth (1:3). With such wealth comes the temptation to **trust in** it instead of God (cf. Prov 30:9; Ps 49:6; Matt 6:24). There was also

---

the "fatherless" of v. 17. Ceresko cites comparative texts like the Kilamuwa Inscription from Phoenicia in support of this translation (cf. Ceresko, *Job 29–31*, p. 138).

[18]Cf. the description of the righteous king Danel of Ugarit in Aqhat II, vv. 5-7; also the above Kilamuwa Inscription (Ceresko, *Job 29–31*, p. 138).

[19]This is exactly what Eliphaz says is the cause of Job's suffering (22:1-11).

the ancient practice of using **gold** and other precious metals to fashion images of gods (Judg 17:3-5; Isa 40:18-20). These twin idolatrous abuses of money may account for Job's putting them in tandem in this portion of his speech. When Job disavows himself of regarding gold as his **security** (מִבְטָח, *mibṭāḥ*), he may be directly responding to Eliphaz's insinuation that he had placed his money above his God (22:24-25). By acknowledging that confidence in money is misplaced and foolish Job embraces a value system identical to that of ancient Israel's wisdom tradition (cf., e.g., Prov 11:28; 23:4-5). By denying any **secret** devotion to the **sun** and **moon** and labeling such actions as **sins to be judged**[20] and **unfaithful to God**, Job places himself firmly in line with Israel's prophetic and legal traditions and the theology of the Hebrew Bible (Deut 17:2-3; Ezek 8:16; Jer 8:2).

Job's strong monotheistic tone is especially noteworthy given the identity assigned to him in the prologue. There he is portrayed as one of the "sons of the East" (i.e., a non-Israelite), living outside of Israel, presumably in pre-Mosaic, patriarchal times. Whatever Job's identity — whether a non-Israelite or a Jew living outside of Israel, before Abraham or after him — he is throughout the book portrayed as a monotheist of the highest order. Not only does this speech make this clear, his entire theological struggle over his suffering presumes that there is but one God who presides over all of life.

Vindictiveness and Inhospitality (31:29-32)

[29]**"If I have rejoiced at my enemy's misfortune / or gloated over the trouble that came to him— / [30]I have not allowed my mouth to sin / by invoking a curse against his life— / [31]if the men of my household have never said / 'Who has not had his fill of Job's meat?'— / [32]but no stranger had to spend the night in the street, / for my door was always open to the traveler—**[21]

31:29-30 Job denies ever having been vindictive or retaliatory toward his **enemies**. The Hebrew word for "enemy" here literally

---

[20]עָוֹן (*āwōn*), a crime potentially punishable by stoning (cf. Deut 17:2-5).
[21]At this point in the oath there is a slight change in literary style with three conditional clauses (vv. 29-33) that have a protasis beginning with "if" (*'im*) but no apodosis stating the prescribed punishment for each offense. Gordis treats such constructions as interrogatives expecting a "no" answer.

means "the one who hates me." Though it is human nature to respond in kind to such derision, Job insists that he is above this. His forgiving attitude is akin to that enjoined by Israel's wisdom and legal traditions (Prov 24:17-18; 17:5; 20:22; Exod 23:4-5; cf. also Matt 5:43ff). The Hebrew Bible contains several examples of people **invoking a curse** upon their enemies (cf., e.g., Jer 11:20; 12:3; Ps 69:23-29[22-28]; 137:7-9). Job claims to have never **allowed** his **mouth** (lit., "pallet"; חֵךְ, *hēk*) to utter such curses.

31:31-32 Job disavows himself of inhospitality toward any **stranger** or **traveler**. He asserts that all the **men of** his **household** can readily bear witness to this fact. This latter phrase (lit., "men of my tent") may refer to Job's kinsmen or to the invited guests themselves. Though such travelers might have sought lodging in the **streets** or public square (Judg 19:17) Job would not allow this and was diligent to supply the standard hospitality of food and lodging.

A Summary Claim of Innocence from Secret Sins (31:33-34)

> [33]**if I have concealed my sin as men do,**[a] [22] / **by hiding my guilt in my heart** / [34]**because I so feared the crowd** / **and so dreaded the contempt of the clans** / **that I kept silent and would not go outside**
>
> [a]*33* Or *as Adam did*

31:33-34 As noted above, most commentators treat these verses as the last in the list of sins of which Job disavows himself — the sin of hypocrisy or hiding some unseemly behavior. It is our opinion, however, that, rather than representing the final sin in Job's long list, these verses actually constitute a summary of the entire list and provide us the clue to just what it is that all of these sins have in common. Namely, they are all behaviors which could be **concealed** and remain unknown to the community. Having already claimed his innocence of any obvious sinful behavior that would merit the suffering God has brought upon him, Job now goes a step further and claims his innocence of any private sins as well. Job has already undermined the friends' unfair indictment of him by insisting that they name his sin. He now seeks to do the same thing to God. By inviting God to immediately punish him for any secret sin knowable

---

[22]Some interpreters take אָדָם (*'ādām*) to refer to the Adam of the Genesis account (3:1-13) who hid from the presence of God in the garden.

only to God, Job seeks to expose the unfairness of God's indictment of him. In this his final defense Job seeks to prove himself innocent of any behavior, public or private, that might merit the "punishment" that God has inflicted upon him.

Closing Plea and Challenge to God (31:35-37)

[35]("Oh, that I had someone to hear me! / I sign now my defense—let the Almighty answer me; / let my accuser put his indictment in writing. / [36]Surely I would wear it on my shoulder, / I would put it on like a crown. / [37]I would give him an account of my every step; / like a prince I would approach him.)—

31:35 Having disavowed himself of even private, secret sins knowable only to God, Job now closes his final defense with a direct invitation to God — **let my accuser put his indictment in writing!** Job's words represent both a plea and a challenge. His opening words (**Oh that;** מִי יִתֵּן, *mî yitten*) also appear in three of his previous speeches. In each case they express some intense desire for something seemingly impossible to yet happen (14:13; 19:23; 29:2). Characterized by some interpreters as "fantasy," "hope," or even "faith" this expression (lit., "Oh, if only") has introduced Job's most heartfelt wishes. For Job, nothing could be more heartfelt than the desire to establish his innocence. It is the thing for which he has contended most earnestly throughout the speeches. Now, he seeks to establish it once and for all. In language that is highly forensic, Job closes his case by formally **signing** his **defense**[23] and inviting the **Almighty** (his accuser) to appear in court and give him a fair **hearing** — that he **answer** Job's countercharges of injustice and formally **indict** him of any sin of which he might be guilty.[24] Earlier Job had invited God to "reply" to him and to "show him his offense" (13:22-23). Since God has refused to respond, Job is now swearing a legal oath in order to compel his heavenly accuser to formally indict him

---

[23]The Hebrew expression representing Job's "signature" is the final letter of the Hebrew alphabet, *taw*. In ancient times it was written like the English letter X. Even an illiterate person could sign a document by the use of this symbol.

[24]For a detailed study of the legal terms used in this final appeal cf. M. Dick, "Legal Metaphor in Job 31," pp. 47-49; also Habel, *Job*, pp. 438-439.

and substantiate the charges. If God chooses to remain silent, then all will know that Job has been falsely accused.

31:36-37 Job's confidence that he is indeed not guilty is reflected in the sarcastic tone of verses 36-37. Job insists that should God actually formally charge him, he would flaunt any such bill of indictment like a badge of honor, proudly wearing it as a royal cape or a **crown**. In language that borders on irreverence the innocent Job says that, given the opportunity, he would boldly take God on in court appearing before him **like a prince**.[25] Job, of course, will finally have his face-to-face meeting with God. Instead of boldly flaunting his innocence, however, he will ultimately retract his case and "repent in dust and ashes" before the God of the whirlwind (42:6).

A Final Oath (31:38-40)

[38]**"if my land cries out against me / and all its furrows are wet with tears, / [39]if I have devoured its yield without payment / or broken the spirit of its tenants, / [40]then let briers come up instead of wheat / and weeds instead of barley."**

The words of Job are ended.

31:38-40 The placement of this final oath has challenged the interpreters. Most moderns consider it misplaced and anticlimactic given the drama of the preceding declaration of innocence.[26] It may, instead, be viewed as a rhetorical reprise — a final vow intended to punctuate this entire oath of innocence.[27] At one level this particular oath could be construed as simply a denial of having committed some kind of environmental sin by exploiting the soil. Evidence of Israel's concern for conservation can be found in the biblical laws of the sabbatical year (Leviticus 25) and the year of release (Deuteronomy 15; cf. also Lev 18:24-28; 19:19). The **land** (אֲדָמָה, *'ădāmāh*), however, is often a symbol of far more than the tillable soil. It is

---

[25]נָגִיד (*nāgîd*) was sometimes used to refer to the king in Israel (1 Sam 9:16; 2 Sam 5:2; 1 Kgs 1:35).

[26]Pope places these verses after v. 8, Budde after v. 12, Dhorme and Kissane after v. 32, and Holscher after v. 7. NIV places the preceding declaration of innocence (vv. 35-37) in parenthesis and seems to treat it as an aside.

[27]Terrien treats these verses as a further example of the author's use of afterthought as in 3:26; 9:32; 14:13.

often personified to represent a kind of "moral ground." The land was "cursed" in punishment of Adam's sin (Gen 3:18). It is "defiled" by the shedding of innocent blood (Gen 4:10-12; Num 35:33-34). It "laments" when Israel sins (Jer 12:4; Hos 4:1-3). In the covenant theology the land is "witness" to God's treaty with his people (Deut 30:19), and Israel's continued presence and prosperity in the land is tied to observance of God's laws (Leviticus 26). So Job's reference to the ground in this final oath serves to call it as a final witness to his innocence by inviting it to **cry out** against him if he has defiled it. Job calls for it to produce **briers** and **weeds** against him as it did against the sinful Adam. When it fails to do so, Job will offer this as final proof of his innocence.

JOB 32

B. THE SPEECHES OF ELIHU (32:1–37:24)

At this point in the book the plot has reached a climactic moment. Job's dramatic avowal of innocence has left the friends speechless and brought an end to the debate. Wearied by the inability of the dialogue to solve Job's dilemma the reader, like Job, is ready for God to appear and settle the issue once and for all. But once again, as it has done at nearly every turn, the book surprises us. It is not God who appears to speak but a heretofore unknown character, the "angry, young man" Elihu.

So surprising is this unexpected development in the story that many commentators reject it as "unoriginal" — a distracting and unfortunate addition to the book.[1] Most moderns regard Elihu as an early "reader" of the book of Job and his speeches as its "first commentary."[2] Others, arguing on literary grounds, have defended the originality of these speeches.[3] As with other challenges to the unity of the book it should be remembered that there is absolutely no textual evidence for the existence of any version of Job that omits the Elihu speeches.

If we assume the originality of the speeches, there remains the challenging task of determining their purpose in the overall composition of the book. Here, too, opinions vary. By some Elihu is regarded as a pompous buffoon who provides "comic relief"[4] to the tension of the plot while, by others, he is assigned the significant role of "forerunner" of Yahweh.[5] In the text Elihu presents himself as a

---

[1]Cf. discussion of these views in the "Introduction," pp. 30-31.
[2]Cf., e.g., Andersen, *Job*, p. 50; Zuckerman, *Job the Silent*, p. 153.
[3]Cf., e.g., the commentaries of Budde, Gordis, Habel, Janzen.
[4]Whedbee, "The Comedy of Job," pp. 18-20.
[5]Gordis, *Book of God and Man*, pp. 115-116.

self-appointed arbiter[6] of Job's dispute with God and the friends. He criticizes both Job and the friends and rises to defend the just ways of God. Perhaps believing that God will never personally appear to answer Job's charges, he feels compelled to speak on God's behalf. In the process, while falling short of his presumptuous claims, he does, nonetheless, add theological insight[7] to the debate and prepare the reader for the appearance of Yahweh. Most notably in his final speech he calls Job's attention to an approaching storm as the vehicle of God's "voice," perhaps the very storm from which God will actually speak.[8]

The Elihu section of the book consists of a brief introduction of the speaker (32:1-5) followed by four separate speeches:[9]

Speech One: Elihu's Defense of His Right to Speak (32:6-22);
    God Does Speak to Men (33:1-33)
Speech Two: God Is Just (34:1-37)
Speech Three: God Is Not Answerable to Man (35:1-16)
Speech Four: God's Management of His World (36:1–37:24)

The Elihu speeches show a connection both with what has already been said in the debate and with what Yahweh will say in the closing speeches. On the one hand Elihu frequently cites the words of Job and the friends,[10] while on the other hand he anticipates some of the very arguments that Yahweh will offer in his rebuttal of Job and the friends.

---

[6]The "arbiter" that Job has repeatedly sought (9:33; 16:18-22)?

[7]Cf. Gordis, *Book of God and Man*, pp. 104-116.

[8]Elihu devotes the better part of his third and fourth speeches to interpreting how God works through the "storm" (אֵד, *ʾēd*, 36:26ff.; סוּפָה, *sûphāh*, 37:1ff.). Elihu's final speech contains a description of what appears to be an approaching storm (37:1ff.). The Yahweh-speeches then open with specific reference to "*the* storm" (הַסְּעָרָה, *hassᵉʿārāh*, 38:1) from which God speaks.

[9]Cf. C. Westermann, *Structure of the Book of Job*, pp. 139-147; Fohrer, "Die Weisheit des Elihu," pp. 83-94. D. Friedman ("The Elihu Speeches in the Book of Job," *HTR* 61 [1968]: 51-59) argues that these four speeches were originally distributed throughout the speech cycles with one at the end of each cycle and the fourth after Job's final speech.

[10]The rhetorical technique of quotation in preparation for refutation has already been employed by both Job and the friends in the debate portion of the book.

1. Introduction to the Elihu Speeches (32:1-5)

As is the case with each new development in the book, the appearance of Elihu on the scene is introduced by a brief narrative (cf., e.g., 1:1-3; 2:11-13). In this prose section we meet Elihu and receive an explanation of why we have not heard from him earlier in the debate.

¹**So these three men stopped answering Job, because he was righteous in his own eyes. ²But Elihu son of Barakel the Buzite, of the family of Ram, became very angry with Job for justifying himself rather than God. ³He was also angry with the three friends, because they had found no way to refute Job, and yet had condemned him.ᵃ ⁴Now Elihu had waited before speaking to Job because they were older than he. ⁵But when he saw that the three men had nothing more to say, his anger was aroused.**

ᵃ*3 Masoretic Text; an ancient Hebrew scribal tradition Job, and so had condemned God*

32:1-5 At this point in the story we learn that the debate is over. Frustrated by Job's "self-righteous"[11] attitude, the friends have given up in their attempt to **answer** him. When the author adds that the friends **had found no way to refute Job** and that they **had nothing more to say,** this is his way of telling us that Job has won the debate. The Masoretic Text of the Hebrew Bible has the author offering a further condemnation of the friends as being unfair to Job by adding the phrase **and yet had condemned him** (Job). As the NIV notes there is another textual tradition that renders this phrase "and so had condemned God" or "made God appear guilty." If we took this reading as original, then the author is accusing the friends of being inadequate defenders of God, an assessment later shared by Yahweh (42:7-8).[12]

Yet another defender of God now takes the stage. **Elihu** ("he is my God") is introduced by the rather lengthy pedigree, **son of**

---

[11]LXX reads, "in *their* eyes" for the MT "in his eyes."

[12]The reading of NIV, following MT, is one of the eighteen *Tiqqune sopherim* or "scribal emendations" found in the Hebrew Bible, where the scribes intentionally altered the text to eliminate a reading that they considered offensive or inappropriate.

Barakel the Buzite, of the family of Ram. This genealogical notice
may be important. As the commentators have noticed, Elihu is the
only character in the book of Job with an Israelite name.[13] His ances-
try makes him a relative of Abraham.[14] Since to this point the story
of Job has been located outside of Israel and its major characters
(including Job) have been numbered among the "sons of the East,"
this sudden appearance of an Israelite is significant. It is difficult to
imagine that a character so critical of the words of "foreigners" and
so closely aligned with the words of Yahweh appears "accidentally"
at this late and crucial stage of the book. His presence, rather than
disrupting the flow of the book, decisively redirects it in a way that
adds both drama and insight to its overall meaning and purpose.
Elihu's Jewish pedigree signals the reader that he is being introduced as a representative of Israelite theological tradition and that
he will function as the "forerunner of Yahweh."[15]

What Elihu will say he will say with passion. Above all he is driv-
en by **anger**. He is angry first with Job for **justifying himself rather
than God**. This phrase can also be translated "made himself more
righteous than God." Such a posture, as Eliphaz has already noted
(4:17; 15:14), is impossible for a mortal before God. With this Elihu
agrees, and it deeply offends him that Job should dare to make such
a claim. Elihu is also angry with the friends for their inability to
refute Job. Elihu knows what the readers know. The friends have
lost the debate. Their attempts to defend God before Job's irreverent accusations have failed miserably and amounted to nothing
more than "defenses of clay" (13:12).

As noted above, commentators differ widely over exactly what to
make of Elihu's anger and, for that matter, his whole persona. It is

---

[13]Cf. 1 Sam 1:1; 1 Chr 12:21[20]; 26:7; 27:18). The name Elihu (אֱלִיהוּא,
'elîhû') is very similar to the name Elijah (אֵלִיָּהוּ, 'eliyahu, "Yahweh is my
God"), and some scholars have argued that is its meaning here (cf. J. Mont-
gomery, "The Hebrew Divine Name and the Personal Pronoun Hū," *JBL* 63
[1944]: 161-163).

[14]Buz was the brother of Uz, and a nephew of Abraham (Gen 22:20-21).
In Jer 25:23 a Buz is mentioned in connection with Dedan and Tema, locat-
ed in Edom. Barachel, "Bless, Oh God," is mentioned only here in the
Hebrew Bible. There is a Ram who was an ancestor of David (Ruth 4:19),
while another Ram is associated with Jerahmeel (1 Chr 2:9-10,25,27). The
Targum of Job identifies Ram ("exalted") as Abraham.

[15]Cf. Hartley, *Job*, p. 429.

possible to see him as a gallant youth driven by righteous wrath to take on the arrogant Job and the incompetent friends — a reluctant yet passionate defender of God. On the other hand it is also possible to label him a hothead and a loquacious fool not unlike the man so universally condemned by the Israelite sages (cf., e.g., Prov 12:15-16; 14:27,29). While God condemns the friends for "speaking wrongly of him" and Job for "accusing God," he says nothing of Elihu. Given the fact that much of what Elihu says is echoed by Yahweh, himself, the reader should not be too quick to dismiss him as the arrogant buffoon of some interpreters. Whatever his motives and however presumptuous his claims, he does end up setting the stage for Yahweh to appear and speak.

Finally, this introduction of Elihu offers us an explanation of why we have not heard from him earlier. Out of deference to those **older than he**, Elihu has intentionally held his tongue. Only after they **had nothing more to say**, does he choose to vent his pent up **anger**. Such a disposition is typical of the respect accorded the elders in ancient times. It is only after it became clear that the older friends could not adequately refute Job that he decided to speak at all (32:11-16).[16]

2. Elihu's Defense of His Right to Speak (32:6-22)

[6]**So Elihu son of Barakel the Buzite said:**

"I am young in years, / and you are old; / that is why I was fearful, / not daring to tell you what I know. / [7]I thought, 'Age should speak; / advanced years should teach wisdom.' / [8]But it is the spirit[a] in a man, / the breath of the Almighty, that gives him understanding. / [9]It is not only the old[b] who are wise, / not only the aged who understand what is right.

[10]**"Therefore I say: Listen to me; / I too will tell you what I know. / [11]I waited while you spoke, / I listened to your reasoning; / while you were searching for words, / [12]I gave you my full attention. / But**

---

[16]MT reads that Elihu had waited "with Job" (אֶת־אִיּוֹב, *'eth-'iyôb*) before speaking. While Pope and Tur-Sinai take this as a dittography from the end of v. 3, Gordis argues convincingly that this reading should be preferred. The scene thus depicted is that of both Job and Elihu awaiting a reply from the friends. When none is offered, Elihu decides to break the silence.

not one of you has proved Job wrong; / none of you has answered his arguments. / [13]Do not say, 'We have found wisdom; / let God refute him, not man.' / [14]But Job has not marshaled his words against me, / and I will not answer him with your arguments.

[15]"They are dismayed and have no more to say; / words have failed them. / [16]Must I wait, now that they are silent, / now that they stand there with no reply? / [17]I too will have my say; / I too will tell what I know. / [18]For I am full of words, / and the spirit within me compels me; / [19]Inside I am like bottled-up wine, / like new wineskins ready to burst. / [20]I must speak and find relief; / I must open my lips and reply. / [21]I will show partiality to no one, / nor will I flatter any man; / [22]for if I were skilled in flattery, / my Maker would soon take me away.

[a]8 Or *Spirit*; also in verse 18   [b]9 Or *many*; or *great*

32:6-10 Elihu's opening words confirm what the prose introduction has already told us. Elihu has been standing by during the debate carefully observing what each side has had to say. Being **young in years** he feels the need to offer an apology for daring to speak at all.[17] Elihu says he was **fearful**[18] of interrupting those older and wiser than he. Now that they have had their say, he is finally emboldened to speak. He feels qualified to speak because **understanding** does not necessarily come by age but by the **spirit**, the **breath of the Almighty**. While this may be a claim to some kind of special revelation[19] similar to what Eliphaz said he had received (4:12ff), it is more likely Elihu's way of saying that he possesses the same spirit of wisdom imparted to all humans by God's life-giving breath (33:4).[20] Though not as old or experienced as the friends, Elihu, by virtue of being human, possesses the same spirit that gives them their insight. He, too, is qualified to **understand what is right**. The connection that Elihu makes between wisdom and right ("jus-

---

[17]Cf. the prologue of "The Protests of the Eloquent Peasant" (*ANET*, pp. 407-410) for a similar defense of the right of a lesser to speak in the presence of a superior.

[18]זָחַל (*zāḥal*) is related to Ug. *dhl*, "fear," and Aram. *dehal*, "fear, worship," and appears in its Hebrew form only here in the OT. In its Aramaic form it appears in Dan 2:31; 4:2[5]; 5:19; 6:27[26]; 7:7,19.

[19]Cf. Hartley, *Job*, p. 434.

[20]Cf. Habel, *Job*, pp. 450-451.

tice" or "equity") is crucial for Job's great struggle and consistent
with the values of Israelite wisdom (cf. Prov 1:3; 2:6-10; 8:20). For
Elihu, wisdom that does not result in "justice" and "righteousness"
is no wisdom at all.

32:11-16 Elihu's disappointment with the friends is echoed in
two specific charges he makes against them. First, he accuses them
of incompetence. Though the friends **searched for words**[21] and
offered their best **reasoning**, they have failed to **prove Job wrong**
and been unable to **answer his arguments**.[22] It is the unanimous
opinion of Job, Elihu, and Yahweh himself (cf. 13:1-12; 42:7,8) that
the friends are inadequate defenders of God. Their contention that
God governs his world exclusively by retributive justice simply does
not stand the test of honest observation of life. This is clearly one of
the truths taught by the book of Job.

Not only does Elihu accuse the friends of incompetence, he also
charges them with arrogance. He finds them guilty of simply dismissing Job without answering him, claiming to have **found wisdom**
without being able to successfully apply it in rebuttal of Job's charges
of divine injustice. By saying, **"Let God refute him,"** they have abdi-
cated their responsibility and tried to cover for their own lack of wisdom with an almost childlike petulance. In verse 14 he further suggests that the friends have been personally threatened by the power
of Job's carefully **marshaled** (עָרַךְ, *'ārak*; cf. 13:18) arguments.[23] The
inescapable proof of the friends' incompetence is their **silence**, the
fact that they **stand there with no reply**. They have been **dismayed**
(lit., "broken and shattered"; חָתַת, *ḥātat*; cf. Isa 7:8) by Job. Their
defeat is complete and humiliating.

32:17-22 Where the friends have failed, however, Elihu is convinced he can succeed. He is confident that Job can be refuted by

---

[21]חָקַר (*ḥāqar*) refers to the discipline of learning. Eliphaz says he had
"searched out" his arguments (5:27), and Bildad says the precepts of the
fathers likewise had been "searched out" (8:8).

[22]On the legal dimensions of this language cf. S. Scholnick, "Lawsuit
Drama in the Book of Job," Ph.D. diss., Brandeis University, 1975, pp. 227-
237; Dick, "The Legal Metaphor in Job," pp. 46-47.

[23]Instead of the neg. לֹא (*lō'*), "not" ("Job has *not* marshaled his words
against me," NIV, v. 14) Blommerde (*Northwest Semitic Grammar and Job*,
p 117) reads וּלְאִי אֶעֱרוֹךְ (*ûlᵃ'ê 'a'ārôk*), "I will indeed prepare (my defense),"
treating the *l* as a first person preformative of the verb.

what [he] **knows**. Elihu has punctuated his apologia for speaking by calling attention to *his* knowledge (יֵדַע, *dēʿî*; "what I know," NIV vv. 6,10,17). To some commentators this self-consciousness suggests that he is possessed by an arrogant sense of self-importance.[24] If this is indeed the case, then Elihu is in good company. Throughout the speeches both Job and the friends, in their enthusiasm for their respective positions, have repeatedly indulged in a form of intellectual arrogance. Their speeches have been full of impugning, name-calling, and competing claims to the high moral ground. If Elihu believes he has the "answer," if he dares to judge others as "wrong," if he has the audacity to lay claims to the "truth," then he nicely completes what Job and the friends have begun. This stage is no place for the timid, and timid, Elihu is not.

Above all Elihu is passionate. The **spirit within**[25] him **compels** him to speak. His frustration with Job and the friends has been building for some time, and like a **wineskin ready to burst** (cf. Matt 9:17)[26] he must **find relief**. As fermenting wine expands, so do the skins that hold it. Elihu's growing rage must find a way to get out. Though driven by passion to speak, Elihu insists that his pursuit of truth will be dispassionate and free of any **partiality**. Though sensitive to the superior status of Job and the friends, he insists that he will not **flatter** his elders nor defer to them in his pursuit of what is right. The fact that he will now proceed to take on both Job and the friends will show him true to his intention. It is clear that Elihu sees himself as the final arbiter to this dispute. He intends to settle what Job and the friends could not. In all of this Elihu feels bound by a sense of obligation toward God. If his efforts to defend God should ever become disingenuous, then God himself would **take** [him] **away**.[27]

---

[24]Cf., e.g., Habel, *Job*, pp. 444, 449.

[25]Lit., "in his belly, his viscera [בֶּטֶן, *beṭen*]" or the seat of his emotions. In the OT a person's passions are said to agitate their viscera and compel them to action (cf. Job 20:9). Cf. Wolff, *Anthropology of the Old Testament*, p. 63; *TDOT*, 2:96-97.

[26]NIV "wineskins" (אֹבוֹת, *ʾōbôth*) may mean "wine jars." Cf. A. Guillaume, "An Archaeological and Philological Note on Job XXXII, 19," *PEQ* 93 (1961): 147-150.

[27]The first of many "storm" metaphors in the speeches of Elihu (cf. 27:21).

JOB 33

3. Elihu's First Disputation: God Uses Suffering to Save Humans from Destruction (33:1-33)

Having argued for his right to speak, Elihu now begins his formal defense of God. He seeks to provide here what the friends could not: an adequate rebuttal of Job's charges against God. He begins by countering Job's central complaint that God unfairly afflicts humans and then refuses to offer any explanation of his behavior. Elihu will insist that God's employment of suffering in a person's life is both fair and purposeful. The speech breaks down into three components: a summons to Job (33:1-7); a rebuttal of Job's claims against God (33:8-30); a final challenge to Job (33:31-33).

Elihu's Summons to Job (33:1-7)

[1]"But now, Job, listen to my words; / pay attention to everything I say. / [2]I am about to open my mouth; / my words are on the tip of my tongue. / [3]My words come from an upright heart; / my lips sincerely speak what I know. / [4]The Spirit of God has made me; / the breath of the Almighty gives me life. / [5]Answer me then, if you can; / prepare yourself and confront me. / [6]I am just like you before God; / I too have been taken from clay. / [7]No fear of me should alarm you, / nor should my hand be heavy upon you.

33:1-7 Elihu now turns from the friends to a direct address of Job. His opening words seem to be an attempt to turn the legal tables on Job, to put him on the defensive.[1] Perhaps believing that

---

[1]This same approach will later be used by Yahweh with much stronger language (cf. 38:2-3; 40:7). For a discussion of the legal language in this opening section cf. H. Huffmon, "Covenant Lawsuit in the Prophets," *JBL* 78 (1959): 285-295.

God will never appear to directly answer Job's charges, Elihu challenges Job to **answer me** instead. Just as he did with the friends, Elihu begins his address to Job with an apologia for his right to speak. He does so with three specific claims. First, he contends that he speaks from an **upright heart**. His motives are pure. Second he insists that his **lips sincerely speak**. There is no guile in his words. Elihu's apologia sounds much like the claims of personified wisdom in Proverbs 8:6-8. It may be that by his choice of terms here he is seeking to elevate himself to the status of sage, of official spokesperson of Wisdom itself. Third he argues that, though younger than Job, he is nonetheless a fellow-creature, **made** by the **Spirit of God** and **given life** by the **breath of the Almighty**. These credentials, he argues, qualify him to address Job as an equal. But he is only an equal. Just like Job he has been **taken from clay**. In no way should Job **fear** him or feel intimidated by him. While this language could be dismissed as the ultimate presumption of proud youth, it may rather be understood as a direct response to Job's earlier words. Job had complained that even if he were granted a day in court with God, God's terror would so intimidate him that he would have no chance for a fair trial (cf. 9:34; 13:21). Aware of this Elihu, as God's self-appointed arbiter, reminds Job that he is merely a man and that Job can **confront** him without dread or sense of **alarm**.

Elihu's Rebuttal of Job's Charges against God (33:8-33)

[8]"But you have said in my hearing— / I heard the very words— / [9]'I am pure and without sin; / I am clean and free from guilt. / [10]Yet God has found fault with me; / he considers me his enemy. / [11]He fastens my feet in shackles; / he keeps close watch on all my paths.'
[12]"But I tell you, in this you are not right, / for God is greater than man. / [13]Why do you complain to him / that he answers none of man's words[a]? / [14]For God does speak—now one way, now another— / though man may not perceive it. / [15]In a dream, in a vision of the night, / when deep sleep falls on men / as they slumber in their beds, / [16]he may speak in their ears / and terrify them with warnings, / [17]to turn man from wrongdoing / and keep him from pride, / [18]to preserve his soul from the pit,[b] / his life from perishing by the sword.[c] / [19]Or a man may be chastened on a bed of pain,

/ with constant distress in his bones, / [20]so that his very being finds food repulsive / and his soul loathes the choicest meal. / [21]His flesh wastes away to nothing, / and his bones, once hidden, now stick out. / [22]His soul draws near to the pit,[d] / and his life to the messengers of death.[e]

[23]"Yet if there is an angel on his side / as a mediator, one out of a thousand, / to tell a man what is right for him, / [24]to be gracious to him and say, / 'Spare him from going down to the pit[f]; / I have found a ransom for him'— / [25]then his flesh is renewed like a child's; / it is restored as in the days of his youth. / [26]He prays to God and finds favor with him, / he sees God's face and shouts for joy; / he is restored by God to his righteous state. / [27]Then he comes to men and says, / 'I sinned; and perverted what was right, / but I did not get what I deserved. / [28]He redeemed my soul from going down to the pit,[g] / and I will live to enjoy the light.'

[29]"God does all these things to a man— / twice, even three times— / [30]to turn back his soul from the pit,[h] / that the light of life may shine on him.

[31]"Pay attention, Job, and listen to me; / be silent, and I will speak. / [32]If you have anything to say, answer me; / speak up, for I want you to be cleared. / [33]But if not, then listen to me; / be silent, and I will teach you wisdom."

[a]13 Or that he does not answer for any of his actions   [b]18 Or preserve him from the grave   [c]18 Or from crossing the River   [d]22 Or He draws near to the grave   [e]22 Or to the dead   [f]24 Or grave   [g]28 Or redeemed me from going down to the grave   [h]30 Or turn him back from the grave

33:8-11 Citation for the purpose of refutation is a rhetorical technique employed repeatedly in the book of Job. Job and the friends have both used it against each other throughout the debate. In their final exchange Yahweh and Job will likewise quote (or paraphrase) one another (cf. 40:8; 42:3-4). Elihu uses it here to summarize Job's essential complaints against God. He does so with a combination of direct quotations and general characterizations that reduce Job's argument to four claims of innocence (v. 9) followed by four charges against God (vv. 10-11). Elihu's recollection of Job's claims of innocence may be a bit hyperbolic. While Job has claimed that he was "innocent" or "blameless" (תָּם, tām; cf. 9:20,21; cf. also 1:1,8) and has consistently defended his "integrity" (תֻּמָּתִי, tummātî; 27:5) and his "righteousness" (צִדְקָתִי, ṣidqāthî; 27:6), he has never actually called himself **pure** (זַךְ, *zak*)[2] or **clean** (חַף, *ḥaph*). In fact, it is arguable if Job ever claims to be totally **without sin** (פֶּשַׁע, *pešāʿ*) and **free from guilt** (עָוֹן, *ʿāwōn*).[3] He does, however, claim that he has faithfully kept God's commands (23:11-12) and that God knows him to be "not guilty" (לֹא אֶרְשָׁע, *lōʾ ʾeršāʿ*; 10:7). Further, Job has disavowed himself of having committed even attitudinal sins (cf. 31:24-30) and sins of omission (31:16-17) and has on more than one occasion challenged God to identify any sin of which he is guilty (cf. 13:23; 31:35). So perhaps Elihu's characterization of Job's claims to innocence, though imprecise, is nonetheless generally accurate.

Elihu's rehearsal of Job's charges against God is truer to Job's actual words. The claim that God treats Job as his **enemy**[4] remembers Job's specific complaint in 13:24.[5] In fact Job has repeatedly cast Shaddai in the role of his violent adversary (cf., e.g., 6:4; 7:12,20; 16:11-14; 19:6-12; 30:21). The final two charges — **he fastens my feet in shackles; he keeps close watch on all my paths** (v. 11) — is a direct quotation of Job's exact words in 13:27. These words remember Job's caricatures of God as a brutal oppressor (cf. 7:1-3) and a cosmic spy (cf. 7:8,20). The characterization of Job's first charge, **God has found fault with me**, is interesting. The idea behind the original Hebrew seems to be that Job has charged that God "finds pretexts against me," that is, looks for some excuse to harm him. This may be Elihu's way of remembering Job's claim that God has been devious in his dealings with Job, afflicting him without just cause (cf. 9:11-22).[6]

33:12 Elihu begins his rebuttal of Job's charges against God with the blunt statement, **in this you are not right**. By this Elihu means that Job is simply not qualified to accuse God of anything. **God is**

---

[2]Zophar said Job had called his "beliefs" *pure* (*zak*, 11.4), and Job has called his "prayer" *pure* (*zak*, 16:17). Bildad said that if Job were "pure" (*zak*) and "upright" (יָשָׁר, *yāšār*) God would restore him.

[3]Cf. discussion by Gordis, *Job*, p. 373. All along Job's real argument has been that he has not done anything worthy of the suffering God has visited upon him.

[4]אֹיֵב (*ʾōyēb*) is similar in sound and spelling to Job's name (אִיּוֹב, *ʾiyôb*) and constitutes one suggested etymology for the meaning of Job's name.

[5]As Habel (*Job*, p. 460) notes, this speech of Elihu (33:1-33) has numerous connections with portions of Job's third discourse (13:17-28).

[6]So Habel, following Fohrer.

greater than man. He is in a totally different class from Job, or any other human. By virtue of being God, he is above criticism from mere mortals. Elihu's defense of God thus makes a departure here from the repeated arguments of the friends. While they have been focusing on the moral difference between Job and God, Elihu is focusing on the ontological difference. He does not compare Job's morality to God's morality, he compares Job's humanity to God's divinity. The friends have been focusing on Job's presumed sin and how this makes Job worthy of God's punishment. Job, by contrast, has insisted he is innocent of any such sin and that his integrity gives him the right to accuse God of injustice because he has "punished" Job unfairly. Elihu now seeks to shift the paradigm of divine-human interaction to a model that totally ignores the issue of Job's innocence or guilt. Job's attacks against God are inappropriate simply because Job is human and God is divine. God, by virtue of being God, is not accountable to man. Job, sinful or innocent, is simply not qualified to judge God. This fresh approach to Job's dilemma suggested here by Elihu anticipates the very approach that Yahweh himself will take in the God-speeches.[7]

33:13-18 These verses begin Elihu's rebuttal of another of Job's charges against God — that he **answers none of man's words.**[8] This is presumably a reference to Job's claim that God is unresponsive to his repeated cries for an explanation of what has happened to him (cf., e.g., 19:7). God simply does not speak to humans, Job has contended. To the contrary, insists Elihu, God **does speak** in a variety of **ways**[9] though humans do not always **perceive**[10] that it is God who is communicating. **Dreams** and **visions** were widely recognized as channels

---

[7]In both of his speeches Yahweh does not deal with the issue of Job's guilt or innocence. He does emphasize the vast difference between him and Job in what he knows and can do as creator and manager of the universe.

[8]MT reads "his words" and most interpreters understand the antecedent to be "man." LXX has "my words" which would make this a quotation of Job's earlier words. M. Dahood ("The Dative Suffix in Job 33,13," *Bib* 33 [1982]: 258-259) renders the expression as a participle, "the one who speaks to him."

[9]The Hebrew literally reads "once and twice." Such ascending numerical sequences are often used in the OT to signify "several" (cf., e.g., Amos 1:3ff; Prov 30:15ff). In this chapter it anticipates the "twice, thrice" of v. 29.

[10]The Hebrew root שׁוּר (*šûr*) is used in Num 23:9 in discerning the meaning of Balaam's oracles.

of supernatural revelation in the ancient Near East.[11] In the Bible dreams are only rarely the means of divine revelation, with references to them primarily limited to the stories of the patriarchs and Daniel.[12] It seems though that Elihu has another kind of dream in mind here. Earlier Job had complained of being afflicted by "troubling dreams" (7:14). Elihu is suggesting that God has been trying to tell Job something through his sleep deprivation. Such **terrifying** dreams, Elihu suggests, are God's way of **warning**[13] a person, an attempt to **turn** him from **wrongdoing**. What we might label "wrestling with a guilty conscience" Elihu identifies as God's specific attempts to keep a man from the self-destructive ends of his **pride** and sinful behavior. When Elihu says that God **preserves his soul from the pit**,[14] he does not mean he delivers him from eternal damnation, but as the next phrase suggests he keeps his **life from perishing**. Elihu is suggesting to Job that the negative things God brings into a person's life may have a positive, even redemptive, purpose.

33:19-22 God's corrective discipline may also come in the more severe form of **pain**. Even something as negative as serious illness can serve a positive purpose. This suggestion, which directly addresses Job's dilemma, has already been offered in a slightly different form by Eliphaz (5:17-18). Such suffering, suggests Elihu, is not an end but a means to another end — the eventual repentance and redemption of the afflicted person. Elihu says this with full appreciation of how devastating such suffering can be. The **constant distress in the bones**, the **loathing** of **food**, and the **wasting away** of a sick person can all be instruments of God's **chastening**. The terms **chasten** (הוּכַח, *hûkāḥ*) and **distress** (רִיב, *rîb*) are actually legal terms that can mean "indicted" and "tried" respectively. Elihu is suggesting suffering is a "trial" of sorts by which the sufferer is confronted by God. Job has been clamoring for a day in God's court. Elihu

---

[11]There is an interesting reference to dreams in the Babylonian Ludlul Bel Nemeqi, where the Joblike character is restored to health through messages received in dreams (III.1-60, *BWL*, pp. 49-50).

[12]Gen 15:12-16; 20:3; 28:12-15; 31:24; 41:11-12; Judg 7:13-15; Dan 2:31-45.

[13]מוּסָר (*mûsār*), normally translated "correction" or "discipline" (cf. 5:17).

[14]The "pit" (שַׁחַת, *šāḥath*) should be understood as synonymous with Sheol or the "netherworld" (cf. Ps 103:4). The following phrase, "perishing by the sword" (NIV), may also be rendered "crossing the River" (שֶׁלַח, *šelaḥ*; cf. NIV footnote) and may refer to the mythological river which one crosses to enter the nether regions.

seems to be saying that he is already in that court. Prosecuted by suffering, a man is brought to face his finitude, as he confronts the **messengers of death**.[15] Of course, as the reader knows, Job is going through a "trial" or sorts. But as the reader also knows, it is not to bring Job face to face with his sins, but to test the purity of his piety.

33:23-25 In this trial, suggests Elihu, there is the possibility that a heavenly intercessor may plead the case of the sufferer.[16] This **angel** functions as a **mediator** (מֵלִיץ, *mēlîṣ*) who takes the **side** of the accused sufferer and advises him on a proper course of action, **what is right for him** or what will put him back in good standing before God. Elihu seems to be responding here to Job's earlier hopes of finding a mediator who would rise on his behalf (cf. 9:32-35; 16:18-22; 19:21-27).[17] The expression **one out of a thousand** is probably meant to suggest just how special such a mediator is among the angels of God.[18] In Elihu's scenario, this angel pleads for the deliverance of the sufferer before God claiming that he has **found a ransom for him**. In Israelite society such "ransoms" (כֹּפֶר, *kōpher*) involved payments of money or other compensations to release people from various obligations. It is difficult to speculate what ransom Elihu has in mind, but it is clearly something beyond what humans can provide (cf. Ps 49:8-10[7-9]).[19] The result of the mediator's intercession is that the sufferer finds his **flesh renewed** and his health **restored**.

33:26-30 The restoration of the sufferer, secured by the intercession of God's angel, leads him to gratefully respond to God through formal acts of worship. He **prays to God**. He **sees God's face** and **shouts for joy**. This language is that of ancient Israelite religion. To see God's face is to enter his presence in worship and

---

[15]מְמִתִים (*məmithîm*; lit., "killers"). In later Jewish literature this term was thought to refer to an angel of death who ushered departed human spirits into the next world (cf. discussion by Gordis, Fohrer).

[16]For the biblical background to this idea cf. Ps 34:7-8[6-7]; Zech 3:1-5; cf. also 1 Enoch 9:3ff; 15:2. Cf. also M.A. Canney's discussion in "The Hebrew *melis* (Prov IX 12; Gen XLII 2-3)," *AJSL* 40 (1923): 135-137.

[17]On the identity of such a mediator cf. the discussion of 19:25 and A. de Wilde, *Das Buch Hiob*, OtSt 22 (Leiden: E.J. Brill, 1981), p. 316.

[18]Cf. W. Eichrodt, *Theology of the Old Testament*, trans. by J. Baker, OTL (Philadelphia: Westminster, 1967), 2:23-29, who identifies him with the "angel of Yahweh."

[19]Fohrer (also Dillmann, Kissane) suggests it is the indicted sufferer's anticipated repentance. Habel speculates that it might be the person's past uprightness.

find his favor (Ps 17:15). The "joyful shout" (תְּרוּעָה, *t°rû'āh*) is the exuberant praise offered by those who gather in the worship assembly (Ps 89:16[15]). Having experienced restoration the sufferer makes formal confession (**comes to men and says**) of God's gracious forgiveness of his sins (**I did not get what I deserved**).

The sequence of events depicted here is important for our understanding of Elihu's unique contribution to the meaning of the book of Job as is the shift from the language of the courtroom to the language of the sanctuary. The friends, presuming Job's guilt, have identified confession of sin as the *means* to Job's restoration. Elihu regards such confession as the *consequence* of Job's restoration. The friends have urged Job to reform his ways and trust in his piety to gain his restoration. Job, on the other hand, has contended that he has never compromised his piety and on the strength of that position believes he can force God to acknowledge his integrity and thereby secure his own restoration. According to Elihu, however, it is not Job but the **God who does all these things** who will bring about Job's restoration. It will not be achieved by Job's "righteousness" but by God's "ransom." Job has been clamoring for "justice" that will come from an encounter with God in his court. Elihu is suggesting that his deliverance will instead come from God's "grace" through an encounter with God in his sanctuary. Job comes before God as a proud man demanding what is rightfully his. Elihu invites him to come as a humble man seeking what God graciously bestows.[20]

33:31-33 Elihu's invitation for Job to respond has been viewed by some interpreters as evidence of Elihu's presumptuous posture.[21] While Elihu's assumption of the role as Job's **teacher** and the imparter of **wisdom** does seem to be presumptuous, in the final analysis his claims must be measured by his ability to impart any new insight into Job's problem. Job's refusal to reply could be taken as proof that Elihu has silenced Job[22] or, conversely, that he refuses to give this brash young man the courtesy of a reply.[23] It may simply be that Job, having rested his case and offered his final appeal to God, has chosen to wait for God and God alone to reply.

---

[20]Cf. J.F. Ross, "Job 33:14-30: The Phenomenology of Lament," *JBL* 94 (1975): 38-46.

[21]Cf., e.g., Habel, *Job*, p. 472.

[22]Rowley.

[23]Habel.

JOB 34

4. Elihu's Second Disputation: God Is Just (34:1-37)

At the core of Job's charges against God is the claim that he is unjust. He fails to see to it that the good are rewarded and the wicked are punished. For this, Job argues, God should be held accountable. Elihu's second disputation is designed to defend God against this charge and to expose the absurdity of a human trying to force God to give account for his behavior.

As was the case in his first disputation, it is obvious here also that Elihu has been carefully listening to Job. This second disputation is closely tied to Job's reply to Zophar (cf. 12:13-25) and may be viewed as a direct and ironic refutation of Job's charges against God's unjust rule of his world. For example, the reader should note:

1. Both speeches begin with a claim of God's sovereign rule (12:10 = 34:13-15).
2. Both cite a proverb that compares "hearing" with "taste" (12:11 = 34:3).
3. Both speeches make reference to the "shadowy realms" (12:22 = 34:21-22).
4. Job claims that God abuses his sovereign power; Elihu says God rules for the good (12:14-15 = 34:13).
5. Job accuses God of leading rulers astray; Elihu argues that God holds evil rulers in check (12:17-21 = 34:18-20).[1]

Structurally, this speech may be divided into three major parts: a summons for all to listen (33:1-4); Elihu's disputation (33:5-33); a judgment against Job (33:34-37). The opening (33:1-15) and closing (33:34-37) parts of Elihu's speech are addressed to all who are

---

[1] For these and other insightful literary comparisons cf. Habel, *Job*, pp. 477-478.

present while the main part of the dispute (33:16-33) is addressed to Job.[2]

Mirroring Job's own language this speech is full of legal jargon. Most important is the use of the Hebrew root רשׁע (*rš'*), "guilty, in the wrong."[3] Appearing five times in this speech (vv. 10,12,17,18,29), Elihu employs this forensic term to argue that God, because of who he is, should never be judged the "guilty party" in any dispute with a man. Though Elihu will defend God's just governance of his world, he seems even more concerned with the impropriety of a mere mortal daring to accuse him and trying to hold him accountable.

Elihu's Summons for All to Listen (34:1-4)

[1]Then Elihu said:

[2]"Hear my words, you wise men; / listen to me, you men of learning. / [3]For the ear tests words / as the tongue tastes food. / [4]Let us discern for ourselves what is right; / let us learn together what is good.

34:1-4 The **wise men** whom Elihu addresses may be the friends but this is not likely given his earlier attacks against their incompetence. It is more likely that Elihu is addressing the elders of the community by whom disputes like Job's were commonly heard. This is supported by Elihu's second characterization of them as **men of learning** (יֹדְעִים, *yōdᵊ'îm*; "those who know"). The Hebrew root ידע (*yd'*), "to know," can also mean "to judge," and that is what those addressed are invited to do (v. 4).[4] The proverb Elihu quotes in verse 3 is essentially the same one that Job quoted in an earlier speech (12:11).[5] The idea conveyed by comparing how the **ear tests words** as the **tongue tastes food** is that as the mouth discriminates between good and bad food, so too does the ear make judgments between good and bad words. Accord-

---

[2]Note the shift from second person plural pronouns to second person singular pronouns and back.

[3]Cf. D. Hillers, "Delocutive Verbs in Biblical Hebrew," *JBL* 86 (1967): 320-324.

[4]Cf. 2 Sam 19:36[35]; Jer 29:23 and Gemser, "The RIB- or Controversy Pattern in Hebrew Mentality," pp. 124; S. Scholnick, "Lawsuit Drama," p. 294.

[5]A similar proverb may be found in Ecclus 36:24: "As the palate tastes the kinds of game, so an intelligent mind detects false words."

ingly, Elihu invites his audience to **discern** what is **right** and what is **good**. In this context both of these terms should be understood to define what is "legally correct" and "defensible."[6] Elihu is inviting his hearers to judge between his position and Job's.

Elihu's Disputation (34:5-33)

[5]"Job says, 'I am innocent, / but God denies me justice. / [6]Although I am right, / I am considered a liar; / although I am guiltless, / his arrow inflicts an incurable wound.' / [7]What man is like Job, / who drinks scorn like water? / [8]He keeps company with evildoers; / he associates with wicked men. / [9]For he says, 'It profits a man nothing / when he tries to please God.'

[10]"So listen to me, you men of understanding. / Far be it from God to do evil, / from the Almighty to do wrong. / [11]He repays a man for what he has done; / he brings upon him what his conduct deserves. / [12]It is unthinkable that God would do wrong, / that the Almighty would pervert justice. / [13]Who appointed him over the earth? / Who put him in charge of the whole world? / [14]If it were his intention / and he withdrew his spirit[a] and breath, / [15]all mankind would perish together / and man would return to the dust.

[16]"If you have understanding, hear this; / listen to what I say. / [17]Can he who hates justice govern? / Will you condemn the just and mighty One? / [18]Is he not the One who says to kings, 'You are worthless,' / and to nobles, 'You are wicked,' / [19]who shows no partiality to princes / and does not favor the rich over the poor, / for they are all the work of his hands? / [20]They die in an instant, in the middle of the night; / the people are shaken and they pass away; / the mighty are removed without human hand.

[21]"His eyes are on the ways of men; / he sees their every step. / [22]There is no dark place, no deep shadow, / where evildoers can hide. / [23]God has no need to examine men further, / that they should come before him for judgment. / [24]Without inquiry he shatters the mighty / and sets up others in their place. / [25]Because he takes note of their deeds, / he overthrows them in the night and they are crushed. / [26]He punishes them for their wickedness / where everyone can see them, / [27]because they turned from fol-

---

[6]Cf. Scholnick, "Lawsuit Drama," p. 294.

lowing him / and had no regard for any of his ways. / ²⁸They
caused the cry of the poor to come before him, / so that he heard
the cry of the needy. / ²⁹But if he remains silent, who can condemn
him? / If he hides his face, who can see him? / Yet he is over man
and nation alike, / ³⁰to keep a godless man from ruling, / from laying snares for the people.

³¹"Suppose a man says to God, / 'I am guilty but will offend no
more. / ³²Teach me what I cannot see; / if I have done wrong, I will
not do so again.' / ³³Should God then reward you on your terms, /
when you refuse to repent? / You must decide, not I; / so tell me
what you know.

ᵃ14 Or *Spirit*

34:5-6 Throughout his speeches Job has vigorously claimed to be
innocent (צָדַק, *ṣādaq*; "in the right"; cf., e.g., 9:20; 10:15; 13:18) and
repeatedly charged that **God denies me justice** (מִשְׁפָּט, *mišpāṭ*; cf.,
e.g., 19:7; 27:2). He has also lamented the fact that God has made
him appear to be a **liar** by afflicting him with a suffering that invalidates his claims of innocence and makes him appear guilty (cf., e.g.,
10:17; 16:8; 19:19-21). This very suffering he has characterized as
God's vicious **arrow** that **incurably wounds** a **guiltless** man (cf., e.g.,
6:4; 16:9-14; 19:7-12). By citing these claims Elihu summarizes Job's
"case" against God.

34:7-9 Elihu will now begin his refutation of these charges against
God by labeling them as both irreverent and untrue. They are irreverent because they betray a lack of proper respect for God. Elihu says
Job's repeated attempts to derisively assault the justice of God are
equivalent to a man **drinking scorn like water**. The term "scorn"
(לַעַג, *la'ag*) means to mock all that is holy and good. From Elihu's perspective to accuse God of wrongdoing is the ultimate mockery of
good. Job's charges are untrue, argues Elihu, because they contradict
one of the fundamental principles of God's righteous rule. When Job
says, "**It profits a man nothing when he tries to please God**," he is
charging that God does not care about human piety. Job has repeatedly argued this both on the basis of his own experience and on the
basis of his observations of life in general (cf. 9:22; 10:3; 21:7-16).
This very claim is what the **wicked** say in defense of their evil behavior (21:15), and when Job asserts it, he identifies (**keeps company**)
with them. Elihu will later offer a rebuttal of this claim (35:2-8).

34:10-15 Elihu's rebuttal of Job's charges of divine injustice sounds much like the position that the friends have repeatedly argued (4:7; 8:3,6; 15:20). God **repays a man for what he has done.** He equitably dispenses rewards and punishments to humans according to what they **deserve.**[7] God does this because it is his nature to do so. He is a deity of unimpeachable character. It is, therefore, **unthinkable**, that he could **do wrong** or **pervert justice** (cf. 8:3). This classic restatement of the doctrine of retributive justice counters Job's claims that God's failure to administer justice disrupts the social order and creates chaos on earth. (12:16-25). With a pair of rhetorical questions, each expecting an answer of "no one," Elihu takes exception to the right of Job or any mere mortal to challenge God's management of his world: **"Who appointed him over the earth? Who put him in charge of the whole world?"** Elihu reminds Job that God is the sovereign creator and ruler of the world. He fashioned it according to his own purposes and designs. He alone understands how it works and how it all fits together. Therefore, he and he alone is qualified to rule it. He answers to no one regarding how it is to be managed. Job, like **all mankind**, owes his very existence to God's creative act. It is within God's power to **withdraw his spirit and breath** from his creatures and **return** them **to the dust.**[8] The creature simply has no right to challenge the creator.[9] For Job to do so is absurd and the ultimate presumption.

34:16-20 Again employing a set of rhetorical questions, Elihu continues to press his argument that God is just. Addressing Job directly Elihu asks, **"Can he who hates justice govern?"**[10] Elihu's point is that God could not possibly maintain his management of the cosmic order if he were to abandon all justice. To do so would put the world at the mercy of power-hungry **kings** and **nobles** who would then have open season on a defenseless humanity. The **just One** and the **mighty One** (cf. Ps 99:4) intervenes to see that this does

---

[7]This language echoes the teaching of much of the OT, especially the wisdom literature (cf., e.g., Prov 4:10-19; 12:14; 19:17; Ps 62:12[11]).

[8]There is obvious allusion here to themes addressed in Genesis 1–11 and the absolute power of one true God to create, judge and, if he chooses, to destroy (cf. also Isa 40:12ff); cf. discussion by Habel, *Job*, pp. 482-483.

[9]When Yahweh speaks (cf. 38:5ff), he will make the same argument also built upon his exclusive role as creator and ruler of the world.

[10]חָבַשׁ (ḥābaš), lit., "to bind."

not happen. He judges the powerful, pronouncing them **wicked** and **worthless**[11] holding them accountable for their evil behaviors. As a judge God **shows no partiality** (cf. Deut 10:17; Acts 10:34-35) to the powerful or the **rich**.[12] The qualities of fairness and equity were highly regarded in biblical times as attributes of the ideal ruler. God, the personification of the ideal ruler, treats all men equally as the **work of his hands** (cf. 14:15; Prov 22:2). The fact that the mighty **die in an instant**, or when they least expect it, proves that even the powerful cannot escape God's judgment. Though presumably in control of their destiny and insulated against life's exigencies, the **people** (עַם, *'ām*; lit., "the landed gentry") are still vulnerable to the **hand** of God. **In the middle of the night**,[13] while they feel secure in their own beds, God **shakes** them and they **pass away**.

34:21-25 Job had previously accused God of being a cruel and vindictive "All-seeing Eye" who unfairly spied on humans in order to find occasion to attack them (7:8,17-20; 10:13-14). Here Elihu defends God's scrutiny of human behavior as a necessary and desirable function of his just rule. Nothing that humans do escapes his watchful **eyes**. Not even a **dark place** or **deep shadow** (צַלְמָוֶת, *ṣalmāweth*)[14] can hide men from his scrutinizing view. Because of his "all-seeing" powers, **God has no need to examine men further**,[15] he has no need to bring humans before him for a trial. This line is, no doubt, specifically aimed at Job's continued demand for a day in God's court. Such a trial, argues Elihu, is completely unnecessary, for God already knows all that he needs to know to make a fair and just judgment. The emphasis here and throughout Elihu's defense is

---

[11]בְּלִיַּעַל (*bᵉliyaʿal*), a compound noun in Hebrew, joining בְּלִי (*bᵉli*), "without," and יַעַל (*yāʿal*), "value, worth," to mean something like "scoundrel." This term is used of the worst kind of people in the OT (1 Kgs 21:10,13; 2 Chr 13:7; Judg 19:22; 20:13; Deut 13:14[13]). In later literature it was used as a title for the devil (cf. T. Levi 3:3; 18:12; Jub 1:20); cf. B. Otzen, *TDOT*, 2:131-136.

[12]שׁוֹעַ (*šôaʿ*) appears only here and in Isa 32:5 where it refers to the wealthy upper class.

[13]It was at midnight that the destroying angel smote Egypt's firstborn (Exod 12:29).

[14]This term is sometimes used as a metaphor of "death" in Job (3:5; 10:21).

[15]Verse 23a reads more literally, "It is not for man to set a time to come before God in litigation." Cf. Guillaume, *Studies in the Book of Job*, p. 120.

that humans have no right to demand that God explain or defend any action that he takes among men. Such a demand violates his omnipotence and his omniscience. It is this same point that Yahweh, himself, will make in his speeches (38:5ff).

34:26-28 Because God already knows the sins of the **mighty**, he acts decisively to **overthrow them** suddenly and **sets up others in their place.** This idea that God judges the powerful is in tune with the larger biblical concept that human rulers reign by God's permission and are accountable to him (cf. Deut 17:14-20). In a world where kings answered to no one, this concept represented a major departure from the prevailing autocratic model of human governance. When God judges the powerful, he does it in a way that **everyone can see**. Their oppressive crimes against the **poor,** which they think they are getting away with, are known (**heard**) by God and exposed by his devastating judgment. Thus even the most powerful of men who **turn** from **following** God do not escape his justice.

The emphasis on God's judgment of "kings" and "nobles" in Elihu's speech may also be traceable to an issue more personally relevant for Job. As the prologue makes clear, Job himself was a powerful man, "the greatest man among all the people of the East" (1:3). Further, in his closing challenge to God Job boldly declared that, given the opportunity, he would approach God "like a prince" (31:37). Elihu's argument that God holds the mighty accountable may be framed in terms that are designed to censure Job's personal hubris and humble this man who would dare rise to accuse God.

34:29-30 The interpretation of these verses is made difficult by numerous textual problems.[16] As the NIV translates it, verse 29 seems to be saying that, should God **remain silent** and **hide his face**, i.e., not choose to intervene and punish an unjust ruler, no mortal has the right to **condemn him** for his failure to act. His purposes remain hidden from what humans can **see**. According to Elihu, God's failure or slowness to impose justice in a particular situation does not invalidate the general principle that God exercises his sovereignty over **men** and **nations** to ensure justice and keep the **godless** from exploiting innocent people. While at times God's ways may prove inscrutable, they are nonetheless just.[17]

---

[16]Cf. discussions by Fohrer and Gordis. LXX omits vv. 28-33.

[17]Habel translates the first line of v. 29, "When he silences, who could

It is also possible to take these words as Elihu's characterization of God's refusal to appear and answer Job's challenge. This interpretation would have Elihu arguing that if God is "silent" and "hides his face" from Job and refuses Job's demand to give an explanation of his actions, such a refusal does not invalidate his sovereign and just rule over his world.

34:31-33 This passage, too, is replete with textual difficulties.[18] As NIV translates the opening line of verse 31, this part of Elihu's speech is to be read as a hypothetical argument that **should a man** (Job) confess (**say**) to God that he is "guilty" in an attempt to force God to release him, God would not be obligated by such a ploy, especially in view of the fact that the man (Job) is not truly **repentant** (v. 33).[19] In such a scenario Job would be attempting to set the terms by which God should conduct justice and thus would be infringing upon his sovereignty. God simply will not honor such an approach. This interpretation makes sense in light of Elihu's overall argument and honors the original Hebrew of verse 31.[20] An alternative reading has this entire section as a direct address to Job inviting him to confess.[21] The very difficult verse 33 seems to be a question put to Job designed to expose the absurdity of his attempt to demand that God prove his innocence.

Elihu's Judgment against Job (34:34-37)

³⁴**"Men of understanding declare, / wise men who hear me say to me, / ³⁵'Job speaks without knowledge; / his words lack insight.'**

---

prove him wrong?" Such a rendering would have the second half of the verse proposing a contrast and mean that should God "silence" as an act of judgment against injustice or "hide his face" in anger over injustice, he is still the sovereign and just God (*Job*, p. 485).

[18]For various emendations proposed for these verses see Gordis.

[19]NIV renders כִּי־מָאַסְתָּ (*kî-mā'astā*; lit., "when you reject") "when you refuse to repent."

[20]In the Hebrew הֶאָמַר (*he'āmar*) of MT the הַ (*he*) clearly appears to be an interrogative (cf. Driver & Gray) but is not in the normal grammatical position in the line.

[21]Gordis repoints the first line of verse 31 to read כִּי אֶל אֱלֹהַ אֱמֹר (*kî 'el 'ĕlōah 'ĕmōr*) and understands it to read, "But say instead to God" treating this as a direct address to Job (cf. Tur-Sinai). Pope puts all of these verses in the mouth of the "godless man" of verse 30 and takes it as an example of his disingenuous speech.

/ [36]Oh, that Job might be tested to the utmost / for answering like a wicked man! / [37]To his sin he adds rebellion; / scornfully he claps his hands among us / and multiplies his words against God."

34:34-37 Elihu challenged Job to reply at the end of verse 33. Hearing none he now goes on to formally indict Job. He presumes to speak for the **men of understanding** (cf. v. 2) as if they were rendering this verdict upon Job. Perhaps he has already heard them say this during the long debate. When they accuse Job of being **without knowledge**, they anticipate the very verdict of Yahweh (38:2). But according to Elihu Job is guilty of more than ignorance. He **answers like a wicked man**. By his impious speech and unwarranted attacks upon God he has made himself God's enemy. He should, therefore, **be tested to the utmost**.[22] The expression **Oh, that,** with which Elihu calls for Job to be tested, could be taken as a wish or even, more strongly, as an imprecation.[23] The testing Elihu has in mind may be further physical suffering that God might afflict upon Job or additional rebuttal that Elihu is prepared to offer. When Elihu says that Job **adds** to **his sin**, he is probably referring to the offense that he, like the friends, believes Job has already committed and is being punished for in his suffering. The phrase **scornfully he claps his hands** is not in the original Hebrew but represents an attempt by NIV and others to complete the sense and balance of the poetry.[24] A better rendering of the MT would be "he increases impiety among us."[25] The line seems to be referring to the power of Job's impious words to influence bystanders and foster unbelief among the people. Job's impious speech proves him to be guilty and his suffering to be the just punishment of God.

---

[22]עַד־נֶצַח (*'ad-neṣaḥ*, "until forever") is a superlative meaning, "entirely, completely"; cf. Thomas, "The Use of *neṣah*," p. 108.

[23]For "Oh, that" the MT actually reads אָבִי (*'ābî*), "my father," but this is difficult. Following LXX and Syr., Dhorme reads אֲבָל (*'ăbāl*), "but"; M. Dahood, "Ugaritic-Phoenician Forms in Job 34,36," *Bib* 62 (1981): 548-550, connects it with Ugaritic *'ebi*, "foes," and renders it "my foes." Driver & Gray and Pope take *'abi* as a "wish" particle as does Gordis who ties it to the root אבה (*'bh*), "wish, desire." Habel suggests it should be deleted as dittography for איב (*'yb*), "Job."

[24]Cf., e.g., Budde.

[25]Cf. Gordis, Hartley.

JOB 35

5. Elihu's Third Speech: God Is Not Answerable to Man (35:1-16)

In his third speech, Elihu continues to press his argument that Job has no right to demand vindication from God. He does so by challenging the logic of Job's paradoxical position and exposing the disingenuous nature of his cry for justice. Citing earlier statements by Job, Elihu decries the absurdity of Job's attempt to demand justice from a God whom he has repeatedly accused of being unjust. Elihu insightfully observes that behind Job's conflicting claims is a presumption that God is somehow limited by human behavior. Job is trying to obligate God to a system of moral governance in which he *must* reward the righteous and punish the wicked. Elihu will rebut this assault upon God's sovereignty with two arguments. First, he will insist that no human behavior, good or evil, *requires* a response by God. Job, therefore, has no right to *demand* that God reward his righteousness (35:2-8). Second, Elihu will argue that neither is God required to answer human calls for justice, especially when they are made out of self-interest and pride. This, Elihu explains, is why Job has received no answer from God (35:9-16).

This speech has important connections with both earlier and later portions of the book. Its suggestion that Job's interest in divine justice is motivated purely by the personal benefit he will derive from it remembers the original challenge of the *satan* (1:9-11). Its insistence that God will not be obligated by human righteousness anticipates one of the themes addressed in the speeches of Yahweh (40:8).

God Is Not Obligated by Human Behavior (35:1-8)

¹**Then Elihu said:**
²**"Do you think this is just? / You say, 'I will be cleared by God.'ᵃ"**

/ ³Yet you ask him, 'What profit is it to me,ᵇ / and what do I gain by not sinning?'

⁴"I would like to reply to you / and to your friends with you. / ⁵Look up at the heavens and see; / gaze at the clouds so high above you. / ⁶If you sin, how does that affect him? / If your sins are many, what does that do to him? / ⁷If you are righteous, what do you give to him, / or what does he receive from your hand? / ⁸Your wickedness affects only a man like yourself, / and your righteousness only the sons of men.

ᵃ2 Or *my righteousness is more than God's*   ᵇ3 Or *you*

35:1-3 With his opening words, Elihu challenges the very foundation of Job's case for vindication. By paraphrasing Job's claims of innocence and his challenges to divine justice, he characterizes Job's essential argument as both arrogant and absurd. He asks, "Do you think it is **just** to demand vindication from a God whom you have repeatedly accused of injustice?" As the NIV footnote indicates there is some dispute over how to translate the first quote Elihu attributes to Job (v. 2b). Job is either saying that he expects to **be cleared by God** or that he is "more righteous than God."[1] However one renders the Hebrew, the intent of the language seems to be that Job is claiming that his righteousness obligates God to vindicate him. Though Job has not spoken these exact words, he has essentially taken such a position throughout the debate (cf., e.g., 13:18-19; 23:3-7,10-12; 31:1-40). He has also repeatedly argued that in the world God presides over there is no **profit**[2] in being righteous or any **gain** in **not sinning** (cf., e.g., 9:22; 21:7ff). Elihu's citations of Job's claims are designed to characterize his arrogant presumption that this personal righteousness qualifies him to demand a reward from God or at least an explanation for why he has not received one. Elihu will now proceed to counter both of these presumptions.

---

[1] צִדְקִי מֵאֵל (*ṣidqî mē'ēl*). Various renderings include: "it is my right from God" (Pope); "I am right against El," (Habel).

[2] MT of v. 3a reads, "What profit is it to *you*" (לָךְ, *lāk*). Some interpreters understand this to refer to God (Dhorme, cf. 7:20). Duhm, Budde and others emend *lāk* with לִי (*lî*), "to me" (Job). Gordis and Driver & Gray retain *lāk* but take it as an indirect quotation (3a) coupled with a direct quotation (3b), both referring to Job.

35:4-5 It is interesting to note that Elihu's reply is directed at both Job and the **friends**. From the beginning, Elihu has set himself apart from both parties of this extended debate, claiming to have his own "answer." The neutral and independent position he takes in the dispute becomes clearer in this particular speech. Job and the friends have been arguing from the common theological presumption that God governs his world through a moral *quid pro quo*. He always sees to it that people get what they deserve. Job's "undeserved" suffering has led him to challenge the validity of this theology and wrongly accuse God of being "unjust." The friends, also taught by retributive theology, have been equally wrong in accusing Job of some "sin" that must have precipitated his suffering. By denying that human behavior requires a direct response from God (vv. 6-8), Elihu offers a **reply** that will correct both parties of their errors.

Elihu invites Job to **look up at the heavens** and to **gaze at the clouds so high above** him. This upward look is designed to remind Job just how far removed from him is the abode of the divine and how far above him is the God he seeks to obligate. Not only does this invitation to learn from nature lay a foundation for the intellectual argument that Elihu will make, it also serves to address the deeper spiritual issue that threatens Job's relationship with God — his pride. Drawing lessons from nature is a typical feature of the OT wisdom literature in general and the book of Job in particular Analogy between the cosmic order and the moral order of the universe is also invited by the speeches of Yahweh (cf., e.g., 38:4–39:30).

35:6-8 As it was understood in Job's day, the doctrine of retribution had both a positive and a negative side. In response to human behavior God handed down punishment or reward to man. Throughout the debate the "righteous" Job has accused God of being "unjust" on both counts. Elihu now counters those accusations by insisting that God is in no way obligated by human behavior. God is neither threatened by human **sin** nor blessed by human **righteousness**.[3] Neither behavior has any effect upon him nor requires any response by him.

When Elihu says that human **wickedness** and **righteousness** affect **only the sons of men**, he is not saying that God is oblivious to

---

[3]Job himself once appealed to this idea in his plea for God to release him from his suffering (7:20-21).

human behavior or that human behavior is without consequence. He is saying that the power of that behavior to evoke a response from others is limited solely to the human sphere. In Job's case against God he has been trying to use his "integrity" as a lever to compel God to vindicate him. This was the very purpose of the "oath of innocence" that he swore in his final appeal to God (31:1-40). Elihu is trying to show Job that a transcendent, sovereign God simply cannot be coerced by anything that a mere mortal can do. He alone is in control of the process of dispensing justice. Job's attempts to force God to appear in person and answer his charges are, therefore, futile and absurd.[4]

God Is Not Required to Answer Human Calls for Justice (35:9-16)

[9]**"Men cry out under a load of oppression; / they plead for relief from the arm of the powerful. / [10]But no one says, 'Where is God my Maker, / who gives songs in the night, / [11]who teaches more to[a] us than to the beasts of the earth / and makes us wiser than[b] the birds of the air?' / [12]He does not answer when men cry out / because of the arrogance of the wicked. / [13]Indeed, God does not listen to their empty plea; / the Almighty pays no attention to it. / [14]How much less, then, will he listen / when you say that you do not see him, / that your case is before him / and you must wait for him, / [15]and, further, that his anger never punishes / and he does not take the least notice of wickedness.[c] / [16]So Job opens his mouth with empty talk; / without knowledge he multiplies words."**

[a]*11 Or teaches us by*   [b]*11 Or us wise by*   [c]*15 Symmachus, Theodotion and Vulgate; the meaning of the Hebrew for this word is uncertain.*

35:9-11 Having explained why Job has no right to demand vindication from God, Elihu now goes on to explain why God has not

---

[4]Contrary to Habel (*Job*, p. 492), the Elihu speeches do not present God as a "detached high God." From the prologue to the speeches of Yahweh, God is portrayed as concerned about human piety and personally involved in the lives of his creatures. Elihu's speeches do not challenge this. They do insist, like the rest of the book, that the transcendent and immanent God engages humans on his terms, not theirs. Habel's contention that Elihu's argument "establishes the virtual impossibility of Yahweh's subsequent advent in the whirlwind" (*Job*, p. 490) misunderstands the intent of Elihu's argument.

answered Job's pleas for deliverance. Job has claimed that God does not hear the cries of the oppressed (cf., e.g., 24:1-17, esp. v. 12). Elihu defends God against this charge by explaining that such cries are often offered purely out of self-interest and not out of true devotion to God. The oppressed do not ask, **"Where is God my Maker?"** in genuine submission to God's sovereignty and trust in his providence (cf. Ps 95:6-7). Rather than trusting in God as one who **teaches** through adversity they merely want to use God to get out of their adversity. Unlike the **beasts of the earth** and the **birds of the air** they have not learned to trust in God's providential care (cf. Ps 104:21; 147:9; cf. 12:5-8). They have no interest in God except when they need something from him. Elihu's characterization of God as one who **gives songs in the night** is unique, found nowhere else in the Old Testament. The interpreters differ over exactly what is meant by this phrase. It could mean that God enables believers to find joy and sing even in the midst of adversity (Ps 42:8; Acts 16:25).[5] It could refer to some manifestation of nature in the night sky (38:7).[6] Some interpreters understand the word "song" (זְמִיר, zāmîr) to mean "strength" as in Exodus 15:21; 2 Samuel 23:1; Isaiah 12:2.[7]

35:12-13 These verses continue Elihu's explanation of why God refuses to answer the pleas of humans. The precise meaning of his explanation hinges on how one identifies the **wicked** of verse 12b. If it refers to the oppressors (Dhorme) of the ones who **cry out**, then Elihu is saying that God does not answer those cries because they are made by people who only appeal to God when they need something from him (cf. vv. 9,10). If, however, the "wicked" are the oppressed themselves (Rowley), then it is their own **arrogance** which God is judging by their silence. Either way, the point that Elihu is making is that God cannot be coerced by the plea of any human. Pleas that try to obligate God are **empty** (שָׁוְא, shāw'; "worthless"). This term can also mean "deceitful," and using it here adds to Elihu's argument that such self-interested petitions to God are disingenuous.

35:14-16 The Hebrew of these verses is very difficult, but, reading with NIV, Elihu's closing words seem to represent an application

---

[5]Cf., e.g., Terrien.

[6]Habel, *Job*, p. 493. Dhorme explains the "songs" as crashes of thunder.

[7]Cf. Tur-Sinai, Pope. For further discussion cf. Grabbe, *Comparative Philology*, pp. 108-110.

of his argument for God's silence to Job's particular situation. If God does not respond to the self-interested prayers of the oppressed, why should Job ever expect God to respond to his petitions? Job is not only trying to obligate God, he has repeatedly accused God of **never punishing** the evildoer and taking no **notice of wickedness**. To accuse God of injustice and then demand justice from him constitutes the worst kind of **empty talk**.

It is important to notice here that, unlike the friends, Elihu's condemnation of Job is not focused upon some sin that might have precipitated his suffering. Rather, Elihu is concerned with Job's behavior after the fact of his suffering. He impugns the motives behind Job's attacks upon God and the arrogant presumption behind his demand for vindication. In the Yahweh speeches, God will likewise condemn only what Job does after the fact of his suffering in his defense of his integrity.

JOB 36

6. Elihu's Fourth Speech: The Justice and Sovereignty of God
(36:1–37:24)

In his fourth and final speech Elihu makes an impassioned defense of God's justice and praises his sovereign rule over his creation. In the process he offers an explanation of why God has presided over Job's suffering. Rather than focusing on some sin that might have precipitated Job's suffering, he focuses on the lessons he can learn from it. He invites Job to accept his suffering as divine discipline not just against some sin that he has already committed but also against some latent, potential sin that poses a threat to his spirituality and of which he needs to be warned.[1] The specific sin Elihu has in mind is the spiritual pride that has emerged in Job's defense of his integrity and now leads him dangerously close to the precipice of apostasy (36:10) This suggestion represents a departure from the version of retributive justice taught by the friends and constitutes one of Elihu's major contributions to the theology of the book. Rather than denying that the righteous suffer, Elihu sees such suffering as a source of moral discipline designed to spur the believer on to true piety — piety that loves and serves God in any circumstance, regardless of reward. This is the very kind of piety that the *satan* said Job lacked and which God permitted the suffering of Job to "test."

This speech breaks down into several components. After a brief appeal for patience from his audience (36:1-4), Elihu opens his speech with a declaration of God's justice (36:5-7). He then offers an explanation of how God warns the righteous through suffering (36:7-15) followed by an admonition to Job that he not reject that warning (36:16-21). After briefly extolling the greatness of God as

---

[1]Cf. Gordis, *God and Man*, pp. 112-115.

creator (36:22-25), Elihu goes into an extended lesson on the mysterious ways of God as illustrated by the phenomenon of the storm (36:26–37:24). The rhetoric of this speech balances theological argument with the language of hymnic praise while offering extended analogies from nature.

Introduction (36:1-4)

¹**Elihu continued:**
²**"Bear with me a little longer and I will show you / that there is more to be said in God's behalf. / ³I get my knowledge from afar; / I will ascribe justice to my Maker. / ⁴Be assured that my words are not false; / one perfect in knowledge is with you.**

36:1-4 Imploring his audience to be patient, Elihu insists that **there is more to be said in God's behalf.** Given the exhaustive nature of the debate between Job and the friends, it is difficult for the reader to imagine just what possible new insight Elihu might add to this overargued contest. As the following verses show, however, Elihu does have an original contribution to make. As both Job and his friends have repeatedly done, Elihu once again defends his right to speak. Though personal qualifications he offers seem a bit presumptuous, they are not out of line with the rhetoric of the other speakers (cf., e.g., 4:12ff; 12:3; 15:9,10,17-18). Elihu claims to get his **knowledge from afar.** This could be a reference to his broad awareness of the wisdom traditions of distant lands (cf. 1 Kgs 4:29-34). More likely, it is a claim to having received revelation from the distant abode of God.[2] Coming from God, his words **are not false** (שֶׁקֶר, *šeqer*) or "without flaw." Inspired by God, Elihu's **knowledge** is **perfect** (תָּמִים, *tāmîm*) or "complete."

It is not insignificant that Elihu refers to the God whose justice he seeks to defend as his **Maker** (פֹּעֵל, *pō'ēl*). In the OT wisdom literature God's role as Creator of the physical universe is commonly connected to his just rule of that world (cf., e.g., Prov 14:31; 16:4). In his speech Elihu will go on to suggest that, just as God has created a natural order in the universe, so also has he created a moral order.[3]

---

[2]Hartley, *Job*, p. 468.
[3]This also seems to be a major inference of the Yahweh speeches (cf. Gordis, *God and Man*, pp. 133-134.

Elihu's Defense of God's Justice (36:5-7)

[5]"God is mighty, but does not despise men; / he is mighty, and firm in his purpose. / [6]He does not keep the wicked alive / but gives the afflicted their rights. / [7]He does not take his eyes off the righteous; / he enthrones them with kings / and exalts them forever.

36:5-7 Elihu begins his defense of God's justice with a direct refutation of Job's earlier claims about God (cf. Job 21; esp. v. 7). The Hebrew of verse 5 is difficult, resulting in a wide variety of suggested translations.[4] The intent of the language seems to be that God the **mighty** (כַּבִּיר, *kabbîr*)[5] is actively involved in the world he has made to diligently enforce justice. The connection between the sovereignty of God and the justice of God is also a theme of early chapters of Genesis. The Creator, who has all power, exercises that power morally and justly in the world that he has made. Responding to Job's earlier question, "Why do the wicked live?" (21:7) Elihu argues that God **does not keep the wicked alive** and sees to it that the (righteous) **afflicted** receive their **rights** (מִשְׁפָּט, *mišpaṭ*; "justice"). Even further he rewards the **righteous** by **enthroning** them and **exalting** them like **kings**. Like Joseph the faithfulness of the righteous eventually results in their exaltation (Gen 37:39; 39–50). It is tempting to assign the term **forever** (לָנֶצַח, *lāneṣaḥ*) some kind of eschatological, beyond-the-grave meaning and see in these words of Elihu an Old Testament version of the later New Testament "eschatological solution" to the problem of injustice in the earthly life. Central to this theology is the belief that though justice may not be fully realized in this life, God will see to it that justice prevails in the life to come. This concept is briefly entertained in the Old Testament, though it is never fully developed (cf., e.g., Dan 12:2).[6] Job, himself, had pondered some form of a postdeath vindication in an earlier speech (cf. 14:14-17).[7] It is more likely, however, that the term

---

[4]MT reads literally, "Lo, God is mighty and does not despise, mighty in strength of heart." LXX supplies an object for the verb in 5a (τόν ἄκανον, *ton akanon*; "the innocent"); cf. discussion by Pope, *Job*, p. 232.

[5]Perhaps, "Champion" (Habel) or "the ancient One" (cf. Dahood, *Psalms II*, AB, p. 213).

[6]Cf. also possibly Ps 49:10-15.

[7]Cf. our discussion of 14:14-17. Cf. also ch. 19 and our discussion on vv. 25-27.

"forever" means here, as it does in Isaiah 13:20, "for successive generations" and that Elihu envisions for the righteous not some kind of heavenly reward but a perpetual dynasty of blessed descendants. As the context indicates, Elihu's predictions of divine reward are expressed in terms of prosperity and longevity in this earthly life (cf. 36:11).

God Disciplines the Righteous through Suffering (36:8-15)

[8]**But if men are bound in chains, / held fast by cords of affliction, / [9]he tells them what they have done— / that they have sinned arrogantly. / [10]He makes them listen to correction / and commands them to repent of their evil. / [11]If they obey and serve him, / they will spend the rest of their days in prosperity / and their years in contentment. / [12]But if they do not listen, / they will perish by the sword[a] / and die without knowledge.**

[13]**"The godless in heart harbor resentment; / even when he fetters them, they do not cry for help. / [14]They die in their youth, / among male prostitutes of the shrines. / [15]But those who suffer he delivers in their suffering; / he speaks to them in their affliction.**

[a]*12 Or will cross the River*

36:8-10 Here Elihu returns to a theme he has already addressed — that God disciplines the righteous through suffering (33:19-22). This concept was first introduced by Eliphaz in his opening speech, though he seems to apply it to Job in a strictly punitive sense (5:17).[8] Elihu's doctrine of God's **correction**, however, emphasizes its power to reveal flaws of character and to rescue even the "righteous" (v. 7) from some potentially self-destructive attitude or behavior. The literal rendering of the Hebrew in verse 10a is "He (God) opens their ears to correction."[9] The Hebrew word for **correction** (מוּסָר, *mûsār*; "discipline," v. 10) should be understood in the sense of "warning" in this context as it is in 33:16. In other words, the "discipline" of suffering is used by God not just to correct an existing sin but also

---

[8]Eliphaz characterized Job's suffering as God's "correction" (יָכַח, *yākaḥ*; 5:17), a legal term referring to a judgment made against some offense. It can also mean "to reprove" or "to correct" a wrong behavior; cf. discussion by Budde, *Hiob*, p. xxxvi.

[9]וַיִּגֶל אָזְנָם לַמּוּסָר (*wayyigel 'oznām lammûsār*).

to "warn" of a potential one.[10] As he does through "night visions" (33:16-17), so also does God through suffering attempt to redirect humans from some potentially destructive attitude or behavior. Through **affliction** God purposefully **binds** men and restricts their movement to keep them from going down the path of sin. More than merely punishing sin, God uses suffering to disclose it. By it he **tells** men **what they have done** (lit., "declares to them their deeds"). **He commands them to repent of their evil** or, more literally, "He tells them to turn from iniquity."[11]

It is important to note the way that Elihu characterizes the sin that threatens the righteous. He says they have **sinned arrogantly**. The Hebrew term behind this translation literally means "they made themselves mighty" (יִתְגַּבָּרוּ, *yithgabbārû*; cf. Isa 42:13). It can also mean, when used of humans, "they behaved proudly." The one other place in Job where this particular form of the verb (*hithpael*) appears, it is used to characterize Job's boastful challenge of God (15:25). This seems to be its meaning here.[12] In his speeches, Elihu uses the verb גָּבַר (*gābar*) and its derivative noun גֶּבֶר (*geber*) to call attention to Job's prideful accusations against God (cf. also 33:17,29; 34:7,9,34).[13] In fact, it is this very issue of Job's spiritual pride that most bothers Elihu. Rather than focusing on some sin that Job might have committed to cause his suffering, Elihu's problem with Job is the arrogant disrespect he has shown God in response to his suffering. Unlike the friends, his speeches are not designed to get

---

[10]Cf. Habel, *Job*, p. 468; Gordis, *God and Man*, p. 289.

[11]וַיֹּ֫מֶר כִּי־יְשֻׁבוּן מֵאָוֶן (*wayyōmer kî-yᵉšubûn mēʾāwen*). This phrase can refer to repenting from an existing sin or "turning back from" a potential one (cp. 33:17).

[12]Cf. H. Kosmala, "*gabhar; gebhurah; gebhir; gibbor; gebher*," *TDOT*, 2:367-382; *idem*, "The Term *Geber* in the OT and in the Scrolls," *VTSupp* 17 (1969): 159-169.

[13]In his challenges of Job, Elihu repeatedly refers to him as a *geber*, a term that normally means merely "man" or "male" but in some biblical contexts carries the spiritually positive notion of "godly man" or one who trusts in God (cf., e.g., Num 24:3ff [Balaam]; 2 Sam 23:1ff [David]; Prov 30:1ff [Agur]; Ps 40:5,9-12[4,8-11]; 34:9ff[8ff] and the discussion by Kosmala, *TDOT*, 2:378-380). Kosmala argues convincingly that Elihu uses this term to suggest that a truly "godly man" (*geber*) would never behave toward God as Job has. In this same vein it is interesting to note that Yahweh, too, addresses Job as a *geber* at the beginning of each of his speeches (38:3; 40:7) perhaps to imply the same thing.

Job to repent of his past sins and thereby be restored but to abandon his ill-advised "lawsuit" against God in which he presumes to
judge God as unjust. It is this very issue that God himself will later
take up with Job (cf. 40:6-7). The evil of which the righteous (especially Job) **need to repent** (יְשֻׁבוּן, y^ešubûn; lit., "to turn") and against
which their suffering is designed to "warn" is the very sin of which
the righteous are most susceptible — self-righteous pride.[14] This "pet
sin of the righteous" (Budde) is the very problem that has finally led
Job to do that which he had earlier resisted — accuse God of wrongdoing (1:22; cf. 2:10). Job's suffering has exposed a latent character
flaw that his previously pious life had never manifested.

Trusting in his own goodness, he has the audacity to demand
reward for it and accuse God of being unjust for his failure to deliver it. This arrogant attempt to leverage goodness for gain is very
close to the attitude which the *satan* said Job was concealing all along
and which Job's suffering would expose. It is also this sin of which
Job will finally "repent" in his response to God's appearance (42:6).

36:11-15 The only deliverance from a sin of such presumption is
humble resubmission to God. Only those who learn to **obey** (שָׁמַע,
šāma') and **serve** (עָבַד, 'ābad) God will enjoy his blessing. These
verbs signify the subordination of human hubris that true piety
requires and is the kind of submissiveness God seeks to evoke by his
correction.[15] Conversely, those who refuse correction, who **do not
listen**, will **perish by the sword**[16] and **die without knowledge**. This
latter phrase means to "die for lack of knowledge" (cf. Hos 4:6a) and
in ancient times was used to signify the failure of a party to a treaty
to obey or abide by the terms of that covenant.[17] Even the righteous,
if they refuse to be instructed by God's discipline and refuse to
resubmit themselves to God, will forfeit the promise of God's blessing and face inevitable demise.

---

[14]Cf. also 33:16-17. Note Elihu's use of the noun *geber* to speak of the
"pride" against which God warns.

[15]Cf. Prov 1:2,3,5; 15:33 and discussion by McKane, *Proverbs: A New
Approach* (Philadelphia: Westminster, 1970), p. 264.

[16]Or "cross the river" (of death; שֶׁלַח, šelaḥ).

[17]Cf. H. Huffmon, "The Treaty Background of Hebrew *yada'*," BASOR 181
(Feb. 1966): 31-37; G. Botterweck, *TDOT*, 5:468-476. The contrast of promise
and threat found in vv. 11-12 are typical of the language of certain ANE
covenants and echoed elsewhere in the Old Testament (cf., e.g., Isa 1:17-20).

In verses 13-14, Elihu further describes the power of God's affliction to expose true piety. The **godless in heart** (חַנְפֵי־לֵב, *ḥanpê-lēb*)
reveal their lack of devotion to God by manifesting **resentment**
toward God when he **fetters** them with suffering. This negative
response to God's correction coupled with their refusal to **cry for
help** reveals their innate impiety. Their suffering only intensifies
their hidden antagonism toward God.[18] The fate of the irreligious
and the rebellious of heart is the same premature death assigned to
the "unholy" or "perverse" (קְדֵשִׁים, *qᵉdēšîm*).[19] By contrast, when the
truly righteous suffer, they hear the voice of God **in their affliction**.
Not resenting suffering, they are **delivered** or redeemed by it as it
corrects them and warns them against some attitude or behavior that
threatens their relationship with God. Here, Elihu reiterates his doctrine of divine discipline (cf. 33:28-30) and offers one of his original
theological contributions to the book. Suffering, rather than merely
a punitive tool of divine justice, can actually serve a redemptive purpose as it informs the righteous of some threatening sin and saves
them from its consequences. It both tests and stimulates true piety by
spurring the righteous on to unconditional devotion to God.

As suggested above, this insight by Elihu has important ties to
both the beginning and ending of the book of Job. The answer that
the prologue gives to the question of why God allowed Job to suffer
is essentially the same answer that Elihu gives. For the righteous, suffering is not punishment for sin but a test of piety. By depriving the
righteous of reward for doing good, it reveals just why it is they do
good. Further, it forces the righteous to do good for goodness' sake,
to love God solely for who he is, whether or not it is rewarded. In
similar fashion the climactic Yahweh speeches confront Job with the
same challenge. Job the "righteous," broken in the "dust and ashes"
of his "undeserved" and "unexplained" suffering, without reward
and rationale, is called upon to bow in unconditional surrender
before his Maker. When he does, he finds his "deliverance." When
Elihu says that God "delivers (the righteous) *in* or *by*[20] their suffer-

---

[18]Habel, *Job*, p. 508.

[19]Lit., "holy ones"; RSV, "shame." The NIV translation "male prostitutes
of the shrine" is speculative; cf. S. Hooks, *Sacred Prostitution in Israel and the
Ancient Near East*, Ph.D. dissertation, Hebrew Union College, 1985.

[20]With Pope, Habel; "through their affliction" (Gordis).

ing" (v. 15a), he is very close to explaining the very meaning and purpose of suffering offered by the book of Job.

Elihu's Admonition to Job (36:16-21)

[16]"He is wooing you from the jaws of distress / to a spacious place free from restriction, / to the comfort of your table laden with choice food. / [17]But now you are laden with judgment due the wicked; / judgment and justice have taken hold of you. / [18]Be careful that no one entices you by riches; / do not let a large bribe turn you aside. / [19]Would your wealth / or even all your mighty efforts / sustain you so you would not be in distress? / [20]Do not long for the night, / to drag people away from their homes.[a] / [21]Beware of turning to evil, / which you seem to prefer to affliction.

[a]20 The meaning of the Hebrew for verses 18-20 is uncertain.

36:16-17 Having argued for the disciplinary and redemptive role of suffering in the life of the righteous, Elihu now applies this teaching to Job. The Hebrew text of this section is quite difficult, leading to a considerable variety of translations.[21] It seems clear enough from verse 16 that Elihu sees Job's suffering as an attempt by God to **woo** him away from the path of self-destruction (**the jaws of distress**)[22] and put him on the path to eventual restoration (**a spacious place free from restriction**). This latter phrase is a metaphor of deliverance in the OT.[23] God has a blessed future in store for Job and plans to sit him at a **table laden** (מָלֵא, *mālē'*; "full") **with choice food**. In his present state, however, Job is laden (*mālē'*) with something else — the **judgment due the wicked**. This phrase and the parallel, **judgment and justice have taken hold of you** (17b), have led the interpreters in several different directions to explain them. The Hebrew text literally reads, "And of wicked judgment you are full, judgment and justice take hold." Some interpreters take these lines to refer to God's judgment on Job. In order to discipline Job God has brought on him a judgment appropriate for a guilty man.[24] Others revocalize the text and understand these lines to be a con-

---

[21]Cf. discussions by Tur-Sinai, Pope, Gordis, Fohrer.

[22]"The jaws of distress (מִפִּי־צָר, *mippî-ṣār*)" probably refers to death.

[23]Cf. J. Sawyer, "Spaciousness," *ASTI* 6 (1967–68): 20-24.

[24]Cf., e.g., Hartley, *Job*, p. 474.

demnation of Job's failure to judge the wicked and uphold justice for the "orphan."[25] An alternative reading, closer to MT, would understand the judgment to refer to Job's case against God. Instead of accepting his suffering as God's redemptive discipline, Job has become "obsessed" with an attempt to bring a legal case against God.[26] This misguided attempt to judge God and try to hold him accountable for Job's "unjust" suffering is Elihu's primary issue with Job and the very thing he is trying to get Job to abandon.

36:18-21 Verses 18-21 are extremely difficult in the Hebrew, and any translation of them must be considered tentative. One way to read them is to take them as a further condemnation of Job's failure to secure justice for the poor. Suggesting that Job has been **enticed by riches** and is susceptible to a **large bribe**,[27] Elihu warns him that such perversions of justice will not serve Job in his attempt to escape his **distress**. NIV's rendering of verse 20 (**Do not long for the night to drag people away from their homes**) could also be understood as a further accusation against Job for some mistreatment of the poor. If this reading is correct, then Elihu is accusing Job of the sin that Eliphaz had accused him of earlier (Job 22).

Still another way to read these verses is to understand them as a further condemnation of Job's case against God. Gordis renders verses 18-19:

> Now beware, lest you be seduced by your wealth
> and your ample means for ransom lead you astray.
> Will your possessions keep you from trouble,
> or all your exertions to achieve riches?[28]

In other words, Elihu is exhorting Job to not take the posture of an arrogant rich man in his attempts to get justice from God. Instead of trying to leverage God, Elihu says Job should be submitting himself to God. Instead of coming before God as a "prince" (31:37) he ought to be approaching him as a humble servant. Such

---

[25]Cf. discussions by Tur-Sinai, Pope, Gordis. Pope suggests the reading, "And the case of the wicked you did not judge; the orphan's justice you belied."

[26]Habel, *Job*, pp. 495, 509. Habel translates v. 17, "But you are full of the lawsuit of a guilty man; lawsuit and litigation obsess you."

[27]רַב־כֹּפֶר (*rāb-kōpher*), "large payment, ransom."

[28]Gordis, *God and Man*, p. 295.

an understanding of the difficult language of this text is possible and more in keeping with Elihu's general approach to Job's attempts to accuse God of being "unjust" and to demand vindication from him.

Along these same lines it is possible to see in Elihu's words an impugning of the motive behind Job's demand for vindication. Elihu may be claiming that Job, whose life has been wrapped up in prosperity, is now being **enticed** by it in his demand that his integrity be rewarded (by **riches**). Elihu has already argued that God turns a deaf ear to those who approach him with ulterior, self-serving motives (35:9-13). Elihu may be saying the same thing here. He may be arguing that Job's quest for justice is driven purely by self-interest.

Verse 20 is considered by most critics to be the least intelligible of all. Literally reading, "Do not long for the night, that peoples go up to their place," it is difficult to make sense of it, much less see how it is relevant to the context. Dhorme takes this as a reference to political revolution, in which one people group displaces another. As such, these words could be intended as a warning that Job not rebel against God. Pope and Gordis understand the Hebrew verb עָלָה ('ālāh, "go up") to mean "vanish" and understand this as some kind of death wish on Job's part. As such, Elihu could be ironically warning Job that for him to arrogantly pursue a case against God is the same thing as longing for his own demise.

Verse 21 concludes this difficult section with a warning. Unfortunately here, too, the original language is a challenge to fully understand. The first line, **Beware of turning to evil**, is clear enough, though exactly what "evil" (אָוֶן, 'āwen) Job is warned against is not specified. Most likely it refers to Job's resistance to God's disciplinary measures. The second line, **which you seem to prefer to affliction**, has spawned a wide variety of interpretations. The MT literally reads "for upon this you have chosen from affliction." The Syriac version reads the verb "chosen" (בָּחַרְתָּ, bāḥartā) as "tested" and understands the line to say, "because of this you have been tested by affliction." This makes good sense and would serve as a fitting conclusion to this part of Elihu's speech.[29]

---

[29]Cf. discussions by Pope, Dhorme, Rowley.

Elihu Extols the Greatness of God (36:22-26)

²²"God is exalted in his power. / Who is a teacher like him? / ²³Who has prescribed his ways for him, / or said to him, 'You have done wrong'? / ²⁴Remember to extol his work, / which men have praised in song. / ²⁵All mankind has seen it; / men gaze on it from afar. / ²⁶How great is God—beyond our understanding! / The number of his years is past finding out.

36:22-23 With these words Elihu makes a shift in his argument from defending the justice of God to extolling the incomparable greatness of God. His goal, however, remains the same: to convince Job to abandon his case against God and to humbly submit to God's sovereign rule of his life. The specific purpose of this section is to remind Job of just who it is that he is impugning and daring to challenge. Verse 22, which literally opens with a call for Job to "Behold God" (הֶן־אֵל, *hēn-'ēl*), invites Job to **remember** how great God is in comparison to him. It does so by enumerating several of God's attributes. First, Elihu proclaims him **exalted** in **his power** (cf. Isa 2:11,17; Ps 148:13). He is the self-sufficient ruler of the universe (34:13-15). As such, Job is clearly no match for him. Second, Elihu extols God's role as the supreme **teacher** (מוֹרֶה, *môreh*; cf. Isa 30:20; Ps 25:8-14; 94:12).[30] It is God's "teaching" through the discipline of suffering that Elihu has been trying to get Job to appreciate and accept (36:5-12). Standing above all others there is no one qualified to try to hold God accountable, to **prescribe** his **ways** or accuse him of doing **wrong** (עַוְלָה, *'awlāh*; "wickedness"; cf. Ps 92:16[15]). Elihu is saying here what he had earlier said in his opening rebuke of Job, "God is greater than man" (33:12). God, by virtue of being God, is answerable to no man.

36:24-26 When Elihu calls upon Job to **remember** (זְכֹר, *z^ekōr*) to **extol** God's **work**, he may be offering a direct rebuttal to Job's irreverent call for God to "remember" him as one of his mistreated creatures

---

[30]This term is rare in the OT but found often in postbiblical Hebrew and the Dead Sea Scrolls. LXX renders the term "ruler" (δυνάστες, *dynastes*). Tur-Sinai defines *môreh* as "one who makes rulings in court as to the conduct of man" (*Job*, p. 501). R. Whybray, *The Heavenly Counselor in Isaiah XL 13-14* (Cambridge: Cambridge University Press, 1971), argues that this concept has a background in the mythology of the ancient Near East.

(10:9-12). Job had argued that God's creation had a hidden malevolent purpose behind it (10:13-14). By contrast Elihu argues that creation is a testimony to God's greatness, and it should evoke **praise** from **mankind** rather than suspicion and criticism.[31] Elihu praises two additional attributes of God in verse 26. He is inscrutable, **beyond** human **understanding** (cf. Eccl 8:17), and eternal, **the number of his years is past finding out** (Ps 102:27[26]). His limitless nature and mysterious ways should move Job to praise, not defiance.

The Mysterious and Benevolent God of the Storm (36:27–37:13)

[27]"**He draws up the drops of water, / which distill as rain to the streams**[a]; / [28]**the clouds pour down their moisture / and abundant showers fall on mankind. / [29]Who can understand how he spreads the clouds, / how he thunders from his pavilion? / [30]See how he scatters his lightning about him, / bathing the depths of the sea. / [31]This is the way he governs**[b] **the nations / and provides food in abundance. / [32]He fills his hands with lightning / and commands it to strike its mark. / [33]His thunder announces the coming storm; / even the cattle make known its approach.**[c]

[a]27 Or *distill from the mist of rain*   [b]31 Or *nourishes*   [c]33 Or *announces his coming– / the One zealous against evil*

Primary to Job's case against God is his conviction that he understands how God runs his world. Assuming that all suffering represents some form of divine punishment of human sin, Job has concluded that, in his case, such punishment is unmerited and that God has, therefore, unjustly afflicted him. Elihu now seeks to dismantle this claim by challenging the very assumption that lies behind it. He will contend that in reality Job knows nothing about how or why God acts in his world. To prove his point he will invite Job to explain the meaning of just one form of divine intervention into human life — the meteorological phenomenon of the violent thunderstorm.

Elihu's choice of the storm as a model of God's activity may be influenced by the awe that such storms evoked as they rolled over the steppes of the Near East. Bringing life-sustaining rain and often accompanied by dramatic displays of lightning and thunder, these storms proved a suitable metaphor of divine power. The psalmist

---

[31]Habel, *Job*, pp. 510-511.

regularly saw in such storms the splendor of God (cf., e.g., Psalm 29). It may be that Elihu is taking note of an actual storm forming on the horizon, perhaps the very storm from which Yahweh will speak (38:1).

36:27-33 In this passage Elihu explores the capacity of the storm to reveal and execute the will of God. The hydrological cycle depicted in verses 27-28 describes a process of condensation (**he draws up drops of water**) and precipitation (**distill as rain**). The phrase **to the streams** is variously interpreted to refer either to the place to where the rains flow or the place from which they come ("from the flood," Pope).[32] By describing the rain as **abundant showers** that **fall on mankind**, Elihu is suggesting that such precipitation has a beneficent purpose, given by God to bless humanity. Not only does the thunderstorm serve God's desire to bless humanity by **providing food in abundance**, it also functions as an instrument of God's righteous wrath. God **thunders from his pavilion** and **fills his hands with lightning and commands it to strike its mark** (cf. Exod 15:7-8; Jer 23:19). Elihu's primary interest in the phenomenon of the storm is centered in its capacity to facilitate God's rule over the **nations**. That rule involves both sustenance and censure.[33]

---

[32]The Hebrew term for "streams" (אֵד, *'ēd*) appears only here and in Gen 2:6 and is thought to refer to some kind of subterranean reservoir that has a heavenly counterpart in the form of a great body of water believed by the ancients to surround the earth; cf. M. Dahood, "Eblaite *i-du* and Hebrew *'ed*, rain cloud," *CBQ* 43 (1981): 534-538.

[33]The final phrase of v. 33, as the NIV footnote acknowledges, may be describing the storm as a tool of God's righteous wrath. The term in MT translated "cattle" (מִקְנֶה, *miqneh*) is understood by the Targ. as coming from קָנָא (*qn'*), "zealous wrath" (cf. Gordis).

JOB 37

6. Elihu's Fourth Speech: The Justice and Sovereignty of God
(36:1–37:24, continued)

The Mysterious and Benevolent God of the Storm (36:27–37:13, continued)

[1]"At this my heart pounds / and leaps from its place. / [2]Listen!
Listen to the roar of his voice, / to the rumbling that comes from
his mouth. / [3]He unleashes his lightning beneath the whole heaven / and sends it to the ends of the earth. / [4]After that comes the
sound of his roar; / he thunders with his majestic voice. / When
his voice resounds, / he holds nothing back. / [5]God's voice thunders in marvelous ways; / he does great things beyond our understanding. / [6]He says to the snow, 'Fall on the earth,' / and to the
rain shower, 'Be a mighty downpour.' / [7]So that all men he has
made may know his work, / he stops every man from his labor.[a] /
[8]The animals take cover; / they remain in their dens. / [9]The tempest comes out from its chamber, / the cold from the driving
winds. / [10]The breath of God produces ice, / and the broad waters
become frozen. / [11]He loads the clouds with moisture; / he scatters
his lightning through them. / [12]At his direction they swirl around
/ over the face of the whole earth / to do whatever he commands
them. / [13]He brings the clouds to punish men, / or to water the
earth[b] and show his love.

[a]7 Or / *he fills all men with fear by his power*   [b]13 Or *to favor them*

37:1-5 As Elihu continues to extol the majesty and mystery of
how God works through the storm, one can almost envision a thunderstorm rolling in upon him and Job. Awestruck by this magnificent display of God's power, Elihu reacts first with excitement[1] and

---

[1]In the Hebrew, the verse begins with the emphatic, אַף (*'aph*), "indeed."

then theological interpretation. He invites Job to **listen** to God's voice as it **roars** (רֹגֶז, *rōgez*) in the thunder.[2] Job had used the term (*rōgez*) earlier to characterize the "turmoil" that God had brought upon him (3:26; cf. 14:1). What Job heard only as turmoil Elihu now invites him to hear in another way. The storms that God **unleashes**[3] deliver other messages as well. The meteorological sequence of **lightning** and **thunder**[4] also proclaim God's **majesty** and his **marvelous ways**. They are examples of God's **great things** (גְּדֹלוֹת, *g⁰dōlôth*). Elsewhere in Job this term is used to describe God's creative power and providential beneficence (9:10; 5:9). Such things, Elihu adds, are **beyond our understanding**. The inscrutability of God's ways is a major theme of the Elihu speeches and anticipates one of the major motifs of the Yahweh speeches. By pointing out to Job that humans cannot always know the purpose behind God's actions, Elihu is trying to open Job's mind to the prospect that he has misunderstood the meaning of the suffering that God has brought upon his life. He is also attempting to convince Job that, as a mortal of limited knowledge, he is simply not qualified to bring a case of injustice against God (cf. 37:14-20).

37:6-10 To the peoples of the Near East rain was an important event. In a world largely dependent upon agriculture, precipitation was crucial for the very subsistence of the population. In Israel, as in other ancient cultures,[5] the falling rain was attributed to the direct intervention of God. Sounding that theme, Elihu suggests that the

---

[2]Thunder is commonly called the voice of Yahweh in the Old Testament (cf., e.g., Ps 18:13[12]; 29:3-9; Exod 19:18). A similar idea may be found in the Ugaritic myths describing Baal (cf. *UT* 51:V:68-71).

[3]MT יִשְׁרֵהוּ (*yišrēhû*) is variously explained. It may be taken as an old Hebrew *yaqtalu* (cp. Ug. *srh*) form with an archaic ending rather than the third person singular pronominal suffix (cf. A. Schoors, *RSP*, 1:24-25, no. 18, e.g., for Ugaritic parallels; cf. also M. Coogan, *Stories from Ancient Canaan* [Philadelphia: Westminster, 1978], p. 101). Dhorme and Rowley connect the Hebrew with Aram. *sera'*, "loosen, release." Gordis connects it with the Heb. noun יֹשֶׁר (*yōšer*, "strength, power").

[4]As Habel notes, "lightning" (אוֹר, *'ôr*; lit., "light") and "thunder" (קוֹל, *qôl*; lit., "voice"), along with five different terms for "storm," are used repetitively in this section to denote how God acts in his world (*Job*, pp. 504-505).

[5]Cf., e.g., Baal's role as bringer of the rain in *UT* 51:V:68-71: "Now Baal will begin the rainy season, the season of wadis in the flood; and he will sound his voice in the clouds, flash his lightning to the earth" (Coogan, *Stories*, p. 101).

snow and the **rain shower** serve a revelatory function. God sends them that **all men he has made may know his work.** Their power to **stop every man from his labor**[6] and cause **animals** to **take cover** demonstrate his sovereignty over the earth. An even more impressive display of God's power was the rare and spectacular winter storm with its capacity to **produce ice** and **freeze** the **broad waters.** This is all said to be accomplished by the **breath of God.** According to Elihu, the same "breath" (נְשָׁמָה, *nᵉšāmāh*) that gives life and inspiration (32:8; 33:4; 34:14) also determines the seasons. When Elihu refers to the **tempest coming out from its chamber,**[7] he is echoing the commonly held ANE notion that various meteorological forces are housed in specific locations in the heavens.[8] God is said to have the power to summon these forces from their assigned places to come upon the earth (cf. also Ps 135:7; Jer 10:13; 51:16).

37:11-13 In these verses Elihu suggests to Job that God's **direction**[9] of the **clouds** to **do whatever he commands** is directly tied to his moral purposes on earth. They are used to **punish** men or **show** [them] **his love.**[10] The word for "punish" (שֵׁבֶט, *šēbeṭ*) literally refers to a "rod," and may have been chosen by Elihu as a direct rebuttal

---

[6]MT literally reads, "With the hand of every man he seals." Duhm and Pope emend בְּיַד (*bᵉyad*) with בְּעַד (*bᵉʿad*) on the basis of Job 9:7 and Gen 7:16. The sense is still the same. Through the storm God restricts men in their normal activity, that is the suspension of agricultural activities in the winter (Gordis). Habel offers a different understanding, suggesting that the storm serves as "a seal/sign/signature" of God's work (*Job*, p. 500, n. 7).

[7]חֶדֶר (*ḥeder*). In 9b the rare term מְזָרִים (*mᵉzārîm*; "driving winds," NIV) is variously understood. Greenberg et al., *Job*, connects it with מַזָּרוֹת (*mazzārôth*) in 38:32 and translates, "constellations." Noting the potential parallel of *ḥᵃdārîm* (9a) Driver reads מְזָוִים (*mᵉzāwîm*), "storehouses" (cf. Ps 144:13).

[8]In Mesopotamian cosmology the seven winds are said to have seven storehouses and in Canaanite mythology El presides over seven chambers (Cf. H. and L. Levy, "The Origin of the Week and the Oldest West Asiatic Calendar," *HUCA* 17 (1943): 8-10, 15-21, n. 229, 52f.; Pope, *Job*, p. 242, n. 9a)

[9]תַּחְבּוּלֹת (*taḥbûlōth*), from חבל (*ḥbl*, "to bind"), a navigational term used in the Wisdom literature to describe skill in managing difficult situations (cf. Prov 1:5; 11:14; 20:18; 24:6). See McKane, *Proverbs*, p. 266.

[10]The Hebrew of v. 13 is difficult and the subject of much discussion. Of particular interest is the phrase אִם־לְאַרְצוֹ (*ʾim-lᵉʾarṣô*), lit., "if for his land" (NIV, "to water his earth"). Duhm and Driver & Gray emend to read לִמְאֵרָה (*limʾērāh*), "for a curse," as in Deut 28:20; Prov 3:33. Gordis splits the words into לֹא רָצוּ (*lōʾ rāṣû*), "if they are not willing" (cf. Tur-Sinai, Grabbe).

to Job's charge that the wicked do not feel the "rod" of God's punishment (21:9). The term for God's "love" (חֶסֶד, *ḥesed*) is part of the grace vocabulary of the Old Testament and designates the covenant love and redemptive mercy he bestows upon individuals and nations.[11] The God who created nature uses it to accomplish his purposes on earth.

By defining the storm as an instrument of both God's punishment and his blessing, Elihu offers Job an interesting theological insight. From a human viewpoint it is virtually impossible to say which of these two divine purposes may be behind a given storm. It is even conceivable that the same storm could both punish and bless at the same time — bringing devastation and much needed moisture. Could this be an invitation for Job to reconsider the purpose behind the "storm" that has so disrupted his life? Understandably Job has seen in his suffering a malevolent act by an unjust God — an undeserved punishment. Could that suffering possibly serve some other, more benevolent purpose? As the following verses (14-20) suggest, human ignorance of God's purposes in the "storm" should serve as a caution against charging God with wrongdoing in his moral governance of his world.

Elihu's Closing Challenge to Job (37:14-24)

[14]"Listen to this, Job; / stop and consider God's wonders. / [15]Do you know how God controls the clouds / and makes his lightning flash? / [16]Do you know how the clouds hang poised, / those wonders of him who is perfect in knowledge? / [17]You who swelter in your clothes / when the land lies hushed under the south wind, / [18]can you join him in spreading out the skies, / hard as a mirror of cast bronze?

[19]"Tell us what we should say to him; / we cannot draw up our case because of our darkness. / [20]Should he be told that I want to speak? / Would any man ask to be swallowed up? / [21]Now no one can look at the sun, / bright as it is in the skies / after the wind has swept them clean. / [22]Out of the north he comes in golden splendor; / God comes in awesome majesty. / [23]The Almighty is beyond our reach and exalted in power; / in his justice and great

---

[11]Cf. H.-J. Zobel, "*ḥesed*," *TDOT*, 5:44-64.

righteousness, he does not oppress. / [24]Therefore, men revere him, / for does he not have regard for all the wise in heart?[a]"

[a]*24 Or for he does not have regard for any who think they are wise.*

37:14-18 By inviting Job to **listen** and **consider**, Elihu calls upon Job to acknowledge the magnificence and mystery of **God's wonders**[12] and to abandon his presumptuous claims against God's justice (vv. 19-24). In both content and form, the tactic Elihu employs anticipates the very tactic Yahweh will later use when he speaks to Job out of the storm.[13] Bombarding Job with a series of rhetorical questions he knows Job cannot answer, Elihu will expose Job's ignorance (**Do you know how God controls the clouds . . . ?**) and his powerlessness (**Can you join him in spreading out the skies . . . ?**) before the wise and sovereign God. According to Elihu the storm, as a model of God's management of the cosmos, testifies to the existence of a God who is **perfect** (lit., "complete") **in knowledge** (תְּמִים דֵּעִים, *tᵊmîm dēʿîm*). By this he means that, unlike Job, God has full comprehension of the grand design of the universe and how it all fits together to accomplish his intended purposes. God is also able to manipulate nature to accomplish his sovereign wishes. He **controls** the clouds (v. 15) and **spreads them out**[14] (v. 18) to bring relief from the **south wind**[15] and its oppressive heat — something Job could never do.

37:19-20[16] These verses disclose the purpose behind all of Elihu's speeches, the goal of his argument with Job. Because of Job's ignorance and impotence he is simply no match for God. He is not qualified to **say** anything **to him**, much less **draw up** a **case**[17] against him.

---

[12]נִפְלָאוֹת (*niphlᵊʾôth*, "marvels"); cf. 9:10.

[13]Cf. N. Snaith, *The Book of Job*, pp. 72-91; D. Freedman, "The Elihu Speeches in the Book of Job," *HTR* 61 (1968): 51-59.

[14]שְׁחָקִים (*šᵊḥāqîm*, "dust, cloud") makes it clear that what is being described here is the spreading out of the "clouds" across the sky to provide relief from the heat, not to the creation of the "heavens" which the NIV seems to imply by its use of the term "skies"; cf. (36:28; 38:37 and Habel, *Job*, p. 501, n. 18a).

[15]Elsewhere in Job the sirocco is described as the "east wind" (15:2; 27:21; 38:24).

[16]Habel sees the alternating use of "we" and "I" in these verses as an ironic shift between Job as plaintiff and Elihu as self-appointed arbiter (*Job*, p. 515).

[17]עָרַךְ (*ʾārak*, "order, arrange") usually appears with מִלִּין (*millîn*, "words")

He should, therefore, abandon his misguided and inappropriate attempt to try to make God answer to his demand for justice. NIV takes the normal meaning of בָּלַע (*billā'*), "devour," when it translates verse 20b, **Would any man ask to be swallowed up**? Many interpreters, in light of the parallel **because of our darkness** (19b), render *billā'* with the term "confused" and translate, "Can a man speak when he is confused?" This rendering is attractive and seems preferable in this context.[18] A mere human, whose way is obscured by "darkness" and whose thinking is clouded by "confusion," should not attempt to challenge God.

37:21-24 With his closing words, Elihu draws a final contrast between Job and God. It represents his final effort to convince Job that he has no hope of confronting God in court. Comparing God's **golden splendor** to the **brightness** of the **sun** in the clear **sky**, Elihu proclaims that **no one can look upon** him. No mere mortal could survive an encounter with such a God. The phrase **Out of the north he comes in golden splendor** (22a) has been variously understood. Most scholars see in these words a borrowing from Canaanite mythology that speaks of Baal coming from his heavenly council in the "northern mountain." Such language is also used of Yahweh in the Old Testament.[19] The term **majesty** (הוֹד, *hôd*) refers to the overwhelming splendor of God before which men stand in awe.[20] Awe, not irreverence, is what Job should be rendering to his God.

In verses 23-24 Elihu pulls together all the major themes of his speeches as he extols three major attributes of God. First, he asserts that God is **beyond our reach**. As he argued in chapter 35, Elihu reminds Job that God is a transcendent deity who is unaffected by anything that mortals do or say. Second, Elihu describes God as **exalted in power**. Picking up on a theme he had explored earlier (cf., e.g., 36:5,22) Elihu insists that God's power puts him in a class far above humankind. Finally, and most important for Job, Elihu affirms God's **justice** and his **great righteousness**. He is completely

---

or מִשְׁפָּט (*mišpāṭ*, "justice, legal case") in Job to mean "prepare a case"; cf. 13:18; 23:4; 32:14.

[18]Cf. Isa 28:7; Gordis, Habel.

[19]Cf. Isa 14:13; Ps 48:2[1]; R. Clifford, *The Cosmic Mountain in Canaan and the Old Testament* (Cambridge, MA: Harvard University Press, 1972), pp. 55-79.

[20]G. Warmuth, "*hodh*," *TDOT*, 3:353-355.

innocent of any charges of injustice that Job would bring against him (cf. 34:17; 36:3).[21]

The NIV renders the last phrase of verse 24 as a question, **for does he not have regard for all the wise in heart?** If this is correct, then the "wise of heart" are to be regarded as parallel to the **men** who **revere him** in the first part of the verse. The entire verse should be understood as an invitation for Job to revere God as one of the wise (cf. Prov 1:7). As the NIV notes, however, the last line of verse 24 can also be read as a declaration, "for he does not have any regard for the wise of heart" (or "for those who think they are wise"; cf. 9:4). In that case the second line of the verse contrasts the first and serves as a warning against the proud.[22] Taken as such, this final phrase could be addressing what Elihu believes is the real issue behind Job's assault on God's justice — his human pride. Whichever reading is correct, these final words of Elihu invite Job to approach God with a spirit of reverence.

---

[21]Habel argues on the basis of LXX that the final phrase of v. 23, "he does not oppress [לֹא יְעַנֶּה, lō' yᵊʻanneh] " should be read "he does not answer [יַעֲנֶה, yaʻăneh]." He regards this as a fitting conclusion to Elihu's argument that Job abandon his demand that God answer him in court.

[22]Cf. Pope, "he respects no clever mind" (*Job*, p. 240); also Dhorme, Leveque. LXX and Syr. make "wise of heart" the subject of the verb. Following LXX, Hartley goes on to treat לֹא (lō', "not)" as asseverative לֻא (lu', "indeed") and takes the phrase to mean, "indeed, all the wise of heart see him" (*Job*, pp. 483-484).

JOB 38

C. THE YAHWEH SPEECHES AND JOB'S RESPONSES (38:1–42:6)

At last, the transcendent deity, who has orchestrated Job's suffering from his heavenly throne and silently waited while his ways were debated, finally steps forth to have his say. This is the moment Job has both desperately sought and deeply feared. The God whom Job has accused of being unjust and from whom he has demanded an explanation will answer. In a way that once again will surprise the reader (and confound many an interpreter), these divine words will somehow provide a solution to Job's great dilemma and at the same time reconcile him to God.

The Yahweh speeches take the poetic artistry of Job to a whole new level. Rhetorically and theologically they constitute the climax of the book and stand as one of the finest examples of ancient Hebrew literature. Nature-hymns presented in the form of a disputation,[1] they constitute what could be called a "creation theology."[2] Their purpose is "not the glorification of nature but the vindication of nature's God."[3] Bombarding Job with a series of rhetorical ques-

---

[1]Cf. H. Richter, "Die Naturweisheit des Alten Testaments im Buche Hiob," *ZAW* 70 (1958): 1-20. Fohrer sees the hymn genre dominant in the speeches as does Westermann (*Structure of the Book of Job*, pp. 105-123).

[2]H. Rowald, "Yahweh's Challenge to Rival: The Form and Function of the Yahweh-Speech in Job 38–39," *CBQ* 47 (1985): 199-211. As such they are similar to the so-called "trial speeches" of Isaiah (41:1-5,21-29; 43:8-15; 44:6ff; 45:20-25). In Isaiah, the contest is between Yahweh and the other gods. Here it is between Yahweh and Job. In both contexts the answer to God's rhetorical questions ("Who created?" "Who measured?" cp. Job 38:4,5 to Isa 40:12,26) is "Yahweh alone." Cf. C. Westermann, *Isaiah 40–66*, trans. by D.M.G. Stalker (Philadelphia: Westminster, 1969), p. 15.

[3]Gordis, *God and Man*, p. 117.

tions that he has no hope of answering, the speeches of Yahweh expose Job's ignorance and impotence while extolling God's great wisdom and power. They reposition Yahweh as the sovereign in his dispute with Job and, at the same time, offer Job insight on how God manages the world he has made. These two speeches (38:1–40:2; 40:6–41:34) each begin with a charge against Job followed by a prolonged interrogation of this mortal who has dared to challenge God. The first speech exposes Job's ignorance of how the creation is ordered and the second speech challenges Job's ability to manage the powerful forces at work in God's world. Following each speech Job makes responses (40:3-5; 42:1-6) that acknowledge God's superior wisdom and power and effectively end his dispute with him.

Though many scholars have argued that the Yahweh speeches make no effort to address the issues that Job has raised in his speeches, a careful reading of Yahweh's three charges against Job suggests otherwise. The opening charge accuses Job of obscuring God's "counsel" (lit., "design"; עֵצָה, 'ēṣāh; 38:2) or the master plan behind his creation. Job has repeatedly challenged God on this point (cf., e.g., 10:8-14; 12:13-25). The second charge, coming at the end of the first speech, has to do with Job's audacious attempt to take God to court (40:2). This, of course, has become Job's grand obsession (cf., e.g., 9:14-20; 23:1-7; 31:35-37). The final charge, which begins the second speech, addresses Job's attempt to "discredit [God's] justice" (40:8). The issue of divine justice has been at the heart of Job's accusations against God (cf., e.g., 9:21-24; 21:7ff; 27:1-6). It is clear that Yahweh has been listening to Job.

It is less clear how God goes about answering Job. What exactly is Yahweh saying to Job, and why does he say it in the way that he does? There has been no shortage of attempts to answer these questions.[4] The following survey illustrates how widely the opinions vary on the meaning and purpose of the Yahweh speeches:

1. **The speeches are designed to humble Job.** Yahweh does not answer Job, he assails him. He backs him down from his self-appointed role as God's accuser by exposing Job's ignorance

---

[4]Cf., e.g., R. MacKenzie, "The Purpose of the Yahweh Speeches in the Book of Job," *Bib* 40 (1959): 435-445; S. Terrien, "The Yahweh Speeches and Job's Response," *RevExp* 68 (1971): 497-509; Tsevat, "The Meaning of the Book of Job," pp. 73-106; Gordis, *God and Man*, pp. 123-134.

and powerlessness before the wise and powerful deity. So humbled, Job confesses his incompetence to judge God and resubmits himself to his maker.[5]

2. **The speeches are designed to comfort Job.** By his willingness to personally appear to Job, God reassures him that he has not abandoned his struggling servant but has been present in his suffering. Overwhelmed by having "seen God" (42:6) Job's problem is not solved, but transcended by a personal encounter with the divine.

3. **The speeches are designed to evade Job's issue.** Job's primary question ("What is the meaning of undeserved suffering?") is ignored by God because there is no satisfactory answer. Humans can only endure the mystery of suffering by faith.[6] A variation of this theory suggests that by refusing to answer Job's question Yahweh is shifting the emphasis on the "Why?" of suffering to the "How?" Humans must learn to face the mystery of suffering through submission to the sovereign God, trusting in his management of his world.[7]

4. **The speeches are designed to refute Job's claim that there is no moral order in God's world.** Through an analogy, Yahweh suggests to Job that just as there is a physical order to the universe, there is likewise a moral order. It is simply beyond the capacity of humans to comprehend it. Job, admitting he really does not "know" how God runs his world, repents of his presumptuous accusations against him.[8]

---

[5]Some scholars characterize Yahweh's encounter with Job as an example of *tremendum* (cf. Rudolf Otto, *The Idea of the Holy: An Inquiry into the Non-Rational Factor in the Idea of the Divine in Its Relation to the Rational* [Oxford: Oxford University Press, 1923], pp. 74-84). Job, in the presence of the glorious creator is overawed. When confronted by God's holiness and splendor Job's existential circumstance no longer matters to him (cf. Carol Newsom's discussion of what she calls "the tragic sublime"; *The Book of Job*, pp. 252-256). Other scholars go in a radically different direction and characterize the God of the Yahweh speeches as a "cosmic bully" who adds insult to the injury he has already inflicted on Job by brutally attacking him. In response, Job is said not to "repent" before God but feels "loathing and contempt" for God. He remains defiant against the God who has abused him (cf. J.B. Curtis, "On Job's Response to Yahweh," *JBL* 98/4 (1979): 497-511.

[6]Pope, *Job*, p. lxxv.

[7]G. Fohrer, *Job*, p. 558.

[8]Gordis, *God and Man*, p. 133.

5. **The speeches are designed to teach Job that God is not just.**
   In the world God created there is inequity and even chaos. A
   survey of the created order suggests that there is no operative
   principle of retributive justice at work in God's world. Acknowledging this, Job is able to move on, realizing that life is
   not always fair. God is not just. He is just God.[9]

6. **The speeches are designed to vindicate Job.** By his appearing
   Yahweh acknowledges that Job's main contention — that he is
   innocent of any sin meriting such suffering — is valid. Noteworthy in the speeches is that God does not accuse Job of
   being "guilty" but of being "ignorant." So vindicated, Job does
   not "repent" but simply "retracts," and he ends his case
   against God.[10]

7. **The speeches are designed to educate Job on the true nature
   of God's justice.** Divine justice is far more sophisticated than
   that which the simplistic doctrine of retribution would suggest. As God makes special allowances and pursues agendas
   other than mere retribution in nature, so also does he pursue
   other agendas in the realm of human affairs. This explanation
   is said to agree with that of the prologue which explains the
   suffering of Job in terms of God's decision to test the genuineness of his piety. God, as the sovereign judge, has the
   right to do this without being called "unjust."[11]

This brief survey of the major views on the purpose of the
Yahweh speeches illustrates the difficulty of assigning them a specific meaning. Some of these theories are not mutually exclusive and
explore valid implications of this climactic portion of the book. In
the final analysis the Yahweh speeches may not be explainable on
the basis of a single agenda. Just as the rest of the book addresses
the problem of undeserved suffering on two levels — philosophical
and spiritual — so also do the speeches of Yahweh. While providing
an "answer" to Job's great dilemma, they also seek to personally reconcile this tortured creature to his creator.

---

[9]Tsevat, *The Meaning of Job*, pp. 98-106.

[10]Some scholars compare Job to Prometheus and go so far as to suggest
that Job, by his integrity and by the power of his argument, has forced God
to appear and to acknowledge his innocence.

[11]Cf., e.g., G. von Rad, *Theology of the Old Testament*, 1:414f.

1. Yahweh's First Speech and Job's Reply (38:1–40:2)

The God who first set this grand drama in motion will now bring it to an end. Having endured Job's irreverent attempts to impugn his providence and challenge his management of human life, Yahweh will now have his say. Whereas Job's words have been primarily directed at God's governance of the moral order of the world, however, Yahweh chooses to speak of his governance of the natural order. The sovereign God leads his defiant creature out into his world and challenges him to explain just how it all fits together, the purpose and design behind his creation. Though modern westerners might not see the immediate connection between Yahweh's answer and Job's questions, an ancient Semite would. Finding no distinction between the natural order and the moral order of the universe, the people of Job's day saw them as part of one grand design.[12] The same God who set the physical world in place and assures that it runs smoothly, in like manner presides over human affairs. Through an argument that is more than mere analogy, Yahweh will make it clear to Job that just as there is order and harmony in the natural world, there is also order and meaning in the moral sphere.[13] Job, being a mere mortal, is simply incapable of fully comprehending it.

Yahweh's first speech begins and ends with a direct challenge of Job to "answer" him (38:1-3; 40:1-2). In between he bombards Job with a series of questions about the cosmic (38:4-38) and the biological (38:39–39:30) realities of creation. The first portion of the speech addresses the design behind the universe, emphasizing its "dimensions" (38:5), "fixed limits" (38:10), "places" (38:12,20), "ways" (38:19;24), "times" (38:23), and "laws" (38:33).[14] Yahweh then turns to the animal kingdom and asks Job questions about a number

---

[12]Cf. J. Assmann, B. Janowski, M. Weller, "Richten und Retten: Zur Aktualität der altorientalischen und biblischen Gerechtigkeitskonzeption," in *Gerechtigkeit: Richten und Retten in der abendländischen Tradition und ihren altorientalischen Ursprüngen* (Munich: Wilhelm Fink, 1998), pp. 9-35; S. Geller, "Where Is Wisdom? A Literary Study of Job 28 in Its Settings," in *Judaic Perspectives on Ancient Israel*, ed. by J. Neusner, B. Levine, E.S. Frerichs (Philadelphia: Westminster, 1985), pp. 120-137.

[13]Gordis, *God and Man*, p. 133.

[14]Cf. Habel, *Job*, p. 532.

of creatures that were generally regarded as beyond the control of man and whose ways evoked a sense of mystery and awe.[15]

Introduction and Yahweh's Challenge of Job (38:1-3)

¹**Then the LORD answered Job out of the storm. He said:**
²**"Who is this that darkens my counsel / with words without knowledge? / ³Brace yourself like a man; / I will question you, / and you shall answer me.**

38:1 Out of the storm (הַסְּעָרָה, *hassᵊ'ārāh*), perhaps the very storm that Elihu referred to as the vehicle of God's voice (37:1-5),[16] God now speaks. Such storms are often said to attend the coming of God in the Old Testament. At Sinai, the Lord spoke to his people from the midst of lightning and thunder (Exod 19:16-20). The prophets predicted God's coming in a tempest to judge the wicked (Isa 29:5-6; Jer 23:19; 25:32; 30:23; Ezek 1:2-4; Nahum 1:3; Zech 9:14-17). The Psalmists commonly employed the storm motif to describe the phenomenon of theophany (Ps 77:17-18[16-17]; 18:8-16[7-15]. God's choice of this vehicle for his appearance may also serve to tie this climactic event to other parts of the book. It was a mighty wind (רוּחַ גְּדוֹלָה, *rûaḥ gᵊdôlāh*) that killed Job's children (1:19). In one of his speeches Job had feared that if God should appear to him he would "crush [Job] with a storm" (*sᵊ'ārāh*, 9:17). To his surprise Job will now witness the appearance of God in the storm not to destroy him, but to correct and instruct him.

---

[15]Scholars have gone in a variety of directions in search of an explanation for the list of animals used here. One approach ties it to the ancient Near Eastern motif of the royal hunt which describes kings subduing some of the animals mentioned in this list. Another suggestion ties this list to the Mesopotamian iconic motif commonly known as "Lord of the Animals" where a divine figure is depicted as grasping such animals by his hands demonstrating his control over them (cf. Othmar Keel, *Jahwehs Entgegnung an Ijob*, FRLANT 121 (Göttingen: Vandenhoeck & Ruprecht, 1978), pp. 71-73. A biblical background (Psalm 104) to the list is proposed by Carol Newsom, "Book of Job," *New Interpreter's Bible*, pp. 596-597.

[16]It is possible that the author, by employing the definite article (*hassᵊ'ārāh*, "*the* storm"), means for the reader to connect this storm to the preceding context (37:1ff) where Elihu, functioning as a "forerunner of Yahweh," possibly observing an actual storm forming on the horizon, directs Job's attention to it in preparation for Yahweh's appearance.

For the first time since the prologue, God is identified by his personal name, **Yahweh**. Throughout the dialogue Job and the friends have referred to God as El, Eloah, and Shaddai.[17] In the Old Testament, Yahweh is the personal name of the God of the covenant, who appears to his people and speaks to men. His appearance to Job is reminiscent of his face-to-face encounters with Abraham and Moses (cf., e.g., Gen 19:16-33; Exod 32:7-14,31-34). The author employs the name here to remind us that the same deity who first set Job's great struggle in motion now personally appears to bring it to an end. Yahweh comes to **answer** (יַעַן, yāʿan) Job. The use of this term remembers Job's repeated appeals for a divine reply (cf., e.g., 9:16-17; 31:35) and suggests to the reader that Yahweh's words are intentionally designed as a direct response to the issues Job has raised.[18]

38:2-3 Yahweh's opening challenge addresses the first of two issues he wishes to take up with Job. He accuses Job of **darkening** [God's] **counsel** (עֵצָה, ʿēṣāh; lit., "design").[19] By his accusations against God Job has obscured the grand design by which he governs his world (cf., e.g., 9:5-13; 10:8-14; 12:13-25). Job has accused God of being a ruthless destroyer who has created a world without order and justice. This constitutes a misrepresentation of the true design behind the created order — an order that God will now vigorously defend. Job's obfuscation of God's governance is done **with words without knowledge**. As several commentators have duly noted, Yahweh, unlike the friends, never accuses Job of being sinful, only ignorant. Job's accusations against God's "injustice" do not grow out of any evil intent to slander God. They grow out of his misunderstanding of God's design for his management of Job's life. As the

---

[17]The one exception, 12:9 is commonly regarded as a textual error. *'Elōah* is attested in some manuscripts in the place of *Yahweh* (cf. *BHS*). It should be noted that the wisdom literature of the Old Testament rarely employs the personal name of God. Like the wisdom literature of the ancient Near East it refers to the deity in more general terms (R. Gordis, *Poets, Prophets, and Sages* [Bloomington, IN: Indiana University Press, 1971], pp. 159-168).

[18]For a detailed survey of how Yahweh's words relate to Job's cf. Habel, *Job*, pp. 530-532.

[19]*ʿēṣāh* is used in connection with "plan" (מַחֲשָׁבָה, maḥăšābāh, Ps 33:10; Prov 19:21) and "wisdom" (חָכְמָה, ḥokmāh, 12:13; Prov 8:14) in the Old Testament to describe the design behind God's creation; cf. J. Lévêque, *Job et son Dieu*, Etudes Bibliques (Paris: Gabalda, 1970), 2:510-513.

prologue made clear, there was a purpose behind Job's undeserved suffering. Job is simply unaware of it.

Yahweh's problem with Job, however, goes beyond their disagreement over how God has ordered his world. There is also the issue of how Job has behaved toward his creator. In defense of his integrity Job has arrogated himself to the level of God's equal. "Like a prince I would approach him," Job declared as he demanded a day in court with God (31:37). In his spiritual pride he has impugned God's providence, accused him of being unjust, and demanded that God reward him for his piety. Yahweh's opening words, **"Who is this?"** capture his indignant attitude toward Job's presumption.[20] He then challenges Job to **Brace** (himself) **like a man** (lit., "gird your loins like a hero"). "Girding the loins" (gathering the robe into the belt) means to prepare for some vigorous activity such as a battle (Isa 5:28) or running (1 Kgs 18:46). Following Cyrus Gordon, a number of scholars have understood this language to be an invitation to a wrestling match.[21] This phrase coupled with the following, **I will question you and you shall answer**[22] **me**, demonstrates that Yahweh sees himself as Job's adversary in a dispute and that Yahweh will now assume the dominant position in the struggle. Up to this point Job has been interrogating God. Yahweh's rebuke announces his intention to reverse those roles. Yahweh's use of the word גֶּבֶר (*geber*), "hero, champion" (**man**, NIV) to describe Job shows the reader that God is aiming his rebuke not just at Job's ignorance, but at his arrogance.[23]

Questions about the Inanimate World (38:4-38)

The Foundations of the Earth (38:4-7)

4"Where were you when I laid the earth's foundation? / Tell me, if you understand. / ⁵Who marked off its dimensions? Surely

---

[20]Habel sees in these words a formal legal summons that constitutes the beginning of Yahweh's rebuttal of Job's charges (*Job*, p. 536).

[21]Gordon, "Belt Wrestling in the Bible World," pp. 131-136. H. Ginsberg, "Interpreting Ugaritic Texts," *JAOS* 70 (1950): 158, offers another view.

[22]הוֹדִיעֵנִי (*hôdî'ênî*, "make known to me"), as the following questions will make clear, indicates that Yahweh is interested in more than mere legal rebuttal from Job. He intends to explore just what Job really knows about God's world and how he runs it.

[23]Terrien sees the use of this term as a play on Job's presumptuous desire to meet God as a prince, i.e., on virtually an equal footing.

you know! / Who stretched a measuring line across it? / ⁶On what were its footings set, / or who laid its cornerstone— / ⁷while the morning stars sang together / and all the angelsᵃ shouted for joy?

ᵃ7 Hebrew *the sons of God*

38:4-7 Yahweh's initial questions are designed to expose Job's ignorance of how the world was created. They take Job back to the time when God, the master builder, **laid the earth's foundations**, **marked off its dimensions**, and **stretched a measuring line across it**. The metaphor of creation as the construction of a building is a common one in the Old Testament.[24] These particular descriptions of the creative process suggest that creation was the result of careful planning and attests to a grand design. According to Proverbs 8:22-31 "wisdom" was present at creation, functioning as God's "craftsman" (cf. Job 28:24-27). Yahweh ironically questions if Job might have been there as well. The sarcastic **Where were you?** (v. 4) and **Surely you know!** (v. 5) reveal the exception God has taken to Job's presumptuous impugning of his governance of the world. What qualifies Job to be the judge of God? What does Job really **understand** of how God governs his world? Yahweh's choice of words (יָדַע בִּינָה, *yāda' bînāh*) challenges Job's ability to "discern" or "comprehend" the true nature of things or just how it is that the natural order works. The reference to the celebration of the **angels** or the **morning stars**[25] at the laying of the earth's **cornerstone** alludes to the common ancient practice of formal ceremonies accompanying the construction of a great edifice.[26] This text clearly suggests that the angels, unlike Job, were actually present at creation.

The Boundaries of the Sea (38:8-11)

⁸"**Who shut up the sea behind doors / when it burst forth from the womb, / ⁹when I made the clouds its garment / and wrapped**

---

[24]Cf., e.g., Ps 24:2; 89:11[10]; 102:25[24]; 104:5; Prov 3:19; Isa 48:13; 51:13.

[25]In the ANE the morning stars were worshiped as deities. Here, as the poetic parallelism suggests, they are used figuratively to refer to the "sons of God," i.e., the angels.

[26]When the temple was reconstructed in the time of Zerubbabel, the laying of its foundation was celebrated with music (Ezra 3:10-12) and the setting of its capstone with shouting (Zech 4:7).

it in thick darkness, / ¹⁰when I fixed limits for it / and set its doors and bars in place, / ¹¹when I said, 'This far you may come and no farther; / here is where your proud waves halt'?

38:8-11 Turning next to the creation of the sea, Yahweh questions Job on just how it was set in place. The relationship of the sea to dry land was a matter of great interest in ancient Near Eastern cosmogony. In both Mesopotamian and Canaanite myths, the sea was described as a violent goddess subdued by a creator deity who wins the right to rule by defeating her.[27] In contrast to this mythical model, the Old Testament describes the sea with its threatening waves as a chaotic force held in check by Yahweh (cf., e.g., Ps 77:16[15]); 104:7-9). Before Yahweh the fierce sea is no more than a mere infant (**burst forth from the womb**), swaddled in baby clothes (**clouds** [cf. 26:8-9, 37:11,15], **thick darkness** [cf. 22:13]), placed in a playpen (behind **doors** and **bars**[28]), and told to stay there ("**This far you may come and no farther**").[29]

It is possible that the wording of Yahweh's initial question (**Who shut up** [יָסֶךְ, *yāsek*] **the sea behind doors?** v. 8) is intended as an ironic response to Job's original challenge to Yahweh's providence. In his opening soliloquy Job used the same verb to suggest that God had "hedged in" (יָסֹךְ, *ysk*) the way of man (3:23).[30] Whereas Job used the term to suggest some malevolent intent of God to restrict humans, Yahweh uses it to describe his limitation of the sea for the benefit of humans. Any **limits** God places on creation are not designed to hinder humans but help them.

---

[27]Cf., e.g., the Babylonian *Enumah Elish* and the *Baal Cycle* from Ugarit.

[28]Cf. *Enumah Elish* IV,139-140; *ANET*, p. 67, where Marduk, after defeating Tiamat, is said to have imprisoned her behind bars.

[29]Habel, *Job*, p. 538. A birth metaphor of creation is also found in Ps 90:2.

[30]Blommerde (*Northwest Semitic Grammar and Job*, pp. 132-133) reads for וַיָּסֶךְ (*wayyāsek*, "and he shut up [the sea]") וַיֻּסַּךְ (*wayyussak*), "when [the sea] poured out," a passive of נָסַךְ (*nsk*). Hartley (*Job*, p. 493) speculates that the expression may derive from סָכַךְ (*skk*, "to weave, knit [the sea] together") and that it is referring to the growth of the fetus in the womb (cf. Ps 139:13b) and serves as a parallel to יָצָא (*yāṣā'*), "burst forth" (from the womb, v. 8b), with both parts of v. 8 describing the birth of the sea.

The Dawning of the Day (38:12-15)

¹²"Have you ever given orders to the morning, / or shown the dawn its place, / ¹³that it might take the earth by the edges / and shake the wicked out of it? / ¹⁴The earth takes shape like clay under a seal; / its features stand out like those of a garment. / ¹⁵The wicked are denied their light, / and their upraised arm is broken.

38:12-15 Yahweh now challenges Job's authority over the cycle of light and darkness. In antiquity darkness symbolized the powers of evil, and under its cover the **wicked** were most active (cf. 24:13-17). Light, by contrast, is associated with goodness and with God himself (cf. Ps 27:1; Isa 60:19-20). The regular appearance of the **dawn** not only regulated the rhythms of time, it also put restraints on the power of evil. It **denied** the **wicked** their **light** (their opportunity to act) and **broke** their **upraised arm** (their power to do harm). Dawn, with its revealing light, has the power to **take the earth by the edges and shake the wicked out of it**. As its breaking light causes the contours of the earth to **take shape** and its colors to **stand out**,[31] it likewise exposes the deeds of the wicked and forces them to flee. All of this, Yahweh insists, happens by his **orders**, not Job's.

Yahweh's characterization of the power of the dawn to limit evil has direct implications for Job's repeated challenges of God's governance of human behavior. According to Job, God presides over an unjust moral order that favors the wicked. He permits them to prosper and allows them free reign in their oppression of the innocent (cf., e.g., 9:22-24; 12:5-6; 21:7-21). Yahweh now counters these claims by reminding Job that in something as basic as the daily rising of the sun God sees to it that evil is restrained. As the divinely appointed boundary of the shore limits the activity of the violent sea, so also does the divinely ordained dawn limit the evil done under the cover of night.

The Extremities of the World (38:16-21)

¹⁶"Have you journeyed to the springs of the sea / or walked in the recesses of the deep? / ¹⁷Have the gates of death been shown

---

[31]For MT וְיִתְיַצְּבוּ (wᵉyithyaṣṣᵉbû, "they stand out") Dhorme reads וְתִצָּבַע (wᵉthiṣṣāba', "it is dyed"). Fohrer reads וְתִצְטַבַּע (wᵉthiṣṭabba', "it becomes colored"); cf. also *BHS*.

to you? / Have you seen the gates of the shadow of death[a]? / [18]Have you comprehended the vast expanses of the earth? / Tell me, if you know all this.

[19]"What is the way to the abode of light? / And where does darkness reside? / [20]Can you take them to their places? / Do you know the paths to their dwellings? / [21]Surely you know, for you were already born! / You have lived so many years!

[a]*17 Or gates of deep shadows*

38:16-21 Continuing his cross-examination, Yahweh explores Job's knowledge of the deepest recesses and the ultimate boundaries of existence. In antiquity the **deep** (תְּהוֹם, *tᵉhôm*) was regarded as one of the primordial extremities of the created world. It constituted the source or **springs of the sea** (cf. 28:14; Gen 7:11). Another extremity of which Yahweh questions Job is the realm of **death**, the shadowy netherworld where all mortals eventually descend (10:21-22; 30:23). Job had longed to go there in his opening lament, believing it to be a place of quiet and rest from his trouble (3:16-19; cf. 14:13-15). Yahweh responds by reminding Job that he has never actually entered its **gates**[32] and thus his perceptions of death are no more than mere speculation. Neither has Job fully explored the **vast expanses of the earth**. His criticisms of God's management of life on earth are made without full knowledge of how it all fits together.

Moving from earth's depths to its horizons, Yahweh quizzes Job on his knowledge of the **abode of light** and **darkness**. In Job's day these cosmological realities were deified and said to preside over their own competing realms. Employing similar language Yahweh personifies (not deifies) these cosmic forces and challenges Job's knowledge of their assigned **places** and **paths**. In his opening soliloquy Job had wished that the day of his birth be "turned to darkness" (3:4) and asked why "light" was given to "those in misery" (3:20). In response Yahweh challenges what Job even knows about how light and darkness come and go. With stinging sarcasm Yahweh punctuates this portion of his cross-examination with the repeated, **Surely you know** (cf. v. 5). Of course, Job does not know. To have

---

[32]The Sumerian myth, *The Descent of Inanna* and its Akkadian equivalent, *The Descent of Ishtar* describe the goddess passing through seven gates on her way to the netherworld (*ANET*, pp. 52ff; 106ff).

such knowledge he would need to have been **already born** at the beginning of creation. Only God, who was present at creation and who alone knows the way of wisdom (28:23-27), could be aware of such things. Job's repeated challenges of God's justice have been made on the basis of what he claimed to "know" about how God runs his world. Through Yahweh's vigorous cross-examination of Job, it becomes obvious that he actually knows very little of God's world and he is, therefore, not qualified to be God's judge.

The Mysteries of the Sky (38:22-33)

²²**"Have you entered the storehouses of the snow / or seen the storehouses of the hail, / ²³which I reserve for times of trouble, / for days of war and battle? / ²⁴What is the way to the place where the lightning is dispersed, / or the place where the east winds are scattered over the earth? / ²⁵Who cuts a channel for the torrents of rain, / and a path for the thunderstorm, / ²⁶to water a land where no man lives, / a desert with no one in it, / ²⁷to satisfy a desolate wasteland / and make it sprout with grass? / ²⁸Does the rain have a father? / Who fathers the drops of dew? / ²⁹From whose womb comes the ice? / Who gives birth to the frost from the heavens / ³⁰when the waters become hard as stone, / when the surface of the deep is frozen?**

³¹**"Can you bind the beautifulᵃ Pleiades? / Can you loose the cords of Orion? / ³²Can you bring forth the constellations in their seasonsᵇ / or lead out the Bearᶜ with its cubs? / ³³Do you know the laws of the heavens? / Can you set up ⌞God'sᵈ⌟ dominion over the earth?**

ᵃ*31* Or *the twinkling*; or *the chains of the*   ᵇ*32* Or *the morning star in its season*   ᶜ*32* Or *out Leo*   ᵈ*33* Or *his*; or *their*

38:22-30 Turning to the skies, Yahweh begins to question Job's knowledge of various meteorological and astronomical phenomena and the purposes that they serve. Speaking first of **snow** and **hail**, he describes them as celestial ammunition stored up for use in **days of war and battle**. Hail and snow could prove troublesome and even deadly for troops in the open field (cf., e.g., Josh 10:11; Ps 68:14[13]). God uses them as weapons in **times of trouble** (Exod 9:18-26; Ps 78:47-48). In the grand design of God's world these potent meteorological forces are said to be kept in **storehouses** at God's disposal for his use at the **times** of his choosing. Likewise the violent **thunderstorm** with its potent **lightning**[33] is not a random, uncontrolled event but a divinely appointed agent with its own appointed **place** and designated **path**. God **disperses** it to accomplish his purposes. In contrast to the snow and hail, the **rain** is said to have a benevolent, even gracious purpose, **watering a land where no man lives** and causing **grass to sprout** in a **desolate wasteland**. Job has accused God of malevolent intent in his management of precipitation (12:15). Yahweh counters that he directs the rain to fall not only on the habitable places of the earth but even on a **desert with no one in it**. Job, because of his limited human perspective and his preoccupation with his own suffering, has failed to appreciate the extravagance of God's grace. He brings blessings even where there are no humans to witness it. God, not Job, is the **father** of the life-giving **dew** and the mother whose **womb**[34] gives birth to the **frost from the heavens** that can turn the **waters hard as stone**. God and God alone gives rise to these powerful forces and he alone knows their purposes. The grand design behind all of these phenomena remains a mystery to humans but by God they are fully understood.

38:31-33 The sudden shift here to astral phenomena may seem out of place to a modern westerner, but from the perspective of the ancients they were seen as sharing the same sky. The constellations mentioned in 9:9 are referred to here. The identification of the first two with **Pleiades** and **Orion** is commonly accepted though there is much debate over the precise meaning of the vague term used to describe Pleiades (מַעֲדַנּוֹת, *ma'ădannôth*; **beautiful** in v. 31a). Many interpreters follow Pope in connecting this term with the root עַנד (*'nd*), "bind," taking this expression to mean "chains, fetters of Pleiades" and forming a parallel with **cords of Orion** in verse 31b.[35]

---

[33]MT, אוֹר (*'ôr*), "light." A number of scholars searching for a better parallel to "east wind" (קָדִים, *qādîm*, v. 24b) have proposed emendations or alternative etymologies. Duhm reads אֵד (*'ēd*, "mist, water reservoir") for *'ôr* (cf. also Dhorme, Pope, Rowley). Gordis sees *'ôr* as a Heb. equivalent for ἀήρ (*aēr*), "air, air currents." Tur-Sinai connects *'ôr* to Akk. *amurru*, "land of the west wind" and translates "west wind" seeing it as a parallel to "east wind."

[34]This is one of the few female metaphors of God in the Old Testament.

[35]Cf. Pope, *Job*, p. 254. *Ma'ădannôth* is commonly thought to be an error of metathesis for מַאֲנַדּוֹת (*ma'ănaddôth*), "bonds" (cf. Dhorme, Tur-Sinai, Driver & Gray, Gordis). Brueggemann speculates that the expression "cords of Orion" may allude to the myth of Orion where he is bound to the sky (cf. "Orion," *IDB*, 3:609).

The reference to the **Bear with its cubs** is generally thought to be connected with the Great Bear and the Little Bear (Dhorme) or as Leo and its encroachment on Cancer.[36] Somewhat of a mystery is the term **constellations** (מַזָּרוֹת, *mazzārôth*; v. 32a). NIV seems to follow those translators who see it as a variant of מַזָּלוֹת (*mazzālôth*, "constellations"; cf. 1 Kgs 23:5) and take it to refer to some or all of the southern constellations of the zodiac.[37] The Vulgate renders it *Lucifer,* and some interpreters follow taking it as a designation of Venus, the morning and evening star. Of particular interest is Yahweh's use of the expression **laws of the heavens** in verse 33. The noun translated "laws" (מִשְׁטָרוֹ, *mišṭārô*) is a hapax legomenon evidently derived from שׁטר (*šṭr*) which literally means to "write, inscribe." This expression is often compared to the Akkadian idiom *šiṭir šamē*, "the writing of the heavens" or the "starry sky." In Mesopotamian mythology as in modern astrology there was a common belief that the patterned movement of the stars affected events on earth.[38] By contrast here the idea is that this patterned movement of the stars is all part of a grand design that is controlled by the same God who has **dominion over the earth.**

Control of the Clouds (38:34-38)

[34]**"Can you raise your voice to the clouds / and cover yourself with a flood of water? / [35]Do you send the lightning bolts on their way? / Do they report to you, 'Here we are'? / [36]Who endowed the heart with wisdom / or gave understanding to the mind[a]? / [37]Who has the wisdom to count the clouds? / Who can tip over the water jars of the heavens / [38]when the dust becomes hard / and the clods of earth stick together?**

[a]*36 The meaning of the Hebrew for this word is uncertain.*

38:34-38 It is not accidental that the God who appeared in a cloud ends his survey of the inanimate world by asking Job if he can control them. Do the clouds pour out their **flood of water** at the command of your **voice**, Yahweh inquires of Job. Do **lightning bolts**

---

[36]Cf. the Arab. cognate *'ay(y)ut*, "lion" for עַיִשׁ (*'ayiš*) (Pope, *Job*, p. 255).

[37]Pope, *Job*, p. 255. Dhorme suggests Corona Borealis, linking the noun to נֵזֶר (*nēzer*, "crown").

[38]Cf. J. Hirschber, "Jobe XXXVIII 31," *REJ* 99 (1935): 130-132.

report to you? No mere human has the power to summon the clouds or require them to release their thunder and rain. Neither does a mere mortal have the **wisdom** necessary to **count the clouds**. Keeping track of them and ordering them to water the dry earth is something only God can do. Verse 36 employs a pair of obscure terms to denote that which God has **endowed with wisdom** and to which he has **given understanding**. The NIV, evidently following the Vulgate, translates the first term (בַּטֻּחוֹת, baṭṭuḥôth) as **heart** and the second (לַשֶּׂכְוִי, laśśekwî) as **mind** (cf. Ps 51:8[6]). Another approach treats these terms as two different kinds of clouds.[39] An alternative proposal is to see these terms as referring to two different types of birds — the **ibis** and the **cock** — birds which in the ancient world were associated with both wisdom and the changing of the weather.[40] So rendered, verse 36 would read, **Who endowed the ibis with wisdom or gave understanding to the cock**? This would fit nicely with the immediate context and serve to anticipate Yahweh's survey of the animal kingdom beginning in the next verse.

Questions about the Animate World (38:39–39:30)

The Lion and the Raven (38:39-41)

[39]"**Do you hunt the prey for the lioness / and satisfy the hunger of lions / [40]when they crouch in their dens / or lie in wait in a thicket? / [41]Who provides food for the raven / when its young cry out to God / and wander about for lack of food?**

38:39-41 Yahweh's interrogation of Job's knowledge of his world now turns to the animals that inhabit it. He will question Job on the habits of the lion, the raven, the mountain goat, the hind, the wild ass, the wild ox, the ostrich, the horse, and birds of prey. In the Old Testament these animals are associated with the uninhabited steppes and desert regions. Some of them are also said to inhabit the desolate ruins left behind by war (cf. Isa 34:8-15; Ezek 34:8). These

---

[39]טֻחוֹת (tuḥôth) is said to be derived from טוּחַ (ṭûaḥ, "plaster, cover"); while שֶׂכְוִי (śekwî) is thought to be from שׂכה (skh=skk), "cover, screen" (cf. BDB, pp. 376, 967).

[40]Cf. discussion by Hartley, Job, p. 501, and O. Keel, "Zwei kleine Beiträge zum Verständnis der Gottesreden im Buch Ijob (xxxviii 36f., xl 25)," VT 31 (1981): 220-223.

creatures are among the wild animals that, with the exception of the horse, are not capable of being tamed by man. In the Old Testament and in other ancient literature they stood as symbols of the uninhabited and the dangerous places (cf., e.g., Isa 34:8-15).[41] This may be Yahweh's point in bringing them to Job's attention. These wild creatures, existing in total independence of humans, yet have a place in God's world and are under his providential care. Though their behaviors may not be understood or may even seem unfair, absurd, or even threatening to humans, they are yet a legitimate part of God's created order. They become a further illustration of what Job does not "know" about the grand design of God's world.

The first pair of animals, the **lion** and the **raven** is not only wild, their existence often depends on the death of another creature. The lions **hunt for prey** and **lie in wait** for their food. Ravens likewise prey upon small animals and carrion. The predator-prey relationship is also mentioned in the concluding line of Yahweh's first speech as he completes his survey of the animal kingdom (39:30). The repetition is intentional, and its meaning is important for Job's intellectual struggle. God presides over a world where some creatures eat others in order to survive. It is hard to fit this biological reality into a system where "justice" always prevails. By making Job aware of the fact that "undeserved" suffering and death are part of the given realities of the animal world, he invites him to consider them as givens of human existence as well. Life is not always "fair." The creatures of God's world do not always get what they "deserve."

As Habel suggests, the language employed in this part of Yahweh's speech remembers some of the very expressions Job had earlier used in his criticisms of God's providence.[42] Job had accused God of "hunting" (צוּד, ṣwd) him down like a lion (10:16; cf. 16:9). Yahweh counters by claiming that he hunts (ṣwd) prey for the lion (v. 39a). Job had charged that God refused to heed his "cry" (שׁוע,

---

[41]As Othmar Keel observes, these animals and the wild lands they inhabited were viewed as a threat to humans and served as symbols of the fearful beyond (cf. O. Keel, *Jahweh's Entgegnung an Ijob*, pp. 70ff.). Keel sees a connection between Yahweh's description of the animal kingdom and the Mesopotamian iconic motif of the "Lord of the Animals," where gods are depicted as grasping wild animals in a gesture of conquest or control, bringing them under divine power.

[42]Habel, *Job*, p. 544.

šw‘) for vindication (19:7). Yahweh insists he hears even the **cry** (*šw‘*) of the fledgling **raven** (v. 41). Far from being the Opponent of his creatures, God is their great Provider (cf. Ps 104:14,21; 145:15-16). He offers his provision even for creatures that humans might look upon with fear or revulsion like the lion or the "unclean" raven. He likewise provides for all humans (cf. Matt 6:25-26).

JOB 39

1. Yahweh's First Speech and Job's Reply (38:1–40:2, continued)

Questions about the Animate World (38:39–39:30, continued)

The Mountain Goat, Hind, Wild Donkey, and Wild Ox (39:1-12)

[1]"Do you know when the mountain goats give birth? / Do you watch when the doe bears her fawn? / [2]Do you count the months till they bear? / Do you know the time they give birth? / [3]They crouch down and bring forth their young; / their labor pains are ended. / [4]Their young thrive and grow strong in the wilds; / they leave and do not return.

[5]"Who let the wild donkey go free? / Who untied his ropes? / [6]I gave him the wasteland as his home, / the salt flats as his habitat. / [7]He laughs at the commotion in the town; / he does not hear a driver's shout. / [8]He ranges the hills for his pasture / and searches for any green thing.

[9]"Will the wild ox consent to serve you? / Will he stay by your manger at night? / [10]Can you hold him to the furrow with a harness? / Will he till the valleys behind you? / [11]Will you rely on him for his great strength? / Will you leave your heavy work to him? / [12]Can you trust him to bring in your grain / and gather it to your threshing floor?

39:1-4 God's management of his wide creation is now illustrated by his care for two creatures of the steppe. The **mountain goat** (יַעֲלֵי־סָלַע, *ya'ălê-sala'*) or Nubian ibex and the **doe** (אַיֶּלֶת, *'ayyālāh*) or hind are among the shy creatures that inhabit the steep cliffs of the wilderness. Small herds of both species can still be found in the regions of Sinai, En Gedi, and Qumran. They are also mentioned together in Proverbs 5:19.[1] These elusive creatures live far away from

---

[1]Cf. also in the Ugaritic literature *RSP*, II:6, no. 2.

the towns and cities, and in Job's day their habits were not commonly known to people. They were, however, known to Yahweh. Acting
as their midwife he sees these creatures through their reproductive
process — through **months** of gestation and the moment of **birth**. All
of this happens out of the sight of humans and without their help.
Yahweh, and Yahweh alone, watches over them and cares for **their
young**. Yahweh's reference to the **time** (עֵת, *'ēth*) when **they give birth**
suggests that such events are a part of his grand design, happening
just as he had planned, though completely unbeknownst to humans.
The theme of the natural order working in ways beyond human comprehension is illustrated by the hidden "times" of creation as it is by
its hidden cosmic structures and patterns (38:4-33).

39:5-8 Next, Job is questioned about the **wild donkey**.[2] Unlike its
domesticated counterpart, the wild donkey or onager roamed the
wilderness (עֲרָבָה, *'ărābāh*) and the **salt flats** (מְלֵחָה, *məlēḥāh*)[3] avoid-
ing humans. Fleet of foot, its speed made it difficult for people even
to observe much less capture (cf. Jer 2:24). The emphasis of this
pericope is that this wild animal, created by Yahweh, is **free**.[4] These
wide-roaming beasts existed independently of those who lived in
towns. They could not be domesticated and made useful for human
beings. There was no **driver** to **shout** at them or put **ropes** on them,
yet they had a rightful place in God's world. By God's providence
they were able to flourish in barren places where they had to **search**
for **any green thing** to eat. They had an existence that was of no benefit to any human, yet they had a legitimate place in God's world.
There is much in God's world that does not revolve around Job or
any other man. By reminding Job of this, Yahweh invites him to consider that God's providence is about far more than seeing to it that
everybody or everything gets what it "deserves."

39:9-12 Continuing the theme of beasts that no man can tame,
Yahweh questions Job about the **wild ox** (רֵים, *rêm*) or water buffalo.[5]

---

[2]The text of v. 5 uses two separate terms to describe the same animal, פֶּרֶא
(*pere'*), and its Aramaic equivalent, עָרוֹד (*'ārôd*; cf. P. Humbert, "En marge
du dictionnaire hébraïque," *ZAW* 62 (1949–50): 202-206; cf. also G.S.
Cansdale, *Animals of Bible Lands* (Exeter: Paternoster, 1970), pp. 94-95.

[3]These terms may be referring specifically to the region of the Dead Sea.

[4]The expression "go free" (שִׁלַּח חָפְשִׁי, *šillah ḥopšî*) is used in Deuteronomy
to describe the release of a slave (Deut 15:13,18).

[5]Cf. Cansdale, *Animals of Bible Lands*, p. 83.

These powerful creatures were legendary in ancient times and were even hunted by kings (cf. Num 23:22; 24:8; Ps 22:22[21]).[6] As suggested by Yahweh's opening question, **Will the wild ox consent to serve you?** these beasts defied any attempt to domesticate them. They would never submit to a **harness** or **till** the soil. Nor would they ever become dependent upon a **manger** (feeding trough) for their sustenance. Yahweh's challenge for Job to tame these animals anticipates his later challenge for Job to rein in Behemoth and Leviathan (cf. 40:1ff). In the vast creation exist creatures and forces that humans cannot comprehend or control. They serve no utilitarian purpose for humankind and can even pose a threat to them. Yet God made them and gave them a legitimate place in his world. God's world is far more complex than the one-dimensional place suggested by Job's simple model of divine justice.

The Ostrich, Horse, and Birds of Prey (39:13-30)

[13]**"The wings of the ostrich flap joyfully, / but they cannot compare with the / pinions and feathers of the stork. /** [14]**She lays her eggs on the ground / and lets them warm in the sand, /** [15]**unmindful that a foot may crush them, / that some wild animal may trample them. /** [16]**She treats her young harshly, as if they were not hers; / she cares not that her labor was in vain, /** [17]**for God did not endow her with wisdom / or give her a share of good sense. /** [18]**Yet when she spreads her feathers to run, / she laughs at the horse and rider.**

[19]**"Do you give the horse his strength / or clothe his neck with a flowing mane? /** [20]**Do you make him leap like a locust, / striking terror with his proud snorting? /** [21]**He paws fiercely, rejoicing in his strength, / and charges into the fray. /** [22]**He laughs at fear, afraid of nothing; / he does not shy away from the sword. /** [23]**The quiver rattles against his side, / along with the flashing spear and lance. /** [24]**In frenzied excitement he eats up the ground; / he cannot stand**

---

[6]The Egyptian Pharaoh Thutmose III bragged that he once killed seventy-five such creatures. In the Baal Epic, the god is described as hunting the wild ox in the marshes of Shamak, located north of the Sea of Galilee (*UT* 76:II:9,12); cf. also, A.H. Godbey, "The Unicorn in the Old Testament," *AJSL* 56 (1939): 256-296. There is evidence that these creatures populated the marshes of the Jordan well into the second millennium B.C.

still when the trumpet sounds. / ²⁵At the blast of the trumpet he snorts, 'Aha!' / He catches the scent of battle from afar, / the shout of commanders and the battle cry.

²⁶"Does the hawk take flight by your wisdom / and spread his wings toward the south? / ²⁷Does the eagle soar at your command / and build his nest on high? / ²⁸He dwells on a cliff and stays there at night; / a rocky crag is his stronghold. / ²⁹From there he seeks out his food; / his eyes detect it from afar. / ³⁰His young ones feast on blood, / and where the slain are, there is he."

39:13-18[7] In ancient times the **ostrich**[8] was considered a carica-ture of comedic stupidity.[9] Its physiology and its habits evoked laughter. A bird that can't fly, it **joyfully**[10] **flaps wings** that can never take it aloft. The mother ostrich seems to possess no protective instincts to shelter her young. She **lays** her **eggs on the ground** instead of building a nest, exposing them to various creatures that might **crush** or **trample** them. In a seemingly heartless fashion she appears to **treat her young harshly, as if they were not hers.** To the casual observer of Job's day the ostrich appeared to be lacking in **good sense** and denied **wisdom** by **God.** We now know that the ostrich is much more protective of her young than this description suggests.[11] The characterization given here is a poetic rehearsal of popular lore. It is a characterization that Yahweh will go on to rebut. Even a creature seemingly as senseless as the ostrich, reminds Yahweh, is endowed by God with the capacity to easily outrun the

---

[7]The LXX omits this section and many interpreters see it as an interpola-tion. It does not use rhetorical questions, and God is referred to in the third person (v. 17). Some scholars (Kissane, Hartley) restore the interrogative to open v. 13.

[8]רְנָנִים (rᵊnānîm, "one that cries out, shouts") is not the normal term for the ostrich (יָעֵן, yā'ēn, Lam 4.3). The term used here may be an attempt to iden-tify it with its screeching call. Gordis considers it to be a euphemism ("the singing one"). Ostriches once inhabited the wilderness regions of southern Palestine, Arabia, and northern Africa. Cf. Cransdale, *Animals*, pp. 190-192; also Driver, "Birds in the Old Testament: II. Birds in Life," pp.: 137-138; *idem*, "Birds in the Old Testament: I. Birds in Law," *PEQ* 87 (1955): 5-20; J. Doehmer, "Was ist der Sina von Hiob 39 13-18 an seiner gegenwartigen Stelle," *ZAW* 53 (1935): 289-291.

[9]Cf. discussion by Pope (*Job*, pp. 260-261).

[10]עָלַס ('ālas, "rejoice") is found only here, in 20:18 and Prov 7:18.

[11]Pope, *Job*, p. 262.

horse and rider. Job is thus exposed to yet another incongruity of the natural order, an inexplicable mystery of God's design. This invites him to consider that there might be mysteries in the moral order as well.

39:19-25 In contrast to the ostrich the **horse** (סוּס, *sûs*) was universally regarded to be a noble and majestic animal in Job's day. Its impressive appearance with its **flowing mane**[12] captured the imagination of ancient peoples. Imported from the steppes of central Asia around 2000 B.C. they played a significant role in ancient Near Eastern warfare.[13] It is that function that is emphasized in this passage. At the **scent**[14] of battle the horse boldly **charges into the fray**.[15] He **laughs at fear, afraid of nothing**. Carrying the **quiver**, the **spear**, and the **lance**,[16] he **cannot stand still when the trumpet sounds**.

Just why does Yahweh include the horse in this list of animals? All of the other animals he names are wild, mysterious, and beyond the control of humans. The horse, by contrast, is commonly domesticated and responds to human control even in the heat of battle. Some scholars have suggested that the terms used to describe the horse are meant to portray him as "godlike" and serve as a metaphor for God himself.[17] Yahweh's opening questions (**Do you give the horse his strength?** and **Do you make him leap?**), each expecting a "no" answer, could then be understood to suggest that just as the

---

[12]רַעְמָה (*ra'ămāh*, lit., "thunder, quivering") takes the meaning "mane" from the context and has the support of LXX.

[13]Because horse and chariot brought such tactical advantage to the battle, Israelite kings, called upon to trust in God rather than military might, were commanded not to accumulate them (Deut 17:16; cf. Prov 21:31; Ps 33:17). Departing from this divine standard, Solomon imported many of them and developed a corps of cavalry and chariots (1 Kgs 10:28-29).

[14]On this term cf. P. de Boer, "*wmrhwa yryh mihmh* – Job 39:25," in *Word and Meanings: Essays Presented to David Winton Thomas*, ed. by P. Ackroyd and B. Lindars (Cambridge: Cambridge University Press, 1968), pp. 29-38.

[15]נֶשֶׁק (*nešeq*), "weapon."

[16]Or perhaps "sword" (כִּידוֹן, *kîdôn*); cf. IQM vii. 2 and K. Kuhn, "Beitrage zum Verständnis der Kriegsroll von Qumran," *TLZ* 8 (1956): 29-30; G. Molin, "What Is *Kidon*?" *JSS* 1 (1956): 334-337.

[17]Cf. Habel, *Job*, p. 547. "Strength," "terror," "proud snorting," e.g., are also used of God in Job and elsewhere in the Old Testament. Observing this, Carol Newsom speculates that this constitutes a subtle attempt to describe Yahweh (*The Book of Job*, p. 247). Newsom sees the same intent to be involved in Yahweh's description of Leviathan (41:1ff).

horse is what it is without any contribution from Job, so Yahweh is likewise not in any way indebted to Job for his existence.[18]

39:26-30 Yahweh concludes his survey of the animals by questioning any role that Job had in enabling the **hawk** (נֵץ, nēṣ; perhaps the "sparrow hawk" or "falcon") to **take flight** or the **eagle** (נֶשֶׁר, nešer; perhaps the "golden eagle" or "griffon vulture") to **soar**. A third term, perhaps identifying yet another bird (כִּי, kî, not translated by the NIV), appears in verse 27 and is variously identified with the "falcon,"[19] the "vulture,"[20] the "ibis,"[21] and even the "pelican."[22] Unlike the ostrich the hawk possesses the **wisdom** (בִּינָה, bînāh; "understanding") to migrate (**to the south**, v. 26). Also unlike the ostrich the eagle is able to take wing and **build his nest on high**, far from any danger (cf. Obad 4; Jer 49:16). As Yahweh's rhetorical questions suggest, Job has nothing to do with these behaviors. Yahweh, and Yahweh alone, empowers these birds. Their capacity to insure their own survival is part of his design for the world.

As noted above, this survey of the animate world (38:39–39:30) ends as it began with a reference to the predator-prey relationship. In the world that God made and over which he presides, some animals die so others can survive. The birds of prey **feast on blood** and consume the **slain**. Such a biological system cannot be explained in terms of what is "equitable" or "fair." If, as many scholars argue, this survey of the natural order is designed as a model to explain the complexities of the moral order, then this first speech of Yahweh does address Job's intellectual problem. It suggests that not everything in God's world is designed to be "just." Such an idea flies in the face of the retributive theology of Job and the friends and constitutes one of the unique theological contributions of this great book.[23]

---

[18]It is interesting to note that Yahweh precedes his survey of each animal with different questions. "Do you know when the mountain goats give birth?" (v. 1); "Did you let the wild donkey go free?" (v. 5); "Will the wild ox serve you?" (v. 9); "Does the hawk take flight by your wisdom?" (v. 26). The common theme suggested by all of these question is that the animals exist totally independent of either Job's knowledge or his power.

[19]Qumran, Targ.

[20]LXX.

[21]G.R. Driver, "Job 39:27-28: The KY-Bird," *PEQ* 104 (1972): 64-66.

[22]J. Reider, "Etymological Studies in Biblical Hebrew," *VT* 4 (1954): 294.

[23]Cf. M. Tsevat, "The Meaning of the Book of Job," pp. 98ff.

JOB 40

1. Yahweh's First Speech and Job's Reply (38:1–40:2, continued)

Yahweh's Closing Challenge (40:1-2)[1]

¹The LORD said to Job:
²"Will the one who contends with the Almighty correct him? /
Let him who accuses God answer him!"

40:1-2 Yahweh's first speech ends as it began, with a personal challenge to Job. The prose formula that introduces Yahweh's direct address to Job, **The LORD said to Job** (lit., "The LORD answered Job and said"), repeats the language of 38:1. It serves to separate the content of the first Yahweh speech from this dialogic conclusion. It is interesting to note that, though Yahweh is doing the talking, he refers to deity with the same terms that Job and the friends have been using — **Almighty** (Shaddai) and **God** (Eloah).[2] This is yet another indicator of the patriarchal setting of the story, in a time when humans had yet to learn of God's personal name (cf. Exod 6:3).

The precise meaning of Yahweh's closing challenge in verse 2 is disputed. Commentators generally agree that the opening expression (v. 2a) is intended to identify Job as **one who contends** (MT רֹב, *rōb*).[3] Habel, noting the relation of this term to רִיב (*rîb*, "lawsuit"), translates more specifically, "one with a lawsuit."[4] The final term,

---

[1]The chapter division is an unfortunate one. The LXX and Vulgate include these verses in ch. 39.

[2]These terms, along with "El" are used by Yahweh in both speeches (cf. 38:41: 39:17; 40:9,19)

[3]A hapax variously understood as an infinitive absolute (Fohrer) or an archaic spelling of the participle (Gordis).

[4]Habel, *Job*, pp. 520, 548.

rendered by NIV as **correct** (MT יִסּוֹר, *yissôr*), has been variously interpreted. Many commentators emend to יָסוּר (*yāsûr*), "he will cease, yield," and read the line, "Will the contender with Shaddai yield?"[5] Whichever is correct, it is clear that Yahweh is taking exception to Job's challenge that God is in the wrong and in need of refutation. The language of Yahweh's penetrating question has an ironic tone and represents a contrast to the initial assessment of Job in the prologue where it is said that he "did not sin by charging God with wrongdoing" (1:22). All of that, of course, has changed with Job's passionate defense of his integrity. From his opening soliloquy forward Job began to accuse God of doing wrong, not only in Job's particular life but also in his general management of his world. Yahweh's challenge of Job's presumption continues with the parallel, **Let him who accuses** [or "arraigns"; מוֹכִיחַ, *môkîaḥ*] **God answer him** (v. 2b). As he did in the opening of his first speech (cf. 38:3), Yahweh turns the tables on Job. The God whom Job has been interrogating, now becomes the interrogator. Having exposed Job's ignorance of the design by which God governs his world, Yahweh now challenges Job to defend his right to judge God.

2. Job's Reply (40:3-5)

[3]**Then Job answered the LORD:**
[4]**"I am unworthy—how can I reply to you? / I put my hand over my mouth. / [5]I spoke once, but I have no answer— / twice, but I will say no more."**

40:3-5 These verses contain the first of two responses (cf. 42:1-6) Job makes to the speeches of Yahweh. In this first response Job concedes that he is in no position to answer Yahweh. Job's opening words, **I am unworthy** (lit., "I am small, light"; קַלֹּתִי, *qallōthî*) represent an admission that he is no match for his Grand Inquisitor. When used in the Qal, this verb carries the meaning of being "humbled" or even "reviled" (cf., e.g., Gen 16:5; 1 Sam 2:30). It sometimes appears as the opposite of כָּבֹד (*kābōd*; lit., "heavy") which carries the idea of "glorious, honored, exalted," sometimes referring to the

---

[5]Cf. Pope, Dhorme, Kissane.

"essence of personality."[6] Job had hoped to retain his "honor" for all
of his days on earth (29:20). In one of his earlier complaints he
bemoaned the fact that God "has stripped me of my honor" (19:9).
But that which he once clung to and resented losing, he now volun-
tarily surrenders in response to Yahweh's challenge. No longer does
he approach God "like a prince" (31:37). Having had his ignorance
of God's grand design exposed, he confesses[7] his insignificance
before the creator and admits that he is simply not qualified to be
God's judge. Seeing he is no match for the omnipotent and omnis-
cient deity, he announces his intention to bring his disputation to a
halt. In a gesture of dumbfounded astonishment (cf. 21:5) and surrender to his superior (cf. 29:9) Job declares, **I put my hand over my
mouth . . . I will say no more**. The Job who once silenced the friends
by the power of his arguments (32:1,3) is now himself silenced by
both the appearance and the "answer" of God. Yahweh, however,
has even more to say.

3. Yahweh's Second Speech (40:6–41:34)

Though Job has announced his intention to end his dispute,
Yahweh subjects him to another round of interrogation. Whereas
the first speech challenged Job's knowledge of the grand design
behind God's creation, the second speech challenges Job's right to
question God's just management of his world. "Would you discredit my justice?" God asks. After an opening challenge for Job to
demonstrate his power to enforce justice on earth (40:6-14), Yahweh
then invites Job to rein in the fierce creatures Behemoth (40:15-24)
and Leviathan (41:1-34). The reply that Job makes to this final
speech (42:1-6) then brings this final dialogue of the book to an end.

It is important to note that just as Job's questions address his
struggle at two different levels, so also does the deity's response.
Beyond the philosophical implications of Job's dilemma, there is
also a spiritual one. In his relentless quest for an "answer" and his
impassioned defense of his "integrity" Job has arrogated himself to

---

[6]Cf. discussion by Tsevat, "Meaning of the Book of Job," p. 91.

[7]Contra Rowley and Habel who understand Job's words as a "complaint"
rather than a confession.

the level of God's judge. Acting as God's superior he has dared to impugn him and demand vindication from him. This is considered the ultimate presumption by the deity, and he will not let it stand. Though the Yahweh speeches are designed to offer an "answer" to the question of how God manages his world, they are also designed to address the irreverent spirit of the questioner. Yahweh is determined to remind Job of the ultimate reality of his grand design — God is God and man is man.[8] Whatever happens in the universe and whatever human response is made to it, God remains in control of the world he created. The Yahweh speeches reassert his sovereignty over his rebellious subject by exposing Job's ignorance and impotence before the all-knowing and all-powerful God.

This second speech of Yahweh breaks down into two basic movements: questions about Job's power to govern (40:6-14); Yahweh's power to govern Behemoth (40:15-24) and Leviathan (40:25–41:26 [41:1-34]). Continuing with a flurry of rhetorical questions, Yahweh exposes Job's powerlessness to rule over the world and then compares that impotence to God's ability to subdue even the most fearsome and powerful of creatures. The identities of Behemoth and Leviathan and the purpose behind Yahweh's depictions of them have been the subject of considerable scholarly debate. The following excursus explores the various theories that have been proposed.

---

[8]Fohrer, *Job*, p. 535, n. 6.

EXCURSUS

THE IDENTITIES OF BEHEMOTH AND LEVIATHAN
AND THE PURPOSE
OF YAHWEH'S DEPICTIONS OF THEM

1. The identities of Behemoth and Leviathan.
   a. Behemoth and Leviathan are actual creatures. Behemoth[9] has
   been identified with the red hippopotamus that once occupied
   the marshes of Egypt and Canaan.[10] The diet ("grass," 40:15) and
   habitat ("under the lotus plants," "among the reeds of the
   marsh," 40:21) assigned this creature in the text support such an
   identification. Likewise, Leviathan (לִוְיָתָן, *liwyāthān*) has been
   identified by many with the crocodile[11] which was common to the
   same marshes.[12] According to one ancient tradition, a town north
   of Caesarea bore the name Crocodilopolis.[13] There are numerous
   depictions of the pharaoh and the god Horus hunting these creatures in Egyptian iconography.[14] There was also a festival known
   as "Harpooning the Hippopotamus" in ancient Egypt.[15]

---

[9]LXX renders בְּהֵמוֹת (*bᵉhēmôth*), evidently the plural of בְּהֵמָה (*bᵉhēmāh*,
"beast," "cattle,") with θηρία (*thēria*, "animals"); cf. also Targ., Vulg,. and
Syr. transliterate the word and take it to refer to a single animal. It has been
suggested that the Hebrew term derives from the Egyptian *p'-ih-mw*, "the ox
of the water," but this has never been substantiated; cf. E. Ruprecht, "Das
Nilpferd im Hiobbuch: Beobachtungen zu der sogennanten zweiten
Gottesrede," *VT* 21 (1971): 209-231.

[10]Cf., e.g. , Andersen. Driver, however, identifies it with the crocodile; cf.
Studie orientalistici, Levi della Vida Festschrift (1956), I:234ff; cf. NEB.
Thomas Aquinas identified Behemoth as the elephant. It has also been identified with the water buffalo; cf. G. Haas, "On the Occurrence of Hippopotamus in the Iron Age of the Coastal Area of Israel (Tell Qasileh)," *BASOR*
132 (Dec. 1953): 30-34.

[11]G.R. Driver (*Book List, Society for OT Study* [London: Society for OT
Study, 1972], p. 18) identifies Leviathan as the "whale"; cf. NEB.

[12]G. Gray, "Crocodiles in Palestine," *PEQ* (1920): 167-176.

[13]Strabo (6:27).

[14]Cf. O. Keel, *Jahwehs Entgegnung an Ijob*, p. 125ff. Dhorme refers to a
painting on the ceiling of the Ramesseum depicting a hippopotamus with a
crocodile on its back. Herodotus (2:68-71) refers to the crocodile and hippopotamus together.

[15]Cf. Ruprecht, "Das Nilpferd," pp. 211-218; T. Save-Soderbergh, *On*

The term בְּהֵמוֹת (bᵉhēmôth) occurs numerous times in the Hebrew Bible without any hint of mythological overtones (cf., e.g., Ps 8:8[7]; 49:13[12]; 50:10; 73:22; Joel 1:20; 2:22; Hab 2:17).[16] In these texts bᵉhēmôth is clearly being used as the plural of בְּהֵמָה (bᵉhēmāh) and means simply "beasts, cattle." The same cannot be said, however, of the term liwyāthān. While Psalm 104:26 uses the term nondescriptively to refer to one of the sea creatures, Psalm 74:14 says this creature has several "heads," while Isaiah 27:1 calls it a "gliding, coiling serpent." These descriptive phrases seem to be referring to something other than a crocodile.[17] Those who view Behemoth and Leviathan as actual creatures understand the extraordinary descriptions of them in this speech (cf., e.g., 40:17,18; 41:18-21) to be poetic hyperbole.

b. Behemoth and Leviathan are the biblical equivalents of mythological creatures referred to frequently in Canaanite, Mesopotamian, and Egyptian religious literature.[18] In the myths these creatures personify the forces of chaos that are subdued by some god or king. In Egyptian mythology, for example, Seth assumes the form of a hippopotamus and a crocodile in his epic battle with Horus. Horus defeats Seth and thereby establishes his kingship.[19]

The Behemoth of this speech has been variously identified with "the ferocious bull of El" mentioned in the Canaanite myths and the "Bull of Heaven" referred to in the Gilgamesh Epic of Mesopotamia.[20] Perhaps originally identified with the water buffalo, this ferocious creature assumes a larger-than-life character in the ancient Near Eastern myths. It is possible that

---

Egyptian Representations of Hippopotamus Hunting as a Religious Motive (Upsala: Gleerup, 1953).

[16]In these texts, however, *behemoth* is clearly being used as a plural of *behemah* and refers simply to "animals."

[17]The Talmud (*Baba Bathra* 74b) explains that there were originally two Leviathans, one of each sex, who might have mated and taken over the universe. Therefore, God castrated the male and killed the female, preserving her in salt to be enjoyed in the great eschatological feast by the righteous.

[18]Cf. H. Gunkel, *Schöpfung und Chaos*, pp. 41ff.; Pope, *Job*, pp. 268ff.

[19]Cf. the work by V. Kubina in *Die Gottesreden im Buche Hiob* (Herder, 1979), pp. 68ff.

[20]Cf. discussion by Pope, *Job*, pp. 268-270.

the author of Job is doing the same here. Knowing that his readers were aware of this legendary creature he appropriates it as a symbol of ferocity and chaos capable of being tamed by Yahweh. The author's use of the intensive plural (*b⁹hēmôth*) instead of the singular (*b⁹hēmāh*) to describe this creature suggests that he wants the reader to think of it not just as any "beast" but as "the great Beast" or "The Beast" beyond all others.[21]

As noted above, the term Leviathan (*liwyāthān*)[22] is arguably never used in the Hebrew Bible to refer to an actual animal. Isaiah 27:1 and Psalm 74:12-14 portray Leviathan as a seven-headed, serpentine creature who is slain by God. This clearly seems to be an allusion to the seven-headed marine monster referred to in the Canaanite myths (cf. also Job 3:8; Ps 104:26).[23] It is interesting to note that in several Jewish postbiblical sources Behemoth and Leviathan are mentioned together as they are in Job. In 4 Ezra 6:49-52, for example, both beasts are designated as food for the righteous in the Messianic age. Many scholars argue that this eschatological model serves to confirm the mythological character of these creatures.[24] The fact that Behemoth and Leviathan are treated as special creations by God in several postbiblical works also lends credence to this view.[25]

Throughout the book the author of Job employs the popular myths, well known to his readers, as rhetorical models to communicate and illustrate various motifs.[26] It is probable that he is doing the same here. Such an understanding does not, however, rule out the possibility that Behemoth and Leviathan were also identifiable with actual animals. It is typical of the ancient myths to take real creatures

---

[21]Cf. Habel, *Job*, pp. 564-565.

[22]LXX renders Leviathan with "dragon" (δράκοντα, *drakonta*); the Targums render it with תַּנִּין (*tannîn*; cf. also Ezek 29:3; 32:2).

[23]Cf., e.g., Pope, *Job*, pp. 276-278. In the Canaanite Hymn to Baal (3:1:1) Baal is said to have dispatched Leviathan: "When thou smotest Leviathan the slippery serpent and madest an end of the wriggling serpent, the tyrant with seven heads" (trans. by Driver).

[24]Pope, *Job*, p. 269.

[25]Cf., e.g. Enoch 40:7-9; Apocalypse of Baruch 29:4.

[26]Cf., e.g., Sheol (7:9; 14:13; 17:13; 21:13; 24:19); Tannim (7:12); Rahab (9:13); Yam (26:12).

and then assign them a supernatural identity, often embellishing their various powers and capacities.

2. The author's purpose in employing these depictions of Behemoth and Leviathan.

    a. These creatures, real or mythic, are designed to show Job that he is no match for Yahweh. Job is invited to subdue these powerful creatures (40:24; 41:1-9,13) in a manner similar to Yahweh's earlier invitations for Job to explain the mystery behind other beasts that Yahweh had made (38:29–39:30). Whereas the first set of challenges exposed Job's ignorance of the creative order, this second set exposes his powerlessness to act in his own defense and disqualifies him as God's opponent. Whereas Job cannot rein in these dangerous creatures, Yahweh can (40:19). He alone is qualified to govern the earth.[27]

    b. These creatures, real or mythic, invite comparison with Job as a would-be opponent of God.[28] Behemoth is introduced as one "which I [Yahweh] made along with you [Job]" (40:15). Though formidable in power, Behemoth and Leviathan are yet easily tamed by God. If these ultimate examples of ferocity and power cannot stand before Yahweh, what makes Job think that he can successfully do so (41:10b)? Job is just another "proud beast" over whom God has ruling power.

    c. These creatures are intended to represent the "proud" and "wicked" men who challenge God's just rule. Yahweh's second speech to Job begins with a challenge to "bring low the proud" and "crush the wicked" as proof of his qualification to impugn divine justice (40:8-14). Behemoth and Leviathan serve as additional and even greater examples of "dangerous" creatures which threaten the safety and tranquility of humans. Job, of course, cannot control them. He is, therefore, not qualified to sit in judgment of the God who does.[29]

    d. These creatures are presented to answer Job's questions about divine justice and inform Job of the true nature of the order

---

[27]Hartley, *Job*, p. 534.

[28]J.G. Gammie, "Behemoth and Leviathan: On the Didactic and Theological Significance of Job 40:15–41:26," in *Israelite Wisdom*, ed. by J.G. Gammie et al. (Missoula, MT: Scholars Press, 1978), pp. 217-231.

[29]Keel, *Jahwehs Entgegnung an Ijob*, pp. 413-414.

by which God governs his world. Whether understood as mythic personifications of chaos and malevolence or threatening beasts, Behemoth and Leviathan are described as "creatures" made by God, having an inherent and legitimate role in creation (40:15; 41:11). The existence of such creatures demonstrates that the world God made is dynamic and multifaceted. By design it contains elements of tranquility and chaos, beneficence and malevolence, suffering and felicity. God, who created it and who alone understands how it all fits together, manages it in ways and for purposes that are beyond human comprehension. The doctrine of retributive justice cannot adequately explain the rationale behind God's rule of his world. In his world God does more than simply see that everything and everyone gets exactly what they deserve.[30]

e. These creatures invite comparison with God, himself. Powerful and unconquerable by man they serve as models of the divine. Since Job is totally incapable of gaining power over them, how could he ever expect to gain power over God? As he stands in awe of them, so should he stand in awe of Yahweh.[31]

f. Referring to mythic powers, the author employs Behemoth and Leviathan to depict Israel's historical enemies defeated by Yahweh. These texts are taken to be examples of the historization of myth by the Old Testament (cf. Isa 27:1; 30:7; 51:9-10).[32]

As argued above, the Yahweh speeches are designed to address Job's dilemma at two different levels: the intellectual and the spiritual. Not only do they attempt to answer Job's difficult questions, they also demand Job's resubmission to the sovereign creator. Both of these agendas seem to be in play in this second speech. Yahweh's depictions of his power over Behemoth and Leviathan are clearly designed to show Job that he is no match for Yahweh. This is made apparent from: 1) the opening challenge ("Do you have an arm like God's?" [40:9]); 2) the repeated questions of the speech ("Can you

---

[30]Habel, *Job*, p. 564. As such they may be the ultimate examples of Yahweh's earlier depictions of the animals (ch. 39) that Job can neither control or understand.

[31]Newsom, *The Book of Job*, pp. 250-253.

[32]Cf. Ruprecht, "Das Nilpferd," pp. 209-231.

pull in leviathan?" [41:1], "Who then is able to stand against me?" [41:10b], "Who has a claim against me that I must pay?" [41:11]); and 3) Job's final response ("I know you can do all things; no plan of yours can be thwarted." [42:2], "Therefore I despise myself and repent in dust and ashes." [42:6]). Acknowledging God's superior status, Job resubmits himself to his Maker.

But Job's final response indicates that he got something more from Yahweh's speeches than a mere dose of humility. He also received a new perspective on God's management of his world. When Job says that he "spoke of things I did not understand, things too wonderful for me to know (42:3)," he is doing more than confessing his ignorance of the created order. He is also reflecting upon new insight that he has gained concerning how God rules his world. There is a sense in which the portraits of Behemoth and Leviathan inform Job of the true nature of God's "just rule" (מִשְׁפָּט, mišpāṭ, "justice" [NIV, 40:8]) — one of the very things this speech is designed to address. Just as the animal kingdom illustrates that the "unfair" (e.g., predator and prey) and the "inexplicable" (e.g., the mysterious habits of the beasts) exist in God's world, so also these untamable, larger-than-life beasts demonstrate that the "chaotic" and the "threatening" are present in God's world as well. God's "just rule" of his creation requires far more than simply seeing to it that evil is always punished and good is always rewarded. It involves his management of a complex universe in ways that are simply beyond the power of any human to fully understand.

Questions about Job's Power to Govern (40:6-14)

⁶**Then the LORD spoke to Job out of the storm:**
⁷**"Brace yourself like a man; / I will question you, / and you shall answer me.**
⁸**"Would you discredit my justice? / Would you condemn me to justify yourself? / ⁹Do you have an arm like God's, / and can your voice thunder like his? / ¹⁰Then adorn yourself with glory and splendor, / and clothe yourself in honor and majesty. / ¹¹Unleash the fury of your wrath, / look at every proud man and bring him low, / ¹²look at every proud man and humble him, / crush the wicked where they stand. / ¹³Bury them all in the dust together; / shroud their faces in the grave. / ¹⁴Then I myself will admit to you / that your own right hand can save you.**

40:6-8 Since Job has not yet withdrawn his case against God, Yahweh continues his cross-examination of his accuser. This second divine speech begins exactly as the first (40:7=38:3). Job is challenged to **brace** himself **like a man** and **answer** Yahweh. The symmetry produced by this repetition signals the reader that this second speech serves a purpose similar to that of the first. Assuming the position of a sovereign Yahweh continues to demand answers of Job. The questions of the first speech explored Job's knowledge of the grand design behind God's creation (40:8). Job's inability to answer (cf. 40:4-5) demonstrated that he really knew very little about the divine design that he had so sharply criticized. As verse 8 indicates, this round of questions will explore a different subject. It will challenge Job's right to **discredit** (God's) **justice** (*mishpat*) or to "impugn" God's "just rule" or "just governance" of his world. In his vigorous defense of his innocence, Job has accused God of behaving unjustly toward him and, in the process, has **condemned** God in order to **justify** himself. At issue in this speech is Job's right to do this.

40:9-14 It is obvious from Yahweh's opening words that he is determined to show Job that, as a mere mortal, he is not qualified to set himself up as God's judge. He is simply not in the same class with God. With anthropomorphic language Yahweh asks Job if he has an **arm like God's** or a **voice** that can **thunder like his**. In the Old Testament the "arm" (זְרוֹעַ, *zᵉrôaʿ*) of God is often a symbol of his redemptive power and his just rule (cf., e.g., Exod 15:16; Ps

89:14[13]). He is also said to demonstrate his power to rule through his "thundering voice" (cf., e.g., Psalm 29). God's **glory** and **splendor** refer to his awe-inspiring appearance in the heavens (Ps 96:6; 104:1). Job is being challenged to match God's power and his ability to impose his will upon his world. Verses 11-13 serve to clarify the particular sphere of divine activity that Yahweh has in mind.[33] Job is being invited to demonstrate his capacity to function as the enforcer of justice upon the earth. By calling upon Job to **unleash the fury of** [his] **wrath**, Yahweh is challenging Job to judge the earth. Job had accused God of failing to do this (21:30); now God calls upon Job to do it. **Fury** (עֶבְרוֹת, *'ebrôth*) and **wrath** (אַף, *'aph*) are used elsewhere in Job to characterize the day of God's judgment upon the **wicked** (20:28; 21:30). The wicked are equated with the **proud** (גֵּאֶה, *gē'eh*) here as they were earlier by Job (cf. 21:28ff). The **dust** or the **grave** (בַּטְמוּן, *baṭṭāmûn*; lit., "hidden place") is the destiny of the wicked man, and to **bring him low** or **humble him** may be seen as a retributive response to his arrogance. The verb **crush** (הֲדֹךְ, *hādak*; lit., "trample") completes Yahweh's description of God's capacity to hold the wicked accountable. As in Isaiah (cf., e.g., 2:12,17; 5:15; 10:33) God's humbling of the proud is presented here as evidence of his power to judge.

Yahweh's challenge ends with an offer to **acknowledge** Job's power to **save** himself, if he can demonstrate his capacity to act as God and execute justice against evil humankind. In some Old Testament texts the verb **save** (יָשַׁע, *yš'*) carries the connotation of "to gain victory" over an adversary (cf., e.g., Judg 7:2; 1 Sam 25:33). This seems to be its meaning here. In his contest with God Job had sought to win his case by proving him "unjust." Yahweh is now saying that if Job can demonstrate his capacity to render perfect justice, he will acknowledge the validity of Job's claim against him and pronounce him the victor in their dispute.[34]

---

[33]The author employs almost an identical parallelism in the wording of 11b and 12a.

[34]A. Brenner ("God's Answer to Job," *VT* 31 [1981]: 129-137) argues that this passage constitutes an admission by God that he can no more dispose of the wicked than Job can. The purpose behind Yahweh's words, however, is not so much to admit his failure to execute justice as it is to invalidate the principle of retribution as the model by which God governs his world (cf. Habel, *Job*, p. 546).

God's Power over Behemoth (40:15-24)

[15]"Look at behemoth,[a] / which I made along with you / and which feeds on grass like an ox. / [16]What strength he has in his loins, / what power in the muscles of his belly! / [17]His tail[b] sways like a cedar; / the sinews of his thighs are close-knit. / [18]His bones are tubes of bronze, / his limbs like rods of iron. / [19]He ranks first among the works of God, / yet his Maker can approach him with his sword. / [20]The hills bring him their produce, / and all the wild animals play nearby. / [21]Under the lotus plants he lies, / hidden among the reeds in the marsh. / [22]The lotuses conceal him in their shadow; / the poplars by the stream surround him. / [23]When the river rages, he is not alarmed; / he is secure, though the Jordan should surge against his mouth. / [24]Can anyone capture him by the eyes,[c] / or trap him and pierce his nose?

[a]*15 Possibly the hippopotamus or the elephant   [b]17 Possibly trunk*
[c]*24 Or by a water hole*

40:15-18 The term **behemoth** (בְּהֵמוֹת, *bᵉhēmôth*) is plural, normally meaning "beasts, cattle" (35:11; Joel 1:20; Ps 8:8[7]). Here it is used as an intensive and carries the meaning of "the super beast," "the great beast."[35] The phrase **which I made along with you**[36] is important for at least two reasons. First, it denies Behemoth the status of deity. Though Behemoth is probably referring to the famous beast of the ancient myths, Yahweh's words limit it to the status of a mere "creature."[37] It is not a god and remains subordinate to Yahweh. Second, this phrase connects Behemoth to Job. In terms of their origin, at least, these words put Job and Behemoth in the same class.[38] Perhaps Yahweh is inviting Job to compare himself to Behemoth as another

---

[35]J. Gammie ("Behemoth and Leviathan, pp. 217-231) argues that Behemoth is also found in 12:7 as the beast who could instruct the friends in God's ways.

[36]J.V. Kinnier Wilson ("A Return to the Problem of Behemoth and Leviathan," *VT* 25 [1975]: 1-14) translates this phrase "which I have made with your help," and suggests that Behemoth's creation was a joint project by God and Job. But such a rendering makes no sense in this context. LXX omits this phrase altogether.

[37]According to the Apocalypse of Baruch (29:4) both Behemoth and Leviathan were created on the fifth day.

[38]According to Gen 1:24ff, the *behemah*, "land animal" was made along with man on the sixth day.

proud "beast" made by Yahweh and answerable to him.[39] If the mighty creature Behemoth can be "captured" (v. 24) or "subjugated" (with a "sword," v. 19) by Yahweh, what chance does Job think he has in opposing God? The author's expanded description of Behemoth in verses 16-18 employs poetic hyperbole to make this creature seem larger than life. Some interpreters have taken the references to Behemoth's **loins, thigh,** and **tail**[40] to be descriptions of his virility.[41] The dominant theme of the poet's description, however, is the animal's legendary **strength.** The characterization of Behemoth's **limbs** as **rods of iron** may be a play on the mythological description of the Egyptian god Seth, symbolized by the hippopotamus and a further indicator of the mythological background of this depiction.[42]

40:19 The primary emphasis of this continuing description of Behemoth is on the power of God to subdue this powerful beast. The characterization of Behemoth as the **first among the works of God** has received a number of interpretations. A comparison with Proverbs 8:22 suggests that the term **first** (רֵאשִׁית, *rē'šîth*) may refer to the primary position which Behemoth held in the actual process of creation. So understood, this phrase places Behemoth in the primordial realm reaching back to the very beginnings of creation.[43] While "wisdom" is the first principle which God employs in the process of creation (28:24-27; Prov 8:22), Behemoth is the first of his created **works.** If, as some have suggested, the figure of Behemoth is drawn from the mythic creature who personifies chaos, this passage could be echoing the ancient Near Eastern motif of creation as the conquest of chaos and the subsequent fashioning of order.[44] The term **first,** however, can also mean the "greatest" or the "preeminent"[45] of God's works. So understood, Behemoth stands atop the animal world and is being portrayed as the beast *par excellence.* He completes the list of the animals which Job can neither comprehend nor control (cf. Job 39).

---

[39]Cf. Terrien.

[40]In later Hebrew זָנָב (*zānāb*) is used to refer to male genitals.

[41]Cf., e.g., Pope, Terrien.

[42]B. Lang, "Job 40:18 and the 'Bones of Seth,'" *VT* 30 (1980): 360-361.

[43]Cf. B. Vawter, "Prov 8:22: Wisdom and Creation," *JBL* 99 (1980): 205-216; Habel, "Symbolism of Wisdom," pp. 154-156.

[44]Kubina (*Hiob*, p. 89) equates Behemoth with Yam the Canaanite god of chaos, who bears the title "the darling of El."

[45]Cf. Gordis.

As with the characterization of Behemoth as a creature "made (like Job) by God" (40:15), so also now does the identification of God as its **Maker** limit Behemoth's status to that of a mere "creature." Whether he is regarded as an actual animal or the larger-than-life personification of chaos spoken of in the ancient Near Eastern myths, Behemoth owes his existence to God and is subordinate to God. This, it would seem, is the purpose behind Yahweh's insistence that he **can approach** this powerful creature **with his sword**. Though such language could suggest Yahweh's power to slay this formidable beast, it is more likely meant to speak of Yahweh's power to subordinate Behemoth and keep him under control.[46]

The designation of Behemoth as "creature" made by Yahweh may suggest another equally important idea. In this speech Yahweh insists that Behemoth, fierce and untamable by any man, is present in the world as a result of God's creative activity. The very existence of such a beast should open Job's mind to the prospect that God's management of his world is far more complicated than merely rewarding or punishing human behavior. If, as many have argued, Behemoth symbolizes the chaotic forces of the earth, then this text is suggesting that even chaos itself has a place in the created order and is part of God's design. It is one of many "evils" (like the "wicked," 40:12) that the sovereign God must subordinate in his governance of his world. Job, who has repeatedly impugned God's just rule, is now being shown the complex and multifaceted nature of what that rule entails. It involves far more than balancing sin with suffering. It also involves balancing the cosmic forces of chaos and order — holding in check dangerous, threatening[47] creatures and forces that threaten the peace and harmony of the world.[48] Such a balancing act Job is not capable of performing. He is, therefore, not qualified to "judge" God.

40:20-23 Yahweh's description of Behemoth now celebrates his status as the "king of beasts" before whom the rest of nature bows. The **hills bring him their produce**[49] like tribute to a king.[50] The **wild**

---

[46]Cf. Hartley, Habel.

[47]The threatening nature of Leviathan is specifically mentioned in 41:25.

[48]Cf. Brenner, "God's Answer to Job," pp. 129-137.

[49]בּוּל (*bûl*), understood by most interpreters as a shortened form of יְבוּל (*yᵊbûl*), "produce, tribute" (Gordis).

[50]Kubina (*Hiob*, p. 89) compares this line to the accounts of tribute being

animals play nearby[51] like subjects under the protective care of their sovereign. His habitat is framed by **poplars** and the **lotuses** provide him shade. The marshes of Egypt and Palestine were once the habitat of both the water buffalo and the hippopotamus.[52] Such language also resembles that of Ezekiel 29:3 where the "streams" of Egypt are described as the habitat of the "great monster" (Tannin). As king of the water, the **rage**[53] of the **river** and the **surge** of the **Jordan**[54] does not **alarm** him. If, as many argue, this language is echoing themes from the Canaanite myths of Yam, then Behemoth is being characterized as the lord of the chaotic waters.

40:24 As the opening verse of this section (v. 15) portrays Behemoth as a "creature" of Yahweh, this closing verse portrays him as a "captive" of Yahweh.[55] While the question **Can anyone capture him . . . or trap him . . . ?** exposes Job's (or any human's) inability to subdue Behemoth, it also suggests that Yahweh clearly can. The image here is one of Yahweh leading Behemoth around by the nose, like a monstrous pet.[56] Like the kings of the ancient near East, Yahweh is being portrayed as "Lord of the animals" whose ability to subdue wild animals demonstrates his greatness and power.[57]

It is also possible to see in this depiction of Yahweh's conquest of Behemoth a veiled reference to Yahweh's subjugation of Job. Yahweh's control of Behemoth's nose and mouth may be intended to imply his intent to control Job's. Job like a "proud beast" has repeatedly raged against God. Yahweh will now "rein him in" just as he reins in Behemoth and Leviathan.[58]

---

brought to the sea god Yam, the chaos monster of the Canaanite myths (cf., Baal III.B.35-36).

[51]Gordis translates this line "the beasts of the hills sing for him."

[52]Cf. Couroyer, "Qui est Béhémoth: Job 40:15-24?" *RB* 82 (1975): 418-443.

[53]עשׁק (*šq*, "oppress") here means to "act violently, rage" (Dhorme).

[54]The term "Jordan" can refer to any violent river. Here it probably describes the Nile at flood stage (cf. Rowley, Tur-Sinai, Dhorme).

[55]Habel.

[56]Ruprecht, "Das Nilpferd," pp. 209-213, sees in this language reference to the way the hippopotamus was hunted by piercing its nose forcing it to breathe through its open mouth down which a spear could be thrown.

[57]Keel, *Yahwehs Entgegnung*, p. 71.

[58]Gammie, "Behemoth and Leviathan," p. 219.

JOB 41

3. Yahweh's Second Speech (40:6–41:34, continued)

In this final portion of his speech, Yahweh confronts Job with
Leviathan, yet another powerful creature that is beyond the capacity of humans to subdue or control. As noted above the identity of
Leviathan is debated. While some scholars identify him as the crocodile, most interpreters regard him as the legendary serpentine
monster of the deep that personifies the chaotic forces of evil.
Mentioned often in the ancient Near Eastern myths,[1] the Old Testament makes occasional reference to Leviathan as well. He is the
seven-headed monster of the deep which Yahweh slew at creation
(Ps 74:14).[2] He is the "gliding serpent" that Yahweh will again defeat
in his final battle against evil (Isa 27:1). His appearance here constitutes another biblical use of popular ancient myth as a vehicle for
spiritual instruction. Yahweh confronts Job with Leviathan as a
potential opponent for whom Job is no match. He then asks him
what possible hope he has for successfully challenging the beast's
Creator. This final part of Yahweh's second speech breaks down
into the following components: 1) a challenge to subdue Leviathan
(41:1-11); 2) a portrait of the unconquerable Leviathan (41:12-34).

---

[1] In Canaanite literature he is known as Lotan, a seven-headed creature
slain by Baal (*UF* 67:I:1-3).

[2] Some interpreters see this portion of Psalm 74 as a description of the
exodus and the parting of the Red Sea with Leviathan serving as a symbol
of the defeated Pharaoh; cf. discussion and literature in M. Tate, *Psalms
51–100* (Dallas: Word Books, 1990), pp. 250-252. Of particular interest in
this discussion is a line in "The Hymn of Victory of Thutmose III" which
depicts the king's majesty as that of a "crocodile, the lord and fear of the
water, who cannot be approached" (*ANET*, p. 374).

A Challenge to Subdue Leviathan (41:1-11)

[1]"Can you pull in the leviathan[a] with a fishhook / or tie down his tongue with a rope? / [2]Can you put a cord through his nose / or pierce his jaw with a hook? / [3]Will he keep begging you for mercy? / Will he speak to you with gentle words? / [4]Will he make an agreement with you / for you to take him as your slave for life? / [5]Can you make a pet of him like a bird / or put him on a leash for your girls? / [6]Will traders barter for him? / Will they divide him up among the merchants? / [7]Can you fill his hide with harpoons / or his head with fishing spears? / [8]If you lay a hand on him, / you will remember the struggle and never do it again! / [9]Any hope of subduing him is false; / the mere sight of him is overpowering. / [10]No one is fierce enough to rouse him. / Who then is able to stand against me? / [11]Who has a claim against me that I must pay? / Everything under heaven belongs to me.

[a]1 Possibly the crocodile

This section on Leviathan is connected to what precedes it through the common theme of human inability to subdue powerful and imposing creatures (cp. 40:24). By speaking of Behemoth and Leviathan, however, Yahweh takes this theme to a new level. These creatures (real or mythic) are wild beasts *par excellence*. They stand as the most extreme examples of the fierce and uncontrollable "beasts" that no human, especially Job, can tame. Verses 1-8 repeat the pattern of Yahweh's first speech by asking a series of questions designed to challenge Job's ability to overpower one of God's creatures (cf. 39:9-12). In this second speech, however, Yahweh supplies the answer to his own questions by clearly stating, "any hope of (Job's) subduing him (Leviathan) is false" (v. 9). This fact exposed, Job is then invited to consider how useless it is for him to confront the Maker of such a creature (vv. 10-11).[3]

41:1-7 The kings of the ancient Near East are sometimes depicted capturing wild beasts like the hippopotamus and the crocodile.[4]

---

[3]There is a difference in the numbering of the verses between the Hebrew Bible and the English versions beginning here (Heb. 40:25–41:26 = Eng. 41:1-34). We will refer to the English numbering as in the text quoted above the section.

[4]Cf. Keel, "Zwei kleine Beiträge zum Verständnis der Gottesreden im

The **fishhook** and the **rope** were regularly used in this process as were **harpoons** and **fishing spears**.[5] The capture of Leviathan, the mythic monster of chaos, however, is beyond the power of any human to subdue. Any attempt to capture him would not be met with **gentle words** or **begging for mercy** by this formidable beast. In verses 4-6, Yahweh employs three metaphors to show how absurd it would be for Job to attempt to tame Leviathan. First, he challenges Job to make him a **slave for life** like ancient conquerors often did of their defeated foe.[6] Next Yahweh invites Job to turn Leviathan into a **pet** that could be **put on a leash** for children to lead around like a tamed **bird**. The final metaphor, drawn from the realm of commerce, asks Job if he can reduce Leviathan to a commodity that can be **bartered** for by the **merchants**.

41:8-11 In verses 8-9 Yahweh provides his own answer to the questions he has put to Job about his power to overcome Leviathan. If Job even attempted to **lay a hand on him**, he would definitely **remember the struggle** and **never do it again!** Such a struggle would only invite disaster. **Any hope of subduing him is false.** Further, **the mere sight of him is overpowering**.[7] This portion of the second Yahweh speech has connections to earlier parts of the book. The term "sight" (or "appearance"; מַרְאֶה, *mar'eh*) was used of the supernatural form that appeared to Eliphaz in his dream (4:16). When

---

Buch Ijob," pp. 223-225. In the ancient Near Eastern world kings were sometimes depicted as "Lord of the Animals." The royal hunt symbolized the king's ability to protect the land from hostile forces. In view of Job's bold intent to approach God "like a prince" (31:37) Yahweh's invitation for Job to subdue Behemoth and Leviathan like a king hunting ferocious prey constitutes an appropriate challenge to Job's presumptuous claims. By exposing Job's inability to capture these great beasts he disqualifies Job as a challenger of the God who can.

[5]Ibid., pp. 134-135, 142; cf. also Pope's citation of Herodotus II.70. According to Kubina (*Hiob*, p. 93) the harpoon and spear are the weapons which Horus used in his battle with Seth; cf. *ANET*, p. 16.

[6]Cf. 1 Sam 27:12 and David's attempt to serve Achish.

[7]This final line of v. 9 has received a wide variety of translations. NIV has the support of Kissane. With a slight revocalization of the Hebrew Gunkel reads, "his appearance casts down even a god [אֵל, *'ēl*]." Similarly Cheyne ("The Text of Job," *JQR* 9 [1896–97]: 579) reads "even divine beings the fear of him brings low." Pope, who preserves the interrogative particle in MT, renders, "Were not the gods cast down at the sight of him?"

Yahweh adds that **no one is fierce enough to rouse** (עוּר, *'wr*) Leviathan, he seems to be responding directly to Job's call for Leviathan to be "roused" (*'wr*) in his opening curse (3:8).

With the challenge **Who then is able to stand against me?** (10b) the point of Yahweh's second speech becomes clear. If Job has no hope of successfully competing against Leviathan, what possible hope does he have of successfully competing against Yahweh? This language, too, has important connections to earlier parts of the book and reminds the reader of just what it is that Job is seeking from God. The expression "to stand before, against" (hithpael of יצב, *yṣb*) is a legal idiom designating the act of "presenting a case" (cf. 33:5). The expression "against me" (lit., "before my face"; לְפָנַי, *l⁰phānay*) likewise remembers Job's desire to argue his case against God directly "to his face" (23:4). Yahweh is thus responding to Job's demand to personally confront God in court.[8] This is also the idea behind the parallel question, **Who has a claim against me that I must pay?** (11a).[9] Job's attempt to "make a claim" (lit., "confront"; הִקְדִּים, *hiqdîm*) against God in order to hold him accountable or force him to concede is at the heart of Yahweh's problem with Job. This is something which no mere mortal has the right or the power to do. Job is simply not qualified to require anything of God because God owes no man. Indeed, **everything under heaven belongs to** him. No match for God, Job's presumptuous attempt to defeat Yahweh in court would be even more futile than trying to subdue Leviathan.[10]

A Portrait of the Formidable Leviathan (41:12-34[4-26])

[12]**"I will not fail to speak of his limbs, / his strength and his graceful form. / [13]Who can strip off his outer coat? / Who would approach him with a bridle? / [14]Who dares open the doors of his**

---

[8]Habel, *Job*, pp. 570-571.

[9]Lit., "Who confronts me that I must requite?" LXX renders this line, "Who will confront me and remain (survive, be safe)?" Some interpreters read third person ("Who will confront him") instead of first person here and take this as a reference to Leviathan.

[10]J. Gammie ("Behemoth and Leviathan," pp. 217-231) suggests that this passage invites a comparison between Leviathan and Job. He argues that Yahweh's question, "Who then is able to stand against me?" expects the answer: "neither Leviathan nor Job."

mouth, / ringed about with fearsome teeth? / [15]His back has[a] rows of shields / tightly sealed together; / [16]each is so close to the next / that no air can pass between. / [17]They are joined fast to one another; / they cling together and cannot be parted. / [18]His snorting throws out flashes of light; / his eyes are like the rays of dawn. / [19]Firebrands stream from his mouth; / sparks of fire shoot out. / [20]Smoke pours from his nostrils / as from a boiling pot over a fire of reeds. / [21]His breath sets coals ablaze, / and flames dart from his mouth. / [22]Strength resides in his neck; / dismay goes before him. / [23]The folds of his flesh are tightly joined; / they are firm and immovable. / [24]His chest is hard as rock, / hard as a lower millstone. / [25]When he rises up, the mighty are terrified; / they retreat from his thrashing. / [26]The sword that reaches him has no effect, / nor does the spear or the dart or the javelin. / [27]Iron he treats like straw / and bronze like rotten wood. / [28]Arrows do not make him flee; / slingstones are like chaff to him. / [29]A club seems to him but a piece of straw; / he laughs at the rattling of the lance. / [30]His undersides are jagged potsherds, / leaving a trail in the mud like a threshing sledge. / [31]He makes the depths churn like a boiling caldron / and stirs up the sea like a pot of ointment. / [32]Behind him he leaves a glistening wake; / one would think the deep had white hair. / [33]Nothing on earth is his equal— / a creature without fear. / [34]He looks down on all that are haughty; / he is king over all that are proud."

[a]15 Or *His pride is his*

This closing portion of the second Yahweh speech has been variously understood. Many interpreters regard it as either misplaced[11] or unoriginal, a later addition to the book.[12] More recent interpretations of the Yahweh speeches have argued for their literary unity.[13] Assuming this section is original, the reader is yet challenged to explain exactly why Yahweh goes on to offer such an extensive

---

[11]Cf., e.g., B.D. Eerdmans, *Studies in Job* (Leiden: Burgersdijk & Niermans, 1939), pp. 27ff. Eerdmans assigned only 41:1-9 to Leviathan and considered the remainder of the chapter to be a misplaced description of Behemoth.

[12]Cf., e.g., G. Fohrer, "Zur Vorgeschichte und Komposition des Buches Hiob," pp. 249-267; Westermann, *Structure of the Book of Job*, pp. 105-123.

[13]Cf., e.g., V. Kubina, *Die Gottesreden im Buche Hiob*; Habel, *Job*, pp. 561-562; Hartley, *Job*, pp. 31-33.

description of Leviathan to end his final speech to Job. An answer may be found in the connection that Yahweh's closing speech has with Job's opening speech. In his opening soliloquy Job uttered a curse against the day of his birth (3:3-10) desiring to cancel it and thus "undo" his existence. As part of that curse Job called upon "those who are ready to rouse Leviathan" to return the night of his birth to the oblivion of chaos (3:8; cf. pp. 86-87). Having distinct mythological backgrounds, the expression "to rouse Leviathan" means to summon the supernatural forces of chaos with all their havoc and ruin. This final portion of the Yahweh speeches responds to Job's bold and reckless words in two important ways. First, by demonstrating that Job is no match for Leviathan, he exposes the presumption of Job's curse. As a mere mortal, Job has no power to summon Leviathan, to invoke the so-called "supernatural forces of chaos" for his own purposes ("no one is fierce enough to rouse him," v. 10a). Any such encounter with Leviathan would have only disastrous consequences for Job (vv. 8,25-26). Job's presumptuous effort to summon Leviathan anticipates the even greater presumption of his attempt to summon God (vv. 10b,11). But this second speech of Yahweh exposes yet another and more serious fallacy in Job's opening speech. Job's attempt to summon Leviathan was the equivalent of inviting some supernatural force to undo what God had done (= grant Job his very existence, 3:3-10). In this portion of his speech Yahweh counters this assault on his sovereignty by denying to Leviathan the status of a god. He acknowledges that chaos, like a fierce beast, is indeed formidable and capable of overpowering any human attempt to control it. But, he insists, it is not supernatural. It is merely a "creature" (41:33), a natural force in God's world. Not a god, it has been "made" by God (like Behemoth, 40:15) and, like "everything (else) under heaven, belongs to" God (41:11). Leviathan, like Job, a mere creature and no more, has no power to "thwart" any "plan" of God. (cf. 42:2).

41:12 The Hebrew of this verse is extremely difficult and the subject of much debate. The rendering of NIV is the generally accepted one and has the support of the major English versions (e.g., KJV, RSV). It announces Yahweh's intent to **not fail to speak** about Leviathan's **limbs**, **strength**, and **form**. As such it serves to introduce the prolonged description of Leviathan's prowess which follows (vv. 13-34).

There are, however, other ways to render MT.[14] Of special note is the translation of Norman Habel:

> Did I not silence his [Leviathan's] boasting,
>   His mighty word and persuasive case?[15]

This radically different translation, which the Hebrew does permit, understands this verse to be a declaration of Yahweh's victory over Leviathan. Though such a victory is implicit in the preceding interrogation of Job (41:1-7) and echoes the thought of Yahweh's claim to approach Behemoth "with his sword" (40:19), only this verse (so translated) explicitly affirms Yahweh's defeat of Leviathan. As such it also has potential connections with other portions of the book. Of special importance is the final term of the verse עֵרֶךְ ('erek; "case," **form** [NIV]) which Habel connects with the root עָרַךְ ('rk), "prepare a case" (cf. 13:18; 23:4; 32:14). So understood, this verse invites a comparison between Leviathan and Job as litigants against God. Yahweh's silencing of Leviathan's claims anticipates his silencing of Job's claim (cf. 40:4).[16]

As it appears in the MT, however, this verse is actually not presented as a question[17] but a declarative statement. It describes either something Yahweh has not done or will not do. As such it could also be read:

> I will not silence/have not silenced his boasting,
>   his proud talk and his bold assertions/array.[18]

This more literal translation confronts the reader with an entirely different idea. Leviathan the violent, Leviathan the untamable, Leviathan the ultimate symbol of all that is chaotic in the world has not been and will not be censured by God. Like Behemoth (40:15)

---

[14]Cf., e.g., Jewish Study Bible: "I will not be silent concerning him or the praise of his martial exploits." JPS: "Would I keep silence concerning his boastings, or his proud talk, or his fair array of words?" Moffatt: "No hunter would survive to boast and brag of his exploits and his fine arms." Cf. discussion in Pope, *Job*, p. 283.

[15]Habel, *Job*, p. 551; cf. p. 555. Habel follows Pope, Tur-Sinai.

[16]Ibid., p. 571. Habel identifies Leviathan's claim or "case" with Yam's (the sea god) claim to kingship in the Canaanite myths (cf. Baal III*.B).

[17]Declarative statements can be understood as questions in Hebrew, depending upon the context.

[18]For the meaning of this final expression (וְחִן עֶרְכּוֹ, *weḥin 'erko*) cf. Tur-Sinai and the discussion by Pope, *Job*, p. 283.

he is a creature made by God (41:33) and as such has a legitimate place in the universe. Rather than judging Leviathan and the threat he poses to humans, Yahweh goes on to celebrate his unconquerable prowess and declare him "king over all that are proud" (v. 34). In so doing, Yahweh addresses Job's great dilemma on two important levels. On an intellectual level Job is confronted by a creature whose very existence shatters his simplistic doctrine of retribution. Leviathan's exalted position on earth is simply not explainable on the basis of what is "just" and "fair." In the world that God rules the competing forces of good and evil are allowed to coexist. Opposing forces of order and chaos, happiness and trouble, health and sickness, wealth and poverty, life and death interplay in ways that are unexplainable and known only by God. His management of his world involves far more than merely seeing to it that justice is enforced. On a spiritual level Leviathan is employed by Yahweh to address the pride that has pitted Job against his Maker. He confronts Job with a creature far superior to him and over whom he has no hope of prevailing. This, in turn, serves as a model for Job's encounter with an even greater Creator over whom he has even less hope of prevailing — a Sovereign before whom he can only bow and "repent in dust and ashes" (42:6).

41:13-17 The prolonged description of Leviathan, which begins here and continues to the end of the chapter, focuses on the invincibility of Leviathan. With this extended portrait Yahweh is thus continuing the primary theme of the opening verses of the chapter (41:1-11). As a potential opponent Leviathan is fierce and unconquerable. His defenses are impregnable, like **rows of shields, tightly sealed together** (v. 15). He cannot be successfully attacked through his **outer coat**[19] or his **mouth**. In ancient Egypt a baited hook was often used in hunting for crocodiles, dragging them to shore so a fatal blow could be struck with a sword or spear (cf. also v. 26).[20] This creature, however, cannot be so **bridled**. Its teeth are **fearsome** (lit.,

---

[19]Or "outer coat of mail" (LXX); MT רִסְנוֹ (risnô, "halter") is undoubtedly an error of metathesis for סִרְיֹנוֹ (siryōnô; cf. BHS).

[20]Keel, ("Zwei kleine Beiträge," pp. 223-225) cites a scene from the Papyrus of Cha (1430 B.C.) that depicts a man controlling a crocodile by a rope which comes from the animal's mouth. Cf. also Herodotus 2.70 for a similar description.

"surrounded by terror"; אֵימָה, 'ēmāh, 14b). Elsewhere in the book this term is used to describe the "terror" Job anticipated experiencing should he ever have a direct encounter with God (cf. 9:32-25; 13:20-21). If Job cannot endure the "terror" of Leviathan, what hope does he have of successfully facing Yahweh?

41:18-21 Employing poetic hyperbole and echoing mythic language, Yahweh goes on to describe the fiery terror that emanates from within this larger-than-life monster. His nose **throws out flashes of light**, full of fiery breath. His **eyes** are aglow like the **rays of dawn**.[21] His **mouth** shoots out **sparks**[22] **of fire**. In the Babylonian creation myth Enumah Elish the god Marduk manifests his glory by fire coming forth from his lips.[23] Similarly, the angry Yahweh is said to display his splendor with smoke from his nostrils and fire from his mouth (Ps 18:9[8]). Those who tie this to the actual behavior of the crocodile take these verses as exaggerated descriptions of the beast expelling water vapor glistening in the rays of the sun.

41:22-24 The **neck** is often regarded to be the seat of **strength** in the Hebrew Bible (cf., e.g., Ps 75:6[5]). The word for **dismay** (דְּאָבָה, d^e'ābāh)[24] occurs only here and comes from a root that means "become faint, languish." It **goes before** (lit., "dances [דּוּץ, dûṣ] before") Leviathan in the sense of spreading terror that invites dismay. The Hebrew term translated variously as **firm** and **hard** (יָצוּק, yāṣûq) is used three times in verses 22-24 to emphasize the impenetrable nature of Leviathan's hide. Likewise the comparison to a **lower millstone** which bore the weight of the upper millstone and the pressure of grinding, speaks of how rigid and hard is Leviathan's skin.

41:25-29 The first line of verse 25 may be rendered (with NIV), **when he rises up, the mighty are terrified**. So translated it describes an aggressive move by Leviathan that causes even rulers[25] to fear.

---

[21]Hartley observes that in Egyptian hieroglyphs the eyes of the crocodile depict the red of the early morning sun (*Job*, p. 532, n. 42).

[22]כִּידוֹד (*kîdôd*) is a hapax but has an Arabic parallel that means "flame, spark."

[23]*ANET*, p. 62.

[24]F. Cross ("Ugaritic *db'at* and Hebrew Cognates," *VT* 2 [1953]: 163) emends to דבאה (*db'h*) and connects this to a Ugaritic term for "strength." LXX apparently connects this to the term אֲבַדּוֹן 'ăbaddôn, "destruction."

[25]Cf. Ezek 31:11; 32:21. Syr., Targ., Sym. all take 'ēlîm to refer to earthly leaders. Vulg. translates it as "angels."

The same line, however, may also be rendered "at his majesty (מִשֵּׂתוֹ, *missēthô*) the gods (אֵלִים, *'ēlîm*) are terrified (יָגוּר, *yāgûr*)." This translation understands the phrase to be a description of Leviathan's godlike splendor. Elsewhere in the book this same term (*missēthô*) is employed as a noun to describe the frightening "splendor" of God himself (cf. 13:11; 31:23). Elsewhere in the Hebrew Bible the term **mighty** (*'ēlîm*) is commonly used to refer to the "gods" of the foreign peoples (cf., e.g., Exod 15:11; Isa 43:10; Ps 44:21). If that is the case here, this line could attest to a mythological background to the passage involving a depiction of Leviathan's prowess that causes other "gods" to shrink back in fear. (cf. Pope).[26] In the hands of humans, the **sword, spear, javelin, arrows,**[27] and virtually every other weapon are of no use in any contest with Leviathan. It should be remembered, however, that the Maker of Behemoth did successfully approach that mighty beast with "his sword" (40:19). The "laugh" motif, used to describe the disdain which God's creatures have toward humans, culminates in verse 29. Leviathan **laughs at the rattling of the lance.** He joins the "wild ass" (39:7), the "ostrich" (39:18), and the "horse" (39:22) as beasts which "laugh" (שָׂחַק, *śāḥaq*) at feeble humans.[28] The term connotes the idea of God's creatures at play in the world in which he has placed them (cf. Prov 8:30-31). Leviathan was created by God to "frolic" in the "sea" (Ps 104:26).

41:29-32 These verses focus on the impact that Leviathan has upon the earth or, more specifically, the **sea.** By identifying Leviathan with the **depths** (תְּהוֹם, *tᵊhôm*; cf. also 28:14; 38:16,30) and the **sea** (יָם, *yām*; cf. also 7:12) he locates this legendary creature in the same primordial abyss (cf. Gen 1:2) assigned him by the Canaanite myths, rather than the rivers and marshes which formed the normal habitat of crocodiles. The Psalmists also assign Leviathan to the "sea" (Ps 74:13-14; 104:25-26). The **glistening wake** that trails Leviathan produces a froth that gives the sea an appearance like an old man with **white hair.** Elsewhere in Job and the Old Testament, the breaking "waves" being described here are a symbol of tumult and chaos (cf. Job 38:12; Ps 65:7; Jer 51:55; Ezek 26:3). This denizen of

---

[26]For other translational challenges presented by this verse cf. Rowley, *Job*, p. 263.

[27]Lit., "sons of his quiver"; cf. Lam 3:13.

[28]Habel, *Job*, p. 573.

the deep is thus being portrayed as the source of these threatening forces of chaos.

41:33-34 This final summation of Leviathan's prowess is important for understanding just why it is that Yahweh chooses to end his response to Job in the way that he does. Verse 33 completes the portrait of Leviathan as a beast without **equal** that **fears** no one. Job, confronted by the fact that as he has no hope of subduing Leviathan, must realize that he has even less hope of winning a confrontation with the God who made him. But this text does more than summarize the exalted status of Leviathan. It also depicts his limitations. Leviathan, for all his ferocity and invincible strength, is at last nothing more than a **creature** (עָשָׂה, *'āśah*, "that which is made"), a beast of the **earth** (lit., "on dust"). In the book of Job "dust" does not mean the "land" as opposed to the "sea" or even refer to the "planet" in general. Rather it symbolizes that which is "mortal" in contrast to the God who creates all things (cf. 4:19). Leviathan, which is the **king** of all **proud** beings, and Behemoth, "the first among the works of God," (40:19) owe their existence to the creative acts of God and, like "everything else under heaven," belong to Yahweh (cf. 41:11). This concluding thought has direct implications for Job and the spiritual problem that has emerged in his defense of his integrity.[29] In a sense Job is like Leviathan, a "proud beast" who, like chaos, challenges God's sovereign rule.[30] He does to the moral order what Leviathan does to the material order. He rises up to contest the Creator and the grand design by which God governs his world. His actions threaten the peace and stability God has built into his world. He rises up against God as if he were his equal — a god unto himself. But, like Leviathan, he is no god nor does he "have an arm like God's" (40:9). A mere "creature" of the "dust" he can neither "crush the wicked" (40:12) nor subdue the malevolent forces of chaos. He is not qualified to "play God" or, for that matter, even to approach God with any "claim" (41:11).

---

[29]Notice the emphasis in the speeches of Elihu given to God's response to the "proud" (33:17; 37:24).

[30]Cf. Gammie, "Behemoth and Leviathan," pp. 220-225.

JOB 42

4. Job's Reply to Yahweh (42:1-6)

This final chapter of the book brings Job's epic struggle to a close in three separate but related events. These events, presented in reverse order of related events recorded at the beginning of the book,[1] resolve the remaining tensions of the plot. The first part of the chapter (42:1-6) ends Job's struggle against God. This tension, which began with Job's opening soliloquy (ch. 3) and continued throughout his speeches, is effectively ended with Job's reply to Yahweh. The second part of the chapter (42:7-9) resolves the tension between Job and the friends over the causes behind Job's suffering. The friends, first introduced in 2:11-13, came to offer sympathy, but they quickly assumed the role of Job's moral superiors and judged him guilty of some offense against God (Job 4ff). The verdict which Yahweh pronounces against them invalidates their false accusations and vindicates Job at their expense. Job's intercession for the friends and their acceptance of it completes their reconciliation. The final portion of the chapter (42:10-17) addresses the matter of Job's undeserved suffering that so brutally undid the bliss of his earlier existence (1:1–2:10). Yahweh's restoration of Job's fortunes by twice the amount he originally possessed not only validates Job's claim that his suffering was "undeserved," it also restores him to the original status he enjoyed as a good man blessed by God.

[1]Then Job replied to the LORD:

[2]"I know that you can do all things; / no plan of yours can be thwarted. / [3]⌐You asked,⌐ 'Who is this that obscures my counsel without knowledge?' / Surely I spoke of things I did not under-

---

[1]Cf. Habel, *Job*, pp. 34-35, on the correlation between the end of the book and its beginning.

stand, / things too wonderful for me to know. / ⁴⌐You said,⌐ 'Listen now, and I will speak; / I will question you, / and you shall answer me.' / ⁵My ears had heard of you / but now my eyes have seen you. / ⁶Therefore I despise myself / and repent in dust and ashes."

Job's final response to the speeches of Yahweh clearly constitutes the climax of the book and brings an end to Job's epic struggle against his Creator. In this brief reply Job: 1) acknowledges God's unchallengeable rule over his world, 2) admits his ignorance of God's ways, 3) personally submits to Yahweh's sovereignty over him, 4) acknowledges Yahweh's appearing, and 5) retracts his case against God.

As the two quotations of Yahweh's words by Job suggest (vv. 3,4), Job's reply is directed at the challenges Yahweh has put to Job in his two speeches (38:2; 40:7; cf. 38:3). As noted above (cf. discussion of 38:2-3), Yahweh's first speech contested Job's knowledge of the design or master plan behind God's creation and management of his world. Throughout his speeches Job impugned that design as "unjust" and even malevolent. In his reply to Yahweh Job confesses that those claims were inappropriate and made out of ignorance. Yahweh's second speech challenged the presumption of Job's attempt to interrogate God and force him to answer Job's accusations like some defendant in a court case. In his reply Job acknowledges that he is not qualified to be God's accuser and resubmits himself to his Maker.[2] Acknowledging the new insight and sense of vindication he has gained from God's appearing he recants his earlier position and resubmits himself to God.

42:1-2 Job's reply to Yahweh begins with an acknowledgement of God's sovereign will as the controlling force behind all things. When Job says **I know** (v. 2a), he literally means "I acknowledge."[3] This same expression occurs frequently in the Psalms as the initial response of the psalmist to God's promised or anticipated deliverance from some foe (cf., e.g., Ps 20:7[6]; 41:12[11]; 56:10[9]). In these contexts the expression amounts to a confession of faith in God's power to

---

[2]Explicit in the language of v. 2 and implied by his quotation of Yahweh's determination to be the interrogator of Job (v. 4).

[3]Some scholars (e.g., Habel, *Job*, p. 581) consider Job's acknowledgement of God's unalterable ways to be a grudging one and the use of *mezimma*, "scheme" (v. 2b) to be indicative of a still resentful attitude toward God by Job.

save.[4] Here, Job "confesses" his faith in God's role as the uncontestable Lord of the universe. He is the one who **can do all things**.[5] Further, that which God does cannot be contested or altered. This is what Job means by his assertion that **no plan of yours can be thwarted** (v. 2b). Job's use of the word "plan" (מְזִמָּה, *məzimmāh*) is interesting. In the Old Testament this term can refer to the "plans" of God (cf. Jer 23:20) or the plans of humans (cf. Job 21:27). In some contexts it is best translated by the word "scheme" denoting that which has evil intent (Ps 139:20) and merits divine condemnation (Prov 12:2). Such a negative connotation is not contained in the root meaning of the term, however, and must be derived from the context. In the other two texts where God is the subject of *məzimmāh* (Jer 23:20; 30:24) it describes the unalterable plans of Yahweh which come to pass without fail.[6] In these two identical verses, Jeremiah connects God's "purposes" (*məzimmāh*) with his "anger," the meaning of which will only be fully understood at a later time. This meaning fits nicely here as an expression of the new perspective that Job has only recently gained about God's ways. He, like the friends, once thought he was the object of God's anger in the form of punishment for some sin. Knowing of no sin in him that might have warranted such punishment, Job declared God "unjust." He has now learned, however, that God's management of his world involves far more than merely rewarding good and punishing evil and that there is not necessarily a direct correlation between sin and suffering. But he now understands even more than this. By declaring that none of God's purposes can be "thwarted" (בָּצַר, *bāṣar*), he is acknowledging that there is no power, heavenly or earthly, that can keep God from fulfilling his will — not Behemoth, not Leviathan, not Job. Implied in this statement is Job's acknowledgement of God's specific power over *him*. Job's second reply to Yahweh thus continues the thought of the first. As an opponent of God, Job acknowledges that he is simply "unworthy" (40:4).

---

[4]These psalms describe deliverance from a "foe" (Psalm 20; 56) or "sickness" (Psalm 41); cf. discussion by Tate, *Psalms 51–100*, pp. 60-64.

[5]Or "You prevail over all" (כֹּל תּוּכָל, *kōl tûkāl*), and perhaps preferred here in parallelism with 2b, "no plan of yours can be thwarted." For יָכֹל (*yākōl*) meaning "to prevail" cf. Ringgren, *TDOT*, 6:74.

[6]Cf. Steingrimsson, "zmm," *TDOT*, 4:88-89.

42:3-4 Job begins each of these verses with a reference to Yahweh's challenges against him (cf. 38:2,3; 40:7).[7] He thus identifies his response with specific issues raised by God. The first quotation, **Who is this that obscures my counsel without knowledge?** comes from Yahweh's first speech and contests Job's ignorant misrepresentation of the design (עֵצָה, 'ēṣāh) or master plan behind God's creation and his management of the world. Throughout his speeches Job impugned that design as unjust and even malevolent. In this his final reply, Job confesses that those claims were inappropriate and made out of ignorance. He had spoken of that which he **did not understand, things too wonderful for** him **to know.** By this latter phrase Job is acknowledging that God's ways are ultimately beyond human comprehension. This echoes one of the major themes of the book (cf. 9:10; 28:23; 37:5,14).

It has been noted by many interpreters that Job does not confess to any sin here, only to ignorance. Consequently, this verse is often interpreted as yet another protest of Job's innocence of any crime against God, either before his suffering or even after it in his defense of his integrity.[8] But do these words of Job really invite such a conclusion? Considered in the context of the Yahweh speeches that Job references and the larger context of the book, this statement could indeed by taken as an admission of wrongdoing by Job — a confession of a "sin" anticipated by the prologue and finally challenged by Yahweh. In two related statements, the prologue characterized Job's pious responses to the affliction Yahweh brought upon him by noting, that "In all this, Job did not sin by charging God with wrongdoing" (1:22), to which the author added after the second round of suffering and Job's subsequent defense of God's actions, "In all this Job did not sin in what he said" (2:10b). Clearly these repeated phrases confirm Job to be innocent, his initial response to

---

[7] These may be regarded as quotations (though not verbatim) much in the style of the rest of the book (cf. Gordis, *God and Man*, pp. 169-189, esp. pp. 185-188.

[8] This is said to be supported by Yahweh's subsequent verdict pronouncing Job "right" and the friends "wrong" in what they said about him (42:7-8). As we will argue below, that verdict is not intended to be a condemnation of all that the friends said any more than it is to be a confirmation of all that Job said. It is rather limited to one specific issue of whether or not Job is suffering because he has sinned.

be pious, and his suffering, therefore, to be "undeserved." Therein, of course, lies the plot of the book.

But these repeated affirmations of Job's innocence also clearly imply that if Job were to "accuse God with wrongdoing" such would indeed be a sin. By suggesting such a possibility these affirmations of Job's innocence also serve to prepare the reader for Job's eventual loss of innocence. In defense of his integrity Job not only impugns God's providence and "accuses" him of "wrongdoing," he virtually arrogates himself to the level of deity and dares to demand an "answer" from God. The Yahweh speeches clearly indicate that God considers these challenges against his just rule to be misleading and impious. They are misleading because they misrepresent the true order by which God governs his world. They are impious because they challenge God's sovereignty and attempt to make God answerable to humans. Yahweh's first challenge of Job (38:2), which Job specifically references in preparation for his reply (v. 3a), addresses the first of these two improprieties. It represents nothing less than a divine judgment against Job's inaccurate and misguided characterizations of his **counsel** ('ēṣāh, "design, plan"). Job's recasting of Yahweh's opening challenge thus constitutes an admission of the legitimacy of Yahweh's charge against him. His reply (v. 3b) is not only an explanation of why he so **spoke**, it is also a *mea culpa* of sorts — a personal acknowledgement of the wrongness of his words. To be sure, Job's obfuscation of God's plan for his world was made on the basis of his lack of information, not some high-handed, deliberate attempt to profane his Maker.[9]

Job's quotation of Yahweh's second challenge of Job, **I will question you and you shall answer me** (v. 4), addresses the second impropriety of Job's words against Yahweh — his impious attempt to interrogate his Maker and try to make God answerable to man. As noted above (cf. discussion of 38:3) the purpose of Yahweh's words was to turn the tables on Job and reverse the roles created by Job's demand for an "answer" from God. By reclaiming the role of interrogator and requiring Job to do the "answering," Yahweh has reclaimed his rightful place as a Sovereign confronting a subject.

---

[9]Yahweh, himself, acknowledged this in his choice of words by which to characterize Job's challenges against him ("Who is this that obscures my counsel *without knowledge?*").

Job's quotation of this divine sanction thus signals his willingness to accept this reversal of roles and announces his intent to resubmit himself to God.

42:5 At the heart of Job's quest to find vindication from God was his desire to have a personal encounter with his Maker and "see" him with his own "eyes" (cf. 13:24; 19:26-27; 23:9,15,17). With Yahweh's appearance in the storm Job's wish has been granted.[10] In these, his closing words, Job acknowledges the power of that encounter to reshape his view of God. He draws a contrast between the God his **ears had heard of** and the God **his eyes have seen**. The God Job has "heard of" was the God of theological tradition — the God of retributive justice who rules his world by always seeing to it that people get what they deserve. Job has tried to make this God a servant of his own system and require him to give account of why justice has not been properly carried out in his own life. By contrast, the God Job "has seen" will not be bound by any such system and refuses to be held accountable by any human. He rules a complex universe and the purposes behind his management of his world are simply beyond human ability to comprehend, much less challenge. When he intervenes in human life, either to act or to appear, he does so on his own terms as the uncontested sovereign of the world he has made.

It is important to note, however, that the same God who reasserts his sovereignty over Job also demonstrates his responsive nature as a God who cares about his struggling children. By choosing to appear and "answer" Job Yahweh demonstrates that he has not abandoned his troubled subject and still values him as his "servant" (cf. 42:7,8). Like Abraham Job is honored by Yahweh's appearance and his willingness to endure even the impugning of his ways (cf. Gen 18:16-33). Job had feared that a personal encounter with God would mean his undoing, his annihilation (cf., e.g., 9:16-17). In reality it has resulted in a form of "vindication" — an acknowledgment of Job's importance to God.[11] Though Job has been censured by Yahweh's speeches, he has also been redeemed.

---

[10]In some ways this theophany resembles that of Yahweh at Sinai, when he veiled himself in the "cloud" (Exodus 19).

[11]Habel argues that Yahweh's appearance represents an acknowledgement that Job is a "hero" whose "case could not be ignored" (*Job*, p. 582).

42:6 Overwhelmed by Yahweh's dramatic appearing, and humbled by Yahweh's reaffirmation of his sovereignty, Job resubmits himself to his God. Confronted by the Lord of all creation, he proclaims, **I despise**[12] **myself**[13] **and repent**[14] **in dust and ashes.**[15] Though challenged by recent interpreters,[16] NIV's rendering of Job's final words with its portrait of a contrite, submissive Job has the support of the ancient versions and most major translations.[17] In what amounts to a total "retraction" (JB) of his case against God, Job "abases" himself (Gordis) before his Maker and "recants" (Pope) his presumptuous challenges to God's just rule.

In our view Yahweh's appearance is not mandated by the legitimacy of Job's claim or the weight of his integrity but, like all other theophanies of the Old Testament, is the act of a sovereign deity who both initiates and presides over his self-disclosure.

[12]אֶמְאַס *'em'as* either a transitive verb from מאס (*m's*, "despise, loathe") with the object supplied by the context, or an intransitive verb from מסס (*mss*, "melt, sink down").

[13]The object is not present in the MT and must be supplied from the context. Habel and others argue from Job 31:13 that *m's* here means "reject" or "repudiate," and the implied object is Job's "case" against Yahweh.

[14]נָחַם (*nāḥam*) is not the usual word for "repent" (שׁוּב, *šûb*). When used, as it is here, with the preposition עַל (*'al*), it can mean "change one's mind about" as in Exod 32:12,14; Jer 18:8,10; cf. D. Patrick, "The Translation of Job XLII 6, *VT* 26 (1976): 370; H. Parunak, "A Semantic Survey of *NHM*," *Bib* 56 (1975): 512-532.

[15]Usually a symbol of mortality in Job (cf., e.g., 4:19) and connotes a sense of self-negation and worthlessness (cf. 30:19; Gen 18:27); cf. Habel, *Job*, pp. 582-583.

[16]Opinions of the meaning of Job's final words range from a description of Job's complete surrender to the will of God (Terrien) to a portrait of Job's final defiance of God (J. Curtis). For a summary of the various interpretations of this verse see Habel, *Job*, pp. 577-578. The debate swirls around the meaning of two key verbs, *'em'as* and *nāḥam*, and the supporting grammar. For a thorough discussion of the meaning of this verse cf. W. Morrow, "Consolation, Rejection, and Repentance in Job 42:6," *JBL* 105/2 (1986): 211-225; also D. Patrick, "Translation of Job XLII 6, pp. 369-371; L. Kuyper, "The Repentance of Job," *VT* 9 (1959): 94. For an alternative view cf. Curtis, "On Job's Response to Yahweh," pp. 497-511.

[17]Cf., e.g., RSV, NASB, NEB, NKJ. LXX renders: "Therefore, I despise myself and I melt, and I consider myself dirt and ashes"; 11QtgJob renders: "Therefore, I am poured out and dissolved; I am become dust and ashes." For a discussion of the translations of LXX and Targ. cf. Morrow, "Consolation, Rejection, and Repentance," pp. 211-213; de Wilde, *Hiob*, pp. 396-400.

Job's encounter with God has afforded him more than intellectual enlightenment. It has resulted in his spiritual transformation. The
overwhelming force of the sublime presence of God has scattered the
self-presence of Job[18] and reduced his complaints to insignificance.[19]
His problems have not been solved, they have been transcended.
Like Isaiah before the heavenly king (cf. Isa 6:5), Job's encounter with
God results in the dissolution of self.[20] The pride that had emerged
in his struggle for vindication melts away. Standing finally in the personal presence of the God who gave him everything, then took it all
away, Job — still deprived of his children, still sick unto death, still the
victim of undeserved suffering — bows humbly before the Lord of his
life. At the end of his bitter struggle for vindication, the Job who submits to his Maker is again the Job of the prologue. Truly pious, he
does not serve God because it pays. He serves God because he is
God. Satan's charge against him is invalidated and Yahweh's confidence in him is affirmed (cf. 1:8-11; 2:3-6).

D. YAHWEH'S VERDICT AND THE RESTORATION OF JOB
(42:7-17)

1. Yahweh's Verdict (42:7-9)

[7]After the LORD had said these things to Job, he said to Eliphaz
the Temanite, "I am angry with you and your two friends, because
you have not spoken of me what is right, as my servant Job has. [8]So
now take seven bulls and seven rams and go to my servant Job and
sacrifice a burnt offering for yourselves. My servant Job will pray
for you, and I will accept his prayer and not deal with you according to your folly. You have not spoken of me what is right, as my
servant Job has." [9]So Eliphaz the Temanite, Bildad the Shuhite and
Zophar the Naamathite did what the LORD told them; and the LORD
accepted Job's prayer.

Job's submissive response to Yahweh has ended his struggle with

---

[18]Newsom, *Job*, p. 254.
[19]Hartley, *Job*, p. 537.
[20]S. Terrien, "The Yahweh Speeches and Job's Reply," *RevExp* 68 (1971):
505.

God. But what of Job's struggle with the friends and the undeserved suffering that has deprived him of his happiness? These two remaining issues are now resolved in the narrative of the epilogue. By returning to the prosaic style of the prologue, the author invites the reader to see the connections between the close of the story and its beginning. The correlations are many. Yahweh's verdict that Job spoke the truth about him (42:7,8) echoes the earlier assertions that Job did not sin in what he said (cf. 1:22; 2:10). Job's intercession for the friends (42:9b,10a) remembers his intercession for his family (1:5). The consolation offered Job by his friends and family (42:11) corresponds to the consolation first offered him by the friends (2:11). The restoration of Job's health, wealth, and family (42:12-17) returns him to where he was before his ordeal began (1:2-3) and vindicates Job as a good man blessed by God (1:1,8; 2:3).

42:7 As the opening verse of the verdict suggests, the friends have not only been in conflict with Job, they have also been in conflict with the God whom they sought to defend. Their vigorous apologia not only did not please God, it **angered** him. It angered him because they **have not spoken of** God **what is right** (נְכוֹנָה, *nᵉkônāh*), what is "true" or consistent with the facts (cf. Deut 17:4; 1 Sam 23:23). But what exactly have they said that is so wrong, and, by contrast, what has Job said that is so right (7b,8b)? If one were to answer "everything," then this verdict would represent a total invalidation of the friends' speech and a total affirmation of Job's. But the accusations against Job's words in the Yahweh speeches (38:2; 40:2) clearly show that this cannot be true. Job has accused God of being malevolent and vindictive in what represented a serious challenge to his sovereignty (cf., e.g., 7:17-21; 10:4-14). In his speeches to Job, Yahweh pronounced these presumptions wrong and of them Job recants. Further, the friends have said some things about God that Yahweh himself affirms. He is indeed all powerful (cf., e.g., 25:2) and his ways are inscrutable (cf., e.g., 5:9; 11:7-9). The verdict pronounced here, therefore, does not invalidate everything the friends have "spoken." Neither does it endorse everything Job has said. Yahweh's words are specifically aimed at the crucial issue addressed in the debate between Job and the friends. Is Job's suffering an expression of divine justice? Is God punishing Job for some sin? This verdict, like other portions of the book, answers that question with a resounding "no!" By insisting that Job's suffering is the result of God's punishment of Job's sin the

friends have slandered Job and misrepresented the purposes of
God's rule over his life. Such a contention is not consistent with the
facts and represents a form of **folly** (נְבָלָה, *nᵊbālāh*, v. 8).[21] By contrast,
Job's denial that sin is always punished by suffering and that he is
innocent of any offense against God represents what is true and correct. As the prologue made clear, Job was not being punished for
some sin he had committed.[22] The suffering that God permitted in
his life was instead a "test" designed to explore the sincerity of his
piety (1:9-12; 2:3-6). Yahweh's verdict thus confirms two related truths
that are important for our understanding of the book. First, it confirms the innocence of Job. Neither in his speeches nor in his verdict
does Yahweh accuse Job of some sin that might have merited his suffering. Second, it invalidates the doctrine of retributive justice as the
sole moral order by which God governs the universe. The simplistic
notion that God sees to it that people always get what they deserve is
not true for Job and it is not true for the world as a whole. As the Old
Testament elsewhere teaches, in the world that God rules bad things
can happen to good people.[23]

By limiting this verdict to the specific issue raised in the debate
between Job and the friends one may also find an explanation to
one of the noted mysteries of Yahweh's verdict — the absence of any
condemnation of Elihu. Though Elihu did subscribe to some of the
views of the friends regarding the justice of God, he differed from
them in at least one important way. Like Yahweh, he never accused
Job of any sin that might have precipitated his suffering (cf. comment on 36:8-15). To the contrary, Elihu's condemnations of Job
were limited to his behavior after the fact of his suffering as he pre-
sumptuously impugned God in protest of his innocence.[24] By refusing to accuse Job of a sin that merited his suffering, Elihu is thus not

---

[21]This term implies that which is "shameful." Job used this same word to
characterize his wife after she invited him to "curse God and die" (2:9-10). As
if to anticipate this divine verdict Job had warned the friends that their disingenuous defense of God would ultimately be judged by him (cf. 13:4,7-11).

[22]By judging the friends wrong for accusing Job of sin, the verdict illustrates yet another connection between the epilogue and the prologue.

[23]For examples, Rowley notes Abel's murder by Cain and the execution of
the innocent Naboth by Ahab and Jezebel.

[24]It was this very issue that Yahweh himself addressed in his speeches to
Job.

guilty of false accusations against Job and avoids being singled out for condemnation in God's verdict.

42:8-9 As Yahweh had reversed the roles between himself and Job in the God-speeches (cf. 38:3; 40:7; cf. 42:4), he now reverses the roles between Job and the friends in his verdict. The **folly** of which the friends are guilty places them in jeopardy of judgment by God. In a twist of masterful irony the accusers become the accused. They who had offered to intercede on behalf of Job's "sins" now need intercession from him on behalf of their sins. At Yahweh's direction this intercession will involve two propitious acts: the **sacrifice** of a **burnt offering** and **prayer**. The gravity of their offense is suggested by the extent of the sacrifice. **Seven bulls and seven rams** was a very costly offering (cf. Num 23:1,14,29). Job's prayer will prove efficacious because it comes from Yahweh's **servant**[25] whom he personally **accepts** (פָּנִים נָשָׂא, *nāśā' pānîm*; lit., "lift up the face"). Yahweh's words and actions thus contribute further to the vindication of Job. By having Job intercede for the friends all doubt is removed concerning Job's innocence.

The divinely ordained intercession of Job on behalf of the friends also serves to further invalidate their erroneous doctrine of retribution. According to the friends sin against God merits, indeed requires, punishment. But with a merciful stroke of redemptive irony God offers the sinful friends forgiveness instead of judgment. Not bound by some code of retribution, God is free to graciously provide for their redemption. This invalidation of their systematic theology not only corrects their mistaken doctrine, it results in their salvation. Humbled by Yahweh's verdict, receptive to his offer of pardon, and submissive to Job's mediation, the friends **did what the LORD told them and the LORD accepted Job's prayer**. Job's intercession for the friends and their acceptance of it demonstrates that reconciliation has been fully achieved, not just between the friends and God, but also between the friends and Job.

---

[25]The term "my servant," used four times in vv. 7-8, is a special title reserved for some of the most important leaders set apart by God (cf. discussion of Job 1:8).

2. The Restoration of Job (42:10-17)[26]

[10]After Job had prayed for his friends, the LORD made him prosperous again and gave him twice as much as he had before. [11]All his brothers and sisters and everyone who had known him before came and ate with him in his house. They comforted and consoled him over all the trouble the LORD had brought upon him, and each one gave him a piece of silver[a] and a gold ring.

[12]The LORD blessed the latter part of Job's life more than the first. He had fourteen thousand sheep, six thousand camels, a thousand yoke of oxen and a thousand donkeys. [13]And he also had seven sons and three daughters. [14]The first daughter he named Jemimah, the second Keziah and third Keren-Happuch. [15]Nowhere in all the land were there found women as beautiful as Job's daughters, and their father granted them an inheritance along with their brothers.

[16]After this, Job lived a hundred and forty years; he saw his children and their children to the fourth generation. [17]And so he died, old and full of years.

[a]*11 Hebrew *him a kesitah*; a kesitah was a unit of money of unknown weight and value.*

This closing portion of the book returns Job and the reader to the point where the story began. It completes the restoration of Job. Though this passage is rejected by many critics as unoriginal and even contradictory to the message of the speeches, it is attested in all manuscript traditions of the book and is affirmed by the New Testament (Jas 5:11). The focus of scholarly debate over this text centers upon the reason for Job's restoration. Proposed answers include:

1)   because of Job's repentance.
2)   because he passed the "test."

---

[26]Many interpreters see this final passage as a later addition designed to reaffirm the justice of God. As such it is said to mar the book and undo its challenge to the theory of retribution. This view, however, misunderstands the basis of Job's restoration. Just as his initial suffering had nothing to do with any sin that he committed, this restoration has nothing to do with any piety that he displayed. The divinely ordained suffering was a "trial" of Job to see if his piety was self-interested. That trial has now ended and Job's piety has been proven true. The purpose of Job's suffering having been achieved, it is now being removed (cf. Rowley, *Job*, pp. 266-267).

3) because he forgave and prayed for his friends.

4) in order to restore him to his original state.

5) in order to vindicate Job's integrity.

6) as an act of grace by God.

Though some of these views are mutually inclusive, the answer that best fits the overall message of the book is the one given in the New Testament book of James: "As you know we consider blessed those who have persevered. You have heard of Job's perseverance and have seen what the Lord finally brought about. The Lord is full of compassion and mercy" (Jas 5:11).[27] James does not connect Job's restoration with his integrity or his pious acts but with his perseverance — his "patience in the face of suffering" (Jas 5:10). He characterizes the divine response not as "reward" but as an act of "grace," motivated by "compassion" and "mercy." Though the restoration of Job was not meritorious, it does contribute to his vindication. Coming on the heels of Yahweh's verdict (42:7-9) it confirms that Job was not the "enemy" of God.

In a sense Job's restoration also vindicates Yahweh. The close parallels between this portion of the epilogue and the prologue serve to validate the stated purpose of Yahweh's affliction of Job offered at the beginning of the story. According to the prologue, Job's suffering was not a "punishment" for some sin but a "test" of his piety (cf. 1:8-12; 2:3-6). Job has now passed that test. Though he has challenged God's justice and impugned his rule of his world, Job has never "cursed" God or abandoned his faith. Satan's accusation against Job (cf. 1:9-11; 2:4-5) has been invalidated and Yahweh's confidence in Job has been affirmed (1:8; 2:3). Having served its purpose, the "suffering" of Job is now brought to an end.[28] The portrait of God presented by the book is now complete. Though he may test the saints, he does not maliciously persecute them. He is not some malevolent tyrant who capriciously afflicts his subjects, but a righteous sovereign whose rule is exercised with moral purpose and in the best interest of his children. While he may permit the suffering of the faithful, he is at last predisposed to bless them.

---

[27]For a discussion of James's interpretation of Job, cf. Zuckerman, *Job the Silent*, pp. 13-15, 33, 176-179, n. 7, n. 105.

[28]Cf. Rowley, *Job*, pp. 266-267.

42:10-11 After (not "because") **Job had prayed for his friends, Yahweh made him prosperous again**. This latter phrase (שָׁב אֶת־שְׁבוּת, *šāb 'eth-šᵊbûth*; lit., "returned the fortunes") elsewhere in the Old Testament describes the restoration of Israel from captivity (cf., e.g., Jer 30:3,18; Ezek 16:53). Because of this some interpreters have understood the suffering of Job and his struggle to find meaning in it to be symbolic of Israel's attempt to understand their captivity. In this more general use of the expression, the author seems to be suggesting that Job is brought back to where he was at the beginning of his great ordeal.[29] When Yahweh gives him **twice as much as he had before**, he is not rewarding him for his piety but signaling his full acceptance of Job. The loss of his family and possessions had been interpreted by the friends as proof of God's judgment against him. His bountiful restoration proves this to be untrue. As such it serves to further vindicate Job. This vindication is formally acknowledged by his family and acquaintances (יֹדְעָיו, *yōdᵊʿāyw*) as they come and **eat with him in his house**. The belated **comfort** and **consolation** they offer reminds the reader of the earlier visit by Job's friends which began with sympathy and quickly turned to judgment and accusation (cf. 2:11).[30] By sharing a meal with Job and giving him **silver** (קְשִׂיטָה, *qᵊśîṭāh*)[31] and **gold** they indicate that they now believe him to be an innocent victim of **all the trouble the LORD had brought upon him** (11b). The epilogue thus affirms what the prologue first proclaimed. Job's suffering could not have happened if Yahweh had not so willed it. This repetition of Yahweh's role in Job's affliction constitutes yet another reminder of the fact that Job had not brought this suffering upon himself as deserved punishment for some sin (cf. 2:3).

42:12-15 By affirming that **Yahweh blessed the latter part of Job's life more than the first**, the author invites the reader to connect Job's restoration with his earlier trial. Though an act of grace, the doubling of Job's original possessions suggests that Yahweh too

---

[29]Cf. E. Preuschen, "Die Bedeutung von *sub sebut* im Alten Testament," *ZAW* 15 (1895): 1-74; E. Baumann, "*sub sebut*, ein exegetische Untersuchung," *ZAW* 47 (1929): 17-44; B, Schlogel, "*swb sbwt*," *WZKM* 38 (1931): 68-75; R. Borger "Zu שׁוב שׁבות/ית," *ZAW* 66 (1954): 315-316.

[30]Cf. G. Fohrer, "Zur Vorgeschichte und Komposition des Buches Hiob," pp. 30-31, 40-41.

[31]An unspecified weight of money, perhaps silver.

wishes to console Job of his suffering and confirm that it was undeserved. The number of Job's children is not doubled, perhaps indicating that people cannot be treated like commodities.[32] Others have suggested that it does actually represent a doubling because Job's original children still lived on in the afterlife. The special attention given to Job's daughters, stating their **names**[33] and celebrating their **beauty,** indicate the public acknowledgement of Job's status as a great and prosperous man. In a man's world, even Job's daughters achieved notoriety. Job's **granting** of an **inheritance** to his daughters also demonstrates that Job's beneficent spirit and sense of social justice went well beyond that of his times.[34]

42:16-17 Job lived **one hundred and forty years** and saw his descendants to the **fourth generation**. This age span may refer to his entire life or to that portion of it which he enjoyed after his suffering.[35] Long life was considered to be specific proof of a person's righteousness (cf. Exod 23:25,26). Likewise, seeing one's children unto successive generations represented the fullest example of a blessed life (cf. Ps 128:6; Prov 17:6). Job's epitaph, **And so he died, old and full of years**, places Job in the same class as the biblical patriarchs and other notable "servants" of God (e.g., Abraham, Gen 25:8; Isaac, Gen 35:29; David, 1 Chr 29:28). The story of Job is thus brought to a suitable end. This final portrait of Job is much like the first (1:1-5). He remains the exemplar of the righteous man blessed by God (cf. Ezek 14:14,20).

---

[32]The number "seven" (שִׁבְעָנָה, *šib'ānāh*) is written in an unusual form. Dhorme, following the Targ., considers the ending to be a dual and translates "fourteen sons." N. Sarna ("Epic Substratum in the Prose of Job," p. 18) takes it as an archaism related to Ug. *sb'ny*.

[33]Jemimah means "turtle-dove," a symbol of beauty and love (cf. S of S 2:14). Keziah is related to "cassia," a plant used in perfumes (Exod 30:24; Ps 45:9[8]). Keren-happuch probably means "horn of antimony," referring to a black powder used for highlighting the eyes (cf. 2 Kgs 9:30; Jer 4:30).

[34]In Israel, a daughter would inherit her father's estate only if there were no sons to succeed him (cf. Num 27:1-8).

[35]The LXX reads that Job lived 170 years after his trial, which he suffered when he was 70.